Shakespeare

His World and His Work

Shakespeare

His World and His Work

Revised Edition

M. M. Reese

Edward Arnold

© M M Reese 1953, 1980
First published 1980 by
Edward Arnold (Publishers) Ltd
41 Bedford Square, London WC1B 3DQ
First edition, 1953
Reprinted 1958, 1964

British Library Cataloguing in Publication Data
Reese, Max Meredith
  Shakespeare. – Revised ed.
  1. Shakespeare, William – Criticism and interpretation
  822.3'3   PR2976

  ISBN 0-7131-6255-4
  ISBN 0-7131-6256-2 Pbk

Printed in Great Britain by Spottiswoode Ballantyne Ltd
Colchester and London

Contents

Hereafter in a better world than this
I shall desire more love and knowledge of you
AYLI I ii 296.

Preface

A revised edition of a book first published more than twenty-five years ago requires a few words of explanation. When, after two reprintings, the original version quietly expired a short while ago, it was felt that a shortened form of the book would be more acceptable in a less leisurely age. Some of the material has therefore been reduced. On the other hand, there are also changes and additions. Shakespearean study has not stood still in the intervening years, and in some matters one inevitably changes one's mind.

In essentials, however, it is still the same book, with the original object of providing anyone interested in Shakespeare with a fairly full and uncomplicated account of his age, his life and his work. It still needs, therefore, the two apologies that accompanied it on its first appearance.

First there is the problem of method: whether the material should be treated chronologically or in sections devoted to particular themes. I have preferred the second method, but the divisions that I have adopted necessarily overlap and the reader must excuse a certain amount of repetition. While each chapter aims to be complete in itself, I have tried to link it with all the other chapters that are associated with it; and this has sometimes obliged me to refer again to matters that have been more fully discussed in another place. Thus the history of certain Elizabethan companies cannot be divorced from the theatres in which they played; an account of the theatres for which Shakespeare wrote his plays, and of the actors who performed in them, leads to some consideration of his stagecraft, and his stagecraft is an important facet of his dramatic art; or again, the study of his mind and thought that is attempted in Chapter XI often infringes the study of his artistic method. My classifications, then, are not as rigid or as exclusive as they might appear. Indeed they are only approximate, as each chapter, beginning with a brief general discussion of its subject, leads in the end to Shakespeare, and the intention is that each chapter should be more or less self-contained.

Secondly, most of the book's suggestions and conclusions are only tentative. But, like Hamlet, many of Shakespeare's commentators know not *seems*, and I have tried always to indicate where a statement rests upon no certain evidence. Much, therefore, has had to be introduced with a *maybe*, and if the result is sometimes blurred and unsatisfactory, I may plead that it is the more honest.

> Upon thy certainty and confidence
> What darest thou venture?

Sometimes far too much.

Any book of this kind owes a debt to previous scholars that is too large and various to be precisely acknowledged. In matters of fact the monumental work of Sir Edmund Chambers has been supplemented and brought up to date in Professor S. Schoenbaum's *William Shakespeare: a Compact Documentary Life* (1977), and Miss Muriel Bradbrook's *Shakespeare* (1978) is the fruit of a lifetime's study of the Elizabethan theatre. Although relatively brief and on some matters superseded, Peter Alexander's *Shakespeare's Life and Art* (1939) is perhaps the book that most Shakespearean critics wish they could have written. Reference to some of my other sources is included in the text and the notes.

Hindhead, October 1979.

Part I
Beginnings

Chapter I
Shakespeare's Youth

Like one that stands upon a promontory,
And spies a far-off shore.

3 Hen VI III ii 135.

The Warwickshire town of Stratford had its beginnings when the Romans carried a road across the Avon and built a military post to police the Celtic tribes that had taken refuge in the wooded valleys of the great forest of Arden. In Saxon times the district came under the authority of the bishops of Worcester, and a little colony of houses grew up around a monastery that was built near the site of the present church. At the Norman Conquest it was an agricultural community numbering about 150 inhabitants, and so it remained until, at the very end of the twelfth century, one of its bishops transformed it into a little town by encouraging building, laying out primitive streets and obtaining a charter for a weekly market. This was soon followed by royal charters sanctioning fairs at which local produce was displayed and sold.

Slowly Stratford grew in importance through the energy and initiative of its citizens. About a hundred years later the remarkable man known as John de Stratford left his midland parsonage for the dangers and responsibilities of a larger service to Church and State. As Bishop of Winchester he first attempted to reconcile Edward II with his enemies; and when reconciliation proved impossible, with the pragmatism characteristic of medieval prelacy he gave his support to the party which seemed likelier to prevail and he helped to remove Edward from the throne as decorously, but also as rapidly, as possible. His brief appearances in Marlowe's *Edward II* do not represent his historical importance during this crisis. In the new reign he became Archbishop of Canterbury and Lord Chancellor of England, and until he quarrelled with Edward III and defied the secular power, he was for ten years the trusted adviser of the throne, travelling on important diplomatic missions. His brother Robert, Bishop of Chichester, also held the Great Seal; and Ralph de Stratford, probably Robert's son, became Bishop of London. While the people of Stratford presumably drew good example from the swift rise of this family, they also profited from the

1

material benefactions which accompanied it. The beautiful church of the Holy Trinity, where Shakespeare was baptized and buried, took its present form chiefly through the gifts of John de Stratford, who enlarged the original building and endowed a chantry to say Masses for his soul. Ralph built a stone house for the residence of the chantry priests, under whose control the church came to be known as the Collegiate Church of Stratford.

But a mark of the sturdier medieval towns was their insistence upon withdrawing their civic affairs from ecclesiastical domination, and Stratford was run neither by the collegiate priests nor by its bishop. Although dedicated by its origins to the simple performance of religious rites and duties, the thirteenth-century Guild of the Holy Cross soon became the principal administrative body of the town. A medieval guild exercised a vast paternal authority. The fixing of wages and prices and the general supervision of a town's economic pursuits were only one part of its responsibilities. It framed and administered sumptuary laws which detailed the clothing held to be appropriate to each class, prescribed the people's diet and regulated their pastimes; it sent the children to school, paved and swept the streets, gave charity to the poor and decreed the privileges and obligations of visiting merchants and travellers. The wide range of its activities invested it with a considerable civil jurisdiction, so that towns with an energetic and efficient guild were the first to outgrow the restraints of feudal and ecclesiastical control and virtually to become self-governing communities. In Stratford all citizens of any standing belonged to the guild. It was richly endowed and had its own chapel and school. The foundations of the chapel were laid by Robert de Stratford, and it was rebuilt and enlarged in 1496 by Sir Hugh Clopton, a Stratford man who went to London to seek his fortune and, in story-book fashion, prospered as a mercer and became sheriff and lord mayor. The school was founded in 1427 to give a free education to children of the guild's members, and its generous endowments enabled it to take its place among the free grammar-schools, some three hundred in number, which were scattered over England as a reminder that not all medieval learning was monastic.

Thus at the end of the Middle Ages Stratford was already a flourishing little town. Baconians (and some others) have used words like *oaf* and *peasant* in reference to Shakespeare, in the belief that his birthplace was a benighted hamlet whose rude inhabitants toiled from sunrise to nightfall in the less exacting tasks of the agricultural round. At the time of the Reformation Stratford had a population of about 2000, but neighbouring Coventry, one of the half-dozen largest cities in England, had only 7000. The stone bridge with fourteen arches which Sir Hugh Clopton had built over the Avon disputed the town's architectural pride with the Collegiate Church and the Guild Chapel. The little stucco houses, with their timbered beams and thatched roofs, mostly had their own kiln-houses for brewing and yeling-houses for cooling the beer, their apple-chambers, powdering-tubs and bolting-houses, all marks of an energetic independence. They were occupied by weavers, woolmen, tanners, millers, maltsters and the like, together with sprinkling of men of more specialized accomplisment. Stratford, described by Camden as *'emporiolum non inelegans'*, did not depend for its prosperity merely on farming and the marketing of agricultural produce. Many of its citizens were engaged in glove-making, weaving, dyeing, rope-making, leather-dressing and similar crafts, and the complexities of this trading required the presence of professional men competent to adjudge the legal niceties and keep the accounts. The town's economic life as well as its civic life reflected an active, resourceful and essentially mature community.

The English Reformation was unusual in being one of the few revolutions in history to be initiated by a ruling class, and in a place like Stratford it took the form, at least in its earlier stages, of a series of arbitrary changes decreed by an external authority whose impact had seldom been experienced. The concept of a sovereign law-giving power being theoretically unknown in the Middle Ages, these changes were little understood at first and, whether they were understood or not, were largely resented. In Stratford, as elsewhere, religious innovation was accompanied by social interference that struck at the root of the town's traditional life. Because the saying of perpetual Masses seemed to Protestants to arrogate to man the Almighty's prerogative of forgiveness, the chantry college was suppressed and the house built by Bishop Ralph de Stratford became a private residence which was occupied in Shakespeare's day by his friend Thomas Combe. Charitable guilds too were denounced as nurslings of superstition, and the Guild of the Holy Cross was dissolved, its school dispersed and its property appropriated by the Crown. The town was bereft not only of education but of its organs of self-government.

But Stratford was more fortunate than some. In 1553, after a few years of confusion and uncertainty, Edward VI gave the town a charter which revived the old guild as the new Corporation of Stratford. In the meantime the Bishop of Worcester had forfeited his two Stratford manors to the Duke of Northumberland. On their reverting to the Crown, they were transferred in 1562 to his son Ambrose Dudley, Earl of Warwick, who was lord of the manor for the first twenty-six years of Shakespeare's life.

In the long run, therefore, the early changes of the Reformation did not seriously interrupt Stratford's steady growth in importance and prosperity. The chantry priests were gone, but maybe they were not much missed: perpetual Masses tied up money whose worldly uses might be more conspicuously efficacious. The people were still christened, wed and buried at Holy Trinity, as most of them always had been, and the new corporation at once resumed the powers and duties of the vanished guild. King Edward's charter endowed it with the guild's properties in the chapel, guildhall, school, almshouse and sundry holdings in real estate; the guild's former officers became municipal officers sitting on the new corporation, or town council, and Stratford became once more a community allowed in the main to direct its own affairs. The progression of offices soon to be held by Shakespeare's father would show the long reach of its paternal activities. Wages and prices were controlled and local industry was protected — quite literally protected when the corporation equipped an armed force to repel the traders of Coventry: the commercial feud between Ephesus and Syracuse, in which Aegeon's life might be forfeit, was the sort of thing that Shakespeare knew on his own doorstep, although he would colour it for dramatic purposes. Provisions for the public health imposed penalties for those who fouled the streets with refuse (John Shakespeare himself was fined the considerable sum of one shilling for leaving a *'sterquinarium'* outside his house, and his friend John Sadler fined for winnowing peas in Chapel Lane and offering the chaff to his pigs) or left their dogs unmuzzled or let their ducks wander unrestrained. Growing Protestant influence on the council was to be seen in the fines levied for profanity, card-playing and similar infractions. At the same time the guild's old school was re-founded as the King's New School of Stratford-upon-Avon (to persist in the whim of acknowledging Edward VI as its pious founder), with funds to provide the schoolmaster with a house and a salary of £20 a year. This was double the emolument of masters of most comparable schools and larger than that of many university Fellows. He had still to be in holy orders and to receive a licence from the bishop, and he still taught the fortifying discipline of classical studies that had been the staple nourishment of grammar-schools since grammar-schools began. So having repossessed themselves of their traditional forms of education and the only form of government they could remember, by the date of Shakespeare's birth the citizens of Stratford had recovered the familiar pattern of their useful lives.

In the middle years of the century — certainly before 1552, when he was fined for leaving garbage outside his house instead of using the 'common muckhill' provided — John Shakespeare, a farmer of the neighbouring village of Snitterfield, came to live in Stratford. Tradition has declared him to have been, among other things, a butcher, wool-merchant, corn-chandler and maltster, but principally he traded as a glover and whittawer, or dresser of white leather: a skilled craft in which he sold not only gloves but soft leathers like aprons, belts and purses. His son grew up in the shop and the plays attest his knowledge of the business: he could distinguish the uses of the various hides and skins, as that cheveril, the skin of kids, made the finest gloves because of its softness and flexibility, and men of a certain sort would have a 'soft cheveril conscience' (*Henry VIII* II iii 32). But in the modern phrase John Shakespeare evidently 'diversified' his interests. He had no wish to continue as a farmer because on his father's death in

1561 he parted with the copyhold of the substantial property at Snitterfield, but he appears to have traded in wool, malt and timber. Indeed the eastern wing of the house in Henley Street was for long known locally as the Woolshop. This was probably the house which, along with another in Greenhill Street, he bought in 1556, having previously lived as a tenant at the adjoining house to the west. These two properties, the traditional Birthplace, were joined together at some later date unknown.

A year or two later John married Mary, youngest of the eight daughters of Robert Arden of Wilmcote. The Shakespeares have not been traced farther back than John's father Richard, who was a prosperous yeoman farmer, but the Ardens claimed a lineage which stretched back beyond the Norman Conquest. The Saxon Turchill accommodated himself to the new settlers and avoided the confiscation of his estates. Adopting the Norman practice of taking a surname, he chose the name of Arden from the forests where his ancestors had lived, and in this he is recorded in the Domesday survey as a holder of land. It has not been established to which branch of this important family Robert Arden belonged, but possibly he took his descent from a minor branch of the Ardens of Park Hall, which was near Coleshill. With his father Thomas he bought an estate at Snitterfield in 1501, and Richard Shakespeare was his tenant in one of his holdings there.

Through her family connections, however distant, Mary Arden was of a higher social class than her husband, and she could bring to the house in Henley Street the advantages of birth and an assured inheritance. At his death in 1556 her father had left her, the youngest of his daughters, the largest of his Wilmcote properties, Asbies, as well as other land in the parish. It often happens that in the parentage of genius the mother is the stronger partner and a woman of commanding personality, but Mary Shakespeare has remained in the shadows. Her involvement in the vicissitudes of her husband's career is unknown. She bore him eight children, seemingly acquiesced in his mortgaging of her inherited property, and outlived him by seven years. We may wonder about her influence upon her famous son, but we wonder in vain.

Having established his business and his marriage, John Shakespeare undertook a career of public service of a kind to be expected of a substantial citizen. His first municipal appointment, in 1556, was to the post of ale-conner, reserved for 'able persons and discreet', who had to see that brewers, and also bakers, sold goods of prescribed quality and price. In 1558 he was made a constable and was reappointed in the following year, when the duties of affeeror, who assessed penalties for offences for which no punishment was prescribed by statute, were added to him. Elected then as a burgess on the town council, from 1561 to 1563 he served two terms as chamberlain, with responsibility for borough property and accounts. He was diligent in restoring dilapidated property, so long as it was not ecclesiastical, and in raising money for people in distress, and on the expiry of his term he was deputed to assist his successors. In 1565 he became an alderman and in 1568 he attained the highest office that the town could offer, that of bailiff, or presiding officer of the corporation. In this role he also served the borough as coroner and Justice of the Peace. His year of office was touched by important national events. Mary Queen of Scots, the focus of Catholic revolt, was detained in the midlands, and the recruiting-officers of the Earls of Leicester and Warwick were mustering soldiers for the army that would suppress the Northern Rebellion. By way of diversion Stratford was visited for the first time by professional companies, the Queen's Men and Worcester's Men, and John Shakespeare as bailiff granted them licences to act in the guildhall. For some years yet his prosperity was on a rising tide. In 1571 he was chief alderman and deputy-bailiff to his friend Adrian Quiney, and four years later he paid £40 for two houses in Stratford, one of them possibly the western house in Henley Street where previously he may have been only the tenant. In 1576 he proposed to set a crown upon his career when he applied for a coat-of-arms and the status of 'gentleman'.

Thus the home to which William Shakespeare was born was blessed with material prosperity and the esteem due to active and disinterested service. His mother was of gentle birth and came from an old and distinguished Warwickshire family; his father, although of yeoman stock, had developed a successful business in the town and by virtue of his public service and his connections through marriage might reasonably aspire to attain the same social level as his wife. John Shakespeare was not a rough, unlettered tradesman. His habit of signing official documents not with his name but with a mark — usually a drawing of his glover's compassess — led the eighteenth century to believe that he was illiterate; but a mark of this sort was commonly set on public documents and was thought to be somehow more authentic than an autograph signature. We do not know whether William grew up in an atmosphere of books and cultured intercourse; probably he did not. But his father was a man of enterprise and practical ability, and of a higher social standing than, for instance, Marlowe the shoemaker or Jonson the bricklayer; his status was nearer to that of Spenser the clothier, Greene the saddler or Lodge the grocer — or even Milton the scrivener.

William was not the eldest child of the marriage. First came two girls, Joan and Margaret, who died in infancy; and when William was hurried to his baptism on 26 April 1564,[1] his parents probably feared that within a few weeks they might be following another little coffin to the churchyard.

1 It is merely a convention which accepts 23 April, St George's Day, as the date of his birth. In days of high infant mortality it was customary to have babies christened as soon as possible, and this was the date — the beginning of a child's spiritual life — usually entered in the registers.

At the end of the long, meatless winter April was the cruellest month; and in 1564 Stratford was gripped by a plague which carried off nearly 250 people within six months. But the child survived, and a certain physical toughness must have been born in him: the Elizabethan theatre was no place for weaklings. Five more children followed: Gilbert in 1566, a second Joan in 1569, Anne in 1571, Richard in 1574 and Edmund in 1580. All but Anne outgrew the dangerous years of childhood, but only Joan out-lived William.[2]

So far the picture is firm and definite. We know surprisingly *much* about Shakespeare's background, about his family, the town where he was born and the avocations of his fellow-citizens. It is a very ordinary picture, and in its surface features his life continued to be ordinary, presenting the familiar tale of one who went to London to seek a living, achieved the sort of material sucess that could be recognized in his own lifetime, and in due course retired to his home town to make careful testamentary provisions on behalf of his family. Of course this is not quite what his destiny should have been. He should have gone to the grammar-school, apprenticed himself to his father's craft and eventually, having married a Sadler or a Quiney or a Rogers, have as the eldest son taken over the business in Henley Street, possibly enlivening the unchanging years with an occa-sional turn of municipal office. But his future had a different pattern, and it is disappointing that after the stage has been set, as it were, in full view of the audience, the curtain should fall just when the action is due to begin. We are faced now with two mysteries which have not yet yielded their secret: there is no certain explanation of the sudden change in John Shakespeare's fortunes after 1576, and we know nothing of the formative years which ended in his son's going to London to become a common player. After the record of his baptism in 1564 the next certain fact about Shakespeare is that in 1582 he was granted a licence to marry. Ten years later a well-known London dramatist wrote of him as one who had begun to make a name as actor and playwright. Of the years between there is no trace.

The Shakespeare boys would have been expected to go to the King's New School, where most of the sons of Stratford were educated, and probably they did. Visitors today, especially if they are American, are sometimes shown the very desk at which William sat and the horn-book at which he acquired the alphabet and the Lord's Prayer, but the registers of the period are missing and there is no evidence that he attended the school at all. If he did not, it may have been because he had the singing voice and presentable appearance which could earn country boys a place in the choir of some nobleman's household; or maybe his mother, with ambitions to

2 All eight children were baptized at Holy Trinity and all but Edmund, the youngest, were buried there. Only William and Joan were married, neither at Holy Trinity.

remove him from his apparent destiny in the glover's shop, importuned her father's family to use their influence to this effect. Against this, however, it is evident that at some time in his life Shakespeare acquainted himself with the formal routine of grammar-school studies, even if they brought him, by Ben Jonson's standards, 'small Latin and less Greek'.

Education began, at the age of four or five, at the petty school, where an '*abecedarius*', an unqualified usher, gave instruction in the three Rs. At the grammar-school an Elizabethan schoolboy's lessons, enforced by not infrequent 'jerks of the breech', continued from seven in the morning until five in the afternoon. The curriculum consisted chiefly of Latin, and its hard core was Lyly's *Grammatica Latina*, which by royal decree was the sole authority for use in schools. Having mastered the rudiments of grammar, the pupils went on to read certain approved works and authors, such as the fables of Aesop, the maxims of Cato, the eclogues of Virgil and Baptista Spagnolo (the 'good old Mantuan' beloved of Holofernes), Cicero, Sallust, Horace, Ovid and the *Copia Rerum et Verborum* of Erasmus. They learned little else. They had a smattering of arithmetic, but they were not seriously troubled with French, which was the language of the traditional enemy. Perhaps they had sufficient Greek to read the New Testament in the original, but they would be more familiar with the Bishops' Bible, an English version prepared early in the reign under the direction of Matthew Parker, or possibly, in towns which like Stratford came increasingly under Puritan influence, with the Geneva Bible, a tendentious version compiled by Calvin and a committee of Marian fugitives.

For all its rigidity, this austere curriculum provided a common stock of legend and story that gave enrichment to the lives of many diverse men, and its solid grounding in classical history was held to furnish statesmen with a fund of warnings and examples sufficient for the conduct of public affairs. But its most valuable achievement was that its objective and undeviating investigation of all the arts of language — not its grammar and syntax merely, but its use as an instrument of reason or a key to unlock the heart — taught its pupils an unrivalled mastery of expression.

If Shakespeare did not receive this discipline at the Stratford school, it is surprising. His plays and poetry seem to reveal an intimate familiarity with the whole process of education as it existed in his youth. It is not just that he could at will illustrate his work by allusion to the myths and heroes of classical antiquity, for no writer of the Renaissance period could help doing that. He seems to be always giving indications of having in the first instance acquired his Latin and little Greek at the feet of Holofernes himself, and of having failed to relish the experience. The study of the *Grammatica Latina*, which Elizabethan schoolboys had to learn by heart, is recollected in the scene (*MWW* IV i) in which Sir Hugh Evans puts young William through his paces; Holofernes and Sir Nathaniel litter their speech with snatches of grammar, as the sublimely absurd 'A soul feminine saluteth us', and of the formal phrases of the *Sententiae Pueriles* (*LLL* IV ii and V i). From *King John* the lines

'I shall beseech you' — that is *Question* now.
And then comes *Answer*, like an absey-book:
'O, sir,' says *Answer*, 'at your best command:
At your employment; at your service, sir'

KJ I i 195.

are founded on the students' Primer. Again, Katherine's 'Fair as a text B in a copy-book' (*LLL* V ii 42) refers to the exercises by which schoolboys were taught to write the 'old English' script that was fashionable at the time. Everywhere Shakespeare's attitude to the aridities of professional Logic and Rhetoric is that of a man who has been obliged to submit to their discipline rather by compulsion than by choice. We need not attach much importance to his

whining schoolboy, with his satchel
And shining morning face, creeping like snail
Unwillingly to school,

AYLI II vii 145.

or to such remarks as

Love goes toward love as schoolboys from their books,

RJ II ii 157.

as a man does not need to have gone to school himself to know that most schoolboys would rather be elsewhere. But we do seem to find evidence of a positive dislike of the pains attendant on a formal education and of the sort of man who enjoyed being 'a domineering pedant o'er the boy'. It has frequently been observed that schoolmasters were the only class of being whom he excluded from his capacious sympathy. He appears to have found them ridiculous. Sir Hugh, who combined teaching with his pastoral duties, is a strutting bantam, Pinch a superstitious ass; and Holofernes, named after one of whom 'it is declared through the whole earth that only thou art excellent and of a wonderful knowledge,' struggles to a fleeting humanity only when the courtiers have punctured his self-esteem.

Shakespeare could have acquired this outlook if, as some commentators believe, he was for a time a teacher himself, but he had other opportunities of studying the habits of the profession. In a little town like Stratford the dominie, although not necessarily respected, was something of a personage. The first schoolmaster whom he might have known when a very young boy was Walter Roche, who arrived in 1569 but resigned two years later to practise law in the town although apparently retaining an ecclesiastical living at Droitwich. Later he was a neighbour of the Shakespeares in Chapel Street. His successor at the school was Simon Hunt, who has been identified, though not with total assurance, as the Simon Hunt who went to Douai in 1575, became a Jesuit and died in Rome. If this was the man and Shakespeare was his pupil, it would have been between the ages of seven and eleven: hypotheses on which bold and far-reaching constructions have been founded. After Hunt came Thomas Jenkins, a man of humble origins who in 1579 seems to have bought himself out of the post in order to become a soldier. His name and presumed ancestry have helped to identify him with Sir Hugh Evans, even with Fluellen, but by birth he was a Londoner and there was a Welsh actor available to the London companies at the time of these creations. Having to find a replacement as a condition of his departure, Jenkins chose John Cottam, who resigned, or was dismissed, after two years. He was a Catholic recusant, brother of Father Thomas Cottam who was arraigned before the same tribunal as Edmund Campion (when a principal informer for the Crown was the play-wright Anthony Munday) and martyred in 1582. All these four school-masters were Oxford graduates, which shows the calibre of man that Strat-ford could afford, but the God-fearing Puritan town was less than blessed when two of them — or one at least — proved to be obdurately Catholic.

After this sequence of rapid changes the school acquired a master who reigned for more than forty years. This was the locally-celebrated Alexander Aspinall, again an Oxford graduate and, like Roche and Cottam, a Lancastrian. His academic attainments were combined with a shrewd capacity for civic and commercial affairs. He held various municipal offices, serving as chamberlain and alderman, and he conducted successful transactions in wool, yarn and malt. In recognition of this versatility, and perhaps of the vast esteem in which he held himself, he was known in Stratford as 'Great Philip Macedon'. He is the likeliest model for Holofernes. Shakespeare certainly knew him because he married a widow who lived nearby in Henley Street. Perhaps he generalized a distaste for Aspinall's academic conceit into a distaste for the whole profession. But all this is conjecture. In the absence of the registers we do not know whether Shakespeare went to the grammar-school or whether he did not; and if we think it probable that he did, it is safer to base the supposition on the common practice of citizens' sons in Stratford than on a version of his schooldays derived from selected passages from the plays.

When Shakespeare was about thirteen, some unexplained disaster fell upon his father. In January 1577 the prosperous alderman who had just applied for a coat-of-arms missed a meeting of the council for only the second time since his election some twenty years earlier; and apart from an appearance in 1582 to support the election of his friend John Sadler as bailiff, he did not attend again before he was expelled in 1586. In 1578 he mortgaged part of his wife's estate at Asbies to her brother-in-law Edmund

Lambert for £40 and conveyed other property in Wilmcote to the Webbe family who were related to Mary Shakespeare through her father's second marriage. Next year, for a meagre £4, he sold her share in the Snitterfield estate to her nephew Robert Webbe. It all suggests a desperate need for ready money.

Other seeming evidences of financial embarrassment have been discovered. Early in 1578 he was assessed at 3s.4d., half the normal rate, for a levy imposed to raise extra pikemen and gunmen against the machinations of the Pope, and although with nine others he was presented for non-payment, it is unlikely that the money was ever extracted from him. Although he was assessed as low as 4d. a week for the poor-rate, he would not pay that either, and he seems to have been excused the customary fines for non-attendance at the council. He had leased one of his Henley Street houses to William Burbage, but for some reason the arrangement had broken down and Burbage sued him for the refund of the fine of the lease. The sum was only £7, but the proceedings dragged on for ten years and it is unlikely that it was ever paid. In 1585 he was sued for a debt by John Browne, a woollen-draper; Browne gained the verdict but reported that the defendant 'had nothing whereon to distrain.' Again, John made himself surety for £10 of a debt owed by his brother Henry to a money-lender named Nicholas Lane. Henry failing in his obligations, Lane at length sued John for the money. With the verdict again going against him, John was arrested, released on securities provided by a friend and once more taken to court. He succeeded in getting the case referred to the Queen's Bench, where its outcome is unknown. Finally, in 1592 he was among a small group of men presented for recusancy with the appended excuse that 'these last nine come not to church for fear of process for debt.'

Up to a point this is a credible picture of a man in severe financial straits. John Shakespeare had the sort of business initiative in which risks were inevitable, and he had been sued for debts even in the prosperous days; he traded in several commodities and his house purchases suggest that he speculated in property; in hospitality and other outgoings he may have overspent in his work for the council; the midlands was undergoing an economic recession. All this may have built up into what would now be called a 'cash-flow problem', and unfortunately his son, who was at home at least during the earlier years, has left no light upon it.

Yet John Shakespeare continued to be a man of some substance. He disposed of his house in Greenhill Street at some time before 1590, but he occupied the property in Henley Street until his death, bequeathing it to William; and even while he was refusing to make various quite modest payments, he was ready to spend larger sums for other purposes. In 1580 he tried to recover possession of Asbies by repaying Lambert the money raised on it, but apparently Lambert refused to allow the mortgage to be redeemed until Shakespeare had discharged certain other debts allegedly due to him. On Lambert's death in 1587 Shakespeare, citing his wife and son as fellow-claimants, made another attempt to recover it and brought the new occupier, Lambert's son John, before the Queen's Bench at Warwick. This claim must have been unsuccessful because in 1597 he filed a suit in Chancery, but it is unlikely that Asbies was ever recovered by the Shakespeares. The point is, however, that a man who was reported to have nothing on which to distrain was able to afford legal proceedings to try to establish his right to spend £40 on the recovery of an alienated property.

In 1580, also, at the very time when he was trying to redeem Asbies, he was summoned to Westminster to be bound over to keep the peace. The occasion for this summons is unknown but it means that in the eyes of the government John Shakespeare was a man who for some heterodoxy of thought, or maybe some hastiness of speech or action, needed to be brought to London to give assurances of good behaviour in the future. The authorities regarded him as a man of means, because when he failed to answer the summons he was fined £20 and his two sureties were fined £10 each. Nor was that all. When one of these sureties, Robert Awdley of Nottingham, was likewise summoned and likewise did not appear, Shakespeare, who in his turn had gone bail for Awdley, was fined a further £20. A total of £40, the value of Asbies, was a considerable sum, but in the absence of further proceedings this may have been a debt that he did pay. In 1586, again, when his creditor John Browne was vainly seeking satisfaction, Lane, a professional money-lender, was accepting him as adequate security for £10 of the loan made to his brother Henry; and in the same year his recognizances were accepted for the same amount by the Coventry magistrates on behalf of Michael Pryce, a tinker of Henley Street, who had been arrested for felony. In 1591 and 1592, when professedly he was lurking in his house in fear of the constable, he was in fact serving in the courts as a juryman and was being employed with other citizens in preparing inventories of the goods of two Stratfordians lately deceased. When, finally, in 1596 he renewed his application for a coat-of-arms and the degree of gentleman, he claimed that he had 'lands and tenements, of good wealth and substance £500.' In the following year his eldest son bought the largest property in the town.

John Shakespeare's troubles, then, were not wholly financial, for although he would not pay certain minor debts, he was wealthy enough to stand surety on a number of occasions and he still owned the house and shop where he carried on his business. He could not have renewed his application for a coat-of-arms, this time successfully, if anyone could have charged him with any serious misconduct, financial or other. In fact he continued to have the respect of his fellow-citizens. His colleagues on the council sympathized with his misfortunes, whatever their nature or cause, because they did not fine him for his continued absence and they kept his place open for him for nearly ten years before striking him from the list of aldermen, giving as their reason that 'Mr Shakespeare doth not come to the halls when they be warned, nor hath not done of long time.' Six years later they were still defending him, for when ordered to present the authorities with a list of recusants, they excused his absence from church on the ground that fear of arrest for debt kept him at home: as though it were only on Sundays and feast-days that a man might be arrested.

But recusancy possibly touches the heart of the matter, because the pressure of the times compelled men to decide their allegiances. When John Shakespeare first took municipal office, and therein swore allegiance to his sovereign and the form of religion by law established, Protestantism was being fertilized by the blood of Mary's martyrs. The heroism of these few, most of them very humble folk, dulled for a while the memory of the greed and destructive fanaticism of the previous reign. Stratford men learned of the ring of fires with which Mary had encircled the town. John Rogers, the first of her victims, was a Warwickshire man; so was the second, Lawrence Saunders, who was burned at Coventry; the third was Hooper, recently Stratford's bishop; Hugh Latimer, one of the Oxford martyrs, was another former bishop of the diocese and he was known and loved in the district, where he had once championed a little nest of Protestants at Hampton Lucy. As the fires blazed in Leicester, Northampton and Banbury, and in the cathedral cities of Coventry, Lichfield, Gloucester and Oxford, the Stratford records tell of widening religious divisions in the town, of brawls in the streets and diminishing respect for the law and its officers.

John Shakespeare was constable at the critical time when Queen Mary died and her half-sister Elizabeth succeeded her. Elizabeth decided to steer a course midway between the competing infallibilities of Rome and Geneva and draw up a settlement which should purge the faith of Romish corruptions without jettisoning the cultural heritage of western Europe. Her compromise was essentially English in its freedom from the restraints of logic or consistency, but since it was devised for the use of Englishmen, that was no great matter: Anglicanism became the least fanatical and the most traditional of the reformed faiths. But her immediate aim was to make her settlement less a repository of spiritual truth than a test and symbol of national unity. 'We never had any meaning or intent that our subjects should be troubled or molested in any matter of faith...as long as they shall show themselves quiet and conformable.'

Quiet and conformable the English Puritans were not disposed to be. For them the quest for spiritual truth was a compulsion which dismissed as irrelevant the political anxieties the Queen could not so easily ignore. The first phase of the English Reformation was an administrative revolution, anti-papal rather than distinctively Protestant, conducted by the government on the sixteenth-century principle of '*cuius regio, eius religio*'; but its second phase, which occupied all Shakespeare's lifetime and beyond, sought to force the government to 'purify' the makeshift arrangements of 1559. Stripped of the doctrinal differences which split its adherents into mistrustful sects, the movement known as Puritanism gathered together all those men who rejected the Elizabeth settlement because it was founded on political expediency rather than the Word of God; and the dominant issue of the reign, invading its political, diplomatic and constitutional history, was whether expediency should continue to prevail.

In Stratford Roger Dyos, the priest who baptized the first of the Shakespeare children, had Catholic leanings and as he refused to resign, the corporation disposed of him by witholding his stipend. Seventeen years later he sued them for the accumulated arrears and recovered it with damages. The influence of the powerful neighbouring families of Dudley and Lucy released the Protestant impulses of a district where the Elizabethan settlement was unacceptable. The first manifestation of Puritan activity had been a campaign to do away with 'the relics of the Amorites', or those externals of the country's traditional worship that were held to be godless survivals of Popish superstition. 'The scenic apparatus of worship is now under agitation,' Bishop Jewel had reported to his German friends, and in their final shape, strongly influenced by Puritan voices in the Privy Council and the Commons, the Injunctions of 1559 gave authority for the removal of 'Popish peltry' from the fabric of the churches, namely images, shrines, pictures and 'all other monuments of feigned miracles, pilgrimages, idolatry and superstition.' This commission was splendidly wide for men with a mood to destroy, and a later worshipper was to find 'bare ruined choirs where once the sweet birds sang.' For the gratification of 'Germanical natures' roods were defaced and the lofts pulled down, chancels converted into sties for incumbents' pigs and playgrounds for their children, altar-stones carried away to serve as aldermen's dinner-tables, vestments used to make robes for municipal wives or sold to strolling players, organ-pipes and the lead wrappings of the dead melted down to serve the humblest domestic uses. Marston's Malevole expressed in his own sour fashion the aspirations of the zealous Calvinist:

> I mean to turn pure Rochelle Churchman, I... Because I'll live lazily, rail upon authority; deny King's supremacy in things indifferent, and be a Pope in mine own parish...I ha' seen a sumptuous steeple turned to a stinking privy: more beastly, the sacredest place made a dog's kennel: nay, most inhuman, the ston'd coffins of long-fled Christians burst up, and made hog's troughs.
>
> *The Malcontent* II v 128.

Because they feared the Cloptons, who were Catholic, the Stratford Corporation for a time held their hand. But this restraint was removed when Sir William Clopton fled abroad in 1563, and John Shakespeare was chamberlain when the rood-loft was taken from the guild chapel, a wooden table substituted for the stone altar, the pictured saints disfigured and the nave divided from the chancel. His adventurous year as bailiff, when Mary Stuart was watchfully held at Coventry during the rising of the Northern Earls, brought close to Stratford the perilous implications of Catholic conspiracy. An immediate result was the hurried departure of the new vicar, William Butcher, and his curate, who were suspected of being deficient in Protestant righteousness. In 1570 came the Queen's excommunication, and in Paris two years later the Massacre of St Bartholomew. Each year it became harder to be neutral, or undecided, or indifferent; and each year more men were persuaded to reject as humiliating and dangerous the government's policy of buying Catholic acquiescence at the price of refusing any further concessions to the Protestants. Although generalization at once breaks down in the divisions that existed within every town and village, and often within the individual family, the midlands were broadly Puritan in conviction. Illustrating the long association between nonconformity and the textile industry, the town of Banbury, then a centre of the cloth trade, was so strong in the faith that Puritans were often known as 'Banbury men'. In Stratford itself most of the leading citizens were energetically Puritan, and in 1571 — when John Shakespeare was deputy-bailiff to Adrian Quiney — the Romish vestments in the church were inventoried and sold for the use of councillors and their ladies. It is possible that young William Shakespeare had a cope as coverlet for his bed.

So far these destructive employments had received no discouragement from the bishops, Edwin Sandys (1559-70) and Nicholas Bullingham (1571-6). Bullingham was one of the worst of Elizabethan bishops. After despoiling the see of Lincoln by sundry lootings and the alienation of ecclesiastical property, he came to Worcester with similar intent. He was in full cry when he died, and John Whitgift, a very different sort of man, was appointed to put the diocese in order. In his personal convictions Whitgift was a moderate Calvinist. He regarded episcopacy itself as 'a thing indifferent', rejecting the Anglican belief in its divine institution; and in the Lambeth Articles drawn up under his supervision in 1595 assent was given to Calvinist theories of grace and reprobation. Doctrinally this was the position of many of the bishops who defended the Elizabethan settlement. They regarded the settlement as erroneous in many serious respects, but in face of the Counter-Reformation they thought it was no time for Englishmen to be exchanging blows in dogmatic controversy. The law was the law, and it must be obeyed, if only to persuade all good Protestants to form a united front against the Pope who was their common enemy.

It must be significant, or else a startling coincidence, that in the year of Whitgift's appointment John Shakespeare ceased to attend the council, and that thereafter he acted like a man anxious to avoid the penalties of recusancy without compromising his conscience. He had reason to be apprehensive as recusancy had become a serious matter. In 1576 the Queen's Ecclesiastical Commission was empowered to imprison and punish by sequestration persons 'wilfully and obstinately absenting themselves from church.' Shakespeare's expedient of conveying the Asbies estate to Lambert was typical of the stratagems by which recusants sought to avoid confiscation. Lands were devised to tenants, and goods entrusted to the safe-keeping of neighbours, in the hope that the ecclesiastical Visitors would believe that the cupboard was bare. Shakespeare's actions at this time were all of a piece. Having, as he hoped, arranged for the safe conveyance of his Wilmcote properties, he felt secure enough to defy the government; and when he was bound over to give sureties to keep the peace, he took the further precaution of distributing his sureties over three dioceses to make their recovery more difficult. In this he was not altogether successful and his gesture of defiance probably cost him £40, but he may have found some oblique satisfaction in it. Even his refusal to pay his assessments for pikemen and the relief of the poor may have proceeded from his determination to defy authority at all points, because the pikemen were to be mustered 'for the defence of the realm, against attempts both inward and outward,' against, that is, religious dissentients of whom the government disapproved; and the poor-rate was composed in part of fines extracted from recusants.

His refusal to pay his other creditors, Burbage, Browne and Nicholas Lane, cannot, so far as we know, be attributed to conscience, but it may not be altogether surprising. It is a reasonable inference that Shakespeare was under heavy strain at this time, and his mood far from normal, inducing a certain perversity of behaviour.[3] He bore his troubles more hardly than most. Other dissentients in Stratford were firm in their recusancy and took steps to devise their property beyond the reach of the inquisitors, but they did not go to the extreme of absenting themselves from public business. The long forbearance of his colleagues, in the expectation that in due course he would return to the council, suggests that they felt he was carrying his protest farther than was necessary. Nor did other recusants allow their zeal to bring them into open conflict with the Queen's Bench if they could conscientiously avoid it.

If this interpretation of John Shakespeare's difficulties is the right one, we have still to decide whether he was marked by the authorities as a Protestant recusant or a Catholic, and of this again there is no positive evidence. When the known facts will fit either conclusion, the matter may be urged either way. While in office he acquiesced, at least, in the destruction of the externals of Catholic worship, and he may have taken an active part in it: which would point to his having had Protestant sympathies at

---

3 Perversity seems to have run in the family. At various times John's brother Henry, who farmed nearby at Hampton Lucy, was fined for an affray, imprisoned for trespass, excommunicated for not paying tithe, fined for wearing a hat instead of the cap prescribed for Sundays and feasts, fined for 'not labouring with teams for amending the Queen's highway'. He was frequently in debt, but when he died in 1596 there was plenty of money in the house. The parallels are obvious.

any rate until 1571. Even this apparently safe inference must, however, be qualified by the Tudor attitude to the holding of office, which was vastly different from the modern attitude. Office, from the highest to the lowest, was a sacred trust. Authority in the state had been expressly instituted by God for the well-being of mankind, and kings and magistrates, being God's representatives, were delegates not of the general will of the people but of a divine plan. Thus the sixteenth century was unacquainted with the act of resignation. A minister did not resign if the law bade him execute a policy of which he disapproved. It is only necessary to consider the example of Thomas Cranmer, whose conscience was often in conflict with his master's policies: a dilemma which led him in the last days of his life to his agonized recantation of what the law decreed as heresy, followed by the withdrawal of that recantation and the acceptance of death. Whitgift and many of the better Elizabethan bishops faced the same sort of problem when they administered a religious policy with which in many respects they disagreed. These high-sounding principles may seem somewhat remote from the municipal affairs of Stratford-on-Avon, but office was held on no other condition and hundreds of Tudor servants found themselves giving public endorsement to policies which their private judgment disliked. It may be relevant that John Shakespeare never resigned from the council; he merely absented himself until he was dismissed from it.

Thus it is possible, although the modern mind has difficulty in acccepting it, that even in the earlier days he did not approve of the religious policy of the corporation whose servant he was. He may even then have known a conflict between his public duty and his private conscience, and it was one that he could only resolve by dropping out of civic life. On the other hand, if he was a Protestant in 1571, he may not have been still a Protestant a few years later. In the confusion of the times such revulsions were not uncommon, particularly when Puritanism came to be seen as a threat to peace and unity. The violent actions, unbalanced language and emotional intransigence of the lunatic fringe at first alarmed and then alienated many who had once looked to Puritanism to light the way to truth. The stronger the original hope, the deeper the disillusion, and perhaps Shakespeare was one of those who turned away and sought refuge in the traditional faith. Some of his behaviour after 1577 was not entirely that of a man who felt that in defying Whitgift and his 'trotting paritors' he had the support and approval of the people among whom he lived. For a time at least, he seems to have been less afraid of defying the authorities than of facing his fellow-men. To have been a Puritan recusant would not, in Stratford's view, have disabled him from serving the community, but he gives the impression of having absented himself because his attendance would have been an embarrassment to his friends. In this he would have been wrong, for Warwickshire Puritans, much as they hated Papists, hated Whitgift more. Whitgift's campaign for the extermination of heresy, whether Protestant or Catholic, broke down in Stratford before the passive resistance of those whose duty it was to present offenders for examination. His Visitors were provided only with the helpless riff-raff of the gaols, and when they tried to lay hands on recusants with property and influence, they were put off with transparent deceits and excuses — as that eminent citizens dare not venture forth on Sunday for fear of being arrested for debt.

It may appear strange that the officers of a Puritan town could have been willing to defend a Catholic from the law, but the bishop, the enemy in their midst who was trying to put down the righteous, was more to be feared than the remoter enemy overseas. They were able to accommodate themselves quite peaceably with Catholics whom they had known all their lives, and a Catholic named George Badger was even appointed bailiff in a year when the national hunt for Papists was approaching hysteria. When external pressure was unduly strong, the council might hand over one or two contumacious Catholics, men suspected perhaps of having Jesuit affiliations, but recusants of whatever colour who stayed quiet in the armour of their personal convictions were safe in their hands.

The picture is endlessly confusing,[4] and no explanation fits all the facts. John Shakespeare's fortunes went into sudden eclipse. The cause was almost certainly not financial, for he retained most of his property; it is unlikely to have been some personal disgrace as he continued to have the respect or sympathy of his fellows. Probably, then, he fell foul of Whitgift and took his religious convictions so seriously that he was disinclined to play his former part in public life. But he might have been a Puritan or a Catholic; and to have shown that despite superficial appearances it was possible for him to have been a Catholic does not necessarily mean that he was not in fact a Protestant. We have to leave it at that.

Whatever their cause, these events must have made some impression on the young Shakespeare and may have been partly responsible for his leaving home. The traditional portrait of his father has had to be revised. It originated in one of the earliest biographical sketches of the family, the

4 Nor perhaps is it clarified by the document known as John Shakespeare's 'Spiritual Last Will and Testament', which was discovered under the tiles at Henley Street in 1757. It was known to the eighteenth-century critic Edmond Malone but has since vanished. It was a Catholic profession of faith in fourteen articles, a formulary by Cardinal Borromeo. If we could be sure that it was in the house in John Shakespeare's time and that he cherished it and believed it, his religious opinions would no longer be in doubt, but S. Schoenbaum, *William Shakespeare: a Compact Documentary Life*, 45-54, concludes that 'too many questions remain teasingly unanswered.' E.I.Fripp, *Shakespeare Studies*, 81-98, argues that he was a Puritan recusant, but for the view that he had reverted to Catholicism, or had never abandoned it, see *Shakespeare Survey* III 5, J.H. de Groot, *The Shakespeares and 'The Old Faith'*, P.Milward, *Shakespeare's Religious Background*. But many writers continue to believe that his troubles were financial — despite evidence of the assets he obviously retained. The gnomes must be at work.

notes collected by John Aubrey shortly after the Restoration. These were based on talks with the actor William Beeston, son of the Christopher Beeston who was a boy player in Shakespeare's company and later a theatre-owner and actor-manager, so that at least they have a playhouse source. Aubrey wrote that John Shakespeare was a butcher, and added:

> I have been told heretofore by some of the neighbours, that when he was a boy he [William] exercised his father's trade, but when he kill'd a calf, he would do it in a high style and make a speech.

Here is the basic error from which others have sprung: John Shakespeare was not a butcher, leather-sellers not being allowed to sell meat. There has long been a folk conception of butchers as plump and jovial men, and among the papers of Thomas Plume, Archdeacon of Rochester, who died in 1704, were found some jottings on Elizabeth drama. One of these says that William

> was a glover's son — Sir John Mennis saw once his old father in his shop — a merry-cheek'd old man — that said Will was a good honest fellow, but he durst have cracked a jest with him at any time.

As Mennis was only three years old when the father died, this jocular recollection has little value, and many of the most potent items in the Shakespeare Apocrypha have been founded on second-hand chatter of this kind. Often they are derived from the gossip of Stratford people in the century following the poet's death, and it is natural that the natives should have embellished the memory of the town's most famous son. They still do.

Aubrey and Mennis/Plume have created a picture that dies very hard of an apple-cheeked, almost Falstaffian parent who matched his son in extemporal wit, but it is not in focus with the surviving documents. These suggest a zealous public servant and enterprising man of business who conducted his retreat from Whitgift with sound tactical skill. His withdrawal from public life was the action of a man obedient to a standard of behaviour that he has prescribed for himself. He was stubborn and intransigent, and possibly he had something of Brutus's capacity for finding himself always in the right. He may not have been an easy man to live with.

If William did take the usual course at the grammar-school, he would have left in about 1578-9, when the shadows were gathering about his home. Nicholas Rowe's biography early in the eighteenth century said that on leaving school, which he had to do prematurely on account of the family's straitened circumstances, he was taken into his father's employment. From Aubrey, who was an indomitable gossip, comes the version, again attributed to Beeston, that 'he had been in his younger years a schoolmaster in the country.' It is possible. The classical models of his early work, chiefly Plautus, Seneca and Ovid, were authors with whom a young schoolmaster would have acquainted himself, and much of this work had the stamp of a literary ambition so far founded on books rather than on life. But if he taught in Stratford, this would surely have been remembered in the town when Aubrey visited it; so that if he ever was a teacher, it must have been elsewhere 'in the country'. He would in any case have been only an '*abecedarius*', or non-graduate assistant, as a qualified teacher required a university degree, holy orders and a licence from the bishop, and no one has yet vested Shakespeare with this particular equipment.

There are many other occupations he may have tried for a time, and here speculation has been misled by his apparent mastery of many crafts. On internal evidence from the plays he might have spent a term in an attorney's office, although his law is not as good as that of dramatists whose training was more strictly academic; his casual command of the technical terms of seamanship has the familiarity of one who had sailed before the mast, but a similar argument makes him a soldier who served under English captains in the Netherlands. On the other hand, his knowledge of horses and dogs, woodcraft, falconry and the discipline of the hunt, a lore too deep to have been acquired in London or among the middle-class avocations of Stratford, suggests a period of service on some large country estate. This lends colour to the theory, seductive to all who prefer romantic solutions, that he was brought up in a nobleman's household, first perhaps as a singing boy in the choir and later as companion and tutor to a son of the family. But unless he pursued all these different activities, which is plainly impossible, their very variety throws doubt on the source from which they come. That source is the plays. The argument always runs on the same lines: because the plays reveal a working knowledge of this craft or that, a knowledge inaccessible to a youth who spent his early years in a little town like Stratford, then he must have studied that craft professionally. But genius grows where it will. The creative imagination is master of all crafts and the secrets of all sorts of men.

Rowe was probably nearer the truth than most when he said that Shakespeare apprenticed himself in the glover's shop. When all else is conjecture, we must make what we can of the single unassailable fact that at the age of eighteen he was granted a licence to be married. But here too there are mysteries. On 27 November 1582 the register of the Consistory Court of the diocese entered the issue of a licence to William Shakespeare and Anne Whateley of Temple Grafton. By strict ecclesiastical law there were certain prohibited seasons in which banns might not be proclaimed, the calling of the banns being the usual way of establishing that there was no impediment to the proposed union. From 2 December to 13 January was one of these periods, and it was to be presumed that there were special reasons why the marriage in question should be performed before it was over. One of the conditions of special licences was the production of a bond, by the bridegroom or other surety on his behalf, indemnifying the bishop and his officers against the consequences of any irregularity that might later be shown against the marriage. On the following day, 28 November, this bond was duly produced, the sureties, who pledged themselves for the very considerable sum of £40, being neither the bridegroom (who was a minor) nor his father (who perhaps had his own reasons for not wishing to present himself at Whitgift's Consistory Court) but two Warwickshire farmers, Fulk Sandells and John Richardson. In acknowledgment the court allowed that if four specified conditions were fulfilled, 'William Shagspere' was to free to marry, with a single calling of the banns, 'Anne Hathwey of Stratford in the Diocese of Worcester, maiden.'

That Shakespeare did marry Anne Hathaway is not in question, but no one has discovered when or where: it was not at Stratford. But what became of Anne Whateley of Temple Grafton, who here makes her solitary recorded appearance in the story of Shakespeare's life? Some biographers have it that there was no such person; she exists only as a clerical error. Thus the bishop's clerk often made mistakes, the register was carelessly kept, inconsistent spellings and inaccurate entries fill its pages, and so Anne Whateley of Temple Grafton was a misprint for Anne Hathaway of Stratford. The confusion between Whateley and 'Hathwey' is easier to understand than the confusion between Stratford and Temple Grafton. It may be that Temple Grafton, a village five miles from Stratford, was the place intended for the ceremony, but its incumbent at the time was elderly and regarded as 'unsound' in religion, meaning that he was Papistically inclined, and he was allowed to celebrate marriages only on very stringent conditions. Local report, for what it is worth, said that the ceremony took place in the chapel at Luddington, which was within the Stratford parish. But why not at Holy Trinity, the natural choice for an alderman's son and heir? This may have been another occasion when the bridegroom's father was reluctant to meet his fellows.

Writers of moralistic bent have supposed that Shakespeare intended to marry Anne Whateley but Anne Hathaway's friends had knowledge of it just in time to prevent him. Anne Hathaway was twenty-six, eight years older than her husband, and she was already pregnant: her eldest child was baptised in Holy Trinity the following May.

> Good name in man and woman, dear my lord,
> Is the immediate jewel of their souls.
>
> *Oth* III iii 155.

It does not follow, however, that Shakespeare's good name was already lost, for a church ceremony might often be the formal solemnization of a union already recognized and publicly contracted. The long survival of actions for breach of promise proceeded from the custom of regarding an 'engagement' as a binding contract in token whereof the man usually gave the woman a ring. 'It is certain, corporal,' Bardolph tells Nym, 'that he is married to Nell Quickly, and certainly she did you wrong, for you were troth-plight to her.' In *Measure for Measure* Angelo imposes his austere legalism against a couple thus pre-contracted, but a union so pledged might be consummated at once and the Church and the law would regard the offspring as legitimate without further ceremony. The high authority of Thomas Cranmer acknowledged the troth-plight as 'perfect matrimony before God', and hundreds of marriages had no other sanction. But a service in church had the advantage of giving a further authority to the union and of advertising it to those outside the immediate family circle. Possibly, therefore, Shakespeare's union with Anne Hathaway had been pledged before their families some months earlier, and their haste to get a licence from the Church showed an understandable wish for a public ceremony before their child was born.

Alternative theories may be only the fruit of romantic and insubstantial fancy and Anne Whateley has no better warrant for her existence than the congenital carelessness of the bishop's clerk. It would certainly be surprising if the licence issued on 27 November were allowed to do duty for Shakespeare's marriage to a person not named in it: the clerk's genial improvidence would hardly have stretched as far as that. Indeed, apart from the disparity in age, the marriage with Anne Hathaway was of the sort known as eminently suitable, a good match between equals. Her family came from Shottery, a little village a mile from Stratford and possibly older than the town itself. They lived in a twelve-roomed farmhouse called Hewlands,[5] a large dwelling for those times, and they farmed some 70 acres. In 1566 John Shakespeare had stood surety for Anne's father, Richard Hathaway, which makes it likely that the families were old friends. Richard's will, drawn up in September 1581, suggests that a marriage was in contemplation, so that if Shakespeare was then the intended husband, it was not the hasty affair that a superficial reading of the ecclesiastical documents would indicate. Moreover, Richard died in the summer of 1582 (which explains why Sandells and Richardson, respectively an executor and a witness of his will, came forward with the £40 bond required by the Consistory Court), and it may be that his death provided the main reason for a postponement of the public celebration of the union.

But some doubts will always linger. If they feed themselves on the supposition that the marriage was an unhappy one, they are over-hasty because this rests on inferences that can be interpreted another way (see

5 Previously held on a lease, Hewlands was bought by Anne Hathaway's brother in 1610. It remained in the direct male line until 1746 and was occupied by the family until 1838. The Shakespeare Trust bought it in 1892 for £3000 and to-day, as 'Anne Hathaway's Cottage', it is the most convincing of the local memorials. Some of the furniture and fittings were there in Shakespeare's day.

pages 254-5). Even if it was not the marriage that Shakespeare intended — of which there is no certain evidence—it lasted until his death. On the other hand, although the troth-plight was still common practice, there is no certain evidence that these two so bound one another and maybe it is an assumption that comes conveniently to explain Shakespeare's lapse from Victorian morality. Moreover, it is at odds with one of his most deeply held convictions.

Here we confront a difficulty that will occur again and again in this book just as it occurs in any study of Shakespeare: selective quotation from the plays. However conscious one may be of the unwisdom of inferring biographical data or personal opinions from the casual remarks by his characters, it is not easy to resist the temptation to extract sentences which seem to reflect upon his experience or beliefs. Of such a kind may be Lysander's warning against love that is 'misgraffed in respect of years' (*MND* I i 137) or Orsino's commonplace

> let still the woman take
> An elder than herself.
>
> *TN* II iv 30.

Shakespeare has made countless observations on love and marriage. Some are well-known aphorisms, some arise from the dramatic context, some may be the fruit of deep meditation: it is absurd to make a choice of any of them as his own considered belief. It is another matter when he goes on saying a thing, giving it to a wide variety of characters in a wide variety of contexts and often working it into the texture of his plots. Then we may begin to suppose that he was expressing something that had value and significance for himself, especially when it seems to occur almost as a reflex of subconscious imagery, like his association of spaniels with flattery and disagreeable habits at the table. His ridicule of schoolmasters, already mentioned, is another example of what seems to have been a rooted conviction in him. Others are more important: his respect for gratitude and loyalty, his insistence upon the quality of 'kindness', obedience to constituted authority in the state, the difference between reality and the outside appearance.

A reading of the plays discloses the further conviction that intercourse outside wedlock brings no happiness to man or woman. The troth-plight will do for Mistress Quickly but not for the young lovers of the comedies. Shakespeare brings before his audience an unashamed procession of bawds and pimps, procuresses and bastards, and he anatomizes love in all the shapes in which it may appear to men; but he demands of his lovers an undefiled purity until they have come together before a priest. He insists upon this with an urgency that far transcends the restraints put upon him by the convention of the boy actor. There are perhaps half a dozen adulterous or illicit relationships in all his plays, and they are formed by persons who are objects of hatred and contempt.[6] The hot-blooded passion that is impatient of control is not an indulgence that he favours — Romeo and Juliet are rebuked for it. The characters he seems to admire, and wants us to admire, have to await the Church's sanction before they may enjoy the rights that are theirs by love. Touchstone and Audrey are relieved by the arbitrary appearance of a hedge-priest in the forest of Arden, a poor thing but a priest nonetheless, and without him their predicament would have been uncomfortable. Since he is not in any other way necessary to the plot and serves no other function but this, his appearance gives an insight into Shakespeare's mind: he comes because Shakespeare, as well as Touchstone, has need of him. In a play written a dozen years later Prospero is speaking to Ferdinand, who has pledged his troth to Miranda:

> Then, as my gift, and thine own acquisition
> Worthily purchased, take my daughter: but
> If thou dost break her virgin-knot before
> All sanctimonious ceremonies may
> With full and holy rite be minister'd,
> No sweet aspersion shall the heavens let fall
> To make this contract grow; but barren hate,
> Sour-eyed disdain and discord shall bestrew
> The union of your bed with weeds so loathly
> That you shall hate it both: therefore take heed,
> As Hymen's lamps shall light you.
>
> *Tem* IV i 13.

Ferdinand dutifully replies that as he hopes for 'quiet days, fair issue, and long life' no promptings of his 'worser genius' shall ever

> melt
> Mine honour into lust, to take away
> The edge of that day's celebration.

Florizel assures Perdita that his desires run not before his honour, nor his lusts burn hotter than his faith (*WT* IV iv 33).

We may suppose that, after the fashion of the times, Shakespeare took his bride to live in his father's house and it was there that their first child, Susanna, was born in May 1583. Some twenty months later, on 2 February 1585, twins were baptized in the church, named Hamnet and Judith after

---

6 *Antony and Cleopatra* may seem an obvious exception to this, but in a semi-historical play Shakespeare was in essentials bound by his sources. In a strange way the intense passion is never explicity sexual. Although Cleopatra teases the deprived Mardian and comments on the felicity of being Antony's horse, this is, unexpectedly, one of the least bawdy plays in the canon. Antony and Cleopatra are mature enough to keep their intimacies private, and the play's passion is of a different kind. If we dare not call it spiritual, at the end it transcends mortality.

the family's friends and neighbours, the Sadlers. Seven years after that Shakespeare was earning fame in London, but why or when he left home is as dark a mystery as his occupation before his marriage or the circumstances of the marriage itself.

Tradition supplies one answer: he went because he had made Stratford too hot to hold him. He had stolen deer from Sir Thomas Lucy's park at nearby Charlecote and, after being punished with a whipping, had lampooned him in a scurrilous ballad. The story originated in some notes made late in the following century by Richard Davies, Archdeacon of Coventry and formerly rector of the Gloucestershire parish of Sapperton. He wrote that the young Shakespeare

> was much given to all unluckiness in stealing venison and rabbits from Sir Lucy who had him oft whipped and sometimes imprisoned and at last made him fly his native country to his great advancement, but his revenge was so great that he is his Justice Clodpate and calls him a great man and yet in allusion to his name bore three louses rampant for his Arms.

Notwithstanding the archdeacon's difficulty with pronouns and his confusion of Justice Shallow with a character from Shadwell's *Epsom Wells* (1673), his anecdote appeared, with amplifications, in the biographical sketch which Nicholas Rowe printed with his edition of the plays in 1709. Rowe speaks of the ballad that Shakespeare wrote to avenge his 'ill usage' by Lucy,

> and tho' this, probably the first essay of his poetry, be lost, yet it is said to have been so very bitter, that it redoubled the prosecution against him to that degree that he was oblig'd to leave his business and family in Warwickshire, for some time, and shelter himself in London.

Rowe also describes Shakespeare's further revenge:

> Amongst other extravagances, in *The Merry Wives of Windsor* he has made him [Falstaff] a deer-stealer, that he might at the same time remember his Warwickshire persecutor, under the name of Justice Shallow.

The story gathered momentum through succeeding generations, and the first essay of Shakespeare's poetry, which Rowe declared to have been lost, was supplied by eighteenth-century fabrications. Many stanzas of the supposed ballad are now in existence.

A great deal is wrong with this story. There is nothing improbable or discreditable in the charge that Shakespeare went poaching, a sport common in adventurous youth.

> What, hast not thou full often struck a doe,
> And borne her cleanly by the keeper's nose?
>
> *TA* II i 93.

Probably Shakespeare had. But it is less probable that he should have reacted to discovery and punishment by composing doggerel so malevolent as to have compelled him to desert his family and take to his heels. The surviving versions of the ballad are not of a nature that a great landowner would have needed to take very seriously; nor do they suggest the authorship of a major poet. But this tale of a literary revenge, always a popular theme, gained a little colour from the early scenes of *The Merry Wives of Windsor*, where Justice Shallow not only accuses Falstaff of poaching his deer but is made the victim of the ancient and disreputable pun on *louse* and *luce*. The luce was a pike and frequently an emblem in heraldry. Sir Thomas Lucy bore three in his arms, and Shallow a dozen: which was enough to prompt many early commentators to identify the scene (*MWW* I i) as a further paying-off of an old score. If so, Shakespeare waited long enough for this second revenge as the play was written ten or twelve years after his departure from Stratford, and he had neglected the opportunities available in the presence of Sir William Lucy, an ancestor of Sir Thomas, in *1 Henry VI* or of the serving-wench Luce in *Comedy of Errors*. The Shallow episode has been convincingly explained by Professor Leslie Hotson's discovery, in *Shakespeare versus Shallow*, that William Gardiner, with whom Shakespeare had some sort of quarrel, was married to a Frances Luce, or Lucy, and quartered the Lucy arms. But the pun was a hardy annual on the Elizabethan stage and is unlikely to have made much impression.

In any case the deer-stealing tradition does not stand up to the test of fact.[7] In Shakespeare's youth Lucy had no park. His grandson was licensed to enclose a park in 1618, but Lucy himself brought venison to his table from his wife's estate in Worcestershire. Nor were the alleged penalties permissible in law. Shakespeare was not a homeless vagabond and therefore could not have been punished summarily. If then he was tried by established forms of law, Lucy could not have sat in judgment in a suit to which he was party; and anyway whipping was not a statutory punishment for poaching. Finally, Shakespeare was not by habit so unsubtle as to ridicule in the fatuous person of Justice Shallow a sober knight who was the friend of Ralegh and Sidney, high sheriff of his county, a weighty voice in the Commons and twice host to the Queen on her costly progresses at the expense of her loyal subjects. Lucy would have been a dangerous target, but if Shakespeare had wished to strike, his aim would have been more accurate.

Depriving a tradition of its particulars does not necessarily deprive it of its essential truth. Many writers have felt that Shakespeare's youth may have been somewhat shiftless and unsatisfactory. It is possible that he turned restlessly from one occupation to another, meanwhile indulging in adventures of which the deer-stealing legend, or even the seduction of

7 For an exhaustive demolition see J.S.Smart, *Shakespeare: Truth and Tradition*, 1928: a pioneering work in the exploding of various Shakespeare myths.

virgins in the woods by Shottery, may be sufficing symbols. An impulse towards poetry must have been present in him from the beginning, and perhaps Stratford was not the place for its full expression. As always, we should be wary of reading too much into random statements in the plays, especially as Shakespeare here may only be echoing the frustrations of young men of higher families whom he met when he first went to London, but an early comedy, *The Two Gentlemen of Verona*, seems to make a plea for young men whom ambition drives into a larger world:

> Some to the wars, to try their fortune there;
> Some to discover islands far away;
> Some to the studious universities.

TGV I iii 8.

The play opens with a call to adventure:

> Home-keeping youths have ever homely wits...
> I rather would entreat thy company
> To see the wonders of the world abroad,
> Than, living dully sluggardis'd at home,
> Wear out thy youth with shapeless idleness.

TGV I i 2.

At the end of his career Shakespeare makes an old shepherd exclaim:

> I would there were no age between sixteen[8] and three-and-twenty, or that youth would sleep out the rest; for there is nothing in the between but getting wenches with child, wronging the ancientry, stealing, fighting.

WT III iii 60.

Although we do not have to take this literally as the poet's confession of his own misdeeds, his references to man's adolescent years are usually touched with a sense of frustration and wasted opportunity. This may have no significance whatever, or it may reflect remembrance of a choice he had once to make himself. Youth's a stuff will not endure. But the warning goes deeper than that. The fleeting years, he seems to say, will pass unprofitably if spent no farther than at home, where small experience grows. There is a decision to be made, a nettle to be grasped, or it is too late.

His own decision may have been impulsive or long matured. He may have seen the great Mystery cycle at Coventry, performed for the last time in 1579, or attended the revels at Kenilworth, to which the populace were admitted, when Leicester entertained the Queen in 1575. Minstrels,

---

8 The Folio reads 'ten', and the emendation is typical of the literal-mindedness of editors who do not trust their author. 'Ten' would be a deliberate comic exaggeration in keeping with the speaker's character.

jugglers, acrobats and mummers performed at the Stratford fairs, and the town became a popular 'date' for the larger professional companies. After the Queen's and Worcester's Men came in 1569, when John Shakespeare was bailiff, twenty-two similar licences were issued in the next eighteen years. At any time there might have been a vacancy for a stage-struck young man who talked with the actors in the taverns.

Two other theories have been promoted to account for his entering the professional theatre. One has identified him with a William Shakeshafte who in 1581 was mentioned in the will of Alexander Houghton, of Lea in Lancashire. Houghton kept a company of players and musicians, and he recommended Shakeshafte to heirs who had similar theatrical interests. But there are many objections to this identification[9], not least that Shakespeare never shows any familiarity with the Lancashire countryside. Stratford and London and the Cotswolds come alive in the plays with a sharpness of detail that insists upon personal acquaintance, but if he ever went north of the Trent, it has left no mark upon his poetry. Of the distant strongholds of Scroop and Percy and the warrior barons of the north he writes only as one who has read of them in the chronicles.

The second theory is that he went away with Lord Berkeley's company, who played in Stratford in 1581 and the two following years. This is more attractive because of the Cotswold connection that comes out so strongly in *Richard II* and *Henry IV,* but the drawback, as also to the theory that puts him in Lancashire before and after 1581, is that his domestic history makes it unlikely that he was for long away from Stratford in the early eighties when he was wooing Anne Hathaway — maybe Anne Whateley too—, marrying and begetting a family. If he was ever resident in Lord Berkeley's household, whether as chorister or player or tutor, it was at an age when most Stratford boys were at school, or else much later in his career.

The most persuasive suggestion, although unproven, is that he left with the professionals in 1587. Five companies came to Stratford that year, and the two strongest, Leicester's and the Queen's, were in difficulties. Leicester disrupted his troupe when he took some of them for his entertainment when he commanded an English force in the Netherlands in 1585-7. The misfortunes of the Queen's Men were less predictable and perhaps more recent. When they were playing at Thame in the summer of 1587, a quarrel broke out between William Knell, their leading straight actor, and another of the company, John Towne. In the fracas Knell was mortally wounded. Did they recruit a replacement when they moved on to Stratford?[10]

9   See Schoenbaum, *op.cit.,* 112-15.

10   See M.Eccles, *Shakespeare in Warwickshire,* 82-3. It is acknowledged that the flaw in this appealing conjecture is that the Stratford records do not give the precise date of the Queen's Men's visit to Stratford. It may have preceded their doom-laden visit to Thame. But the incident is otherwise interesting on two counts. This sort of violence, common enough in the

In this unsatisfactory state we must leave the fragmentary account of Shakespeare's youth. We do not know when or how or why he left his home. The certain facts are few, and the illumination that they shed is often puzzling; the traditions are contradictory and in their detail demonstrably false; and the evidence to be inferred from the plays is to be trusted only when it betrays a steady and recurrent knowledge or conviction. At some time he decided that he would be no longer 'dully sluggardis'd at home' and entered the theatre. We may suspect that his father's strange intransigence made his home not a happy one to live in, and possibly this was the strongest motive in his decision to leave it; or maybe he could not stand having babies around the place, mewling and puking in the nurse's arms. Most of the great questions go unanswered. We should like to know for certain about his schooling, his first ventures in earning a living, his reputation among his fellow-townsmen as a boy; it would be reassuring if we could lay for ever the oddly persistent ghost of Anne Whateley; we would know something of the women whose voices are never heard, Mary Shakespeare and Anne Hathaway. Above all, we should like some insight — a Wordsworthian *Prelude*, for example — into the thoughts and preoccupations of his mind throughout these years; for not the least of the Shakespearean mysteries is that one of the great creative geniuses of the world apparently wrote little or nothing until he was approaching twenty-five.

Although for a time he left it, Stratford and its surrounding fields and woodland remained a dominant influence in his life. 'He was wont to go to his native country once a year,' Aubrey says. Probably his visits became more frequent, and for the last five years of his life, if not for longer, he again became a resident, visiting London only when he must. As soon as he had money to spare, he began to invest in land and houses in Stratford. The chief end of his earthly ambitions, more compelling than the 'fame that all hunt after in their lives,' was to provide his descendants with a patrimony in the town where he was born.

In a sense this man whose mind was as broad as the universe remained provincial all his days. All his larger affections were bounded in the little town whose background he portrayed in *The Merry Wives of Windsor*. Page and Ford were typical citizens of the Elizabethan provincial town, with their warehouses and small estates, their sport with hawk and hound, their lively, well-dressed wives (who, be it noticed, could read and write), the small son at school and the friendly, slightly patronizing relationship with the parson-schoolmaster. Whatever else Shakespeare learned from friends and books about other social groups, this was the norm to which all his characters in some part belonged. He is always betraying his own origins and affinities by putting into the mouths of princes and noblemen the sentiments and turns

---

acting profession, did not occur in Shakespeare's company during his association with it; and Knell's widow married John Heminges, whom we shall meet again.

of thought appropriate to the Tudor middle-class. It is not only the unprivi-
leged characters who utter the earthly wisdom of the country town, the great
ones do it too. The Capulets, persons of much consequence in Verona,
harass their flustered servants like anxious Stratford housewives: 'Hold, take
these keys, and fetch more spices, nurse'; 'Sirrah, fetch drier logs'; 'Sirrah,
go hire me twenty cunning cooks'; 'Look to the baked meats, good Angelica:
spare not the cost.' Desdemona's father was a senator of Venice, a much
greater man than Master Ford or Master John Shakespeare, but it was many
days before she had leisure from her household chores to listen to the end of
Othello's story 'whereof she had by parcels something heard.'

> This to hear
> Would Desdemona seriously incline;
> But still the house-affairs would draw her thence;
> Which ever as she could with haste dispatch,
> She'd come again.
>
> *Oth* I iii 145.

The picture is not so much of a senator's daughter as of Mary Shakespeare
hurrying through her household work to listen to the solemn fancies of her
eldest son.

From Stratford came the experience and the values that Shakespeare
carried with him throughout his life. He saw there the bustle of the market,
the ducking-stool, the pillory, the vagrants whipped and branded at the
High Cross; he knew of friends brought to suffering by fires and floods and
plague; through them he felt the impermanence of wealth, the insolence of
office, the hatefulness of persecution and man's countless inhumanities to
man. From friends and neighbours he even borrowed names to give his
characters: Bates, Court and Williams all come in the Stratford records at
this time, and a William Fluellen and a George Bardolph were cited as
recusants in the very list that contained his father's name in 1592.

In the farms and villages beyond the town he found 'good yeomen whose
limbs were made in England.' Tom dragging logs across the frozen snow to
the low-ceilinged kitchen where greasy Joan keeled her pot, the country
hospitality immortalized in the sheep-shearing revels in *The Winter's Tale*,
for which the shepherd's boy set out to buy

> three pound of sugar, five pound of currants, rice...
> I must have saffron to colour the warden pies, mace...
> nutmegs, seven; a race or two of ginger — but that I may beg: four pound of
> prunes, and as many of raisins o' the sun:
>
> *WT* IV iii 40.

and the mistress of the house was

> both pantler, butler, cook,
> Both dame and servant: welcomed all, served all:
> Would sing her song and dance her turn.

WT IV iv 56.

These people and their lives he observed too faithfully ever to sentimentalize them or, at the other extreme, belittle them with easy satire.

Stratford, then, counted for much in Shakespeare's life and writing, and critics no longer suppose that his origins were primitive. Nor was he the only citizen of his day to move into the larger world and make a name elsewhere. Among men who were contemporaries of his father or himself, Richard Field went off at the age of fifteen to apprentice himself to a London printer, married his master's widow and put up his own sign; it was he who printed *Venus and Adonis* and *The Rape of Lucrece*. Abraham Sturley, a doughty Puritan who studied under Cartwright, was a celebrated lawyer and Latinist; Richard Quiney, who corresponded in Latin with his eleven-year-old son, and John Sadler both acquired plantations in Virginia; John Lane traded in the far Levant, and the mercer William Smith, whose brother was Bishop of Winchester, was employed by the Czar in Moscow. So it was not particularly unusual for a son of a leading citizen to break away from home and put his fortunes to the test, for there blew in Stratford 'such wind as scatters young men through the world.'

It was less usual for a young man to enter the theatre, which was an ill-regarded profession. Before we take up Shakespeare's story in 1592, we must look at the world into which he was moving. He was to find the London theatre, now organized on a professional basis and slowly establishing itself against its enemies, very different from anything he had previously known. He was to find, too, that the theatre had lately been penetrated by a group of writers who were transforming the possibilities of poetic drama. He was fortunate in his time.

Part II
Shakespeare's Predecessors

Chapter II
Miracle Plays and Moralities

The Vice is of a great kindred; it is well allied.

MM III ii 108.

The English professional theatre originated in the ritual of a Church that was hostile to acting. A hundred years before the Norman Conquest Bishop Ethelwold of Winchester recorded the simple scene when the three Marys come to the tomb to seek the risen Jesus, and in this brief enactment lay the origins of a native liturgical drama that grew independently of similar developments on the continent. From the antiphons sung and humbly acted in church at Christmas and Easter there evolved a series of representations to accompany the supreme events of the Christian story; a veil falling to show the rending in the temple, a piece of linen torn when Christ's raiment was parted, a few simple actions to make more vivid the Crucifixion and the Resurrection. In time the scope of these actions was enlarged to include not only the principal events of Christ's life on earth but also the more dramatic episodes of the Old Testament, such as the Creation, the Flood or the tempting of Eve by the serpent. In due course they took in the whole range of Christian history and the lives of the saints.

Although they were acted in Latin, these episodes told stories well known to the congregation, and they were performed by priests whose vocation instructed them in the mastery of histrionic effect. This unadorned representation of the cardinal events in the Christian story awakened an emotional sympathy, and even a new sort of understanding, in minds which the subtleties of dogma could not penetrate. Its influence, so long as it was held within bounds, must have been almost wholly good. But inevitably the bounds were broken. At the great festivals the congregations crowded into the churches mainly to see the plays, their enthusiasm disturbing the dignity of the service and vulgarizing the purpose for which the plays were presented. Partly to prevent disorder inside the churches, but mainly to accommodate the crowds who came to watch, the plays moved outdoors and were acted on scaffolds specially built in the churchyards. Even this did not satisfy the demands of an ever-growing popularity, and at length, probably in the middle of the thirteenth century, they moved into the streets.

To the streets the clergy did not follow them, or not officially. The Miracle plays[1] passed into the control of the guilds, and thus occurred the first step in the secularization of English drama. The Church, which has cradled all the arts, has allowed them early escape from the cloister to find varied forms in the world beyond, often with the disapproval of the mother who gave them birth. Whatever the backslidings of individual clerics — as men of literacy and learning they obviously continued to write many of the plays, and Chaucer's Joly Absolom 'playeth Herodes in a scaffold high' — the Decretals forbade the clergy to take part in secular performances. The guilds eagerly took up the responsibilities the Church had discarded, and the rivalry between the crafts brought greater elaboration and better equipment. Acting now in English, members of a single guild would present an appropriate incident, the shipwrights building the ark, the mariners playing Noah and his crew, the bakers enacting the Last Supper or the butchers the Crucifixion. In time these incidents were combined into a cycle telling an unbroken story from the Creation to the Judgment.

These cycles were usually presented at Corpus Christi (Whitsun at Chester) and in the more ambitious of them movable stages presented an episode to onlookers assembled at a particular point in the town and then passed on to the next gathering. At York there were twelve stations in different parts of the city, and forty-eight scenes were played and repeated in sixteen hours, the actors being warned to be up and ready by 4.30 in the morning. Texts have survived of thirty-two scenes at Wakefield (the so-called Towneley plays) and thirty-two in the *Ludus Coventriae*, which did not belong to Coventry at all but to some other town, possibly Lincoln. Coventry had its cycle, perhaps the most famous of them all, and two of the ten plays have survived. It is known that Beverley had thirty-six plays, Newcastle and Norwich each twelve, and it is likely that in the fifteenth century every town and all the larger villages had one or more plays — in Essex alone there were twenty-one. Some districts, notably Cornwall, had small amphitheatres, known as rounds. These were open arenas surrounded by wooden stands or banks in which steps were cut to accommodate the spectators.

The stages used for the plays and cycles were called pageants, and in some respects they determined the structure of the permanent theatres when they came to be built in the latter part of the sixteenth century. A spectator of the Chester plays in 1594 thus described the pageants:

> The manner of these plays were every company had his pageant, or part, a high scaffold with two rooms, a higher and a lower, upon four wheels. In the lower they apparelled themselves, and in the higher room they played, being all open on the top, that all beholders might hear and see them.

1 Miracle plays were also known as Mystery plays, not because the craftsmen who performed them were members of a mystery or trade but because 'Mystery' was a word applied to certain sacramental rites of the Christian religion or to incidents in the lives of the saints believed to have mystical significance.

The detail varied, but in general the pageants consisted of simple platforms with a tent at the back from which the actors made their appearance, and, underneath, the tiring-house where they changed, since there was considerable 'doubling' of parts. The more elaborate stages had roofs from which 'angels' descended by ladders, and in all of them the tiring-house also represented hell.

The method of these plays was a homely realism spiced with comedy. In telling the Bible story the performers added topical detail and dialogue in which they ignored artistic decorum in favour of incidents reflecting the habits and outlook of their own daily lives. The shepherds of Bethlehem talked as shepherds do talk, complaining of the weather and (in the Towneley cycle) expressing a liking for Ely ale; Noah becomes a hen-pecked husband ruled by a termagant wife; Joseph is a real carpenter, worried by high taxation and disposed, as a cuckolded husband, to a caustic view of marriage. In one of the Towneley plays on the Nativity the peasant Mak steals a sheep from the waiting shepherds and, to avoid discovery, his wife swaddles it in a cradle and vows she has just given birth. Faithful craftsmanship is honoured in God's instructions to Noah in a York pageant given by the shipwrights. The ark is to be made of boards,

> Thus thriftily and not over thin,
> Look that thy seams be subtly seen
> And nailed well, that they not twin:
> Thus I devised it should have been;

and Noah promises that

> It shall be clinched each ilk and deal,
> With nails that are both noble and new.

Even a murderer is allowed his kinship in a Chester play. Cain enters with his plough and says,

> A tiller I am, and so will be;
> As my daddy hath taught it me
> I will fulfil his lore.

Such characters were more convincing on the stage than those who came from the higher walks of life. Kings, high priests and lawyers spoke in language as stiff and unreal as their conventional costume: and for the supernatural the guildsmen's imagination did not stretch beyond the figures shown in gargoyles, images and stained-glass windows. Sacred characters wore contemporary costumes indicative of their status: angels in surplices, apostles in rich gowns and gilt beards, the Almighty in a tiara, a white cope and gloves.

It would be wrong, however, to dispose of the Miracle plays as crude, inartistic stuff little deserving the name of drama. It is true that dramatic conflict was only formal, because there was never any doubt under whose banner a man appeared, nor questioning why one was good and another bad. The causes of human behaviour were not investigated, and character appeared, unsubtly, in unmistakable colours. Again, a play was just a series of incidents, lacking dramatic structure; and such emotion or tension as it achieved was either accidental or inseparable from the story. The humour was boisterous and physical, and the dialogue, mostly in rhyming doggerel and erratic metres, had small savour of style or rhetoric.

But such criticisms do not state the whole matter. The Miracle plays may have outraged most of the principles of artistic decorum, but when Isaac went wonderingly to the sacrifice or the Blessed Mary lay in sorrow at the foot of the cross, they achieved tenderness and pathos in their own despite. They unfolded the testament story in a language and setting that ordinary folk could associate with their daily lives, and often there was artifice in the seeming simplicity. So strong was the hold of this early dramatic convention that it powerfully influenced the development of a professional drama in the Elizabethan age. The stage itself retained the scaffold structure so familiar in the medieval streets; the actors continued to heighten the illusion by wearing rich and elaborate costume however unsuitable (the craftsman's expenditure of '2d. for God's gloves' or '2s.1d. for the Holy Ghost's coat' would be paralleled time and again in Henslowe's accounts), or by introducing such awesome effects as 'Hell-mouth, the head of a whale with jaws worked by two men, out of which devil boys run'; and tragic and comic effects would still be mixed haphazardly in defiance of the canons of classical playwriting. The shearmen and tailors of Coventry performed a Herod play which Shakespeare himself may have seen as a boy[2] with the generosity that knew that no imperfections are too serious for imagination to amend them.

The last full cycle at Conventry was played in 1580 and the Miracle plays did not survive much longer. Already for more than a hundred years they had been losing favour to Morality plays, Interludes and other manifestations of an astonishing theatrical energy. 'Mumming' is an embracing word that contains, beside the more familiar sorts of dramatic production, the sumptuous rituals of the tournament, the drama of the lawyers and the schools, the folk plays given in the villages and the more ambitious festival productions in the towns, the pageants[3] staged to welcome royal processions,

2 Cf. *Hen V* III iii 41 and *Ham* III ii 16.

3 In Tudor times pageants were tableaux or mimic entertainments usually presented in honour of a royal progress or on celebrations like the Lord Mayor's Show. Vehicles resembling the pageant carts of the Miracle plays were used, and in water pageants, especially popular on the Thames, boats were used instead. Fireworks often added to the excitement. Londoners loved their City pageants, which were allegorical in content and required elaborate staging. Dekker, Middleton and even the fastidious Jonson were among the dramatists who

or the 'disguisings' popular among the courtly classes. The Muscovite caper in *Love's Labour's Lost* (V ii) is a typical 'disguising'; 'maskers' come to dance with Capulet (*RJ* I v), and in order that he may dance with Mistress Anne, Henry VIII and his friends come to Wolsey's banquet 'habited like shepherds' (I iv). The highly formal speeches at the barriers before the duel in *Richard II* (I iii) may have been the practice of an earlier age, but by Tudor times the joust had added a wealth of artistic embellishment to its cumbrous mimic warfare. The champions now fought according to a script based on an allegorical situation, perhaps defending the Church against the infidel or wrestling with the seven deadly sins. Rich costumes, music and scenic devices made this a very spectacular and costly entertainment in which the stage staff were able to display their virtuosity. At a tournament in 1501, at the wedding of Prince Arthur, the knights entered the arena in portable tents of which one represented 'a red dragon, led by a great giant having a great tree in his hand', another 'a mountain of green with many rocks, trees, stones and marvellous herbs on the side, and on the height a goodly young lady in her hair, pleasantly beseen.' At an indoor entertainment on the following day 'a castle of singing boys' was drawn into the hall by two lions, a hart and an elk; each animal propelled by a man in its forelegs and another 'in the hinder part, secretly hid and apparelled, nothing of them seen but their legs, which were disguised after the proportion and kind of beasts that they were in.' Although this has little to do with drama in the higher sense, it has its distant affinity with Snug the joiner in the role of lion and it suggests the variousness of the Tudor appetite for theatrical shows.

The Morality developed from the Miracle play in response to the need for works that required fewer actors and less elaborate staging, while retaining the essential quality of seeking a moral purpose. Medieval drama was faithful to its origins as an offshoot of the liturgy, and the Morality was initially a personified sermon imparting a doctrinal message instead of just telling a story as the Miracle plays did. The Middle Ages could force a jest from most things, even from the Devil himself, but they could never make a jest of death. Thus the Morality recorded man's passage from the cradle to the grave, reminding him that the toothless skull was the favour to which he must ultimately come, that all earthly goods are 'contrary to the love everlasting' and cannot save him. During his mortal journey personified abstractions struggle for possession of his soul. The usual pattern was for the 'hero' to forget the good advice given him in infancy by such characters as Temperance, Truth and Fortitude, and fall victim to the enticements of various of the deadly sins; until after a timely repentance in the closing stages, an embodiment of Mercy or Contrition or Good Deeds takes up his cause at the throne of judgment and has some success in

wrote scenarios, but Shakespeare was not. His nearest contribution was the Pageant of the Nine Worthies in *Love's Labour's Lost*, which in its modest way was typical of the mode.

mitigating the trials of purgatory. The best-known of the Moralities is *Everyman*, a fifteenth-century translation of a Dutch play, wherein Everyman is brought by Knowledge to an acknowledgment of past misdeeds and the need for repentance; and then, after all his mortal powers have gradually deserted him, only his Good Deeds remain to intercede at the final Judgment. The theme was the Psychomachia, the battle for the soul, which goes at least as far back as Prudentius, a contemporary of Augustine and the first great poet of the Latin Church.

The earliest surviving English Morality was *The Castle of Perseverance*, dated about 1425. Tempted first by Luxuria, Humanum Genus is saved by Poenitentia and brought in safety to the castle; there he is tempted again by Avarice and finally only Pity and Mercy save him from perdition. The earlier plays retained this ethical and sermonizing purpose, but with the growing secularism of the drama of the sixteenth century, the comment, while still keeping the allegorical mode, became increasingly social and political. *Respublica* (1553), possibly by Nicholas Udall, was a Morality on the abuse of power and the Protestant vandalism under Edward VI, and Avarice, 'alias Policy', is named as 'the Vice of the play'. The Vice became the Morality play's most significant legacy to the later drama. Originally just one of the misleaders of youth, he came to be the mainspring of the action and, appearing now in his own name and not as an abstraction, he gave the plays a new comic emphasis. Fingering the dagger which was his emblem, he established a quick rapport with the audience by his shameless avowal of his mischievous purposes; and although the proprieties were satisfied by his eventual overthrow, he was a more robust and theatrically effective figure than the shadowy personifications around him. His language became coarser and his deceptions more ingenious, and it is significant of his new importance that in later Moralities his was the only part that could not be doubled.

Shakespeare acknowledges the potency of the Vice in his very first tragedy, *Titus Andronicus*, where Aaron soon reveals his unscrupulous intentions: 'Away with slavish weeds and servile thoughts!' Richard III's sardonic pleasure in his own intrigues communicates itself to the audience, and his characterization gives shape and purpose to what otherwise might have been only a chronicle. The Morality structure of the play is further established when Richmond appears as the saviour of the much-abused Commonweal: 'Make us thy ministers of chastisement.' In terms of the same tradition Falstaff is properly rejected, however much it may offend us. There are specific references in *Henry IV* which identify him as 'the tutor and the feeder of my riots', 'villainous and abominable misleader of youth', reverend Vice, grey Iniquity, father Ruffian, Vanity in years. Such too was Riot, the unprincipled rogue in *Youth*, an allegory acted in about 1520 and popular enough to have been printed in five editions before Shakespeare's birth, so that he is likely to have read it even if he did not see it on the stage. For Falstaff, however, he significantly reversed the common formula. Whereas most Morality 'heroes' are corrupted through their own folly and weakness, Hal makes it clear from the first that he recognizes his would-be seducers and will indulge them only for as long as it pleases him:

> I know you all, and will awhile uphold
> The unyok'd humour of your idleness.
>
> *1 Hen IV* I ii 217.

This alters the whole balance by almost making Falstaff the victim of a Morality abstraction called Calculation; and so we may feel sorry for him if we wish.

Shakespeare's most surprising and unexpected projection of the Vice is Iago. It is unexpected because by 1604 he was an experienced playwright, accustomed to presenting characters in a human and naturalistic mode, and Iago is a throwback to an earlier convention. In *Shakespeare and the Allegory of Evil* Professor Bernard Spivack has persuasively demonstrated that to regard Iago as the Vice is the only explanation of the 'motiveless malignity' that has puzzled Coleridge and many other critics. There is no moral explanation of his conduct because he is not a moral being. Rational motives are for other people, and the motives with which he chooses to beguile the audience merely show his talent for comic improvization. It does not occur to him to plead them when his villainy is discovered. His frankness and jocularity and his readiness to take the audience into his confidence are all qualities of the Vice, and *Othello* is a 'hybrid' play because Iago is a denial of the human principles that control the lives of the other characters.

It was not the only play of its kind, because the Morality structure persisted long after a more realistic convention had established itself. In a play by Dekker and Ford, *The Sun's Darling*, written in about 1623, Raybright rejects the innocent pleasures offered by Spring, Health, Delight and others, and is led by Humour and Folly to the pursuit of sensual pleasure; and finally the Sun, in passing judgment on this wasted life, takes occasion for a generalized commentary on the doomed perversity of human kind. Chiefly, however, the allegorical mode was used to stress the importance of good education and filial obedience and to denounce the covetousness of monopolists, 'projectors' and confidence men. The context became less abstract and moral, more specific and social, with harsh words for citizens who became the dupes of these new tempters. The message of *A Looking-Glass for London and England* (*c.*1590), by Greene and Lodge, is that London, like Nineveh in the play, must repent. In Jonson's *The Devil is an Ass* (1616) the old Vice Iniquity is refused permission by Satan to visit London because his outmoded deceptions would be unavailing in the wickedness of the age: 'You are not for the manner, nor the times.'[4]

The Interlude grew up alongside the Morality and gradually superseded it as the allegorical and homiletic element weakened and the emphasis moved from edification to entertainment. On occasions the Interlude occupied a digestive break during the long medieval banquets. Henry Medwall's *Fulgens and Lucrece* (*c*.1494) was originally played in two parts to fill two such intervals; and in *Sir Thomas More* (written in about 1593 but describing what might have happened in the time of Henry VIII) the play is broken off while the guests go to the feast, with a promise that it shall be resumed later (although in fact it is not). Interludes may also have been short pieces performed in the intervals of longer plays; or the term may simply indicate a *ludus*[5] in which two or more men take part. These are obscure matters, and for practical purposes it is probably safe as well as convenient to regard the Interlude as any sort of play that marked the transition from the Moralities to the Elizabethan drama, although it may be interchangeable with either.

Usually it was shorter than the Morality, about 1000 lines, and initially it was more commonly performed in courts, private houses and colleges than in open spaces; its tone was secular and comic, and it was written in doggerel verse; but although human types and figures became more prominent, allegorical personification never entirely disappeared and the two kinds might be found in the same play. Quince's version of *Pyramus and Thisbe* shows that Interludes were acted by humble rustics as well as by the more accomplished troupes kept by royal and noble patrons, and it indicates the technical problems encountered in these amateur presentations. On festal occasions there was a wide choice of such entertainments, for Theseus chose Quince's 'device' in preference to three others which Philostrate, at least, rated more highly. Although consisting only of 'four men and a boy', the more professional players in *Sir Thomas More* offered a selection of seven Interludes, and the one chosen, *The Marriage of Wit and Wisdom*, contains a Vice called Inclination, played by the leading member of the company. Things did not always go right even for the more experienced players, and More himself speaks the lines when one of the actors proves to have forgotten his beard and has to go to the costumier to fetch it. These two episodes were written from the retrospective viewpoint of the Elizabethan professional theatre, but the satire is affectionate and there is mention of the importance of having a kindly patron. 'I would there were more of his kind,' the beardless actor says of More: 'he loves our quality. And yet he's a learned man, and knows what the world is' (III iii 339).

4 For this play see also p. 88.

5 For the close association between 'play' and 'game' see V.A.Kolve, *The Play Called Corpus Christi*, especially pp. 8-32.

John Heywood, a court musician during the 1520s, wrote two of the earliest surviving Interludes, *The Play of the Weather* and *The Four Ps*, full of rough humour. Their didactic element is so unobtrusive that they are secular comedies rather than Moralities. *Thersites*, perhaps by Udall, was played at court in 1537 to celebrate the birth of the Prince Edward. It seems an odd choice for an event so long awaited by the hopeful father, the theme being that the loudest boasters are not always the best doers; but despite the moralizing bent of this message, the spirit again is comic in its exposure of the *miles ingloriosus*. But in other extant plays of the earlier sixteenth century the Morality element is almost unadulterated, as in *Wit and Science*, written by their master, John Redford, for the St Paul's choir-school. John Bale, born in sea-threatened Dunwich, was a moralizer too, and among his copious polemical writings was *King Johan* (*c.* 1539). Once a Carmelite monk, Bale had been converted to the new outlook, and his play was primarily an exercise in psychopathic Protestantism depicting John as a morning star of the Reformation and his country's champion against Rome. In Morality fashion John protects 'the widow England' (she is widowed of the true faith), while Verity defends his own name against generations of traducers. But a more realistic method keeps on turning the abstractions into real people. Thus Sedition becomes Stephen Langton, Dissimulation becomes the scheming monk of Swinstead, the Pope takes over as Usurped Power and Private Wealth turns into Cardinal Pandulph. For all its humourless absurdity, it is possible to see here the first English historical play, or at any rate a powerful transitional influence. Transition was taken a stage further in *Respublica*, which was a reply or antidote to Bale. Although it has the Vice Avarice and other abstractions, it is a much maturer play with an eye for comic situations. The propaganda is conveyed through the dialogue, not by declamation, and the abstractions are fleshed as differentiated characters.

It has been suggested that between 1540 and 1580 the native drama changed from being mainly allegorical to being mainly secular, but such progress was too erratic, and too many plays have been lost, for any generalization to be very secure. *Dr Faustus*, the first great English tragedy, was a Morality when the form was supposedly dead. With so many dramatic forms and themes and influences, when Shakespeare came to London almost anything was still possible, and it was as easy to be a bad playwright as a good one. Flat sermonizing might accompany, within a single play, attempts to probe the nature of sin and suffering and achieve a proper tragic mode. Subtler comic plotting and characterization would still lapse into the bawdy knockabout that gave the stage a bad name among its enemies, aesthetic as well as clerical.

But changes there were. Metrical experiment substituted quatrains, with alternating rhymes, for the laboured fourteeners, and shorter lines meant faster and more dramatic speech. The small casts of the Interludes, with many parts being doubled, meant that fewer abstract figures were paraded, so that the dramatic focus was sharper and the message more explicit. The Vice lost some of his farcical qualities and developed into a more consistent villain, the embodiment of evil rather than of mischief. A proclamation in 1559 warning playwrights off religious controversy diverted their attention to the secular evils of the day and the creation of recognizable social types. Finally, the native drama was influenced by the drama of the schools. In the process of infiltration and absorption that then followed, the popular theatre responded to new themes and treatments and acquired, up to a point, some necessary disciplines, but it rejected much that was alien in thought and manners. Fundamentally it preserved its own character and it refused to submit to academic pedantry.

Chapter III
Seneca and Others

O, this learning, what a thing it is!

TS I ii 160.

At the Renaissance English drama went to school. In medieval times it had evolved without benefit of theory, unaware of what had been written about acting during the classical period. Although there was a strong dramatic tradition with roots in the public taste, there were no good medieval plays and not much speculation about drama's function and technique. But when Humanism promoted the study of drama in the schools and proclaimed, within limits, its social and educational possibilities, the universities, the Inns of Court, the grammar-schools and the choir-schools began to evolve a drama, based on classical models, that was much more formal and self-conscious than the haphazard productions of the public stages. It was in this academic company that Polonius acted Julius Caesar, and perhaps that does not much commend it; but as far as its influence was allowed to extend, class-ical drama would have a salutary influence on the professional theatre, disci-plining its worst extravagances, imposing some sort of unity, and teaching useful lessons about plot, characterization and style.

In spite of Plato's well-known condemnation of drama, Renaissance Humanism was favourable to it as an activity which displayed man in rela-tion with his fellows and his destiny, reflected on the sources of his conduct and warned him against wrongdoing. Erasmus recommended the study of plays, especially those of Plautus, Terence and Seneca, for the moral lessons to be drawn from them and the emotional stimulus that relieves the mind 'from sordid cares'. Pleading the theatre's social function, Sir Thomas Elyot argued in *The Governor* (1531) that so far from being 'a doctrine of ribaldry', comedy was a mirror of life 'wherein evil is not taught, but discovered', and the ever-ready 'promptness of youth to vice' discouraged by example. In *Jephtha*, a Senecan tragedy written in Greek in 1546, John Christopherson, Master of Trinity College, Cambridge, declared the glories of tragedy to be its grandeur of style, the wisdom to be learned from its *sententiae*, and the warnings to be derived from the fall of great men from power and prosperity.

For a short period in the sixteenth century there even emerged a religious drama based on secular themes. In part this was a reaction against

Renaissance secularism and its enthusiasm for classical models, but primarily it was an attempt by the champions of Protestantism to use the theatre for doctrinal propaganda, as in Bale's fantasy about King John. The Morality form lay ready to hand as an instrument of religious conversion as well as ethical instruction. Bucer's *De Regno Christi*, which would have turned England into a Genevan theocracy, recommended the Bible as a source of countless good plots replete with moral edification. George Buchanan, tutor to the young King James, also saw possibilities in religious drama, but except in the numerous plays written round the theme of the Prodigal Son, it never took hold of the popular theatre. The alliance of stage and pulpit was unnatural and short-lived. It suited neither Tudor policy nor Calvinist inclination. Once she had made her settlement of religion, Elizabeth forbade playwrights to meddle with themes which might arouse doctrinal bitterness; and the next generation of Protestants mistrusted secular learning even when it might serve their own interests. Armed with Calvin's words of condemnation, the Puritans launched an attack on the Elizabethan theatre that nearly overwhelmed it.

While Humanist approval gave drama some intellectual respectability, the crucial influence on its development was the rediscovery of classical technique. The makers of medieval plays had known nothing of Aristotle's doctrine of *mimesis* which is the essence of creative art. *Mimesis* does not mean the literal imitation of a thing, which is barren and lifeless. It rather means representation, in the sense, for instance, in which music represents something in symbols of its own being. Art's concern is with the thing itself, not with its outward form. What matters is not this outward form but the artist's feeling about it, not the sunset as it appears to the naked eye but the sunset which Turner felt ought to be. Thus the truest poetry, as Touchstone said in another context, is 'the most feigning'. 'And for the authentical truth of either person or action, who (worth the respecting) will expect it in a poem, whose subject is not truth, but things like truth?' In these words (in the dedication to *The Revenge of Bussy d'Ambois*) Chapman stated what Aristotle meant by *mimesis*; and when a playwright could write thus about his work, drama had come a long way from the crude episodic realism of the Middle Ages.

The Renaissance brought to light also the classical conception that it was the business of comedy to occupy itself with types. In *De Arte Poetica* Horace wrote that every category of mankind has its professional form in which it should be represented on the stage; this having been the practice of Plautus and Terence, who derived it from their Greek originals. Thus every comedy had a selection of stock characters—the sighing lover, the cantankerous old father, the cunning servant, the braggart soldier, the scholar pedant and so forth. This enabled the plot to get swiftly into action without time being spent on establishing the characters. These types were instantly recognizable, their function was known and invariable, and they pandered to the comforting notion that certain people always behave in a certain way. The pattern was simple: in a setting that might reflect on contemporary manners the disagreeable characters came under the lash of ridicule and in the end the young lovers found that they had not sighed in vain. Because men's vices were thus exhibited for laughter, comedy was able to claim the ethical purpose of censuring folly in so pleasurable a way that the lesson was all the likelier to be effective. Through their affinity with the personified abstractions of the Morality the stock figures of classical comedy, revived in the Italian Renaissance, soon flourished on English soil, and the tradition persisted throughout Elizabethan drama. On a creative writer the convention could be cramping, and Shakespeare, although he used it frequently, was never at ease with it. Like much else that he inherited, he adapted and transformed it. Whereas Pistol and Fluellen are recognizable examples of the *miles gloriosus*, it is only one of the elements that go to the making of Falstaff. Shakespeare's fully realized characters never submit to a simple classification. They are themselves alone.

The classical theorists strove also to impose on the developing English drama the approved doctrines of the unities and decorum. Aristotle is popularly believed to have insisted that a play should observe the three unities of place, time and action; and Dryden, rebuking Shakespeare, brought the story of Antony and Cleopatra within this discipline. In its most austere form, as practised in the classical drama of France, this doctrine requires that a play should be localized in a single city; that the events represented should occupy no longer time than the play takes to perform, with no lowering of the curtain to indicate the passing of days or years; and there should be no sub-plot to diversify or reinforce the central theme. In fact neither Aristotle nor the Athenian playwrights observed these laws strictly, and pedantic adherence to them imposes intolerable restraints on the writer. As Johnson pointed out in the preface to his edition of Shakespeare, 'he that can take the stage at one time for the palace of the Ptolemies, may take it in half an hour for the promontory of Actium'; and as for time, it is 'of all modes of existence, most obsequious to the imagination'. In its milder and more acceptable form the doctrine is simply a plea for artistic discipline free of a jumble of episodes sprawling over time and space and of irrelevant sub-plots and comic interpolations that weaken the prevailing mood of the play. A play must preserve a unity of mood or impression, what Coleridge called its 'predominant passion'. In this respect the public stages had much to learn.

The ancient writers' plea for decorum was similar in purpose. Decorum means, roughly, that both play and characters shall be recognizable for what they are. A play that sets out to tell a tragic story in a serious way should continue to be serious until its end, and not diminish into farce like *The Jew of Malta* or resolve into an implausible 'happy ending' like *Measure for Measure*. Likewise, a character should use language appropriate to his status and should not stray beyond the limits prescribed by his essential qualities, a garrulous old man turn statesman or a boastful coward become a phlegmatic man of action. Again, if pressed to academic extremes this is a doctrine that enforces unnatural restraints by forbidding the dramatist to deal in the variety and unexpectedness of life and confining him to rigid categories of individual and event. But it has to be viewed in the light of the excesses which in the sixteenth century the purists were seeking to moderate: inconsistent and irresponsible characterization, the sacrifice of plausibility to theatrical tricks, the gallimaufry of tragedy and comedy, violence and farce.

If drama was to make good its claim to be the mirror of life, then its people must behave as people do behave, and display, as John Fletcher put it, only such 'actions and passions...as may agree with their natures'. In the Prologue to *Damon and Pythias* (*c*.1564) Richard Edwards said that if comedy's business is to delight, and by delighting to instruct, then the playwright must 'frame each person so that by his common talk you may his nature rightly know'. Another dramatist, George Whetstone, said that drama had a bad name because writers lacked judgment. Too much was sacrificed just to raise a laugh, and in defiance of decorum there was no differentiation between characters, and 'a crow will ill counterfeit a nightingale's sweet verse'. In the Prologue to his *Promos and Cassandra* (1578) Whetstone complained that 'Your Englishman first grounds his work on impossibilities; then in three hours he runs through the world, marries, gets children, makes children men, men to conquer kingdoms, murder monsters, and bringeth gods from heaven and fetcheth devils from hell.'

The dominant figure in the classical vogue was Seneca. Seneca was a Spanish-born philosopher and statesman who lived in Rome in the days of Caligula, Claudius and Nero, and he took refuge in a Stoic philosophy of undefeated despair. Finally Nero tired of him and he was ordered to take his life by opening his veins. This he did with great Socratic courage but without true Socratic detachment: he appeared to be acting a scene from his own plays. His output in philosophical works was vast and he diversified it by writing nine tragedies, sombre works profuse in rhetoric but devoid of poetic quality. In 1559 his *Troas* was translated by Jasper Heywood, John Heywood's son, who later was driven abroad for his religious opinions and became a Jesuit. He translated two more of the tragedies, and during the 1560s there was a spate of translations and 'original' Senecan plays written by English academics. It is likely that many of these were exercises in literary imitation not intended to be acted. Their dedications tended to apologize for the inadequacy of the English tongue to achieve true Senecan sublimity, but they claimed to be exhibiting 'sound matter that beateth

---

1 An extreme view of this occurs in Thomas Rymer's *Short View of Tragedy* (1692). He condemns Shakespeare's portrayal of Iago on the ground that Iago is 'not like other Soldiers of our acquaintance', namely bluff and hearty and genuinely 'the honest Iago'. Because Horace had said that a soldier on the stage should be '*impiger, iracundus, inexorabilis, acer*', so must all soldiers be for evermore.

down sin, loose life, dissolute dealing and unbridled sensuality'.

The appeal of Senecan tragedy to the early Elizabethans is one of the curiosities not only of literary history but of the history of thought and manners. It was congenial to the age in its concentration on the dilemma of the individual, regardless of hour and place. In the turmoil of violence, murder, incest and revenge it was the individual tragedy that mattered. For the hero, wordily dramatizing himself as his fate unfolds, there is no earthly consolation to be had from wealth or power or love or friends; only the resolution which stands undefeated among the wreckage of mortal hopes, the vain defiance of pitiless and crushing destiny. Suffering itself brings no discipline, teaches no lesson, offers neither hope nor reconciliation. All that Stoicism could give its burdened disciples was a pride that rose from the ashes of humiliation to enable the victim to join himself with the universe and there retain his indestructible individuality. '*Medea superest*' finds its echo in 'I am Duchess of Malfi still'.

'*O nos dure sorte creatos.*' The mood which left man with nothing to do but make a mouth at ineluctable destiny was commoner among the early Jacobeans, and if one looks for a reason why it appealed to mid-century academics, possibly the explanation is simply that they were academics. They were more interested in literary form and imitation than in the nature of human existence. To the Jacobeans time seemed to be running down and soon must have a stop, so that their involvement was more immediate and personal. Shakespeare's position, as always, is at once comprehensive and ambiguous. With refinements of his own he was very Senecan in *Titus Andronicus*, but he found no dramatic consequence in the megalomaniac aspirants of Marlowe and Chapman. On the other hand, the individual predicament is the essence of his tragedy: not the causes of it, but the response.

Thematically, then, Senecan tragedy had some correspondence with the medieval view of man's helplessness in his sinful state, so awesomely depicted in the fall of great ones from prosperity to ruin. It was the theme of Lydgate's *Falls of Princes* (c.1430), which he based on Boccaccio's *De Casibus Virorum Illustrium*, and Chaucer stated it in the Prologue to the Monk's Tale:

> Tragedie is to seyn a certeyn storie,
> As olde bookes maken us memorie,
> Of him that stood in greet prosperitee
> And is y-fallen out of heigh degree
> Into miserie, and endeth wrecchedly.

In Seneca such falls are usually due to the operations of a blind fate that is malicious and unpredictable and appears to rule by its own arbitrary laws. When in the middle of the sixteenth century George Cavendish wrote his account of the fall of his master Wolsey, he attributed it to no fault in the man but to 'the wondrous mutability of vain honours'. It happened because fortune at length 'thought she would devise a mean to abate his high port', and Wolsey was Senecan in his acceptance of the inevitable. Only in his readiness to meet death courageously can the individual overcome his fate.

What is surprising is to find such attitudes still current when Humanism had asserted man's personal responsibility for his fortunes. But Seneca also appealed to the academic mind in other ways. His plays were full of *sententiae* — lofty moralizings and aphorisms — and they were written in an elevated, bombastic diction that was a challenge to literary ingenuity. The violence of the theme had to be matched by an appropriate force of rhetorical expression. Other Senecan characteristics were the division of the play into acts; a Chorus to comment on the action and underline the moral; frequent use of stichomythia[2]; the presence of ghosts calling for revenge; and, '*ne pueros coram populo Medea trucidet*', the enaction of horrors off-stage but with a gory account of them given on-stage by messengers introduced for the purpose.

Until the production of the very Senecan *Misfortunes of Arthur* in 1588 this was the general pattern of academic tragedy, and comedy was guided by the principles of Plautus and Terence. But it was only a pattern, not a rigid convention, and even in the relatively few plays of the period that survive there were numerous variations. In its austerest forms the classical vogue was short-lived. The famous passage about Hecuba spoken by the First Player at Elsinore burlesques Alleyn and may also give Shakespeare's idea of what the tragedy of the schools was like. In his preface to Greene's *Menaphon* (1589) Thomas Nashe said that Senecan tragedy yielded 'many good sentences', but the satisfaction to be had from that was 'soon exhausted'. Seneca's imitators might make good use of his technical devices and achieve a passable echo of his sonorous style, but his devitalized tragedies lacked passion and conflict. In real tragedy the hero has something noble about him, and there is some error in himself or his society that makes him, and not chance alone, in some degree responsible for his fate. Superficially Seneca's plays revealed the working of sin and retribution, but with no understanding of what nemesis meant to the Greeks, nor of the hubris that invoked it. Without this spiritual foundation they became mere 'thrillers' of revenge, arousing horror but no tragic pathos.

Closet drama persisted in academic institutions, and from Thomas Legge, Master of Caius College, Cambridge, it produced, apart from Bale's negligible extravaganza, the first English historical play. Elephantine even of its kind, his *Ricardus Tertius* (1579) was in Latin and its fifteen acts took three days to perform. A few dramatists, among them Daniel and Fulke Greville,

---

2 Literally 'line-by-line' dialogue, a device to quicken and intensify the action frequently used in Attic drama, especially in exchanges with the Chorus. Shakespeare used it in his earlier work, e.g. *3 Hen VI* III ii, *R III* IV iv, *CE* III i, *LLL* II i, *KJ* III i.

both scholarly men, remained faithful to classical principles of composition; but neither of these was very successful on the stage, and their work shows what might have become of the theatre if classical precept had not been diluted by public taste. It is difficult to imagine Shakespeare writing for it. What fortunately happened was an instinctive process of cross-fertilization between classical themes and disciplines and the cruder native tradition of the popular stages. A few academics retreated into disapproval of an increasingly professional theatre that existed to entertain and make money, but only conscribed audiences watched their plays. Others used their experience to write for the professionals, no doubt at diminishing cost to their artistic conscience, and at the choir-schools it was the same. At these institutions — Windsor, St Paul's and the Chapel Royal — acting was part of the curriculum, with music naturally integral to the production, and many of their plays were written as well as directed by their masters. Although little of their work has survived, such men as Richard Farrant, Richard Edwards, William Hunnis, John Redford and Sebastian Westcott may have been among the prolific dramatists of the age. As they were writing for boys under training, their work might have been expected to be classical and educational in conception, as indeed it often was. But the boys were too well accustomed to appearing in public shows and pageants to be indifferent to popular demands, and in 1576 Farrant showed his commercial instinct by leasing a theatre in Blackfriars where the boys gave performances for profit. Besides, the boys competed with the professional companies for the privilege of appearing at court, and the Queen was not disposed to sit through *Ricardus Tertius*.

Thus both in comedy and tragedy the classical drama had to adapt itself to popular fashion. In the native tradition the Morality influence was still powerful. Whether the theme was English history or classical legend or Italian romance, the audience expected the moral to be plain and pointed, and at the same time pungently seasoned with farce. The didactic purpose remained although the allegorical element was being assimilated into more realistic settings and would not always be conveyed by personified abstractions. A more recent strain in popular drama was the romance, inspired by the Italian *novelle*. Stories of love and adventure by Boccaccio, Bandello, Giovanni Fiorentino and Cinthio were translated in William Painter's *Palace of Pleasure* (1566) and Geoffrey Fenton's *Tragical Discourses* (1567), books which for many years were a rich quarry for dramatists.[3] The attempt to fuse these romantic tales with other dramatic elements encouraged the growth of tragi-comedy, which to purists was a bastard form. A play, Sidney declared, should not 'match horn-pipes and funerals'. Tragi-comedy is

3 Shakespeare's sources are impossible to trace precisely but there is an apparent debt to Boccaccio for *All's Well that Ends Well*, Bandello for *Much Ado about Nothing* and *Twelfth Night*, Giovanni for *The Merchant of Venice* and Cinthio for *Othello, Measure for Measure* and possibly *Cymbeline*.

difficult stuff to handle because it so easily fails to achieve unity of impression. A somewhat naive definition of it was offered by John Fletcher, one of its most fertile exponents, in the preface to *The Faithful Shepherdess* (1609): 'A tragi-comedy is not so called in respect of mirth and killing, but in respect it wants deaths, which is enough to make it no tragedy, yet brings some near it, which is enough to make it no comedy'. This is not much of a recommendation, and the appalling levity of which tragi-comedy was capable may be illustrated by *Philaster*, which Fletcher wrote with Francis Beaumont in 1611. The basic situation is Hamlet's. A young prince is told by the usurping king to be better-tempered; 'the bravery of his mind' is admired by the populace, who are in arms on his behalf; he is possessed by his dead father's spirit and reminded that he is a king; he is suspected by the court of mental derangement. But in the resolution of the play he solves his problems by marrying the usurper's daughter. The fault of tragi-comedy is so to raise great issues and resolve them by mechanical contrivances. Comedy declines into sentimentality, and tragedy declines into sensationalism. Yet not all tragi-comedy was irresponsible, and after describing it as 'the common mistake of that age', Nicholas Rowe, in the preface to his edition of Shakespeare (1709), admitted that it 'is indeed become so agreeable to the English taste that tho' the severer critics among us cannot bear it, yet the generality of our audiences seem to be better pleas'd with it than with an exact tragedy'. The editors of the First Folio were not being deliberately disingenuous when they divided Shakespeare's plays into comedies, histories and tragedies, but 'tragi-comedy' would be a fitter description of many of them.

With all the conflicting strains seeking accommodation, mention of a few of the surviving plays of the pre-Shakespearean era will show a mingling of styles in 'pastoral-comical, historical-pastoral, tragical-historical, tragical-comical-historical-pastoral'. Even *Gorboduc* (1562), the most celebrated extant play in the Senecan style, was not wholly Senecan. It was written for the Inner Temple by two learned and serious-minded young men, Thomas Norton, who was married successively to a daughter and a niece of Archbishop Cranmer, and Thomas Sackville, later Earl of Dorset. Both were members of the so-called 'Puritan choir' which in the 1560s harried the government over clerical vestments. *Gorboduc* introduced the dumb-show to compensate the want of action by providing spectacles in mime; the plot is taken not from classical legend but from the chronicles of Geoffrey of Monmouth; it develops the idea of tragedy as punishment for individual sin; the explicit conflict of good and evil derives from the Morality; and there is an overt political moral on the dangers of a divided succession. The real importance of *Gorboduc* is that like George Gascoigne's Senecan *Jocasta* (1566), it was written in blank verse, but of that more later.

The unknown John Pickering credited as the author of *Horestes* (1567) may have been Sir John Puckering, a lawyer of Lincoln's Inn who later became Speaker of the Commons and Lord Keeper. The play is typical in its failure to rise to a great tragic theme, or even to treat it in a strictly classical way. The story of Clytemnestra's murder by her son to avenge her killing of her husband had inspired one of the noblest of the Greek tragic cycles, but in Pickering's hands it became a bourgeois tragi-comedy with the hero's personal dilemma reduced to the flat simplifications of the Morality. Horestes in his agony confronts good and evil counsellors, with the Vice (here a villain, no longer a comic figure) urging revenge and Nature trying to restrain him from the impiousness of matricide.

The plot of *Apius and Virginia* (1567) comes from Livy, and Macaulay was to write a sententious lay about it. Chaucer adapted it in the Physician's Tale, which probably was the source used by the anonymous Elizabethan author, R.B. It is the story, used with modifications by Whetstone in *Promos and Cassandra* and Shakespeare in *Measure for Measure*, of a girl who dies at her own father's hands rather than be deflowered by a wicked judge. The title-page of the printed edition (1575) calls it a 'tragical comedy' but shows its Morality origins by going on to claim that it expresses 'a rare example of the virtue of chastity'. The Vice Haphazard not only plots the destruction of Virginia but provides the comedy by corrupting the servants. His introductory speech in the second scene illustrates the many guises which the Vice might adopt to practise his deceptions. The dramatist, who was a conscientious craftsman, sought to heighten the emotion by reference to classical figures who had the same feelings as his characters, all drawn from works fashionable in the schools, but the effect is declamatory and academic and true tragedy is frustrated by the closing scene in which various abstractions promise that the fame of Virginia and her father shall live eternally as an *exemplum*.

Cambyses (printed in 1569 but acted earlier) styled itself as 'a lamentable tragedy mixed full of mirth'. The author, Thomas Preston, was a Cambridge scholar who disputed theology with Cartwright, and he was to become Master of Trinity Hall and vice-chancellor of the university, but he could not write a play. With drunken orgies, shootings, embraces and executions, mostly enacted in view of the audience, the story describes the reign of the Persian king; but there is some crude comedy from the Vice Ambidexter and his retainers Huf, Ruf and Snuf, while Cruelty and Murder present more sinister abstractions. The play became proverbial for its grandiloquent bombast (*1 Hen IV* II iv 25), and its only importance in the evolution of drama is that the Morality element is secondary to the historical narrative — and even that may not have been deliberate. *The Misfortunes of Arthur*, written by a gaggle of Gray's Inn lawyers that may have included Francis Bacon, is more sophisticated in this respect. It has all the Senecan apparatus, with ghosts at the beginning and end, a Chorus to comment on each phase of the action, and stichomythia to vary the longer conversational exchanges. But the play has a sense of historical causation, albeit conventional in its ethics, and its political moral is up-to-the-minute. In general terms it denounces rebels as'the seminary of lewd Catiline, the bastard covey of Italian birds', but more specifically it commends firm action in rulers who are threatened by their own flesh and blood. This was a few months after Elizabeth at last sanctioned the execution of her cousin, Mary Queen of Scots. On the other hand, the versification suggests the legal profession's inaptitude for poetry. Energy is sought by unskilful alliteration, so that in a battle scene 'boist'rous bangs with thumping thwacks fall thick' and Mordred scours the field 'all fury-like, frounc'd up with frantic frets'. Queen Guenevara stokes her emotion by proclaming that her heart throbs, her liver boils: 'somewhat my mind portends, Uncertain what; but whatsoever, it's huge'.

Comedy based on classical models similarly found it difficult to find a satisfactory form and was restlessly experimental. The structure of Roman comedy was too spare and strict to accommodate the abstractions and the profusion of homely characters that thronged the native drama, and the playwright's difficulties increased when he tried to season the mixture with Italian romance. The traditional inclination to allegory was at odds with low-life realism. But the comic writers saw it as their chief duty to amuse, and only incidentally to instruct. Udall's *Thersites* was written to entertain a court celebration, and in *Ralph Roister Doister* his aim was to write a genuinely native comedy using Latin techniques. The date is uncertain. Some critics put it as early as about 1540 when Udall was headmaster of Eton, but more probably it belongs to his final years when he returned to favour under Queen Mary. Ralph is the *miles gloriosus* of Plautus but the mischievous Matthew Merygreek has a touch of the traditional Vice and there is a virtuous widow who keeps her pledge to the absent sea-captain to whom she is betrothed. Among a supporting cast of truly English rustics is the figure of Madge Mumblecrust, a nurse. In its healthy boisterousness the play is similar to *Gammer Gurton's Needle* of approximately the same date. A bishop and the head of a Cambridge college have been canvassed as the 'Mr S., Master of Art' who is named as the author. Although classical in structure, it is a swift-moving farce with no moral pretensions and it is chiefly famous for its drinking-song in praise of beer. The first English comedy in prose was Gascoigne's *Supposes* (1566), but before Lyly this experiment seems to have had few imitators. Although produced for the revels at Gray's Inn, the play was taken from Ariosto, with all the action in Ferrara, and Gascoigne made no attempt to introduce English characters or customs. The plot centres on a master and servant who exchange indentities, a device which Shakespeare used in *Comedy of Errors*, except that he doubled the technical difficulties by having two sets of mixed identity. As entertainment *Supposes* is burdened by some obtrusive moralizing about the importance of sound education and filial obedience.

Among extant plays there is relatively little pure comedy, the fashion being for tragic themes or *mélanges* of tragedy, romance and chronicle. As a final example of the inartistic confusions which this fashion produced we may note *Sir Clyomon and Sir Clamydes*, an anonymous play of the 1570s that at one time was attributed to George Peele. Written in fourteeners, it is a romance of chivalry featuring knights who bear golden and silver shields, but somehow the historical character of Alexander the Great finds a place in it, along with Subtle Shift (a Vice), Corin (a rustic clown) and the abstractions Rumour and Providence. (It was perhaps the first play, however, to use the device of a girl waiting upon her lover in the disguise of a page.) With so much shapeless work of this kind, the English drama in 1580 had still to find its direction, and in his *Apology for Poetry* Sir Philip Sidney complained of its artistic indiscipline. Even *Gorboduc*, which he praised as 'full of noble morality, which it doth most delightfully teach, and so obtain the very end of poesy', was 'very defectious in the circumstances' of time and place.

> But if it be so in *Gorboduc*, how much more in all the rest? where you shall have Asia of the one side, and Afric of the other, and so many under-kingdoms that the player, when he cometh in, must ever begin with telling where he is: or else the tale will not be conceived. Now ye shall have three ladies walk to gather flowers, and then we must believe the place to be a garden. By and by, we hear news of a shipwreck in the same place, and then we are to blame if we accept it not for a rock...While in the mean-time two armies fly in, represented with four swords and bucklers, and then what hard heart will not receive it for a pitched field? Now of time they are much more liberal, for ordinary it is that two young princes fall in love. After many traverses, she is got with child, delivered of a fair boy, he is lost, groweth a man, falls in love and is ready to get another child, and all this in two hours' space.

Sidney turned next to the reckless breaches of decorum:

> But besides these gross absurdities, how all their plays be neither right tragedies nor right comedies: mingling kings and clowns, not because the matter so carrieth it, but thrust in clowns by head and shoulders, to play a part in majestical matters, with neither decency nor discretion. So as neither the admiration and commiseration nor the right sportfulness is by their mongrel tragi-comedy obtained.

Sidney did not live to see *King Lear*, where a clown plays a part in majestical matters without giving artistic offence, and these are the views of a man with an inflexibly fastidious and classical mind. While many academics were withdrawing in distaste and becoming very critical of the public theatre, he sought to purify the drama according to the highest principles, and by his own standards he had a case. But it was not a case that the practical journeymen of the theatre were willing to accept. The pathetic *Sir Clyomon* was typical of its time in the clumsy fusion of disparate influences, and yet for better or worse this was the soil from which the great Elizabethan drama was to grow. Traces of the Morality, the romantic, the classical and the purely local may be found in the majority of Elizabethan plays, not least in Shakespeare's. So far, however, the theatre was lacking in guiding principles and common standards of criticism. It rejected the stricter precepts of the scholars — as in the future it would ignore the chidings of Ben Jonson — and in avoiding the restraints of the 'scene individable' it would lose itself in the formlessness of the 'poem unlimited'.

Thus the English theatre, ten years before Shakespeare began to work in it, presents an expansive, disorderly picture of an immensely popular activity that ranged from minstrels, jugglers and little bands of strolling players setting up a booth in the market-place to the liveried professionals in the great houses, the scholars in their colleges, the lawyers in the Inns and the singing boys in the choir-schools. What would become of all this dramatic energy was not immediately foreseeable. By preserving its natural growth from classical pedantry it had won its first important victory to exist and develop in its own way; a second struggle, with Puritanism supported by soured and disapproving classicism, was only just beginning. But its real battle had to be with the disintegrating forces within itself. English drama might so easily have been destroyed by the vigour and variousness of its growth. The craving for violence, novelty and undiscriminating effects might have brought it to the level of bull-baiting and the bear-garden, driven men of taste and judgment from the theatre altogether, and created an unbridgeable gulf between a degraded public stage on the one side and a lifeless, inbred academic drama on the other. Indeed it was likely that this would happen; Sidney was sure that it would, and for the good name of poetry hoped that it would. But somehow it did not happen. A group of young men, not untainted by the world, suddenly brought an artistic purpose to the writing of plays for the public theatre and guided English dramatic literature almost unheralded into its greatest age.

Chapter IV
The University Wits

I doubt not but this populous city will
Yield many scholars.

Per IV vi 198.

'The University Wits', a term applied to a small group of Oxford and Cambridge men who worked in the theatre approximately between 1584 and 1593, is obviously misleading if it suggests that they were the first university men to write for the public stages. Several academic dramatists had produced popular plays, sometimes under the tactful concealment of initials or possibly pseudonyms, and they found no discredit in working for the boy companies. Nor were the University Wits a homogeneous group, still less a school of dramatists consciously obeying common principles or pursuing common purposes. They were not even scholars in the strictest sense, because universities were regarded as production-units for the Church and these men had left their colleges and, without benefit of academic theory, were trying to earn a living by the pen. This was the link between them, that they were part of the literary industry of London, accepting all its hazards of insecurity, backbiting and dissipation. They knew each other and sometimes, though not always, admired each other, but plays were only one stream in their frantic and necessitous output. To earn a livelihood they would write pageants for the City guilds, turn out sonnets, lyrics or longer poems, translate works that had become fashionable in Europe or hire themselves to anyone who wanted a pungent pamphlet on some passing issue.

For men in their condition drama had a commercial appeal now that the professional actors were in possession of their own permanent theatres. This must have been a powerful factor. It meant that the companies were better organized and no longer had to fight the innkeepers as well as the Puritans, the local authorities, epidemics and the weather. They could provide a more dependable market for plays. The University Wits therefore entered the theatre on the theatre's own terms, not as academics proposing to reform it. The professionals on their side were not unreceptive, because they must have been aware of the volume of classical precept directed at their shortcomings, and already they had an art of their own, a forceful and pragmatic one that calculated the likely response during performance. These new playwrights elevated the drama by a superior artistic instinct that may have belonged to themselves or may have been already latent in the theatre for which they wrote. The eventual gain was a new realism in plot and character, along with a style in prose or verse in which it could be dramatically expressed.

John Lyly, George Peele and Thomas Lodge were at Oxford, Robert Greene, Christopher Marlowe and Thomas Nashe at Cambridge; Lyly (b.1554) was the eldest, Nashe (b.1567), 'tender juvenal', the youngest. Although he is usually bracketed with them, Thomas Kyd stands slightly apart from the others because he was not a university man and they may have looked down on him. Like Milton, he was a scrivener's son and it seems that for a while he followed his father's occupation. In the epistle to Greene's *Menaphon* (1589) Nashe wrote of him much as Greene himself would later write of Shakespeare. Nashe complained of men who 'leave the trade of *Noverint*, whereto they were born, and busy themselves with the endeavours of art'. It is an educated man's sneer at one whom he chooses to regard as an unlettered upstart, but Nashe soon changed his mind about the actors, whom at this time he treated as parasites, and in the literary world such outbursts are usually as short-lived as they are frequent. Kyd did more for the development of dramatic art than Nashe himself or Lodge, whose chief importance is that they defended the theatre against Puritan attack.

Nashe, who wrote 'as fast as his hand could trot', was primarily a satirist and pamphleteer, but *The Unfortunate Traveller* has its place in the history of the novel as the first picaresque romance in England. The title-page claims him as a collaborator in Marlowe's *Dido Queen of Carthage* but his only surviving play is a curious pastoral comedy *Summer's Last Will and Testament* (1592), described by one of the characters as a show rather than a play. He also wrote the lost *Isle of Dogs* (1597) which the Privy Council found to contain such 'seditious and sclanderous matter' that all the theatres were closed and the actors imprisoned, including Ben Jonson, who was named as part-author. Nashe escaped to Norfolk, and he died in 1601.

Lodge was too variously gifted to do anything supremely well, and he had interests outside literature. Son of a Lord Mayor of London, he studied law at Lincoln's Inn before a period of intense activity during which he wrote plays, translations, pamphlets, romances, satires, sonnets and verse epistles. Perhaps none of it was very profitable because in 1588 he was on a freebooting voyage to the Canaries and three years later he sailed to South America with Thomas Cavendish. To beguile the time on the first of these expeditions he wrote, 'when every line was wet with surge,' the novel *Rosalynde: Euphues' Golden Legacy'*, which was the only source for *As You Like It*. He is linked with Shakespeare again through his *Scilla's Metamorphosis* (published in 1589), which freed Ovid of the didactic and allegorical interpretations that medieval writers had laid upon him and was the first attempt to claim ancient mythology as a fit subject for courtly poetry and the love complaint. The poem inspired a fashion to which Shakespeare's contribution was *Venus and Adonis*. Probably Lodge wrote more for the theatre than the two pieces that survive: *The Wounds of Civil War* (c.1588) and *A Looking-Glass for London and England* (c.1590), in which he collaborated with Greene. *The Wounds of Civil War*, based on Plutarch, faithfully records the story of Marius and Sulla, rivals in second-century Rome. Although stiffly written in verse reminiscent of *Gorboduc*, the play concentrates the historical narrative on the clash of personal ambitions — until, that is, Marius dies, whereupon Lodge sacrifices dramatic unity by dragging out the story until the death of Sulla.

At some time Lodge was converted to Roman Catholicism, turned to the study of medicine and for the last twenty years of his life (he died in 1625) practised among his fellow-Catholics. During this period he compiled translations and memoirs of Josephus, Seneca and du Bartas. Lodge was not a very creative writer and it is unlikely that any lost plays would have shown much dramatic talent; but his fundamental seriousness dignified everything that he touched, and his championship of the theatre was the better respected because he was free of the personal vices and frivolities of which the profession was accused.

Compared with the rest of the University Wits, John Lyly was a rather superior person. He was the grandson of William Lily, famous grammarian and the first high-master of St Paul's School; he may have held a post in Burghley's household before becoming secretary to the Earl of Oxford; in about 1597 he had hopes, not fulfilled, of succeeding to the lucrative office of Master of the Revels, and his work always has the self-conscious elegance of a courtier. What especially distinguishes him from his fellows is that all his plays were written for the boy companies for performance in a private theatre in Blackfriars. In the early eighties he was principal organizer of a mixed company of the Chapel Royal, St Paul's and Oxford's boys, and when this amalgamation broke up he wrote for the Paul's boys alone until in 1590 they were suppressed because 'the players take upon themselves to handle in their plays certain matters of Divinity and of State unfit to be suffered'. Apparently they had made indiscreet allusion to the Marprelate controversy, in which Lyly, like Nashe, wrote pamphlets on the side of the bishops.

Before he began to write plays Lyly already had a literary reputation for his two-part romance *Euphues* (1578-80). For some of the characteristics of 'euphuism' Lyly borrowed from George Pettie's *Petite Palace of Pettie his Pleasure* (1576). As well as alliteration this peculiar style revelled in antithesis, often pursued regardless of sense; classical and mythological allusions that have little point other than that they are allusions; and similes and correspondences fetched from history, fable, horticulture and the medieval bestiaries.

Whereby I noted that young swans are grey, and the old white, young trees tender and the old tough, young men amorous, and growing in years, either wiser or warier. The coral plant in water is a soft weed, on the land a hard stone: a sword frieth in the fire like a black eel; but laid in earth like white snow: the heart in love is altogether passionate; but free from desire altogether careless.

From Letter Commendatory to Watson's *Hecatompathia*.

Or here is an extract from the preface to the first part of *Euphues*:

Gentlemen use books as gentlewomen handle their flowers, who in the morning stick them in their heads, and at night straw them at their heels. Cherries be fulsome when they be through ripe, because they are plenty, and books be stale when they are printed, in that they be common. In my mind printers and tailors are bound chiefly to pray for gentlemen: the one hath so many fantasies to print, the others such divers fashions to make, that the pressing iron of the one is never out of the fire, nor the printing press of the other at any time lieth still. But a fashion is but a day's wearing and a book but an hour's reading: which seeing it is so, I am of a shoemaker's mind who careth not so the shoe hold the plucking on, nor I, so my labours last the running over.

Polonius had read his *Euphues*, even to the matter as well as the manner. His famous admonition to Laertes paraphrases the advice given by Euphues to Philautus; 'Be valiant but not too venturous. Let thy attire be comely, but not costly', and so on.

It is a hardened stomach that can receive much of this, a disciplined concentration that can hold to the twisting thread of meaning, especially when it is transferred to the stage. The application of Lyly's technique to English comedy,which had not progressed since *Ralph Roister Doister* and *Gammer Gurton's Needle*, had an effect similar to the first application of Senecan principles to crude episodic tragedy: it turned the spectator's attention from the action to the words. In tragedy this by now had become sterile, and Senecan sentences would no longer suffice; comedy, likewise, could not long thrive on Lyly. But for the moment he was an immensely civilizing influence. The dialogue — much of it in the vernacular despite its convolutions, and full of homely illustrations — concealed the thinness of the plots and allowed him to dispense with buffoonery, knockabout and indecency. He dared to proclaim style as the prime attraction of a play and he invited his courtly audience to enjoy the subtlety of word-play, repartee and polished language.

For instance, Sir Tophas, the braggart soldier of Endimion, burlesques the type to which he belongs:

Tophas. I was the first that ever devised war, and therefore Mars himself has given me for my arms a whole armoury: and thus I go as you see, clothed with artillery; it is not silks nor tissues, nor the fine wool of Ceres, but iron, steel, swords, flame, shot, terror, clamour, blood and ruin that rocks asleep my thoughts, which never had any other cradle but cruelty. Let me see, do you not bleed?

Dares.   Why so?
Tophas.   Commonly my words wound.

Endimion I iii 48.

But in a moment the rapier rusts and the drum is still, for their master is in love and is for whole volumes in folio: the submission of martial vigour to the gossamer yoke of love was one of Lyly's favourite themes. Here is Hephaestion chiding Alexander the Great for having 'become the subject of Campaspe, the captive of Thebes':

> Beauty is like the blackberry, which seemeth red when it is not ripe, resembling precious stones that are polished with honey, which the smoother they look, the sooner they break. It is thought wonderful among the seamen that mugil, of all fishes the swiftest, is found in the belly of the bret, of all the slowest, and shall it not seem monstrous to wise men that the heart of the greatest conqueror of the world should be found in the hands of the weakest creature of nature — of a woman, of a captive? Ermines have fair skins but foul livers, sepulchres fresh colours but rotten bones, women fair faces but false hearts. Remember, Alexander, thou hast a camp to govern, not a chamber; fall not from the armour of Mars to the arms of Venus, from the fiery assaults of war to the maidenly skirmishes of love, from displaying the eagle in thine ensign to set down the sparrow.

Campaspe II ii 54.

So Lyly saunters on, creating his verbal arabesques, minding little where the journey will end if there be flowers to gather on the way. Shakespeare dealt him fearful blows, but the parody in *Love's Labour's Lost*, incomparably more brilliant than the work of the victim, was partly a tribute of respect and affection, and Shakespeare would fall into 'a trick of the old rage' for as long as he could hold a pen. When his company was suppressed in 1590 Lyly was already in the Commons and he wrote no more. He sat in the last four parliaments of the reign, and politics perhaps engrossed him. For a while he had many imitators both in prose and drama, but we do not know how his plays, written for select audiences and probably all performed at court, were received when, if ever, they were seen in the public theatres. His plotting was perfunctory and his characters never come to life in their remote romantic settings. But he has his place with Congreve, Sheridan and Wilde as a writer of high comedy. His use of prose as its medium (only one of his eight surviving plays, *The Woman in the Moon*, is in verse) was a significant advance in the drama of his time, and there was much else in his comedy that others were glad to imitate: the lyrical songs that intersperse the action, although probably he did not write them; the pastoral background for his romantic intrigues; the theatrical effectiveness of sex disguises; even the introduction of fairies. All this is very Shakespearean. In breaking with Latin models in comedy he excused the English 'gallimaufrey', the mingling of tears and laughter, on the ground that English playwrights had to write for mixed audiences, not just for the judicious. He believed, contrary to the classical purists, that the purpose of comedy is 'mere pastime', not to reform manners but to give pleasure, a pleasure unalloyed by clowning and coarseness. 'It is wit that allureth'. In the Prologue to *Sapho and Phao* (1584) he wrote a fitting description of his art:

> Our intent was at this time to move inward delight, not outward lightness, and to breed (if it might be) soft smiling, not loud laughing; knowing it to the wise to be as great pleasure to hear counsel mixed with wit as to the foolish to have sport mingled with rudeness.

Marlowe was the first great English poet to write plays. Before him, as Swinburne has said, 'there was neither genuine blank verse nor a genuine tragedy in our language'. History seldom moves in cataclysms, but the appearance of *Tamburlaine the Great* in 1587 translated English drama from the medieval to the modern idiom. Marlowe had the Greek dramatists' power of projecting his whole being into the central character and motivating it with his own passion and imagination: so that for the first time a play concerned itself with what goes in a man's mind, and the audience was admitted to an inner conflict as well as to the pressure of external circumstances on an individual destiny.

This is the sort of thing that Elizabethan audiences had been wont to hear when they went to a tragedy. Videna, the spouse of King Gorboduc, thus laments her fate:

> Why should I live, and linger forth my time
> In longer life to double my distress?
> O me, most woeful wight, whom no mishap
> Long ere this day could have bereaved hence.
> Might not these hands, by fortune or by fate,
> Have pierc'd this breast, and life with iron reft?
> Or in this palace here, where I so long
> Have spent my days, could not that happy hour
> Once, once, have happ'd, in which these hugy frames
> With death by fall might have oppressed me?
>
> *Gorboduc* IV i 1.

And so on for another seventy lines. Yet *Gorboduc* had been revolutionary in its hour as the first play to be written in blank verse, a measure introduced into England in the Earl of Surrey's translation of two books of the *Aeneid*. It soon became the normal medium for popular drama and the University Wits used it freely. But older measures still lingered, whether fourteeners or rhyming couplets or any jingle that took a writer's fancy. In a song from *Horestes* courtiers thus bid farewell to the tranquil mind as they march to battle:

> Farewell, adieu, that courtly life,
> To war we tend to go;

It is good sport to see ths strife
Of soldiers in a row:
       How merrily they forward march
       Their enemies to slay:
       With hey trim and trixie too,
       Their banners they display.

Now shall we have the golden cheats
When others want the same;
And soldiers have full many feats
Their enemies to tame:
       With cocking here, and booming there,
       They break their foes' array;
       And lusty lads amid the fields
       Their ensigns do display.

In all that has survived from the dramatic literature of this period, some of it better but much of it worse, there is nothing to suggest that this was about to happen:

Zenocrate, lovelier than the love of Jove,
Brighter than is the silver Rhodope,
Fairer than whitest snow on Scythian hills...
A hundred Tartars shall attend on thee,
Mounted on steeds swifter than Pegasus;
Thy garments shall be made of Median silk,
Enchas'd with precious jewels of mine own,
More rich and valurous than Zenocrate's.
With milk-white harts upon an ivory sled
Thou shalt be drawn amidst the frozen pools,
And scale the icy mountains' lofty tops,
Which with thy beauty will be soon resolved.
My martial prizes with five hundred men,
Won of the fifty-headed Volga's waves,
Shall we all offer to Zenocrate, —
And then myself to fair Zenocrate.

1 Tamburlaine I ii 88.

This still less:

What is beauty, saith my sufferings, then?
If all the pens that ever poets held
Had fed the feeling of their masters' thoughts,
And every sweetness that inspir'd their hearts,
Their minds and muses on admired themes:
If all the heavenly quintessence they 'still
From their immortal flowers of poesy,
Wherein, as in a mirror, we perceive

The highest reaches of a human wit;
If these had made one poem's period,
And all combined in beauty's worthiness,
Yet should there hover in their restless heads
One thought, one grace, one wonder, at the least,
Which into words no virtue can digest.

V i 60.

The first of these two passages merely shows that here is a great lyric poet, a maker of music. There is nothing essentially dramatic about it, and Marlowe lets the lyric impulse run away with him: the pictures multiply but the hold on the reader's attention weakens. It is the second passage that sets him apart from his predecessors in the drama. It has relaxed the stiffness of Anglo-Saxon prosody and allowed blank verse to become the instrument of living thought. In the extract from *Gorboduc* the regular iambic beat is unvaried, with a pause after the fourth syllable. Marlowe, by emphasizing some of the stressed syllables, usually the first, third and fifth, substitutes a more natural rhythm in which the rhetorical stresses subdue the mechanical beat. As Shakespeare would develop it, this becomes a sort of vocal counterpoint that gives the effect of a speaking voice. Shakespeare, too, would give further variety by the use of enjambment and feminine endings, whereas Marlowe mostly adhered to the end-stopped line which after a while sounds declamatory and inhibits the naturalness of ordinary speech.

Technical advances of this kind spring from the inner necessities of the creative artist. Marlowe wrote thus because of emotional pressure that broke through the rigidity of strict Senecan verse. All his great creations were superhuman figures, high-aspiring men who needed to express themselves in high astounding terms since their passion could not be content with less. The plays concentrate all the interest in a single character, and always this character is a man who challenges fate to give him more than his due, more indeed than any mortal should aspire to; but so intense is his passion, and so splendid the language in which he tells of his lawless hopes, that the listener — and here is the great difference between Marlowe and the Senecans — is won to share his emotions, to reach with him for the stars and fall with him to ruin. From the little that we know of Marlowe's short and restless life it might seem that he poured into his heroes something of his own intellectual compulsion to overstep the limits of power and knowledge. The vision which beckoned his Scythian shepherd was of a world lying conquered at his feet:

Is it not brave to be a king, Techelles!
Usumcasane and Theridamas,
Is it not passing brave to be a king
And ride in triumph through Persepolis?

1 Tamburlaine II v 50.

Barabas must have gold, 'wearying his fingers' ends with telling it', seeking to enclose 'infinite riches in a little room'. Even in *The Massacre at Paris*, a wretched, ill-organized pot-boiler on a contemporary theme, Guise reveals the 'deep-engender'd thoughts' that will not let him rest happy until he has won the crown of France:

> Oft have I levell'd, and at last have learn'd
> That peril is the chiefest way to happiness,
> And resolution honour's fairest aim.
> What glory is there in a common good
> That hangs for every peasant to achieve?
> That like I best that flies beyond my reach.
> Set me to scale the high Pyramides,
> And thereon set the diadem of France...
> For this, hath heav'n engender'd me of earth,
> For this, the earth sustains my body's weight,
> And with this weight I'll counterpoise a crown,
> Or with seditions weary all the world...
> Give me a look that, when I bend the brows,
> Pale death may walk in furrows of my face;
> A hand that with a grasp may gripe the world;
> An ear to hear what my detractors say;
> A royal seat, a sceptre and a crown;
> That those which do behold them may become
> As men that stand and gaze against the sun.
>
> I ii 37.

Young Mortimer, another disciple of Caesarism, has as his device

> A lofty cedar tree, fair flourishing,
> On whose top branches kingly eagles perch.

For such men the hour will come when they can aspire no longer, and they meet it defiantly and unrepentantly, 'For Tamburlaine, the scourge of God, must die.' As he is led away to execution Mortimer acknowledges that in Fortune's wheel

> There is a point to which, when men aspire,
> They tumble headlong down: that point I touch'd,
> And seeing there was no place to mount up higher,
> Why should I grieve at my declining fall?
> Farewell, fair queen: weep not for Mortimer,
> That scorns the world and, as a traveller,
> Goes to discover countries yet unknown.
>
> *Edward II* V vi 60.

They have no immortality but this, that they rose as high as man may rise on earth.

> Nature, that fram'd us of four elements,
> Warring within our breasts for regiment,
> Doth teach us all to have aspiring minds:
> Our souls, whose faculties can comprehend
> The wondrous Architecture of the world,
> And measure every wand'ring planet's course,
> Still climbing after knowledge infinite,
> And always moving as the restless spheres,
> Will us to wear ourselves and never rest
> Until we reach the ripest fruit of all,
> That perfect bliss and sole felicity,
> The sweet fruition of an earthly crown.
>
> *1 Tamburlaine* II vii 18.

In *Dr Faustus* the hero strives for nothing less than intellectual mastery of the world, the power to bend the laws of Nature to his will. The sweet fruition of an earthly crown is not enough. 'Go forward,' his Evil Angel bids him, 'be thou on earth as Jove is in the sky, lord and commander of these elements.' In form *Dr Faustus* is a straightforward Morality play. Good and evil angels struggle for his soul; Mephistophilis wrestles with his innate human goodness to bring him captive to Lucifer; he meets the seven deadly sins; and his fearful death is followed by a few quiet lines which point the conventional moral:

> Cut is the branch that might have grown full straight,
> And burned is Apollo's laurel bough
> That sometime grew within this learned man.
> Faustus is gone. Regard his hellish fall,
> Whose fiendful fortune may exhort the wise
> Only to wonder at unlawful things
> Whose deepness doth entice such forward wits
> To practise more than heavenly power permits.

But Marlowe advanced the Morality convention by showing the conflict as not merely the external struggle for a human soul but as also a struggle within that soul itself. Faustus is not just the abstract figure of Everyman; he is a human being tortured by his conscience, aware of what he is doing and of the dreadful consequences of it. He wants to repent, 'abjure this magic, turn to God again', but Mephistophilis returns to lure him with the promise of power and knowledge infinite. His last anguished cry is the cry of a man whose soul has been laid bare to us; of one damned knowingly and by his own fault, but familiar alike in his weakness and his fundamental goodness, and therefore claiming our sympathy. The play consummates the transition from the Morality abstractions to the tragic hero who fights his battle in his own conscience and therefore takes responsibility for what is to come.

No dramatist before Marlowe could have written the lines in which Mephistophilis speaks of hell. Twice Faustus presses him to say where hell is and how its pains are to be recognized, but hell is no longer located through a trap-door under the stage.

> Why, this is hell, nor am I out of it.
> Think'st thou that I, who saw the face of God
> And tasted the eternal joys of heaven,
> Am not tormented with ten thousand hells
> In being deprived of everlasting bliss?

iii 77.

And again:

> Hell hath no limits, nor is circumscrib'd
> In one self place; for where we are is hell,
> And where hell is there must we ever be:
> And, to conclude, when all the world dissolves,
> And every creature shall be purified,
> All places shall be hell that is not heaven.

v 121.

Hell is in the mind, in the burden that the guilty conscience must drag with it wherever it goes. Mephistophilis, servant of fallen Lucifer, suffers pains 'as great as have the human souls of men'; and for consolation, '*solamen miseris socios habuisse doloris*', the comfort of the wretched is to have fellows in misfortune. The conception of tragedy has altered since painted devils sprang on stage to bear away their victims. It is instructive, too, to compare on the one hand Faustus's soliloquy during his last hour on earth, when his agony probes to the core of human terror and he implores the heavens to cease their wonted movement, and the last sunset he will ever see appears to him as Christ's blood streaming in the firmament; and on the other, the lines in which, only some twenty years previously, King Cambyses had ended his turbulent course[1]:

---

1 Yet this absurd piece is full of echoes and anticipations. In line 2 Cambyses alludes to the sudden chance by which kings fall from ruin, and this is followed by the conventional, although vain, appeal for rescue, divine or human; lines 4-6 denounce faithless courtiers, a theme of almost every history play; in lines 7-9 Cambyses praised his own bravery, as Marlowe's heroes would, and Macbeth, and then he shows the audience his painted wound; the closing lines suggest most of all the death of Pyramus/Bottom, but there is a hint of the fell sergeant and of 'the rest is silence'; and finally there is a routine Morality repentance.

Out! Alas! What shall I do? My life is finished.
Wounded I am by sudden chance; my blood is minished.
God's heart, what means might I make my life to preserve?
Is there nought to be my help? Nor is there nought to serve?
Out upon the court, and lords that there remain!
To help my grief in this my case will none of them take pain?
Who but I, in such a wise, his death's wound could have got?
As I on horseback up did leap, my sword from scabbard shot,
And ran me thus into the side — as you right well may see.
A marvellous chance unfortunate, that in this wise should be!
I feel myself a-dying now; of life bereft am I;
And Death hath caught me with his dart, for want of blood I spy.
Thus, gasping, here on ground I lie; for nothing do I care.
A just reward for my misdeed my death doth plain declare.

Here, says the stage-direction, 'let him quake and stir'. But he is not done with yet, and a few lines later he is back to speak the Epilogue, pray for the Queen's continued prosperity and dismiss a satiated audience to their homes.

Marlowe, born some three moths earlier than Shakespeare, died before he was thirty, squalidly and uselessly in a tavern brawl. He has been described as a government spy, which may have meant no more than common informer; and it has been suggested that his death was deliberately staged when the authorities were embarrassed by his proclaimed atheism and other deviations. Such things are not unknown in the history of governments, and certainly his killer was pardoned on a plea of self-defence.

In his lines 'To Henry Reynolda, Esq.' Michael Drayton said of Marlowe that he 'Had in him those brave translunary things That our first poets had.' Shakespeare's debt to him is obvious, especially in his development of blank verse as a flexible instrument for dramatic poetry. But compare *Tamburlaine* with Shakespeare's later work, *Tempest* and *Winter's Tale*, or even with the verse of *Hamlet*: the difference may not be as great as that between Marlowe and *Gorboduc*, but it is vast. Again, Marlowe succeeded in focusing all the dramatic interest on the struggle of one character to achieve his proud ambition. But his heroes are not fluid, they do not develop. Early in his career, by the time he had finished *Richard III*, Shakespeare had discovered that men like this, men who proclaim their ambitions and relentlessly pursue them, imprisoned in the formula of 'I am that I am', are dramatically insufficient. After two whole plays we know no more of Tamburlaine than we knew at the beginning, whereas every word of Hamlet's is a continuous self-revelation.

Marlowe knew and cared too little about ordinary men. He lacked Shakespeare's balance, his unvaried acceptance of the moral order and the immutable laws of the universe, his humorous familiarity with all sorts of men in their everyday doings.[2] Whereas Shakespeare writes with complete artistic detachment, in Marlowe we feel that the story is being kept alive by his own passion, that only his own poetic energy is holding it together. In *Edward II*, which structurally is his best play, he made some attempt to observe conventional principles; but although his genius breaks through from time to time — as in the terrible suspense before the king's death, in an occasional phrase like 'But what are kings, when regiment is gone, But perfect shadows in a sunshine day?' — the weight of the historical material seems to oppress him and crush the splendour from his verse. He is happiest when the Scythian shepherd is poet as well as conqueror and speaks from a poet's heart of far-off, unattainable things, of Damascus and the Egyptian fields and of Helen who drew a thousand ships to Tenedos. His heroes come from outside the common range of humanity. All of them are rebels against belief and custom and the tacit sanctions which men must accept if they are to live with one another. Their 'looks do menace heaven and dare the gods', and these tempestuous figures, lacking humour and strangely isolated in their pride and aspiration, pall after a time.

So too does their language. There are long stretches of rant and bombast in which the poet swells his sails but makes no dramatic progress. Shakespeare in his early days was guilty too. His martial noblemen and wailing women puff windily through their castles, and when he felt the need to write bombast, he could never do it as well as Marlowe. On the other hand, he drew his imagery from a much wider range of feeling and association. Marlowe's imagery is of the sun, the stars and the oceans, painting a scene of celestial and spatial magnificence which he adorned with garnishings from his favourite Ovid. It is very splendid in these heights above the world, but it is chilly too. One longs for a touch of 'human-kindness', of plain earthy humour. In an anonymous Cambridge play, *Second Return from Parnassus* (*c.*1601), Furor Poeticus, whose usual function is to mock the verbal excesses of Marston, seems here to be looking at Marlowe:

> You gransdire Phoebus with your lovely eye,
> The firmament's eternal vagabond,
> The heaven's promoter that doth peep and pry
> Into the acts of mortal tennis balls,
> Inspire me straight with some rare delices...
> Or I'll dismount thee from thy radiant coach
> And make thee a poor Cutchy [coachman] here on earth.

2 The artistic and temperamental difference between the two men is evident again in a comparison between *Venus and Adonis* and *Hero and Leander*. The broad humanity of Shakespeare's treatment is at odds with the artificiality of myth, and the poem does not have the artistic unity of the Ovidian original. But Marlowe's consistency of tone amounts to a single-minded absorption with the spectacle that ignores the moral implications of the tale. '*Desunt nonnulla*': significantly, he never finished the poem (which was completed later by Chapman) and he disregarded the moral present in his source that 'Love compels not Fate'.

Ingenioso (who is Nashe): replies: 'Thou hast a very terrible roaring muse, nothing but squibs and fireworks' (*2 Return 1310*). Pistol frequently burlesques him too, particularly in *2 Henry IV* II iv where his talk is full of misquoted tags from earlier plays.

Within fifteen years of his death the Jacobean playwrights were thinking of Marlowe as a primitive, his 'bragging blank verse' as exciting to raptures that were all air and fire and lacked the earthy components demanded by more serious men. But it is one thing to realize Marlowe's limitations, and to believe that his lack of the common touch would have prevented him from increasing his stature if he had lived longer; and quite another to forget, as his successors and debtors rapidly did, what the drama owed to his brief and astonishing career. In his hands the writing of tragedy became an art; and, in the form in which he wrote it, an art indigenous in its blending of the native and the classical traditions. Stage revivals and reprinting of his plays and poems prove his popularity in a commercial sense. He had taught Elizabethan audiences to attend with all their faculties to tragedy that involved them in a human predicament.

The fame of Thomas Kyd depends upon a single play, *The Spanish Tragedy*, even whose date is uncertain: most critics suppose that it was later than *Tamburlaine*, but some have put it earlier. It does not much matter, because they are quite different achievements and neither may be thought to have borrowed from the other. Kyd also wrote *Cornelia*, a wooden adaptation of a French play about the daughter of Pompey the Great. Other attributions, inevitably including his hand in Shakespeare's first plays, are uncertain.

Kyd's paradoxical achievement was to give new life to Senecan tragedy just when Marlowe might have killed it. *The Spanish Tragedy* was the forerunner of many similar 'revenge' plays, *Hamlet* not the least, and itself it continued to be so popular that for later revivals it had to be doctored and updated by Jonson and possibly other dramatists. It was acted by both the Chamberlain's and the Admiral's Men, so that Hieronimo was a powerful part for Burbage as well as Alleyn. The background is as recent as the Spanish annexation of Portugal in 1580, and on its inferior levels the play introduces much of the Senecan apparatus of blood, ghosts, revenge, horrors, stichomythia and sententious maxims. What is not Senecan, however, is the supple competence of the blank verse (apart from some rather obtrusive rhyme), the ordering of the action through cleverly-contrived suspense towards a surprise climax in a play-within-the-play, and the presentation of Hieronimo as a man who, when not maddened by his grief, is a real and sympathetic figure. Much of his speech is gusty rhetoric, but he has intervals of self-analysis and reflection and he commends himself by his patient determination to be certain who killed his son before planning his revenge. The embodiment of Revenge who introduces the play and appears between the acts is not a restless perturbed spirit clamouring for action; he is rather the embodiment of nemesis coolly awaiting the appointed hour:

> Thou talk'st of harvest when the corn is green:
> The end is crown of every work well done;
> The sickle comes not till the corn be ripe.
>
> II vi 7.

Kyd's admirable stagecraft, much superior to Marlowe's, makes significant advances. The action moves by controlled stages, with low-key pauses where the tension is relaxed; it is not just a jumble of episodes exploding into an unprepared climax, and there is much dramatic irony while the audience waits, as in *Hamlet*, to discover whether the climax will ever be reached at all. Unusually, too, Kyd moves the crisis — the deed that initiates the subsequent action — towards the middle of the play. In *Gorboduc* and most Senecan tragedy, and again in *Hamlet*, it occurs in the first scene or even before the play has started, when it becomes harder to sustain interest without recourse to irrelevant interludes. Here the characters are given time to establish themselves before Hieronimo discovers his murdered son. Finally, Kyd enacted his horrors on the stage, and this is important too. Lyly's diversion of comic interest from action to the polished elegance of the style was salutary for a while and it uplifted the tone of comedy, but not all comic playwrights, or their audiences, could exist for ever on that exalted plane. So it was with Seneca in tragedy. The rhetorical thunder had exhausted itself, and the audience needed to be shown what the pother was about. It is brutal but true that tragic catharsis cannot depend on words and attitudes alone: there must be an element of physical action and visual horror. Shakespeare was quick to take the point in furnishing the grisly contents of the pie in *Titus Andronicus*; and Gloucester's blinding ('Out, vile jelly!....dark and comfortless') is not for the faint-hearted.

Kyd's poetry lacks Marlowe's grandeur but it suffices to keep the story moving and enable the characters to explain themselves credibly. It is most pleasing when the touch is lightest, as when the lovers Bellimperia and Horatio arrange to meet:

> Then be thy fathers's pleasant bower the field,
> Where first we vow'd our mutual amity;
> The court were dangerous, that place is safe.
> Our hour shall be when Vesper 'gins to rise,
> That summons home distressful travellers:
> There none shall hear us but the harmless birds;
> Haply the gentle nightingale
> Shall carol us asleep, ere we be ware,
> And singing with the prickle at her breast,
> Tell our delight and mirthful dalliance:
> Till then each hour will seem a year and more.
>
> II ii 42.

Not many dramatists have been able to rest their reputation on a single play, but in *The Spanish Tragedy* there is real achievement. In 1593 Kyd was arrested on a charge of 'lewd and mutinous libels' of an atheistical kind, and although he was released, he died in poverty, possibly a victim of the plague, in the following year. The text of a pre-Shakespearean *Hamlet* attributed to him has not survived.

Peele and Greene are the last of the University Wits to be considered because while Lyly is associated with comedy and Marlowe and Kyd with tragedy, they defy classification because they tried their hand at everything. Although he was probably an actor as well as a playwright, Peele was an indifferent dramatist, weak at plotting and unable either to sustain any narrative interest or to focus strongly on his characters. His plays are remembered only for their melodious versification: Nashe, in the preface to *Menaphon*, called him 'the chief supporter of pleasance now living, the Atlas of poetry, and *primus verborum artifex*'. The commendation is excessive because Peele was not a major poet and he had not anything very important to say. Charming and musical as it is, his verse is too experimental and inconsistent to be suitable for drama. In *The Arraignment of Paris*, for instance, the metre varies, sometimes within a single speech, between heroic couplets, blank verse pentameters, rhyming heptameters and alternate hexameters and heptameters rhyming together. In his less irresponsible moments, however, there is some poetic felicity, as in the well-known lines from *David and Bethsabe*:

> Now comes my lover tripping like the roe,
> And brings my longings tangled in her hair.
> To joy her love I'll build a kingly bower,
> Seated in hearing of a hundred streams,
> That for their homage to her sovereign joys
> Shall, as the serpents fold into their nests
> In oblique turnings, wind the nimble waves
> About the circles of her curious walks,
> And with their murmurs summon easeful sleep
> To lay his golden sceptre on her brows.
> Open the doors and entertain my love,
> Open, I say, and as you open, sing,
> 'Welcome, fair Bethsabe, King David's darling'.

115.

Like Marlowe, Peele had learned to vary the iambic rhythm, but there is a sense of strain even in these pleasant lines, a compulsion to squeeze each image until it will yield no more At times the effect is ludicrous and painful, as when (1.1473 sq.) Absalon is strung up by his hair and multiplies verbal conceits while waiting to be stabbed.

The Arraignment of Paris is a pastoral play that ends in gross flattery of

Queen Elizabeth, before whom it was performed, and the presence of some thirty characters, together with the nine Muses, Cupids, knights and shepherds, shows Peele's lack of dramatic concentration. *David and Bethsabe* is interesting in being derived from a Biblical source, but to the royal romance is added the story of Absalon's insurrection. *Edward I*, which some critics have regarded as a stage in the transition from chronicle to history play, is even more diffuse. With proper patriotic intent Peele wished to celebrate the 'mere English' qualities of the king, but the play also includes 'the life of Llewellyn, rebel in Wales; lastly, the sinking of Queen Elinor, who sunk at Charing Cross, and rose again at Potters-hithe, now named Queen-hithe'. Regardless of dramatic unity, Peele has chosen three focal points in the expectation that this would treble the interest of the play as a whole. It was a mistaken view from which English drama had been suffering for many years. *The Old Wives' Tale*, written mainly in prose, was intended as a satire on popular romantic drama, featuring the magician Sacrapant. But satire demands an intellectual control that Peele did not possess, and temperamentally he was not averse to the sort of work he was ridiculing. Thus his play, although allegedly inspiring Milton to write *Comus*, is a confused and ordinary little comedy with too many characters and none of them adequately deployed. This fault is damaging also in his attempt to emulate *Tamburlaine* in *The Battle of Alcazar*. He took a contemporary topic, the defeat and death of Sebastian of Portugal in a war against the Moors in 1578, and at least he disciplined himself by cutting out comic interludes and extraneous incidents and sticking to the main story. Even the verse is regular, seeking the effect of Marlowe's 'mighty line'. But any competent dramatist must have perceived that Marlowe's strength lay not so much in the powerful rhetoric of the verse as in his concentration on the character who speaks it. As a tragedy *The Battle of Alcazar* is a failure because it has no dominant central character, the interest being tepidly diffused among a number of participants in the story.

Peele died in 1596, reputedly 'by the pox' after a life of dissipation. There is a lack of personality, even a spinelessness, in his numerous patriotic and gratulatory odes as well as in his plays, and the most that can be said for him is that he had a humanizing influence, showing that a play of modest aims might sufficiently commend itself if its characters were pleasant and its diction graceful and melodious. He did little to amend the faults of earlier drama and it is unlikely that Shakespeare learned very much from him.

Greene too wrote some pot-boiling hack-work that in itself did little to improve the quality of contemporary drama, but he had certain intuitive gifts in a medium he seems to have despised. Unless some of his work has been lost, it was only between 1587 and 1592, in the final years of a spendthrift and unhappy life, that his exigencies obliged him to write plays. Previously he had poured out romances, novels (including a continuation of *Euphues*), pamphlets and social satires, many of which he decorated with some pleasing verse. He could work very fast. Nashe records that 'in a night and day would he have yerked up a pamphlet as well as in seven year, and glad was that printer that might be so blest to pay him dear for the very dregs of his wit.' Journalism of this kind requires some awareness of current trends, and in his plays Greene made use of anything that happened to be fashionable. In *Alphonsus* he plunged at once into competition with *Tamburlaine*, as Peele had done, and its failure on the stage may have confirmed, or perhaps originated, his contempt for the profession. He had much to learn about dramatic propriety. In a tale about a contemporary Turkish sultan it is strange to find Medea a visitor to his court or Venus enclosing the action attended by the nine Muses. The play's high-flown language was intended to astound more than in fact it does. Like Kyd, Greene wrote best when he did not try to raise his voice, and when he wrote beyond his powers, the effect might be comic. Here is the way of a man with a maid:

Alphonsus.	Nay then, proud peacock, since thou art so stout
	As that entreaty will not move thy mind
	For to consent to be my wedded spouse,
	Thou shalt, in spite of
	Gods and Fortune too,
	Serve high Alphonsus as a concubine.
Iphegena.	I'll rather die than ever that shall hap.
Alphonsus.	And thou shalt die unless it come to pass.

V ii 48.

In *A Looking-glass for London and England* Greene — or his collaborator Lodge, but Greene is the likelier — still wants to pass as a poor relation of Tamburlaine:

The lovely trull that Mercury entrapp'd
Within the curious pleasure of his tongue,
And she that 'bash'd the sun-god with her eyes,
Fair Semele, the choice of Venus' maids,
Were not so beautiful as Remilia...
Lordlings, I'll have my wedding sumptuous,
Made glorious with the treasures of the world:
I'll fetch from Albia shelves of margarites,
And strip the Indies of their diamonds,
And Tyre shall yield me tribute of her gold,
To make Remilia's wedding glorious.

Looking-glass I i 73.

The rhythms and imagery of Marlowe appear again in *Orlando Furioso*, a play so peculiar that readers have wondered whether Greene had not by this time passed from imitation to burlesque. He had by this time conceived some personal hostility to Marlowe, and it may well be so. But in Sacripant he drew an Iago-like figure who undermines true love by forged allegations of infidelity, and in Angelica he made his first sketch of the gentle, trusting maidens who were to be his principal remembrance.

So far Greene had written nothing characteristic, but now he abandoned imitative melodramas full of martial noises and oriental glamour and in *Friar Bacon and Friar Bungay*, *James IV* and *George-a-Greene* (not certainly his, but if it was not, he too could inspire a faithful imitation) he found his proper vein. These plays are similar in structure. The defeat of the Spanish Armada had borne a patriotic enthusiam that sought vicarious gratification in plays and stories about former events in English history. With an eye on the takings, Greene hastened to meet this demand. The three plays all introduce royal and noble personages in episodes that have no factual excuse and only by skilful plotting are brought into relation with the main theme. The imposture was most audacious in *James IV*. Greene founded the play on an Italian novel by Cinthio, and in order to attract an unlearned audience he gave some of the characters of the Italian fiction the names of real people and called the result *The Scottish History of James IV, slain at Flodden*. Despite this title it is not a history play at all.

The interest of these works — apart from what they disclose of the opportunism of dramatists and the gullibility of audiences — lies in their pastoral setting and their simple, unaffected romance. The place-names and the titles may be ignored; the setting is the English countryside and the lives of English countryfolk, and homely realism is imposed on classical and mythological stories. In this pleasant country air Greene introduced some felicitous clowns: Ralph the fool, Miles the serving-man and Cuddy the yokel are not unworthy companions for Shakespeare's own comic creations. But it is the heroines who matter most. Margaret, the keeper's daughter of Fressingfield, and Ida and Dorothea of the Scottish court have no predecessors in English drama. Other plays have a love interest, but the heroines are lay figures appointed to stand and listen to the impassioned rhetoric of their suitors and reply, more briefly, in sentiments similarly over-emphatic. Greene's women are real women: charming, modest and natural, endowed with their own individuality. It is possible to see in them Rosalind, and Viola, and Perdita at the sheep-shearing.[3]

In these plays the spirit of Arcadia, hitherto confined to verse and novels, found a habitation on the stage. In *George-a-Greene* (if it is really his) Greene even managed to deny himself the customary adornment of classical and mythological allusion. The story is taken from the popular ballads about Robin Hood, and the countrymen refrain from literary references beyond their learning. By this time Greene had mastered the elements of his craft. Contemporaries acknowledged his skill as an architect of plots, and *Friar Bacon* was one of the landmarks of pre-Shakespearean drama for its ingenuity in weaving two distinct plots into a single story. Greene's method

3 His *Pandosto* was a source for *The Winter's Tale*.

was to provide an abundance of characters and incidents, so that the plays present a continuous flow of pictures, but in the end he gathered all the varied issues into a tidy and acceptable conclusion. This was achieved at the expense of the gradual evolution of events towards a climax that is the essence of the greatest drama, and it set an example for complex sub-plots which to Shakespeare was a challenge but to less skilled practitioners only brought confusion. Greene nonetheless had an instinctive sense of theatre. If it was only through his haste to proceed to the next incident, he understood the value of restraint; his comic interludes are not overdone, and Sidney could not have said of his clowns that they were dragged into places where they did not belong. He used only themes that were popular with the audience, but he assimilated the chronicle play — or at least a pretence of it — and a tale of the English countryside into some kind of unity: the perfection of Shakespeare's *Henry IV* grew out of materials sketched by Greene. Above all, his psychological insight, especially into the nature of women, showed how character might be unfolded on the stage with sensitiveness and restraint. The wretched story of his personal life has been told by himself in the exaggerated terms that often accompany belated repentance, and the acrimony of his pamphleteering stung his contemporaries. This cannot diminish his achievement in the theatre. His friend Nashe said what needs to be said on this matter: 'Why should art answer the infirmities of manners?'

Greene brings us very close to Shakespeare. Shortly after his death in September 1592 there appeared a book with the title *Greene's Groatsworth of Wit, bought with a million of Repentance*, which included an unfinished novel, a fable and some letters — all the manuscript that an eager printer could find among the remains of a man who died in such squalor that his estranged wife had to pay off his landlady. One of the letters was 'To those Gentlemen, his quondam acquaintance, that spend their wits in making plays', and it warns them to what straits scholars and gentlemen may be reduced if they debase their talent by writing for the common stages:

> Base-minded men all three of you [perhaps Marlowe, Lodge and Peele], if by my misery you be not warned: for unto none of you (like me) sought those burrs to cleave: those Puppets (I mean) that spake from our mouths, those Antics garnished in our colours. Is it not strange that I, to whom they all have been beholding: is it not like that you, to whom they all have been beholding, shall (were ye in that case as I am now) be both at once of them forsaken? Yes, trust them not: for there is an upstart Crow, beautified with our feathers, that with his *Tiger's heart wrapped in a Player's hide*, supposes he is as well able to bombast out a blank verse as the best of you: and being an absolute *Johannes fac totum*, is in his own conceit the only Shake-scene in a country. O that I might entreat your rare wits to be employed in more profitable courses: and let those Apes imitate your past excellence, and never more acquaint them with your admired intentions...yet, whilst you may, seek you better Masters; for it is pity men of such rare wits should be subject to the pleasure of such rude grooms.

Greene is here saying three things. First, he is regretting on general grounds that men of education should put themselves at the mercy of the players; secondly, these 'peasants' and 'painted monsters' are men of base ingratitude and have abandoned him in his need; and thirdly, he suggests that the reason why the players are no longer commissioning work from scholars like himself is that they have found in their own ranks a man who supposes he can do the job better, a '*Johannes fac totum*' who presumes that he can write plays as well as act in them. The identity of 'Shake-scene' is reinforced by a parody of his line 'O tiger's heart wrapped in a woman's hide' (*3 Henry VI* I iv 137), and this is the real importance of the passage. Otherwise it may not be very significant: deathbed utterances of dis-illusioned men seldom are. Greene's relationship with the actors may never have been very close. The unusually detailed stage-directions for *Alphonsus* suggest that he had done his part by writing the play and he had no intention of going to the theatre to assist in its performance. The actors may not have much cared for him either. He was accused of selling *Orlando Furioso* to two different companies, and maybe that was why they did not help him.

Whatever the particulars, Greene does, however, seem to have been right in his general prediction. A new race of dramatists was emerging from within the theatre itself, linked professionally with the men for whom they wrote. Ousted by these upstart crows, the scholars had to look elsewhere for their bread, and the *Parnassus* plays suggest that they did not easily find it. The three plays were acted at the turn of the century by the students of St John's College, Cambridge, and in mock-rueful style they lament the plight of scholars when men of money have no taste and men of learning have no money. "'Tis a shame indeed', says a character in the *Second Return*, 'that there should be any such privileged places for proud beggary as Cambridge and Oxford are'.

After taking their degress, two innocent cousins go forth into the world confident that their academic laurels will bring them a handsome livelihood. Ingenioso Nashe, a scholar who lives precariously by serving up hack-work for the printers, warns them that they will be disappointed: learning is 'the nearest way to poverty'. He has just been on Parnassus and found it 'out of silver pitifully', with Apollo having to borrow money from Pluto 'for his commons'; and trooping sadly down the hillside he has met 'a company of ragged vicars and forlorn schoolmasters' scratching their unthrifty elbows. The cousins discover that Ingenioso is right. Having several shabby and unrewarding employments, they fall to the lowest shift of all when they offer to prostitute their learning by writing for the theatre.

And must the basest trade yield us relief?
Must we be practis'd to those leaden spouts
That nought do vent but what they do receive?

2 Return 1846.

The cousins meet Burbage and Kempe, and in Kempe's opinion 'Few of the university men pen plays well; they smell too much of that writer Ovid, and that writer *Metamorphosis*, and talk too much of Proserpina and Jupiter'. The young men soon realize that their talents will be unappreciated even in the theatre, and after an unsuccessful attempt to grow rich as fiddlers (perhaps a reference to Kempe's triumphant dance to Norwich[4]), they withdraw into Kent to devote their scholarship to the tending of sheep. Specifically this scene with the actors is concerned with the the the recent *Poetomachia*[5] but it contains an envious and bitter attack on the profession:

> But is't not strange these mimic apes should prize
> Unhappy scholars at a hireling rate?
> Vile world that lifts them up to high degree,
> And treads us down in grovelling misery.
> England affords those glorious vagabonds,
> That carried erst their fardels on their backs,
> Coursers to ride on through the gazing streets,
> Sooping [sweeping] it in their glaring satin suits,
> And pages to attend their masterships:
> With mouthing words that better wits have framed,
> They purchase lands, and now esquires are named.
>
> 2 *Return* 1918.

It is a curious fact, which may have no significance at all, that these plays were acted at St John's, the college of which Nashe and Greene had been members.

Scholars and university men did, of course, continue to write for the theatre. Chapman, Greville, Thomas Heywood, Massinger, Daniel, Ford, Marston, Fletcher and Beaumont were all at Oxford or Cambridge. But mostly they had to conform to the wishes of their paymasters, and it could be a hard and impecunious life. John Day was a Cambridge man, although he was sent down, and he has been suggested as the author of the *Parnassus* trilogy. He was one of the playwrights employed by Henslowe to turn out plays at such a rate that collaboration was unavoidable. Such men almost worked on a treadmill. The point which the *Second Return* underlines is that mere learning is not enough. It may be an advantage, but it is better if it is worn lightly and does not obtrude itself in superfluous references to Proserpine and Jupiter; and in any case the players have in their own ranks men who can get along without it.

To summarize the achievement and importance of the University Wits is not easy. In the past both have possibly been exaggerated, and it would be wrong to suppose that within a few years the English theatre was suddenly

4 See page 155.
5 See pages 152-4.

transformed and set upon more decorous courses. Certainly the things that Sidney hoped for were not achieved. Poverty, not fame, was the spur, and these men produced much shoddy stuff that only ministered 'to penny-knaves' delight'. In some respects their example was unfortunate because it set standards to which inferior dramatists were unequal. Ranting echoes of *Tamburlaine* grew emptier and more monotonous; Kyd's success led to catchpenny imitations of the revenge theme, Greene drew the unwary into the pitfalls of tragi-comedy and Peele gave sanction to formless comedies put together by anyone who thought he could write a musical line. On the other hand, critics have sometimes wondered whether they set any example at all. Many of the old crudities persisted, and Henslowe's records show his hirelings churning out plays too hastily compiled, often by necessitous authors working in tandem, to have had any artistic merit.

So far as they had any cohesive identity, the University Wits were literary men who accepted the commercial theatre as one of the outlets for their work and were willing to accommodate themselves to its demands. That in itself was important, especially as their academic training was refreshed and strengthened by their experience of other literary forms. This versatility made them a forcing-bed of late Elizabethan literature.

To the theatre they brought an artistic control that went some way towards resolving the confusion in which they found it. They found the old Interludes in the course of growing into full-length plays with a coherent division into acts and scenes and a concern for appropriate metrical expression. Plays were made up of the three semi-independent strains of Morality, classical and romantic, and by the 1580s there had come the further intrusion of the chronicle or history form that was trying to bolster contemporary confidence by evocation of England's heroic past. The better plays of the University Wits showed how some order might be brought to these confusions, notably by pruning the classical and legendary allusion and by so modifying and assimilating the Morality element that dramatists could focus on the crisis of the individual character. The careful arrangement of the action to lead towards a logical climax was also a quality of the better plays, but we have to be thankful that the process of fusion and assimilation was not taken too far. Creative writers rejected the formalism of the schools and used only so much discipline as they felt to be desirable dramatically. The multitudinousness of Shakespeare may have offended the Augustans but his mastery of all the components of Elizabethan drama is one of the excitements of his work.

It is tempting but idle to speculate what Shakespeare would have achieved in the theatre if the University Wits had not preceded him there. The certainty is that he would have arrived in it, notwithstanding plague or Puritans or the feeling of social-moral-aesthetic disapproval that he understood and partly shared. Coleridge made sure of this during his discussion (*Biographia Literaria*, chapter XV) of *Venus and Adonis*. In the poem he found an imaginative consistency which 'reduces multitude into unity of effect', an essential quality of a dramatist; and, further, an intuitive power that works by an unbroken chain of images to provide a 'visual substitute' for the language used by actors on the stage.[6] Shakespeare was a dramatist because that was the way that his mind and imagination worked, and as a young man nothing would have kept him out of the theatre.

Being in, he no doubt found that his immediate predecessors had done several things as he would have wished to do them himself. In every one of his early plays he explored a fashion already known to be popular. Problems of authorship and dating make it impossible at times to say which of two plays came first, or even who wrote them; and the possibility of subsequent revision by other hands is a further complication, so that even at this early stage we cannot always be certain whether Shakespeare is creating or imitating. In *Edward II* Marlowe has probably been impressed by the success of *Henry VI*, but in *Henry VI*, and occasionally in later work, Shakespeare was trying to write like Marlowe, to manage the 'bombast' which in those days was a compliment to a poet's ingenuity, if not to his taste. It was akin to the literary art of 'amplification', the extension of an idea by rhetorical devices. *Richard III* completed a tetralogy of history plays, something that no English dramatist had attempted previously, and in Richard himself Shakespeare made a study of the sardonic Machiavellian rogue much more consistent than Marlowe's Barabas. *Titus Andronicus* adds further horrors to Kyd's recipe, but here again Aaron is a Machiavellian sketch and Shakespeare added something peculiarly his own in Lucius's promise 'to heal Rome's harms and wipe away her woe': the horrors are ended and ordinary life must continue. *Comedy of Errors* is based on the Latin models used by Lyly and resembles his *Mother Bombie* as a 'comedy of intrigue' exploiting disguise and changed identities; *Love's Labour's Lost* was designed for the courtly circles where Lyly had his vogue, whereas *Two Gentlemen of Verona* is more characteristic of Greene and the romantic plays which borrow an Italian novel and an Italian background but tell an English story of clowns and lovers.

Shakespeare's 'borrowings' are plain enough: from Lyly the attraction of sheer style, of elegant diction cured of excess; from Greene the large romantic canvas and the lively heroines who particularly adorn it; from Kyd the stagecraft through which it is possible to sup full of horrors and not be nauseated: from Marlowe the revelation of individual destiny through the medium of the highest poetry. It has often been pointed out that in 1594 Greene, Marlowe and Kyd were dead, Peele and Nashe would not write

---

6   The poem is consistently visual and dramatic. In six lines the opening stanza sets the scene and establishes essential facts about the two characters, just as in his plays Shakespeare gets the action moving in a few informative sentences; brief descriptive passages resemble the scene-setting devices of the theatre; and the characters reveal themselves through speech — 623 of the 1194 lines are dialogue.

much more for the theatre and Lodge and Lyly had already turned to other interests. This did indeed leave the way clear for Shakespeare, but it is more to the point that by 1594 he was already developing and improving upon the work of these men and he might have welcomed their continued competition as a stimulus. Possibly his chief debt to the University Wits is that they were too varied and independent to try to reduce English drama to any rigid and exclusive form. Shakespeare was left to enjoy complete freedom of topic, mode and treatment, so that as late as *Othello* he could reintroduce the Vice and in his last play of all take more notice of the dramatic unities than on any previous occasion.

Part III
The Elizabethan Stage

Chapter V
London

I'll hence to London on a serious matter.

3 Hen VI V iv 47.

In the days when monarchy was essentially personal, the seat of government was to be found wherever the monarch happened to be. At any time and in any place the councillors attendant upon him might constitute themselves the appropriate body for any particular act of government, whether administrative, legislative or judicial; and even when the Crown needed to function through the weightiest of its courts, the High Court of Parliament, the session was as likely to be held in some provincial town as in the capital in London. It is true that since the twelfth century certain courts and administrative departments had established a permanent base at Westminster and developed into permanent institutions; but London, although the largest and most important city in the kingdom, was slow to become the unifying centre of government or the focus of social life.

Its ultimate pre-eminence was advanced by Tudor centralization: the new dynasty from Wales settled in London and seldom left it. All the great Tudor parliaments met at Westminster, and perhaps this helped as much as anything to establish the city, to a degree hitherto unknown, as the true capital and focal point of the nation. It became the channel through which England absorbed the new European culture with its rich and eccentric fashions in dress and its sometimes stranger innovations in religion. With the Church now having less to offer as an employer of able men, the court and its patronage held out better prospects of a career. So to London came the adventurers, the men of ambition, the poets, the country gentlemen with money to spend, the innocents hopeful of enlarging the 'small experience' available in their provincial homes. One such innocent, almost certainly, was William Shakespeare.

Economic difficulties, combining with the Tudors' success in establishing a mainly peaceful and orderly society, created for the first time a serious problem of unemployment. Labourers who had rejected the constrictions of the manorial economy now found themselves deprived of its compensating security. The sort of men who formerly wore their lord's livery and fought his private battles no longer had extended periods of foreign war as an alternative outlet for their energies. They could not all be absorbed into the crafts or agriculture, which had problems of their own, so that they too sought a livelihood in the multifarious activities of the capital.[1] One consequence of the growing size and importance of London was the development of the professional theatre. With a large potential audience at their doors, the actors abandoned the inns where they had formerly played, built their own theatres and organized themselves into companies to cater for the endless demand for entertainment.

London in 1600 had a population of some 200,000, of whom about half were cramped within the boundaries of the old City and half in the suburbs spreading over the countryside outside it. The next largest city was Norwich with a population of 15,000, followed by Coventry and Bristol. The City was still bounded by its old battlemented wall, which extended from the Tower in the east to Fleet Ditch in the west (although the jurisdiction of the Lord Mayor stretched as far westwards as Temple Bar). Its most northerly point was Cripplegate, and the seven 'gates', from Aldgate to Ludgate, were still gateways through which the main highways passed to the suburbs beyond. The streets and dwellings of the City were insanitary and overcrowded. Most of the streets were only narrow lanes, unpaved and sodden with refuse, deprived of light and air by the over-hanging houses. Where they were able to bear coaches and carts, the press of traffic, on wheels and on foot, blocked the way. Dekker tells how

> in every street, carts and coaches make such a thundering as if the world ran upon wheels: at every corner, men, women and children meet in such shoals, that posts are set up of purpose to strengthen the houses, lest with jostling one another they should shoulder them down. Besides, hammers are beating in one place, tubs hooping in another, pots clinking in a third, water-tankards running at tilt in a fourth.
>
> *Seven Deadly Sins of London.*

Overcrowding was aggravated by official policy. Alarmed at the growth of London's size and potential influence, the Crown forbade any further building on unoccupied sites inside the City or within three miles of its walls; so that the only way to accommodate the extra population was to build in gardens, and thereby increase the congestion and further darken the scene. Plague was the terrible consequence.

In these circumstances the Londoners' main throughfare was the river,

---

1   A picture of the streets and life of Elizabethan London may be found in the plays of the period, especially those by Dekker, Thomas Heywood and Middleton, and in other contemporary writings, e.g. William Harrson, *Description of England*; Stow, *Survey of London*; Fynes Moryson, *Itinerary*; Greene, *Groatsworth of Wit*, *Notable Discovery of Cozenage, Second Part of Coney-Catching*; Dekker, *Gull's Horn-Book, Seven Deadly Sins of London*; Lodge, *Wit's Misery*; Nashe, *Pierce Penniless*; John Earle, *Microcosmography*; Philip Stubbes, *Anatomy of Abuses*.

'the glory and wealth of the city'. It was as yet unpolluted and full of fish, and as well as royal barges, merchants' argosies and foreign visitors borne in from Gravesend, it carried a constant traffic of ordinary folk going about their business in ferries and small boats. On its way to the sea the Thames was the vital artery of London life. It flowed through the fields of Chelsea, 'so called of the nature of the place, whose strand is like the chesil which the sea casteth up of sand and pebble stones', past Westminster and the gardens of Whitehall to the splendid palaces which lined the Strand: York House, where Francis Bacon was born; Durham House, the home of Sir Walter Ralegh; Somerset House, occupied now by Lord Hunsdon, cousin to the Queen and patron of the players; Exeter House, once the home of Leicester and now of the Queen's last favourite, the Earl of Essex. Next came the gardens of the Temple, and then Whitefriars Stair, the river exit from the ill-famed district of Alsatia, a refuge of criminals; King John's old palace of Bridewell, now a prison; then the liberty of Blackfriars, where the hall of a disused monastery would presently become a theatre. From Baynards Castle, home of the Earl of Pembroke, the river came to the busy traffic of the London wharves before flowing through the arches of London Bridge, on to the Custom House and the Tower Steps; and finally out into the country and the suburbs again, until it reached the palace of Placentia at Greenwich, the Queen's birthplace and her favourite residence.

Outside the City lay the fields and gardens which made London, despite the fetid congestion within the wall, still a country town. Houses lined Shoreditch beyond Bishopsgate; there was a cluster of buildings at Clerkenwell and a tiny isolated hamlet at Charing Cross; Hampstead and Islington were villages on the distant hills; north of Kentish Town was still an uncleared forest. Here the citizens took their sport and their exercise. They hunted in the area of Hyde Park and hawked in Liverpool Street, practised archery in Finsbury Fields and artillery in Bishopsgate Without, shot wild duck at Islington Ponds; in the meadows round Finsbury and Paddington 'velvet-guards and Sunday citizens' took their ease and comfit-makers' wives swore the genteel oaths that displeased Hotspur. In the fresher air of the northern suburbs small farms produced the vegetables and fruit which supplied the population massed within the City.

The suburbs south of the river had a bad reputation. They were reached by ferry or on foot across London Bridge. This was the only bridge across the Thames, and it filled Londoners with pride and foreign visitors with admiration. Its twenty arches were built on woolsacks, and its narrow width was flanked by houses and shops; in the middle was a drawbridge whose gatehouse displayed the warning of some thirty human heads rotting in the salty air. The bridge led into Southwark and the splendid chuch of St Mary Overie, and westward from Southwark to the Bankside. On Bankside lay the pleasure resort of Paris Garden, where bulls and bears were tormented by dogs, and the stews and taverns which ministered to diversions of a less overt kind. Here stood, in gloomy menace, five prisons; and here, the Globe would presently be built.

This was the London where Shakespeare lived the greater part of the year for perhaps twenty years: for some of the time in the City, in Bishopsgate and, later, by St Olave's, and for some of the time over the river in Southwark. Although he never tried his hand at the popular citizen comedies which dramatists like Dekker, Heywood and Middleton supplied for the gratification of London pride, his work is full of incidental touches which sketch the scene he knew so well: the scent of flowers in Bucklersbury at simple-time; the windmill in St George's Fields where Falstaff and Shallow lay all night; the Boar's Head in Eastcheap and the dark delights of the 'manor of Pickt-Hatch'. Even when his plot is set in Italy, its real background is the varied pageant of Elizabethan London, with the measured life of courts and noble houses and on the other hand the turbulent life of the streets, where round any corner Tybalt and a band of serving-men might be waiting to pick a quarrel that would end in death.

Socially as well as spiritually, St Paul's was the hub of London life. Its wooden spire, destroyed by lightning in 1561, formerly rose above the spires and steeples of 120 other churches in the City and its environs, and in its central aisle, known familiarly as 'Paul's Walk', the visitor would find 'the land's epitome...the whole world's map'. It was at once mart and throughfare and club, Here the 'lisping hawthorn-buds' paraded in the newest fashion, loose women plied for hire, tailors waited with their tape-measures, merchants and lawyers met to discuss their respective business. 'They say this town is full of cozenage.' Antipholus of Syracuse spoke of the darker side of this street of adventure, where came the coney-catchers, the wide boys looking for easy money, nips, foists and confidence-men seeking the unwary visitor from the country. Mingling with the strains of the organ and the chanting of the choir could be heard the specious talk of those hoping to 'dine with Duke Humphrey': the tomb of Humphrey of Gloucester having become the spot where men of luxurious and recondite imagination hoped to beguile the credulous into buying them a meal. Here gathered travellers with tales of 'Pyrenean and the River Po' and of men with heads beneath their shoulders; here Falstaff would have bought Bardolph into his service and have met Pistol with patches over the scars allegedly won in Gallia's wars, and 'all th' unsettled humours of the land', their 'fierce dragons' spleens' cowing the listener into an awed suspension of belief.

In his *Dead Term* Dekker thus described the scene:

> ...   Foot by foot and elbow by elbow shall you see walking the knight, the gull, the gallant, the upstart, the gentleman, the clown, the captain, the apple-squire, the lawyer, the usurer, the citizen, the bankrupt, the scholar, the beggar, the doctor, the idiot, the ruffian, the cheater, the Puritan, the cut-throat.

In this terse catalogue Paul's Walk is made to epitomize the vigour and variety of life in Elizabethan London and, more particularly, the unity that underlay its diversity. The contrasts were somehow less important than the unity of taste and mental habit that depended, in despite of the rigid distinctions of status, creed and occupation, upon a landed economy and the possession of a common language and religion. In later generations the distinctions were to become much more divisive, the community of taste correspondingly weaker. Perhaps television, more potent than any political or sociological theory, is the leveller that has brought the people as close together under the second Elizabeth as they were under the first. In Shakespeare's time the stage had much of the function that television has today. Puritans hated the theatre, but they and the dramatists were brothers under the skin, alike in their surrender to the intoxication of words, in their passion of spirit, in the ecstasy which they both sought after, however different it might be in externals. Stage and pulpit have always been at war, but they have always been children of the same family; since, as Keats perceived, the pursuit of beauty and the pursuit of truth arrive at much the same goal at the end of the journey. The Elizabethans were brothers in that every class basically had the same satisfactions. Thus the drama of the age was healthy and vital and splendid so long as it was written to be enjoyed by every sort of audience. As soon as there arose a visible distinction between the plays written for courtly coteries and those written for the popular theatres, it sickened and died, and it has never yet recovered its former authority. Even today theatre-going is looked on as a bourgeois habit.

In some respects, however, Elizabethan London, in the days when Shakespeare was making his career, was not altogether a happy place. Popular phrases about 'Merrie England' and 'the spacious days of Queen Elizabeth' evoke a picture of men idling in a golden haze as their sun sank slowly beneath the horizon, but those who lived through the last years of the reign did not feel life to be merry at all and their anxieties allowed them no time to relax. They were worried about the succession. In face of her subjects' repeated petitions that she find a husband and perpetuate her line, the Queen had never married. Her refusal even to nominate a successor seemed to invite the recurrence of civil war, with the additional danger of foreign intervention. The historical plays and poems of the nineties, Shakespeare's especially, reflect the nation's anxiety in their insistence on the duty of obedience and on the sinfulness of rebellion against the anointed ruler which might

> open
> The purple testament of bleeding war...
> Change the complexion of her maid-pale peace
> To scarlet indignation, and bedew
> Her pasture's grass with faithful English blood.

R II III iii 93, 98.

The Queen herself had outgrown her time. King James VI, waiting impatiently in Scotland, complained that she seemed likely to 'continue as long as sun and moon,' and Essex said that her mind was grown as crooked as her body. The court, which many fancy to have echoed with the praises of grateful poets, was as mean to scholars and artists as to the sailors who beat the Spaniards, with Spenser denied 'maintenance for his dear relief' and Lyly sighing 'Thirteen years your Highness's servant, but yet nothing... A thousand hopes, but all nothing.' The Tudor harmony of Crown and Parliament was wearing thin, and the clash over monopolies in 1601 was the culmination of increasingly bitter division over religion, finance and foreign affairs.

In the 1590s, too, there was a constant background of war. The defeat of the Armada in 1588 was not, as faulty perspective has sometimes made it seem to be, the moment when England emerged from the long shadow of danger. The splendour and unexpectedness of this performance were in fact something of a landsmen's myth, for English seamen had been beating the Spaniards in many waters for many years and in 1588 — while landsmen humbly gave thanks to God — they cursed the storms that had allowed so many of the invading ships to get away. The repulse of a single attack was no guarantee of lasting safety because if Philip of Spain could fulfil his designs in France and the Netherlands, he would be able to launch a much more dangerous attack from the Channel ports. For some years, therefore, English contingents were sent to assist the Dutch rebels and the Huguenots in France, and naval expeditions, most of them unsuccessful, attempted to harass Spain in the Atlantic and the Caribbean. The Spaniards retaliated with raids of their own, in 1595 setting fire to Plymouth and Falmouth and in 1601 landing a force in rebellious Ireland.

Thus Shakespeare's London saw the bustle and stir of warlike preparations. The importunity of Pistol, Bobadill and Captain Tucca waxed in time of war, and as well as being militarily ineffective, socially they were an embarrassment to the authorites. Apart from these swaggering professionals, the unwilling recruits for Elizabethan enterprises were those 'cankers of a calm world and a long peace' with whom Falstaff had to make shift. There was no exaggeration here. Elizabethan armies were gathered by any expedient that unscrupulous ingenuity could devise. For Essex's voyage to Cadiz in 1596 impressment officers surrounded churches during the Easter services and marched off the able-bodied members of the congregation. The social and intellectual uneasiness caused by this indeterminate state of war was visible in the history plays of the period, with their deliberate appeal to the triumphs and unified purpose of former times. The presence of English volunteers when Maurice of Nassau defeated the Spaniards at Turnhout in 1597 was celebrated in a popular play, *The Battle of Turnhout*, which drew the appropriate lessons, but there were more occasions for alarm than for patriotism. *King John* closes with an appeal for patriotism and unity:

> This England never did, nor never shall,
> Lie at the proud foot of a conqueror,
> But when it first did help to wound itself...
>   nought shall make us rue
> If England to itself do rest but true.
>
> *KJ* V vii 112.

The nation's anxiety deepened when rebellion broke out in Ireland in 1598. In *Henry V* Shakespeare, with a direct topicality seldom found in his work, contrasted the splendid memory of Agincourt with current misgivings about Essex's expedition against Tyrone, as though recollection of the past might furnish inspiration against the dangers of the present. But it was not to be. Essex failed, and the pent-up frustrations of a decade culminated in the tragic futility of his rising in 1601. The affair was half-hearted and ill-conceived, but Essex was popular with the disgruntled of all parties, especially the Puritans and the profesional soldiers, and his outbreak was symptomatic of all sorts of discontents.

At first the accession of James of Scotland brought widespread relief. To contemporaries it was an unlooked – for miracle that he should have come to the throne without a mouse stirring. His escape from the Gunpowder Plot was felt to be equally miraculous, and there was a Messianic aura in the figurative language in which he congratulated the nation and himself upon his deliverance. But it was soon evident that the new reign would bring difficulties of its own. Although James had much to say about the privileges and responsibilities of kingship, he lacked the royal qualities which had redeemed the Tudors even in their mistakes. He was soon quarrelling with the Commons; his handling of the religious problem alienated the Puritans without reconciling the Catholics; and he aroused native prejudice by lavishing offices and titles on the avaricious Scots who had followed him to England. Life at court became a sordid scramble for rewards, and its moral standard was relaxed by horseplay, drunkenness and immorality. Even in her tantrums Elizabeth had commanded loyalty and admiration, and those who grew most restive under her meanness and caprice usually returned to her compelling orbit. But poets and statesmen alike could find nothing to earn their respect in James's uncouth ways and empty values. They felt, like Gloucester, that 'we have seen the best of our time' and they transferred their loyalty to the heir to the throne, Prince Henry, 'our English Marcellus'. In Chapman's *Bussy d'Ambois* (1607) Henry III speaks in admiration of the court of Elizabeth:

> ...that's a court indeed,
> Not mixt with clowneries used in common houses,

But, as courts should be, th' abstracts of their kingdoms,
In all the beauty, state and worth they hold;
So is hers, amply, and by her inform'd.
The world is not more contracted in a man,
With more proportion and expression,
Than in her court her kingdom.

                                                                        I i 265.

He goes on to contrast with it 'our French court'. Dramatists had to disguise some of their popular allusions, but many of the London audience would know that James and his courtiers were the target.

                    Our French court
Is a mere mirror of confusion to it:
The king and subject, lord and every slave,
Dance a continual hay; our rooms of state
Kept like our stables; no place more observed
Than a rude market-place.

Moral indignation was also aroused by the consequences of economic troubles that were beyond the control or understanding of the contemporary mind. England was painfully emerging from the medieval economy of subsistence towards a capitalist economy of production and credit. Money, rather than land or goods, was the new measure of wealth, and Jonson's Lady Pecunia became 'the Venus of the time and state.' This is not the place to discuss the causes of the change. It is sufficient to note that men had become aware of various puzzling phenomena, such as that money was not purchasing as much as it had formerly, that merchants could outbuy the landowner, that there were many cozening schemes abroad to rob a man of his money, that there were jobbers who bought and sold land just as though it were a commodity, that trade and agriculture were liable to sudden inexplicable bouts of depression and unemployment. The dislocation of economic life by bad weather, ruined harvests or the plague was something with which men were familiar, although the years between 1590 and 1610 seemed to experience it with more than usual severity. But these other phenomena were new and unwelcome and perplexing. The emergence of an acquisitive middle-class, depending on the production of plenty and the expansion of credit, was altering the pattern of social life; and the change was taking place in an age whose moral and political thinking was still medieval and traditional.

During the sixteenth century prices more than quintupled, and the inevitable search for scapegoats explains the outburst of poetic and dramatic satire which began in Elizabeth's closing years. This literary protest, like the laws passed by the government, was unavailing because its diagnosis was incorrect. The statutes which composed the Elizabethan Poor Law made a brave effort to overcome the problems of poverty, vagabondage and unemployment. But the law-makers did not perceive that the causes were different; they merely offered sedatives to lessen suffering until the medieval norm should be restored. The satirists, likewise, assumed that all would again be well once men had reverted to the neighbourly Christian customs of the good old days. In default of the means to make an economic analysis, they made a moral one. They took the fine old-fashioned standpoint, the standpoint of the preacher, that the cause of man's misfortunes was man's own wickedness. They knew no jargon of statistical trends which bound economic life to the operation of inexorable laws. Convinced that man was, as he always had been, perilously liable to the sin of avarice, they allowed no appeal from human fallibility to the impersonal mechanism of change. Even plague and tempest merely signified God's displeasure with sinful man.

The economic problem of the period affected the choice and treatment of dramatic themes. The patriotic plays popular in the nineties gave place at the turn of the century to bitter, disillusioned tragedy or domestic and citizen comedies which depicted the contemporary scene.[2] Shakespeare took curiously little part in this: he was never primarily a satirist. This is not to say that he understood the economic situation better than anyone else, but he held up a wider mirror to the age than his fellows could encompass. But as an actor with his company he appeared in many plays of the kind and he was aware of the attitude they expressed.

Many of these plays, and in particular the work of Ben Jonson and Massinger, occupied themselves explicitly with the sin of acquisitiveness. In the over-simplified thinking of playwrights and satirists the social troubles of the time could be reduced to two fundamental causes: greed and the abandonment of status. The villain is the man who wants to get rich at the expense of others: not the usurer only, who in Dekker's phrase 'lives by the lechery of money and is bawd to his own bags,'but the promoter (the contemporary term was 'projector'), the swindler, the confidence-man, the whole tribe of those who believed that 'wealth is lord of all felicity' (Tourneur, *The Atheist's Tragedy* I i 30). The standard pattern of Middleton's comedies was to show the beast of prey confounded by his own intrigues. Massinger's *New Way to Pay Old Debts* arraigned two government jackals, Mompesson and Michell, who in 1621 were impeached for

---

2 Even for that prolific age the output of satire was unusually voluminous. Donne's *Satires* were circulating after 1593, and the disenchanted turned their milky minds to gall: 'My pen a sharper quill of porcupine, My stained paper thin sin-laden earth' (*2 Return from Parnassus* 2115-6). Examples were Lodge's *Fig for Momus* and *Wit's Misery*; Joseph Hall's *Virgidemiarum*; Marston's *Scourge of Villainy*; Everard Guilpin's *Skialetheia*; Samuel Rowlands's *Letting of Humour's Blood*; the *Epigrams* of John Weever, Sir John Davies, Thomas Bastard and others. In June 1599 the Privy Council ordered that 'no Satires or Epigrams be printed hereafter', and the satirical impulse was diverted to the stage or to the more urbane 'prose character' in imitation of Theophrastus, as in the work of Overbury, Hall and Earle. See Chapter XII below.

their racketeering. In *Volpone* Jonson exposed the shifts and abasement to which men would resort to grasp a dying man's fortune; in *The Alchemist* a man has only to pretend to the secret of making gold to have all London at his door; in *The Devil is an Ass* Pug the Devil finds the world a dirtier place than hell, made so by the schemes of projectors and monopolists. Meercraft, the projector in this play, has countless ingenious schemes for raising money: he would make gloves from dogskin, wine from blackberries, wool from egg-shells, grass from marrow-bones; he would serve the whole state with toothpicks and have the government make their use compulsory. Jonson spared no one. His Tribulation Wholesome is the man who can be acquisitive with a good conscience and scriptural support. Indeed he became so deeply obsessed by the theme of avarice that many of his plays were simply Moralities on the power of money.

Merciless to the exploiters, the dramatists had little sympathy for the exploited, They did not hide their exasperated contempt for those who allowed themselves to become victims of the unscrupulous: the gull, like the cuckold, earned only ridicule on the stage. The swindlers could not operate their schemes if there were not a supply of dupes wanting to get rich the easy way: the charge of cupidity was lodged with both parties. The moralists' remedy for the victims was that they should be satisfied to remain in the station to which God had called them, and cease to try to mount where they did not belong. Insistence on status was one of the bastions of medieval life. Each man, like the planets and all other works of Nature, had his appointed place, and the well-being of society depended upon his being content to remain in it. The cause of present troubles was that everywhere status was dissolving, calling neglected and degree overturned. Merchants were seeking titles, landlords were making fortunes in the City, riff-raff of all sorts (including certain actors) were applying for a coat-of-arms and the rank of gentleman.

The comic mode accordingly made heroes of characters who embodied the traditional virtues, were dutiful and neighbourly and walked contentedly in their vocation; and correspondingly pilloried the fortune-hunters, the social climbers, the sparrows in jays' plumage. Dekker's Simon Eyre was generous to his workpeople and showed a proper sense of station by refusing to buy a country estate and masquerade as a landed gentleman; another exemplary citizen, Heywood's Tanner of Tamworth, refused the offer of a patent from Edward IV. The objects of censure, on the other hand, were members of landowning families who neglected their responsibilities, spent their revenues on luxury and came to London to repair their fortunes. All would be well again when the landed gentry recovered their former sense of obligation to their tenants, to their class, to the community. This decline in social responsibility was regarded by the satirists, whether in drama or in poetry, as a principal cause of the evils they deplored. How could humble folk contentedly serve their calling when the great ones failed in example?

The satirical moralists, again in drama and in verse, were vehement in their denunciation of luxury, especially luxury in dress, and here they were of the same mind as their own Puritan critics. Extravagant expenditure on the newest fashions was supposedly a main reason why the prodigal sons of the gentry fell into the hands of the usurers and the promoters and had to forfeit their estates. Middleton tells in *Father Hubbard's Tales* of a 'young landlord accoutred in such a strange and prodigal shape that it amounted to above two years' rent in apparel': apparel that included breeches 'full as deep as the middle of winter, or the roadway between London and Winchester.' Shakespeare makes a similar comment when Buckingham refers to the improvidents who have pledged their estates to buy new fashions and so 'have broke their backs with laying manors on 'em' (*Henry VIII* I i 84). Of Falconbridge, 'the young baron of England,' Portia says: 'How oddly he is suited! I think he bought his doublet in Italy, his round hose in France, his bonnet in Germany and his behaviour everywhere' (*MV* I ii). In *Bussy d'Ambois* the French have this opinion of the English:

Never were men so weary of their skins,
And apt to leap out of themselves as they;
Who when they travail to bring forth rare men
Come home deliver'd of a fine French suit.
Their brains lie with their tailors, and get babies
For their complete issue; he's sole heir
To all the moral virtues that first greets
The light with a new fashion, which becomes them
Like apes disfigur'd with the attires of men.

I i 288.

Extravagance in dress was additionally objectionable because it obliterated the necessary distinctions of degree. William Harrison, whose *Description of England* (1587) was spiced with a forthright parsonical bias, complained that this 'fantastical folly of our nation' debauched all classes, 'even from the courtier to the carter': there was none who did not spend his substance in the vanities of dress or curled beards or pearls in the ears. 'How much cost is bestowed nowadays upon our bodies, and how little upon our souls!' In *Christ's Tears over Jerusalem* Nashe was apostrophizing London:

Scandalous and shameful is it, that not any in thee (fishermen and husbandmen set aside) but live above their ability and birth; that the outward habit (which in other countries is the only distinction of honour) should yield in thee no difference of persons; that all thy ancient nobility (almost) with this gorgeous prodigality should be devoured and eaten up, and upstarts inhabit their stately palaces...No land can so unfallibly experience this proverb, *The hood makes not the monk*, as thou; for tailors, serving-men, make-shifts and gentlemen in thee are confounded.

This summary account of some of the major anxieties of Shakespeare's age will be expanded in later chapters, but for the present it should have achieved two things. It should have readjusted the familiar image of the 'nest of singing-birds' stretching their throats in untroubled ease through halcyon days. Perhaps it was the almost continuous visitation of plague between 1592 and 1594 which divided the glory of their April-singing years from the disenchantment that followed. Once the rosy illusions were put away, their zest for life found its obverse in a preoccupation with vanity and corruption.

Secondly, we have been able to see the response of the dramatists to the dfficulties that troubled them. They did not run away from these difficulties and content themselves with being mere entertainers, though they always had to be that as well; nor did they merely hold up a mirror to the age and be its abstract and brief chronicle. They interpreted their social function more seriously than that. Their diagnosis may have been defective, but they led an appeal to the nation's conscience. As spokesmen of the traditional order they anatomized the pains and follies of the time and urged the remedies in which they believed. None of them was expressing in his work a purely personal set of values. What they felt they felt in common with each other, with preachers and writers in other fields, with the authorities, with all sections of the audience. Here, then, is one of the clues to the virility of Elizabethan drama. It was rooted in the deepest feelings of the age, and it knew itself to be in some sense a response to a vital challenge.

Chapter VI
The Theatres

Here is my space.

AC I i 34.

The buildings[1] in which the Elizabethans performed their plays did not differ in essentials from the stages used in medieval times by strolling-players all over Europe. Medieval troupers — maybe four or five men and a couple of boys — arrived at fairs and markets and set up their simple apparatus: a platform on trestles, high enough for a ring of spectators to get a clear view, with a decorated tent at one end to serve as tiring-house. The same design was used in the pageant-cars of the Miracle plays, and it lent itself to dramatic variety by providing three levels of staging. Most of the action took place on the platform, which usually was unlocalized but could be transformed by simple properties: a throne set before the tiring-house converted it into a palace, or God's judgment-seat, a bench made it a garden outside a house. The curtained space beneath the platform might be the hold of a ship or a dungeon or, most frequently, hell. A fourth acting area might be found in the street itself. The Coventry Cycle has a direction, 'Here Herod rages in this pageant, and in the street also'.

While there continued to be travelling groups performing in this traditional manner, professional actors came to require a more durable setting than a booth in the market-place, one where they could charge for admission. In London plays were sometimes given in the Beargarden south of the river, but the place was unsavoury, spectators were unruly and the proprietors demanded the best days for their own activities. A more satisfactory home was found in the yards of the larger inns. Where the yards of the old coaching-inns still exist in something like their former state, as at Gloucester and Huntingdon, it is possible to reconstruct the scene. Round

---

1 The basic facts in this chapter are drawn from E.K.Chambers, *Elizabethan Stage*: inns and public theatres are discussed in II xvi; private theatres in II xvii; structure in II xviii; staging in III xx, xxi. For further interpretation of the facts, much of it conflicting, see among others J.C.Adams. *The Globe Playhouse*; J.Q.Adams, *Shakespearean Playhouses*; M.C.Bradbook, *Elizabethan Stage Condtions*; C.W.Hodges, *The Globe Restored*; L.Hotson, *Shakespeare's Wooden O*; R.Watkins, *Moonlight at the Globe*; G.Wickham, *Early English Stages*; A. Gurr, *The Shakespearean Stage*.

three parts of the yard staircases led to balconies which gave on to the bedrooms. The actors built their platform at the enclosed end; their tiring-house, with a curtain hung before it, was in the stabling or ground-floor rooms behind their stage, and the gallery above it enabled them to incor-porate a new acting area. Spectators paying a larger fee occupied the galleries along the two sides, and others stood in the yard. For a period this became almost a permanent structure in certain inns, and the term 'inn theatre' is not inappropriate.

This was the setting of popular Elizabethan drama in its formative years where the Morality was finally secularized and a new drama evolved from the old mumming and miming of the Church. The surroundings did not lend themselves to psychological subtlety or quietist effects. The attack had to be loud and direct, the emotion simple and unvarnished. The first perfor-mances recorded in inns took place at the Saracen's Head, Islington, and the Boar's Head in Aldgate, in 1557.[2] Since plays attracted crowds and therefore were good for trade, innkeepers were willing to finance structural alterations to improve the facilities. There are records of playing at the Bell in Gracechurch Street, and nearby at the Cross Keys where in the eighties 'Bankes his curtal', a performing horse, danced and did mathematical calculations and other prodigies. Along with the Bell, the Bull at Bishopsgate was assigned to the Queen's Men for their first winter season in 1583; at the Bel Savage, on Ludgate Hill, the Admiral's Men were reputed to have acted *Faustus,* and at the Red Lion, outside the City jurisdiction at Stepney, the stage and seating were built as a speculation by the grocer John Brayne, later to be a partner in the building of the Theatre.

The use of so many stages indicates abundant dramatic activity, but it also suggests that the players were moving from one inn to another in search of satisfactory arrangements. Playing at the inn-yards had the disadvantage that the landlord's rent (some of which he had to give in donations to the poor, as a kind of entertainments tax) absorbed too much of the takings, and he took all the profit from the sale of tobacco, ale and fruit. At some of the inns the actors had to share the arena with acrobats, players of 'prizes' (fencing) and performing animals, and carriers from the provinces would wish to use the inn at certain times in its accredited purpose as a post. The innkeepers, for their part, were less than whole-hearted as they might be held liable for any illegalities or disturbances occurring among the audience. It was inevitable that sooner or later the actors should build permanent structures of their own, and the final impetus was provided by the mayor and aldermen of the City. Their zeal as the civic authority responsible for health and good order was quickened by the Puritan conviction that stage-playing was reprehensible anyway, and on 6 December 1574 they decreed that no innkeeper 'nor any other person whatsoever within the Liberties of

---

2 Not Falstaff's Boar's head, which was in Eastcheap.

this City' should permit 'any play, interlude, comedy, tragedy, matter or show which shall not first be perused, and allowed'.

It was part of a long story of antipathy and friction, and the players' best recourse was to build a playhouse. James Burbage, an unsuccessful joiner who had become an actor with Leicester's company, leased the site of a disused Benedictine priory in the parish of St Leonard's, Shoreditch, to the north of Bishopsgate. It was in the Liberty of Holywell and could be approached from the City by way of Finsbury Fields, a playground for Londoners since early in the fourteenth century. Burbage rented the site on a twenty-one-year lease for which he was to pay a fine of £20 and an annual rent of £14; he undertook to spend at least £200 on improving the site, but these improvements were to be his own property. With freedom to put up whatever sort of building he pleased, he simply used the traditional features of the public stages, erecting a platform with the tiring-house at its back and constructing an amphitheatre with galleries around it. He preferred the circular shape of the Beargarden to the rectangle of the inn-yards, but otherwise there is no evidence that he added any feature or device with which the actors were not already familiar. Thus the Theatre did not interrupt the development of the drama on traditional lines. The players built it to get away from the cupidity of innkeepers and the interference of the City Corporation, not because they were dissatisfied with the technical conditions in which they had been working. Indeed, they still found it convenient to use the inns at certain times, and as late as October 1594 Shakespeare's company were using the Cross Keys as their winter quarters. It was not until 1596 that the Corporation obtained the consent of the Privy Council to the banning of all acting within the City.

The Theatre cost Burbage more than he had anticipated. When he had put all his available capital into it, including what he could raise by pawning his wife's clothes, he borrowed from his brother-in-law, John Brayne, a successful grocer: an arrangement leading to subsequent bitter litigation with both Brayne and his widow. The cost was about £700, more than the Fortune a quarter of a century later, and much of the money seems to have been spent on elaborate decoration, the sumptuousness of the new playhouses being a frequent object of Puritan censure. But as proprietor Burbage must have done quite well on his (and Brayne's) investment, Leicester's, the Queen's, the Admiral's and the Chamberlain's being among the companies that played there during the twenty years of the Theatre's existence.

The Curtain, just to the south of the Theatre, must have been built very soon afterwards as it was complained of by the Puritan John Northbrooke in 1577. It was named after Curtain Close, the land on which it stood, and its builder was probably Henry Laneman, who rented property in the area. In 1585 Burbage made a seven-year agreement with Laneman to use it as an 'easer' to the Theatre and share the profits. The Chamberlain's Men almost certainly used the Curtain in the period between the abandonment of the

Theatre and the opening of Globe in 1599, in which case it was the 'wooden O' for which Shakespeare apologized in *Henry V*. In 1600 the Privy Council were assured that it would be 'ruinated or applied to some other good use', but it survived this threat just as it survived others. Worcester's Men were playing there in 1603 and it was still standing in 1627. Although probably used in later years for prize fights and spectacles rather than for plays, the Curtain had a longer continuous existence than any other Elizabethan theatre.

The first playhouse to be built on the Surrey side of the river was at Newington Butts, a village about a mile from the bridge, near to 'the south suburbs at the Elephant'. It was separated from Bankside by the popular resort of St George's Fields where wrestling, bowls and other sports were enjoyed. The theatre was in use at least as early as 1580 but it was too remote ever to be successful. When Strange's and the Admiral's played there for a short season in 1594, Henslowe's share of the takings averaged only 9s. a performance. By the end of the century it had been either destroyed or converted to other purposes, its limited usefulness having come to an end with the building of the Rose in 1587.

This famous playhouse, on a site that had formerly been a rose garden, was in the Liberty of the Clink, in the parish of St Saviour's, Southwark, and it was conveniently close to the river, the Beargarden and the Bankside stews. It was built by John Cholmley, like Brayne a grocer, and Philip Henslowe. Cholmley's interest was confined to an exclusive right to sell food and drink to the audience, and he seems to have died soon after the agreement was made, leaving Henslowe as sole landlord.

Henslowe was one of the most remarkable figures in the Elizabethan theatre, and his *Diary*, really an account-book for the years 1592-1603, throws light on the theatrical practice of the times.[3] Son of the Master of the Game in Ashdown Forest, he was as a young man in the service of Viscount Montague's bailiff. With characteristic opportunism he married the bailiff's widow and employed her fortune in buying property in Southwark, where they came to live. He became the owner of slum tenements and brothels and financed his clients by acting as money-lender and pawnbroker, although documents describe him as 'citizen and dyer of London' and he seems to have been a respected vestryman and churchwarden at St Saviour's. He acquired the lease of the plot at the corner of Rose Alley in Maiden Lane in 1585, by which time it is possible that he already had some interest in the Curtain and the playhouse at Newington Butts: it was after Burbage's agreement to use the Curtain in conjunction with the Theatre that he decided to create a new centre of dramatic interest on Bankside.

3 Henslowe's *Diary* and *Papers* were edited by W.W.Greg (1904-8). A more recent edition of the diary by R.A.Foakes and R.T.Rickert (1961) takes a kindlier view of Henslowe's character and motives.

Perhaps he saw it as a sound investment, perhaps he was obeying some baffled artistic longing, but for thirty years he applied his business acumen to the professional theatre. Until his death in 1616 there was scarcely an acting company (always excepting the Chamberlain's Men) with which he did not at some time have dealings, and scarcely a theatre (always excepting those controlled by the Burbage family) in which he did not have an interest. His relationship with players and playwrights was that of banker, business manager and money-lender, and it was not always a happy one because he callously exploited their necessities. In a formal indictment in 1615 they alleged that 'within three years he hath broken and dismembered five companies'. His partnership with the actor Edward Alleyn, who in 1592 married his stepdaughter John Woodward, was a formidable combination because Alleyn was a fine swashbuckling tragedian and as shrewd a businessman as Henslowe. (In 1604 they bought jointly 'the Mastership of his Majesty's Game at Paris Garden', which gave them a monopoly of 'all and every our bears, bulls and mastiff dogs' supplied for the 'pastime' of baiting. This must have contributed substantially to the munificence of Alleyn's educational endowments.) It is impossible to know whether Henslowe had any artistic judgment or any voice in the policy of his theatres. The players leaned on him because he could finance them, but with Alleyn to lead them, their acting policy is likely to have been their own.

The Rose was built just in time to share in the outburst of play-writing that followed *Tamburlaine*: Tamburlaine himself, Hieronimo, the Jew of Malta and Faustus were all famous Alleyn roles. Henslowe was always shrewd enough to improve the value of his investment and in 1592, when some combination of Strange's and the Admiral's were playing, he spent £108 on additions and repairs, and in 1595 — rather obscurely — he made 'a throne in the heavens'. From June 1594 until they moved to the Fortune in 1600 the Admiral's Men played continuously at the Rose, but that was the end. The theatre could not compete with the Globe planted so challengingly and so dauntingly within a stone's throw, and there are no records of performance after 1603.

Theorizing about the structure of Elizabethan theatres would have been much simpler if Francis Langley, a London draper and pawnsmith, had not built the Swan on Bankside in 1595 and if a pastor from Utrecht, Johannes de Witt, had not sketched a performance there. Built in 1595, the Swan stood in Paris Garden to the west of Bankside, and de Witt described it as the largest and most magnificent of the London theatres, but professionally it seems to have been unsuccessful. Langley failed to find a company willing to occupy it regularly until early in 1597 he leased it to Pembroke's Men, who had latterly been touring without much success but now had recruited two actors from the Admiral's and contracted to play for a year in London. Langley spent £300 on the playhouse and apparel, but Pembroke's performed the unfortunate *Isle of Dogs* which so enraged the Council that they forbade further playing and ordered the theatres to be pulled down. Even when the dust had settled and playing was resumed in the autumn, they did not lift the ban on Pembroke's or the Swan and they decreed that only two professional companies should be licensed to play in London. Five members of the Pembroke company deserted to the Admiral's and it was futile for Langley to sue them because they pointed out that his theatre no longer had a licence. Thereafter the Swan was occupied, if at all, by acrobats, fencers and miscellaneous entertainers, and although in the next reign Lady Elizabeth's company played there for a while under Henslowe's management, there is no record of its use after 1621. For scholars the importance of the Swan is the debate about its structure, and this is discussed below.

Meanwhile James Burbage's lease of the Theatre was due to run out in 1597 and Giles Allen, the landlord, was putting difficulties in the way of its renewal. The Corporation had at last succeeded in preventing the use of inns, and as Burbage did not own the Curtain, he was in danger of finding himself without a theatre. Accordingly he made a speculation which he thought would solve his problems. For £600 he bought part of the premises of a disused Dominican priory in Blackfriars and at further expense constructed an indoor theatre. (This would be the 'second' Blackfriars theatre, the first having been another hall in the same building used between 1576 and 1584 by boy companies, Lyly's early comedies being acted there.) But as soon as the residents of Blackfriars realized that there was a scheme to open a professional theatre in their midst, to be the resort of the dregs of the City and Bankside, they petitioned the Council to rescue them from 'this very great annoyance'. Lord Hunsdon, patron of the company, was among the petitioners and in the autumn of 1596 the Council 'forbade the use of the said house for plays'.

In the following February Burbage died, bequeathing his problems in a lordly way. To Cuthbert, his elder son, he left the Theatre, whose lease was due to expire in two months; and to Richard, the younger, principal actor in the Chamberlain's Men, the hall in Blackfriars that was not to be used for plays at all. James Burbage had been known to contemporaries as 'a stubborn fellow', and fortunately for English drama, his sons inherited his spirit and pugnacity. Allen's proposal to increase the annual rent from £14 to £24 was after twenty-one years only mildly exorbitant in view of sixteenth-century inflation, and James Burbage had agreed to this. What he could not accept was a mere five-year extension of the lease, after which the landlord would pull down the theatre and 'convert the wood and timber thereof to better use'. After the *Isle of Dogs* disaster Allen sensed a chance to force the inexperienced Cuthbert into even more stringent conditions. A desperate situation found a bold and desperate remedy. First the Burbages leased a plot of ground. They chose their pitch on Henslowe's doorstep, within knocking distance of the triumphant Rose. Their site, for which they had a thirty-one-year lease, was in Maiden Lane, Southwark, under the shadow of St Mary Overie. (Mrs Thrale was sure she lived on the exact spot, but as Dr Johnson later decided, she was not always dependable in matters affecting the emotions. Recent conjectures have located the site in Park St., Southwark, some twenty yards east of the commemorative plaque.) The next step was to convey their present building across the river. They hired a master carpenter, Peter Street, and shortly after Christmas 1598 a dozen of his workmen began to dismantle the Theatre and re-erect it on Bankside. They behaved, Allen later alleged, 'in very outrageous, violent and riotous sort', but he failed in his suit against the actors because by the original lease James Burbage became the owner of any improvements he made on the site.

Such was the manner of the building of the Globe, the home of one of the best organized and most successful companies in the history of the English theatre. There is no evidence that any company but the Chamberlain's Men (after the accession of James I the King's Men) ever played there. It was probably ready by the late summer of 1599 as a Swiss traveller, Thomas Platter, saw *Julius Caesar* there in September. It was burned down during a performance of *Henry VIII* on 29 June 1613, and the players decided at once to 're-edify the same', this time of brick. In 1642 all the London theatres were closed by a provisional government not representative of the nation, and two years later the Globe was destroyed 'to make tenements in the room of it'.

As the most easterly of the Bankside theatres, and the first to be reached across the bridge, the Globe was too much for Henslowe and the Admiral's Men, especially as in 1597 the great Alleyn had 'left playing'. They hastened to get out of reach of such embarrassing competition, and before the end of the year they had bought a site in the growing suburb of Cripplegate, to the northwest of the City. Then they summoned Peter Street and gave him twenty-eight weeks to build a theatre, to be called the Fortune, surpassing the Globe in size and magnificence. Alleyn paid £240 for the lease but only £520 for the building and painting of the theatre. Objections from the residents were overcome and the Fortune was ready by the end of 1600, with Alleyn emerging from retirement as its principal attraction. Burnt down in 1621, it was rebuilt of brick at a cost of £1000 and it was still being used by the same organization in 1642.

Henslowe's papers contain the contract which he made with Street, and since he was at pains to specify that in almost every respect the Fortune should take the Globe as its model, its structure and dimensions tell us a good deal about an Elizabethan play in performance. The first conclusion to be drawn is that the actors, on the evidence of their two leading companies, were satisfied with their conditions. In building anew, both companies had the opportunity, if they wished, to make innovations, but they did not so wish. They retained the familiar design of the inn-yards and the essential features of the older theatres. Galleries still encircled an unroofed yard, and the platform still thrust into the yard, where the groundlings stood close enough to touch the actors.

Elizabethan theatres were mostly round in shape. Some contemporary maps depicted them as hexagonal or octagonal, but the maps seldom agree with one another about either the shape or the site of a particular building. The many references to 'wooden O', 'thronged round', ring, circumference and circuit are sufficient to establish that the general design was circular even if the outer wall was angled. In this respect the Fortune differed from the norm, the contract requiring 'the frame of the said house to be set square', and the auditorium likewise; but when rebuilt after the fire, it was circular, which suggests that experience had shown the usual shape to be the most satisfactory. Each of the outer walls measured eighty feet; galleries and the tiring-house lined the inner walls to the depth of twelve and a half feet, leaving an auditorium fifty-five feet square. Half the auditorium was occupied by the stage, which extended twenty-seven and a half feet into the yard and was forty-three feet wide; probably it tapered to leave a narrow corridor on either side. The building was forty feet high and the galleries were divided into three storeys, 'with four convenient divisions for gentle-men's rooms and other sufficient and convenient divisions for twopenny rooms, with necessary seats to be placed and set as well in those rooms as throughout all the rest of the galleries'. The frame, stage and staircases were tiled but otherwise the structure was of wood, of 'good and sufficient new deal boards of whole thickness where need shall be'.

The striking feature of these arrangements is the smallness of the dimen-sions. To suggest two simple comparisons, the stage at its widest point was only two-thirds the length of a cricket-pitch, sixty-six feet; and its depth corresponded to the base line of a singles court at lawn tennis, twenty-seven feet. Thus the Elizabethan playhouse was a tiny enclosure and its stage a platform on which a dozen actors would have very little room to manoeuvre. In the calculations of Professor Alfred Harbage (*Shakespeare's Audience* p. 23) the Fortune when full to capacity held about 2350 spectators, of whom 800 were packed in the yard. The Rose accommodated a similar number, the Globe rather fewer, about 2050, and the Theatre only 1500. According to de Witt, the Swan 'accommodates in its seats about three thousand persons', but de Witt was wrong in many of his observations about this theatre and he was almost certainly wrong in this. It is not impossible, however, that the Swan held 3000 sitting and standing. What clearly emerges is that when full, especially with its cylindrical design, an Elizabethan theatre had an atmosphere of claustrophobic intimacy.

Admission at the doors cost one penny, with a further penny or twopence for seats in the galleries. Privileged spectators sat in the more expensive 'lords' rooms', equivalent to boxes in later theatres. These were set at an angle to the tiring-house facade and in the older theatres may have been directly above it. Admission cost sixpence or a shilling, and all prices might

be doubled at the first performance of a new play. After about 1596 the practice grew up of allowing the *élite* to sit on stools on the stage itself, where they
would advertise their eminence in various tiresome ways, flaunting their
disapproval of the play or nudging the actors and engaging them in conversation. 'You will thrust and spurn,' Jonson complained in the Prologue to
The Devil is an Ass, 'and knock us on the elbows...If you'll come to see new
plays, pray you afford us room.' Dekker, on the other hand, blamed the
'covetousness' of the theatre managements who let the stools at such a profitable rate that the lords' rooms are 'now but the stage's suburbs'.[4] This charge
is not inconsistent with the steady propaganda directed from the stage at the
'penny groundlings' for being groundlings and refusing to pay more for
their pleasure.

Henslowe's detailed instructions to Street about the building of the stage
have not survived. There is to be 'a shadow or cover over the said stage',
namely the canopy or 'heavens' from which apparitions were lowered, but
instead of giving particulars of the structure and fittings of the tiring-house
facade (the back wall of the stage), the surviving document says only that the
stage is 'to be in all other proportions contrived and fashioned like unto the
stage of the said playhouse called the Globe'. In this crucial matter we have
therefore to depend upon inferences made from spectators' reports, stage-
directions and the prologues and prefaces attached to contemporary plays.
These prologues are often full of detail, particularly Jonson's; and the stage-
directions supplied by some dramatists, notably Marston, give many indications of the way a play might be acted. But the total evidence defeats generalization, for the details often conflict and we do not always know whether the
text that happened to survive was of a performance at court, in a nobleman's
house, an inn, a public theatre or a private theatre. A successful play might
in its time be acted in all five of these settings, and for each it would require
some measure of adaptation. Again, a text may be a dramatist's 'foul papers',
his original version of a play before it had been prepared for the stage. The
only indisputable evidence is that Elizabethan actors had to be quick and
versatile because the presentation of a play would vary with the resources of
a particular building or the number of men available at a particular time.
Nor were stage-directions, like some of Marston's hopeful effects or
Greene's instructions for *Alphonsus*, necessarily carried out.

Of evidence supplied by spectators the most famous, and the most controversial, is de Witt's account of a performance at the Swan in 1596. His own
description and sketch of the theatre are lost but a copy was made by a
former schoolfellow at Leyden, Arend van Buchel. The sketch, therefore,
that has caused so much trouble is only a reproduction of one which itself
may have been made from memory rather than on-the-spot observation. It
shows spectators sitting in boxes above the rear facade, which excludes any

possibility of action 'above' on a balcony or battlements; and the facade itself, set with two doors, has no inner stage or recess in which characters may
be 'discovered'. The sloping roof above the rear part of the stage blocks the
view of spectators in the higher galleries; so that this roof would have been
flatter and its supporting posts higher. The platform is set on trestles, presumably in order that it may be removed to make room for bear-baiting or
other non-dramatic spectacles; but the sturdy posts holding up the roof
mean that it could not have been removed. When in 1613 Henslowe and
Alleyn pulled down the Beargarden in Bankside and built the Hope, they
stipulated that the stage should be movable, 'to be carried and taken away,
and to stand upon trestles', so that the new theatre might be 'fit and convenient in all things, both for players to play in, and for the game of bears and
bulls to be baited in the same', and accordingly 'the Heavens all over the said
stage' are to be 'borne or carried without any posts or supporters to be fixed
or set upon the said stage'. In the course of these directions to the builder
Henslowe and Alleyn implied that in general he was to take the Swan as his
model. The stage as sketched by de Witt is deeper than it is wide, and wider
at the front than at the back. A structure above the roof would accommodate
the pulleys for flying apparitions, but there is no trap in the floor of the stage
for descents into nether regions. Finally, a trivial point, the man at the
summit who blew a trumpet to summon people to the theatre appears to be
blowing it while the play is in progress. In his written description of the
building de Witt said that it was constructed of 'a mass of flint stones',
whereas this was an effect created by a surface of lime and plaster over wood.

Yet critics are reluctant to believe that de Witt was wholly wrong in what
he supposed himself to have seen. They agree that the omission of the trap is
an error, but the crucial areas are the balcony and the inner stage. It is
beyond dispute that on certain stages these resources did exist in some form,
however rudimentary. If not a balcony with a formal setting there must at
least have been space above the stage, unencumbered by spectators, where
Juliet might speak to Romeo, Henry V scale the battlements of Harfleur,
Berowne like a demigod sit in the sky, Richard III enter aloft 'between two
bishops', Antony be drawn up to Cleopatra's monument, Richard II appear
on the castle walls and descend like glistering Phaethon. There must, too,
have been some inset where Ferdinand and Miranda were discovered playing chess, the caskets were kept at Belmont, Titania lay in her bower or the
imprisoned Malvolio was taunted by Sir Topas. The mistake, perhaps, is to
assume that these were elaborately staged in a recess behind a traverse, or
curtain. A mere suggestion may have been enough, and the opening of one of
the large doors in de Witt's sketch would serve for it. Another device, inheri-
tant from the Miracle plays and sometimes used in indoor performances at
the lawyers' Inns, was a multiple setting in which localities were indicated
by 'houses', frames covered with painted canvas. But on some stages few of
these resources were available and the actors, who were endlessly adaptable,

had to improvise as best they could. They would be realistic in their staging if it were possible, but they could get along without it, and at no time would they allow it to hold up the continuous flow of the action.

The conclusion would seem to be that in the employment of scenery, properties and effects the Elizabethans ranged from lively attempts at realism to the naivest forms of make-believe; wherein they adopted the habit of the theatre at all times. The most realistic drama, so far gone in realism that it pretends the audience does not exist, rests on the convention of the 'fourth wall': a convention which the Elizabethans did not contemplate and is as naive as any they did adopt. But they were quite elaborate in some of their devices, and in the Prologue to the revised version of *Every Man In His Humour* Ben Jonson affected to despise them for it, offering instead a play

> Where neither chorus wafts you o'er the seas,
> Nor creaking throne comes down the boys to please;
> Nor nimble squib is seen to make afeard
> The gentlewomen; nor rolled bullet heard
> To say it thunders; nor tempestuous drum
> Rumbles, to tell you when the storm doth come.

Flats or a painted backcloth must have been used for Henslowe's 'cloth of the Sun and Moon', or the 'City of Rome' he had made for *Faustus*. In an inventory of properties belonging to the Admiral's Men he listed, among many other items:

> i rock, i cage, i tomb, i Hell mouth.
> i tomb of Guido, i tomb of Dido, i bedstead.
> i pair of stairs for Phaeton.
> i heifer for the play of Phaeton, the limbs dead.
> Phaeton's limbs and phaeton's chariot; & Argus' head.
> Old Mahomet's head.
> Kent's wooden leg.
> Iris head, & rainbow.
> i boar's head & Cerberus' iii heads.
> i Caduceus; ii moss banks, & i snake.
> Bellendon stable ; i tree of golden apples; Tantalus' tree.
> i chain of dragons.
> i lion; ii lion heads; i great horse with his legs.
> i wheel and frame in the Siege of London.
> i frame for the heading of Black Joan.
> i cauldron for the Jew.

These contrivances could be quite expensive: for 'poles and workmanship for to hang Absalom' Henslowe paid 'xiiij d.' They mean that the audience were not expected to piece out all the action in their imaginations, and nothing was spared in scenes of hanging, beheading, torture and mutilation.

Spectators inured to the work of the public executioner demanded to have these things faithfully portrayed. The severed heads of Cloten or Macbeth, the blinding of Gloucester, the assassination of Caesar were displayed *coram populo* without any Senecan inhibitions. There were special tricks to create the illusion of bloodshed. *Cambyses* specifies 'a little bladder of vinegar pricked', and Peele in *The Battle of Alcazar* required 'three vials of blood and a sheep's gather'.

Pictorial effect was futher enriched by the splendour of the costumes. The wardrobe was the largest item of expenditure. By acting nearly all their plays in contemporary Elizabethan dress, irrespective of place or period, the companies saved the expense of having to provide new costumes for each play. He that played the king had to make do with the same robes on several occasions. But the vanity of their kind bade them dress splendidly, on the stage and off it, and in the theatre this splendour heightened the illusion they were trying to create. They were assisted by the Elizabethans' susceptibility to changes of fashion, which furnished them with a supply of yesterday's novelties passed by the spendthrift gallants to their servants, who sold them cheap to the actors; and Henslowe's companies could be equipped from his pawnshops. Even so, the outlay was immense, particularly in relation to other costs. For a play about Cardinal Wolsey in 1601 the Admiral's Men paid £21 for the materials alone, apart from the cost of having them made up by 'our tireman'; 'two pile velvet of carnadine' cost 20s. a yard, cloth of gold 10s., and for one play they bought eight yards of it. A doublet and gown of branched velvet cost £6, and for a 'black velvet cloak with sleeves embroidered all with silver and gold' Alleyn paid £20 10s. 6d. To put this sum in proportion, it was more than a third of the price Shakespeare paid for the largest house in Stratford. It is small wonder that the Puritans complained of the actors' 'overlashing in apparel'. But this finery adorned some dazzling stage pictures. For a royal procession, a coronation, a wedding, the actors, even the least of them, must wear robes of velvet, silk and cloth of gold; not stage reproductions put together by the tireman's needle, but the real thing. The magnificence of the spectacle on these ceremonious occasions impressed the majesty of kings and beguiled the eye in compensation for the lack of painted scenery.

The Elizabethans had also a surprising range of sound effects. Battles, small and mimic things on the tiny stage, were made more exciting by gunfire and 'alarums', which were a combination of voices, trumpets and drums. In the modern theatre a call of trumpets, seldom varied, serves a number of purposes, but Shakespeare had at his disposal a variety of sounds, each with a special meaning. Thus the 'flourish' of the stage-directions was a long blast of trumpets sufficiently protracted to allow a character to descend from the upper stage to the platform; the 'sennet' was sounded on cornets to denote a processional entrance by royalty, whereas the 'tucket' announced the coming of a messenger or foreign envoy; and banquets, masques, dumb-shows and the like were usually accompanied by hautboys. The regular beat of drums denoted an army on the march, and for battles there was a recognized series of signals, the alarum, the retreat, the charge, the parley, each of them with meaning to an audience accustomed to listen for them.

Musical accompaniments were almost always integral to the play. When the Elizabethans used music to establish a mood, as in the opening scene of *Twelfth Night* or Ford's *The Broken Heart* V ii, it was played by musicians who were part of the action. There was no 'background music' played by an invisible orchestra. The accompaniment might come from above the stage or behind it or below it, but almost always — in Shakespeare's work at any rate — it was commanded by a character on the stage and it continued until it was ordered to stop; or if it came from an unknown source, like the mysterious music below the ground in *Antony and Cleopatra* IV iii, it was heard and commented on by everyone present and was not an independent communication from the orchestra to the audience. When 'solemn music' was required in the heart of a Welsh forest, Shakespeare was at pains to invent for Belisarius an 'ingenious instrument' to play it. This is not a very significant matter perhaps, but it shows the Elizabethans demanding greater realism than modern audiences who accept without question the convention that music shall sound, often unheeded by the actors, whenever the dramatist requires it. Few modern dramatists would put Lorenzo to the trouble of sending Stephano to the house to fetch musicians (*Merchant of Venice* V i 53) and of bidding them play when they arrive (66); and they continue to play until Portia tells them to stop (109). In similar circumstances most modern plays would give the conductor a cue and the actors would listen to the music, and even comment on it, without wondering where it came from. The versatility of Elizabethan actors made it easier for them to do without an orchestra. Many of them were skilled instrumentalists as well as vocalists, and when required to sing they were able to accompany themselves: Lucius, for instance, when he played himself to sleep, or Ophelia in her madness, or Marina singing to the distracted Pericles.

Let us try, therefore, to reconstruct the staging of a play in the open-air theatre of the Elizabethans. A flag with the theatre's symbol of swan or globe would fly from the turret to announce that a play was to be given that day, and the trumpeter's summons would become more urgent as the time drew near. On entering the theatre the audience would be able to tell what sort of play to expect. The First Part of *Henry VI* opens with the line 'Hung be the heavens with black...' and it is likely that this refers to the draping of the tiring-house with black cloth to indicate a tragedy. Plays began at two o'clock in the winter and probably rather later when the days lengthened. The Prologues to *Romeo and Juliet* and *Henry VIII* state clearly enough that the performances will take two hours, in which case they must indeed have been spoken trippingly on the tongue. References to the two hours' traffic of the stage are puzzling. The length of Shakespeare's plays ranged from *The*

Comedy of Errors with 1777 lines, and *The Tempest* and *Macbeth* with just over two thousand, to *Hamlet* with nearly four thousand. The average was about 2750 lines, and *Henry VIII* (2819) and *Romeo and Juliet* (3050) were both in excess of this. Although the closeness of the actor to his audience permitted a more rapid delivery than is possible in a large theatre, it is hard to believe that blank verse can have been spoken at the rate of some fifteen hundred lines an hour with time left for 'business', fights, processions and other diversions. It is true Ben Jonson estimated that *Bartholomew Fair* (4344 lines) could be played in two-and-a-half hours 'and somewhat more', but his later plays were shorter, by as much as a thousand lines on average, and he may have realized that he had been writing more than his actors could conveniently speak or his audience willingly hear. It would seem to be a fair guess that a play lasted for about two-and-a-half hours, including intervals, if any, and the jig with which the performance ended.

The jig was originally a dance, but skilled comedians like Tarleton and Kempe developed it into a musical farce in rhyme, sung and danced to a ballad measure. Thomas Platter noted in 1599 that at the end of *Julius Caesar* 'two of the actors in men's clothes and two in women's clothes performed a dance, as is their custom, wonderfully well together'. The jig was so popular that the players had difficulty in preventing its expansion into undue length and prominence. When the indecency of the notorious 'garlic jigs' at the Fortune obliged the Middlesex Justices to forbid their performance at the end of the play, the company evaded the ban by staging them in the middle of the perfomance.

With some fifteen or twenty minutes thus occupied by the jig, there can have been little time for intervals in the play itself. Whether there were intervals at all is a matter of debate, and the evidence , as so often, is scanty and conflicting. Probably the practice varied with the play and the theatre. Platter observed that 'in the pauses of the comedy food and drink are carried round amongst the people, and one can thus refresh oneself at one's own cost'. Refreshments there certainly were — nuts, fruit, beer and tobacco — and it was to the proprietors' interest to see that they were sold. They were carried among the spectators before the play began and it is more than likely that they were available during the performance, intervals or not. What does Platter mean by 'the pauses of the comedy'? With so many lines to be spoken in so short a time, he can hardly have meant the sort of interval that breaks the illusion in the modern theatre. Other considerations apart, there was not time.

The division of a play into acts and scenes was a sophistication seldom found before the middle of the sixteenth century, and Shakespeare seems never to have bothered with it. The act divisions were supplied by the editors of the First Folio, and they seldom sub-divided the acts into scenes. Shakespeare wrote his plays so that they might be performed continuously. The emptying of the stage and the immediate arrival of fresh characters, opening their dialogue before the others have fully departed, is his way of changing the scene, and when a lapse of time or a significant change of locality needs to be indicated, it appears in the dialogue. 'Barkloughly Castle call they this at hand?' conveys in a single line that Richard II is back from Ireland and is in the west, where we have seen his enemies gathering. Time is made to pass by a comic interlude, or a short linking-scene of citizens meeting in the street or carriers gossiping in an inn-yard, or sometimes a song. This was the purpose of the hay danced by Dull at the close of *Love's Labour's Lost* V i, or of 'It was a lover and his lass' in *As You Like It* V iii. In the previous scene Rosalind has arranged to pair the lovers on the morrow, and a night must pass. Shakespeare's device is to bring two unlikely Pages into the forest, give them a beautiful song to sing, and add the information that Touchstone and Audrey are to join the country copulatives, Martext's ministrations having been deemed insufficient. In the modern theatre actors need to rest and audiences to stretch, but Shakespeare required no intermissions in performance because he wrote all the necessary 'intervals' into the text. The chorus speeches of Gower and Time are a way of dealing with the special problems of *Pericles* and *Winter's Tale*, and we feel them to be clumsy compared with his normal practice. The Elizabethan stage freed itself of the tyranny of time and place which classical purists regarded as so important.

Henslowe's list of properties shows that within the limits of their resources the Elizabethans achieved what realism they could. With their fogs, their gunpowder and explosions, trapdoors in the floor and pulleys in the roof, the shipwrecked mariners dripping with actual water, their real animals and counterfeit animals, the contraption which ejected Jonah from the belly of the whale, and the 'quaint device' by which Ariel caused a laden banquet to disappear, they were particular in their search for visual effects. But on the open stage, with no curtain, no lighting, few painted flats and only a minimum of furniture, they soon came to the point beyond which realism was impossible. They relied instead on the spoken word. The technical restrictions of their theatre were the source of its real strength. Too much striving after realism eventually impoverished the drama by diminishing its imaginative power, and perhaps there was some ironic justice in the destruction of the Globe in 1613 when a spark from the 'chambers' (charges inserted into the breech of a gun) ignited the thatched roof of the canopy.

Shakespeare's view of the place of realism in the theatre is revealed in *A Midsummer Night's Dream*. 'There is two hard things,' says Quince: 'that is, to bring the moonlight into a chamber' and to make a wall 'through which the fearful lovers are to whisper'. Quince and his company are devotees of realism, and their solution is that characters shall come on to present Wall and Moonshine, so that no strain shall be put upon the auditors' imagination. Likewise, being realists, they must have prologues to assure the ladies, lest they be affrighted, that Pyramus is not really dead, being Bottom the weaver who is very much alive, and the roaring lion is not really a lion, being

Snug the joiner. In Quince's Interlude — and again in the pageant of the Nine Worthies, where there must be 'an apology for the purpose' of explaining how the diminutive Moth comes to be presenting Hercules: he shall present Hercules in infancy — Shakespeare is gently mocking the problems of dramatist and producer, and incidentally laying bare the mechanics of his own stagecraft. 'Moonshine and Lion are left to bury the dead,' Theseus remarks at the close of the Interlude, glancing at the dramatist's difficulty in getting corpses off the stage when there was no curtain to bring down on them. While Quince and Bottom are puzzling how to bring moonlight into the palace, Shakespeare is showing them how to do it. The bulk of the play's action passes in a summer wood at night. Actually it passes on the boards of a theatre open to the London air, in the afternoon, perhaps on a summer's day, perhaps in rain or in the greyness of November. Shakespeare's problem is the same as Quince's. He has to persuade the audience that the steady daylight which they see around them is a summer darkness illumined by the moon. In his mockery of the production devices of Quince and Holofernes he is implicitly condemning the cruder devices of the theatre, such as the display of a sign-board to indicate a change of locality or the use of a choric interpreter to explain every detail of the action. The right way to bring moonlight into the open theatre is to create the illusion by the spoken word. Thus in the first two scenes of the play Shakespeare prepares the audience for their visit to the moonlit wood: the recurrence of *night*, *moonlight* and *moon* wins our acceptance even before the wood is reached. In the wood itself we are at once in the company of the immortals, and when Oberon speaks his harsh and arrogant greeting to his fairy queen, 'Ill met by moonlight, proud Titania', our surrender to the illusion is complete. By the time the mortals come into the wood (II i 188), *moon* has occurred twelve times, *moonlight* four times and *night* twelve times. Looking over Shakespeare's shoulder as he writes, we see how the trick has been done.

Of course Shakespeare does use properties and mechanical devices. They would save him trouble, and he was seldom averse to taking short cuts when they were convenient; and it is likely that his colleagues insisted upon introducing simple spectacles to gratify the groundlings. A stage-direction in *King Lear* bids the 'drummers make thunder in the tiring-house, and the twelve-penny hirelings make artificial lightning in the heavens'. But such resources are always secondary to the poetry. The real storm in *King Lear* is in the characters themselves: it is Lear who creates it, and it would rage just as fiercely with no twelve-penny hirelings to give it mechanical impetus. Kent greets Lear's Gentleman on the stormy heath in words that at once give a picture of a man struggling head-down against wind and rain. 'Who's here, beside foul weather?', and the Gentleman shouts his reply into the roar of the storm, 'One minded like the weather, most unquietly'. The short dialogue between them (III i) further sets the scene and prepares us for the cosmic reflections that follow. Shakespeare here, and on countless occasions

elsewhere, is using the bareness of the Elizabethan stage to establish poetically the physical situation that he requires in order to tell his story. But he is
using it simultaneously in order to convey the characters' feelings and intensify the emotional response. The two activities are inseparable. In the little
scene on the heath it is not only the weather that is 'unquiet': there is mutiny
in the soul of man.

When Shakespeare wanted the audience to see a physical picture, his relationship with them was similar to Edgar's with the blinded Gloucester (*King
Lear* IV vi), where a few touches create the scene: the crows flying below the
cliff are no bigger than beetles, there is the tiny figure of the man gathering
samphire, the fishermen on the beach below appear like mice. Gloucester,
like the audience, believes what he is told. The chatter in the inn-yard at
Rochester, remarkably circumstantial, creates both scene and mood for the
Gadshill robbery; and a mere forty lines at the opening of *Hamlet* could
persuade an audience in the sultry London heat that out on the battlements
it is raw and cold and dark and terrible events are stirring. In Horatio's 'A
piece of him' it is impossible not to see the man pulling his cloak about his
freezing body and thawing his fingers at the sentry's brazier.

In these descriptive passages Shakespeare conveys mood and emotion as
well as the physical detail. Frequently he uses the motif of storm and shipwreck to reflect the turmoil of the heart, the endurance of its perils seeming
to ease the burden of the mind and guide it to illumination or reassurance
or decision.

> The seaman's whistle
> Is as a whisper in the ears of death,
> Unheard.
>
> *Per* III i 8.

When Othello is carried through the storm to Cyprus he greets Desdemona
in lines whose cadence tells of his relief and happiness even as it echoes the
rise and fall of the billowing waves:

> O my soul's joy!
> If after every tempest come such calms,
> May the winds blow until they have waken'd death!
> And let the labouring bark climb hills of seas
> Olympus-high, and duck again as low
> As hell's from heaven!
>
> *Oth* II i 186.

In *Julius Caesar* I iii and II i the characters speak of a night shaken with
thunder, prodigies and whizzing exhalations. This disturbance in Nature
reflects the torment in the mind of Brutus as he struggles with his
conscience. At length Cassius and Brutus whisper apart, and the night

seems to fall calm again as two of the conspirators idly wonder where lies the east and Casca's sword points ominously at the Capitol. When they have done, Brutus has made his decision.

Dramatic necessity was always compelling Shakespeare to write lines descriptive of nightfall or daybreak, and here again the technical obligation became an artistic opportunity, the lines being made appropriate to the character and the occasion. In his early work, when Marlowe provided the spur, he might not do it very well:

> The gaudy, blabbing and remorseful day
> Is crept into the bosom of the sea,
> And now loud-howling wolves arouse the jades
> That drag the tragic melancholy night;
> Who with their drowsy, slow and flagging wings
> Clip dead men's graves, and from their misty jaws
> Breathe foul contagious darkness in the air
>
> *2 Hen VI* IV i 1.

Certainly the lines portend the murder that is about to be committed, but they tell us nothing of the mercenary sea-captain who speaks them and in their would-be poetic afflatus they are scarcely appropriate to his condition. It is otherwise when two other characters in their different fashion welcome the coming of night:

> Gallop apace, you fiery-footed steeds,
> Towards Phoebus' lodging; such a waggoner
> As Phaethon would whip you to the west,
> And bring in cloudy night immediately.
> Spread thy close curtain, love-performing night.
>
> *RJ* III ii 1.

> Come, seeling night,
> Scarf up the tender eye of pitiful day,
> And with thy bloody and invisible hand
> Cancel and tear to pieces that great bond
> Which keeps me pale. Light thickens, and the crow
> Makes wing to th' rooky wood:
> Good things of day begin to droop and drowse,
> Whiles night's black agents to their preys do rouse.
>
> *Macb* III ii 46.

This is echoed at once by the assassin hired to kill Banquo:

> The west yet glimmers with some streaks of day:
> Now spurs the lated traveller apace
> To gain the timely inn.
>
> III iii 5.

The evocative power of these lines is extraordinary. The listener shares the stranded traveller's haste to reach the warmth and lights and company of the inn, beyond the reach of the evil now embodied in Macbeth.

Daybreak too might be greeted in characteristically individual ways. To the sober Horatio dawn was a sober visitant 'in russet mantle clad', russet meaning grey, or at most a dull reddish-brown. For fussy, complacent Friar Laurence, whom probably Shakespeare did not like,

> The grey-ey'd morn smiles on the frowning night,
> Chequering the eastern clouds with streaks of light,
> And flecked darkness like a drunkard reels
> From forth day's path and Titan's fiery wheels.
>
> *RJ* II iii 1.

It is fustian, and typical of the man. Here, not long afterwards, is Romeo, regretting that the night is gone, but lyrical, exultant:

> It was the lark, the herald of the morn,
> No nightingale: look, love, what envious streaks
> Do lace the severing clouds in yonder east:
> Night's candles are burnt out, and jocund day
> Stands tiptoe on the misty mountain tops.
>
> III v 6.

Yet again there is a graver, gentler beauty, a sense of sorrows endured and a happier day to come, in the words of Don Pedro after Claudio has made what amends he can at the empty tomb of Hero:

> Good morrow, masters, put your torches out.
> The wolves have preyed, and, look, the gentle day,
> Before the wheels of Phoebus, round about
> Dapples the drowsy east with spots of grey.
>
> *MAN* V iii 24.

One last example will show how Shakespeare used a necessary piece of description as a means to ethical and dramatic comment, thus guiding the emotional response of the audience. Duncan and his train arrive before Macbeth's castle at Inverness.

> *Duncan.*   This castle hath a pleasant seat; the air
> Nimbly and sweetly recommends itself
> Unto our gentle senses.
> *Banquo.*   This guest of summer,
> The temple-haunting martlet, does approve,
> By his loved mansionry, that the heaven's breath
> Smells wooingly here; no jutty, frieze,

> Buttress, nor coign of vantage, but this bird
> Hath made his pendent bed and procreant cradle;
> Where they most breed and haunt, I have observed
> The air is delicate.
>
> *Macb* I vi 1.

It is a charming description and it sets the scene, but the dramatic irony shocks the audience. The pleasant aspect of the castle, and Duncan's unaffected gladness in being there, stand in contrast to the crime that is being plotted within, and Macbeth's treachery is blacker than if these lines had never been spoken. As Banquo speaks we remember the words of Lady Macbeth only a few moments earlier:

> The raven himself is hoarse
> That croaks the fatal entrance of Duncan
> Under my battlements.
>
> I v 39.

When Shakespeare himself has done so much, it is idle for producers to crowd the stage with elaborate scenery or employ lighting and sound effects that distract attention from the poetry. We do not need live rabbits in an Athenian wood or live birds twittering in the eaves of Macbeth's castle. An artificial reddening of a painted sky when for Faustus Christ's blood streams in the firmament does not heighten the emotion, it merely leads to bathos.

Although Shakespeare used exact description when it served his purpose, it was a further advantage of his stage that a scene did not have to be localized at all. The bane of the picture stage with its formal scenery is that it has to be somewhere. It cannot, as the stage of the Globe could, suddenly turn itself into a locality undefined; it cannot, conveniently, although it is often obliged to try, shrivel distance, so that armies may camp at either side of the platform and make their preparations unaware of one another. Editors who have tried to localize the battle scenes, shifting them from 'Caesar's camp' to 'the Plain', from 'Antony's camp' to 'Another part of the Plain', have mistaken Shakespeare's purpose and diminished his art. In the action of a play he anticipated the technique of the cinema, 'cutting' from one incident to another so as to isolate the episodes that were dramatically significant.

The same fluid convention gave theatrical point to scenes containing eavesdropping, ambushes or concealed observers, where two or more groups are on stage and, in defiance of strict naturalism, suppose themselves to be alone. On such occasions the two pillars were accepted as providing the required concealmeant and isolation. Clarence's murderers did not commit the solecism of jesting in the presence of their sleeping victim, for they both were and were not in the room with him. All eavesdroppers were lawful espials, and Oberon was not the only character who could make himself invisible simply by telling the audience that he was so. The duping of

Malvolio or the trick played on Beatrice and Benedick need to be acted for all they are worth in simple acceptance of the Elizabethan convention, whatever the outrage to realism. In *Love's Labour's Lost* the central scene of the comedy (IV iii) is all the funnier if the hidden lords are not always popping out jack-wise but stand where the audience can see them and continuously read their expressions. The technical advantages of Shakespeare's unlocalized multiple stage are evident in the remarkable scene in *Troilus and Cressida* (V ii) where Cressida and Diomed steal perjured kisses and are observed on the one hand by Ulysses and the deserted Troilus and on the other by Thersites, the eternal scavenger of filth. Here the poet is not merely presenting three separate phases of the action, he is offering simultaneously three distinct dramatic styles. There is sentimental comedy in the age-old coquetry of the faithless lover, romantic tragedy in Troilus's shocked disillusion, and contemporary 'railing' satire in the comments of Thersites, who finds equal relish in the wantonness of Cressida and the suffering of Troilus. The scene is a *tour de force* that the audience will not properly enjoy if they are worrying whether or not it could really happen in just that way.

To complete this account of the staging of an Elizabethan play we must return to its controlling feature, the smallness and intimacy of the theatre. An actor at the front of the platform stood at the exact centre of the tiny 'circle' with spectators at his feet, on either side of him and looking at him from different angles on three sides of the building. The larger the theatre, the more difficult it is to unite an audience in that common passion that is a playgoer's most exhilarating experience. It must have happened quite frequently at the Globe when poetry cast its spell. The actor stood among the audience, could watch their changing expressions, nudge them, speak individually to them, include them in the action. Hamlet told them of his innermost thoughts, engaging them to reflect with him on transcendental matters; Richard III or Iago favoured them with sardonic asides, inviting them to enjoy the discomfiture of the credulous; Falstaff joked with them and did not allow them to overlook his cleverness; Macbeth made them see a dagger, Antony talked them into avenging Caesar, Henry V had them pouring through the breaches into Harfleur. The soliloquy and the aside, awkward matters on a proscenium stage, were an economical means of advancing the plot and directing a response. The speed of the action, unbroken by lengthy intervals or striking of a heavy set, kept interest at a high pitch once it had been aroused; and the technical problem of clearing the stage without dropping a curtain meant that a play ended, as artistically it should, with a gradual lowering of tension and quietness at the close. Nothing is gained by trying to send the audience home in a muck-sweat. This intense intimacy, sustained by swift action and undemanding conventions, was the outstanding difference between the Elizabethan theatre and subsequent developments. It generated an emotional excitement that perhaps can never be attained when actors are obliged to pretend that the audience is not there.

But fashions were changing even in Shakespeare's lifetime, and for those who could afford it the indoor theatre was more comfortable and had certain advantages. The custom of presenting plays indoors had, of course, a long history at court, colleges and private houses and also in the semi-public performances given before select (but paying) audiences by the boys of the choir-schools. Such performances did not receive the same disapprobation as a performance in the public theatre of the same play by the same author. We have already seen how James Burbage's bid to instal a professional company in his expensive conversion at Blackfriars was defeated by the residents, but in 1600 his sons leased it to Henry Evans, a Welsh scrivener who had become business manager for the Children of the Chapel Royal. To this the residents had less objection as the audience would be of a higher class and the performances less crude. A year earlier the Children of St Paul's had been revived under the partronage of the Earl of Derby, and for a while the 'little eyases' offered serious competition to the adult professional.[5] But the novelty wore off, and after various irregularities the Chapel children lost the favour of the court and in 1608 Evans returned the Blackfriars lease to Richard Burbage. His company being now under royal patronage as the King's Men, there was little the residents could do about it.

Within a few years the enclosed theatre had become the vogue with four more opening in the next twenty years; and the Fortune was probably roofed when it was rebuilt in 1623 and the Red Bull when it was enlarged in 1632. London's theatreland thus moved again from Bankside to the western suburbs and Liberties of the City, which were more accessible for the court, the lawyers and the great houses in the Strand. The Rose fell into disuse, the Swan was never a success, and until the Southwark Beargarden was rebuilt for theatrical purposes in 1613 and named the Hope, the Globe, which was always the summer home of the King's Men, was the only theatre whose flag flew across the river. With the change in the structure of the playhouse came inevitable changes in theatrical procedure.

The indoor stage was still small. The auditorium at Blackfriars was only sixty-six feet by forty-six feet, holding some 600-700 spectators, all of whom had seats. The dimensions of the Salisbury Court, off Fleet Street, opened in 1629, were 140 feet by forty-two, the intervening years having shown a long rectangular shape to be most suitable for indoor performances. At Blackfriars there was seating along three sides of the building and prices ranged from 6d. to 2s.6d. It is probable that the stage extended the full width of the hall, so that gallants might sit on the stage without unduly confining the acting space.

5 See p. 150-5.

The crucial change that came in with the private theatre was an increase in music and spectacle, and the sort of entertainment which before 1600 had been the privilege of small courtly audiences came in time to be the staple recreation of a much wider and less discriminating circle. The windows could be covered and the stage artificially lit by candles and torches: whence the popularity of 'nocturnals', plays like Marston's *Antonio and Mellida* that were written to be performed in murky darkness faintly penetrated by flickering lights. The stage-directions in plays known to have been written for indoor performance show how often action was interrupted for some spectacular effect, like a procession or a dumb-show. Marston particularly was in love with such diversions. Act II of *Antonio's Revenge* opens with these instructions:

> The cornets sound a sennet.
> Enter two mourners with torches, two with streamers: Castilio and Forobosco, with torches; a Herald bearing Andrugio's helm and sword: the coffin: Maria supported by Lucio and Alberto, Antonio by himself: Piero and Strozzo, talking: Galeatzo and Matzagente, Balurdo and Pandolfo: the coffin set down: helm, sword and streamers hung up, placed by the Herald; whil'st Antonio and Maria wet their handkerchers with their tears, kiss them, and lay them on the hearse, kneeling: all go out but Piero. Cornets cease, and he speaks.

The dumb-show had been a device much used by Senecan imitators but it had gradually disappeared. Before 1609 Shakespeare had used it only once, in *Hamlet* when he was burlesquing an outmoded style. But with the mechanical resources of the indoor theatre it returned, and dramatists used it who had no need of it. *The Changeling*, by Middleton and William Rowley, was much too strong play to be interupted by the empty show that begins the fourth act, with De Flores smiling until 'Alonzo's ghost appears to him in the midst of his smile, and startles him, showing the hand whose finger he had cut off'. A direction in Jonson's *Cynthia's Revels* says simply, 'A Mute divides the act with a dumb-show, and exit'.

As well as spectacle there was much more music. Music played for an hour before the performance, and there was a regular intermission — song, dance or unaccompanied melody — between the acts. The play itself would be interrupted with songs having no relevance to the character or the circumstances. For each act of *Antonio and Mellida* Marston wrote in directions for a song without any indication of the tune, the theme or even the first line, so that any dramatic significance it might have was accidental. Dramatic relevance was not what the playwright was seeking. The boy companies for whom Marston chiefly wrote had some charming singers, the audience wanted to hear them and the playwright merely had to give them the opportunity. But Shakespeare's songs are so tightly woven into the texture of the play that to transfer them to another scene or another character or even another play is to lose much of their value.

Enthusiasm for music and spectacle culminated in the masque, a form of entertainment which subordinated character and action to the less exacting pleasures of song and dance. Already fashionable as a courtly accomplishment among the nobility, who liked to perform as well as watch, it became in James's reign one of the accepted diversions of the professional theatre. The masque might be a complete entertainment in itself or it might be intruded in an abbreviated version within the framework of a play. Elizabethan masques had usually been 'disguisings' for the most part mimed, and the Muscovite episode in *Love's Labour's Lost* is of this sort, with Moth as the 'presenter' who gave such explanation as was necessary. But Jonson enlarged the function of song and dialogue, and with Inigo Jones to design the settings, Jacobean masques were sumptuous and expensive. At best they were a mongrel sort of entertainment that moved away from poetic drama, from the unfolding of plot and character that is the theatre's eternal business.

The influence of the indoor theatre, then, was in many ways unfortunate. The entr'acte diversions, the musical turns, the pomps and spectacles were artistically as indefensible in their different way as the horseplay of the common stages, and more insidious because they appealed to spectators who ought to have been more discriminating. Playwrights discovered that they might achieve success by mechanical means instead of poetry and the sweat and gristle of dramatic contruction The labour that is saved by a dumb-show or a song and dance is labour ill lost.

The success of the Blackfriars theatre stirred rival companies into emulation. More ambitious effects were attempted on the open stages of the Fortune and the Red Bull in Clerkenwell, built about 1604 and the home of Worcester's Men. It is likely enough, too, that Shakespeare's company employed some of the new methods at the Globe. Thomas Heywood, a level-headed and industrious professional, illustrates the change in his four mythological *Ages* plays (1611-14), a sequence of episodes between the reign of Saturn and the fall of Troy. Even the choice of such a theme suggests a deliberate intention to exploit the legends of gods and heroes for purposes of spectacle. Here are some of Heywood's directions:

> Hercules sinks himself: flashes of fire; the devils appear at every corner of the stage with several fireworks ....fireworks all over the house.

> Two fiery bulls are discovered, the fleece hanging over them, and the dragon sleeping beneath them: Medea with strange fiery-works, hangs above in the air in the strange habit of a conjuress.

> Jupiter above strikes him with a thunderbolt, his body sinks, and from the heavens descends a hand in a cloud, that from the place where Hercules was burnt brings up a star and fixeth it in the firmament.

What is happening here is not a change in kind but a change in values and emphasis. The use of a few simple properties, and of painted canvas 'houses' or 'mansions' as symbols of locality, was an unbroken tradition from the

Miracle plays that continued into Shakespeare's drama. At court the Master of the Revels kept a stock of scenic aids that provided the players with 'houses', chariots, painted trees, monsters, etc., so that court performances, and to a lesser degree all indoor performances, were more spectacular than those given in the open air. But once the actors had acquired their own indoor theatre for commercial presentations there was a shift of emphasis towards the use of spectacle for its own sake, and the popularity of masques was to the disadvantage of legitimate drama. All this culminated in the excesses of the nineteenth century. At Covent Garden in 1823 Charles Kemble presented *King John* in dresses, armour and settings scrupulously faithful to the period: a ludicrous feat of pedantic antiquarianism in an essentially Elizabethan play. At Her Majesty's in 1899 Beerbohm Tree staged a tableau of King John signing Magna Carta, a constitutional event in which Shakespeare was not interested. Tree had a weakness for tableaux of this kind, introducing a large-scale representation of the battle of Shrewsbury and of Bolingbroke riding into London on Roan Barbary. At the Princess's in 1857 Charles Kean employed 140 stage-hands for his production of *The Tempest*. Irving too went in for huge spectacular scenes like the 'disguisings' in *Henry VIII*, and even Benson, who normally was more conscientious, played all the Venetian scenes in *The Merchant of Venice* before moving to the splendours of Belmont.

After the opening of the Blackfriars theatre Shakespeare's dramatic output fell to a single play a year, and the event may have hastened his retirement. His company still used the Globe during the summer months and it is impossible to know whether, as he wrote the four romances with which he ended his career, he had in mind the new stage at Blackfriars or the old bare platform that he knew so well. As a theatre manager it was his business to gratify the public taste, and the secret of the strange, unearthly atmosphere of the final plays may lie no deeper than an attempt to find a successful formula for the new venture. There is a definite concession to music and spectacle. It is equally possible, however, that a distaste for the new manner of playwriting may have concluded his professional career earlier than he had intended, that the company's new recruits, Beaumont and Fletcher, could handle the fashion as skilfully as himself and better enjoyed doing it. It may be that the elaborate stage-directions that appear in the Folio edition of the last plays were thus detailed less because he was exploiting the scenic resources of Blackfriars than because he had already retired to Stratford and he would not be present during rehearsals.

The present century has reacted against Tree and Irving by reverting to methods that permit the continuous flow of the action with a simple permanent setting; and the prohibitive cost of spectacular productions makes it likely that this trend will continue. But there is a *caveat* here. Some thirty years ago, after the war, there was a brief revival of poetic drama, led by T. S. Eliot, Christopher Fry and others. This movement petered out, for reasons which literary historians may be able to explain when they stand farther from the event. There was also an attempt, more sustained and successful, to continue the revival of Elizabethan principles of staging started by William Poel and Harley Granville-Barker a generation previously. Theatres were built or adapted for playing 'in the round', with no proscenium or orchestra-pit and the actors brought closer to the audience. Much has been gained from this, especially in speed and naturalness, and it is suitable for plays which, like Shakespeare's, depend much on dialogue. But latterly there have been signs of a withdrawal from this style of presentation, an acknowledg-ment of its limitations. We know, or should know, that no cosmetic methods will restore Shakespeare's own theatre or rediscover the impact of his plays as they were first presented. No one seriously wants to revive the boy actor,[6] but there is more to it than that. Society has changed, audiences are different, the nature and economics of playgoing are different. The miracle of Shakespeare's art has bridged the generations, but his people were not as we are. Besides, three hundred years of the picture stage have established theatrical customs of which, except perhaps by artistic intuition, he was unaware. For the modern playgoer 'theatre in the round', with its wide spaces and diffused lighting and actors making free of the auditorium, destroys illusion by its constant reminder that the actors are just actors. Seated round three parts of the stage, the audience can also see each other, which is now a total disadvantage. All this produced a different experience at the Globe, but the Globe itself belongs to a vanished world. To-day a darkened theatre and a framed stage may best supply that 'distant enchant-ment of the view' upon which theatrical illusion has come to depend.

6 For whom, see pp. 176-9.

Chapter VII
The Players

The best actors in the world, either for tragedy, comedy, history...

Ham II ii 414.

1. The Struggle for Status.

The status of the sixteenth-century actor was not high, nor was his life easy. Some of his difficulties originated in the legislation that followed the Black Death, when a serious shortage of labour obliged the government to try to put every able-bodied man to work; and unless a man could prove that he had a master whom he served, he might be classed as a vagabond, punished, and directed into a useful occupation. All wandering entertainers, whether clowns, tumblers, jugglers, minstrels or players of Interludes, were mistrusted by the authorities because they belonged to no guild, sold no visible commodity and might become a charge on the parish. Thus they were classed (not always unjustly, as many of them were deserters from guild or manor) as 'masterless men', and they could not practise their 'quality' without a nobleman willing to act as their patron. A statute of 1572, part of the Tudor Poor Law, branded as rogues and vagabonds all 'fencers, bearwards, common players in Interludes and minstrels' not authorized by a baron or person of higher degree. Such patronage was not hard to get as many noblemen had minstrels and interluders to perform in their houses, and the cost of maintaining them was defrayed if they were allowed to give public performances as well. It is possible that the severe regulation of 1572 was approved, even encouraged, by companies who were fortunate enough to have obtained patronage and consequently wanted to limit the competition.

Patronage did not, however, free the actors from the restrictions imposed by local regulation. By medieval law and custom the civic authorities were responsible for the health, order and general well-being of their districts, and as this included the regulation of popular amusements, visiting

---

1 For the basic facts of this chapter see Chambers, *Elizabethan Stage* and *William Shakespeare*. The actors' struggle for recognition is discussed in *Eliz.St.* I viii-x and the relevant documents are in IV App C and D; the history of the boy companies is in II xii, of the adult companies in II xiii. The history of Shakespeare's company is given in greater detail in *WS* I iii and II App A viii.

entertainers could not perform without a licence. This might not be obtainable if the corporation believed that the gathering of audiences endangered health and public order and also kept apprentices from their trades and labourers from their rural tasks. Thus the actors were at the mercy of small-town prejudice and policy, with many local corporations hostile to stage-playing as unscriptural and idolatrous. They did not achieve recognition and a relative stability in their profession until controversy became so heated that the Crown and Privy Council at length decided the issue in London, where it mattered most. If plays were to be controlled, as everyone agreed they must be, the Crown would be the final authority in their regulation.

But the contest was bitter and exhausting. The City of London was in some respects a self-governing republic, and there was no constitutional ground for the direct intervention of Crown or Council in matters of purely local significance. The City claimed that their traditional right to control and license entertainments had been confirmed by the royal proclamation of 1559 which prohibited plays on controversial issues of religion and politics. The government naturally shared the Corporation's concern for health and public order, and they had no wish to encourage idleness or sedition. The real issue was that the authorities in London, as in many other towns, were predominantly Puritan and wanted to suppress the theatres altogether.

This policy was embarrassing to a government already disturbed by Calvinist hostility to the Prayer Book and the Established Church, and they were reluctant to give official support to any such energetic manifestation of Puritan opinion as the City Corporation's hostility to plays. Drama was not the only matter in contention: the Council would disregard regulations prohibiting Sunday games, bowling-alleys, cards, dice and other popular diversions. But in drama a special consideration was the Queen's insistence on having plays at court during the Christmas revels and at certain other times. She required these to be efficiently and lavishly presented without herself having the expense of maintaining actors within the royal household. As boys from the choir-schools could not alone satisfy her demands, professional companies must be allowed a regular and active existence, 'as well for the recreation of our loving subjects as for our solace and pleasure when we shall think good to see them'. After 1575 the professionals appeared at court more frequently than the boys, and on more than one occasion temporary bans on the public theatres were lifted or disregarded as the Christmas season drew near. When in 1600 there was local opposition to the building of the Fortune, the Council decreed that

the use and exercise of such plays not being evil in itself may with a good order and moderation be suffered in a well governed estate, and...her Majesty being pleased at times to take delight and recreation in the sight and hearing of them, some order is fit to be taken for the allowance and maintenance of such persons as are thought meetest in that kind to yield her Majesty recreation and delight.

Provision for 'her Majesty's solace' was crucial in the players' struggle for recognition.

Puritan opposition to the theatre may seem tainted and parochial but there were precedents for it in the sumptuary legislation of the Middle Ages and it was similar in spirit to the Roman Index. Both Calvinism and the Counter-Reformation represented a reaction against the bold assertions of Renaissance Humanism, with the consequence that Humanist energy was gradually confined to narrow considerations of classical style and form. These were safe when discussion of the fundamentals of man's existence was not. The Renaissance had lost its early bravery when manner became more important than matter and, for example, a man of Lyly's intelligence could devote himself so whole-heartedly to the pursuit of stylistic elegance.

The Marian fugitives had returned to England in 1559 with the dangerous zeal of first-generation converts sharpened by a sense of grievance. They regarded England as an important prize to be won over to the Swiss way of doing things, and the first wave of their assault fell upon those outward forms of the Anglican faith that still savoured of Catholic practice: what Tribulation Wholesome called 'the menstruous cloth and rag of Rome' (*The Alchemist* III i 36). Drama was feared and detested because, like vestments and church ornaments, it was associated with the ritual of the Catholic Church and indeed originated when 'the great scarlet-coloured whore of Babylon...set the church door wide open for sundry sports and plays to enter freely into the House of God'. Idolatrous vestments and images could be destroyed for ever, but in drama the human voice might still give life to Catholic doctrine and worship. To minds appropriately conditioned even a Miracle play was an artifact of Satanic wickedness because it reached illiterate auditors who could not comprehend liturgical finesse or the parson's saws but were responsive to simple stories simply enacted. Miracle plays were suppressed but drama persisted in its secular forms and it was abhorrent to men who condemned the Mass because the priest was 'acting Christ'. The virulence of Puritan hatred of the theatre is explicable only in terms of deep spiritual or emotional conviction.

This meant that the City Fathers were consistent in their affirmations and their actions. Suppression was their long-term policy, and their occasional permits were hedged with conditions whose breach would instantly renew the demand for total closure of the theatres. The Council, on the other hand, were not consistent, and the ambiguousness of their attitude to the players must at times have made the City Fathers feel that they were on the point of victory. Prominent councillors like Burghley, Knollys and Mildmay had Puritan sympathies, Mildmay to the extent of founding Emmanuel College as a Puritan seminary; concern about health and discipline was genuine; and the actors did not help themselves by putting on some plays that were indiscreet and by failing to prevent disturbances in their theatres. The Queen's solace perhaps was the great imperative, and in 1574 a royal patent sidestepped the Corporation by authorizing the company patronized by the Earl of Leicester to perform 'throughout our Realm of England' on the licence of the Master of the Revels, who was a court official.

The Corporation appear to have realized where this might ultimately lead because later in the year they replied with a weighty summary of 'the great disorders and inconveniences' consequent upon stage-playing. These included 'frays and quarrels, evil practices of incontinency in great inns'; 'inveigling and luring of maids to privy and unmeet contracts'; 'the publishing of unchaste, uncomely and unshamefast speeches and doings'; together with the keeping of people from divine service, robberies and purse-picking, 'uttering of popular busy and seditious matters', the hazards to life by plague and infection by 'sundry slaughters and mayhemings' caused by 'ruins of scaffolds, frames and stages, and by engines, weapons and powder used in plays'. The exaggerations in this blanket indictment at least reveal the Corporation's ultimate purpose, and they accompanied it with six regulations upon which, with penalties, they insisted if acting in the City was to continue. James Burbage responded by building the Theatre outside the City's jurisdiction, and when this was followed by the building of the Curtain, and then of the theatre at Newington Butts south of the river, the contest entered a new and more acrimonious phase.

With theatres now operating outside their immediate control the Corporation had to change their tactics. If at present they could not suppress the actors, men who 'should by their profession be rogues', they might bleed them to death by depriving them of their audiences. Having tried, with only limited success, to convert the more lenient Justices of Surrey and Middlesex to their own intolerant attitude, they sought to mobilize public opinion against the stage. Preachers in the City pulpits threatened perdition to anyone who entered a playhouse; writers were commissioned to denounce the theatre in pamphlets; and the Corporation appealed to the freemen of the London guilds not to allow their apprentices or servants to visit plays.

Already, in 1574, Geoffrey Fenton, whose translation of Bandello's novels supplied the drama with so many good plots, had attacked the theatre in *A Form of Christian Policy*, basing himself on the sanctity of the Sabbath and on early Christian denunciations of Roman stage-playing in circumstances very different from those of Elizabethan London. (Unhistorical citation of patristic writings condemning the practices of pagan Rome was a regular feature of Puritan protest.) In the same year Thomas Norton, part-author of *Gorboduc*, had urged the Corporation to prohibit 'unnecessary and scarcely honest resorts to plays', and after 1576 complaints grew more bitter when the actors built their own 'gorgeous playing places' and walked the streets wearing fine clothes and looking more prosperous than vagabonds ought. In a sermon at St Paul's in 1577 Thomas White produced a remarkable syllogism to connect the theatre with the spread of infection: 'The cause of plagues is sin...and the causes of sin are plays'. There can be no real answer

to that kind of thing. Plays were listed among the evils of the age in maledic-
tory works like John Northbrooke's *Dicing, Dancing, Vain Plays or Interludes* (1577) and Philip Stubbes's *Anatomy of Abuses* (1583), and there was a
general Puritan consensus that theatres endangered public health and
morals, corrupted the 'transvestites' who played the women's parts (for had
not Calvin, in his interpretation of Deuteronomy xxii 5, blasted all who,
even for innocent amusement, put on the costume of the opposite sex?),
offered entertainment that was violent and salacious and — not least — kept
people from divine service. A preacher lamented that a trumpet announcing
'a filthy play' at the theatre would 'sooner call thither a thousand than an
hour's tolling of a bell bring to the sermon a hundred'. In *Virtue's Commonwealth* (1603) Henry Crosse, no lover of drama, contrasted the swift,
enveloping movement of the theatre with sermons and sacred exercises
wherein 'all the senses are mortified and possessed with drowsiness'.

Some of the criticism came from men who themselves had been associated
with the theatre and probably were hired for the purpose by the Corporation
or their friends. Certainly neither Stephen Gosson nor Anthony Munday
was a Puritan in the strict sense, although both could take up the idiom well
enough, and both had to struggle to make a living in London's literary
jungle. Gosson's *School of Abuse* (1579), dedicated to Sidney, was concerned
for the fate of poetry as well as drama, and Sidney wrote his *Apology* in reply.
Plays Confuted in Five Actions (1582) was a more powerful and specific
attack on the theatre, possibly because the players had responded to the first
pamphlet by reviving some of Gosson's own dramas. Meanwhile there had
appeared in 1580 *The Second and Third Blast of Retreat from Plays and
Theatres*. The second blast was a medieval diatribe and the 'Anglo-Phile
Eutheo' who wrote the third is thought to have been Munday. Previously an
actor and subsequently a dramatist, Munday was a typical Elizabethan hack
who would sell his pen or his principles to any paymaster. Apart from his
delation of Edmund Campion he is chiefly remembered for his pastoral play
about Robin Hood, written for the Admiral's Men, which inspired a
comedy with the disdainful title *As You Like It*. In their arguments and their
language these two men with theatre experience were indistinguishable
from Stubbes, who sincerely believed that the times were out of joint. For
him the theatre was only one of the 'notable vices and imperfections' of a sick
society, the others including dancing, football, usury, astrology, the state of
the prisons and sartorial extravagances like the wearing of starched ruffs.

The language of these complaints is hyperbolic and monotonous and a few
brief extracts will give their flavour. Gosson admitted that he had written
plays, which he described as piglets born of his own sow, and he allowed that
a few plays might be regarded as innocent in themselves. One of these was an
exemplary piece called *The Jew*, a lost play that may have been a source for
The Merchant of Venice. But in general theatres are 'a market of bawdry' and
the actors 'caterpillars of the commonwealth', 'uncircumcised Philistines',

'dancing chaplains of Bacchus'. To the drama's claim to be a schoolmistress of life he replied that

> the argument of tragedies is wrath, cruelty, incest, injury, murder, either violent by sword or voluntary by poison; the persons gods, goddesses, furies, fiends, kings, queens and mighty men. The ground-work of comedies is love, cozenage, flattery, bawdry, sly conveyance of whoredom; the persons cooks, queans, knaves, bawds, parasites, courtesans, lecherous old men, amorous young men...What schooling is this?

Munday protested that the theatre fills 'our hearts with idle cogitations...our ears with filthy speech, unhonest mirth and ribaldry'. It gives 'our whole bodies to uncleanness; our bodies and minds to the service of the Devil'. We attend it only to feed on vanities:

> The notablest liar is become the best poet; he that can make the most notorious lie, and disguise falsehood in such sort that he may pass unperceived, is held the best writer...Our nature is led away with vanity, which the author perceiving frames himself with novelties and strange trifles to content the vain humours of his rude auditors, feigning countries never heard of; monsters and prodigious creatures that are not, as of the Arimaspi, of the Grips, the Pigmies, the Cranes, and other such notorious lies.

From later editions of *The Anatomy of Abuses* (significantly a very popular book) Stubbes withdrew his original admission that plays might be 'very tolerable exercises' so long as they exalted virtue and gave good example and wholesome instruction. He described them as 'sucked out of the devil's teats to nourish us in idolatry, heathenry and sin'. Indeed there are examples to be learnt from them

> if you will learn falsehood; if you will learn cozenage;...if you will learn to play the hypocrite, to cog, to lie and falsify;...if you will learn to become a bawd, unclean, and to devirginate maids, to deflower honest wives...to practise idleness, to sing and talk of bawdy love and venery...and finally, if you will learn to contemn God and all His laws, to care neither for Heaven nor Hell, and to commit all kinds of sin and mischief.

The academic playwrights of the universities had come to look down upon the common stages but their own work was no longer immune. At Oxford William Gager of Christ Church wrote Latin comedies, with at one time some assistance from Peele in their presentation, and he defended the exercise on the ground that acting not only trains the memory and the faculties of speech and movement but also 'tests what mettle is in everyone, and of what disposition they are of'. He was attacked by John Rainolds, or Reynolds, a fellow of Corpus Christi, which was Gosson's college, celebrated for his Latin orations and lectures on Aristotle. As a student he had acted a teenage Hippolyta, later he would be a principal Puritan spokeman at the Hampton Court Conference and translator of the prophets for the Authorized Version.

It is significant of the age[2] that this man of scholarly and capacious mind should fall to pamphleteering about the drama and should find special affront in plays taken from sacred themes. When watching one of Gager's plays at Oxford in 1592 the Queen rebuked Rainolds for his 'obstinate preciseness' in objecting to such harmless entertainment, but in his *Over-throw of Stage Plays* (1599) he turned from academic drama and attacked on a broader front.

The dramatists might have replied to the critics that present mirth has present laughter and 'Dost thou think, because thou art virtuous, there shall be no more cakes and ale?' Udall in fact had said this in the Prologue to *Ralph Roister Doister*. His comedy was to deflate vainglorious boasting, but honest mirth, 'wherein all scurrility we utterly refuse', is purgative in itself:

> For mirth prolongeth life, and causeth health;
> Mirth recreates our spirits, and voideth pensiveness,
> Mirth increaseth amity, not hindering our wealth;
> Mirth is to be used both of more and less,
> Being mixed with virtue in decent comeliness —
> As we trust no good nature can gainsay the same.

But this was written in Queen Mary's time, before the Puritans had mustered the assault. It would no longer be a valid defence in the 1580s, when men of ill nature were gainsaying the virtues of healthy laughter and, with hats pulled tight around their brows, had no intention of being voided of their 'pensiveness', which then carried a sense of heavy distaste and foreboding. It would not be sufficient to confess that the purpose was to entertain and to invite the disapproving to stop away. Drama had a strong didactic tradition, and the actors thought that the surest way to the favour of the authorities was to convince them that the theatre was healthy in its effects: not for recreation only but as a source of uplift and moral improvement. Apart from Jonson, no one in this controversy was much concerned with drama as an artistic form. The arguments were social and ethical, the actors contending that the stage invariably displayed the triumph of virtue, with violence perishing by the sword and cozenage ending in the stocks. They defended themselves by quoting Horace's view that the most effective reformer is he who mixes profit with pleasure, delighting the reader as well as instructing him. Both sides, too, resorted to unedifying personal abuse. Mincing Puritans and busybody magistrates were ridiculed on the stage and were represented as hirelings of the brothels and taverns whose custom was being attracted to the playhouses.

2 Significant, too, of the sad divisiveness of the age's religious conflicts that Rainolds's brother William became a Catholic and went abroad to teach at the English College at Rheims.

Replying to Gosson in his *Honest Excuses*, or *A Defence of Poetry, Music and Stage Plays* (1579), Lodge tried to dignify the argument by taking a Humanist standpoint, asserting the divine inspiration of poetry and reminding critics of the respect due to allegory throughout all medieval literature. In tragedy the instructive stories of the fall of princes warn us against the crimes that turn prosperity to disaster; and comedy, which Cicero described as 'the imitation of life, the mirror of custom and the image of virtue', rebukes vice through pleasurable representation of the ways of men. To Gosson's question how spectators would derive profit from the elaborate exhibition of villainy Lodge replied with Plutarch that 'those of judgment can from the same flower suck honey with bees, from whence the spiders take their poison': which seems to leave much of the question unanswered.

A less philosophical defence of the theatre appeared in Nashe's *Pierce Penniless* (1592), an allegorical dissection of the follies of the age. He shows how each of the seven deadly sins has won disciples in contemporary England, and the theatre is presented, somewhat surprisingly, as an influence likely to resist the corrosion of Sloth. The enemy of Sloth is emulation, and in the theatre men are stirred to emulate great deeds. The long Elizabethan peace has left our martial spirits unoccupied, and 'if they have no service abroad, they will make mutinies at home'. People with time on their hands will devote themselves to pleasure, and of drinking, dicing, whoring or playgoing, playgoing is the least harmful. Nashe even claims that it is more than innocent recreation, it may be 'a rare exercise of virtue'.

> First, for the subject of them (for the most part) it is borrowed out of our English chronicles, wherein our forefathers' valiant acts (that have laid long buried in rusty brass and worm-eaten books) are revived, and they themselves raised from the grave of oblivion, and brought to plead their aged honours in open presence: than which, what can be a sharper reproof to these degenerate effeminate days of ours?

He goes on to refer specifically to the success of a recent play on Henry VI, probably the first part of Shakespeare's trilogy, and from this unheroic reign he extracts a heroic theme.

> How would it have joyed brave Talbot (the terror of the French) to think that after he had lain two hundred years in his tomb, he should triumph again on the stage, and have his bones new embalmed with the tears of ten thousand spectators (at several times), who in the tragedian that represents his person imagine they behold him fresh bleeding.

Following this unusual argument, Nashe offers the more familiar justification of plays as 'sour pills of reprehension, wrapped up in sweet words'. No play 'encourageth any man to tumults or rebellion, but lays before such the halter and the gallows'; and as for the argument that the theatre keeps men from honest work, that is just an invention of the innkeepers, who if there were no plays 'should have all the company that resort to them lie boozing and beer-bathing in their houses every afternoon'.

Such talk is spirited but we may feel it to be spurious. Ben Jonson is a more convincing witness because he really meant what he said when in the Introduction to *Every Man Out of His Humour* his Asper promised to 'strip the ragged follies of the time' and hold up a mirror

> Where they shall see the time's deformity
> Anatomis'd in every nerve and sinew,
> With constant courage and contempt of fear.

Jonson could be hectoring and arrogant, but he was trying to reform the contemporary drama on classical precepts and his hard intellectualism is more persuasive than the soft rhetoric of the pulpits and the pamphleteers. His case was the stronger because he admitted the faults which most of the theatre's apologists wanted to conceal: 'nothing but ribaldry, profanation, blasphemy, all licence of offence to God and man'. In dedicating *Volpone* (1607) to the sister universities, he claimed to have 'loathed the use of such foul and unwashed bawdry as is now made the food of the scene', and he had laboured for 'the principal end of poesy, to inform men in the best reason of living'. It was 'the office of a comic poet to imitate justice and instruct to life, as well as purity of language, or stir up gentle affections'. Again in the Prologue to *Every Man In his Humour*, written some years after the first performance in 1598, he said that the comedy presented

> deeds and language such as men do use,
> And persons such as comedy would choose
> When she would show an image of the times,
> And sport with human follies, not with crimes.

But not even Jonson, with his high intentions, is really meeting the Puritan argument. It is true that in his terrifying comedies vice eventually is punished with a savagery that crosses the frontiers of laughter into some darker region; but for most of the plays' duration vice has prevailed with an exuberant relish that makes the imitation of justice look pale and has done little to stir up 'gentle affections'. There is nothing 'gentle' in Jonson's exposure of vanity, greed and credulity.

In the long debate about the theatre's acceptability and survival the two parties were giving a contrary interpretation of the same facts and were responding differently to the nature of drama. It is difficult for anyone responsive to the spell of the theatre to stand outside the question and identify himself with the mind that regards that spell as pernicious; and just as hard for the man whose bones mistrust all manifestations of secular art to look upon the theatre as innocent recreation, still less as inspiration to virtue. Within its own limited terms the debate probably should be decided against the dramatists and their champions because their argument was demonstrably specious. The Vice and his kindred had fixed too firm a hold on Elizabethan stages for them to be accepted as moralizing agents through their eventual and often perfunctory defeat. They had enjoyed themselves too much in the meantime, and provided too much enjoyment for others. The rejection of Falstaff may be conventional and orthodox, but few spectators will have found it an edifying experience; and with this the players' case collapses. On the other hand, neither party was expecting to convert the opposition. An occasional brand might be rescued from the burning, such as Gosson, the former dramatist who was to become rector of a London parish, but the appeal was to public opinion and to the authorities with whom the decision lay.

Decision was hastened by the stridency of Puritan propaganda and the reluctance of the City Corporation to be content with small and tentative advances. In 1574 the Privy Council had overruled the Corporation by authorizing Leicester's Men to perform in the City and the Liberties on the allowance of the Master of the Revels. In 1580 the Corporation tried to take advantage of disturbances at the Theatre by petitioning for the suppression of plays as 'ungodly and perilous', but in the following year the Council appointed the Master to be supervisor of all stage performances throughout the realm. In 1583, when the Corporation managed to bar the actors from the inns and resumed their attempted interference in the Middlesex and Surrey suburbs, the Council issued a warrant for the formation of the Queen's Men, a dozen players recruited from Leicester's and other companies, and forced the City to allow them the use of two inns, the Bull in Bishopsgate and the Bell in Gracechurch Street, during the winter months. Here was a plain hint to the Corporation that the Queen meant to have her solace, and they were soon complaining that all the inns and theatres were 'filled with men calling themselves the Queen's players'.

With the lesser companies thus sheltering behind the privilege given to the Queen's Men, the players, so long as they behaved themselves, were now reasonably sure of their position despite the Corporation's efforts to hedge them with restriction — no playing on Sundays and holidays, or during Lent, or after dark, and so on. But in 1584 Whitsuntide riots by the apprentices gave occasion for a prolonged closure until in November the Queen's demanded to be allowed to practise for the winter season. During the Marprelate controversy some of Lord Strange's company were imprisoned for defying a prohibition against playing in the City, and when the Puritan Lord Cobham was Lord Chamberlain for a few months in 1596-7 the Corporation went again on the attack. It was during this period that Burbage was refused permission to use his new theatre in Blackfriars; and the magistrates won a still more substantial victory when they at length and finally barred the players from the City inns.

When in July 1597 the Pembroke company's performance of *The Isle of Dogs* at the Swan prompted the direct intervention of the Privy Council, the

Corporation's campaign against the theatre seemed to be on the verge of total success, but the outcome was contrary to their expectations. As the government ordered all copies of the play to be destroyed, the exact cause of offence is unknown. Probably it satirized some public persons in too transparent a disguise. The Corporation took occasion to petition for the 'present stay and final suppressing' of all the theatres, and their letter summarized all the objections they had been raising over the years.

> Neither in polity nor in religion are [plays] to be suffered in a Christian commonwealth, specially being of that frame and matter as usually they are, containing nothing but profane fables, lascivious matters, cozening devices and scurrilous behaviours, which are so set forth as that they move wholly to imitation, and not to the avoiding of those faults and vices which they represent.

In the first heat of anger the Council ordered all the theatres to be pulled down, 'and so to deface the same that they may not be employed again to such use', and for the summer at least the players had to go on tour or be idle. But as the angry shock wore off, the patrons began to intercede for their servants' livelihood and once again the Queen's Christmas recreation had to be provided for. By October the players were back in London and their houses reopened. During a revision of the poor laws the players were brought still more strictly within the statutes relating to vagabonds, and thus more directly under central control. With an order from the Privy Council licensing only two companies, the Chamberlain's and the Admiral's, to perform in the suburbs, the goverment assumed full authority over stage-playing in London. This restriction was renewed when permission was at length given for the building of the Fortune in 1600, but it seems to have been little observed. The Rose and the Curtain were soon in use again, and early in 1602 the Council sanctioned the formation of a new company, Worcester's Men, to play at the Boar's Head. In theory, too, plays were to be given only twice a week, but soon the companies were performing every weekday.

So the Corporation had finally failed to win control, and in 1601 they had the further mortification of seeing the Chamberlain's Men weather a crisis that might have cost some of them their heads. In February the Earl of Essex, the rotten apple of the Queen's declining years, raised a rebellion in the London streets; and Augustine Phillips, a principal member of the company, was summoned before the Council to explain why on the day before the rising they had acted at the Globe Shakespeare's *Richard II*, a play about the deposition of a king. He was able to convince the Council that when the players had accepted a fee from certain of Essex's friends to revive this old piece from their repertoire, they had had no idea what was being planned. As a macabre token of royal forgiveness they were commissioned to play at court on the night before Essex was executed.

On the accession of James I the noble patrons were superseded and all the companies, both adults' and boys', were taken directly under royal control.

The Chamberlain's Men became the King's Men, licensed under letters patent from the Crown, and as liveried grooms of the household they were free of molestation. By a similar arrangement the Admiral's became Prince Henry's Men and Worcester's became Queen Anne's. Royal authority, already approximate, thus became formal and absolute, and the City magistrates had to be content with the Blasphemy Act of 1606 'for the preventing and avoiding of the great abuse of the Holy Name of God in stage plays'. Thenceforth the name of Jove was substituted for that of the Almighty. But the new and glamorous status of the companies did not mean that they had achieved an unfettered liberty to do as they pleased. Constitutionally this was just another episode in the extension of royal control over men's social activities; and one day it would be unfortunate for the players, because when in 1642 the Puritans possessed themselves of the machinery of government, they were able to close the theatres. Meanwhile the companies found James no more indulgent to criticism than Elizabeth had been. The Children of the Queen's Revels forfeited their royal patronage when in 1606 *Eastward Ho*, a comedy by Jonson and Chapman, was uncomplimentary to the Scots. Two years later, when James's personal mannerisms were ridiculed on the stage, and at the same time Chapman's *Biron* plays brought complaints from the French ambassador, the government imposed a general prohibition on all the companies and withdrew it only on payment of a heavy fine. The players were harassed too by their old enemy the plague, which made London almost uninhabitable in the early years of the reign and continued to be very severe until 1609. They had, however, established their right to practise their profession, so long as they practised it discreetly, in the knowledge that royal favour protected them from the malice of the local authorities. With licences now freely and unconditionally granted, theatres and companies multiplied; and although the Puritans did not give up the fight, and never would, their heavy artillery was reduced to spasmodic sniping.

This sniping set off another skirmish in the pamphlet war. In 1612 Thomas Heywood published *An Apology for Actors*, to which 'J. G.', an unidentified clergyman, replied three years later in a specific *Refutation*. Heywood's defence covered familiar ground, praising the theatre for having 'taught the unlearned the knowledge of many famous histories', commemorated the valour of our heroic ancestors, and shown 'the fatal and abortive ends' of those who practise evil: 'we present men with the ugliness of their vices'. Comedy 'entreats of love, deriding foolish inamorates' or displays 'the harmless love of shepherds diversely moralised'. Heywood points out that 'playing is an ornament to the city' that attracts visitors, and he also claims that it is refining and standardizing the English language, so that 'many nations grow enamoured of our tongue (before despised)'. It is the usual specious case with the usual overstatements, but there is an interesting passage in which Heywood defends the players against the charge that they led immoral lives. There are some, he admits, whom he would like to see excluded from the profession, but

> as we are men that stand in the broad eye of the world, so should our manners, gestures and behaviours savour of such government and modesty to deserve the good thoughts of all men, and to abide the sharpest censures even of those that are the greatest opposites to the quality. Many amongst us I know to be of substance, of government, of sober lives and temperate carriages, house-keepers, and contributory to all duties enjoined them equally with them that are ranked with the most bountiful.

All this was true, and it needed to be said.

In terms that again are familiar 'J. G.' complains of the theatre's 'sundry inventions which infect the spirit, and replenish it with unchaste, whorish, cozening, deceitful, wanton and mischievous passions': the which passions he tabulates in considerable detail. In a spirit of scriptural fundamentalism he makes a specific reply to the actors' claim to 'instruct men what vices to avoid...and what virtues to embrace'. They had no divine commission for this purpose. 'God only gave authority of public instruction and correction but to two sorts of men: to his ecclesiastical ministers and temporal magistrates; he never instituted a third authority of players, or ordained that they should serve in his ministry', and in claiming such authority they 'assume an unlawful office'.

To us it is surprising that Shakespeare's plays should have been regarded by many of his contemporaries as the worthless offerings of idolatry and sin, but the debate was significant in its time and it left its mark on the theatre and those who wrote for it. Although tedious and vexatious, the long jar with the Puritans was not altogether a misfortune for the Elizabethan stage. It has sometimes been suggested that the theatre would have been more gracious if churchmen, both high and low, had been more liberal in their attitude towards it, that their patronage would have refined its crudities and elevated its tone. But patronage has an insidious way of enervating the object of its interest, and probably the divines did the theatre more good by opposing it. Their criticism was at least a challenge, and something was lost to the drama when opposition weakened with defeat. It had kept alive the didactic tradition that was in danger of languishing as the drama became more secular, and in a sense the Puritans achieved the opposite of what they intended because their hostility forced the theatre to raise its standards. The players took notice of what was urged against them, and they tried to keep order in their houses and, as far as possible, to avoid giving offence. Their criticism of one another's imperfections had a wider application than the satirical in-jokes and personal feuding that have always been dear to the profession. There was, at least among the better of them, a conscious striving for quality, for seriousness of theme and dignity of language. Thus plays were written that might sincerely claim to edify. No enemy of the theatre could honestly say, for instance, that *Dr Faustus* was a play to persuade an onlooker that to sell his soul to the devil was to make a good bargain: the horror of the deed and the awfulness of the penalty so much outweigh the somewhat infantile satisfactions Faustus received from it. Puritanism is entitled to some of the credit for this because in the theatre, as in many other walks of life, it was a tonic to the Elizabethan genius. Together with the older classical strain, which demanded decorum, good example and a high sententiousness, it helped to discipline the extravagances of a popular and potentially demoralizing form of entertainment.

Fortunately, however, the Puritans failed in one respect where the academic critics also failed: they could not clip the wings of Elizabethan fancy. Puritans and classicists alike complained that the theatre's weakness for fabulous and romantic adventures, its irrelevant clowning, its sacrifice of historical truth to tawdry histrionic effect, vitiated its pretence to teach by good examples. To this the theatre's apologists offered only the limp excuse that the incidents do not matter so long as a fitting moral is presented at the end: an argument that cannot have impressed anyone who witnessed the debauches of which the theatre was capable. But it would have been calamitous if this failure to reply adequately to the Puritan case — and Sidney's case as well — had been allowed to curb that freedom of fancy which, for all its extravagance, was one of the glories of Elizabethan drama. Rational critics and moralists will make little of the plot of *King Lear* and are likely to dismiss it as a foolish fond story of a foolish fond old man. *Hamlet* contains all the ingredients which Gosson contemptuously identified as 'the argument of tragedies', namely, 'wrath, cruelty, incest, injury, murder, either violent by sword or voluntary by poison'. It is a fantastic compound of melodramatic incidents. Yet it can scarcely be held, as the Puritans would hold it, to encourage spectators to a like violence: rather does it purify the mind of the passions that incline men to such disorders.

The artistic imagination transforms base materials into inspiring examples. Inferior workmanship can make nothing of the finest materials, however honest the intent, but an artist fashions beauty from whatever lies to his hand. The test lies not in the externals of theme and plot but in the poet's controlling vision: and once they were free of the obligation to counter Puritan objections by spurious ethical arguments, the dramatists were at pains to insist on this. In his dedication to *The Revenge of Bussy d'Ambois* Chapman said that the poet's subject 'is not truth, but things like truth', and the spectator should not demand 'the authentical truth of either person or action...Poor envious souls they are that cavil at truth's want in these natural fictions'. In a note to the reader which he printed at the head of his *Sophonisba* Marston gave the warning that 'I have not laboured in this poem to tie myself to relate any thing as an historian, but to enlarge every thing as a poet'; and the poet need not bind his fancy to the things of every day. *Ficta voluptatis causa sint proxima veris.* He may tell of 'monsters and prodigious creatures that are not, as of the Arimaspi, of the Grips, the Pigmies, the Cranes', and his vision may still be a true vision.

2. The Chamberlain's Men.

When in September 1592 Robert Greene complained on his troubled death-bed of an insolent actor-dramatist regarding himself as 'the only Shake-scene in a country', the theatres had already been closed by plague and except in a few brief and frustrating intermissions they would remain closed until the early summer of 1594. A stoppage of virtually two years was shattering for the professional companies, who hitherto had more or less agreed with the authorities that an excess of fifty deaths a week in London would justify a complete prohibition. Figures can only be conjectural but it is said that there were nearly 11,000 plague deaths in London during 1593 alone.

> the dead man's knell
> Is there scarce asked for who, and good men's lives
> Expire before the flowers in their caps,
> Dying or ere they sicken.
>
> *Macb* IV iii 170.

When the theatres reopened, or very soon afterwards, Shakespeare became a leading member of the Lord Chamberlain's Men. In December he was named, with William Kempe and Richard Burbage, as payee for the company's court performances, and to be bracketed with these two players suggests that he was already of some eminence in the profession. As a comedian Kempe had been described by Nashe as 'the vice-gerent general to the ghost of Dick Tarleton', and Burbage would soon rival Alleyn as the age's 'complete tragedian'.

How Shakespeare arrived at this position is a mystery buried somewhere in the tangled thicket of London's theatrical history between 1592 and 1594, and it is unlikely that the truth will ever be discovered.[3] His name is never mentioned in connection with any particular company, and probably his career began at a time when new companies were taking shape after the decline of the Queen's Men. On their formation the Queen's recruited leading players from other companies and between 1583 and 1590 they gave twenty-one of the thirty adult performances chosen for the court. Although they had many talented actors, their real strength lay in their privileged position and in the highly individual genius of Richard Tarleton. The story goes that when tending his father's pigs in his native Shropshire, Tarleton fell into conversation with a servant of the Earl of Leicester and made such an impression by his saucy speed of wit that he was brought to court as a

---

3 An attempt was made in the original edition of this book, 185-207; see also Schoenbaum, 159-183. But all is dark and speculative.

royal jester. There, according to Thomas Fuller in his *Worthies*, he would 'un-dumpish' the Queen when she was out of humour, and courtiers used him 'as their usher to prepare their advantageous access unto her. In a word, he told the Queen more of her faults than most of her chaplains, and cured her melancholy better than all of her physicians'. On the stage he was equally master of the situation. He had the sort of ugliness which by acceptance may be turned to comic account. He was almost a dwarf, with curly hair, a squint, a flat nose and something of a hump; and he came on stage in the traditional costume of the simpleton, 'in a foul shirt without a band, and in a blue coat with one sleeve, his stockings out at heels, and his head full of straw and feathers'. Tarleton was essentially the 'stand-up comedian' of the English music-hall, whose conventions he did much to create. He was a solo turn making a direct and intimate appeal to the audience; always himself, whatever the role assigned to him, gifted with extemporal wit and a happy knack of coining rhymes. Like the Vice whom he succeeded, he was apt to steal the play, and he gave the clown's part a disproportionate ascendancy of which Shakespeare would complain in *Hamlet*. But contemporary records leave no doubt of his wide and original talent and his personal likeableness. If, as is generally supposed, he played Mouse in *Mucedorus*, it suggests his skill in bringing a trivial tale to popular success by an inventive personality. In the Induction to *Bartholomew Fair*, Jonson, who as a boy at Westminster might have seen him play, testifies to the potency of his performance; probably he was the 'pleasant Willy' of Spenser's *Tears of the Muses*; and possibly some reference was intended in Yorick, although Shakespeare is less likely than Jonson to have seen Tarleton on the stage and Kempe, his former friend and colleague, may have been nearer to his mind.

Tarleton's death in September 1588 coincided with the Queen's Men's involvement in the Martin Marprelate debate, and they never recovered. John Singer, Tarleton's fellow-comedian, left them for the Admiral's, and the engagement of John Symons, famed for his acrobatic 'activities', did not compensate for the loss of Tarleton's particular talents. Their political indiscretion cost them favour at court, where they appeared only once in 1591-2 and in the following year not at all; and although they were the only company to play before the Queen in the plague-ridden winter of 1593-4, it was for the last time. In April they began a season with Sussex's Men at the Rose, but after nine days the plague struck again and they 'broke and went into the country to play', selling seven of their play-books to meet their expenses. In their short existence the Queen's Men had a significant place in stage history as the first professional company to maintain some coherence of policy, organization and personnel. Ten years is not a long time, and there were some changes in their membership, but they were firmer in their allegiance than Elizabethan actors had formerly been, and their brief history reveals a discipline and a corporate spirit previously unknown in the professional theatre.

The company to take advantage of their decline was a curious amalgamation of Strange's and the Admiral's Men.[4] Both these companies are traceable in London and the provinces before, in the autumn of 1589, they were forbidden the use of the City inns and certain of their members combined and went to play at James Burbage's Theatre outside the boundaries. They were joined by a few members of the Queen's Men, including Singer, and also by one or two from Hunsdon's. Although most of the members belonged to Strange's Men and the combination was usually known by this name, the dominating figure was Edward Alleyn, who was rare in his time and place by having organizing ability as well as a compelling power as a tragic actor. Alleyn was, and always remained, a servant of the Admiral, but he had bought out several of his former colleagues and between 1590 and 1594 the Admiral's Men, at least as a London company, were embodied in himself and he seems to have had the disposal of their plays, properties and apparel. With these resources added to the stocks and repertoire of Strange's Men, the new combination overshadowed its rivals and played at court more often than any other company. In the spring of 1591 the imperious Alleyn quarrelled with the ever-contentious Burbage and moved from the Theatre to the Rose, thus acquiring the financial backing and business acumen of Henslowe, who became their accountant as well as their landlord. Henslowe's share of the receipts was half the takings from the galleries, and early in 1592 he began to record in his *Diary* the title of the play performed each day and the portion of the receipts due to himself.

On 19 February 1592 the Alleyn-Strange company began a season at the Rose during which they played six days a week for eighteen weeks (thus evading the ban on playing during Lent), and gave in all 105 performances of twenty-three different plays. The season ended abruptly on 23 June when as a result of anti-alien riots in Southwark the theatres were ordered to close until Michaelmas. By that time London was in the grip of plague and for two years the professional theatre was in confusion. Plague relaxed sufficiently to enable the Alleyn-Strange company to give twenty-six performances at the Rose between 29 December 1592 and the end of January, and also to play at court, and it was the hope that plague would soon abate that kept

4 Sir Charles Howard (1536-1624) became Lord High Admiral in 1585 and was created Earl of Nottingham in 1596, so that his players were known successively as Howard's, the Admiral's and Nottingham's; in 1603 they became Prince Henry's, and after his death in 1612 their patron was the Elector Palatine. Ferdinando Stanley, Lord Strange (a minor poet and possibly Spenser's Amyntas) was patron of Strange's men in the 1580s, and they became Derby's when he succeeded his father to the earldom in September 1593. After his death in the following April the company were for a few weeks known as the Countess of Derby's. In June they found a new patron in Henry Carey, first Baron Hunsdon, who was then Lord Chamberlain. On his death in July 1596 the company passed to his son, George Carey, the second baron, and they were known as Hunsdon's Men until he succeeded Lord Cobham as Chamberlain in the following March. They became the King's Men in 1603 and so continued until 1642.

many of the actors in London rather than risk the 'division and separation' of provincial tours. There was no easy choice between unemployment and bankruptcy in London and tours which broke up companies and destroyed their cohesion. Companies under the patronage of Pembroke and Sussex tried their luck in London and the provinces, and there were groups touring in the livery of the Admiral and Lord Strange that were independent of the Alleyn combination. In May 1593 Alleyn himself had to take to the road and play in towns 'where the infection is not', his associates named in the warrant, Kempe, Pope, Heminges and Bryan, all being Strange's men and all subsequently colleagues of Shakespeare.

The easing of the plague in the spring of 1594 allowed a gradual return to more normal conditions. Alleyn then began to revive the Admiral's Men as a separate London company and in May they opened at the Rose, only to be barred after three days by a brief recurrence of the plague. From 5 to 15 June the Admiral's and the Chamberlain's Men (formerly Strange's) had an unsuccessful season together at Newington Butts, Henslowe's takings averaging only 9s. a performance, and then the two companies finally separated, the Admiral's to Henslowe and the Rose, the Chamberlain's to James Burbage and the Theatre.

It is frustrating that there is no reference to Shakespeare in any of the records of this complicated period. He was not in the cast of *The Seven Deadly Sins*, a play by Tarleton revived by Strange's Men in about 1590, and he was not named in the licence to tour issued to Alleyn and others in May 1593; nor was he mentioned in the surviving letters written by Alleyn during this tour to his wife, whom he had married in October 1592, or to Henslowe, now his father-in-law. Seventeen actors are referred to during the years of the Alleyn-Strange partnership, and Shakespeare is not among them. Yet nearly all the principal members of the Chamberlain's Men when the company organized itself in 1594 had previously been with Strange's, and there must be a strong inference — although it is only an inference — that Shakespeare had played with them at some time, as a hired man, not a shareholder. We might suppose that he had written plays for them too, but there is no positive evidence of it.

Traditions about his first steps in the theatre are as late in origin and as misleading as those surrounding his Stratford boyhood. It is said that he began by holding horses outside the playhouse: a story which, according to the first man to set it down, Robert Shiels in 1753, 'Sir William Davenant told Mr Betterton, who communicated it to Mr Rowe; Rowe told it Mr Pope, and Mr Pope told it to Dr Newton...and from a gentleman who heard it from him 'tis here related'. It tells of the needy youth 'driven to the last necessity' and earning a few pence 'by taking care of the gentlemen's horses who came to the play'. In this role of parking attendant he was so diligent and expert that he had soon more business than he himself could manage, and at last hired boys under him, who were known by the name of Shakespear's boys: Some of the players accidentally conversing with him found him so acute, and master of so fine a conversation, that struck therewith, they recommended him to the house, in which he was first admitted in a very low station, but he did not long remain so, for he soon distinguished himself, if not as an extraordinary actor, at least as a fine writer.

This story was accepted, even embellished, by Dr Johnson, who perhaps should have known better. A few years later Edmund Malone reported a persistent tradition that Shakespeare entered the theatre as a call-boy or prompter's attendant, to warn actors when their presence was required on stage. Where the truth is unknown, we are entitled to these or other fancies. Chambers believes that Shakespeare began to be a professional playwright in about 1591, and that he first became an actor not more than a year before that (*WS* I 59). If this be so, his reputation was not long in the making as Greene's misquotation from *3 Henry VI* and Nashe's reference to the popular play about 'brave Talbot' both appeared in the autumn of 1592. For once we may be fairly sure of the identifications. The target of Greene's jealous sneer is unmistakable, and Talbot, 'the great Alcides of the field', was undoubtedly the hero of the play printed in the First Folio as *1 Henry VI*, huge liberties being taken with historical fact to make him so. Shakespeare possibly was working on an earlier play, giving shape to the heterogeneous events of chronicle by emphasizing the need for national unity. Despite his valour, Talbot is foredoomed to failure because England has still to expiate the usurpation of the House of Lancaster and his cause is undermined by treachery and division. The introduction of this theme links the play with Parts Two and Three, written earlier. If this was the play recorded by Henslowe as '*Harey the vi*', its success was sensational — as indeed Nashe reported, and it would be natural for him, when seeking to defend the theatre, to quote a recent success on a heroic theme. It was first acted at the Rose on 3 March 1592. It was the first performance of a new play during the season, and Henslowe's receipts were £3 16s. 8d., compared with an average of 23s. 6d. for the previous eleven days. It maintained its popularity so well that it had fourteen further performances before the season ended abruptly in June, a quite exceptional number, and Henslowe's share of the takings averaged 40s. 6d. Nashe's claim that it was seen by 'ten thousand spectators at least' was no great exaggeration.

Greene's diatribe against actor-playwrights had a curious sequel. The copy for his *Groatsworth of Wit* was prepared for the press by Henry Chettle, himself a printer and literary aspirant, and the letter that formed part of the miscellany took occasion to rebuke two other dramatists, believed to be Marlowe and Nashe. Evidently there was an angry protest because in the preface to his *Kind-Heart's Dream*, published at the end of the year, Chettle attempted some amends. He confessed that 'a letter written to divers playmakers is offensively by one or two of them taken', and 'with neither of them that take offence was I acquainted, and with one of them I care not if I never be'. This presumably was Marlowe; but he had since met Shakespeare and 'myself have seen his demeanour no less civil than he excellent in the quality he professes: besides, divers of worship have reported his uprightness of dealing, which argues his honesty, and his facetious grace in writing, that approves his art'. The identity of these 'divers of worship' is unknown, and there is something disingenuous about the whole passage. It has even been suggested that Chettle was the author of the original letter,[5] trying to turn a dishonest penny by attributing semi-libellous opinions to a writer lately dead. Be that as it may, his apology contains the first contemporary reference to Shakespeare as a man, and it is handsome enough.

The first and third parts of *Henry VI*, and by implication the second, are the only plays that can with any certainty be ascribed to him before the summer of 1594, but there are two with Shakespearean titles: a *Titus Andronicus* acted by Sussex's Men at the Rose in January 1594 and published later in the year; and *The Taming of a Shrew*, acted when the Admiral's and Strange's (now the Chamberlain's) played a short joint season at Newington in June 1594, and again published the same year. On the evidence of style and content, subjective but not unconvincing, *Comedy of Errors*, *Richard III* and *The Two Gentlemen of Verona* had also been written by this time. *Comedy of Errors* was acted at Gray's Inn during Christmas 1594, and probably this was a private performance of a play already popular. With its technically brilliant development and fusion of two Plautine situations, it is the sort of piece to have been brought to London by a young academic who had been 'a schoolmaster in the country'. Shakespeare had to wait until 1598 before printed texts of his plays acknowledged his authorship on the title-page. In later years catchpenny publishers would attach his name to plays he had not written, but in the 1590s the dramatist was less of a selling point than the company who had performed his play.

Greene's abuse of the 'upstart crow, beautified with our feathers' was thought at one time to be a charge of plagiarism, accusing Shakespeare of passing off the work of other dramatists as his own. This was given some colour by a sonnet in *Greene's Funerals*, poems by 'R. B., Gent.', published in 1594:

> Greene is the ground of every painter's dye;
> Greene gave the ground to all that wrote upon him.
> Nay more, the men that so eclips'd his fame
> Purloined his plumes: can they deny the same?

If R. B. was Richard Barnfield and he had Shakespeare then in mind, he thought differently when four years later he praised his 'honey-flowing vein' and promised that Venus and Lucrece 'thy name in Fame's immortal book have plac'd'. The charge of plagiarism largely disappeared once it had been established that versions of the second and third parts of *Henry VI* printed in 1594-5 were not original plays that Shakespeare had borrowed and adapted but were themselves corrupt versions of his own work later printed in the First Folio. *Taming of a Shrew*, printed in 1594, is probably in the same category: a much-altered version of Shakespeare's play with the Bianca sub-plot expanded, the chauvinism toned down and Christopher Sly kept on stage until the end.

Plays belonged to the companies that paid for them, not to the dramatists who wrote them, and the companies did not normally wish to see them printed. They were a valuable asset like costumes and properties, and it was poor policy to release them to the printers until their stage life was exhausted. But companies in financial difficulties sometimes had to realize their assets, and in the abnormal circumstances of the plague years this happened all too often. In September 1593 Henslowe wrote a significant note to Alleyn, then on tour: 'As for my Lord of Pembroke's which you desire to know where they be, they are all at home and have been this five or six weeks, for they cannot save their charges [i.e. cover their expenses] with travel, as I hear, and were fain to pawn their apparel for their charge'. They would have pawned their play-books too, as the Queen's had done when they disappeared into the provinces, and Sussex's would do later. The mere fact of going on tour with a skeleton company required the preparation of shortened texts, and the originals might be sold to publishers or to other companies as a means of raising money. Thus we do not have to be surprised that the first published version of *Titus Andronicus* in 1594 said that it had been acted by 'the Right Honourable the Earl of Derby, Earl of Pembroke and Earl of Sussex their Servants'. No doubt it had, and no doubt other plays with a similarly varied history passed quite legitimately into the stock of the Chamberlain's or the Admiral's companies. Some printed versions, how-ever, were less legitimate. Actors in financial straits would sometimes sell to the printer a text compiled not from the original but from their own recollec-tions of the play in performance. Thus the 'bad quarto' of *2 Henry VI* may have been a reported text by the actors who played Suffolk and Cade; and that of Part Three compiled by the actors who played Warwick and Clifford.

In a limited and quite honourable sense, therefore, Shakespeare may have 'plagiarized' whenever he was required to work up an old text that had newly come into the company's possession. *1 Henry VI* may originally have been a Queen's play, as were early versions of *King John*, *Henry V* and *King Lear*. This sort of cobbling or revision was a routine chore of theatrical life, and Henslowe frequently recorded as 'new' a play that had merely been 'newly corrected' or augmented or had only lately come into his possession. Like any dramatist attached to an acting company, Shakespeare must have been called upon for various revisions throughout the whole of his working life, to amend an unsatisfactory speech or revitalize a scene that would not take off. It was part of his function, and at times it might extend to the quite extensive revision of a play acquired from another source. For the period 1592-4, however, it is unsafe to assume that because a play likely to have been his was acted by Strange's or Pembroke's or anyone else, this means that he was an actor with the particular company or wrote it for their use. During these uncertain years he may not have been very closely associated with the theatre at all, being gainfully employed in other matters.

Printed by Richard Field, an old Stratford acquaintance, *Venus and Adonis* was published in 1593 and dedicated to the Earl of Southampton as 'the first heir of my invention': which may mean that Shakespeare wrote it before taking to the theatre or, more probably, that it was the first of his works to be published. Apologizing for his 'unpolished lines', he promised 'to take advantage of all idle hours till I have honoured you with some graver labour'. This labour was *The Rape of Lucrece*, printed by Field in the following year, and that Shakespeare had 'idle hours' in which to write it (it has 1855 lines) suggests that he had not been heavily engaged in the theatre. Again it was an Ovidian narrative on the theme of love, this time taken by force, and again the dedication was to Southampton:

> The love I dedicate to your Lordship is without end: whereof this pamphlet without beginning is but a superfluous moiety. The warrant I have of your honourable disposition, not the worth of my untutored lines, makes it assured of acceptance. What I have done is yours, what I have to do is yours, being part in all I have, devoted yours. Were my worth greater, my duty would show greater; meantime, as it is, it is bound to your Lordship, to whom I wish long life still lengthened with all happiness.

There is of course a conventional language of dedications: the author must protest the worthlessness of himself and his book, and attach his only hope of immortality to the patron's grace in accepting the wretched thing. Shakespeare pays respect to convention without becoming servile, and he can write with greater confidence because Southampton has accepted the earlier poem. He is not pretending to intimacy, but he does seem to be writing in the assurance of some mutual acquaintance and respect. Readers have differed in their response to these lines, but this was not the usual tone in which a common player would have addressed a lord. It lacks the mixture of hyperbole and unctuousness with which Nashe invited Southampton to accept *The Unfortunate Traveller*: 'Your Lordship is the large spreading branch of renown from whence these my idle leaves seek to derive their whole nourishing. It resteth you either scornfully shake them off, as worm-eaten and worthless, or in pity preserve them and cherish them for some little summer fruit you hope to find amongst them'.

Southampton in 1594 was just twenty-one and he had succeeded to the earldom when he was only eight. Until he earned the Queen's disfavour by a forced marriage with one of her ladies, and later by a perilous association with Essex, he was in good esteem at court and with John Florio in his household as Italian tutor, he had some reputation as a patron of the arts. Although the air was heavy with poets lamenting that patronage was in decay and learning condemned to beggary, many of them did in fact find some support in noble households. The relationship was relaxed and undemanding, and although the rewards were not liberal, a writer might expect occasional gifts and congenial working conditions. Of Shakespeare's relationship with Southampton we know only what we may choose to infer from the two dedications, but it is unlikely to have been close enough to establish Southampton as the golden boy of the Sonnets. It has been suggested that Shakespeare spent some months in 1593-4 at Titchfield, Southampton's house in Hampshire, and there wrote the first version of *Love's Labour's Lost*. This at any rate is more probable than Rowe's story, given on the always dubious authority of Sir William Davenant, that Southampton once gave him 'a thousand pounds, to enable him to go through with a purchase which he had a mind to. A bounty very great, and very rare at any time, and almost equal to that profuse generosity the present age has shown to French Dancers and Italian Eunuchs'. Such bounty, probably equivalent to Southampton's full annual income, is so great and rare as to be incredible.

By 1617, only a year after Shakespeare's death, *Venus and Adonis* had gone into eleven editions and *Lucrece* into six, and their immediate popularity may have tempted him to make his future as poet rather than as dramatist. Artistically his imagination visualized the world in terms essentially dramatic, as the deployment of character in a concrete setting, but this does not mean that he was in love with the theatre as a profession. Several of the Sonnets, which he may have been writing at this time, hint at some distaste for it. His natural reticence and his mistrust of emotional display made him shrink from being a motley to the view, subdued to the dyer's hand, a pipe for any man's finger to play upon. Actors were still 'i' the statute', and Shakespeare would chide the fortune

> That better did not for my life provide
> Than public means which public manners breeds.
>
> Sonn CXI 3.

After writing the poetic romance of *Scilla's Metamorphosis*, Lodge swore

> To write no more of that whence shame doth grow,
> Or tie my shame to penny-knaves' delight,
> But live with fame, and so for fame to write.

If Shakespeare was seduced by such thoughts of fame, it was to penny-knaves' delight in the theatre that he nevertheless committed his future, and until a printer got hold of them, even the Sonnets were only circulated among his friends. But the connection with Southampton, even if it was more remote and tenuous than many critics have supposed, brought him to the threshold of an unfamiliar world. The plays he was soon to write seem to bear the impress of a new experience. From Southampton's friends he might hear tales of travel oversea (and pick up some of the geography incorrectly), study at close hand their outlook and their way of life, store his mind with their conversation and their books. If the influence did not come from Southampton, it came from somewhere, because there is a marked change in the character of his work. The classical influences of *Comedy of Errors*, *Titus Andronicus* and the verse romances no longer dominate. His comedies revolve around men who are young and wealthy and adventurous: students, courtiers, heirs to great titles, who dabble in philosophy, jest coarsely, strain the language for conceits and quibbles and lose themselves in love. As a foil to these gallants, whose raillery would grow tedious if there were not danger in the air, he matched them against 'mocking wenches' who vied with them in wit and ultimately conquered them by their steadfast womanly tenderness. With subtle variations this is the pattern of his comedy, and of his earliest tragedy, until the turn of the century. It argues — although it does not prove — that in the plague years the theatre was not his major occupation.[6]

Although doubt and speculation are never wholly absent, after the summer of 1594 the course of Shakespeare's professional life becomes less obscure. Interruptions, for plague or other causes, were less frequent, and the two main companies, the Chamberlain's and the Admiral's, developed a continuing identity which, against all rivalry and change, enabled them to share the supremacy of the Elizabethan stage.

The nucleus of the Chamberlain's company had been with Strange's and the Alleyn-Strange combination. William Kempe, Augustine Phillips, John Heminges and Thomas Pope had been named in the touring permit in 1593; and earlier the cast of *The Seven Deadly Sins*, probably acted by Strange's before the amalgamation, included, as well as Bryan, Phillips and Pope, the names of Richard Burbage, Richard Cowley, Henry Condell, William Sly, Robert Gough, John Sincklo and John Duke. All these men were colleagues of Shakespeare, although the last two never became sharers. In 1594 Richard Burbage took Alleyn's place as the leading tragic actor, and his

---

6   *Willobie his Avisa*, a strange poem registered in September 1594, is prefaced by commendatory verses containing the first literary reference to Shakespeare:

> Yet Tarquin pluck'd his glistering grape,
> And Shakes-peare paints poor Lucrece' rape.

The poem itself contains a teasing reference to the author's 'familiar friend W.S.', who is described as 'the old player' in a fruitless love affair. Some critics has converted 'H.W.' (Henry Willobie) into 'Mr. W.H.' and have found clues for an interpretation of the Sonnets, But the poem's allegory is too elusive to give much clue to anything, see Chambers, *WS* I 568-9, II 191.

absence from the warrant of 1593 is something of a mystery. Possibly it was just a clerical omission as the warrant did not need to name all the actors proposing to tour. On the other hand, when the players quarrelled with James Burbage in 1591 and moved elsewhere, the son may have remained with his father at the Theatre.

The Chamberlain's Men organized themselves rather differently from the Admiral's. Although James Burbage as the landlord took a share of the receipts as his rent, the real controllers and proprietors of the company were the players themselves. They could at any time have abandoned Burbage's theatres, as they did when they played winter seasons at the Cross Keys; or they could again have broken off all relations with him as they had in 1591. The theatrical and financial policy of the company was in the hands of a group of actors known as 'sharers'. In 1594 there were eight of these, Kempe, Pope, Heminge, Phillips, Bryan, Cowley, Richard Burbage and Shakespeare; and in 1604 the number was increased to twelve. To acquire a share the actor paid a sum of money into the common stock (perhaps totalling about £700), and he became a part-owner of the company's assets — its costumes, properties and play-books — and took a proportionate share in its profits and losses. The value of a share rose steadily. When Alleyn bought Richard Jones's share in the Admiral's Men in 1589, he paid £37.10s.; and when the restless Jones again left the company in 1602, the price was £50. By 1613 the value of an Admiral's share had risen to £70, while a share in Queen Anne's company at about the same time was sold for £80. There is no reason why figures for the Chamberlain's Men should have been substantially different, but in the absence of any record we do not know what Shakespeare paid for his share in 1594, nor what he received when he sold it.

The landlord was responsible for the ground-rent and maintenance of the building, for which he took half the gallery takings as his rent, but all the other costs fell upon the sharers. In estimating the expenses of running a professional company we have to depend chiefly on Henslowe, for the reason that his accounts have survived and the Chamberlain's have not. This is slightly hazardous because the two companies developed in different ways. James Burbage, once an actor, was always interested in the theatre for its own sake; and as he was usually in debt, he was in no position to interfere with the policy and development of the company, which was virtually a self-governing corporation. Henslowe, on the other hand, manoeuvred himself into becoming not merely landlord but the Admiral's manager, banker and, for some of the men, employer. He writes now of 'my company', and from 1597 to 1603 his accounts consist of the advances he made for the purchase of plays and apparel and for individual loans made to the actors, his usual rate of interest being 40 per cent. He recouped himself for these advances by appropriating the full takings of the galleries, and he ceased to pay for the upkeep of the theatre. Actors and playwrights were bound to him by individual contracts of service, so that even some of the sharers were little better than his personal hirelings, and he increased their thraldom by lending them money to pay debts due to himself. It was in 1597 that Alleyn 'left playing' for some three years, and in his absence Henslowe was able to tighten his control. In his defence it has been said that actors were thriftless beings only amenable to strict financial discipline, but the Chamberlain's Men did not have these problems and it would seem that he exploited their fecklessness to his own advantage. For him the theatre was only one of several capitalist enterprises.

On the other hand, in professional matters the organization of the two companies was very similar. In the putting on of plays, which was their business, they both had to recruit actors and dramatists, maintain their buildings, attract audiences, build a stock of properties and costumes, placate the authorities. In these respects it is a reasonable presumption that evidence about the Admiral's Men is acceptable for the Chamberlain's too, so long as we remember that Henslowe drove hard bargains and the figures may not exactly correspond.

Between 1597 and 1603 his advances to the Admiral's for the purchase of stock and other expenses totalled £1,338.7s.4d., which Chambers has estimated at £1 for every playing day. About half of this went on fees to dramatists. His payment for a play ranged from £4 to £10, and he usually managed to keep it down to £6. Apparel cost £560, and £100 went in miscellaneous charges such as music, licensing fees, the compulsory annual contribution of £5 for the poor of the parish, and a non-recurring item of 40s. for retrieving the dramatist Dekker 'out of the Counter in the Poultry'. Henslowe's loans did not, however, cover the largest item of expenditure that the sharers had to find, the bill for wages. First the company had to pay the 'hired men', actors who were not sharers and often had no contract of service. At a top rate of about 10s. a week this was less than the average of a skilled craftsman in London, and many of the hired men were paid less: perhaps a shilling a day when they were in work, and often they were not. When Thomas Downton, an experienced actor who served the company intermittently for some twenty-five years, was down on his luck, he bound himself to Henslowe for 8s. a week, which would fall to 4s. if he were not required to play for a fortnight.

Although the boy actors were not apprentices in the strict legal sense, being in theory servants of a nobleman, they were in effect apprenticed to senior members of the company, who housed and trained them and were paid the fee due for their services. It seems that the boys were transferable, as they might be hired out, or even sold, to another company. This may have been rare, but in 1594 Henslowe bought a boy player for £8 and hired him to the Admiral's for 3s. a week, thus getting his money back in little more than a year. Fees paid for the boys when actually performing might go as high as 15s. When their training was complete and their voices had broken, the boys had to face the hazards of the hired man's career, with the hope of one day becoming a sharer, or find another profession. Of the twenty-six sharers in the Chamberlain's company named in the First Folio, Samuel Gilburne, Richard Robinson, William Ostler, Nathan Field, John Underwood and Nicholas Tooley had all been boy players.

Finally, the sharers had to pay a staff of door-keepers (who often absconded with the takings), musicians and stage officials like the prompter, property men and wardrobe men (the Admiral's employed two tailors and a crown-maker). Not long after Shakespeare's death his company were employing as many as twenty-one 'hirelings', of whom only six were actors.

Thus the expenses of running a company were heavy, and Henslowe's record of his share of the takings provides a basis on which to calculate the receipts. As he was entitled to half the receipts from the galleries, the players' share was the same as his, plus the takings from the groundlings who paid a penny to stand in the yard. We can only guess how many of these there were. Nothing was done to make them comfortable, and they were always being urged from the stage to pay another penny and have a seat; but the number who responded to this overt pressure would depend on the weather, the popularity of the play, the space available in the yard and, presumably, the current state of the economy. Henslowe's *Diary* records his receipts between 1592 and 1597, and they averaged about 30s. a performance. It has been estimated that the yard at the Rose accommodated about 870 spectators. In normal circumstances the yard probably filled more readily than the galleries, so that when the galleries were only averagely full, there might be some 800 groundlings. On this assumption we find that when the galleries yielded £3 (30s. to Henslowe, 30s. to the sharers), the yard would yield the same amount or a little more: so that the players' share of an average house was something under £5. The fee fixed for a performance at court was £10 (for other private performances presumably a little less), on the assumption that this was the sum the players would lose by not appearing in their theatre that day; and it also had to cover their expenses in giving a trial performance before the Master of the Revels and in transferring their production to Whitehall. Thus it is a reasonable conclusion that total receipts at the Rose for an average house amounted to a little over £6, and for a popular play they would be higher. On good days, as when '*Harey the vi*' was playing, Henslowe's share might be over £3.

The Theatre and the Curtain were smaller than the Rose and takings for a full house accordingly were less. At the Globe and the Fortune there was perhaps a higher ratio of sitting to standing accommodation, and therefore a larger income on good days, but overheads at these more elaborate playhouses were higher too. Finally, the players acquired revenue from the sale of beer, tobacco, fruit and nuts, and contemporary plays and pamphlets show how blatantly the sale of these refreshments was canvassed from the stage. The practice wounded the artistic sensibility of many dramatists, but chiefly dramatists who were not also sharers in a professional company. Shakespeare made no complaint.

The crisis which led to the move to Bankside and the building of the Globe caused the Chamberlain's Men to carry their cooperative organization a stage further. James Burbage was dead, having left his theatrical property to his sons. Cuthbert and Richard lacked the resources to build the Globe out of their own pockets, and many years later Cuthbert lamented 'the sums of money taken up at interest, which lay heavy on us many years'. As he was speaking in a law-suit in 1635 he may have been exaggerating the weight of the burden, because they made an experiment unprecedented in the history of the English theatre by inviting five of their fellows to share the expenses and the risks and create a joint tenancy. The two Burbages held half the lease and the other half was divided between Shakespeare, Heminges, Phillips, Pope and Kempe. These seven men were known as the 'housekeepers', and their function as housekeepers was distinct from their function as sharers. As housekeepers they became landlords to the company, each member of the syndicate being liable for his proportionate share of the ground-rent (annually £14.10s. for thirty-one years) and the cost of upkeep, and entitled to half the gallery takings. As sharers they continued to receive their proportion of the profits when all expenses had been deducted. They thus had a double interest in the prosperity of the company. Initially Shakespeare's holding as a housekeeper was a tenth of the whole, but Kempe soon afterwards left the company and Condell, Sly and Ostler had become additional housekeepers by 1612. His share then was a fourteenth.

An actor's share in the company was inalienable in that it was not to be held by a sleeping partner or one who did nothing to earn it. When a sharer ceased his active life in the company, whether as player, musician, dramatist or business manager, he resigned his share and it was taken up by a hired man or an actor brought in from another company. It was intended that the housekeepers' holdings should similarly be inalienable, and litigation followed in later years as a result of their being 'dissolved to strangers'. The damage was done when an actor died and his holding passed to his heirs. Thus when Phillips died in 1605, his widow married a spendthrift, John Witter, who went through her capital and was unable to meet his share of the cost of rebuilding the Globe in 1613. Heminges thereupon resumed possession of the holding, which he had leased to the widow, and in 1619 Witter brought an unsuccessful action against him. It was established in law that the interest belonged to the company and not to the individual. Heminges meanwhile had taken the precaution of refusing to allow his own daughter Thomasina to inherit the holding of William Ostler, whom she had married in 1611. When Ostler died intestate in 1614, Heminges witheld the share she had expected to inherit and seems to have kept it although she twice took him to law over it. Ironically, it was Heminges's son William who in 1635 caused legal action by selling holdings in the Globe and Blackfriars theatres to John Shank, a veteran actor who became a sharer just before Shakespeare died. Three members of the company petitioned for the right to buy a share, and Shank was ordered to sell them one in each theatre.

In the course of time, because they outlived their immediate fellows, Heminges and Condell came to possess most of the shares and holdings of the company. They did this not because they were acquisitive but because they wanted to preserve the company's independence from greedy outsiders with no particular interest in the theatre. It is sad that Heminges's son and daughter should not, apparently, have seen things in the same disinterested light. One of many unsolved mysteries in Shakespeare's life is his disposal of his shares and holdings in the company and its two theatres. As they were not mentioned in his will, he must have disposed of them already. He was in retirement in 1613 when the Globe burned down and was 'new builded in far fairer manner than before', at an eventual cost of over a hundred pounds to each housekeeper. This would have been a sensible time for him to have disposed of his interest, but it is mere inference and no particulars have survived. His shares passed eventually to Heminges and Condell, as he and they would have wished, and at least we may think that he took care not to make the sort of bequest to outsiders that might involve his late fellows in litigation. Unless undiscovered records show the contrary, Shakespeare's company only had to go to law against the suits of outsiders. They had no litigation over internal affairs. In a litigious age, with a legal system relatively unsophisticated, this has to be recognized as a remarkable indication of the quality of their fellowship and the success of their cooperative organization.

It was otherwise with the Admiral's, but in the 1590s the one company cannot be considered without reference to the other. They differed in style as well as organization, and their rivalry was stimulating for them both, encouraging them towards experiment and raising their dramatic standards. The Admiral's had the initial advantage that the Rose was larger and better equipped than the older Theatre and Curtain, although it stood on marshy ground and was already falling into disrepair. But in invitations to play at court the pre-eminence lay with the Chamberlain's, who between 1594 and 1603 appeared there on thirty-two occasions, against twenty by the Admiral's and thirteen by other companies. Court officials attentive to the royal solace needed to provide the best, and they could not fail to be aware of the popularity of Shakespeare's work, indicated by the printing of as many as twelve of his plays by 1600. That some were 'bad quartos', imperfect in form and not authorized for publication, shows how strong was the demand: the booksellers could not wait to get his work on the market. Unfortunately the warrants for court performance name the payees (usually Heminges and Pope) but not the plays. It would be surprising if several were not Shakespeare's, because his popularity was the principal reason for the ascendancy of his company.

In September 1598 there appeared *Palladis Tamia*, by Francis Meres, a strange collection of apophthegms on religion, philosophy and the arts expressed in euphuistic similitudes. It included a sort of *cursus honorum* of English writers, who are compared, not to their disadvantage, with the ancients. It is fatuously unselective and uncritical but it is usefully informative about 'mellifluous and honey-tongued Shakespeare', in whose verse romances and 'sugared sonnets' the 'sweet witty soul of Ovid' lives again. With Plautus and Seneca as the standard, he is also 'the most excellent' in both comedy and tragedy, and Meres names twelve plays. This is valuable for the dating of some of the plays, those mentioned being *The Two Gentlemen of Verona, Comedy of Errors, Love's Labour's Lost, Love's Labour's Won, Midsummer Night's Dream, Merchant of Venice, Richard II, Richard III, Henry IV, King John, Titus Andronicus* and *Romeo and Juliet*. Sceptics have noted the absence of *Henry VI* and *Taming of the Shrew*, but Meres may only have lived in London in 1597-8 and not even his rag-bag mind could have absorbed everything. The enigma is *Love's Labour's Won*. The title would suit *Taming of the Shrew*, but a stationer's catalogue, recently discovered, shows that in 1603 he had both plays in stock. A lost early draft of *All's Well that Ends Well*, wherein the winning labour is the bed trick, seems now to be the favourite nomination.[7] Critics are reluctant to concede that *Love's Labour's Won* may have been lost to us for ever, but sadly it is possible. Heminges and Condell confess plainly enough the difficulties they had in assembling all the Shakespearean texts for the First Folio.

If *Julius Caesar* was the first of his plays to be given at the Globe, Shakespeare had also written by that time *Much Ado About Nothing* and *Henry V*, and Elizabethan playgoers should have been — and manifestly they were — dazzled by the richness and variety of what he had to offer them. *Feliciter audax*. The Admiral's playwrights too were experimenting with dramatic novelties, but these were more ingenious than impressive and Henslowe seems to have put more trust in revivals or the machine-made collaborations that he wrung from his necessitous hacks. Compared with the vitality and unexpectedness of Shakespeare's work, the Admiral's recourse to revivals was a mark of insufficiency. Henslowe's *Diary* gives details of three winter and three summer seasons at the Rose between 1594 and 1597, during which the Admiral's played on almost every weekday for 126 weeks. During this period they presented 55 plays which Henslowe marked as 'ne' (new), but as Prospero said to Miranda on a different occasion, 'Tis new to thee'. Henslowe would mark as 'ne' an old play newly revised (however slightly: it need only have been a touring script adapted for the Rose) or a play that had reached him from another company and would, he hoped, be unfamiliar to his present audience. Several of the 55 'ne' plays were not genuinely new. The same records show that by June 1595 the company had

7   See G.K.Hunter in the new Arden edition of *All's Well*.

given no fewer than fifty-one performances of Marlowe's plays. The opening of the revivals of *Faustus* and *1 Tamburlaine* brought higher receipts than the opening of all but one of the plays that Henslowe offered as new. For *Tamburlaine*, either part of it, one exposure to its splendid but suffocating rhetoric might have sufficed. But Henslowe's successes included other old plays from an earlier period, either the property of the Admiral's in their provincial days or relics of defunct companies like the Queen's and Pembroke's; such as *The Spanish Tragedy*, Greene's *Alphonsus*, *1 Tamar Cham* and *Longshanks*, which may have been a resuscitation of Peele's *Edward I*. Only one new play, *Bellendon*, was thought to be worth reviving for a further run after its initial popularity had been exhausted.

In part this dependence on old favourites may have been the deliberate policy of Alleyn, who liked to appear again and again in the famous impersonations his audience never tired of seeing. But he was shrewd enough to realize that he must enlarge his repertoire with new roles of comparable magnificence. His range as an actor seems to have been limited, and in their different ways both Pistol and the Player King in *Hamlet* made fun of his weaknesses. But given a full-blooded plot and some appropriately grandiloquent verse, he must still have been able to create the authentic excitement. It surely argues some poverty of invention among his dramatists that during this period they failed to add a memorable role to his repertoire. It may perhaps have been a cause of his retirement in 1597.

Despite their failure to do the right things for Alleyn, the Admiral's playwrights seem to have been the bolder innovators. It was usually they who launched a new type of play, and the Chamberlain's who watched the results and, according to its success or failure, ignored it or ridiculed it or nursed it into a fashion which they could exploit. In his *Pre-Restoration Studies* W. J. Lawrence made the fascinating, if perhaps fanciful, suggestion that it was Shakespeare's special task to keep an attentive eye on the experiments attempted at the Rose and, if they caught the public taste, reply on behalf of the Chamberlain's. For instance, it was the Admiral's who introduced the 'nocturnal', a play in which night, silent and sable-visaged, 'casts her black curtain over all the world'. To this idea *A Midsummer Night's Dream* offered a deliberate deflation, as was so often Shakespeare's way. Almost certainly he did it again when *As You Like It* was his response to the over-romantic pastoralism of a pair of Admiral's plays about Sherwood Forest and Robin Hood.

Again, it was the Admiral's who got in first with the comedy of 'humours'. Chapman's *Humorous Day's Mirth* being played in the spring of 1597. This was not a mode that Shakespeare found congenial and he contented himself with making fun of it in the character of Nym. Heavier artillery was brought to bear upon it in Jonson's *Every Man In His Humour*, and according to Rowe it was Shakespeare who persuaded the company to take the play after others had 'turn'd it carelessly and superciliously over'. The Admiral's experimented with plays like Chapman's *Blind Beggar of Alexandria* in which the plot revolves round complicated disguises, but this again was a device that Shakespeare rejected. Disguise was a variation in which he found pleasure and profit, but he had no use for plots built on that and nothing else. The tit-for-tat between the two companies must have provided great entertainment for playgoers who followed it closely. Because of uncertain dating we do not know which came first, *Henry V* or Dekker's *Old Fortunatus*, both written during 1599, but the similarity of the Prologues is too close to be coincidence and one was having a typical theatre joke at the other's expense. Shakespeare's apology for the limitatons of his stage is well known. This is Dekker's:

> And for this small circumference must stand
> For the imagined surface of much land,
> Of many kingdoms, and since many a mile
> Should here be measured out, our Muse entreats
> Your thoughts to help poor art, and to allow
> That I may serve as chorus to her senses;
> She begs your pardon for she'll send one forth
> Not when the laws of poesy do call,
> But as the story needs.

The Admiral's suffered more severely than the Chamberlain's from the upheaval that followed *The Isle of Dogs* in 1597. They had already received a serious blow when two of their members, Jones and Downton, defected to the reorganized Pembroke company at the Swan, and for this or some other reason they had to stop playing for three weeks. During the subsequent ban on playing in London both companies had to tour, but whereas the Chamberlain's do not seem to have had any changes in personnel when the theatres reopened, the Admiral's were much reorganized. Alleyn had gone, and also the veteran James Tunstall and Martin Slater, to whom Henslowe had once lent £8 on the understanding that the debt would be doubled if not repaid within a month. The renegades Jones and Downton were readmitted after covenanting to act for the Admiral's and no other company, and their defection may explain why Henslowe now made such tight agreements with those whom he treated as his 'servants'. Similar contracts were made with Robert Shaw, William Bird (or Borne) and Gabriel Spencer, who had all been with Pembroke's, but in a duel a few months later Spencer was 'slain in Hogsdon Fields by the hands of Benjamin Jonson, bricklayer': an event which caused Jonson to take temporary refuge in the Church of Rome. Thomas Heywood, both actor and dramatist, 'came and hired himself with me as a covenant servant for two years', but although in the next three years Henslowe paid for fifty-eight plays that he marked as new, he drove his men too hard to get good work for them. Jonson soon left for the Chamberlain's, and although Chapman wrote a few plays at this time, they were among his least distinguished contributions to a medium that he never held in high regard. It was his affectation that he could never be bothered to see his plays performed. Dekker's natural felicity was dulled by overwork, and Henslowe had to depend mainly on the mechanical productions of Chettle, Munday, Robert Wilson and Samuel Rowley. There was nothing he might not demand from them. In 1602, trying to rejuvenate an old favourite for yet another outing, he paid Rowley and the actor Bird £4 for making additions to *Faustus*. Presumably that is where the funny bits come from.

In the relative poverty of their dramatic resources the Admiral's were quick to exploit their rivals' embarrassment over their 'Oldcastle' play. In *Richard II* Shakespeare had begun a tetralogy in which, without prejudice to his colleagues' insistence on acceptable entertainment, he would examine the nature of political authority. An old Queen's play, *The Famous Victories of Henry V*, was much to his purpose as it dramatized the tradition of the young Henry as a roisterer who underwent a gratifying repentance when responsibility called: a sound Morality theme. In the old play the prince's boon companion was named after Sir John Oldcastle, who had indeed been a friend of Henry until he took to Wycliffite heresies, led a rebellion and finally was 'hung and burnt hanging' in St Giles's Fields. His second wife was heiress to the barony of Cobham, and when *1 Henry IV* came on the stage depicting him as tutor of the prince's riots, the Cobham descendants protested. The protest may have been made by Lord Chamberlain Cobham, who died in July 1597, or by his son and successor, depending when the play was first produced. The family had a case because although self-willed and intransigent, Oldcastle was a brave soldier not given to dissipation. We may wonder why they had not complained sooner as the *Famous Victories* had been a popular play, but their pious ancestor in the role of Falstaff was too much for them to stomach. Such is the potency of art.

According to Rowe, it was the Queen herself who 'was pleas'd to command him to alter it', and by the time the play was printed in 1598 Shakespeare had changed Oldcastle to Falstaff; and for fear of offending other eminent persons, Harvey and Russell had become Bardolph and Peto. Fossils of the original may be found in the amended text, where Falstaff is still called 'my old lad of the castle'. His new name raised objections too. It was taken from Sir John Fastolfe, who had appeared in *1 Henry VI* with a somewhat distorted reputation for cowardice. In 1625 Dr Richard James, a scholar of some distinction, wrote in a letter that the misuse of Fastolfe's name was 'one of those humours and mistakes for which Plato banished all poets out of his commonwealth'. After the Cobhams had procured the removal of Oldcastle, 'the poet was put to make an ignorant shift of abusing Sir John Fastolfe, a man not inferior of virtue, though not so famous in piety as the other'.

It seems a small matter now, but in a period when the stage was so vulnerable we must be surprised at the culpable carelessness of Shakespeare and his fellows in giving offence to persons of rank. In the Epilogue to *2 Henry IV* they had to show real contrition: 'Oldcastle died a martyr, and this is not the man'. The influence of the Cobhams may explain why Falstaff did not fulfil his promise to lard the fields of France as the text of *Henry V* shows that he was meant to do. It is a likelier explanation than Kempe's departure from the company, as it is by no means certain that Kempe played Falstaff. Possibly it was Pope. The Admiral's meanwhile were doing their best to turn the situation to account. Falstaff, by whatever name, had already joined the immortals and crowds were flocking to see him. The company could not have been pleased, either, when Pistol was introduced into Part Two for the apparent purpose of burlesquing the heroic roles and fustian language in which Alleyn found fulfilment: his speech is crammed with mangled scraps of Rose successes. Accordingly they put their team of journeymen to work and in 1599 Drayton, Munday, Wilson and Hathway came up with *The True and Honourable History of the Life of Sir John Oldcastle, the Good Lord Cobham;* and a sanctimonious Prologue announced:

> It is no pampered glutton we present,
> Nor aged counsellor to youthful sin,
> But one whose virtue shone above the rest,
> A valiant martyr and a virtuous peer.

Henslowe paid £10 for this, his top rate, and he was so delighted with the play's success that he added ten shillings 'as a gift' and advanced £4 to Drayton for a sequel. This second part has not survived, but in 1619 the first part was reissued with Shakespeare named as the author.

3. 'Little Eyases'.

At the turn of the century the two companies had more to occupy them than their professional rivalry, which in any case did them no harm. They had both put themselves at risk by building new theatres. In the Chamberlain's Men the burden may have been quite heavy on individual investors who had pledged themselves to the future of their enterprise and the continued felicity of Shakespeare's art. In the Admiral's the capital burden was taken by Alleyn, who recorded later that although the building itself cost only £520, with legal costs, leases, the later purchase of the freehold and the erection of other buildings on the site, his eventual outlay was £1320. Henslowe had a half-share in the building, and some of the working profit went towards capital costs. Alleyn himself returned to the stage, but a report that this was at the personal request of the Queen because she so much enjoyed his acting sounds like an inspiration of the company's public-relations department. His presence was necessary financially if he and Henslowe were to see anything of their money.

Since 1597 the Chamberlain's and the Admiral's had, in theory, been the only two companies licensed to play in London, but there had been evasions. In 1601 a company under the patronage of the Earl of Worcester, the Queen's new Master of the Horse, gave a performance at court and in the following March the earl obtained leave from the Privy Council to play, in association with Oxford's Men, at the Boar's Head. With some experienced actors, including Kempe and two, Christopher Beeston and John Duke, who had been hired men with the Chamberlain's, they represented an organized professional opposition, and they had Thomas Heywood to write for them. His domestic tragedy *A Woman Killed with Kindness*, one of the minor masterpieces of the Elizabethan stage, was played in 1602-3.

> There is, sir, an aery of children, little eyases, that cry out on the top of question, and are most tyrannically clapp'd for't: these are now the fashion, and so berattle the common stages (so they call them) that many wearing rapiers are afraid of goose-quills, and dare scarce come thither.
>
> *Ham* II ii 354.

These lines, spoken by the unregarded Rosencrantz, are meaningless to-day but all the scenes in *Hamlet* concerning the players are illuminating about the contemporary theatre. Rosencrantz is referring to the surprising revival of the boy players, whose shrill voices now dominate the scene and cause gallants to shun the public stages for fear of being ridiculed. Before the rise of the professional companies the boys of the choir-schools had given many performances at court and to private audiences. A succession of able masters — Richard Edwards, William Hunnis, Richard Farrant, Sebastian West-cott, Thomas Giles — had encouraged their dramatic activities and some-times written their plays, and Farrant, followed by Lyly, had admitted select audiences to what in effect were public performances although they were called rehearsals. For various reasons the fashion for this sort of entertain-ment declined, and after the building of the Theatre in 1576 the boys lost favour as the professionals improved their acting standards and began to attract educated playwrights. After 1584 the only serious competition came from the St Paul's choristers under the direction of Lyly, and when their dramatic activities were suppressed in 1590 the adult companies had the theatre to themselves.

In about 1599, however, the Paul's boys started acting again under the mastership of Edward Peers, who brought them to the court in January 1601, and at the same time the Burbage brothers wanted to make use of the indoor theatre at Blackfriars which their father had bought but had been forbidden to use for public performance. In 1600 they assigned the theatre on a twenty-one year lease to Henry Evans, a scrivener, who with Nathaniel Giles, the master, found experienced dramatists ready to supply plays for the boys of the Chapel Royal. Both companies achieved immediate success because — so long as audiences were willing to watch boys taking the part of

male as well as female adults — they had certain advantages over the professionals. They had no difficulty in getting recruits as long-established practice allowed the impressment of choristers for the royal choirs and the
managers took advantage of this to secure the boy players they needed, even
kidnapping them, it was alleged, if they were not amenable to gentler
persuasions. In 1602, when the anxious professionals had enlisted the authorities in their own defence, Giles was accused of abusing his spiritual
privilege in the cause of commercial profit. It was said that he engaged boys
'no way able or fit for singing...to exercise the base trade of mercenary interlude player'. By this means the boy companies were supplied with an abundance of cheap labour, with the result that plays written for them might have
much larger casts (Marston's *Histriomastix* had more than a hundred parts)
than the professionals could afford, and thereby richer opportunities for
processions, dances and elaborate spectacle. Furthermore, the boys were
trained vocalists and musicians, and their performances were a musical
delight. An enraptured visitor reported that the play was preceded by an
hour of melody from 'organs, lutes, pandores, mandolines, violins and
flutes', with singing whose beauty was surpassed only by 'the nuns of
Milan'. Admission charges were much higher at the private theatres, and
since the income did not have to cover a heavy wage-bill for actors, it could
be devoted to music, spectacular staging and the hiring of skilled dramatists.

It was the dramatists who primarily ensured the boys' success. Except for
those bound by contract or other loyalties, nearly all the best playwrights of
the time deserted the professionals and hastened to write for them: Jonson,
Chapman, Marston, Middleton and the grave poet Daniel; Beaumont and
Fletcher in their first play together, and Dekker and Webster also in collaboration. The attraction was not so much the better pay as the greater freedom,
and for this the professional companies must take some of the blame. Greene
in 1592 was not the only dramatist to have resented working for 'an actors'
theatre' where the players — mere puppets speaking the words put into their
mouths — had most of the credit and most of the profit. They also appointed
themselves judge of the conditions, deciding what would be effective on the
stage and what would not; so that the dramatists, often men of superior
confidence and learning, were wounded in their artistic pride when their
plays were chopped about, their learned wit disesteemed and their poetic
flights replaced by pedestrian contributions from the company's journeymen. When they wrote for the boys they did not suffer these indignities. In
the private theatres the dramatic Muse was unfettered and the playwright
was allowed elbow-room for his topicalities and innuendoes, his learning
and his Latinity, his digs at his professional rivals.

Freedom turned to self-indulgence in the foolish *Poetomachia*, or 'war of
the theatres'. The chief combatant was Ben Jonson, who tended to be arrogant and contemptuous towards others and to be over-sensitive when he
thought that he was himself being ridiculed. In *Histriomastix* (1599)

Marston glanced at Jonson as the crusty philsopher Chrisoganus, and there followed a series of satirical comedies with Marston writing for the Paul's boys and Jonson for the Chapel Royal, and Dekker intervening later. The conflict would be easier to pursue if we could be more confident about the order of the plays, but it was a fairly trivial business and literary historians may have made too much of it. Certainly some of the blows were wounding, but the convention in these matters was very different in Elizabethan times when modern laws of defamation did not operate. The writers were keen to show off their wit and subtlety, and their gibes may have been more good-humoured than they seem on the printed page. At the close of the struggle Marston was happy to dedicate *The Malcontent* to Jonson, and the personalities mostly occurred as incidental gags or scenes introduced into a self-contained story. Dekker's *Satiromastix*, for example, which in 1601 was the last shot in the war, was primarily a tale of William Rufus and Sir Walter Terrill upon which the appearance of Jonson as Horace had no bearing at all. Jonson is here ridiculed for the long time he was in labour before producing a play, in retaliation for his own attack on Marston and Dekker as windy plagiarists.

Shakespeare comes into the story because in the third *Parnassus* play (IV iii) the character of Kempe is made to say:

> O, that Ben Jonson is a pestilent fellow, he brought up Horace giving the poets a pill, but our fellow Shakespeare hath given him a purge that made him beray his credit.

It is as certain as such things can ever be that the character in Jonson's *Poetaster* who had lately lost his father and bought himself a coat-of-arms was to this extent — nothing else in the character resembles him — a reflection of Shakespeare; and in the printed version of *Every Man In His Humour*, registered in 1600, Sogliardo's motto 'Not Without Mustard' is too direct a hit to have been a coincidence. What then was the purge that brought Jonson to the seat of repentance? Something there must have been, for *3 Parnassus* is full of theatrical allusions most of which are identifiable. Shakespeare probably was not much troubled by references to himself but he would not accept disparagement of his friends and his profession. The tone of *3 Parnassus* and of plays written for the boys was unsympathetic to the public theatres, and in *The Poetaster* Jonson spoke scurvily of the 'common stages' for which he had lately been writing and the 'common actors' who had lately been his colleagues. Such incivility indeed demanded a purgative and possibly it was administered by the presentation of *Satiromastix* at the Globe simultaneously with its production by the Paul's boys, so that Jonson/Horace, grievously mocked and crowned with nettles, should have his medicine on the public stage as well as in a coterie theatre. If speculation may be allowed its occasional extravagance, perhaps the Chamberlain's Men gave Dekker some help during the writing of the play, and perhaps it was Shakespeare who took the part of Horace at the Globe.[8]

But Shakespeare's principal purgation was of the boys themselves rather than the dramatists who brought them fleeting popularity. For a time they had a vogue. Delivered by these pert and talented children, the topicalities of the *Poetomachia* were daring and, for a limited circle, amusing. So long as they had the gloss of novelty they attracted enough of the fashionable audience to cause the professionals some anxiety. Hamlet is surprised that the players should arrive at Elsinore for a blind date when 'their residence both in reputation and profit was better both ways'. 'The tragedians of the city', perhaps a hint of the melodramatic inclinations of Alleyn's company, had been obliged to tour, but 'Hercules and his load' had suffered too: Hercules shouldering the globe being the proud new badge of Shakespeare's own playhouse. No one complained if the youthful companies were provoked to a dog-fight; in fact, promoters would only pay for plots in which 'the Poet and the Player went to cuffs'. Guildenstern, who hitherto has added nothing to the discussion, agrees, with subtly deflating irony, that indeed 'there has been much throwing about of brains'.

Hamlet's view is that this is an unnatural situation that cannot last. A check would soon be put on Nathaniel Giles's cynical conscription of 'choristers' whose musical training would be secondary to their histrionic performance, and the actors' patrons probably had a hand in this. The precocity of the boys was forced and unnatural, and there was the sad little figure of Salamon Pavey, pressed by Giles and famed for his playing of old men, who died when 'years he numbered scarce thirteen'. Hamlet went to the root of the boys' predicament when he enquired how in future they would be 'escoted', or earn a living.

> Will they pursue the quality no longer than they can sing? Will they not say afterwards, if they should grow themselves to common players (as it is like most will if their means be not better) their writers do them wrong, to make them exclaim against their own profession?
>
> *Ham* II ii 363.

Hamlet is asking what will happen to the boys when they are no longer serviceable to their masters if meanwhile they have belittled the adult companies with whom their hopes of future employment must lie. Youth's a stuff will not endure. The boys' success was disturbing for the professionals while it lasted, but it was of necessity impermanent and sooner or later their indiscretions would get them into trouble. In 1603 the boys of the Chapel Royal were constituted the Children of the Queen's Revels, but in 1606, after their participation in *Eastward Ho*, they lost this title and Giles was instructed that his choristers should no longer take part in plays, 'for that it is not fit or decent that such as should sing the praises of God Almighty should be trained up or employed in such lascivious or profane exercises'.

8 Chambers, *Eliz.Stage*, I 381, III 363-4. *WS* I 71-2.

The Paul's boys appear to have ceased playing at about the same time, and although the Chapel children were later restored to royal favour and appeared occasionally at court, the boy companies were outside the main stream of theatrical development.

4. The King's Men.

English Puritans were hopeful that a monarch brought up in the rigours of Presbyterian Scotland would share their opinion of the iniquity of dramatic performances, but whatever their other shortcomings the Stuarts were generous patrons of the theatre. James I acted promptly and decisively. On 19 May 1603, only ten days after his arrival in London, he issued the patent which made the Chamberlain's Men royal servants. Nine players were named in it, Lawrence Fletcher, Shakespeare, Richard Burbage, Phillips, Heminges, Condell, Sly, Robert Armin, Richard Cowley, 'and the rest of their associates'. It appointed them to be sworn officers of the royal household with the style of grooms of the chamber; and another patent in the following year supplied them with measures of scarlet cloth in which they might do honour to his Majesty in his progress through the capital. They had no household duties beyond the performance of plays when this should be demanded of them, and therefore they received no regular fee; but between 1603 and 1616 they gave 177 performances at court, more than all the other companies combined, and on three occasions James made them an *ex gratia* payment when plague lost them their income from the public stage. In August 1604 they were temporarily attached to the household of the Constable of Castile when he came to London to discuss a treaty for the conclusion of the war with Spain, and although his entertainment was provided by bears and acrobats, Heminges and Phillips received £21.12s to share with their ten associates. The three additional sharers brought the number to twelve, where it remained for the rest of Shakespeare's lifetime.

The new men are thought to have been John Lowin, who came from Worcester's company, Alexander Cooke and Samuel Crosse. Formerly apprenticed to Heminges, Cooke had served the company as a hired man; little is known of Crosse, who died in 1605 and was replaced by Nicholas Tooley, formerly an apprentice of Richard Burbage. The original nine names mentioned in the patent of 1603 show that few changes had occurred in the company since 1594. Pope had left, probably on account of failing health for by 1604 he was dead, leaving his apparel and arms to two of his apprentices; Bryan had probably retired rather sooner as he was mentioned in 1603 as an ordinary groom of the chamber with household duties; and Kempe had been replaced by Armin. Soon after the Globe had opened Kempe left the company to dance his way from London to Norwich. Jigs were his speciality, and his virtuoso performance was so well applauded and rewarded that he repeated it on the continent, where it was less successful.

His appearance in *3 Parnassus* as a colleague of Shakespeare and Burbage is not certain evidence that he had rejoined the Chamberlain's on his return: probably he had not. In 1602-3 he was with Worcester's and then he disappears, perhaps a victim of the plague. Fletcher was a Scottish protégé of the King, a comedian who in the exercise of his quality had earned the civic disapprobation of the elders of Edinburgh. His unheralded appearance in London's leading theatrical company was a minor and relatively harmless instance of James's ill-considered zeal in advancing his fellow-countrymen. Fletcher may never have been a sharer in the company[9] and he is not to be found in the surviving actor-lists, but apparently he remained in London because he was buried at St Saviour's in 1608.

In 1608 the King's Men opened a second playhouse. When deprived of their title of Queen's Revels, the boy company had struggled on as the Children of Blackfriars. But recurrent plague, and perhaps the deterioration of the premises, made it difficult for them to continue, and when a general inhibition on the theatres resulted from Chapman's plays on recent French history, Henry Evans was willing to surrender his lease. Protected now by the royal livery, the Burbages were confident that they might use the theatre as their winter home without provoking the local opposition that had balked them ten years previously. Accordingly they formed a syndicate consisting of themselves, Heminges, Condell, Shakespeare and Sly, with the unknown Thomas Evans representing Henry. As in the earlier arrangement at the Globe, the syndicate were the housekeepers, responsible for rent (£40 a year) and renovations and drawing their share of the takings as landlords to the company. Sly died shortly after the agreement was completed and as a housekeeper he may not have been replaced. The syndicate were involved in litigation with Robert Keysar, a speculating goldsmith, and Edward Kirkham, to whom Evans had sold shares in the premises and assets of the boy company. Keysar contended that the new arrangement was illegal and prejudicial to his interests, and in 1610 he sued for a sixth of the subsequent profit of £1500. The housekeepers challenged his figures and replied that Evans had no business to subdivide the lease. Kirkham alleged in his evidence that a winter season at Blackfriars was bringing the company £1000 more than a winter season at the Globe, and this may not have been much exaggerated. Although Blackfriars held only 700, less than a third of the accommodation at the Globe, the minimum charge was sixpence and attendance at the outdoor theatres always fell away during the winter months.

Apart from interruptions due to plague, these were prosperous times for the King's Men and for Shakespeare personally. In the first ten years of the reign James summoned them to court on an average of thirteen times a year,

9   So it is generally believed, and he is not among the twenty-six 'Principal Actors' named in the First Folio in 1623. On the other hand, in Phillips's will in 1605 he is among the 'fellows' who each received twenty shillings in gold.

compared with the three times a year under Elizabeth's more frugal dispensation, and of the ten plays they presented there during the long Christmas season of 1604-5 seven were by Shakespeare, and *The Merchant of Venice* was given twice. His authorship was usually acknowledged in the registration and printing of plays and he was now receiving the compliment of false attributions, his name appearing on the title-page of works he did not write. With new companies and new theatres springing up in London, playgoing seems to have grown more popular everywhere, but competition was less intense and concentrated than in the 1590s when two companies virtually had the stage to themselves. It may have been keener but because it was more widely diffused, its quality was lower. The King's Men were comfortably pre-eminent.

The Admiral's Men, now Prince Henry's, had freed themselves from their dependence on Henslowe. They still owed him rent as part-proprietor of the Fortune, but in 1604 all other outstanding liabilities were discharged and with the ending of his invaluable records we have little information about his old company. Although retaining a financial interest in the Fortune and its assets, Alleyn finally left the stage in 1604 and returned to the accumulation of one of the largest fortunes amassed in an acquisitive society by a self-made man who was not in the commodity business. (This is not said in denigration of the man, because it was a remarkable achievement. Alleyn's stage reputation was punctured by the pinpricks of Shakespeare and other writers. He acted in a thrasonical style that temporarily was outmoded and he relied overmuch on dramatists who similarly were out of fashion. But it was a style for which the theatre periodically has its uses, and Alleyn was too formidable a person to be a figure of fun. His generous and understanding treatment of his associates in the theatre, the tenderness of his correspondence with his wife and the lavishness of his benefactions all testify to his qualities as a man.) With his departure the company's artistic standards seem to have declined. They now ran themselves as a self-governing group, but although their membership was now more consistent, of the players named in the patent from the Elector Palatine in 1613 only Thomas Downton survived from 1594 and he had been a truant in his time. The company's weakness had always been a want of top-class dramatists. Heywood now was with Worcester's, Jonson returned to the King's whom he had reviled, Chapman was more intent upon completing his translation of Homer, and Marston took holy orders and withdrew to a Hampshire parsonage. Dekker's prolific vein had been exhausted, and the rising playwrights like Beaumont, Fletcher, Webster, Massinger and Middleton mostly took their work elsewhere. Prince Henry's were behind the times, too, in becoming the only professional company without an indoor theatre. The reconstructed Fortune in 1621 was probably roofed, but the change was made too late; and whereas the King's Men rebuilt the Globe from their own resources, the sharers in Prince Henry's could not find the money and had to seek help from a business syndicate headed by Alleyn. Thereafter they were dependants of these capitalist proprietors.

Worcester's, now Queen Anne's, began their London existence at Henslowe's Rose and then at the Boar's Head, but in 1606 they opened their own theatre, the Red Bull in Clerkenwell, which they occupied until in 1617 they moved to the roofed Cockpit in Drury Lane and renamed it the Phoenix. At the Red Bull they played to the lower end of the market, with Richard Perkins tearing passion to tatters in the tragic roles and Tom Greene playing for broad comic effects. Webster wrote *The White Devil* for the Red Bull and commended Perkins for his performance, but it was the King's who acted *The Duchess of Malfi* in 1614 with Lowin as Bosola and Burbage as Ferdinand. Queen Anne's appear to have taken their coarse and noisy style of playing indoors with them, and the Phoenix had a salty reputation among the private theatres.

With Lady Elizabeth's company we are back with Henslowe, whose strange passion for the theatre was seemingly unquenchable. He formed the company in 1611 from defectors from Prince Charles's Men, and among the players who signed agreements with him were William Ecclestone, Joseph Taylor and John Rice, all subsequently sharers in the King's Men. Henslowe then engaged some former members of the Queen's Revels, now grown up, and in 1614 he took this motley combination to the Hope, lately built by himself and Alleyn. There they had to share the premises with bears, whose public baiting was 'a sweet and comfortable recreation fitted for the solace and comfort of a peaceable people'.

They acted Jonson's *Bartholomew Fair*, whose Induction contains a useful guide to two decades of the contemporary theatre, but after little more than a year they were in bitter dispute with Henslowe and his partner, Jacob Meade. Their nine 'articles of grievance and oppression' accused Henslowe of keeping them in financial servitude, even to the extent of periodically disbanding the company in order to re-engage them at lower wages. As with the Admiral's in the 1590s, he had a calculated policy of keeping the players in permanent obligation because 'should these fellows come out of my debt, I should have no rule with them'. Possibly it was a way of maintaining discipline in a profession that still had its quota of 'rogues and vagabonds'. When the players complained that 'we have paid him for play-books £200 or thereabouts, and yet he denies to give us copies of any one of them', we can see his point of view: some of them would have hurried to the printer with any copy they could lay hands on. Henslowe's agreement with the actor Robert Dawes reveals a suspicious nature convinced that he was surrounded by villains. An actor not 'ready apparelled' when the play was due to begin was fined 3s., and for being late at rehearsal 1s.; to be 'overcome with drink at the time when he ought to play' cost 10s., and to be unable to play at all cost £1. The worst enormity was to go to the tavern after performance wearing stage costume (which was Henslowe's property), and the fine for this was £40. In every generation the theatre has had to impose sanctions on the undisciplined and the intransigent; there is a professional code in these matters. But Henslowe's motive, it seems, was not only to protect his property but to impose his authority. Except at the lower end of the scale, his fines existed only on paper, because indigent actors could not afford to pay them; but the existence in the ledgers of even a paper debt further deepened their servitude. Their revolt in 1615 appears to have disrupted the company, for later in the year the Hope was occupied by a collection of players from Lady Elizabeth's, Prince Charles's and the Queen's Revels. After Henslowe's death in 1616 actors from these three companies undertook to play at the Hope until they had discharged to Meade and Alleyn the money supposedly owing to him.

By and large the Elizabethan theatre was a disorganized world that needed a Henslowe to keep it in some sort of order, but it was the world to which Shakespeare the player and dramatist always belonged. The processes of his mind and imagination we may not understand unless we ourselves are poets, and not always then, but he was not a remote genius who composed immortal verse out of some inner necessity unrelated to his working life. Like all playwrights, he sometimes wrote more than was required for the business on hand, and he had to see it removed for stage performance. Probably few of the printed texts set up from his original version were acted just as he wrote them, but as a professional he would respect the judgment of his fellows and agree to their modifications. First and foremost he was a man of the theatre who produced plays for a living.

Thus his career in the theatre is inseparable from his colleagues in the King's Men. They were the instrument on which he played, and although their greatest glory was to have Shakespeare as their principal dramatist, in a lesser fellowship Shakespeare could not have achieved what he did. Their help was necessary to his greatness: not merely in the obvious sense that a play without actors is a dead thing or, if it has life at all, exists in one dimension only and that not properly its own; but in the deeper sense that their understanding of his work, the quality of their interpretation of it, left him free to follow any road where his genius led him. When a play came to its final test, on the boards of a theatre, they would not fail him. Their skill complemented his poetic vision, and either would have been less without the stimulus of the other. If he wrote them a pot-boiler, their competence put a gloss on its defects; if he wrote them a masterpiece, they were equal to it.

Acting is a nervy and testing occupation, and like any group of men who live and work at close quarters, the company must have had their traumas and misunderstandings, perhaps their animosities, but there is no record of it nor even a hint of it in current theatrical gossip. The troubles that afflicted other companies seem not to have touched them. They had a history strangely free from acrimony, desertion or litigation within their own ranks, and they preserved an almost continuous membership which only death could disrupt. Once a player acquired a share in the company, it was rare for him to leave the stage for another occupation, as Bryan did; or, like Kempe, to go off and then join another company; it was even rare for one to go into partial retirement, as Shakespeare did, while he still had life and health. So far as the records give reliable evidence, the hired men had the same sort of loyalty. Some of them, of course, left to better themselves with another company, often returning as sharers when there was a vacancy. Others seem to have remained consistently in the service of the company even when there was small prospect of advancement. John Sincklo, famous for his leanness, played for the company or its various combinations without ever becoming a sharer, and Robert Gough played with them, first as a boy and then as a hired man, for twenty years before his faithfulness was rewarded.

In consequence the King's Men always had a core of devoted, experienced men whose knowledge of each other, and common agreement on aims and policy, created a deep and lasting unity. Richard Burbage, Sly, Heminges, Condell, Cowley and Phillips had been colleagues in Strange's company; and as this first generation gradually passed away, a second generation, tutored under their guidance and taught to respect the same ideals, succeeded them as inheritors of their policy. John Lowin, who came from Worcester's in about 1604, became joint-manager after the death of Heminges in 1630 and was still working when the theatres closed. Subsequently he was host of the Three Pigeons in Brentford, when it was reported that 'his poverty was as great as his age'. In 1647 the Folio of the plays of Beaumont and Fletcher was published to raise money for himself and his old partner as manager, Joseph Taylor, who had joined the company when Burbage died in 1619. Among those who signed the dedication to the Folio were Robert Benfield, a sharer since 1614, and Richard Robinson, who began as a boy player, matured as a comedian and succeeded Cowley as a sharer in 1619. He may be the Robinson who married Burbage's widow. The company had thus preserved the continuity of their membership, and when the Globe was shut and the younger actors went off to fight for their king, their senior colleagues were men who had played with Shakespeare.

The professional ties which bound the King's Men to one another were strengthened by those of personal regard and affection. They were far from being the mountebanks that contemporary Puritanism and an ill-informed posterity have supposed them. The theatre certainly had its rakes and spend-thrifts, its debauchees and petty crooks, but as Heywood seasonably said in his *Apology for Actors* in 1612, if 'there be any few degenerate from the rest in that good demeanour which is both requisite and expected at their hands, let me entreat you not to censure hardly of all for the misdeeds of some'. He named some actors who were worthy of credit:

Gabriel [presumably Spencer], Singer, Pope, Phillips, Sly, all the right I can do them is but this, that though they be dead, their deserts yet live in the remembrance of many. Among so many dead let me not forget one yet alive, in this time the most worthy, famous Master Edward Alleyn.

In the circumstances of the day it is an astonishing fact that, so far as we know, Shakespeare never saw any of his fellows thrown into prison. London's prisons were numerous, and with writs of *habeas corpus* as yet unknown, it was very easy to get into them. Mere suspicion was enough: suspicion of heresy or subversiveness, a whispered report of a word spoken in careless anger, of a hand placed too readily on a sword. Men went to prison for debt, for 'a commodity of brown paper and old ginger', for slander, for rioting in the streets, for drunkenness, fisticuffs or petty theft. They might not stay there very long. For a few days they would lie in foetid dungeons in the company of hardened criminals and then they would be released with a perfunctory examination or no examination at all. Authority believed in the 'cooling off' process. A man had to be very respectable or very cautious, or perhaps just lucky, to spend many years in London without ever being carried off by a nervous bumbledom careless of fine distinctions.[10] Particularly this was so of theatre folk, whose occupation made them prone to the sort of offences, or suspicion of offences, the law was sharpest to rebuke. The long immunity of the King's Men suggests a high standard of personal and professional conduct and a far-seeing discretion in the choice of recruits.

So far, then, from being rootless vagabonds sunk in debauchery and debt, the King's Men were respectable, God-fearing citizens, men of property and enviable domesticity. The absence of scandal about their private and professional lives would almost suggest a conspiracy of silence were it not that their rivals in the theatre would have grown fat on any imputation that came their way. Shakespeare was granted a coat-of-arms, a permission never given without punctual scrutiny, and so too were Burbage, Heminges, Cowley, Pope and Phillips. None of them amassed — nor perhaps would have wished to — the prodigious wealth of Alleyn, who bought a manor in Dulwich for £10,000 and maintained a school there with an annual endowment of £1700, settled £1500 a year on his second wife, John Donne's daughter, and left £2000 in his will. Many of them, however, made considerable investments in property and land. Burbage left real estate worth £300 a year, Pope owned three houses in Southwark, Heminges and his family had a grocery business, Phillips owned a country estate at Mortlake, Cowley an estate in the Cotswolds as well as property and houses in London. After 1596 at least, and possibly sooner, Shakespeare lived an impermanent life in various London

10 Of literary folk known to Shakespeare, either personally or by repute, all these for various causes spent time in prison: Nashe, Kyd, Dekker, Chapman, Jonson, Marston, all dramatists; Donne, Joseph Hall, Thomas Habington, Ralegh, Bacon, Sir John Harington, Sir Thomas Overbury, Lord Herbert of Cherbury, Sir John Hayward. The vulnerability of mere actors, always prone to be improvident or indiscreet, was much higher.

lodgings[11], and his real home, the focus of his earthly regard, was far away in Warwickshire. His fellows made their homes in London. Richard Burbage lived always in his father's parish of St Leonard's, Shoreditch, where he had seven children, and Cowley and his family were neighbours. Gough and Phillips, each the father of five children, lived over the river in Southwark, as did the two bachelors, Pope with his adopted children, and William Sly. Heminges and Condell chose to stay in the sober and non-theatrical parish of St Mary Aldermanbury, where they were churchwardens and parented huge families. These men had interests outside the theatre and they had planted roots in the city where they worked. For anyone meeting them as they walked with their families in Finsbury Fields perhaps only a touch of bizarre splendour in dress or ornament would have distinguished them from the Londoners who flocked to see their own image in the citizen dramas of Heywood and Dekker.

Their professional relationships were founded on the same citizen qualities of integrity, confidence and respect. Over the years considerable sums of money passed through the hands of the company's managers, to be assigned to the various items in the balance-sheet and distributed among the sharers and the hired staff, but there is no trace of the disputes and charges of misappropriation that soured the affairs of other companies. Where we have record of the legacies made in their wills, they speak of continued trust and affection. Phillips appointed Heminges, Burbage and Sly to be his executors, rewarding each with the gift of a silver bowl, and he left gold or other gifts to all his fellows and £5 to be shared among the hired men. Shakespeare, Condell and 'my servant Christopher Beeston' (later the owner of the Cockpit/Phoenix) each received 30s., the other principal members 20s. To 'my late apprentice' Samuel Gilburne he left 40s., some valuable clothing and his bass viol; to his present apprentice James Sands 40s. and three musical instruments, 'to be paid and delivered unto him at the expiration of his term of years in his indenture of apprenticehood'. Although worried at the time by dispositions within his own family, Shakespeare in 1616 remembered his fellows who were still alive and left to Burbage, Heminges and Condell each 'xxvis. viiid. to buy them rings'. Pope made bequests to two actors he had trained as boys. Tooley was a witness to Richard Burbage's will and in his own will in 1623 left gifts to his family; to Mrs Cuthbert Burbage, 'in whose house I do now lodge', he left £10 'as a remembrance of my love in respect of her motherly care over me'; Cuthbert Burbage and Condell were appointed his executors and residuary legatees; he made gifts to Mrs Condell and her daughter and to Joseph Taylor, who had not long joined the company; and he forgave Ecclestone and Underwood, but not Robinson, their debts to him. (Robinson's debt of £29.13s. was not remitted because Tooley wanted to leave the money to a daughter of

11 See pages 239, 245.

Richard Burbage. That three of his associates should be in debt to him is unsurprising in the profession, but the arrangements were kept within the company, with no mention of the usurious interest Henslowe would have exacted in like circumstances; and if it be true that Robinson had lately married Burbage's widow, the obligation to his new daughter-in-law may have been only a paper transaction.) Alexander Cooke appointed Heminges, to whom he was formerly apprenticed, and Condell as his trustees and left them money to bring up his 'poor orphans'. Underwood likewise left Heminges, Condell and Lowin money to buy rings and committed the care of his five children (one of them christened Burbage) to his 'loving and kind fellows'.

As the ultimate survivor of the company's original members Heminges was almost a universal legatee, and he kept alive the tradition by making small bequests 'unto every of my fellows and sharers, His Majesty's Servants', including 20s. to 'John Rice, clerk, of St Saviour's, Southwark', a former apprentice and sharer who left the company in about 1625 to take holy orders. By the time of his death in 1630 Heminges must have been a very old man because it was in 1588 that he married Rebecca Knell, relict of William Knell untimely stabbed at Thame. By her and perhaps some later consort he had at least twelve children. The account of the players' bequests becomes an iterative catalogue but it is significant. If a man's will is in some sort a record of those whom he has loved and trusted in his lifetime, we have in these documents evidence of the harmony that prevailed in the company and the justice of their dealings with one another.

5. The Actor's Art.

At the higher levels of the profession Elizabethan actors had to be very competent. They had to be quick at learning their lines as runs were short, plays were seldom given consecutive performances and at any moment the repertoire must contain half a dozen plays ready for the stage. They must have good memories, helped perhaps by some aptitude for metrical improvization when the prompter had too many responsibilities to be able to give uninterrupted attention to the script. They must be versatile, as the repertoire ranged from tragedy to romantic comedy, from fantasy to farce, and all these elements would sometimes occur in a single play. Finally, they must be strong and fit physically, because the job required the endowment of an athlete. Most Elizabethan plays offered scope for spectacle and vigorous action, to gratify an unsophisticated demand for battles, sieges, duels and dances. Thus the player had to know how to use a sword and look as though he relished it. The modern actor is seldom zestful when the time comes for him to pass from vehemence of speech to vehemence of action. His Macbeth is seldom a man on whom fell deeds sit naturally, his Henry not conspicuously enthusiastic in jumping the walls of Harfleur. But an Elizabethan fencing-match was an accomplished exhibition of sword-play, a battle something to be waged with authentic spirit albeit limited numbers. The actor also had to show some ability in the dance, and at least he must be able to sing if he could not play. Phillips's bequests of instruments to his late apprentices show that musicianship in one form or another was a further attribute of men whose varied talents were summarized in a sketch in general unsympathetic to the profession, T. G.'s *Rich Cabinet* (1616):

> Player hath many times many excellent qualities: as dancing, activity [tumbling], music, song, elocution, ability of body, memory, vigilancy, skill of weapon, pregnancy of wit, and such like: in all of which he resembleth an excellent spring of water, which grows the more sweeter and the more plentiful by the often drawing-out of it: so are all these the more perfect and plausible by the more-often practice.

The most important of these qualities was 'elocution', if by this the writer meant the discipline of speech and gesture known as Rhetoric. As propounded by famous orators like Gorgias and Isocrates (and rejected by Socrates because its purpose was trickery, not truth), Rhetoric was a technique of persuasion that employed every literary and aural device to win an argument. Every Elizabethan schoolboy had a smattering of it because it was part of the edifice built on the foundation of his classical training. It instructed him, first, in the rules governing the cogent exposition of an argument, arraying before him the appropriate uses of metaphor, antithesis, parenthesis, synecdoche and the rest. Secondly, it laid down the rules to be observed in public speaking: the modulation of the voice, the use of gesture, the government of the peroration. In writing and in speaking, Rhetoric was what Elizabethans meant by style, and mastery of its intricate formalities was the touchstone of an artist's worth.

In the theatre Rhetoric created a stylized acting that harmonized also with drama's origins in the rituals of the Christian liturgy. It taught the actor how to use his voice, hold his head, control his feet and hands. In Nashe's *Summer's Last Will and Testament* (1592) a character tells the other actors how to conduct themselves: 'And this I bar, over and besides, that none of you stroke your beards to make action, play with your cod-piece points, or stand fumbling on your buttons when you know not how to bestow your fingers. Serve God, and act cleanly'. It is the professional's perennial rebuke to the amateur whose ineptitudes discredit the mystery. The actor trained in Rhetoric commanded all the effects of which the human voice, by subtle variations of pitch and range and pace, is capable. By power of speech, almost unaided by scenic device, he had to give a location to the bare platform on which he stood, create an atmosphere of darkness or revelry or mounting tension, perhaps embody a picture of something that never existed, of Ophelia's death in the glassy stream, or Cleopatra's barge or the popinjay courtier at Holmedon. By delicate changes of rhythm he could give to each character that articulation that was his and his alone, so that even in the varying moods of anger or passion or acceptance that character would be speaking and none other. If he needed to act not with his voice only but the whole of his body, reinforcing speech with appropriate movement and gesture, here again Rhetoric gave him the necessary instruction.

Rhetoric, however, had its dangers. It happens in any art, and not in art only, that a body of principles formulated out of need and experience hardens into devitalized dogma. The rigidity of Rhetorical disciplines, as professed by some of its devoted but uncritical theorists, could have grotesque consequences. Chaucer had shown this two hundred years ago when in *The Nun's Priest's Tale* he mocked the extravagances of the *De Nova Poetria* of Geoffrey de Vinsauf, an obsessed grammarian of the twelfth century. By 1600 Rhetoric, in its severer forms at any rate, had largely served its turn[12], and there can be little doubt that the twenty years that Shakespeare spent in the theatre saw a movement towards a more natural style of acting. Rhetoric, the matured product of classical precision and medieval love of balance, was never casual and never sought to assimiliate itself with ordinary speech. It was always a special way of speaking, in confident possession of territories where it was the only proper way of speaking. But, once its basic principles had been mastered, giving technical authority in diction, gesture and artistic decorum, was it the only proper way of speaking in the theatre? Alleyn, one suspects, had no doubt that it was. It was King Cambyses's vein: he had been brought up in it and he would persist in it. The style in which a play is written determines the manner in which it shall be spoken and performed, and to look at the text of *Cambyses* is to know how the actors must have delivered their lines. This is evident too in Lyly, Rhetoric's most obedient servant, or in Greene puffing to be a tragedian or in Shakespeare's *Henry VI*, where ranting histrionics would have matched the sound and fury of the writing. But the wind died from the furious sails, bombast went out of fashion and playwrights discovered a style less remote from the speech of ordinary intercourse. (The malapropisms of the Shakespearean clowns of the 1590s reveal the transition from the academic to the popular.) Poetic speech was still heightened, obviously, and classical and mythological allusion still coloured the argument, but it is not only Shakespeare's characters who have discovered a more intimate address to the audience. With this went a change in acting style that allowed Sir

---

12 On the evidence of the handbooks on Rhetoric in which the age abounded, this statement may be open to challenge; and no reader of the sermons of Donne or Lancelot Andrewes would deny that in the pulpits of the great Anglican divines Rhetoric was still golden. But the making of many text-books, the anxious reassertion of supposedly incontestable principles, is often a sign of decay. Rhetoric was already doomed by Francis Bacon, that mighty rhetorician, in his demand for the 'disassociation of sensibility'. The English language was shortly to undergo a revolution, or rather a purgation, as seventeenth-century science insisted that words should cast off all ambiguities and emotional associations and attain a single precise meaning. In such a climate Rhetoric was only a beguiler and a cheat.

Thomas Overbury to write in his *Characters*, published in 1614: the player 'doth not strive to make nature monstrous; she is often seen in the same scene with him, but neither on stilts nor crutches; and for his voice, 'tis not lower than the prompter, nor louder than the foil and target'. Here too *Rich Cabinet* is pertinent: 'Player must take heed of wrested and enforced action: for if there be not a facility in his deliverance, and as it were a natural dexterity, it must needs sound harsh to the auditor, and procure his distaste and displeasure'.

Hamlet has some words upon this matter. In II ii he is speaking in character, at a stage in the play when his mind is disturbed and his response to people and events is uncertain. His warm and princely greeting to the Players, coming close upon his cold reception of Rosencrantz and Guildenstern, reflects the natural courtesy he always displayed to those he did not suspect of having injured him. His interest in the drama and theatre politics is natural to a young man of his tastes and culture, and he reminds Polonius that actors are 'the abstracts and brief chronicles of the time'. His taste in plays is a scholar's taste. He commends a play that was caviare to the general, one planned on classical lines and free alike of affectation and gratuitous bawdry: Ben Jonson, we feel, would have said no less. But then Hamlet allows himself to be moved by the 'Hecuba' speech of the First Player, which is a roaring Senecan burlesque: Senecan in its over-wrought phrasing and in its observance of the convention that violent action may be passionately described but not portrayed. It is the sort of histrionic set-piece for which Shakespeare's company were always laughing at their rivals. It is right that Polonius should applaud it, for it recalled to him the academic drama of his youth, and his taste has not advanced with the passing years. Throughout the play he is shown to be devoted to all the outmoded devices of Rhetoric. His utterances are rebuked for containing more art than matter. He ventures into the pomposities of antimetabole (''tis true 'tis pity...') and agnomination, he relishes phrases like 'mobled queen' and he rolls his tongue round the *sententiae* he delivers to Laertes, borrowing them from Lyly. But Hamlet shares his admiration for the Hecuba speech, and is moved by it to a passionate consideration of his own predicament. Shakespeare seems here to be acknowledging the potency of Rhetoric even its crudest forms.

In III ii it is different. The Hamlet who was moved to feminine grief by the woes of the mobled queen is now warning the First Player against tearing a passion to tatters; and it would appear that for the moment Shakespeare has abandoned his play and its protagonist in order to talk stage politics. *Hamlet* was played at the Globe when the *Poetomachia* was still in contention. We cannot know whether Shakespeare was following his own inclination in making reference to it or whether he did it at the bidding of his colleagues. He has earlier remarked the ascendancy of the 'little eyases', and he is now perhaps defending the style of acting favoured at the Globe against the older fashion of his adult rivals. It would be hard to defend the passage dramatically: it is as clearly 'dragged in' as the previous reference to the boy companies. Whatever its propriety or its motives, it is valuable evidence of contemporary acting styles.

Hamlet wishes that the lines he has written for the players shall be spoken 'trippingly on the tongue';

> but if you mouth it as many of your players do, I had as lief the town-crier spoke my lines. Nor do not saw the air too much with your hand — thus — but use all gently, for in the very torrent, tempest and, as I may say, whirlwind of your passion, you must acquire and beget a temperance that may give it smoothness

After a warning not to outdo the Termagant and Herod who were obstreperous villains of the Miracle plays, Hamlet wants the actors to be 'not too tame, neither' but to be guided by their own discretion:

> suit the action to the word, the word to the action, with this special observance, that you o'erstep not the modesty of nature: for anything so o'erdone is from the purpose of playing, whose end both at the first, and now, was and is to hold as 'twere the mirror up to nature, to show virtue her own feature, scorn her own image, and the very age and body of the time his form and pressure. Now this overdone, or come tardy off, though it make the unskilful laugh, cannot but make the judicious grieve, the censure of which one must in your allowance o'erweigh a whole theatre of others. O, there be players that I have seen play, and heard others praise, and that highly, not to speak it profanely, that neither having th'accent of Christians, for the gait of Christian, pagan nor man, have so strutted and bellowed that I have thought some of nature's journeymen had made men, and not made them well, they imitated humanity so abominably.

The professional receives this admonition from the royal amateur with the laconic hope that his company have reformed these matters fairly well.

These are surprising words from the prince who has lately received a cue for passion in the woes of Hecuba, a speech in which the Player must have shattered every one of the precepts now held up for his better instruction. But we need not trouble any further with Hamlet's contradictions, for it is with Shakespeare's views that we are here concerned and we find Shakespeare behaving, for him, rather strangely. It is not unusual for him to show things in a contradictory light — or, to be more exact, to present the same thing from different angles of vision — but it is seldom that he repeats his effects. In *Hamlet* he makes a double attack on the old school of acting, first by burlesque and secondly by specific renunciation: a heavy concentration of fire from one who normally was so economical and unobtrusive.

The key to the passage is the First Player's quiet assurance that 'we have reformed that indifferently with us, sir'. Actors at the Globe, he seems to be saying, have learned better. They no longer saw the air, roll the eyeballs or mouth lines like the town-crier; they suit their actions to the words and try to conduct themselves like ordinary human beings. It is likely that this claim was well founded. Some have thought that through Hamlet Shakespeare was trying to tell his company how he wished them to act, but it would have been a strange and uncharacteristic method of instruction to require them first to make fools of themselves in public. It is surely more probable that he was giving them credit for a lesson already learned. The lesson, it should be noted, was not that the discipline of Rhetoric had been wholly discredited but that it was not to be carried to unnatural excess. For both dramatist and actor it was too valuable a training to be rejected altogether. Shakespeare himself used it just as he used other things he learned in boyhood, the groundwork of classics and grammar and logic; and at times he would laugh at it even as he laughed at pedantries of grammar in Holofernes or at ill-assimilated logic in the reiterated 'argal' of a clown. There are many passages in the plays that gave more pleasure to an Elizabethan educated in the principles of Rhetoric than they will ever give again; and since we can no longer admire their virtuosity, our response is to that extent impoverished. Less would be heard about the supposed tedium of the casket scenes in *The Merchant of Venice*, for instance, if critics would pause to consider the rhetorical skill with which they are written. Particular dissatisfaction is felt over the scene (III iii) in which Bassanio makes his choice. It is not a dramatic scene because everyone has always known that Bassanio will choose the leaden casket and win his bride. The dramatic tension being slack, Shakespeare calls upon Rhetoric to give unexpected emotion to the scene. To the untutored spectator, impatient for action, Bassanio seems to spend an eternity of words in reaching his predestined choice but, judged rhetorically, it is a beautiful piece of writing and the Elizabethan actor was trained to lose none of its effectiveness. Indeed, when the part of Bassanio is given to an actor of proper accomplishment — and it may have been Burbage's part — the balance of the play is held and Shylock does not over-weight it.

The difference between, say, Enobarbus's account of Cleopatra in her barge and the First Player's account of Hecuba is the difference between Rhetoric used with supreme artistry and Rhetoric running mad. It would seem also to be the difference between the matured art of Shakespeare's company and their earlier habits — habits in which many of their rivals possibly persisted. It is tempting to go on to suggest that it marks also Shakespeare's success in educating his fellows, but this would be unfair to them and would fly in the face of the little we know or can surmise about Elizabethan methods of production. We have to recognize in the King's Men, and indeed in the period's drama as a whole, a continuous development. The difference between the Shakespeare of 1592 and the Shakespeare of 1610 reflects more than the progress of an individual genius in the perfection of his art: it reflects also the progress of the art itself. No doubt Shakespeare's genius was the largest factor in this development, but the simultaneous develop-ment of his fellows in the theatre, whether actors or dramatists, was at once complementary and indispensable to his personal achievement. Even the bickerings between one company and another, between actors and playwrights or actors and their managers, in retrospect so trivial, were fruitful in their time because they helped to establish empirical standards of criticism and to eliminate by salutary ridicule some of the crudities of the older drama. Ben Jonson, for example, contributed more to this end by satire and example than by the hectoring tone of his prologues. But even more effective than ridicule was the disciplined, corporate aspiration of the actors themselves to move steadily forwards in the quality they professed.

An Elizabethan play has to be regarded as a cooperative enterprise to which the actors contributed almost as much as the dramatist — and in poor plays they obviously contributed more. As yet the theatre knew nothing of the 'star' system, still less of the 'tyranny of the director' of which we hear so much to-day. Although Hamlet might have been a different play if Shakespeare had not known that Burbage would be playing the lead, this is not the same thing as saying that it was written just as a 'vehicle' for one man's special gifts. Nor were Elizabethan audiences acquainted with the sort of production in which the chief attraction was the name of the dramatist. The author might consider himself fortunate if he found himself mentioned on the playbill. The Elizabethan theatre, it cannot be too often insisted, was an actors' theatre: a limitation which even Shakespeare had to accept, although, unlike Jonson and several other playwrights, he did not find it a limitation in the least. He conceived his plays in terms of the stage where they would be performed (different kinds of stage, quite often) and the actors who would interpret them. Thus if we would understand his art, we ought to know as much about the King's Men as we know about Blackfriars or the Globe; but whereas the patient reconstruction of scholars has taught us much about the structure and conventions of the theatres, the great acting performances have no memorial. The scanty records of the time do not particularize. From passages of parody and burlesque we learn what styles of acting had become unfashionable and ridiculous, but we have little more than the few comments of Hamlet or the strictures of Jonson to tell us how the good actor was expected to approach his task. We know a great deal more about the bad than about the good.

Perhaps the most vivid piece of contemporary criticism is the story of the local innkeeper who offered to take visitors to the very spot on Bosworth Field where Burbage pledged his kingdom for a horse. Here is a tribute to an actor's mighty spell, although it still does not tell us how the spell was wrought. It would have been fascinating to attend a rehearsal at the Globe and see how the players, having grasped their dramatist's poetic idea, sought to translate it into action, possibly with their own comments and suggestions. For the play had to be adapted to the company, and the company to the play. Shakespeare had to keep in mind the special aptitudes and weaknesses of his fellows, to provide them with parts that would stretch them to the limit of their achievement without demanding the impossible. Thus the play was to some extent a collaboration between him and them, and their contribution to it was not merely to act the parts he gave them but in their turn to inspire him to write parts worthy of their powers. The proof of the ability of Shakespeare's company lies in the parts he gave them to act. When we marvel at Rosalind and Viola and Beatrice, it is a mark of respect for the unknown boy who first created them on the stage: a boy, surely, with gifts and personality that fired Shakespeare's inspiration with a bright particular flame. The part of Falstaff could not have been written unless the man who played it, whether Kempe or Pope or another, had been equal to it, and we shall never know how much of Falstaff may not have been due to the actor's interpretation and development of the lines provided for him — and thus, perhaps, causing *Henry IV* to become two plays instead of one. Without Burbage there would have been no Lear, or there would have been a different Lear. If Burbage was fortunate in having Shakespeare to write for him, Shakespeare too was fortunate in having Burbage to realize his visions. The two men grew up together, and the mighty progression from Richard III to Lear is one that neither could have made without the other.

Such, then, was the world in which Shakespeare chose to work. More than any other dramatist of his time he was a man of the theatre. After 1594 he wrote no more for fame. If in his Sonnets, which apparently were only for circulation among his friends, he seems to have given voice to occasional regrets about his way of life, these private feelings did not divert him from exclusive service to it. Other dramatists, weaker in their devotion to the theatre or in need of that fame that all hunt after in their lives, occupied themselves with works on which their reputation or their worldly comfort might more securely rest. For Chapman plays were the occupation of an idle hour compared with his translation of Homer; Drayton became one of Henslowe's hacks only to feed and clothe himself while he laboured at his clumsy epic, *Polyolbion*; even Heywood, actor and sharer and indefatigable writer of plays, fixed his graver hopes upon his *Troia Britannica* and his translations of Sallust and other classical authors. From playwrights as a body poured a hopeful stream of occasional poems, odes, masques, ballads, translations, verse for pageants, verse commemorative of coronations, weddings, murders, the discomfiture of Papists and the overthrow of the Queen's enemies; but from Shakespeare nothing, or nothing but an untitled 'poetical essay' attributed to him in Robert Chester's *Love's Martyr* (1601), a collection of verse celebrating the wedded life of Sir John Salisbury. This is the poem known as *The Phoenix and Turtle*, and Shakespeare's authorship has been questioned. His silence on the occasion of the Queen's death was sufficiently remarkable to provoke contemporary comment, and he is not known to have contributed to the chorus of song that arose in facile welcome of her successor. After the spectacular success of *Venus and Adonis* and *Lucrece* it is astonishing that in effect he turned away from all forms of writing but the dramatic. Three compulsions persuade men to write and influence their choice of medium: the desire for money, the desire for fame and the search for a literary form that will allow them to express themselves as they must. Money to realize his earthly ambitions Shakespeare certainly found in the theatre. To fame he was perhaps indifferent for he never troubled to have his plays printed; or he may have had some inner conviction that his fame was secure enough. For the last, it was in the theatre, and only in the theatre, that he found the freedom of expression that he needed.

This freedom was not attained at once. The rigid traditional forms of writing and acting which, despite the influence of the University Wits, still held the stage in 1592 were too stiff for the poetic delineation of character in action. Rhetoric, if overstrained, might prove a strait-jacket. Blank verse, although a liberation, was an imperfect instrument so long as it was restricted by the end-stopped line. The old themes of classical heroes, mythology, Moralities and romance could not contain the rich and complex thought of an enlarging inspiration. Thus Shakespeare and his company had to be always moving towards new forms or investing the old forms with a new vitality. Acting outgrew its subservience to traditional types and began instead a direct assault on the emotions; comedy was freed from the inhibiting convention that a play's comic relief must depend on solo improvizations by the company's chief comedian; blank verse carried a new weight of imagery and achieved new harmonies of thought and sound as its rhythms approximated more nearly to those of common speech. All this amounted to a revolution that admitted poetic drama to a larger world, a broader range of human action. The persons of comedy were observed with a sharper eye. The chronicle, with its ill-assembled masses of incident, gave place to studies of the divided nation and the qualities which fit a man to be a king; and in due turn the study of political man yielded to the study of man divided within his own soul, to the writing of tragedy whose themes had the appearance of being universal. The poet had then all the world for his stage and all humanity to people it.

This revolution demanded a new art of acting. Tamburlaine is easy to act, Hamlet is not. The old actor could make his way with the equipment that Rhetoric had taught him. His conceit lay in his hamstring, and he had little need of his imagination. Hamlet's players came to Wittenberg with all the stock types in their repertoire — the clown, the king, the lady, the adventurous knight, the sighing lover — and with a theatrical tradition to tell them how these types should be rendered. The speeches in *The Murder of Gonzago* are full of outmoded devices. With their end-stopped lines and regular beat they are easy enough to deliver; and each speech is a little essay in itself, not dramatically related to the words of the last speaker. In further obdedience to their training in Rhetoric the actors would accompany each emotion with the gestures and movements traditionally recognized as appropriate: a further blow to naturalism.

'Who cannot be proud, stroke up the hair, and strut!' exclaims Piero in *Antonio and Mellida* (Induction 14). When Marston was writing for the boys he took occasion to ridicule the simulated passions of the adult professional:

> Would'st have me cry, run raving up and down,
> For my son's loss? Would'st have me turn rank mad,
> Or wring my face with mimic action;
> Stamp, curse, weep, rage, and then my bosom strike?
> Away, 'tis apish action, player-like.
>
> *Antonio's Revenge* I v 81.

Early in his career Shakespeare recognized how crudely the tragic actor might obtain his effects, and already he was deploring the unspontaneous formality of this style of playing:

> *Gloucester.* Come, cousin, canst thou quake, and change thy colour,
> Murder thy breath in middle of a word,
> And then begin again, and stop again,
> As if thou wert distraught and mad with terror?
> *Buckingham.* Tut, I can counterfeit the deep tragedian,
> Speak and look back, and pry on every side,
> Tremble and start at wagging of a straw,
> Intending deep suspicion: ghastly looks
> Are at my service, like enforced smiles...
>
> *R III* III v 1.

Such 'to-be-pitied and o'er-wrested seeming' might survive in isolated examples as late as Macduff's pulling his hat over his brows in a conventional gesture of grief, but true tragedy demanded a more flexible style and a more fluent speaking of the verse. Both playwrights and actors had to discard conventions dear to their predecessors: the rhetorical set-piece such as that provided by the plangent womenfolk in *Richard III*, the outbreaks of Latinity, the dumb-show, the contrived stichomythia, the irrelevant musical interpolations. Although Shakespeare would at any time use such devices if they happened to serve a dramatic purpose (there is an elaborate stichomythia in *Antony and Cleopatra*), he grew to regard his own apprentice work as subject for laughter. He makes fun of the devil paring his nails with a dagger, of the happy ending which always brought Jack to the arms of his Jill, of the mechanical construction which never varied the sequence of events ('and pat he comes, like the catastrophe of the old comedy'). Launce's dissertation on his shoes, or Gobbo's arraignment of his conscience, simply vary the pious chop-logic of the Morality. But at least these things were easy to act and could be confident of acceptance by an audience quick to recognize them. The adoption of a more natural and realistic style called for a subtler technique of interpretative acting. The achievement of Shakespeare's maturity was the pre-eminence of the poetic idea over the action; and this was not to be realized by actors who, in Greene's incessant gibes, were merely 'pranked with the glory of others' feathers' and for their own part could supply nothing but 'a kind of mechanical labour'.

In so far as the Elizabethan theatre had need of such a function, the direction of a play was probably the responsibility of the author. This was not always possible. When a play came off the production line from a parcel of hacks, or was offered by a poet like Chapman who held himself aloof from the traffic of the theatre, its staging was arranged by the players themselves, who had their own experience and the company's settled tradition to guide them. Companies did not, that is to say, employ a resident director, nor engage outsiders for the purpose. But many dramatists were keenly interested in the production of their work, with Jonson somewhat keener than the players liked. In his Inductions to both *Cynthia's Revels* and *Bartholomew Fair* he has them speaking in disparaging terms of what they, but not he, regarded as the inexpert interference of authors. The stage-keeper in *Bartholomew Fair* complains of these 'master poets' who 'will have their own courses; they will be informed of nothing. He has (sir reverence) kick'd me three or four times about the tiring-house, I thank him, for but offering to put in with my experience'. The pert children in *Cynthia's Revels* congratulate themselves that 'we are not so officiously befriended by him as to have his presence in the tiring-house, to prompt us aloud, stamp at the book-holder, swear for our properties, curse the poor tireman, rail the music out of tune, and sweat for every venial trespass we commit'.

Shakespeare's hand in the direction of a play need only have been slight because he saved himself the trouble by indicating in the text what he wanted his actors to do. Stage-directions were few in those days, at least until the drama began to choke itself on scenic elaboration; and even then they indicated little but the music and lighting cues and the movement of actors about the stage. The subtler indications of the author's design were conveyed through the dialogue. Attentively read, Shakespeare's text is full of clues to his intention, and this is particularly true, in the first place, of a matter apparently as insignificant as the punctuation. The renewal, in recent scholarship, of confidence in the First Folio as in general the most authentic of Shakespearean texts has incidentally revealed that the punctuation, so far from being the haphazard improvization of two semi-literate actors, perverted in due course by the careless ignorance of Jacobean printers, was largely based on Shakespeare's own playhouse manuscripts and therefore showed how he wished his lines to be spoken. The labours of subsequent editors, who altered the Folio punctuation to conform with the written usages of their own day, merely substituted a literary convention for one which was essentially rhetorical and dramatic.

As well as guidance in the delivery of his lines Shakespeare gave the actor sufficient indication of the character he was playing. Sometimes a character lays himself bare in a soliloquy — and Shakespeare's soliloquies have always to be taken at their face value: he never cheats the audience. In revealing speech Richard III, Edmund and Iago leave no doubt what manner of men they are. Nor, on a different intellectual plane, do men like Hamlet and Macbeth, although their speech is oblique and ambiguous beyond the reach of the straightforward Vice-like villains. But many important characters do not significantly soliloquize at all. Coriolanus and Falstaff may represent the diversity here, Falstaff revealing himself through soliloquy only when, as in the 'honour' speech, he appears transparently as the Vice. Many others, good and bad, are seen only in their public aspect, and their nature is revealed partly by their personal choice of imagery (those, for instance, who have no music in their souls) and partly by the comment of other characters. The picture of the 'lean and hungry' Cassius, who is 'dangerous' (which then meant disagreeable, uncompanionable, difficult to get on with), is contributed by Caesar, and the device serves a multiple purpose. It tells the actor playing Cassius how he should present himself; it hints at Caesar's hidden fears; and in quick dramatic terms it contrasts Cassius with the free and open Antony, whose delight in plays and music is deliberately referred to.

Berowne says of Boyet:

> This fellow picks up wit as pigeons peas,
> And utters it again when God doth please...
>   Why, this is he
> That kissed his hand away in courtesy,
> This is the ape of form, Monsieur the Nice...
>   The ladies call him sweet.
> The stairs as he treads on them kiss his feet.

LLL V ii 315.

This tells the audience something of Boyet, whom they have met already. The ironic purpose here is that Berowne's comment reflects back on himself: unconsciously he finds in Boyet a mirror of some of his own qualities. There are many examples of this refracted illumination when a character reveals something about himself as well as the person he is describing.

Here is Ulysses on Cressida:

> Fie, fie upon her!
> There's language in her eye, her cheek, her lip,
> Nay, her foot speaks, her wanton spirits look out
> At every joint and motive of her body.
> O, these encounterers, so glib of tongue,
> That give a coasting welcome ere it comes,
> And wide unclasp the tables of their thoughts
> To every ticklish reader! Set them down

For sluttish spoils of opportunity,
And daughters of the game.

TC IV v 54.

These lines seem to tell the boy actor what impression Cressida should make upon the casual observer, although the character is not as one-dimensional as that. The worldly Ulysses did not perceive those qualities in her that Troilus had been able to love, and this partiality tells us something about Ulysses himself. Is he not 'ticklish', one who would go halfway to greet a 'coasting'? The actor is being instructed that there is more to the character than the crafty politician and the anatomist of 'degree'.

Often Shakespeare visualized his characters not just in general terms of the actor's art but in a particular relation to members of his own company. The Elizabethan dramatist did not have the liberty to write the parts which his fancy decreed and search the whole profession for someone to play them. He had to cast his play from perhaps a dozen sharers, a few hired men and a limited number of boys. So precisely did Shakespeare match his invention to the available resources that a learned student of the period, Professor T. W. Baldwin, has conjectured (*The Organization and Personnel of the Shakespearean Company*) that each member of the King's Men had his particular skill and the plays were written with this in mind. Much of Baldwin's detail is admittedly speculative, and his theory underestimates the versatility of a repertory company. It is easy to forget that the Elizabethan actor appeared in many more plays than the modern professional, and he needed to be able to make a passable attempt at any sort of part. But there is no doubt that Shakespeare often wrote a part with a particular actor in mind. In the Quarto text of *Much Ado About Nothing* (IV ii) Kempe's name appears as a prefix to one of Dogberry's speeches. Obviously there was a Welshman, or a capable imitator of one, who played Glendower, Fluellen and Sir Hugh. Then there was an actor of extraordinary thinness whose presence is detectable in many plays of the period. His name was John Sincklo. Although he had a long career in the theatre, he never became a sharer, so that it is possible that he was not a very good actor — or that he was incapable of holding on to his money. But his leanness was one of those endlessly recurring jokes of which audiences never tire, and the references to it disclose many of the parts he played. He was such a familiar figure that on three occasions Shakespeare names him in the text: in *3 Henry VI*, where he was First Keeper; in the Induction to *Taming of the Shrew*, where he was a player, and in *2 Henry IV* V iv, where he was the 'nuthook' Beadle who held Doll in custody. It is likely that he was Romeo's Apothecary with famine in his cheeks, and Dr Pinch, the 'mere anatomy'; the Induction to Marston's *Malcontent* calls him 'father of maypoles'. Other possibilities that suggest themselves are Starveling, Sir Robert Falconbridge, Old Gobbo. Like the lame actor in Molière's company, he had parts written round his physical appearance. So too did the celebrated pair who adorn the comedies, Helena and Hermia, Rosalind and Celia, Portia and Nerissa, Beatrice and Hero. One of the boys was short, the other tall: so tall to be playing women's parts that apologetic comment has to be brought into the text.

If Shakespeare was concious of any limitation in being obliged to write all his female parts for boys, he never said so. In the plays he alluded critically to several members of the profession, to comedians frequently, to certain types of tragedian, to producers like Quince who use real live Moonshine to do the work of poetry; and he deplored at times the limitation of numbers and the smallness of the stage. But he never spoke ill of the boys. In fact he paid them a supreme compliment when he wrote these lines for Cleopatra:

> and I shall see
> Some squeaking Cleopatra boy my greatness
> I' th' posture of a whore.
>
> *AC* V ii 219.

The audacity of this is astonishing. No boy could have spoken thus, during a highly emotional scene, had there been any likelihood of his rousing the audience to disrespectful laughter. The criticism of later centuries has dismissed the boy actor as one of the hampering conventions that restricted the full expression of Shakespeare's genius, but it is more pertinent to look closely at what he required the boys to do.

They were apprenticed at an early age to the experienced professionals, by whom they were thoroughly trained in their craft. This training was expert and exacting enough to curb any tendencies towards precocity or errant vanity. The boy had to learn to dance, to sing, to play musical instruments, to wear a wig and manage his heavy robes, to master all the devices of gesture and intonation and, above all, to speak audibly in the open air while still saving his voice from the 'mannish crack'. By the time, therefore, that he was judged fit to appear in a professional production he was in his own way a skilled and versatile performer. All the same, a wise dramatist would not set him tasks beyond his intellectual and emotional reach. This was the error of the over-ambitious proprietors of the boy companies. They attempted too much. For a time the novelty was sufficiently appealing to attract audiences away from the adult theatres, but the success of a company consisting only of boys was bound to be impermanent. The boys' immaturity as human beings limited the range of what they should attempt, and when they passed outside that range they became embarrassing and futile. Their virtuosity could make a show at most things, but virtuosity without roots in mind and experience would not attract audiences for long. Perhaps rather desperately, they engaged in topicalities that would have been dangerous for their seniors and finally became dangerous for them.

The wiser members of the adult companies seem to have kept the boys in their place, both on and off the stage, and to have known just what that place should be. Shakespeare's employment of them displays once again the scrupulousness of his art. He made such enormous demands upon them that at first sight it is easy to fail to notice what he did not demand.

It is not true, although it is often said, that he spared them the embarrassment of physical contact. There was not a lot of erotic by-play on the Elizabethan stage, the farthingale being a stout deterrent to it, and when William Prynne, writing in the reign of Charles I, complained of 'more than Brothel-house obscenities' and 'those real lively representations of the acts of venery', he can only have been referring to the practices of the new coterie theatres that he is unlikely to have visited. Things did not happen thus at the Globe or Blackfriars in Shakespeare's lifetime. But it is closing one's eyes to the text to suppose that Romeo and Juliet, Antony and Cleopatra, Cressida with Troilus or Diomed went through their plays without a kiss or an embrace; not to mention the 'flattering busses' that Doll Tearsheet was required to bestow on Falstaff. Romeo and Othello both die upon a kiss — without ridicule or embarrassment.

But while he expected the boys to be capable of a formal embrace, Shakespeare spared them the actual display of sensuality or passion. He was careful to preserve them from the expression of emotional acts or feelings that would have come unnaturally to them. In the scenes where the female characters are concerned, either they are alone together and may reflect on masculine folly or, if they are with men, the burden of the emotion they generate is borne by the adults. Their own emotions are often facile and always static. They are intense in pursuit of their objective, but they pursue one thing only, they know what it is and it does not alter. This singleness of purpose, which is the dominant quality of Shakespearean heroines, makes them easier to act. In the high comedies their aim is to make captive the man they love, and modestly, unaffectedly and wittily they pursue and win him; in the tragedies they are wives and lovers, faithful and innocent; in the later romances (except perhaps Imogen, who has something of Viola as well as Desdemona) they are simple children. When it is necessary that any of them shall be noted for beauty or sensuality or depth of passion, Shakespeare is careful that the point shall be made by someone else.

Thus he is all the time sheltering the boys from the display of feelings they were too young to know about. Much he could leave to their technique and to the vitality and personal attractiveness that most of them must have possessed. They were, within their limits, very accomplished performers. But with extraordinary delicacy Shakespeare contrived that his heroines should meet their lovers on the plane of poetry and wit rather than on the plane of sex. Romeo and Juliet are usually separated by a balcony; Othello and Desdemona are not alone together until he comes to kill her, Antony and Cleopatra not until the early coquetry is forgotten in a deeper passion.

In the same way Shakespeare did not demand of the boys complex displays of emotion. His complex characters are the men, not the women. It is Macbeth who has to search his conscience; his wife is clear and unswerving in her purpose, and it is significant that when her resolution breaks, this occurs off-stage and when she does appear she has found refuge in madness, which is much easier to portray than a scene of agonized remorse. Contrast, again, the spiritual tortures of Angelo with the uncomplicated single-mindedness of Isabella, who has her standard and applies it. Contrast Othello with Desdemona, Claudius with Gertrude, Benedick with Beatrice (when each has been told of the other's love, she responds with simple acceptance whereas he has a vast deal to say), Troilus with Cressida: in each case we are admitted to the man's mind but not to the woman's.

This does not mean that the women display no emotion, for plainly they do. The point is that their emotions are created for them through the poetry they are given to speak, and they do not have to depend on their own inadequate experience. This is true even of the subtlest and most difficult of the heroines, Cleopatra. Her ascendancy over Antony is one of the essential themes of the play, and in different ways most of the characters bear witness to it. But on the stage this ascendancy is more often alluded to than actually displayed; and when it is displayed, the conquest is made by malice and wit and language, not by personality or the allure of sex. Antony's submission, that is to say, exists in his own acknowledgment of it. It does not have to depend on the boy actor, who only has to speak his lines and let them work their spell. In the final scenes Cleopatra has to a rise to a challenge more severe than any other boy actor had to meet. But Shakespeare has lightened the task by writing poetry that carries the scene along; and it must be remembered that the boy passes most of it with only two other boys on the stage with him. It is by deliberate contrivance that Cleopatra cannot be allowed to hold the stage until Antony is dead.

Shakespeare thus overcame the problem of the boy actor just as he overcame the problem of the bare unlocalized stage: by careful technique and the power of language. He suggested the illusion of mature and attractive womanhood just as he suggested the illusion of the storm-tossed ship or the moonlit forest, and he did it so cunningly that we forget we are not seeing the real thing. In some ways, of course, the convention was restrictive, and there are certain themes, particularly some of the relationships between husband and wife or mother and child, whose absence from Elizabethan drama we must feel to be a loss. Domestic and marital themes were not easy to explore, and the theatre was male-dominated for the simple practical reason that adult actors far outnumbered the boys. This problem of availability was certainly troublesome for the dramatist, because in the absence of suitable boys there were certain types of play that could not be written. Often Shakespeare was fortunate. The boy who played Rosalind and similar parts made the 'golden' comedies possible, and later there was another gifted boy — possibly Richard Robinson — whose personality inspired the guileless innocence of Marina, Perdita and Miranda. But there was always the hazard that a boy would grow too big or heavy or — less easy to anticipate — that his voice would suddenly break.

Shakespeare encountered this inconvenience in *Cymbeline*. He knew that Guiderius and Arviragus, two lost princes, would be played by adolescents who until lately had been cast for female parts. They could play young women no longer because their voices had at length betrayed them, but Shakespeare wanted them to sing a dirge over Imogen, their 'brother' who was seemingly dead. It would not be safe for them to sing, or not without a previous apology in anticipation of disaster. So the song is preceded by this short dialogue:

> *Arviragus.*   And let us, Polydore, though now our voices
>   Have got the mannish creack, sing him to the ground,
>   As once our mother; use like note and words,
>   Save that Euriphile must be Fidele.
> *Guiderius.*   Cadwal,
>   I cannot sing; I'll weep and word it with thee;
>   For words of sorrow out of tune are worse
>   Than priests and fanes that lie.
> *Arviragus.*   We'll speak it then.

Cym IV ii 235.

They break into the exquisite melancholy of 'Fear no more the heat o' the sun'; and in small things there is no more striking testimony to Shakespeare's genius than that of all his songs this is the best fitted to be spoken. A musical setting for the singing voice seems rather to adulterate its beauty, and the usual practice in modern productions is for the lines to be spoken, not sung, against the melodic background: a strange consequence of the fleeting accident that two lads in Shakespeare's company happened to be breaking their voices when *Cymbeline* was written.

Another technical difficulty for the dramatist was simply numerical. 'The necessity of the play forceth me to act two parts', says Alberto (doubling with Andrugio) in the Induction to *Antonio and Mellida*. If the dramatist wanted a large cast, he had to take trouble with his arrangements because there was a limit to the number of hirelings a company would engage and a limit to the space in which they could manoeuvre. Doubling was as old as the theatre itself. The little groups of strolling players who went about the country could multiply themselves so ingeniously that four of them could carry a play with a dozen parts. Doubling was taken for granted, too, in academic plays and in the London theatre. There are thirty-eight characters in *Cambyses*, but eight or nine actors could manage it, and six could fill the twenty-five parts in *Horestes*; Marlowe had only about eighteen actors for the enormous cast of *Tamburlaine* and not many more for the thirty parts in *Edward II*; eighteen, again, was the probable number for the forty-seven parts of *2 Henry VI*, and as late as 1599 Thomas Platter wrote that he had seen *Julius Caesar* played by only fifteen actors.

Doubling was never eliminated altogether, but dramatists learned to ease the burden by concentrating their effects and using fewer characters. One device, and a very unsatisfactory one, was to provide a silent substitute when two characters played by a single actor were on stage at the same time. The muffled figure of Claudio in the last scene of *Measure for Measure* probably was one of these, for he does not speak although he and Isabella ought to have had something to say to one another. But Isabella does not speak very much in this scene either, and it is possible that the original Isabella went on to play Mariana: at least the physical similarity would make the bed trick more convincing. If, again, the same boy played Perdita and Hermione (perhaps not very likely in a company with the resources of the King's Men, but *The Winter's Tale* has the unusually large number of six speaking-parts for women, and the boys were liable to sudden casualty), it would explain Perdita's strange silence at the restoration of her mother.

But substitution was a crude expedient, and a commoner way round the difficulty of under-manning was to jettison a character, often arbitrarily, so as to release the actor for another role. The outstanding case is Antigonus. The spectacular manner of his departure has obscured the significance of his departing at all. His loyal service, on a mission that he hated, earned a kindlier fate, and Paulina did not deserve to be thus rudely unhusbanded. Moreover, in a play with a strong emphasis on reconciliation and reunion, one would have expected Antigonus, garrulous but happpy, to be present at the end. The disappearance of Lear's Fool has been questioned too. The supposition that Robert Armin doubled the Fool with Cordelia depends on Lear's 'And my poor fool is hang'd', but 'fool' was a word with many connotations. Besides, prestige entered into these things. The theatre is jealous of its gradations, and with occasional exceptions doubling was a job for hirelings rather than principals. We do not have to suppose that Mercutio was killed in order that the actor might reappear as Friar John or Balthasar, or that Polonius was transformed into the First Gravedigger. Their deaths were dramatically necessary. But we do wonder what became of Adam and whether he recovered the money he lent to Orlando, and we notice that although the Second Gravedigger was sent off in search of ale, he never returned with it. This was the sort of part that had to be doubled, and the hired men had a busy afternoon. The belief that the Bad Quarto of *Hamlet* was based on the recollections of one of the actors has led to speculation about the parts he played. One conjecture claims that he was Marcellus, Voltimand, a Player, a soldier with Fortinbras, the Second Gravedigger, the churlish Priest and an ambassador from England. This would have been asking too much even of an Elizabethan hireling, and a more cautious estimate has suggested that the pirate had access to Voltimand's script and himself acted Marcellus, a Player (possibly speaking the Prologue and the part of

Lucianus), an attendant lord in IV ii, a mourner at the graveside, and a courtier in the final scene. This is a more credible programme, but even to organize this would require hard thinking from the company and the playwright during the staging of the play.

In this discussion of Shakespeare's relationship with his actors, let us see finally how he handled the clown. This was a serious problem because the clown was the *enfant terrible* of the Elizabethan theatre. His popularity was important to the company's success, and his gifts were of a kind to make him independent of his playwrights. Marlowe, who perhaps had no more humour in his composition than the eloquent sentimentalists who dominate his plays, seems to have thought that he was unnecessary. He disdained 'such conceits as clowning keeps in pay', and wrote no scenes of comedy. His reward was that others wrote them for him, and wrote them exceedingly ill. The tradition that even tragedy should be blended with 'most delectable mirth' was too strong for the actors to allow him such independence.

A dramatist who conceived his plays as an artistic whole, and not just a hotch-potch of popular conventions, had to persuade the clown to see himself as one of a team. The obstacle was the enormous prestige that Tarleton had won for himself and consequently for his style of clowning. Lesser comedians saw themselves in Tarleton's mantle and were indifferent to the scruples of dramatists who cared about decorum and dramatic structure. Tarleton's ascendancy was therefore unfortunate in so far as it encouraged the fashion, already deplored by Sidney, of periodically suspending the plot to leave the stage free for comic business. Clowns were admired for their 'extemporal wit', which was only another name for irrelevant gagging; and even when the dramatist tried to provide an adequate script for them, they would add embellishments of their own. A comedy published in 1638, Richard Brome's *Antipodes*, speaks feelingly about these interpolations, and in referring to them as the practice of the 'elder stages' it implies the reforms achieved by Shakespeare, Jonson and others:

Letoy.	But you, Sir, are incorrigible, and
	Take licence to yourself to add unto
	Your parts your own free fancy; and sometimes
	To alter or diminish what the writer
	With care and skill composed; and when you are
	To speak to your coactors in the scene
	You hold interlocutions with the audience.
Byplay.	That is a way, my Lord, has been allow'd
	On elder stages to move mirth and laughter.
Letoy.	Yes, in the days of Tarleton and Kempe,
	Before the stage was purged from barbarism
	And brought to the perfection it now shines with.
	The fools and jesters spent their wits because

The poets were wise enough to save their own
For profitabler uses.

Antipodes II ii.

The printed version of the anonymous *A Knack to Know a Knave* (1594) sought to tempt the reader by promising him 'Kempe's applauded merriments of the Men of Gotcham', but these merriments do not appear in the text, presumably because they owed nothing to the dramatist. One adjunct of the clown's performance was a particular eccentricity of dress, like Tarleton's baggy trousers or Kempe's flapping slippers; another, also popular in the later music-hall, was the catch-phrase repeated over and over again until the iteration brought laughter. The Bad Quarto of *Hamlet* condemns clowns who

> keep one suit of jests as a man is known by one suit of apparel, and gentlemen
> quote his jests down in their tables before they come to the play, as thus: *Cannot
> you stay until I eat my porridge?* and *You owe me a quarter's wages*: and *My coat
> wants a cullisen*, and *Your beer is sour.*

For the unskilled or the hurried playwright this was well enough: he could leave blank spaces in the text and expect the clown to fill them. In the *Pilgrimage to Parnassus* Dromo hauls in a clown on the end of a rope, with the comment that 'clowns have been thrust into plays by head and shoulders ever since Kempe could make a scurvy face'. 'Why, if thou canst but draw thy mouth awry', he tells the clown, 'lay thy leg over thy staff, saw a piece of cheese asunder, lap up drink on the earth, I warrant thee they'll laugh mightily'. The clown himself complains that 'when they have nobody to leave on the stage, they bring me up, and which is worse, tell me not what I should say'. This crude comedy was popular with audiences but it would not do for Shakespeare. With clowning as with so much else in his theatre, it does not seem to have occurred to him to abandon a tradition and start something fresh: that was never his way. The peculiar quality of his genius was to adapt and modify what he found and by some mysterious transmutation make a new thing of it. The First Gravedigger shows the direct influence of Tarleton, who as Yorick may here have received his due of homage; Feste and Lear's Fool were in another tradition; but all were essentially Shakespeare's own creations.

A sudden change in his handling of the clown can be seen from about 1599, when Kempe left the Chamberlain's Men and was succeeded by Robert Armin. A change there certainly was, but it was forced on Shakespeare by events and we have no right to say that he regarded it as a change for the better. Many critics have assumed that because a new style of clowning followed Kempe's departure, therefore his departure was the result of his own dissatisfaction with the parts he was getting or of the company's — and especially Shakespeare's — disapproval of his methods.

Hamlet is quoted in support of this. After his remarks to the First Player about the unnatural antics of tragedians he adds a few words about the clown: words that are quite out of context as there is to be no clowning in *The Murder of Gonzago*:

> Let those that play your clowns speak no more than is set down for them, for there be of them that will themselves laugh, to set on some quantity of barren spectators to laugh too, though in the mean time some necessary question of the play be then to be considered. That's villainous, and shows a most pitiful ambition in the fool that uses it.
>
> III ii 43.

It has been proposed that these words refer to Kempe: which is scarcely more sensible than to think that the preceding lines on the passion-tearing tragedian referred to Burbage. Even if it were true that Shakespeare and his colleagues had grown weary of Kempe and his style, they would not have denounced him in public, especially as many of the plays in which he had acted would be played again and the clown's part could not be radically altered. The lines must surely refer to rival comedians, or at most to a type of comedy that the Chamberlain's Men had outgrown by 1600.

We may assume what we wish, but there are no solid grounds for the notion that Kempe was shown the door by his colleagues. He was indubitably a box-office draw, and he was a sharer in the joint-stock company that built the Globe. Although he is reported to have been dissatisfied with the role of Peter in *Romeo and Juliet*, Shakespeare and other playwrights had written him many fat parts since then. His own explanation is probably the true one, that he 'danced myself out of this world' of the public theatre. His one-man show on the road to Norwich was followed by a less fortunate excursion to the continent, for which he sold his share and his housekeeping rights in the Globe. When he returned he probably had not the money to buy them back, even if this was his wish, and he found Armin well established in his place. Possibly he rejoined the company for a short while in a lesser capacity, until the formation of Worcester's new company promised him a better opportunity of retrieving his former reputation. His death, although unrecorded, must have occurred soon afterwards, because there is no further mention of him. Hamlet's tribute to Yorick may have been added in a later production as Shakespeare's tribute not to Tarleton but to his own dead friend and colleague. He may never have seen Tarleton on the stage, and what would have been the point of reviving his memory, after a lapse of several years, when the company were attempting to refine his individualist style?

It would have been more characteristic of Shakespeare thus to salute the great comic actor for whom, and probably with whom, he had written parts like Costard, Bottom and Dogberry. His 'naturalization' of the clown began long before 1600. The absence of comic relief from *Richard II* and *King John* shows his determination that it should not intrude where it did not belong. The crux of the matter, as Hamlet explained, was to fix the clown within the limits of a character integral to the play. In Shakespeare's early comedies the assimilation is incomplete. Launce and Speed do not really belong to their play and could as easily belong anywhere else. Launce's two big scenes, the discourse on his shoes and his act with his dog, belong to the tradition of the interpolated 'turn'; and Speed is the impudent, word-splitting serving-man whom Lyly had found in the classical comedy of Plautus and Terence. Costard is more at home, but not wholly so: much of his jesting lacks spontaneity, and he has to work too hard at being funny. But suddenly, at the end of the play, he speaks some simple words in defence of Sir Nathaniel, his neighbour and an uncommonly good bowler, and in those words turns himself into a human being, and Sir Nathaniel too; and all their fellows spring to life with them and take on a strange dignity in the wreckage and humiliation of their pageant. 'This is not generous, not gentle, not humble'. 'Sweet chucks, beat not the bones of the buried: when he breathed, he was a man'.

In this scene Shakespeare's mature comedy was born. There would still be times when inspiration would not kindle and he fell back on the dusty conventions of the old style — the jesting of the Gobbos is tired and perfunctory — but he had discovered how to create comic characters who really were characters, belonging essentially to the play that gave them birth and owning a speech that was theirs individually. Next of these creations after *Love's Labour's Lost* was Juliet's Nurse:

> Susan and she — God rest all Christian souls! —
> Were of an age. Well, Susan is with God;
> She was too good for me. But, as I said,
> On Lammas-eve at night shall she be fourteen;
> That shall she, marry; I remember it well.
> 'Tis since the earthquake now eleven years;
> And she was weaned, I never shall forget it,
> Of all the days of the year upon that day
> For I had then laid wormwood to my dug,
> Sitting in the sun under the dove-house wall...
>
> *RJ* I iii 18.

As surely as the lineaments of the Giaconda, these are the accents of eternal woman, as old as the sun in whose warmth she sat. In the years that followed there was born for Kempe and Pope and Cowley and the company's other comedians a succession of comic figures whose like had not been seen on the English stage, and each of them contributed to his play. Bottom is a realist in a dreamlike world, but his very literalness seems to add virtue to those who have been dupes of the dream; Fluellen brings the viewpoint of the professional soldier to a play which, among other things, is a study of war and leadership; Falstaff is incarnate commentary on the great world of 'policy' on whose fringes he moves, and his discourse on honour has a dramatic relevance which the not dissimilar meditations of Launce had lacked. To compare these people with, say, Mouse in *Mucedorus*, a popular Tarleton role, or Hodge, the amusing but rootless clown of *The Life and Death of the Lord Cromwell*, is to appreciate the development that Shakespeare had brought about.

It was achieved, however, without a total rejection of the older ways. Established comedians did not have to abandon all their training, because although the element of horseplay was now subdued, they could still display their musical accomplishments; their disposition to bawdiness was indulged with a wealth of unashamed inventiveness beyond their personal reach; their gift for miming found scope in burlesquing their betters — Falstaff is endlessly acting, whether parodying the King or Pistol or the Lord Chief Justice or Edward Alleyn and his dramatists. Even the stock-in-trade of the Elizabethan clown, his blundering exploration of his mother-tongue, was genially exploited. In the Elizabethan age the language was in its springtime, and when for men of judgment and discretion the coining of new words was a continuous excitement, it blossomed into luxuriant and undisciplined growth. No one found this so exciting as Shakespeare. Speed mocked Launce with 'your old vice still: mistake the word', and Feste, whose jesting was professional, was his mistress's 'corrupter of words'. But when Shakespeare's clowns enjoyed the complete liberty of the Queen's English, they enjoyed it with a difference. Their speech, even at its most outrageous, was appropriate to their characters and their function in the play. The sophisticated clowns, the jesters, were masters of the currency: they patterned words into arabesques worthy of their mastership. The countrymen, on the other hand, were uncomprehending slaves of their vice. The malapropism was not invented by Shakespeare but in his hands it first became a reputable device of comedy. In Mrs Malaprop herself, the eponymous heroine of the trick, it is dramatically inappropriate: she is an educated woman and is not in other ways notably vain or foolish, and the failing sits so incongruously upon her that it is not as funny as it should be. But for Costard, Bottom, Dogberry, Mistress Quickly, Elbow, Dull it is a recognizable quirk of character which the dramatist uses to indicate their station in life and their humble striving to rise above it. It was one of the means he used to transform the clown into a dramatic force.

In this transformation Kempe must have taken a considerable part. As Launce he had a certain freedom to display his talents as a solo entertainer, but as Bottom he could not have exceeded his script without damaging the fragile beauty of the play. It is surely a reasonable assumption that the part would not have been written for him if there had been any danger of his overplaying it. His memory has been unfairly prejudiced by the impression held by many students of the Elizabethan theatre that he was disloyal to his dramatists and ultimately had to be eased out of the company because he was a bad 'trouper'. The position that he won in the Chamberlain's Men refutes it. So does the quality of the roles which Shakespeare wrote for him, and probably he had his share in enlarging the conception of the clown's dramatic function.

He departed nonetheless, and because of his fame and importance it was a serious matter for his company. Probably this was not the reason why Falstaff was included in the first draft of *Henry V* and then replaced by Pistol. The influential Cobhams' sensitiveness about their ancestor is a likelier explanation;[13] and it is not certain that Kempe played Falstaff — Professor Baldwin gives this to Pope and assigns Kempe to Shallow. With Pope soon to retire — possibly he was already in ill-health — the company had to find a new principal comedian. Shakespeare's problem was that the successor was a very different sort of artist.

Robert Armin, who came to the Chamberlain's from a provincial company, Lord Chandos's Men, had been a goldsmith's apprentice in Lombard Street. Subsequently he had been trained by Tarleton, which means that in 1599 he was not a young man and that presumably he had been in the theatre for some years. Tarleton's strength, as we know, lay in a gift for brilliant improvization: like a certain type of orator, he took fire from the presence of an auditory, and his best effects were not studied. Armin, on the other hand, was a student and theoretician; his comedy was born by candlelight. In a modest way he was a writer on his own account. His *Fool upon Fool* was a solemn attempt to embody in dramatic form various theories of comedy; and in *The Two Maids of Mortlake* the comedian wrote a tragedy. Besides plays he wrote a poem, *Phantasma*, and tracts on religious and metaphysical subjects. This sober-minded man was Shakespeare's new partner in clowning, and necessarily the clowning was different. It may or may not have been the sort that Shakespeare had come to prefer, although its undertone of sadness was in harmony with his growing preoccupation with the darker side of life. The immediate creative challenge was to find a new style for the new recruit. His last invention for Kempe was probably Dogberry,[14] his first for Armin Touchstone. The contrast shows his astonishing capacity for adapting himself at need to the requirements of his profession. Whether the new style was better than the old, whether Kempe was a loss or Armin a

13 Falstaff's appeareance in *The Merry Wives of Windsor* was protected by the Queen's wishes, if there be anything in the story, printed by John Dennis in 1702, that the play was written 'at her command, and by her direction', with the added instruction that it be completed within a fortnight. There is, however, a theory that the comedy preceded *Henry IV* and was first produced at the Garter Feast in April 1597, just after Hunsdon had been appointed Lord Chamberlain. See Schoenbaum, 198, who regards it as 'not implausible as such hypotheses go'.

14 In *Phantasma* Armin speaks of being a constable and being 'writ down an ass in his time': from which some have inferred that he joined the company early enough to play Dogberry. That this was originally Kempe's part is attested by a speech-prefix in the text, but it is interesting that Armin may have played it in revivals. It proves his versatility.

gain, are important questions that concern Shakespeare as a poet rather than a working dramatist in the theatre. His swift technical adjustment from one style to the other was remarkable enough.

Armin was the jester in cap and bells, the 'allow'd fool' to be found in courts and great houses. It was right that the banished Duke or Olivia or Lear should maintain him. These fools had some licence to speak freely to their masters — even Thersites, a sombre *reductio ad nauseam* of the species, claimed it for his insolent reviling of the Greek commanders — and although their efforts sometimes won more blows than 'remuneration', they had a useful cathartic function in the households of great persons who daily heard much flattery but little candour.

> The wise man's folly is anatomiz'd
> E'en by the squandering glances of the fool.
>
> *AYLI* II vii 56.

As You Like It and *Twelth Night* call in question the wise man's wisdom that is not seasoned with the folly of the fool. They say that it is a sad world where 'fools may not speak wisely what wise men do foolishly', for 'since the little wit that fools have was silenced, the little foolery that wise men have makes a great show'.

These jesters needed quick wits because, as Viola justly remarked, theirs was practice 'as full of labour as a wise man's art'. It is hit-or-miss stuff often depending on the mood of the recipient, and it could become tedious. *Love's Labour's Lost*, although a deliberate parody, had shown the brittleness of purely verbal repartee, and much as the more sophisticated Elizabethans enjoyed these logomachies, they were not matter for the public stages. Armin's style, like Kempe's, had to be assimilated, and the dramatist's task was again to naturalize the clown and weave him into the texture of the play. Probably the studious Armin assisted him, for *As You Like It*, that brilliant anatomy of folly, has the stamp of a mind that has pondered deeply before deciding that motley is the only wear.

It is not easy, unless one is writing a comedy of manners, to make mere cleverness dramatically effective. The fatal weakness of epigram is that it may be darkly impersonal, just as the brightness of a rocket does not illuminate the man who sets it off. Thus the problem of Armin may have been more disturbing than the problem of Kempe. Kempe's rustics had their setbacks but they never allowed circumstance to master them. Bottom's composed air when giving orders to the fairies is a splendid thing. So is Dogberry's royal indignation:

> I am a wise fellow, and which is more, an officer, and which is more a householder, and which is more, as pretty a piece of flesh as any is in Messina, and one that knows the law, go to! and a rich fellow enough, go to! and a fellow that

hath had losses, and one that hath had two gowns, and everything handsome about him: bring him away!

MAN IV ii 83.

These men are solid as earth and their complacency is justified of itself. The court fool is harder to identify. Beneath the hard shining surface of his wit is a void; his slick repartee is the patter of a society entertainer, not the utterance of a human being. In *As You Like It* Shakespeare takes the jester away from the court that was his professional *milieu* and exposes him to the doubtful consolations of the pastoral life. The keen winds of the forest lay bare the inner man. Touchstone is surprised to catch himself in self-examination. Indeed he is surprised all the time: surprised to meet the strange learned gentleman who would like to be a fool, surprised by the raw aspect of William, most surprised of all to find himself among the country copulatives and looking for a parson. In the end he has discovered a good deal about himself, having in the meantime instructed the audience about the other characters while analysing the nature of folly. In *Twelfth Night* Feste's early appearances are not impressive. Like all his kind, he is a compulsive chatterer, but he does not say very much. He begins to develop individuality only when his facile wit is complemented by the grosser humours of Sir Toby and he is brought into the conspiracy against Malvolio. The temperamental clash between Feste and Malvolio, reaching an eerie climax in the 'Sir Topas' scene, is an underlying motif of the play; and Malvolio's discomfiture, strangely unrelieved by pity, leaves the stage to Feste and the heartache of 'The Wind and the Rain'. In *King Lear* Shakespeare's handling of the clown comes to perfection. Here is the final proof of the tradition, so gravely lamented by the judicious, that even tragedy must have its measure of comic relief. Lear's Fool is all that, professionally, he ought to be: the ingenious quibbler, the unblinkered commentator on affairs of state, and finally the comforter and friend. But he is not permitted, as Fools for their own safety must wish to be, to be a mere watcher on the sidelines. Drawn into the terrible action, he becomes one of its first victims; and his words — and Poor Tom's after him — lighten the darkening scene with a flicker of sanity.

In many ways, therefore, Shakespeare's art was conditioned by the medium in which he chose to work: by the structure of the theatres, by the groundlings in the yard, by changes in public mood and taste, by the actors who interpreted his plays. It would be possible to pursue these enquiries still farther, to wonder whether he sometimes introduced characters that were not in his sources (Beatrice, Dogberry, Jaques, Fluellen) mainly in order to find a part for a particular actor; or to speculate how far the strange mood of the final plays was deliberately attuned to the new resources of the Blackfriars theatre and its cultured audience. External factors such as these constitute the challenge which every creative artist has to face. The sculptor has to work in wood and stone, the composer to orchestrate his music for known instruments, the dramatist to fix in his mind's eye the stage where alone his play will become actual. To try to estimate Shakespeare's achievement in ignorance, or deliberate disregard, of the conditions in which he worked is to mistake the function of the artist, who does not operate in a vacuum; and to deplore those conditions as unworthy of his genius is fatuously to misunderstand their true nature. At the same time one must not, in the excitement of observing at close quarters certain features of Shakespeare's dramatic technique, fall into the trap that is always awaiting realists and forget that he was first, essentially and always a poet. It is not alone the malleable properties of stone that make a sculptor, nor a preordained pattern of rhyme and metre that makes a sonneteer. The casual factors that surround an artist's life — economic pressure, the drive of ambition and prestige, the ferment of his age, the technical laws of his art — remain outward. They do not penetrate into that inner mind where experience acquires a meaning and feeling becomes passion. Firm as the impress of these external matters may be, they do not uncover the mystery of his art. Thus we do not 'explain' Shakespeare by learning something about his working conditions. Although we have no business to think of him at all except in his relation to the theatre, we are not to suppose that the day-to-day exigencies of an acting company tell us all we need to know about the composition of his plays. The study of these things is fascinating because they show how he overcame the lesser challenges he had to meet. But there is more to Shakespearean comedy than the incidental substitution of Armin for Kempe, more to Shakespearean tragedy than the fashionable pessimism of the new reign and the new century, more to *The Tempest* than a technical appreciation of the possibilities of an indoor theatre. Always there are rightnesses that are only a poet's rightnesses.

Chapter VIII
Plays and Playwrights

Remember, the life of these things consists in action.
Marston, The Fawn, Address to the Reader.

The academic amateur who wrote the *Parnassus* plays had small opinion of professional dramatists. He dismissed most of them as 'the bots and glanders of the printing-house' who 'write as men go to stool, for needs, and when they write, they write as a boar pisses, now and then drop a pamphlet' (*1 Return* 320-5). Many of them, if they were honest, would have accepted the judgment, if not the expression of it, because in an actors' theatre they rated little better than the hired men, for whom at least there was the hope of an eventual partnership and a modest security. For the dramatist, unless he were also an actor or had some sort of contract with a company, the material rewards were slender, so that he needed to become poet and pamphleteer as well.

It was the actors who claimed the prizes. The successful among them made money, owned property and wore fine clothes; and, to their further gratification, they stood in the limelight. Although Shakespeare's contemporary reputation was high, he was remembered rather for his poems and for the quotable felicities from the plays than for his more substantial qualities as a dramatist. Shakespeare, moreover, was exceptional. His fellow-poets admired him, as indeed they should, and some of them realized where his true genius lay; but he was also sufficiently well known to the reading public for there to be a profitable trade in the unauthorized printing of mangled versions of his plays and in the ascription to him of plays, many of them worthless, that he did not write. As the publisher of the 1622 Quarto of Othello declared, 'the author's name is sufficient to vent his work'. But no other dramatist was distinguished enough to have false attributions fathered on him with the same liberality, and as a rule the public went to the theatre to see their favourite actors rather than their favourite plays. Whereas the death of Burbage occasioned sorrow from which several famous people declared they would not easily recover, if the death of Shakespeare provoked any contemporary comment, it has not survived.

Because, therefore, playwriting had not yet established itself as a reputable literary form, most plays were composed with the haste and inattention

of ephemeral journalism. The demand, too, corresponded to the requirements of journalism, because the professional theatre was still too young to
have built up a repertory of plays, and not every company shared Alleyn's
enthusiasm for revivals. It is likely that during Shakespeare's working life
some seventy new plays were presented every year, in addition to substantial
revisions and adaptations: which is a very large figure if one bears in mind
the smallness of the whole theatrical operation and the numbers engaged in
it. On the other hand, it was not large enough to keep many writers in regular employment, and most of the theatre's purveyors were freelances with a
variety of literary occupations. They wrote a play when the actors called for
it, when they were in particular need of money, when some national event or
local scandal had aroused sufficient interest to call for its immediate presentation on the stage. Once written, a play was bought outright by the
company and the author had little interest in what became of it. If it were a
moderate success, it would achieve perhaps a dozen performances within a
period of about three months; and then, although the company might keep it
in stock against contingency, in effect it was dead for ever. The author was
protected by no law of copyright. His play might be an outstanding hit and
revived in following seasons; or transferred to another company, or adapted
for a provincial tour; or sold to a printer and published with some success.
Such consequences might please his self-esteem and assist his reputation
among the actors, but they made no difference to his pocket.

These conditions inevitably governed the dramatist's attitude to his work,
and they were not conducive to great art. Although somewhere in the depths
of his being he might acknowledge a primary duty to the theatre as an
evolving art, his only material concern was to supply his paymasters with
work sufficiently stage-worthy to earn him other commissions in the future.
For the fact that the artistic quality of many surviving Elizabethan and
Jacobean plays was nonetheless very high we have to seek other causes.
Possibly the greatest of these was the work of Shakespeare and his actors in
advancing the frontiers of poetic drama into regions hitherto unsought.
Spenser was able to allegorize the uncertainties of his age, with muted reference to his own personal disappointments, in a great poem that had as many
sub-categories as even Polonius would have desired. Just a few years later
drama became the medium that drew creative artists towards the theatre for
the expression of the anguish and aspiration of their troubled times. Ben
Jonson showed himself aware of the adult status that the theatre had
achieved when in 1616 — the year that Shakespeare died — he gathered
together his dramatic pieces, gravely revised and edited them, and gave
them to the world under the impressive title of *Works*. His fellows found this
a laughable demonstration of Jonsonian pretentiousness, for no dramatist
had previously thought to assemble immoment trifles in the dignity and
permanence of a folio. In the address to the reader prefacing *The English
Traveller* (1633) Heywood said that his plays were 'not exposed to the world

in volumes to bear the title of works (as others)', one of his reasons being that 'it never was any great ambition in me to be in this kind voluminously read'. But Jonson was right. His commercial instinct was justified because already there was a public for quarto editions of single plays; and his artistic instinct was equally sound because his comedies, so conscientiously conceived, expressed a positive attitude to society and merited collection as an *opus*. But for his brave example it is unlikely that Heminges and Condell would have assembled the First Folio.

The theatre's drudges could not, however, devote the same care to the subtleties of dramatic composition. Often a play would be commissioned by the actors only a few weeks before it would be needed on the stage. The first stage in its creation would be a tavern conference between the company's representatives and one or more playwrights. Here the general theme was outlined and the playwrights reminded of the actors available and the sort of roles that best suited them. The plot might be suggested by the actors themselves, especially if some event or scandal lately in the news might conveniently be dramatized, or if it were possible to emulate or plagiarize some recent success of a rival company. A writer with a gift for the shaping of a plot (Greene, Munday and Jonson were all recognized to be good 'plotters') would then hammer out a rough scenario, and the actual writing would be distributed among a number of playwrights. The actors were nearly always in a hurry and their insistence on speedy completion explains the extraordinary amount of collaboration to be found in the Elizabethan theatre. Henslowe's records show that between 1597 and 1603 well under half his payments for new plays were made to a single author; and payment to a single author did not necessarily mean that it was his unaided work. In extreme cases as may as five writers contributed to a single play, each writing one act on the lines laid down by the 'plotter'; but this was recognized to be too haphazard even for the Elizabethans, and a collaboration was usually shared between two or three partners. The final result might be revised by a 'dresser' of plays like Dekker, who performed this office for Henslowe and other managements; and we have no means of knowing how often Shakespeare may have been called upon to 'dress' an imperfect piece written for his company. Collaboration was not welcomed by the playwrights because it meant the splitting of the fee, and it was an irksome sign of their bondage to the imperious requirements of the players. It was in such circumstances that Chettle had a hand in forty-eight plays for Henslowe within a period of five years, and Heywood reckoned that in a long career he had 'either an entire hand or at the least a main finger' in 220 plays. That collaboration could have flourished to such an extent was partly a consequence of the general assumption that a play was a perishable thing. The flaws in its motivation and construction would escape notice in a stage performance, and nothing else mattered. It was not expected to survive the cold analysis of the reader in his study.[1]

From the critical point of view the results of collaboration were mostly disastrous, although it was not unknown even in the academic drama. For *Gorboduc*, a singular play in so many different ways, Norton had written the first three acts and Sackville the two last. But in the professional theatre the association of Beaumont and Fletcher, which produced perhaps a dozen plays within about eight years, was rare, and it was founded on some harmony of mind and purpose. For some years before Beaumont's marriage they lodged together on Bankside and, according to Aubrey, not only shared cloak and other clothing but 'had one wench in the house between them, which they did so much admire'. From such domestic felicities successful drama may sometimes grow, but more commonly collaboration was a fortu-itous and impermanent association of two or three men who happened to be available at the moment and in need of quick money; or a writer would be arbitrarily linked with a partner whose gifts were thought to complement his own, a painstaking writer being yoked with one more facile, or a man of sombre mind provided with someone to take care of the comic underplot. These forced marriages were seldom fortunate. The artistic success of *East-ward Ho*, in which Jonson, Marston and Chapman each gave of his best, was an exception. More often the cooperation of men of diverse taste and accom-plishment produced work unflattering to each. Not much, for example, could be hoped from the collaboration of writers as dissimilar as Dekker and Ford, adroit and Protean as Dekker undoubtedly was; nor was it sensible to entrust *The Tragedy of Sir John van Olden Barnevelt*, demanded in haste within a few weeks of the statesman's death, to Fletcher, who believed in divine right, and Massinger, who in the 1640s would have been a parliament man and had all the makings of a Whig. Middleton wrote several plays with the pedestrian William Rowley, probably including *A Fair Quarrel*, *The Spanish Gipsy* and *The Mayor of Quinborough*. Middleton's contribution is in the main responsible and dignified but it is marred by a coarse-grained underplot written without wit or sensibility. This sort of thing has to be accepted as a consequence of the ever-present demand to keep the theatre supplied with plays; and we have also to bear in mind that inconsistencies in structure, style and characterization were not peculiar to collaborations and might appear as frequently in plays by a single author.

Shakespeare's work can exhibit in some degree most of the faults to be found in the drama of the period but he never, or very rarely, involved him-self in the sort of collaboration we have been considering. At various times

---

1 It was sometimes a sad thing for a play if it were. Seeing *Bussy d'Ambois* in the theatre, Dryden found in it the splendour of a falling star; but when he came to read it slowly and attentively, 'I found I had been cozened with a jelly; nothing but a cold, dull mess, which glittered no longer than it was shooting', mere dwarfish thought wrapped up in hyperbole (from the Dedication to *The Spanish Friar*).

he worked on and revised existing work. Source-plays are known or suspected for *Richard III, Taming of the Shrew, King John, Henry IV, Henry V, Hamlet, King Lear* and *Henry VIII* at least, and there may be others. But the adaptation of older work was a common practice in the Elizabethan theatre and it was necessary for practical reasons. A play might have to be shortened for the limited resources of a provincial tour or, conversely, a short piece successful in the provinces might be expanded for a larger London cast; additions might be required to replace musical interludes if a play were transferred from a private to a public theatre, as when Webster was required to augment Marston's *Malcontent*; or a play might be deficient in comedy, so that William Bird and Samuel Rowley, or maybe others, added some knockabout scenes to *Faustus*; or deficient in spectacle, so that excerpts from Middleton's *Witch* were imposed upon *Macbeth*. Adaptation of this professional kind is far removed from collaboration. When Shakespeare went to work on someone else's play, he stamped his own impress on it as firmly as when he borowed the plot of a novel and based a play on that. His style of adaptation may be studied in his resolution of a rambling two-part chronicle, *The Troublesome Reign of King John*, into a close-knit play of 2500 lines.[2]

Collaborators of the familiar kind have, however, been suggested for some of his plays. Even the cautious Chambers, who accepts most of the canon as Shakespeare's authentic and unaided work, finds an unknown collaborator in *1 Henry VI* (*WS* I 289-93), and associates have frequently been proposed to explain the unevenness and imperfections of difficult plays like *All's Well That Ends Well* and *Measure for Measure*. These suggestions are too speculative to allow any presumption that Shakespeare engaged himself to work with a partner in order to get a play ready for the stage. The texts are unsatisfactory, and too many other explanations are possible. Again, it may well be that *Timon of Athens* was completed by another hand from a draft that Shakespeare left unfinished, and that in *Pericles* he took over a play that someone else had drafted and begun to write. Neither of these may properly be regarded as collaborations.

In three plays written after Shakespeare had virtually left the theatre, *Henry VIII*, *The Two Noble Kinsmen* and the lost *Cardenio*, we face a different problem. All three may be dated with some assurance. It was at the first performance of *Henry VIII*, on 29 June 1613, 'set forth with many extraordinary circumstances of pomp and majesty', that the Globe caught fire and 'that virtuous fabric', as Sir Henry Wotton called it, was burnt down; it is on record that *Cardenio* also was performed during the wedding festivities of the Princess Elizabeth; and *Bartholomew Fair*, acted in 1614, refers to 'the play of Palamon' in words that suggest that it was new to the

---

2 For a short account of the differences between the two texts, see M.M.Reese, *The Cease of Majesty*, 265-70. The source is 300 lines longer and has 40 speaking parts compared with 23, and the work of compression and rearrangement reveals Shakespeare's dramatic technique.

tage. Many authorities believe that these three plays, probably written in
612-13, were the combined work of Shakespeare and Fletcher; and if this
e so, Shakespeare was for this brief period engaged in the sort of collabora-
ion that was common in the theatre of his time.

First, there is the circumstantial evidence that although Shakespeare had
lmost certainly retired to Stratford, he was in London for private business
n 1612 and again during the wedding celebrations in the following year;
nd at about the same time Beaumont married and gave up the theatre,
/hich, while possibly leaving Fletcher in sole possession of the wench that
oth so much admired, left him without a collaborator. The inference is that
'letcher turned to Shakespeare for help and inspiration. The details are left
ague, but the theory is that on his visits to London Shakespeare discussed
hese plays with Fletcher, sketching the plot and maybe contributing certain
cenes and speeches. Fletcher may then have sent drafts to Stratford, or gone
here in person, and received further improvements and suggestions. It all
eems rather cumbersome, but if Shakespeare was still a shareholder in the
Xing's Men, he may have felt such chores to be obligatory. Secondly, there
s a certain amount of external evidence. A quarto version of *The Two Noble
Xinsmen* in 1634 gave the names of Fletcher and Shakespeare on the title-
age; and Humphrey Moseley, who later published the Beaumont and
'letcher Folio, omitted *Cardenio* from his collection because, he said, it had
een written by Fletcher in conjunction with Shakespeare, not Beaumont.
'inally, the theory is buttressed by internal evidence of metrical and stylistic
liosyncrasies held to be characteristic of Shakespeare's later work.

None of this amounts to very much beside the solid fact that *Henry VIII*
/as included in the First Folio and the two other plays were not. Professor
Xenneth Muir takes 'the tentative view' (*The Sources of Shakespeare's Plays*,
84) that *Henry VIII* was substantially Shakespeare's but that when the
nanuscript arrived from Stratford, Fletcher 'did a bit of tidying up' and
dded the prologue and epilogue. (The prologue and the play's sub-title *All
s True* were a broadside directed at Samuel Rowley's *When You See Me
'ou Know Me* (1604, reprinted in 1613), a chronicle distinguished for levity
ather than historical truth.) The King's Men may have congratulated them-
elves on persuading Shakespeare to write a patriotic play which they would
:age, with appropriate magnificence, for the festival crowds coming to
.ondon for the royal wedding, but his heart was not in it. He depended
berally on Holinshed, in early days his constant stand-by when inspiration
/as slack, and for this very reason Wolsey's long farewell to all his greatness,
 passage beloved by anthologists, has a sententious vacuity worthy of
'olonius. Shakespeare was no longer interested in affairs of state: all he
/anted to say about that had been said long ago. He could hardly fail to
)uch the fall of Catherine with a noble pathos, but the play is a sequence of
)osely unified episodes. An experienced, almost somnambulist technique
arries it to its perfunctorily patriotic close, and it is characteristic of

Shakespeare's later drama that the infant Elizabeth should embody the promise of regeneration. The play acts better than it reads, but left to himself Fletcher might have made a better job of it.

A contrary process seeks to establish internal evidence of Shakespeare's hand in *The Two Noble Kinsmen*. It is a mildly agreeable tragi-comedy based on Chaucer's *Knight's Tale*, and it bears the acknowledged marks of Fletcher's authorship. Style and situation are ends in themselves. The plot is too elaborate for the adequate display of character, there is a surfeit of spectacle and stage-directions, and the story is told in verse which attains at times to a vague grandeur but always misses the profundity and incisiveness of a true poetic vision. The style is that of a man who has worked long enough with Shakespeare to have charged his brain with echoes of Shakespeare's voice. He has acquired some of Shakespeare's verbal tricks: he makes nouns serve as verbs, as *urn, bride, chapel, ear, jaw*, and he achieves the Shakespearean acceptance of 'Let us be thankful for that which is'. In fact he is an enthralled imitator, and if only there were in the play some trace of Shakespeare's *ordonnance*, we might take him for Shakespeare himself. The reasoning which makes Shakespeare's authorship of *Henry VIII* quite credible argues against his connection with 'the play of Palamon'. *Henry VIII* stayed flat because he was not interested in it; but *The Two Noble Kinsmen* had the sort of plot and atmosphere which, if he had handled it at all at that stage in his career, would have so kindled his imagination that he would have lifted the play to a level which has never been claimed for it. If he had been sufficiently involved to have written as much of it as critics have assigned to him, he would probably have elbowed Fletcher out of it altogether.

On balance the external evidence too must weigh against the theory of collaboration. The Quarto attribution of *The Two Noble Kinsmen* to Shakespeare as well as Fletcher counts for little since printers were always ready to take Shakespeare's name in vain in order to sell their publications and in due course the play found its way — admittedly along with many ill founded attributions — into the second Beaumont and Fletcher Folio of 1679. It is safer to rely on Heminges and Condell, whose evidence is as conclusive as any we are likely to find. The appearance of a play in the First Folio does not guarantee that every word in it was Shakespeare's, nor does the absence of a play prove that Shakespeare had no hand in it. But its inclusion does seem to mean that in conception and execution it was essentially his.

There remains the problem of *Sir Thomas More*, a chronicle play not published until 1844 but probably written in about 1593. Since it failed to satisfy the political scruples of the Master of the Revels, who demanded several amendments, it probably was never acted in Shakespeare's lifetime but on a certain interpretation of the problems of its authorship he appears to have collaborated with three or four other writers, among whom Munday Chettle, Heywood, Kyd, Dekker and even Chapman have been proposed. A much later date, 1600-1, has also been suggested, to accommodate the notion that More's dignified rebuke of the insurgent multitude was in the context of the Earl of Essex's attempt to stir the London rabble. The manuscript is interesting for the light it throws on Elizabethan methods of playmaking. A fair text was prepared, probably by Munday, for submission to the Master of the Revels, Sir Edmund Tilney, although some amendments may have been made in the playhouse before it reached him. Tilney demanded further revisions, among other things instructing the players to leave out the insurrection wholly and the cause thereof'. Even a corrected version failed to satisfy him and the team of writers abandoned the attempt.

The contributor known as 'Hand D', who re-wrote the opening part of II v, is claimed to have been Shakespeare: in which case we have something unique, a fragment of text in his own writing. If this inded be so, the passage does not support the claim of Heminges and Condell to have received his papers with scarcely a blot, for it contains a surprising number of slips of the pen, deletions, emendations and second thoughts. Palaeographical evidence rests upon a comparison of the text with Shakespeare's six surviving signatures, all dated 1612 or later, and it is well known that a man's signature, the sequence of letters he pens more often than any other, acquires a stylized formality which inhibits accurate indentification with his normal handwriting. The evidence from style and content is more persuasive. The scene portrays the Evil May-Day insurrection which broke out in London in 1517 against the menace of foreign workers in English trades, and the citizens, like Jack Cade's followers or the mobs in *Julius Caesar* and *Coriolanus*, are handled with Shakespeare's genial sympathy for them as individuals and his abhorrence of them when in the mass they threaten the settled order of society. More speaks with measured gravity on the high duty of order and obedience:

> For to the king God hath His office lent
> Of dread, of justice, power and command,
> Hath bid him rule, and willed you to obey;
> And to add ampler majesty to this,
> He hath not only lent the king His figure,
> His throne and sword, but given him His own name,
> Calls him a god on earth...

II iv 122.

In terms similar to those of Menenius and Ulysses he warns them against rebellion as a self-destructive process which releases the unbounded waters and causes men to raven upon one another. More's words lack the grand manner, but there is nothing in the vocabulary, metre or pausation to rule out the possibility of Shakespeare's authorship. The sentiments too are undoubtedly his, but not his alone. They were of ancient lineage and in homily, play and pamphlet they were a commonplace of Elizabethan thinking. The scene may well be his, together with another short speech by More that has been copied by a playhouse scribe, but the supposition has much wishfulness in it because it would be agreeable to think that we have a dramatic fragment in his own hand. No one really believes, however, that he was working in a typical playhouse collaboration with the likes of Chettle and Munday. The contention is that the other writers, driven to the wall by Tilney's implacable demands for revision, turned to Shakespeare to help them out of their difficulty. Apparently he did not succeed, which is interesting in itself. But the dating of the play is uncertain, and when, and in what circumstances, would Shakespeare have been asked to come to the rescue of dramatists writing for another company? The time of the Alleyn-Strange combination has been suggested, but this supposition disqualifies some of the other writers presumed to have contributed to the script. Ultimately the authorship of 'Hand D' has to be yet another of the Shakespearean dead-ends.[3]

The demanding hurry that was responsible for so much collaboration among dramatists had likewise damaging effect on plays written by single authors. It meant that a playwright's special virtue was his facility. In Marston's *Histriomastix* the poet to Sir Oliver Owlet's troupe of players is called Posthaste, a gibe supposed to refer to Munday; but although a talent for rapid improvization might be fair game for a jest in the *Poetomachia*, it recognized Munday's usefulness to the professional companies. Elizabethan playwriting developed into a specialized craft, and the way was hard for interlopers who lacked its discipline. Even Jonson, slowed by his laborious striving for classical perfection, was disesteemed in the trade because he took so long to deliver. He seems to have needed about fifteen weeks to write a play, which is not an economic rate. 'You and your itchy poetry'. Captain Tucca told him in *Satiromastix*, 'break out like Christmas, but once a year', and *1 Return from Parnassus* described him as 'so slow an inventor' that he had best return to his brick-laying. At great pains he taught himself to write more rapidly, and he boasted that he had completed *Volpone*, 'without a co-adjutor, novice, journeyman or tutor', in five weeks. Webster was another who complained of the speed at which the actors expected plays to be written. In the preface to the printed text of *The White Devil* he thus defended himself:

> To those who report I was a long time in finishing this tragedy, I confess I do not write with a goose quill winged with two feathers; and if they will needs make it my fault, I must answer them with that of Euripides to Alcestides, a tragic writer. Alcestides objecting that Euripides had only, in three days, composed three verses, whereas himself had written three hundred: 'Thou tellest truth',

---

3 The play is printed, together with all the other Shakespearean attributions, in *The Shakespeare Apocrypha*, edited by C.F.Tucker Brooke, who discusses the problem of authorship in pages xlvii-liv. See also Chambers, *WS* I 500-15, Schoenbaum 214-17.

quoth he, 'but here's the difference — thine shall only be read for three days, whereas mine shall continue three ages'.

A bookseller advertising a selection of Heywood's varied work praised him for being 'very laborious', or hard-working, because 'he not only acted every day, but also obliged himself to write a sheet every day for several years together'. Shakespeare, likewise being an actor, was under a similar necessity, but in comparison with the copiousness of some of the theatre's needy journeymen[4] his output of thirty-six or thirty-seven plays in some twenty years looks meagre. In their famous tribute to their friend and fellow Heminges and Condell declared that 'his mind and hand went together', utterance following immediately upon the thought: thus loyally crediting him with the facility which his theatre held to be a necessary endowment. Ben Jonson sourly commented that he would have done better to blot a thousand lines, but in verses printed with the First Folio he praised Shakespeare for more considered habits:

> Thy Art,
> My gentle Shakespeare, must enjoy a part,
> For though the poet's matter Nature be,
> His Art doth give the fashion. And that he
> Who casts to write a living line must sweat
> (Such as thine are) and strike the second heat
> Upon the Muses' anvil: turn the same
> (And himself with it) that he thinks to frame;
> Or for the laurel he may gain a scorn,
> For a good poet's made, as well as born.
> And such wert thou.

In many Elizabethan plays the felicities were only intermittent because the pressures of the profession compelled their authors to be too fertile to sustain a high level of achievement. Shakespeare is often careless, but the blemishes do not flaw the unity of impression which his plays so remarkably create. It may be that his company did not exact from him the feverish fertility that was demanded of most of his colleagues but gave him time to strike the second heat upon the Muses' anvil.

A play, once written and put upon the stage, had a short life and small hope of posterity. The greatest theatrical sensation of the period was Middleton's *Game at Chess*, which at the Globe in 1624 was played for nine consecutive performances before the authorities suppressed it. It owed its

---

4 Even the copiousness of the Elizabethans shrivels beside the output of a French dramatist, Alexandre Hardi (1569-1631), who claimed to have written 600 plays. He was a member of the company of Valleran-Lecomte, which, like Shakespeare's, was given the title of 'royal'. His fellows likewise tried to keep his plays out of print, but in 1624, possibly influenced by the appearance of the First Folio, he began to publish *Le Théâtre d'Alexandre Hardi, parisien*, and 34 of his plays appeared in the next five years.

popularity to its political timeliness because it satirized in allegorical guise the crippling influence exercised by certain Spaniards at the English court. Many plays had achieved more than nine performances, but hitherto none had achieved a consecutive run. The usual practice, if a play was a reasonable success at its opening performance, was to present it weekly for five or six weeks and thereafter at longer intevals until it quietly expired. Really popular plays were given a second life and revived in a subsequent season, and it was not uncommon for an old play to be re-worked and renovated so that it could be staged with a new title. Dramatists were said to be 'as crafty with old plays as bawds with old faces', and companies sometimes found it more profitable to refurbish an old favourite than to risk something new and untried.

In Henslowe's records the average life of a new play was about twelve performances. Some, the immediate disasters, were never repeated at all, and others perished after three performances. On the other hand, the triumphant *Wise Man of West Chester* was played thirty-two times in three years, *Bellendon* twenty-four times, *A Knack to Know a Knave* twenty-one times. Plays that managed to establish themselves as perennial favourites, like *Mucedorus, The Spanish Tragedy, Faustus* and some of Shakespeare's more emphatic successes (*Titus Andronicus* not the least), were revived regularly and totalled a much higher aggregate; but as a general rule even a successful play ran through its potential audience very rapidly.

Since a play was such a transitory thing, it is not surprising that the rewards were correspondingly meagre. Henslowe's payments ranged from four to ten pounds, and he managed to keep the average fee down to six. For alterations, whether to prepare a play for court or renovate an old one, he paid one pound or two. The experienced Heywood reckoned that throughout his working life he averaged about six pounds a play: and Jonson's estimate that his work for the theatre brought him altogether some £200 roughly conforms with Heywood's figure if we remember that Jonson wrote several plays for the boy companies and Heywood did not. The boy's managers were able to afford higher fees, which was one of the reasons why in their brief heyday they attracted the better writers. For his *Old Joiner of Aldgate* (1602), written for the St Paul's boys, Chapman received £13 6s.8d. Probably the fee was swollen because Chapman wrote the play on behalf of one of the parties in a law-suit that was still in progress, but it was still much higher than Henslowe would have paid for the same work. Henslowe treated his writers much as he treated his actors, binding them to service by allowing them to get into his debt. As soon as a play was commissioned, the wretched author begged for an advance, and thereafter he was doomed. If he failed to complete the play by the date stipulated, his labour was mortgaged for an unforeseeable future; and if in order to get it finished he sought help from collaborators, he had to share the fee. Typical of these dismal transactions was the payment in 1598 of four pounds to Drayton, Dekker, Chettle and

Robert Wilson as an advance for *Earl Godwin and his Three Sons*, with the addition of five shillings for 'good cheer'.

Slender as these payments were, they compared favourably with the fee for pamphlets, for which the booksellers usually paid two pounds. Moreover, the practice grew up of giving the author the profits from the second or third performance as a benefit, and this made a considerable difference to the rewards he might expect and may even have encouraged him to write a better play. In James's reign the basic fee rose too, for in 1613 Robert Daborne reported that he was getting as much as twenty pounds from Henslowe and more from the King's Men. Inflation would explain part of the increase but not all of it.

The dramatist was expected to supply the company with a clean copy of his play, and when this had been amended to the players' satisfaction it went to the Revels Office for licensing. Once the Master of the Revels had made such corrections as he considered necessary and given his 'allowance' to the text, no significant alterations might be made. This 'allowed' version, known as 'the book', was then used for stage performance. (Some of the texts printed in the First Folio were set up from 'the book' and others from Shakespeare's 'foul papers', that is, the uncorrected and unacted draft which he first submitted to the company.) An official known as the book-keeper — or book-holder, as he also acted as prompter — prepared the text for the stage by binding or stitching the sheets together and making notes for the music cues and 'noises off' required in performance. He also prepared each actor's part, together with his cues and stage business. One such part has survived, Alleyn's role in *Orlando Furioso*, and it is in the form of a scroll, six inches wide, pasted to make a continuous strip that the actor could unroll as he spoke it in rehearsal. At the same time an abstract of the play was prepared, called 'the plot'. It was drawn up in two columns, mounted on paste-board and hung in the tiring-house. From this the actors informed themselves of the sequence of the play. It tabulated the scenes in their order, stated the characters, with names of the actors, required in each scene and indicated the cues for their entry. It also provided the stage-keeper with the music and property cues for which he and his underlings were responsible.

It will be noticed that there was only one complete copy of the acting version of the play: the version approved by the Master of the Revels, prepared by the book-keeper, elaborated by a few stage-directions and production notes, and finally put into the hands of the prompter during performance. This meant that the individual actor would be acquainted only with the skeleton summary provided in the 'plot' and with the action taking place when he was himself on stage. The only other text would be the author's original draft, and it is likely that the company locked this safely away or even destroyed it. The object of all these precautions was to ensure that no version found its way to an unscrupulous printer and that no hireling knew enough about the play to be able to transcribe it from memory. A play was a valued possession, because even one that had exhausted its first life on the stage might after a while be doctored and re-presented with a fresh title. It was part of the company's capital stock, and Heywood complained as late as 1633 that some of his plays 'are still retained in the hands of some actors, who think it against their peculiar profit to have them come in print'. The actors tended to believe that once a play had been printed audiences would no longer come to see it on the stage. In this they may have been mistaken since the eagerness of educated men to acquire quarto texts indicated a healthy interest in the drama. The publishers of the 1609 Quarto of *Troilus and Cressida* deplored the unwillingness of the 'grand possessors' of plays to make them available to the reading public. But the actors had a further reason to fear the consequences of printing a play. There being no law of copyright to protect them, they could not prevent rival companies from staging it with a few perfunctory revisions and different names for the characters and a different setting. In their enxiety to safeguard their assets they came to look on printers as greedy scoundrels capable of infinite treachery and deceit.

When, therefore, Heminges and Condell decided to prepare a collected edition of Shakespeare's plays, they were undertaking something that in theatrical circles was neither customary nor welcome. It is true that by 1623 several dramatists had given plays to the printers, furnished with an address to the reader, but many of these were plays originally for the boy companies, whose circumstances were different. The motive was usually a practical one and was little connected with hopes of literary immortality. Jonson's presumption in gathering his 'Works' in folio, a format too dignified to be appropriate for the transitory scribblings of 'proud statute-rogues', was resented even among the dramatists themselves. It was a joke that went on for years, as in Heywood's mocking couplet:

> Pray tell me, Ben, where does the mystery lurk,
> What others call a play you call a Work?

It is difficult now to understand why plays, although they were eagerly read, stood so low in the esteem of the judicious that it was rare, in an age much given to dedication, for one to be offered to the condescending notice of a patron. In dedicating *The Revenge of Bussy d'Ambois* to Sir Thomas Howard, Chapman thought it necessary to inform his patron, by way of apology, that elsewhere things were different, that 'the greatest Princes of Italy and other countries [have not] conceived it any least diminution to their greatness to have their names winged with these tragic plumes, and dispersed by way of patronage through the most noble notices of Europe'. But the English nobility were in no hurry to be honoured in this way. Sir Thomas Bodley sought to have these 'baggage-books' excluded from his library, believing that they would bring only 'scandal' upon his cherished project. In lines which Leonard Digges wrote for the First Folio, although they were not included in it, he congratulated the reader on being put in possession of Shakespeare's plays, but

> thou hast (I will not say),
> Reader, his Works (for to contrive a play
> To him was none).

Leaving aside the probably erroneous view of Shakespeare's methods of composition, we find Digges echoing the general assumption that 'Work' should be reserved for something essentially laborious, and that a play was not deserving of the word.

Heminges and Condell persisted nonetheless, and they had the immediate practical motive of protecting Shakespeare, and the company's interest in his plays, from an unusually impudent case of of false ascription. In 1619 Thomas Pavier, a publisher already notorious for his piracies, joined with the printer William Jaggard to produce a series of Shakespearean quartos. Four of these were reprints of Bad Quartos, *2 and 3 Henry VI, The Merry Wives* and *Henry V; King Lear* was imperfect; and *A Yorkshire Tragedy* and *Sir John Oldcastle* were not by Shakespeare at all. When the King's Men protested to the Lord Chamberlain, Pavier and Jaggard sought to evade the restraint on publication by putting false dates on some of the plays so as to suggest that they had already been printed.

Unless a stop were put to this sort of thing, the company's continuing interest in Shakespeare's work would be damaged, and possibly this was the principal reason for their decision to prepare an authentic canon to establish what was his work and what was not. The enterprise probably began in the following year, and to describe Heminges and Condell as its 'editors' may be something of a misnomer. Their contribution may only to have been to collect and supply the copy, and the collation and editing may have been carried out by Edward Knight, who as the King's Men's book-keeper was professionally equipped for this sort of work. Even their responsibility for the two remarkable prefaces has been questioned. Jonson and Edward Blount, a bookseller who helped to finance the Folio, are among the names that have been canvassed as possible authors, but why Heminges and Condell should not have written them, or why, if they did not write them, the fact should have been concealed, is not apparent. Literary 'ghosting' is much commoner in these days of mass education than it was in Elizabethan times. This theory would seem to be one of the pestilential offshoots of the 'Baconian' belief that no one professionally connected with the Elizabethan theatre was capable of writing a literate sentence.

The first preface was a dedication to the Earls of Pembroke and Montgomery, sons of Sir Henry Herbert, the second earl, who had been patron of London and provincial companies in Elizabeth's reign. Sir William

Herbert, the third earl, touches Shakespeare's story at many points. Some writers have found him to be the beloved youth of the Sonnets, and certainly he begot a child on Mary Fitton, who for many years held the field as the Dark Lady. He was tutored by Samuel Daniel and grew up to be the patron of writers and artists, including Jonson, Massinger and Inigo Jones. Inheriting his father's interest in the theatre, he was well known to Shakespeare's company and they had visited his house at Wilton to act before King James. Since 1615 he had been Lord Chamberlain. His brother Philip, who succeeded to the earldom in 1630, received office and favours from the Stuart kings but deserted them in 1640[5] and was to have the sordid distinction of receiving Charles I on behalf of the parliamentary forces when the Scots delivered him to the English rebels for a cash payment. In 1647 the first Beaumont and Fletcher Folio was dedicated to him in the view that 'There is none among all the names of Honour that hath more encouraged the legitimate Muses of this latter age than that which is owning to your family'. At this time the theatres had been closed, and were still closed, by Pembroke's political confederates.

In their dedication to these furtherers of drama and the arts Heminges and Condell achieved a manner rare in seventeenth-century addresses. Their tone bespeaks gratitude and respect, but they allow themselves no doubt that the honour done to their Lordships in receiving Shakespeare's work is as great as any their Lordships can confer. Shakespeare having died without 'having the fate, common with some, to be executor to his own writings', his friends

> have but collected them, and done an office to the dead, to procure his Orphans, Guardians; without ambition either of self-profit, or fame: only to keep the memory of so worthy a Friend and Fellow alive, as was our SHAKESPEARE.

The preface to 'the great Variety of Readers' begins by urging them to buy, and then follows the crucial paragraph:

> It had been a thing, we confess, worthy to have been wished that the Author himself had lived to have set forth and overseen his own writings; But since it hath been ordained otherwise, and he by death departed from that right, we pray you

5   This sort of thing ran in the family. William Herbert, the first earl, came to his final rest at St Paul's in 1570 after a career of tergiversation startling even in the early years of the Protestant ascendancy. His fortunes were founded on a grant of abbey land at Wilton, and he supported the early religious changes under Edward VI. Backing Northumberland against Protector Somerset was a shrewd investment, but he was less prudent in backing Northumberland against Queen Mary. He managed to change sides in time to help in the suppression of Wyatt's rebellion in 1554, but he was careful to be on good terms with Mary's Catholic husband. A loyal, and well rewarded, Protestant in Elizabeth's early years, he later had to practise the nimbleness of a lifetime of prosperous intrigue to extricate himself after favouring a design to marry the Catholic Duke of Norfolk to Mary Queen of Scots. Like grandfather, like grandson. It was careers like this that coloured Shakespeare's characterization of the barons in his early histories. If their shifts of policy seem unrealistic, Shakespeare had examples near at hand.

do not envy his Friends the office of their care and pain to have collected and published them; and so to have published them as where (before) you were abused with diverse stolen and surreptitious copies, maimed and deformed by the frauds and stealths of injurious impostors that exposed them: even those are now offered to your view cured and perfect of their limbs; and all the rest, absolute in their numbers as he conceived them. Who, as he was a most happy imitator of Nature was a most gentle expresser of it. His mind and hand went together: And what he thought, he uttered with that easiness that we have scarce received from him a blot in his papers. But it is not our province, who only gather his works, to praise him. It is yours that read him. And there we hope, to your diverse capacities you will find enough both to draw and hold you: for his wit can no more lie hid than it could be lost. Read him, therefore; and again and again: And if then you do not like him, surely you are in some manifest danger not to understand him.

The honesty and directness of this address, warmed by their affection for the man they had known, may suggest that they will also prove reliable guides in the textual problems that confronted them. Eighteenth-century editors chose to regard the Folio as a brazen attempt by two semi-literate actors to turn Shakespeare's reputation to their own advantage. Their literacy may be left to speak for itself in the manner of their dedications, and although the Folio has not the perfect accuracy they claim for it, their work was honourably performed.

In 1623 half of Shakespeare's plays had already appeared in print, and sometimes there were good reasons for publication as well as bad. Sometimes companies needed cash and sold some play-books in order to raise it. Thus twenty-three quartos appeared in 1594 when the companies were in difficulties after the long spell of plague; and the publication of another nineteen around 1600 may reflect the competition suffered from the companies together with the pressure on the Chamberlain's and the Admiral's to raise money for their new theatres. Another good reason was to undo the damage caused by the publication of a 'stolen and surreptitious' text by publishing an authentic one — or, similarly, to print a good text in order to forestall a bad one believed to be on the way. In the epistle to *The Rape of Lucrece* (1608) Heywood apologized for having sometimes been driven to this necessity: 'Some of my plays have (unknown to me, and without any of my direction) accidentally come into the printer's hands and therefore so corrupt and mangled (copied only by the ear) that I have been as unable to know them as ashamed to challenge them'. It is on record that Shakespeare protested against the attribution of certain poems in *The Passionate Pilgrim*, but the prevention of the unauthorized printing of his plays was something he could safely leave to his company. Ultimately they conducted this campaign with some success.

Of the eighteen plays already printed four had so far existed in corrupt versions only. These were the Bad Quartos, namely *2 and 3 Henry VI*, *Henry V* and *Merry Wives*, of which authentic texts appeared for the first time in the

Folio. There had also been Bad Quartos of *Romeo and Juliet* and *Hamlet*, but these had been followed by more authentic versions; and the existence of a Bad Quarto of *Love's Labour's Lost* is assumed, although it has not survived, from the words 'newly corrected and augmented' on the title-page of the (Good) Quarto of 1598. That makes seven Bad Quartos in all, with possibly an eighth if *Taming of A Shrew* was a corrupted text rather than, as for long assumed, a source-play.

Two other quarto editions are also suspect. The text of *King Lear* published in 1608 and reprinted in 1619 is much inferior to the Folio text and it has some signs of having been assembled from actors' recollections or even from shorthand transcription. The quarto of *Troilus and Cressida* (1609) is a good text but the prefatory Address to the Reader is written in terms suggesting that publication was not authorized by the company. On the other hand this may have been a smart trick by the publisher to sell his book by hinting at some subterranean traffic. Finally, there is the problem of *Pericles*, which appeared in quarto in 1609 (two editions), 1611 and 1619 but was not included in the First Folio. In general this might have meant one of two things: either that Heminges and Condell did not regard the play as Shakespeare's work or that they could not acquire a satisfactory text. They should have had no difficulty in acquiring a text of some kind as the play was registered to Edward Blount, one of the promoters of the Folio, and there had been four quarto printings.

Pericles was first added to the canon in the second edition (1664) of the Third Folio (1663), along with six other plays rejected by Heminges and Condell and most subsequent editors. It was restored by Edmund Malone in 1790 and thereafter most readers of Shakespeare have accepted at least the last three acts as predominantly his work. The theme of separation and reconciliation is in the prevailing mood of the final plays, and — in so far as such a hazardous test may be applied — much of the writing seems to be characteristic. The squeamish persuade themselves that Shakespeare could not have put his hand to the brothel scenes. 'The poor Transylvanian is dead, that lay with the little baggage': it is ruthless, but Shakespeare was capable of such grim realism when he chose and it is these very scenes which seem to assure us of his presence. Many might have written the pretty and pathetical story of Marina, but no other dramatist could have so pitilessly exposed the timeless indecency of this small dark corner of Mytilene. The Boults of this world are always with us, and at the present time they seem to flourish as never before.

Yet Heminges and Condell did not include *Pericles* when they so easily might have done, and their judgment cannot be ignored. Possibly they considered the existing texts as failing in the accuracy on which they prided themselves. Q 1, on which later quartos were based, was certainly corrupt, the first two acts appearing to be reported, and perhaps the play should be seen as a Bad Quarto of which no satisfactory version was available.

Heminges and Condell may have had some inside knowledge of which posterity is unaware: as, for instance, of Shakespeare's taking up a play in the company's possession (the play which, according to Q 1, 'hath been divers and sundry times acted by his Majesty's Servants at the Globe on Bankside') but only 'dressing' it without making it his own. Whatever the reason, its omission implies that Heminges and Condell were not lacking in critical integrity. It is unlikely that they were deterred because, as Jonson was later to describe it, *Pericles* is a 'mouldy tale'. They did not make their selection on aesthetic grounds; and Jonson is known to have condemned other plays, notably *Titus Andronicus*, that appeared in the Folio nonetheless.

The appearance of Bad Quartos was seldom the work of shorthand reporters, although these ingenious 'brachgraphy men' were much feared by the acting profession. A system of shorthand had been elaborated by the subtle and learned Dr Timothy Bright, whose *Charactery* had appeared in 1588; and it had been followed by a more popular work, John Willis's *Art of Stenography*, in 1602. In a revival of *If You Know Not Me, You Know Nobody* many years after its original performance in 1605 Heywood complained of corrupt texts 'copied only by the ear':

> Some by stenography drew
> The plot; put it in print (scarce one word true).

But it is no longer believed that Elizabethan shorthand was competent to transcribe a whole play during performance, and the first source of Bad Quartos was not necessarily dishonest. Their characteristics were brevity and the transposition of scenes and speeches, and the inference is that they were shortened versions prepared for the smaller companies that took London productions on tour. Provincial companies had not the manpower and resources of the London theatre, and they played to audiences who were less exacting and incapable of prolonged concentration. So the longer soliloquies were shortened and replaced by low comedy; some characters were omitted because there were not enough actors to play them; and scenes and speeches were transposed, to the confusion of sense, in order that some parts might be doubled. The Bad Quarto of *Romeo and Juliet* (1597) was botched in this fashion to accommodate a company that could manage twelve characters but could not rise to musicians; whereas the Good Quarto that followed in 1599 provides for some twenty characters with pages, servants and musicians as well. Probably most of these provincial adaptations were made with the approval of the parent company, and the abbreviated texts were accordingly prepared with access to the prompt-book. It was only when the prompt-book was not available that the actors had to call on their memory of what had been played in London, as seems to have happened in the Bad Quartos of *Hamlet* and *The Merry Wives of Windsor*. This still does not mean that the construction of the provincial text was unauthorized, although sometimes it may have been. The serious offence was to sell the text to a printer when the tour was over.

Issuing a good text in the hope of driving out the bad was at best a makeshift, and the actors discovered a more satisfactory expedient in the 'staying entry' in the Stationers' Register. The Stationers' Company had been incorporated by royal charter in 1556 and all the London booksellers and most of the printers belonged to it. For a fee of sixpence a publisher might enter a book in the register and secure for himself, though not for the author, the protection of copyright; and provided that another entry was duly registered, the copyright accompanied the transfer of a book from one publisher to another. But the registration of a book did not mean that it had to be printed immediately or printed ever at all. What it did mean was that the copyright was safeguarded to the man who made the entry, and no one else might publish the book. Shakespeare's company, who took more care than any of their rivals to keep their plays out of print, adopted the device of the staying entry, which protected their plays from pirate publishers without obliging them to put them into print.

These blocking entries were not wholly effective. They did not prevent the appearance of a Quarto of *Henry V* in the very year when its publication was 'stayed', nor later of *The Merry Wives, Hamlet, Pericles* and *Troilus and Cressida*. But after 1603 there were only four quarto publications of Shakespeare's plays, apart of course from reprints of plays already issued. It is impossible to say how far the blocking entry was responsible for this decline because after 1603 the King's Men were able to invoke the authority of their royal patron. The Privy Council would not have hesitated to revoke the licence of a publisher who could be shown to have injured the interests of the King's servants, and it was royal authority, exercised through the Lord Chamberlain, that frustrated the scoundrelly enterprise of Pavier and William Jaggard in 1619. Their original intention probably was to issue their ten plays as collected 'Works', and Pembroke's intervention established the principle that, publishers' copyrights notwithstanding, plays were the property of the actors and might not be published if they felt that publication was detrimental to their interests. The principle might as yet have no standing in law, but it had the authority of a court official and probably that was more potent. It was an important victory for the players.

The Folio was published by a syndicate of four printers and publishers that included Blount and Isaac Jaggard, whose father had lately died after a long illness during which he was afflicted with blindness: the company seem not to have held him responsible for the bogus 'Works' of 1619. The syndicate's main task was to negotiate for the copyrights which, through registration and blocking entries, belonged to other men, and the Folio was already set up for the press before they could reach an agreement for the surrender of *Troilus and Cressida*. Its insertion as the first play in the 'Tragedy' section of the Folio does not mean that Heminges and Condell so classified the play, nor that they made a last-minute decision to introduce a doubtfully Shakespearean text: the difficulty was a technical one within the publishing business. The syndicate had also to establish their own copyright in the eighteen plays not hitherto printed, and the entry appeared in the Stationers' Register on 8 November 1623. It referred to those of Shakespeare's plays 'as are not formerly entered to other men', and it therefore named only sixteen plays, omitting the (probable) Bad Quarto of *Taming of the Shrew* and the source-play for *King John* because these plays had been registered, and copies had appeared, some thirty years previously.

The Folio does not appear to have followed any consistent editorial policy. Where a Good Quarto was available, it was sometimes collated with other copy, sometimes not. This other copy would be of three main kinds: the author's 'foul papers', his original draft before he made a fair copy (which Shakespeare seldom did); the prompt-book; or a playhouse transcript, which might be a transcript of the prompt-book or of the foul papers. It is impossible to tell why in setting plays not previously published the editors sometimes used more than one of these sources or sometimes used one rather than another: we simply do not know what was available to them. Some of the plays have detailed stage-directions, others very few; the majority are divided into acts and scenes, but six are not even divided into acts and several have act divisions only. *Macbeth* appears in a shortened stage version with interpolations from Middleton; the Folio version of *Hamlet* is shorter than the Good Quarto; in *Love's Labour's Lost* Berowne's long speech in IV iii, in which he says that to be in love is no perjury, is printed in both the original and a corrected version, and Dover Wilson has calculated (in his Cambridge edition, 1923) that in this play the printer corrected 117 errors in the Quarto text but reproduced fifty-nine and added 137 of his own. It is not even possible to speak of 'the Folio reading' of a play, because sometimes there was more than one reading: the printing and binding were so poorly done that there are discrepancies between one copy and another.

The editors are not to be blamed for the vagaries of Jacobean printers, who were a law to themselves: even a Quarto text that supposedly was a reprint of an earlier one seldom corresponded with it. But the editors had other difficulties that were implicit in the nature of their task. It has to be remembered that a play in the theatre, especially a repertory theatre, is a living thing, subject to constant change. Although companies were not supposed to alter a text once 'allowed' by the Master of the Revels, it would not have been realistic to require submission of the minor alterations required over the years with changes in personnel or the differences a play underwent when presented at an inn, at court, at the Globe or at Blackfriars. For their own convenience the actors would keep such changes as small as possible, but changes there were bound to be. At one time during their plays' history there was a Viola who could sing and a Desdemona who could not. We have to remember, too, that when the Folio was being prepared Shakespeare had been out of the theatre for some ten years, and we do not know how many playhouse books disappeared when the Globe burned down. Pavier's attempted piracy in 1619 testifies to Shakespeare's continued popularity in the theatre, but this does not mean that all his plays were still being revived. Several, no doubt, had fallen into disuse, and the Folio editors may have had great difficulty in finding a satisfactory text. Prompt-copies may have disappeared or become worn out over the years. The editors may then have had to call on the actors or the book-keeper to remember what they could. Heminges and Condell were claiming too much when they said they were printing the plays 'cured and perfect of their limbs' and 'absolute in their numbers as he conceived them', but in most cases care was taken when care was possible, and the literary habits of the age did not require them to explain, as modern editors do, the principles on which they worked or the problems they encountered in particular cases.

The emblematic contents of the Folio are likely to have come under the editors' personal attention. Their own two prefaces would have done honour to any book, but the solemnity of the occasion required something more. The dignity of a folio setting demanded a selection of verses sufficiently laudatory to excuse the enterprise: Jonson had provided himself with nine, Beaumont and Fletcher would in the future receive the acclamation of thirty-six. Heminges and Condell were content — or had to be content: we do not know how widely they sought — with four.

Jonson's poem is too long to be quoted in full, and excerpts cannot give the full flavour because every comment is brilliantly edged and balanced. Shakespeare's 'small Latin and less Greek' almost becomes a classical scholar's compliment, but seeming praise finds somewhere or other its qualification. Dryden found it subtly aspersive and every reader must make his own evaluation. As a memorial panegyric it has provoked controversy from the day it was written. Probably Shakespeare himself, knowing and respecting the man who wrote it, would have preferred such praise, even coming so reluctantly that it seems half-strangulated, to the laurels of lesser men.

The other contributions are not of a high order. The best was a grave little poem of only eight lines by 'I. M', believed to have been James Mabbe, an Oxford don known chiefly as a translator from the Spanish. A sonnet on 'the Famous Scenic Poet', complacently inept, came from Hugh Holland, a protégé of Buckingham, and some couplets from Leonard Digges. Digges was a neighbour of Heminges and Condell in St Mary Aldermanbury, and his mother married as her second husband Thomas Russell, a landowner of Alderminster, near Stratford, and an overseer of Shakespeare's will. Digges's initial contribution is interesting for its first-hand testimony to the popularity of some of Shakespeare's characters in the theatre, but he does not seem to have known his author very well as he applauds him for having always invented his own plots and having never introduced phrases from Latin, Greek and the vulgar tongues or borrowed a scene from his friends.

His way of commending Shakespeare was to contrast his success with Jonson's failures. He dismissed *Catiline* as 'tedious (though well laboured)' and *Sejanus* as 'irksome', and declared that *Volpone* and *The Alchemist*, when acted at the insistence of the author's friends, scarcely bore the cost of heating the theatre and paying the door-keepers. Further, if he be read aright, he appears to have categorized Jonson, along with other 'needy Poetasters', as 'vermin'. These not very tactful lines could hardly be included in a volume to which Jonson was a fellow-contributor, and they were later printed in a dubious miscellany of Shakespeare's *Poems* published in 1640, where they accompanied a tribute from Milton. For the Folio Digges was evidently asked to think again, and he submitted a shorter poem in which he refrained from gibes at Jonson but again failed to illuminate the art of Shakespeare. The Folio was completed by the names of the twenty-six Principal Actors in all these plays' (valuable as listing the sharers in the company) and an engraved portrait, possibly of Shakespeare as Old Knowell in *Every Man In His Humour*, by Martin Droeshout, who was only fifteen when Shakespeare died and could not have been expected to produce a convincing likeness. In ten lines accompanying the portrait Jonson advised the reader to look 'not on his picture, but his book'. The poverty of all this commendatory material, apart from Jonson's tribute, has not escaped the notice of critics who have wished to denigrate the Folio on other counts as well.

The Folio measured 13 ⅜ inches by 8 ½ and consisted of 908 pages printed in double columns, in the disapproving words of William Prynne, on 'the best crown paper, better than most Bibles'. The original price was £1, but when the Bodleian Library bought back its original presentation copy in 1906, it was at a cost of £3000. Just before the war a copy changed hands for £8600, and its value in the dilapidated pound of the present day is beyond reasonable speculation.

The first edition of about a thousand copies was followed by a reprint, with some corrections, in 1632. The third Folio (1663) was followed in the next year by a new impression that added *Pericles* for the first time, together with six other plays that had been printed under Shakespeare's name during his lifetime: *Locrine, A Yorkshire Tragedy, Sir Thomas Cromwell, The Puritan Widow, Sir John Oldcastle* and *The London Prodigal*. These attributions also appeared in the Fourth Folio (1685) but were eliminated by eighteenth-century editors.

The admitted defects of the Folio, and the circumstances that caused it, in due course gave birth to the critical exercise known as 'the disintegration of Shakespeare'.[6] The disintegrators argue that there is no such thing as an

See 'The Disintegration of Shakespeare' in Chambers, *Shakespearean Gleanings*. He discusses the authenticity of Shakespearean texts in *WS* I iv-vii. See also W.W.Greg, *The Editorial Problem in Shakespeare*; A.W.Pollard, *Shakespeare Folios and Quartos*; A.Walker, *Textual Problems of the First Folio*.

authentic Shakespearean text. In the Elizabethan theatre there was constant collaboration, with plays being 'mended' or revised, so that when a play was produced some twenty years after its original performance, as many of Shakespeare's were, the changes introduced during the intervening years, small perhaps but cumulative, left it something very different from the original. In its extreme form the doctrine would hold that 'it is doubtful whether any play of Shakespeare's was ever performed twice in his lifetime in exactly the same form': what passes for a Shakespearean text is merely the text which happened to be used on one particular occasion, incorporating the omissions and accretions made in the past but lacking the further changes which would inevitably be made in the future.

The disintegrators argue from their conception of a continuous playhouse copy which was carefully preserved by the company and re-shaped and brought up to date as changes among the actors, the type of theatre being used or fluctuations of popular taste made such rewriting necessary. Sometimes the text was transcribed (a process introducing a rich crop of inaccuracies) and a clean copy made, sometimes it was retained with its accretions thick upon it, the interlineations, marginal insertions, deletions and additional slips; but it was a continuous text, 'the book of the play', and unless the author's original manuscript happened to exist, there was no other. Over the years the copy would fall into the hands of various revisers who bridged the gaps with infelicitous interpolations and in the course of tidying it for stage performance departed farther and farther from the copy which the author had handed to the company long ago. The more popular the play, the likelier it was to be exposed to this treatment. A play-book, on this view, was a theatrical property never free from the meddling intrusion of adapters and stage revisers. It was not a piece of literature, still less the contrivance of deliberated art. It was a dish periodically served at the table by any cook or playhouse scullion who chanced to turn a spoon in it or throw in a pinch of pepper.

The more conservative disintegrators allow that in his own work most of the revisions may have been made by Shakespeare himself, but others have been persuaded by stylistic clues that the plays are full of alien and non Shakespearean matter. The chief of these was J. M. Robertson, who as a young man was an admirer and colleague of Charles Bradlaugh and early in the century an active politician and privy councillor. His passionate solicitude for Shakespeare's good name led him to exclude so much of the canon as unworthy that he concluded that *A Midsumer Night's Dream* was Shakespeare's 'first, and indeed only complete play'. In *Richard III*, which was primarily Marlowe's, he allowed Shakespeare some six or seven speeches; he transferred the 'substance' of *Romeo and Juliet*, *Richard II*, *Julius Caesar* and *Comedy of Errors* to Marlowe, of *The Two Gentlemen of Verona* to Greene, of the three 'problem comedies' to Chapman; and in tracing the genesis of the Folio text of *Henry V* he decided that the first draft was by

Marlowe, with some assistance from two collaborators who may have been Peele and Greene, that it was later revised by some or all or any of Peele, Chettle, Greene, Munday, Heywood, Dekker or Drayton, that the comedy scenes were added by Chapman, and that finally this many-handed structure was overhauled by Shakespeare, possibly aided by Chettle. Such notions result from a whole-hearted application of the doctrines of continuous copy and incessant 'dressing', collaboration and revision. Compared with Robertson, Dover Wilson, the textual editor of much of the new Cambridge edition, is restrained, almost diffident, but after completing his work on the fourteen comedies he allowed only four to have been Shakespeare's unaided work; not including *A Midsummer Night's Dream*, in which he detected three layers of composition.

To accept the disintegrators' basic principles and begin to apply them in detail to the plays is ultimately to sink into impotent indecision and abandon all hope of discovering Shakespeare's artistic intentions. Shakespeare does not need the flattery of our deciding that wherever a play is inferior or uneven, someone else is responsible for it. A major artist is more likely to be uneven in his work than a competent craftsman scrupulously blotting every line. As Dr Johnson wrote in his notes on *3 Henry VI*,

> From mere inferiority nothing can be inferred; in the productions of wit there will be inequality. Sometimes judgment will err, and sometimes the matter itself will defeat the artist. Of every author's works one will be the best, and one the worst. The colours are not equally pleasing, nor the attitudes equally graceful, in all the pictures of Titian or Reynolds.

When we remember the pressure under which Shakespeare worked, and the range and variety of the subjects he treated, it would be foolish to expect a uniform standard of achievement, and Ben Jonson justly said that 'many times he fell into those things, could not escape laughter'. Nor, unlike Jonson, did he personally prepare his plays for the press, and doubtless he would have amended a great deal if he had. Meanwhile three centuries of criticism have been undertaking the work of improvement for him, judging his lines by standards literary rather than dramatic and relieving him of passages unacceptable to the fashions of other times. All his readers have been disintegrators to some extent because it is impossible not to wish that here and there a scene, a trick of plotting , a speech, a line, a phrase were other than it is; and from the wish it is a short step to the supposition, rapidly hardening into conviction, that here we have the blundering hand of the collaborator, the reviser, the printer or the wretched pair of actor-editors.

It is remarkable how fallible these personal exclusions may turn out to be, even when first-class critics make them. Coleridge gave an impressive warning against critics who approach Shakespeare wearing 'the seven-league boots of self-opinion', and yet he wrote of of 'the disgusting passage' of the Porter in *Macbeth*, 'I dare pledge myself to demonstrate [it] to be an interpolation of the actors'. In the same passage in his *Lectures o Shakespeare* he surprisingly said that he could not bring to mind 'a sing pun or play on words in the whole drama'; although *Macbeth* contains wh is perhaps the most famous of all Shakespearean puns:

> If he do bleed,
> I'll gild the faces of the grooms withal,
> For it must seem their guilt.

II ii 5

Pope too was always discovering interpolations by the barbarous player and among the lines of which he accused them was 'the multitudinous se incarnadine...', which he relegated to a footnote, supplying a genteel eme dation of his own: This my hand will rather

> Thy multitudinous seas incarnadine
> And make the green ocean red.

The loss in terror and dramatic power is enormous.

Dr Johnson himself, having very properly rebuked Pope for his insens tiveness in substituting *gory* for *golden* in the line

> His silver skin lac'd with his golden blood,

failed to see the force of another poetic image in the same play. In a paper o 'Poetry Debased by Mean Expressions' he quotes Macbeth's terrible inv cation of the night:

> Come, thick night,
> And pall thee in the dunnest smoke of hell,
> That my keen knife see not the wound it makes;
> Nor heav'n peep through the blanket of the dark,
> To cry, Hold! hold!

Macb I v 5

Of these lines he writes:

> Macbeth proceeds to wish, in the madness of guilt, that the inspection of heave may be intercepted, and that he may, in the involutions of infernal darknes escape the eye of Providence. This is the utmost extravagance of determine wickedness; yet this is so debased by two unfortunate words that while endeavour to impress on my reader the energy of the sentiment, I can scarce chec my risibility when the expression forces itself on my mind; for who, without son relaxation of his gravity, can hear of the avengers of guilt *peeping though a blanke*
> *The Rambler*, No.16

Who now, without some relaxation of his gravity, can read this? It is astonishing that a critic with Johnson's wide reading and percipience should have turned away from such a simple, telling image. Again, as an example of the sort of lapse which 'could not escape laughter' the other Jonson, Ben, chose a passage from *Julius Caesar* whose meaning is clear and forceful:

> As when he said in the person of Caesar, one speaking to him, *Caesar, thou dost me wrong*. He replied: *Caesar never did wrong, but with just cause*, such like: which were ridiculous.
>
> *Discoveries*

If it be necessary to quibble about these lines at all, it would seem that Shakespeare knew the legal meaning of *wrong* and Jonson did not. But on the stage the words are immediately effective; and if Caesar be guilty of an 'o'erleaping thought', as Jonson implies, that is in the character that Shakespeare was presenting.

In these last instances the critics were not expressly attributing the offending lines to actors or other interpolators, but it is this sort of subjective dislike of various lines in Shakespeare that gives birth to theories of disintegration and reaches second childhood in Robertson's ascription of the substance of *Romeo and Juliet* and *Comedy of Errors* to Marlowe. Probably few of us are now much attracted by Prince Hal's teasing of Francis the potman in *1 Henry IV* II iv, but social habits change and we have no right to transfer the scene to Hathway or Chettle or Munday, or maybe a conflation of all three.

The various dogmas of disintegration (in the nature of things each disintegrator must have his own) have a fundamental justification in the habits of the Elizabethan playhouse, where as in all theatres in almost any age, the dramatist's text was not sacrosanct. Clowns put in their gags, certain 'business' became traditional, a scene might be shortened in a private theatre to permit music and spectacle, senior actors died or departed, boys in apprenticeship had differing skills and aptitudes, plays had to be abridged for the short winter afternoons, the author's original manuscript might be too long for the theatre: the opportunities for disintegration are endless, and the disintegrators are right to draw attention to it. To be a Folio fundamentalist is a comfortable attitude as it combines respectability with a dispensation from critical thinking. The great mass of Shakespearean readers and playgoers will not worry anyway: they are content with what they have, and it is unlikely that Shakespeare himself would have wished it otherwise. For the critical student of the texts it would seem that each play needs to be examined independently on the available evidence. This examination may come to involve quarto versions, one or more theories of authorial revision, actors' memorization, playhouse transcription, printers' carelessness: and where in the end is Shakespeare, if not totally disintegrated?

Dr Johnson did not rate Heminges and Condell very highly. He allowed that their 'attestation may be received in matters of fact' (although one wonders what matters of fact he had in mind), but he thought that they superintended their edition 'unskilfully' and that they 'often made strange mistakes by ignorance and negligence'. So it may be, but we do not know how often they, or their assistants in the preparation of the Folio, tracked and excised playhouse accretions or restored omissions. We do not know, that is to say, how much better or worse the Folio text might have been. Dr Johnson is realistic here: 'They who had the copy before their eyes were more likely to read it right than we who read it wholly by imagination'. By 'imagination' Johnson, who was a professional philologist, surely meant an adherence to unproved theories, the medieval usage of the word. It is from this sort of 'imagination' that the accepted Shakespearean canon now needs to be protected.

Quite apart from its inherent subjectivity, with text-tasters debating whether a single image belonged to Shakespeare, Marlowe, Chapman or the ever-obliging Chettle, the theory of disintegration may have exaggerated the possibilities of revision in the Elizabeth theatre. Progressive change there must have been when a play long outlived its first production, but it was in the technical and financial interest of the players to keep this as small as possible. What the disintegrators call 'revision' may have been no more than the minimal adaptation consequent upon changing circumstances. A play due for revival needed to be taken out of store and dusted down with as little inconvenience as possible, so that actors could rehearse it quickly and spectators with long memories would be protected from drastic and unwelcome changes in the company's style. Certainly the company would want to avoid the trouble and expense of going to the Master of the Revels for a new 'allowance'.

The disintegrators and other textual critics have done a useful service in causing it to be recognized that every text in the canon must be treated as a special case because no convenient generalization will cover them all, but in general they have not shaken the testimony of Shakespeare's friends: not of Heminges and Condell merely, whose scholarship and perseverance may not have matched their good intentions, but of Jonson and Heywood and all those other contemporaries, professional rivals as well as admirers and friends, who would not have been put off with an imposture. If the Folio had not been substantially and recognizably Shakespeare's work, we should have heard of it soon enough. Even when the case for disintegration has been stretched to the full and every possible admission made about the editorial problems and the intrusion of playhouse adapters, the Folio speaks with a strange authority. It bears many signs of haste, imprecision and weakening endeavour, but the bad as well as the good contributes to the impression of an overlying unity and a characteristic style.

Chapter IX
The Audience

But our poor dooms, alas! you know are nothing
To your inspired censure; ever we
Must needs submit; and there's the mystery.

Chapman, *All Fools*, Prologue.

In an essay on the influence of Shakespeare's audience Robert Bridges said that 'The foolish things in his plays were written to please the foolish, the filthy and the brutal for the brutal...those wretched beings who can never be forgiven their share in preventing the greatest poet and dramatist of the world from being the best artist.' This merely states in an unusually emphatic and offensive form a view which had already prevailed for three hundred years. The barbarity and ignorance of the Elizabeth audience was a critical assumption too obvious to require discusion, and it has been regularly advanced in mitigation of the crudities in Shakespeare's writing. Indeed he was rare among his contemporaries in not advancing it himself.

Thus Hazlitt qualified a fine tribute to Shakespeare (*Lectures on the English Poets*, 'On Shakespeare and Milton') by regretting that he

> wrote for the 'great vulgar and the small' in his time, not for posterity. If Queen Elizabeth and the maids of honour laughed heartily at his worst jokes, and the catcalls in the gallery were silent at his best passages, he went home satisfied, and slept the next night well... He was willing to take advantage of the ignorance of the age in many things, and if his plays pleased others, not to quarrel with them himself.

His eighteenth-century editors, men of great fastidiousness when not hurling abuse at one another, also knew where to lay the blame for all that offended their taste. Bishop Warburton attributed Shakespeare's 'obscurity' to the Elizabethans' craving for the 'high and turgid'; Theobald wrote with condescending pity of the age's 'reigning Barbarism'; Dr Johnson found the people 'gross and dark' and thought that Shakespeare purposely crowded his drama with 'incidents by which the attention of a rude people was more easily caught than by sentiment or argumentation'.

In the preface to his edition of the plays Johnson wrote:

The shows and bustle with which his plays abound have the same original. As knowledge advances, pleasure passes from the eye to the ear, but returns, as it declines, from the ear to the eye. Those to whom our author's labours were exhibited had more skill in pomps or processions than in poetical language, and perhaps wanted some visible and discriminated events as comments on the dialogue.

We may note here that although a certain amount of spectacle was provided on the open stages, 'pomps and processions' were commoner in the private theatres; and that those who supposedly derived their pleasure from eye rather than ear were accustomed to stand for a couple of hours listening to a sermon. Pope similarly prefaced his edition by saying that as Shakespeare initially had 'no other aim in his writings than to procure a subsistence', he 'directed his endeavours solely to hit the taste and humour that then prevailed'.

> The Audience was generally composed of the meaner sort of people; and therefore the Images of Life were to be drawn from those of their own rank. Thus in tragedy we find the most strange, unexpected, and consequently most unnatural, Events and Incidents; the most exaggerated Thoughts; the most verbose and bombast Expression; the most pompous Rhymes, and thundering Versification. In comedy, nothing was so sure to please as mean buffoonery, vile ribaldry, and unmannerly jests of fools and clowns... It may be added that not only the common Audience had no notion of the rules of writing, but few even of the better sort piqu'd themselves upon any great degree of knowledge or nicety that way.

Here again is much that is wrong. Whatever we may at the moment suppose about the Elizabethan audience, Pope does not give a very convincing account of Shakespeare's drama. 'Verbose and bombast Expression' is an unfortunate term when many of Shakespeare's most moving lines are almost monosyllabic; and 'unmannerly jests' is a foolish description of all the comedy that is essentially courtly and conceited. The remarks on 'the better sort' are foolish too. Renaissance influence had caused educated Elizabethans to be much concerned with literary technique.

Shakespeare, then, 'writ to the People', but Pope will not allow the actors to escape their share of the blame. Shakespeare being himself a player (which in Pope's view was 'to keep the worst of company'), he formed his taste by players' standards, which constitute 'other principles than those of Aristotle'.

> As they live by the Majority, they know no rule but that of pleasing the present humour, and complying with the wit in fashion; a consideration which brings all their judgment to a short point. Players are just such judges of what is right as Tailors are of what is graceful. And in this view it will be but fair to allow that most of our Author's faults are less to be ascribed to his wrong judgment as a Poet than to his right judgment as a Player.

Finally, Dryden, whose Restoration world seemed to be set at a great distance from Shakespeare's, admired the zest of Elizabethan audiences but questioned their taste. Dryden was the first of the Augustans. He valued classical models and literary decorum. So although he realized that the Elizabethans were in love with poetry, he felt that they loved it without much discrimination and were more responsive to its sound than to its sense: 'For Bombast is commonly the delight of that Audience which loves Poetry but understands it not'. Elizabethan writers, therefore — although he absolves Shakespeare from the greater part of this charge — 'have made it their business to ply the ears, and to stun their Judges by their noise'.

Many of the Elizabethans said the same sort of thing, and maybe that is how later critics came to believe in it. But once again we have to remember that the better educated among Elizabethan playwrights never quite reconciled themselves to the indignity of writing for the theatre, and they could not overcome their resentment of the demanding beast whom their necessities forced them to entertain. *Auriculas asini quis non habet?* In the Prologue to *All Fools* Chapman asked:

> Who can show cause why quick Venerian jests
> Should sometimes ravish? sometimes fall far short
> Of the length and pleasure of your ears?
> When our pure dames think them much less obscene
> Than those that win your panegyric spleen?

In the Epilogue to the same play he turned again to the unpredictability and impotence of the audience's taste:

> Since all our labours are as you can like,
> We all submit to you; nor dare presume
> To think there's any real worth in them;
> Sometimes feasts please the cooks, and not the guests;
> Sometimes the guests, and curious cooks contemn them.
> Our dishes we entirely dedicate
> To our kind guests; but since ye differ so,
> Some to like only mirth without taxations,
> Some to count such works trifles, and suchlike,
> We can but bring you meat, and set you stools,
> And to our best cheer say, you all are — welcome.

Middleton's Prologue to *No Wit, No Help like a Woman's* stated the dramatist's problem with similar exasperation:

> Some for mirth they chiefly come,
> Some for passion — for both some;
> Some for lascivious meetings, that's their arrant;
> Some to detract, and ignorance their warrant.

How is't possible to please
Opinion toss'd in such wild seas?

In lines written to commiserate with Fletcher upon the chilly reception of *the Faithful Shepherdess* Jonson referred without affection to

The wise and many-headed bench that sits
Upon the life and death of plays and wits.

In his own *The Case is Altered* he spoke of the hazards that beset an author in his desire to please:

> But the sport is, at a new play, to observe the sway and variety of opinion that passeth it. A man shall have such a confused mixture of judgment poured out in the throng there, as ridiculous as laughter itself. One says he likes not the writing, another likes not the plot, another not the playing; and sometimes a fellow that comes not there past once in five years, at a parliament time or so, will be as deep mired in censuring as the best, and swear by God's foot he would never stir his foot to see a hundred such as that is.
>
> II iv 32.

The theatregoing public has always seemed wayward in its judgment to those who cater for its pleasures, and all that is surprising so far is the naive candour with which this opinion was stated in the theatregoers' own presence: Elizabethan entertainers and their audience were always frank with one another. But rancour came in too, under the strain of trying to keep the public amused and anticipating their capricious moods. Groundlings and gallants alike might find that they had paid their money to hear themselves abused. Dramatists complained that 'while the people generally are very acceptive, and apt to applaud any meritable work' (this surprising admission is Jonson's), their manners were corrupted by two elements 'that most commonly are infectious to a whole auditory'. The first is

> the rude and barbarous crew, a people that have no brains, and yet grounded judgments; these will hiss anything that mounts above their grounded capacities;

and the second 'a few capricious gallants' who

> have taken such a dislike in all things that they will approve nothing, be it never so conceited or elaborate; but sit dispersed, making faces, and spitting, wagging their upright ears, and cry *filthy! filthy!* simply uttering their own condition and using their wryed countenances instead of a Vice, to turn the good aspects of all that sit near them from what they behold.
>
> *The Case is Altered* II iv 53, 60.

Jonson wrote in the same strain in the Induction to *Every Man Out of His Humour*, where he pilloried the gallant who tried to display himself as one of the judicious, and also in the Induction to *Cynthia's Revels*. He seldom made much effort to mollify his critics.

These two elements, the rank-scented groundlings and the perfumed gallants, drew upon themselves the greatest part of the dramatists' scorn. The groundlings were easy game. They paid only a penny, and they would not easily be cajoled or bludgeoned into paying more; and although their mews and hisses could kill a play, they could be condescendingly placated with dumb-shows and trumpets and a few indecencies of the more obvious kind. Thus their uncouth habits, their smell and their meagre understandings could be exhibited to the unkind laughter of the judicious. Even their demand for beer and nuts and tobacco, from which the actors drew a welcome revenue, brought them into the way of further public insult. The dramatist Shirley, eminently a courtier, called them 'penny stinkards', accused them of chewing nuts with the congenital craving of squirrels and warned them to be careful not to crack the benches as well. Marston congratulated the audience who came to see the children at Blackfriars that there

> A man shall not be choked
> With the stench of garlic; nor be pasted
> To the balmy jacket of a beer-brewer.

Jonson said that 'the beast, the multitude...loves nothing that is right and proper. The farther it runs from reason and possibility, with them the better it is'. The publishers of the Quarto of *Troilus and Cressida* introduced it with the recommendation that the play had never been 'clapper-clawed with the palms of the vulgar' nor 'sullied with the smoky breath of the multitude'. It was to the multitude again that Webster ascribed the failure of *The White Devil*, which was rejected by the patrons of the Red Bull in spite of a fine bravura performance by Richard Perkins. The tragedy was first staged

> in so dull a time of winter, presented in so open and black a theatre, that it wanted (that which is the only grace and setting-out of a tragedy) a full and understanding auditory; and...since that time, I have noted most of the people that come to that playhouse resemble those ignorant asses who, visiting stationers' shops, their use is not to enquire for good books, but new books.

However good the play, 'the breath that comes from the uncapable multitude is able to poison it'; for 'detraction is the sworn friend to ignorance'.

According to the jaundiced playwrights, the gallants were almost as incapable of appreciating the finer points of what was set before them. A certain type of fashionable fop, the Osrics of the age, embarrassed the players by an extravagant and undiscriminating devotion to the theatre. This were the men from whom 'doth flow Naught but pure Juliet and Romeo', the men whom Dekker bade 'hoard up the finest play-scraps you can get; upon which your lean wit may most savourly feed'. They hoped that their conversation would acquire a borrowed distinction from the newest gems of playhouse poetry and wit. Typical of these play-cullers was Gullio in *1 Return from Parnassus*, who 'never spoke a witty thing but out of a play'. His appearance on stage is greeted with the warning that now 'we shall have nothing but pure Shakespeare and shreds of poetry that he has gathered at the theatres'. Gullio knows no poet like the 'sweet Mr Shakespeare': he will 'have his picture in my study at the court' and 'to honour him will lay his *Venus and Adonis* under my pillow'.

At the same time the Gullios of Elizabethan London felt that they were conferring great honour on the playwrights in condescending to notice their works. In advertising their favourite writers they were seeking to advertise themselves, and their conduct in the theatre might be insufferable. The most damning evidence of this comes from Dekker's *Gull's Horn-Book*, a satirical homily in which the ass-about-town is followed through all his favourite avocations. Dekker advises 'our feathered ostrich' to sit on the 'very rushes where the comedy is to dance, yea, and under the state of Cambyses himself', where he may make his presence known to everyone in the house and seem to arrogate to himself the responsibilities of an informed and privileged critic.

> If you know not the author, you may rail against him, and peradventure so behave yourself that you may enforce the author to know you...
>
> Present not yourself on the stage, especially at a new play, until the quaking Prologue hath by rubbing got colour unto his cheeks, and is ready to give the trumpets their cue that he is upon point to enter...It shall crown you with rich commendation to laugh aloud in the midst of the most serious and saddest scene of the terriblest tragedy; and to let that clapper your tongue be tossed so high that all the house may ring of it.
>
> If the gallant has a grudge against the author, it is easy to disgrace him if, in the middle of his play, be it pastoral or comedy, moral or tragedy, you rise with a screwed and discontented face from your stool to be gone. No matter whether the scenes be good, or no; the better they are, the worse you do distaste them. And, being on your feet, sneak not away like a coward; but salute all your gentle acquaintance that are spread either on the rushes or on stools about you; and draw what troop you can from the stage after you.

Jonson too was enraged by these 'fastidious impertinents' and 'Plush and Velvet outsides'. The Induction to *Cynthia's Revels* pictures a gallant arriving at a private theatre, busier with lighting his pipe than watching the play:

> Now, sir, suppose I am one of your genteel auditors that am come in...with much ado, and here I take my place and sit down: I have my three sorts of tobacco in my pocket, my light by me, and thus I begin.
>
> 'By this light I wonder that any man is so mad to come to see these rascally tits play here — They do act like so many wrens or pismires — not a fifth part of a good face amongst them all — And then their music is abominable — able to stretch a

man's ears worse than ten — pillories, and their ditties — most lamentable things, like the pitiful fellows that make them — poets. By this vapour, an 'twere not for tobacco — I think — the very stench of 'em would poison me, I should not dare to come in at their gates — A man were better visit fifteen jails — or a dozen or two of hospitals — than once adventure to come near them'.

When Puritan critics denounce patrons of the drama as 'a brood of Hell-bred creatures' and the actor's art as 'only scratching the itching humours of scabbed minds', they are being hardly more censorious than the dramatists themselves, and we have to wonder what lay behind this curious practice of insulting the cash customers. It cannot have been wholly justified or there would have been no Elizabethan drama. Men did not go to the theatre solely for the pleasure of hissing or embarrassing the performances; if they had, there would soon have been no actors or dramatists to gratify them. The prerogative of destroying a play by overt expression of dislike has belonged to audiences since the theatre began, and certainly the Elizabethans exercised it. In their tiny playhouses this damning of a play must have been awe-inspiring and quite final. The Induction to Marston's *What You Will* called attention to the arrival of the 'Knights of the Mew', the terrible trio of Signior Snuff, Monsieur Mew and Cavaliero Blirt, 'three of the most-to-be-fear'd Auditors', who will keep the author on edge lest

> drunken Censure belch out sour breath,
> From Hatred's surfeit on his labour's front...
> Some boundless ignorance should on sudden shoot
> His gross-knobb'd bird-bolt, with *That's not so good,*
> *Mew, blirt, ha ha, light chaffy stuff.*

When occasion demanded, and sometimes when it did not, disapproval might be noisy and malicious.

Nor is it to be doubted that men of fashion sometimes behaved deplorably. The dramatists may have exaggerated, but they cannot have invented, the rehearsed antics which distracted audience and players alike, the affected disdain and the equally artificial obbligatos of appreciation. To some extent it seems to have been required by the manners of the age. *Love's Labour's Lost* and *A Midsummer Night's Dream* both illustrate the ridicule which courtiers and their dependants might bestow upon an Interlude painfully constructed for their pleasure. The plays are acted to a running fire of offensive and patronizing comment. Both Theseus (*MND* V i 82-105) and the Princess of France (*LLL* V ii 516-21) ask that honest endeavour be given a courteous hearing, but their pleas are disregarded. Such a reception must have been common in great men's houses, for in *Taming of a Shrew* Sly says, 'Sim, stand by me, and we'll flout the players out of their coats'.

In the public theatres the audience were well able to administer their own correctives to those whose behaviour displeased the majority. Most people, both high and low, wanted to enjoy the play, and their first inclination was to give it a chance. Although disappointed dramatists sometimes chose to believe that their play had been discredited by a claque of hecklers hired by a jealous rival, it is unlikely that such a group would have much influence if the majority were well disposed. Outbreaks of drunken rowdiness in the yard could be silenced, and the gallants too had to be wary of a hostile reaction. Dekker supplied his Gullio with advice on the correct line of action when the 'scarecrows in the yard hoot at you, hiss at you, spit at you, yea throw dirt even in your teeth: 'tis most gentlemanlike patience to endure all this and to laugh at the silly animals'. But there are times when discretion is the better part of gentlemanliness. 'If the rabble with a full throat cry: Away with the fool! you were worse than a madman to tarry by it: for the gentleman and the fool should never sit on the stage together'.

If we take their written words at face value, the dramatists seem to have protested more vehemently than they needed. In practice their rebukes were probably part of a good-humoured give-and-take between the actors and the audience. Mockery of the spectators' taste and intelligence has always been a popular jest in the music-hall and in any theatre where the actors can make a direct address to the audience. It is only the convention of 'the fourth wall', the pretence that the audience does not exist, that prevents it. In the Elizabethan theatre discipline was a further and important consideration. The actors were responsible for the policing of their premises, with the authorities ever anxious to close them on the least excuse of misconduct or disturbance. To protect their own livelihood the players had to be constantly disciplining the audience by reminding them from the stage that certain standards of behaviour had to be maintained. A fusillade of abuse may seem a curious way of doing this, but if delivered and taken good-humouredly, as probably most of it was, it would achieve its object.

For the rest, the dramatists' railing often sprang from injured vanity. Creative artists often find it hard to preserve a truly democratic respect for the right of personal judgment, and it would seem that the myth of the barbarous and undiscriminating ignorance of the Elizabeth public had its origin in those disappointed authors who saw the pearls of their inspiration sniffed at and rejected by swine from the stews of Alsatia. They never could endure it that the plebs should sit in judgment on them. That dramatists should have to 'stand to a popular censure for any thing they present' is the recurrent, exasperated, half-incredulous theme of their outbursts. Jonson grieved that 'the rankest stinkard of them all will take upon himself as peremptory as if he had writ himself *in artibus magister*'; and Dekker reminded the courtier that the stage allows

> a stool as well to the farmer's son as to your Templar; that your stinkard has the
> selfsame liberty to be there in his tobacco-fumes which our sweet courtier hath;
> and that your carman and tinker claim as strong a voice in their suffrage, and sit to

give judgment on the play's life and death, as well as the proudest Momus among the tribe of critic.

Under the sting of disappointment Jonson was willing to blame anybody, Momus as well as stinkard. In *Cynthia's Revels*, written for a private theatre, he announced that his Muse did not concern herself with

> popular applause
> Or foamy praise that drops from common jaws;

and in the Induction to *Every Man Out of His Humour*, too, he had made his pitch for the higher levels of the market. He would 'scourge those apes' who 'contemn all physic of the mind', and he would write only for such 'attentive auditors' as would

> join their profit with their pleasure,
> And come to feed their understanding parts.

The failure of *Sejanus*, acted at the Globe in 1603 with Shakespeare in the cast, determined him to bid no longer for 'common suffrages', although when he published the play in the following year he alleged that he had had a collaborator whose share had now been excised. Much later, in *The Staple of News* (1625) he declared that it was offered

> as a rite
> To scholars that can judge, and fair report,
> The sense they hear, above the vulgar sort
> Of nut-crackers that only come for sight.

When writing in this spirit, piqued and disappointed dramatists have helped to create the picture of an audience so radically divided between the vulgar and the judicious that no artist could serve them. Jonson was always very bitter towards those playwrights, often men much less talented than himself, who found a formula for successful work in the public theatre, but the 'Attic judgments' whom he flattered were just as unpredictable as the penny stinkards. The stinkards at least could be relied upon to respond to certain well-known stimuli, but a man could never be sure that he had found the secret of appealing to the educated. The judicious should have reprieved *Sejanus*, they should have been the 'attentive auditors' whose understandings, appropriately fed, took physic from *Every Man Out of His Humour*. When he found them unequal to these critical burdens, Jonson brought them, as well as the groundlings, under his lash. Even before the failure of *Sejanus* Dekker had alluded to this ambivalent attitude when in *Satiromastix* he brought on stage Captain Tucca, a character from Jonson's own *Poetaster*, to charge Horace/Jonson with first trying to 'screw and wriggle himself into great men's familiarity' by his blatant flattery, and then denouncing them when they dared to disparage his work: 'when your plays are misliked at Court, you shall not cry mew like a puss-cat, and say you are glad you write out of the courtier's element'.

On the whole the Elizabethan dramatists were unreliable guides to the true nature of their audiences because — like dramatists at any time in the history of the theatre — they were trying to rationalize failures which they would not attribute to any defect in themselves. But one voice is conspicuously absent from these recriminatory pronouncements. Shakespeare's only significant comment on the audience occurs in the scene between Hamlet and the touring players. In its reference to theatre it is an untypical scene because Shakespeare was seldom explicitly topical. He was much too experienced and professional to write plays that would be caviare to the general, and it was Hamlet's opinion rather than his that the censure of the judicious must be allowed to 'o'erweigh a whole theatre of others'. Himself he never harangued the audience in the dyspeptic tones adopted by so many of his associates. Not many of his prologues have survived, although it was probably a regular custom to open the performance with some introductory lines, if only to quieten the audience and tell them that the play was begun. Shakespeare's method was to come at once to the matter in hand. Refraining both from innuendoes about the audience and boastful generalizations about the dramatist's art, his prologues aim to tell the spectators something about the play, contributing to its character and mood. In his epilogues likewise his tone was warm and natural and friendly, neither expostulatory nor patronizing; his only aim to send them cheerfully to their homes. *2 Henry IV* dismisses them with the promise of more fat meat, 'if you be not too much cloyed' with it. The Chorus of *Henry V* concludes in simple words the patriotic appeal of the play:

> Small time: but in that small, most greatly lived
> This star of England.

In *Twelfth Night* and *Love's Labour's Lost* the audience depart on the lovely notes of a song, and Puck awakens them from their dream with his affectionate farewell:

> If we shadows have offended,
> Think but this, and all is mended...
> So good night unto you all.
> Give me your hands, if we be friends:
> And Robin shall restore amends.

Nowhere perhaps does Shakespeare so faithfully reveal his relations with his audience as in Rosalind's valediction at the close of *As You Like It*:

It is not the fashion to see the lady the epilogue: but it is no more unhandsome than to see the lord the prologue. If it be true that good wine needs no bush, 'tis true that a good play needs no epilogue: yet to good wine they do use good bushes; and good plays prove the better by the help of good epilogues. What a case am I in then, that am neither a good epilogue nor cannot insinuate with you in the behalf of a good play. I am not furnished like a beggar, therefore to beg will not become me: my way is to conjure you, and I'll begin with the women. I charge you, O women, for the love you bear to men, to like as much of this play as please you: and I charge you, O men, for the love you bear to women — as I perceive by your simpering, none of you hates them — that between you and the women the play may please. If I were a woman, I would kiss as many of you as had beards that pleased me, complexions that liked me, and breaths that I defied not: and I am sure, as many as have good beards, or good faces, or sweet breaths, will, for my kind offer, when I make curtsy, bid me farewell.

The note here is, above all, tolerant. It shows no fear of the audience, nor any resentment of its sovereign caprice. No one is rebuked or disparaged or sneered at. Shakespeare and his audience seem to have found each other good fellows, parting on humorous and friendly terms and looking forward to their next meeting. He, at least, was content to abide by 'the yea and no of general ignorance'.

What manner of men were they? Obviously it is unwise to give too much credit to the theatre's Puritan enemies or to playwrights momentarily deflated in their self-esteem. But having received the sanction of eighteenth-century critics, their opinions went unchallenged for too long, with the result that editors have felt themselves free to emend the texts, and directors to make cuts and interpolations on behalf of audiences held to be so much more enlightened than the Elizabethans that they must not be expected to receive Shakespeare's work as he actually wrote it. More recent criticism has possibly found in Elizabethan audiences more virtues than they were endowed with, but at least it is no longer believed that they were barbarians whose crudity and ignorance prevented a race of giants from attaining full stature.

In any age the term *audience* is an abstraction used, rather dangerously, to signify a body of diverse people. The danger arises if we try to equate the audience of 1600 with the audience of, say, Dr Johnson's period or our own, for not only were they different people as individuals but they made a very different sort of body in the aggregate. Shakespeare's own audience included at one extreme a number of people who have long ago ceased to go to the theatre at all, and many of these nowadays attend race-tracks, amusement arcades and bingo halls more often than they watch films or television. At the other extreme was a social and intellectual aristocracy whose modern counterparts, while they do not disdain the theatre, visit it much less often and with less knowledge and enthusiasm. There is no element in a twentieth-century audience to match in youth, wit and energy the students from the Inns of Court or the better sort of apprentice. Except at the state-subsidized drama of Athens there probably has never been an audience composed of so many diverse elements, and the drama of Athens was a religious rite where attendance was compulsory.

The particular character of the Elizabethan audience was established by one of those simple acts that have illimitable consequences: when James Burbage opened the first professional theatre, he set the minimum charge at one penny. He need not have done so. In view of the hostility of the authorities, he might well have thought it prudent to exclude the rougher elements that came to the inns, and to welcome only courtiers and the more prosperous and respectable of the citizens and shopkeepers. His decision to put his entertainment within reach of the working-class set his son's company on the path to success and greatness. It also detemined the genius of Elizabethan drama, which lost its virility when it began to cater for coteries rather than the broad mass of the people.

The sum of one penny was aimed at the pocket of the artisan, and it made the theatre cheaper than most of his amusements and some of his necessaries. The best way to discover the value of money in past generations is to enquire how long a penny took to earn and what might be bought with it. In figures Elizabethan incomes seem very small. The Queen's revenue in normal times was less than £250,000 a year, and on this, and on such 'extra-ordinary' revenue as she could squeeze from parliament, she had to govern the nation. Only a handful of Elizabethans had an income of more than a thousand a year, and the number of very rich men would not have filled the Globe for a single performance. Earnings of forty shillings a year seem to have raised a man slightly above the lowest group of wage-earners, but the value of money fell fairly steadily during the sixteenth century and wages lagged behind prices. In London, where wages and costs were higher than in the provinces, the skilled artisan earned perhaps sixteen pence a day and the ordinary workman about a shilling, while the wage for a man who worked in a shop came somewhere between the two, about eight shillings a week. Food prices fluctuated with the yield of the harvest and varied from one district to another. On an average, eggs cost a halfpenny, butter a penny a pound, cream one shilling and sixpence a gallon, a pig a shilling, a sheep six shillings. Ordinary clothing, which was manufactured by domestic craftsmen enjoying government protection, was durable and cheap.

Thus the ordinary Londoner's earnings would provide him with his necessaries in reasonable abundance without leaving a great deal for his pleasures. An afternoon in the tavern might be expensive as although he could have a quart of small beer for a penny, ale cost fourpence a quart and sack eightpence, with a pipe of tobacco costing a further threepence. For men of different inclination there were dogs and bears mauling each other in Paris Garden, and this show was to be had at about the same price as a visit to the theatre. Cut-price drabs could be hired for sixpence, but money might have to be spent on their further entertainment. On the other hand, if money were short, the Londoner could see a flogging or an execution for nothing, or take the air in Finsbury Fields and watch the archers display their skill.

A visit to the theatre would therefore be chosen in preference to several alternative recreations, and although it was less expensive than most of them, it was not so cheap that the artisan could afford to go whenever he pleased, even supposing him to have had the time. If he took his wife and son, the outing would cost him about a shilling by the time he had bought refreshments for them and ale or tobacco for himself. In that sense the admission charge was delusively low, for it was never the management's intention that the spectator should get away with paying that and nothing else. So at least in the cheaper parts of the house, the audience consisted of enthusiasts who went to the theatre, at some sacrifice, because they enjoyed it. In the thirties of the present century, we are told, sixty-five Americans in every hundred went to the cinema at least once a week. In face of this numbing statistic the Elizabethan theatre was only sparsely attended; but when in 1613 the Watermen's Company petitioned the Privy Council for the return of all the theatres to Bankside, they estimated the daily attendance to be between three or four thousand, or some twenty thousand a week. This means that about ten per cent of Londoners went to the theatre weekly, although the figure obviously included visitors; and this despite the attraction of many alternative amusements and despite charges which, low as they were, were high enough to prevent the ordinary artisan from taking his family more than once in a while.

These matter-of-fact considerations dispose of much of the cant and misrepresentation about Shakespeare's audience. Wherever crowds gather, the 'wide boys' will gather also: they accompanied Moses out of Egypt and Xenophon to the sea, and they find work to do at race-meetings and fairs. The theatres attracted their proportion of pickpockets, confidence-men, harlots and miscellaneous undesirables; but these folk, intent upon their professional concerns, did not all stand in the yard, and in any case outbreaks of disorder were not in their interest. Occasionally a bunch of drunken roughs were spoiling for a fight, but not nearly as often as the authorities pretended. Fear of disturbance was always present in the minds of those charged with the duty of keeping the Queen's peace. The unlighted streets were dangerous after dark; on holidays the apprentices might be looking for trouble; bands of serving-men pursued obscure feuds, and the street scenes in *Romeo and Juliet* would be familiar enough to Londoners. Another well-known play, *Sir John Oldcastle*, opens with the followers of the Lords Herbert and Powis cutting each other to pieces in the streets of Hereford. But these disturbances were likelier to occur in the streets, the public play-grounds and the taverns than in the tight-packed theatres, where the majority were bent on watching the play. Although the authorities were eager for any opportunity to close the theatres after a riot, it is remarkable how few opportunities were afforded them. Moreover, the audience had their own sharp way with felons and pickpockets when they caught them, and they could be trusted to carry out their own policing. Rough and unlettered they may have been, but the groundlings in the yard paid their money to hear the play. If they wanted to fight or drink or play cards, their needs were abundantly supplied elsewhere.

The regular patrons of the galleries were the more prosperous citizens and their wives, sober, industrious folk like the pair who brought their apprentice Ralph to the theatre and saw him play *The Knight of the Burning Pestle*. Their tastes were simple, inclining to patriotic chronicles, citizen comedy and romance. Their participation seems to have been warm, and they were not incapable of intelligent appreciation. By their side in the galleries must always have been numbers of people who, because they were not inhabitants of London, found a visit to a real theatre a novel and exciting experience. Travellers from abroad, seamen home after a long voyage, wide-eyed country-folk marvelling at the pageant of London life, found the theatre too unfamiliar to be blasé or disaffected in their response to it.

Two other groups, the apprentices and the lawyers from the Inns of Court, contributed a higher proportion of young manhood than is normally to be found in a modern playhouse. What was written about 'the clamorous fry' from the Inns suggests that their reactions were outspoken and uninhibited, but youthful exuberance did not dull their responsiveness to fine issues. It has been said that the four London Inns constituted England's third university, intellectually on a level with Oxford and Cambridge and socially more influential. The young law-students came mostly from the landed gentry through whom the Tudors governed the country. Because they were young their taste was not flawless, and some of their enthusiasms and prejudices were hastily conceived; but their studies sharpened their wits, and their values were nurtured on the traditions and responsibilities of a governing class. Later they would form the hard core of resistance to Stuart folly, and their sons would fill the benches of the Long Parliament. In the meantime they were an audience for whom a young dramatist might fitly stretch his powers. The apprentices, too, were apt and lively. Nearly all the guilds required a fair standard of education, and their appprentices were mostly youths of Shakespeare's own class, with the solid foundation of a grammar-school training.

Finally, occupying the lords' rooms in the galleries (and, according to de Witt, above the stage) and in some theatres sitting on the stage itself, were the courtiers and the sons of the nobility. Here again youth may have been predominant, but the influence of this element of the audience is difficult to estimate. Some of the dramatists disliked them, or affected to, and it seems that at times a handful of gallants behaved objectionably. On the other hand, Gullio is not easily identified with the 'divers of worship' who spoke for Shakespeare against Chettle and Greene and seem to have stepped on the stage to grace his early comedies. Nor is it very helpful to observe that there were foolish courtiers as well as wise ones and that Gullio was among the foolish. So, no doubt, he was; but so, in a superficial regard, was Osric, who despite his mincing ways seems to have held a responsible position at the court of Claudius, and Claudius was not a fool. Their faults, so easy to exaggerate for comic effect, seem to have been the faults of their class, a social quirk of the age. We have already noticed how disdainfully they would treat a simple entertainment honestly prepared for their recreation, and however much Shakespeare may have admired their wit and elegance, he was not blind to the brutal heartlessness of some of their habits. High spirits took a dangerously ugly shape when a group of lordlings fell to hounding Shylock and thought the loss of his daughter to be the best joke Venice had known. This craving for cruel sensation might in time become the restless appetite of Tybalt, which must have blood for its satisfaction. Shakespeare was not alone in sensing this. Much of Fletcher's tragi-comedy might have been written expressly for Tybalt.

In the theatre, then, the virtues of the gallants were qualified by the inherited or social weaknesses of their caste. Their sense of *noblesse oblige* was not large enough to restrain them from attempting to distract actors and audience by a display of bad manners, but the sport would have lost its savour for them as soon as everyone joined in: which may go some way towards explaining the dramatists' pointed references. In most respects they must have provided an admirable audience. They were picturesque, cultured and amusing, they loved poetry, they brightened the theatre with their colour and charm. They were not entertained by the cruder sort of clowning, nor did they care to wade aimlessly through a sea of blood and pronounce *Titus Andronicus* to be Shakespeare's finest play. They were guilty rather of a vitiated taste that leaned towards the more sophisticated cruelty that was a dark stain on Renaissance culture. This developed into the tortured abnormalities of Jacobean tragedy, where sensation rather than passion drives the play forward. Their vaunted love of poetry, too, may have been partial and insincere. They wore it like a badge, and although Gullio in his way was an enthusiast for the theatre, it was a narrow way and not altogether free of affectation. He picked a line of poetry for his tablets rather as he picked a ribbon for his bonnet or a jewel for his ear, and equally he regarded it as a personal adornment.

It is rash to generalize about a coherent and influential class. Many Elizabethan noblemen had fine and civilized minds, and Shakespeare was not the only playwright to benefit from their patronage and their interest in the theatre. But we shall misunderstand the Elizabethan theatre if we look only to the courtiers in the audience for the leavening of the judicious whose influence, if supposedly it had not been overweighed by baser judgments, would have elevated and purified the popular drama. The patronage of court and nobility gave the actors political and financial advantages without which they might have found it difficult to survive. How far it stimulated them artistically is more doubtful. One or two plays may have been commissioned for private performance on particular occasions, but they were adapted for the public theatre afterwards. The plays which the actors took to the court had already proved themselves on a larger stage, and if the Queen really did demand to see Sir John in love, this may well reflect the critical capacity of herself and her close adherents. The truly judicious were those in the audience who were capable of a full response to a wide-ranging play; and these belonged to all ages and classes, not to one class only.

From an audience so diverse in character a dramatist could only expect a mixed response, and it was Shakespeare's particular art to unify it. On occasion the whole body would be moved as one man by a dramatic situation, an outburst of poetry or the tense unfolding of passion. In his lines on the Red Bull Dekker wrote:

> Give me that man
> Who ...
> Can call the banish'd auditor home, and tie
> His ear with golden chains of melody:
> Can draw with adamantine pen even creatures
> Forg'd out of th'hammer on tip-toe to reach up,
> And from rare silence clap their brawny hands
> T'applaud what their charm'd soul scarce understands.

This is the rare and authentic theatre magic, but for the most part the response may have been more fragmentary, with each section of the audience awaiting its particular gratification. Not everyone wishes to listen to Henry IV when Falstaff is waiting in the wings, and the playwright could not hope to be pleasing all the people all the time. He had to provide the simpler forms of poetry for the sonnet-loving Gullio, dumb-show and action for the groundlings, rhetorical bombast and classical allusion for the 'termers' of the Inns, topicality for the London-proud citizenry, and bawdry for everyone, ranging from the broad jesting of the clowns to the recondite indecencies which Mercutio shared with the scholars and the courtiers. Shakespeare often, and in their better moments some of the others, wove these varied materials into a texture that had a recognizable pattern. In his hands the scattered, fragmentary response of a disparate cross-section of the people merged into a single, unified response to a work of art, and the reader who troubles to take apart any of the greater plays, breaking it into its component parts, may see how it was done. *Romeo and Juliet*, usually dismissed as only an apprentice tragedy, was a tale of star-crossed love with an appeal to simple sentiment. Into it Shakespeare put Mercutio's sharp unsentimental wit, but added the Queen Mab speech for Gullio to put down in his note-book; brought to earth the lyrical transports of Romeo by setting against them other and contrasted notions about love — the bloodless, cynical bawdry of the serving-men, the bourgeois calculations of the match-making Capulets, the earthy sexuality of the Nurse; for the groundlings he provided street-fighting and a mortal duel, for the politically conscious some sobering reflections on the injuries brought to the community by a family vendetta: all this, and more, transmuted into art by poetry and passion.

We cannot deplore the taste of an audience that made demands of this kind upon a great writer; we should instead be grateful for the eager appetites which insisted upon so much. The diversity of the Elizabethan audience, over which some scholars have grieved, was the source of its strength. The penny admission brought into the theatre a vertical cross-section of the whole nation. The only absentees, apart from the rural poor, were those — again a vertical division, not horizontal — who accepted some part or other of the Puritan opposition to the drama. Their absence was to be regretted because it meant that there was an important part of the community whom the dramatists were unable to address. But everyone else was there, without distinction of age or sex or class or income. The theatre is not to be measured only by the entertainment it provided on the stage. It meant also colour, warmth of feeling, a place to meet one's friends and rub shoulders with one's betters, a forum for debate, a sounding-board for gossip and the latest news. It was a place, above all, where one participated in something.

Yet in spite of its diversity, an Elizabethan audience was in some important respects remarkably homogeneous. Although distinctions of status were marked and jealously guarded, the nation was bound together by a cultural unity that made these divisions in the last analysis merely formal. The basic assumptions were common to all men. They loved and obeyed the Queen; quarrelsome as they were about the externals of worship and the reverence due to bishops, they were united on the necessity of being religious; all were agreed on the high destiny of their country; only a few sceptics as yet were questioning the medieval assurance of man's place in the universe midway between the beasts and the angels. In an organic community a man's worth was still judged by the contribution he made in his work and his play to the community's good. The probings of science had not yet disturbed all moral values, and capitalism was only just beginning to disturb men's traditional relationships. Whatever the differences of birth or education, all men were brought up on the same legends and traditions, the same interpretation of history, the same fundamental sense of the ties that bound men to one another and all men to their Creator.

Moreover, everyone used a similar language. When even men of high birth unaffectedly spoke the dialect of their native shires (Ralegh's west-country burr was notorious), there were no barriers of accent, and there-fore no standard pronunciation to embarrass those unable to achieve it. Shakespeare characterized the speech of his yokels not by suggesting that words sounded differently in their mouths but by giving them the freedom of a vocabulary which they could not master. Words are the vesture of ideas and common usages, and it follows that the possession of roughly the same ideas will require the use of roughly the same words. Thus the language of Shakespeare was the language of a whole society, a society deriving its rights, privileges and obligations from a landed economy that had not yet been challenged. Men spoke to each other in the same way because they spoke about the same things and attached the same meanings to the words they used. The language did not lend itself to intellectual subtleties or fine-drawn abstractions, and the new school of 'metaphysical' poets had to practise new tricks with it. Still less was it an instrument of scientific precision, and Bacon knew that for purposes of science and philosophy he would practically have to make a new one. But in daily intercourse it was supremely a language for poets. The imagery of the Elizabethan poet was intelligible to all of his audience since he was able to draw it from occupations and experiences that all of them shared. Prose and poetry were idiomatic and alive, finding their similitudes in the daily routine of buying and selling, in the rural activities in which even townsmen participated, the sports of the countryside and the universal business of ploughing and threshing and bringing in the harvest. Everyone had knowledge of the primary means of production even if he was not personally concerned in it, and the city financier had a countryman's awareness of birds and flowers and the unchanging rhythm of the seasons.

When Bacon, a courtier and a scholar, was seeking an effective generalization about the distribution of wealth, he wrote 'money is like muck, not good unless it be spread': instinctively turning to the rustic task of dunging to express an economic proposition in language intelligible to himself and all his readers. To Shakespeare the fickleness of love found natural expression as 'the uncertain glory of an April day', and throughout the Sonnets love in all its forms presents itself in a profusion of natural images. Nature, again, supplied him with an image for the perils of public life:

> This is the state of man: to-day he puts forth
> The tender leaves of hopes; to-morrow blossoms,
> And bears his blushing honours thick upon him;
> The third day comes a frost, a killing frost,
> And when he thinks, good easy man, full surely
> His greatness is a-ripening, nips his root.

Hen VIII III ii 352.

On the maintenance of law and order in the state he writes:

> We must not make a scarecrow of the law,
> Setting it up to fear the birds of prey;
> And let it keep one shape till custom make it
> Their perch, and not their terror.

MM II i 1.

Most of his imagery was drawn in this way from the sports and activities of the countryside, the weather, the trees and animals, the bodily occupations of men and women whose life was lived close to Nature. With dramatic simplicity he would employ some everyday experience to give shape to a subtle conception difficult to express in the limited language of Elizabethan metaphysics; and the homely metaphor lends the thought the force and comfort of the familiar.

This concentration of a whole society upon a limited range of pursuits and satisfactions, together with a fast-evolving language to express it, presented the creative writer with a remarkable opportunity. It may be that it was a unique opportunity. It may be that the achievement of Shakespeare and his fellows in the art of poetic drama was possible only when the nation was passing from medievalism into a rather frightening world in which each class would develop its own systems of thought and habits of life and would ultimately produce its own particular ways of speech.[1] All art is communication, and to the dramatist language is all-important. Shakespeare's supreme advantage was the certainty of being understood. He could give life and dimension to his characters through simple illustrations which all his hearers would recognize. In those days there was only one way of writing, and playwrights who experimented with artificial words and a bookish style were laughed at by their fellows. This pretentiousness was one of the themes of the *Poetomachia* and it was rebuked in other literary debates of the day.

Thus the audience's emotional participation in the poetry enacted before it was important creatively for the dramatist. Always in the search for Shakespeare we have to be conscious that we are missing something. Even if a company could exactly reproduce the architecture and acting conditions of the Globe, we should not recapture the effect his poetry had upon those who heard it first. Because many of them could not read, they were better listeners than we are. The spoken word, written to be understood at speed, was the essence of poetic drama, and the Elizabethans gloried in the jewelled utterance and high astounding terms that sounded on the stage. Perhaps they were not very critical in their appreciation, and Dryden was right to suspect that they loved poetry better than they understood it, roaring their approval of much bombast they would have been better without. But they were not afraid of passion. They saw life's main issues clearly and they could weep for the tragic consequences of error without expecting sin to be clouded in a mist of psychological explanations. Familiarity with fell deeds had not choked all pity in them, for *King Lear* was not written for the insensitive: savages would just have laughed to see the old man helpless in the storm. They preferred their drama, or most of it, to be larger than life and to

1   This view is developed by L,C.Knights in the early chapters of his *Drama and Society* in *the Age of Jonson.*

concern kings and princes above their station, but they faced issues that a politer mode of playgoing prefers to shirk. As soon as the professional theatre began to bid for an audience that was not universal, the drama began to decline.

Nor did the court make any specific contribution to drama as an art. Elizabeth saw as many plays as her anxious thrift would allow. James was a lavish patron, and possibly discriminating when he was sober enough to follow the scene, but his court also enjoyed the music and spectacle of the masque, where poetry became stylized and less significant. Charles I and Henrietta Maria were enthusiastic. The Queen actually took part in 'theatricals' at the court, which earned her the censure of William Prynne (although it would have been her portion anyway). Charles is known to have had a special sympathy for the predicament of Malvolio, and he had some feeling for Parolles too: there is scope for an imaginative thesis here. But the court's role was strangely passive throughout. It appears to have been content with the standards of the professional companies, whose status it did much to preserve. But unless we are to accept theories about the assistance provided for the professional authors by Bacon and other courtiers, it offered no positive inspiraton (other than for Sir John in love).

In time the court's taste declined and its interests narrowed. In the twenty years following Shakespeare's death plays were written more and more for the court, the gentry and the universities, at the expense of the broad-based audiences of the common stages. The Crown too was losing the sympathy and understanding of the people, and court and poets withdrew together into the sand. When poetry was touched with the blight of Caroline escapism, it evaded the great questions it had boldly faced not so long ago. Caroline verse, exquisite minor poetry, is heavy with fragance, but it is the fragrance of flowers strewn on a coffin. When the Catholic armies were pressing to the Baltic and the Protestant cause had shrunk to a few beleaguered garrisons, the court poets piped in tremulous voices of the peace which seemed to bless their sheltered land.

> White Peace (the beautifull'st of things)
> Seems here her everlasting rest
> To fix, and spreads her downy wings
>   Over the nest.

Richard Fanshawe, An Ode (1630).

It was not a time to sing of hock-carts, wassails, wakes and cleanly wantonness, for poetry should have weightier themes in years heavy with postponed crisis.

Since it was breaking the popular associations from which it had once drawn its strength, these were sorry days for the drama too. In the lonely mind of the King, Shakespeare was sovereign still, but the Queen and her entourage found refreshment in the graceful, empty verse of Fletcher and Shirley. In the winter of 1630-1 the King's Men acted twenty plays before the court. Ten of them were by Beaumont and Fletcher, and only one, the light-weight *Midsummer Night's Dream*, was Shakespeare's. A new race of 'university wits' arose, Thomas Randolph, William Cartwright, William Strode, Peter Hausted and others, men who were resident in Oxford or Cambridge and liked to persuade the professionals to perform their plays. Various courtly amateurs joined them in paying for public performance of their work. Although the years had softened Jonson's asperity, this was altogether too much for him. In the Induction to *The Magnetic Lady* (1632) he turned upon the 'poets, poetaccios, poetasters, poetitos...all haberdashers of small wit' whose birth, money or superior education won them a footing on the stage.

Shakespeare did not live to see these events. The audience for which he learned his trade was the many-headed monster of the public theatres, and he did not remain long in the business after the Blackfriars opened. The special quality of his drama was its appeal to an audience diverse in its parts but united in submission to his spell. Always we seem to come back to James Burbage and his penny fee. Without it, drama might have remained a courtly and academic exercise, and Shakespeare might never have left Stratford.

Part IV
Shakespeare Personally

Chapter X
London and Stratford

Yet hath my night of life some memory.

CE V i 314.

Writing towards the close of the eighteenth century, the editor George Steevens observed that

> all that we know of Shakespeare is that he was born at Stratford-on-Avon; married and had children there; went to London, where he commenced actor, and wrote plays and poems; returned to Stratford, made his will, and died.

Even in Steevens's own day more of Shakespeare's story was known than this, and what men did not know they showed much fertility in inventing: his biography has never been barren of conjecture. The second half of his life is better documented than the first, and over the years scholars have patiently accumulated scraps of information which have enabled them to date many of the plays with reasonable certainty and to build a fragmentary picture of his life in London and Stratford. By 1594, as we know, he was a sharer in the Lord Chamberlain's company of players, in whose fellowship he was to continue for the rest of his professional career; but the present chapter is concerned less with his public life than with the life he lived outside the theatre.

The first record of him after 1594 is a sad one: the burial at Stratford on 11 August 1596 of his son Hamnet, one of the twins born in 1585. What this meant to Shakespeare the following pages will reveal. In addition to the personal loss, he had to abandon his hopes of one day devising an estate upon the son of his body. Anne had borne him no children for the past eleven years and it was unlikely now that she would conceive again. In those days of swift and sudden mortality the life of a single boy was a poor insurance against the future, and the death of Hamnet can never have been wholly unexpected. Thereafter Shakespeare would have to base his deferred hopes on the posterity of his daughters, and there too he was to be disappointed.

Several critics have found evidence of Shakespeare's anguish in the lamentation of Constance over the dead Arthur (*KJ* III iv). But although *King John* was almost certainly written at about this time, this display of grief is unlikely to have been the expression of a personal and private emotion. This was never Shakespeare's way. The Lament was the accepted medieval mode for the statement of tragic feeling. Constance's formal exaggeration of her distress, with the elaborate conceit of her invocation of the 'odoriferous stench' of death, exasperated her hearers, politicians reared in the new school of Commodity. They bade her bind up her dishevelled hair and roundly told her, in language that Claudius and Laertes were to use of Hamlet, that her excessive grief was a form of madness. Their taunts at last drew from her a dignified reply: 'He talks to me that never had a son'; but this was the only line in the whole performance that spoke of genuine natural feeling, and King Philip assured her that she was as fond of grief as of her dead child. It does no honour to Shakespeare's sorrow to identify it with the parade of a theatrical convention.

The consequences of Hamnet's death are possibly to be found in Shakespeare's leaving his lodgings in the parish of St Helen's, Bishopsgate, and buying a house in Stratford. In spite of containing the Bethlehem ('Bedlam') hospital for the insane, this was quite a fashionable district that at various times accommodated Sir Thomas Gresham, a Lord Mayor of London and the musician Thomas Morley: the common player had found a 'desirable area' to live in. In October 1596, for the purpose of a parliamentary subsidy, Shakespeare was assessed at 5s. on goods valued at £5. Twelve months later this had not been paid, the collectors reporting that he was among those who had defaulted because they were presumed to have died or left the district. Following a new subsidy in 1597, Shakespeare was marked down for 13s. 4d., but this too was unpaid, and it was eventually referred to the Bishop of Winchester's Liberty of the Clink on Bankside, where presumably satisfaction was obtained. Further evidence that Shakespeare left Bishopsgate at about this time is to be found in a document of November 1596 in which William Wayte sought sureties of the peace, 'for fear of death', against Shakespeare, Francis Langley, Dorothy Soer and Anne Lee. A few weeks earlier Langley had sought similar sureties against Wayte and his step-father, William Gardiner, a Justice of the Peace in Surrey and an unscrupulous landowner. Langley was the financier and speculator who built the ill-fated Swan, and this establishes a theatrical connection that might somehow involve Shakespeare. But we do not know how Shakespeare, by all reports a most peaceable man, or the two ladies came to be involved in the quarrel, if indeed he was involved at all. Wayte was a small-time rogue previously described as 'a certain loose person of no reckoning or value', entirely under the thumb of his step-father. It is significant, however, that the writ of attachment against Shakespeare was issued to the Sheriff of Surrey.

This suggests that he had moved to Bankside by the end of 1596, a year before the Theatre was demolished and his company were looking for other

1 See L.Hotson, *Shakespeare versus Shallow*; Schoenbaum 198-9.

quarters. Even if, as has been suggested, they played at the Swan for a while before the Globe was ready, that does not explain why he moved as early as he did; and in any case it is more probable that they used their 'easer' at the Curtain. Then in May 1597 he bought New Place, the second largest property in Stratford. The house was built sometime after 1483 by Sir Hugh Clopton, Lord Mayor of London, opposite the Guild Chapel that he had 're-edified'. The Cloptons did not live there very much, and during the 1540s it was leased to the King's physician and former president of the College of Physicians, Dr Thomas Bentley. In 1563 the Cloptons surrendered the title to William Bott, formerly of Snitterfield, who four years later sold it to a Warwickshire lawyer, William Underhill, for £40. When Shakespeare bought it from Underhill's heir, also William, for £60, the property had acquired sinister associations from its recent owners. Although he was never charged with the murder, Bott was suspected locally of having poisoned his own daughter in order to secure her husband's inheritance, and the deed may have been committed at New Place; and the second Underhill was poisoned by his eldest son, who was duly hanged.

Shakespeare paid a further sum when the sale was confirmed in 1602, but the property was in bad repair and he at once spent money on renovations and improvements. A load of stone sold to the Corporation in 1598 was presumably material remaining over. The house had a fine frontage of 60 feet, a depth of 70 feet, and no fewer than ten fireplaces, a sure mark of wealth and distinction as fireplaces were a taxable indulgence. The gardens, comprising nearly an acre, contained barns and orchards.

This handsome purchase occurred a few months after John Shakespeare renewed his application for a coat-of-arms, suddenly abandoned twenty years previously. The renewal may have been suggested and promoted by the son, but it had to proceed on the father's merits because substantial citizens with a record of service were more highly esteemed than play-wrights. The application was approved by Garter King-at-Arms in October 1596, by virtue of John Shakespeare's having been a Justice of the Peace and 'the Queen's officer and chief of the town of Stratford-upon-Avon', possessing lands and property to the value of £500, and having married 'a daughter and heir of Arden, a gentleman of worship'. In 1599 a further application was made for the right to impale the Arden bearings with those of Shakespeare, but for some reason the scheme was abandoned. Evidently, however, the cloud over John Shakepseare's name had lifted and he was regarded again as a man of property and good reputation. It is not impossible that the one-time 'debtor' helped financially in the purchase and develop-ment of New Place.

The immediate object of the purchase was presumably to provide a home for Anne Shakespeare and her two daughters, but we have to wonder why it happened just when it did, only a few months after Shakespeare left the house in Bishopsgate. Tradition asserts, in the absence of any evidence to the contrary, that during the 1580s Shakespeare went off to London, leaving his family behind. Apart from the mention of a small debt owing to a Hathaway dependant, there is not a single record of Anne's existence between the baptism of her children and the drafting of her husband's will, and perhaps this very silence has led to the assumption that their relationship over the years was indifferent, if not hostile. Yet the making of adequate provision for his family was the first of Shakespeare's worldly ambitions, and from the plays there emerges a sense that the companionship of wife and children is a happiness that every man should wish for. Cynics may say that Shakespeare was here idealizing a condition that he himself never knew, but it is undeniable that he devoted himself to the accumulation of the material supports upon which domestic contentment is often found to rest. There is not a scrap of evidence for it, but in face of all the traditions and all the assumptions it has to be possible that as soon as he had established himself in the London theatre, he brought his family to join him. But when Hamnet fell ill, and was taken to Stratford to die, he would no longer expose his daughters to the same dangers. The house in Bishopsgate now had unhappy memories, and also it would have been too big for his needs.

One of the more persuasive items in John Aubrey's gossip is that Shakespeare 'was wont to go to his native country once a year', and after the purchase of New Place his visits no doubt became longer, (Aubrey also tells the story of Shakespeare's frequently breaking his journey at the Crown at Oxford where Mistress Davenant, the taverner's wife, was not only very beautiful but 'of conversation extremely agreeable'. William Davenant, born in 1606, claimed to be Shakespeare's godson, and later in life was willing, even proud, to be thought his natural son as well.) Nicholas Rowe said in his biographical sketch that

> The latter part of his life was spent, as all men of good sense will wish theirs may be, in ease, retirement and the conversation of his friends. He had the good fortune to gather an estate equal to his occasion and, in that, to his wish; and is said to have spent some years before his death at his native Stratford.

For many people in the modern world 'retirement' means a precise cut-off date, but it is unlikely that his fellows in the theatre could have named any particular moment at which he might be said to have retired or not retired. His 'cousin' Thomas Greene, apparently a kinsman, was a lawyer who in 1603 was appointed clerk to the Stratford Corporation. He and his family were for an unknown period guests or tenants at New Place, and in 1609 he was able to accept a delay in the purchase of his own house 'because I perceived I might stay another year at New Place'. From this it has been inferred that Shakespeare did not come into final residence at his home until early in 1611, where he spend the summer months writing *The Tempest*, acted at court in November. Prospero's farewell to his art therefore was his own.

It is a tidy 'explanation', which most Shakespearean explanations are not, but Prospero's valediction has a well-known source in Ovid and in its context it has a dramatic appropriateness irrelevant to Shakespeare's personal affairs. Various purchases and legal transactions show him to have been in Stratford frequently before 1611, and between 1612 and 1614 he had occasions to be in London. His retirement was a gradual withdrawal from the active life of the theatre. So long as he remained a sharer and house-keeper, his company had a right to expect some participation from him, but with Jonson now writing for them regularly and Beaumont and Fletcher proving industrious and profitable apprentices, they had less need of him than formerly. Except when he provided a festival pot-boiler in *Henry VIII*, the character of his later work suggests his growing detachment. The plays are longer, perhaps too long to have been performed without abridgment, and he seems to be writing less 'as you like it' than as he liked it. His stage-craft never failed him — these final plays conquered new territories for drama — but he was intent upon some personal vision which lay beyond the immediate requirements of the King's Men. The domestic arrangements of Thomas Greene are unlikely to have had much influence on his decisions.

The records of these Stratford years show a steady acquisition of property, insistence on protecting his legal interests and a cool reluctance to bestir himself in local crises that agitated his fellow-citizens. The death of his father in 1601 left him the owner of the houses in Henley Street, of which he had no need in his own family. He left the western house (the Birthplace), where presumably his mother still lived, in the possession of his sister Joan, who at some unrecorded date had married 'William Hart, hatter'. The eastern house (the Woolshop) appears to have been let to Lewis Hiccox, who converted it into an inn, the Maidenhead. In 1602 Shakespeare paid William Combe[2] and his nephew John £320 for 107 acres of arable, with twenty acres of pasture, at Old Stratford; the deeds being delivered, presumably during his own absence in London, to his brother Gilbert. Later in the same year he acquired a copyhold cottage in Chapel Lane, facing New Place: convenient for a gardener or servant — or even as a love-nest for the

---

2   The Combes were a wealthy and influential family. The mother of William (d.1610) was the widow of a Quiney; a lawyer, he was High Sheriff of Warwickshire and a M.P., and he married the widow of Sir John Puckering, Lord Keeper and possibly the author of *Horestes*. His nephew John (d.1614) was a bachelor living at Welcombe, and from money-lending and land speculation he amassed a large fortune which he mainly devoted to religious and charitable purposes. Among his bequests he left £5 to Shakespeare and remitted a shilling in the pound to all his 'good and just debtors'; but he had a hard name as a usurer and Shakespeare is credited with doggerel that survived, in numerous versions, about him and his brother Thomas (*WS* II 139-40, 246, 251, 253, 269, 294). Thomas (d.1609) lived at the College House near the church, formerly occupied by the chantry priests, possibly the only house in Stratford larger than New Place. It was his sons, William and Thomas, who took over the movement to enclose the Welcombe fields. Shakespeare bequeathed his sword to this younger Thomas, and as he was always friendly with the Combes, it is unlikely that he lampooned them.

Dark Lady, whose occupancy has yet to be proposed, although doubtless it will be.

In 1605 he made the boldest purchase of a prudent career when he paid Ralph Hubaud £440 for a leasehold half-interest in tithes in the neighbouring hamlets of Old Stratford, Bishopton and Welcombe. Annual rents totalling £22 were due to the Corporation as ultimate holders and to descendants of the original legatee, and in about 1611 Shakespeare helped to initiate a complaint against other lease-holders who by defaulting on the rent might concede a right of re-entry. When in 1625 the Corporation recovered Shakespeare's interest from his heirs, it was valued at £90 annually, subject to £22 in rent.

Incidents recorded in the town's annals suggest the close attention to practical affairs of a man who was not as civic-minded as his father had been. John Shakespeare's last service to the town, not long before his death, was in helping to draw up the council's case against Sir Edward Greville of Milcote, whose family had bought the lordship of the manor on the Earl of Warwick's death in 1590. Greville was thought to be interfering overmuch in local affairs and even to be menacing the town's chartered right to self-government. Meanwhile Shakespeare himself had been returned by the Stratford justices as a hoarder of malt. Three very wet summers in the mid-nineties (that of 1594 is commemorated in *A Midsummer Night's Dream*) had led to a scarcity of grain, with the usual consequence of hoarding and, in some cases, of releasing it for sale when prices had come to famine level. A return at the end of 1595 disclosed substantial stocks being held by Stratford citizens. Those two staunch Puritans Richard Quiney and Abraham Sturley were of their number, Quiney holding forty-seven quarters of barley and thirty-two of malt. In 1597 the Privy Council called on local authorities for further investigation of the engrossers, 'wicked people in conditions more like to wolves and cormorants than to natural men'. A survey taken in February 1598 discovered that much less corn and barley was now being held by private citizens and that stocks of malt, although considerable in the aggregate, were widely distributed. Altogether 689 quarters of malt were found, but the largest individual holding was only eighteen: from which it would appear that with connivance the largest offenders were prudently spreading their stocks. Shakespeare's holding was ten quarters: hardly enough to brand him as wolf and cormorant. His neighbours realized, however, that he was a man with money to invest or lend. Sturley and Richard Quiney had previously tried to interest him in the purchase of tithes, to find him as yet unready, and in the autumn of 1598 Quiney was in London to petition the government for financial relief to a town lately afflicted by ruinous harvests and two devastating fires. From his inn Quiney wrote a letter asking Shakespeare for a personal loan of £30 to help him with his London debts. For some reason this letter was never delivered. The only surviving letter written to Shakespeare, it was found in Quiney's papers when he died. Probably the two men met in London and the matter of the loan was settled — one way or the other.

Small entries in the Stratford Court of Record show Shakespeare to have been insistent on enforcing his rights. In 1604 he sued the apothecary Philip Rogers for £1 15s., the balance of an unpaid debt, and in 1608-9 he instigated a long-drawn suit against John Addenbrooke for a debt of £6 and, Addenbrooke having moved outside the court's jurisdiction, against his surety Thomas Hornby, a local blacksmith, for the debt plus 24s. in costs and damages. Such petty actions were common at the time and do not suggest that Shakespeare was particularly heartless or grasping, but he was a shrewd man of business and he was quick to protect his interests in the great enclosure dispute that divided the town in 1614.

Ever since Thomas More had declared sheep to be devourers of men, the enclosing landlord had figured in pamphlet and sermon as the symbol of black-hearted oppression. Tudor paternalism had tried to preserve the medieval system of agriculture, but without much success as the gentry responsible for enforcing the law were the likeliest to break it. Enclosure for sheep-farming certainly did cause depopulation and unemployment and raise the price of bread. Enclosure with the object of improving the inefficient agriculture of the open-field system was a different matter, but overheated opposition refused to discriminate between the one kind and the other, and the scientific farmer was classed with the capitalist sheep-farmer as the tyrant of the fields. Enclosure during the sixteenth century affected less than three per cent of England's agricultural land. The outcry was out of all proportion to the real suffering.

Through his purchase of land and tithes Shakespeare had a personal interest when Arthur Mainwaring, steward to Lord Chancellor Ellesmere, and his cousin Walter Replingham prompted a scheme to enclose certain fields in the manors of Welcombe, Old Stratford and Bishopton,[3] and were joined in the enterprise by the younger William Combe. Combe, who already had considerable property in Welcombe, had much to gain if he could extend it by enclosure and his motives were single-minded and mercenary. Other holders of land or tithe, including Shakespeare, stood to gain if enclosure improved the agricultural yield but to lose if the land were only cropped by sheep. In October Shakespeare entered into an agreement with Replingham, who acted as attorney for the promoters, compensating himself or his heirs for any loss ensuing 'by reason of any enclosure or decay of tillage there meant and intended'. Thereafter he was able to preserve his usual detached neutrality even though he was courted by both parties in the dispute and ceaselessly importuned by his 'cousin' Thomas Greene. A third terrible fire, destroying fifty-four dwellings and numerous stables and barns, had struck the town just before the enclosure scheme was opened and

3 See *WS* II 141-9, Schoenbaum 281-5.

it found the Corporation rattled and apprehensive. They decided to oppose the scheme, which would be 'the undoing of the town' and a cause of greater loss than all three fires. This was embarrassing for Greene, who had recently invested £300 in tithes and had a holder's interest but as town clerk had to forward the council's policy. He seems to have depended upon Shakespeare to advise or procure him a way out of his dilemma, writing him letters, all lost, and on one occasion calling upon him in London. Greene is not remembered in Shakespeare's will.

The controversy ended in desperate actions akin to farce. Before the end of the year Combe and his men were digging trenches at Welcombe preparatory to enclosure, but the Corporation mustered angry citizens to fill them in again. Even when the Corporation obtained an order at Warwick Assizes prohibiting enclosure, Combe harried the Welcombe tenants and pursued his design with the intensity of a maniac. A few weeks before Shakespeare's death the case was brought before the Lord Chief Justice, the imperious Coke, who told Combe that he 'should never enclose nor lay down his common arable land'. Shakespeare seems to have been non-committal throughout, and he was not given to making gestures in matters of this kind. His own interests were safeguarded and although he had friends in the council, he was also friendly with Combe. Nor can the issue itself be simplified as the intended oppression of a hapless peasantry. Combe was greedy and he intended to convert some of the land to pasture, but enclosure would benefit those estates left under the plough and he offered solid and reasonable compensation for losses sustained. The interested freeholders would not suffer from loss of tithe. There was a case for enclosure, and doubtless Shakespeare was aware of it when he quietly evaded the Corporation's pleas that he use his influence on their behalf.

On the other hand there is a pleasant story of his journeying to London in 1612 to pay the dues of friendship. Sometime after the turn of the century he had left Bankside and gone to live with Christopher Mountjoy, a Huguenot tire-maker, in Silver Street in the parish of St Olave's, Cripplegate. In 1604 Mountjoy and his wife had asked Shakespeare to persuade Stephen Belott, their former apprentice, to marry their daughter Mary; such persuasion being necessary, as it turned out, because Belott was determined to have a satisfactory financial settlement before he would acknowledge any romantic feelings. He alleged that he had been promised a dowry of £60 and a further £200 in Mountjoy's will; and he went to law in 1612 because he had received only £10 and some paltry household items and had no assurance of getting any more. Since Mountjoy disputed these claims, it was necessary to find witnesses who might remember the negotiations that preceded the marriage. In view of the kindly assistance he had given to the young lovers, Belott sent a friend to ask Shakespeare to give evidence, and in his deposition before the court Shakespeare agreed that Mistress Mountjoy did 'solicit and entreat' him to 'move and persuade' Belott into the match. He remembered too that Mountjoy had promised his daughter a dowry, but on the vital detail his memory failed him: 'what certain portion he remembereth not, nor when to be paid, nor knoweth that the defendant promised the plaintiff two hundred pounds with his daughter Mary at the time of his decease'. A financial settlement was just the sort of thing he would remember, and it seems that his habitual caution was asserting itself, with a disinclination to take sides when both parties had been his friends. When the case was eventually referred to the overseers of the French church in London, they took the view that both parties were undeserving and awarded Belott an ignominious £6 13s. 4d.

Early in 1613 Shakespeare was in London again when the Princess Elizabeth was married to the Calvinist Elector Palatine. The entertainment was even more lavish than at James's coronation nine years previously, and again it was a happy time for the actors, the King's Men receiving £93 6s. 8d. for fourteen plays, four of them Shakespeare's, performed during the wedding celebrations. The marriage was followed by further junketings to commemorate the anniversary of the King's accession, and here Shakespeare found a new role. The Earl of Rutland, newly succeeded to the title, took part in a tournament in which the chosen knights rode into the lists splendidly arrayed, their display including an *impresa*, a symbolic picture painted on the shield and bearing a motto to explain its significance. Rutland, who was a patron of poets and playwrights, chose Richard Burbage to paint the design and Shakespeare to write the motto, rewarding each of them with 44s. Their work has not survived, but examples of *imprese* may be found in the tournament scene in *Pericles* (II ii).

In the same month of March 1613 Shakespeare made another purchase of property. From Henry Walker, 'citizen and minstrel of London', he bought the gatehouse of the Blackfriars Priory, a house darkly associated with secret passages, priests' holes and Catholic intrigue. The price was £140, of which he paid £80 and took up a mortgage for the balance. Although the house was only a short distance from the Blackfriars theatre, he seems to have bought it purely as an investment without intending to live in it. When he made his will one John Robinson was living there as his tenant, and the will appeared to expect that he would continue to do so. The mystifying feature in this transaction is that Shakespeare appointed three trustees to watch over his interests: John Heminges, his old friend and fellow who was accustomed to receiving such commissions from the King's Men; John Jackson; and William Johnson, landlord of the Mermaid tavern in Bread Street. The effect of this, whether intended or not, might have been to exclude his widow from any dower interest in the property; whereas in his will he did not specifically deprive her of dower right in any of his possessions. Probably there is no need for subtle or tendentious explanations. Shakespeare may not have expected to be in London very often in the future, and that would be sufficient reason for asking friends to watch over his affairs.

He would have been in London, however, when *Henry VIII* was acted at the Globe in June. Tradition says that he coached John Lowin in the part of the King and that he himself spoke the Prologue that welcomes 'the first and happiest hearers'. When a spark from the stage ordnance ignited the thatch and the whole theatre burnt down, with narrow stairways and limited exits the fire must have been terrifying for some of the spectators. Puritans rejoiced at the evidence of divine intervention, however tardy, but within a year a new Globe stood on the same site, with tiled roof and brick exterior. Since their lease obliged them to repair and maintain the building, the cost fell upon the sharers, and an original estimate of some £60 per head proved, in the way of such matters, to be optimistic. Shakespeare's holding in 1613 was a fourteenth, or a seventh of the moiety not held by the Burbages. That he had disposed of his holding when he made his will in 1616 is virtually certain. The will has no specific mention of it, and it could hardly have been contained in the portmanteau allocation, following the detailed bequests, of 'all the rest of my goods, chattels, leases...' Even if the busy lawyers could construe these words to embrace a theatrical holding, Shakespeare was a theatre man and a company man, and the King's Men seldom disposed of their shares outside the profession. But when and to whom, and for how much, he gave up his holding is unknown. The destruction of the Globe may have confirmed him in a decision he already had in mind. He may have made the decision at once, or it may explain his presence in London in November 1614, with winter setting in and (unless it be lost) no new play of his own to set upon the stage. He was accompanied by his son-in-law, Dr John Hall, and we know of this visit only because Thomas Greene, pursuing the business of the Welcombe enclosure, took opportunity to call on him: 'At my Cousin Shakespear coming yesterday to town, I went to see him how he did'. The variousness of English idiom is unhelpful here. Greene may have meant only that he went, as it were, to pass the time of day; or he may have been enquiring after his cousin's health. Like so much else in the Shakespeare story, it is only conjecture, but possibly Shakespeare came to London in that early winter in order to complete the disposal of his shares; and because he had not been very well, his doctor son-in-law came with him.

In the spring of 1614 Shakespeare received from the Corporation 20d. for a quart of sack and a quart of claret for the entertainment of a visiting preacher come to deliver one of the endowed sermons with which the citizens were regularly edified. This meant that the visitor was accommodated at New Place, and if he was of the Calvinist inclination favoured by the civic authority, his exchanges with his host may have been no more than courteous. Biographers have found it difficult to reconcile the London Shakespeare, to whose sweet and amiable disposition so many friends have testified, with the Stratford Shakespeare, who appears to have been uncooperative and not very amiable. Certainly he did not have his father's zest for parochial involvement. In 1611 his name was added in the margin to a list of seventy-one people willing to share the cost of presenting a parliamentary measure 'for the better repair of the highways'. The bill was stillborn, like others of its kind, and the signatories may not have had to contribute very much. This was not a particularly impressive gesture, but it was the only one of its kind that has so far come to light. His pursuit of Rogers and Addenbrooke for minor debts has been held against him, but the Elizabethans had to go to court on issues that in later times would have been settled in a solicitor's office. A 'fine', which to-day has punitive associations, was then a mode of 'conveyance', an amicable composition. Whereas to-day a suitor goes to court because things have gone wrong, Elizabethans went to court in order that they should not go wrong. In the absence of evidence that Shakespeare ever extracted his dues from Rogers and Addenbrooke, his motive may only have been to establish in law that the debts existed.

Tradition supplies a more agreeable picture which, however uncertain the detail, may for once be more plausible. In a supplement to Johnson's edition of the plays George Steevens tells of an acquaintance who assured him that 'at his house in Warwickshire he had a wooden bench, once the favourite accommodation of Shakespeare, together with an earthen half-pint mug, out of which he was accustomed to take his draughts of ale at a certain public house in the neighbourhood every Saturday afternoon': potations which, if taken only weekly and from a half-pint mug, stop well short of dissipation. Rowe said that 'His pleasurable wit and good nature engag'd him in the acquaintance, and entitled him to the friendship, of the gentlemen of the neighbourhood'. Although Rowe gives no authority for saying this, it may well be that Shakespeare was welcomed in some of the larger houses of the neighbourhood where his true quality would have been better understood than in the more restrictive society of Stratford itself. One such house was Beauchamp Court, the home of the poet-dramatist Fulke Greville, who in one report (David Lloyd, *Statesmen and Favourites of England since the Reformation*, 1665) desired 'to be known to posterity under no other notions than of Shakespeare's and Ben Jonson's Master'. Another was Clifford Chambers, the home of Sir Henry Rainsford, where Dr Hall was physician and Michael Drayton a frequent guest. Ironically, Shakespeare may also have been an esteemed visitor at Charlecote.

Every biographer must have his own conceptions, but this seems a more persuasive picture than the Shakespeare fallen into uncommunicative senescence:

> 'Let me not live', quoth he,
> After my flame lacks oil'.

AWW I ii 58.

In this version of the final years the flame burns low and the old poet, exhausted, written-out and disillusioned, sits idly in his garden, half in love with easeful death and seeking some apothecary's magic that

embalms and spices
To the April day again.

Tim IV iii 40.

He would seem to have avoided the Seventh Age of Man. The dramatist who was singularly out of love with the weaknesses of foolish old men would have had the humour and detachment not to cultivate them in himself. Happiness in chosen friends may have rewarded the long years of creation that lay behind.

The greater happiness that he enjoyed, or hoped to enjoy, in his family was scarred by various disappointments: by a long toll of bereavement and the infertility that afflicted most of his kin. Of the eight children of John and Mary Shakespeare, William and Joan were the only survivors and the only ones with children of their own. Edmund, youngest of the family, died in 1607. He had followed his brother to London and become an actor. Although he is unremembered in the annals of the profession, he was only twenty-seven when he died and it may be that William had designed him to inherit his own share in the King's Men. Edmund was buried in the chancel of St Saviour's, Southwark, his passing marked by 'a forenoon knell of the great bell'. The fee for the bell was 8s. and for burial within the church a further 20s. This was exceptional treatment for a lesser member of an unregarded profession, and it seems to indicate that Shakespeare had some influence with the ecclesiastical authorities. It suggests also that by 1607 he had quit the Mountjoy *ménage* and returned to Bankside.

Mary Shakespeare, that 'gracious silence' of whom we know so little, died in 1608. Gilbert, who had taken legal delivery of his brother's purchase in Old Stratford, was buried at Holy Trinity in 1612, and Richard, who has found no place in the story, in 1613. Although a base-born son of Edmund was buried at St Saviour's a few months before his father, none of Shakespeare's brothers appears to have married, so that the direct male line was already extinct. Joan Hart, however, had four children. A daughter died in childhood, but three sons survived.

Shakespeare's own hopes for the future were founded on the marriage in 1607 of his elder daughter Susanna to Dr John Hall, described as *medicus peritissimus*. Himself a doctor's son, Hall graduated at Cambridge and came to Stratford in about 1600. His medical notes, which apparently he did not begin to compile until after his father-in-law's death, record his zeal in treating all kinds of maladies in all kinds of persons, and his services were sought, even by 'such as hated his religion', far beyond Stratford. His equable relationship with Shakespeare is suggested in the medical references in the plays, which after 1607 become more frequent and also more professional, and probably it was only in later years that his Puritanical convictions became obsessive. He perhaps was instrumental in bringing from Evesham Thomas Wilson, who was vicar from 1619 to 1638. Their

Calvinist and anti-Laudian bigotry was too strong even for Stratford burgesses to stomach. Wilson kept pigs and poultry in the newly-restored chancel, which he also regarded as a fit place to dry the washing of his six children. As churchwarden Hall conducted himself like a Genevan lay elder, reproving citizens for 'loitering forth of church on sermontime', 'sleeping in the belfry, with hat on, on the Sabbath', sitting unreverently in church and 'laughing and rumbling' during the sevice. Urged by his fellows to join the council, he was eventually expelled from it, partly for non-attendance and partly for 'his continual disturbances' when present.[4]

His non-attendance he fairly explained by the demands of his practice. Some of his prescriptions contained ingredients favoured by the Witches in *Macbeth* but he was in advance of his time in discovering that plant-juices with vitamin C were effective in the cure of scurvy, a widespread disease caused by over-consumption of salted beef in the winter months. His 'scorbutic beer' was a sovereign remedy. He was sufficiently eminent to be marked down by the financial advisers of Charles I as one who might be mulcted by the offer of a knighthood. The fees payable for this honour were so heavy that it was cheaper to pay £10 'in distraint', as Hall did in 1626. Epitaphs make indifferent evidence as a rule, but much of the character of Susanna and her husband may appear in the opening lines of the memorial that stands over her grave in the chancel of Holy Trinity:

> Witty above her sex, but that's not all,
> Wise to salvation was good Mistress Hall.
> Something of Shakespeare was in that, but this
> Wholly of him with whom she's now in bliss.

In one thing, however, the marriage was a grievous disappointment, there being only one child of it, and that a daughter: Elizabeth, born in 1608. Shakespeare's greatest hope was never realized, although the detailed provisions of his will show that he had not relinquished it. Some women who keenly desire a son are tempted after a time to look outside wedlock for a man to give them what they need. Although Susanna's reputation should have protected her from such aspersion, in 1613 John Lane, whose family were gentry of Alveston on the outskirts of Stratford, was saying that she 'had the running of the reins [meaning that she had contracted gonorrhea] and had been at naught with Ralph Smith'. The Halls sued Lane for slander and when the case was heard at the Consistory Court at Worcester, he did not appear and was duly excommunicated. He had been in trouble before for minor misdemeanours. Ralph Smith, a haberdasher in the town, was not associated in the action and seems to have left it to Susanna to clear his name

---

4 For Hall and other Stratford worthies see C.M.Mitchell, *The Shakespeare Circle*; E.I.Fripp, *Shakespeare's Stratford* and *Shakespeare Studies*; M.Eccles, *Shakespeare in Warwickshire*; Schoenbaum 278-319.

as well as her own. The slander seems to have been nothing more than the invention of an irresponsible young man in his cups. Subsequently Lane was to make an attack upon the vicar Thomas Wilson. Maybe he just did not like Puritans.

Meanwhile Judith Shakespeare, born in 1585, was still unmarried. She must have been singularly independent or singularly unattractive, because marriage was a woman's appropriate function, she was aware of her father's hopes, and every fortune-hunter in the district knew that she would be a substantial heiress. In the last months of her father's life she announced that she was going to marry Thomas Quiney, a vintner five years younger than herself. He was the third son of the Richard Quiney, a Stratford mercer and an old friend of the family, who had asked Shakespeare for a loan in 1598, but he had not the qualities either of his father or of his eldest brother, also Richard, who was to be a prosperous grocer in London and buy a plantation in Virginia. The marriage, in February 1616, had an unfortunate start as Quiney failed to obtain a licence for the ceremony to be performed during a prohibited season. He was excommunicated, but the offence was regarded as only technical because a son, named after his maternal grandfather, was baptized at Holy Trinity before the end of the year. More serious and more shameful was Quiney's appearance before an ecclesiastical court in March to answer a charge of having carnal knowledge of Margaret Wheeler, who had died in childbirth and her infant with her. Quiney admitted the offence, presumably committed while he was courting Judith, and was sentenced to do open penance in church on three sucessive Sundays. Perhaps out of regard for his new wife and her parents, he was spared this public display of contrition. He was fined 5s. and ordered to make private confession before the minister of Bishopton.

Judith's marriage and its attendant circumstances caused Shakespeare to amend his will, of which a first draft had been prepared in January. On the day before Quiney's appearance in court he sent for his lawyer, Francis Collins, to make some fairly substantial alterations. First, however, it would be pertinent to try to discover how much he had to leave. Some estimates have been fantastic, such as William Davenant's story of his receiving £1000 from the Earl of Southampton, or the statement of John Ward, a vicar of Stratford soon after the Restoration, that for writing two plays a year for the London stage he 'had an allowance so large that he spent at the rate of £1000 a year, as I have heard'. All the purchases he is known to have made during his life did not total much more than £1000. His holding in the two theatres varied slightly with the number of sharers and housekeepers at a particular time. His original interest in the Globe was one-tenth and one-seventh in Blackfriars, but the proportion changed as others came and went: when Ostler became a sharer in 1612 Shakespeare's interest in the Globe was only a fourteenth. During the litigation that occurred within the company in 1635 it was stated that in the year from May 1634 each sharer made a profit of about £90; and in addition each of the sixteen housekeepers at the Globe made £25 and each of the eight housekeepers at Blackfriars a further £90. Thus Shakespeare, as sharer and housekeeper in both theatres, would in that year have received £205. In the intervening years profits may have risen and the value of money may have fallen. On the other hand, his holding as house-keeper was larger than a sixteenth and an eighth respectively, and it seems reasonable to accept £200 as the average yield of his theatrical earnings in a good year. In bad years, bedevilled by plague and inhibitions or by excep-tional outlay on renovation, it would have been less; and it also has to be remembered that the company had Blackfriars as their winter house for a relatively short time in his professional career.

This £200 would have represented his net share in the profits of the company and the housekeepers, and he could not have expected much further income from theatrical sources. In some estimates his receipts have been inflated by fees for court performances, fees as Groom of the Chamber, fees for each play that he wrote, fees for the apprentices that he trained, and so forth. But the King's Men were grooms without fee: any fees paid to them were for specified services, and these, together with any receipts for court or private performances, were added to the gross takings of the company and eventually distributed as part of the profits. There is no evidence that Shakespeare ever had any apprentices, who in any case paid no fee to their masters and were a liability until they could be hired to the actors. He would have had no profit from the publication of his plays, which were the property of the company; nor in his later years was he entitled to any special payment for supplying the company with a play. Earlier, when he was acting regularly, he may have done, and there may be some truth in the eighteenth-century story that he received £5 for *Hamlet*. But he does not appear in any of the surviving actor-lists after 1603, and although this is unlikely to have been his last performance, it has to be inferred that his appearances became less and less frequent. Sharers served the company in other duties besides acting, and Shakespeare's arrangment with his fellows was probably that, while he might sometimes act in plays with large casts, his essential duty was to supply them with a couple of plays a year, rehearsing them and putting them into performance. Possibly he was allowed the 'benefit' usually granted to the author on the second or third performance of a new play, but that is all.

His income from other sources was not spectacular in cash terms, although of course his investment in land and houses made him a man of solid wealth. The Stratford tithes brought him £38 a year, but his remain-ing profits, from rents, leases and interest on loans, would not have aver-aged more than a further £20 or £30. In actual money, then, his total income was around £250 a year, and that was only when he had established him-self and had money to invest. The disposal of his theatre holdings — always assuming that he did sell them — reduced his devisable income to a relatively small figure. The value of the cash bequests in his will was about £350.

The will consists of three sheets, of which the first is a fresh sheet replacing the first page of the original draft, and the other two are scored with cancellations and insertions. The signatures authorizing the revisions suggest a growing physical weakness, and failing mental powers have been held to account for the considerable number of afterthoughts and apparent changes of mind. This may be so. Unless there were earlier drafts now lost, Shakespeare did not make a will until he felt death close to him. On the other hand, the intentions of the document are firm and clear; and unless Francis Collins had unusual abilities for a country lawyer, this was the work of the testator.

In some ways Judith was easier to provide for now that she was married: it was no longer necessary to devise contingent arrangements for a spinster who might one day became a wife. She was to receive £150: £100 as a marriage portion and £50 on condition of her surrendering to Susanna her interest in the small copyhold property in Chapel Lane. She was also to have the interest on a further £150. If she died without issue within three years, the capital would go to Susanna's daughter Elizabeth (£100) and Joan Hart (£50). But if she were still alive after three years, the capital would pass to her husband, whether Quiney or another, on condition that he settled upon her lands equivalent in value; failing that, she might have the interest, but the principal would be held in trust. Judith was also to receive his 'broad silver-gilt bowl', the only item in his plate that was not left to Elizabeth Hall.

Shakespeare has often been cast in the role of Brabantio towards his younger daughter's marriage. He must have been delighted in her marrying at all after these years, and in her uniting herself with a family he had known and respected all his life, but there was much in the particular circumstances to distress him. The provisions of the will have been interpreted as discriminatory against the Quineys' interest: as indeed they were, and would have been whomever Judith had married, because Shakespeare was first of all ensuring that if Susanna should have a son, he should inherit the bulk of the estate. Otherwise he is giving Thomas every chance. The will requires that he shall be able to take care of his wife and family, and the main proviso is not necessarily directed at Quiney at all. If Elizabeth Hall were to die unmarried, the whole estate might one day revert to Judith and her heirs, and the will protects her from greedy but penniless suitors if she should be left a widow.

Meanwhile the bulk of the estate passed to Susanna for her lifetime. On her death it would go to her eldest male issue and his heirs; in default of male issue, to Elizabeth Hall 'and the heirs males of her body lawfully issuing', and then to Judith and her heirs males. The legacy embraced New Place, the Henley Street houses and other dues in Stratford and the neighbourhood; the house in Blackfriars presently occupied by John Robinson; and 'all the rest of my goods, chattels, leases, plate, jewels and household stuff'.

His sister Joan Hart was to live in Henley Street for the rest of her life at a nominal rent of 1s. a year; she was also given a sum of £20 and all the testator's wearing apparel — perhaps for the use of her three sons, who also received £5 each. To Elizabeth Hall Shakespeare left his plate; to the poor of Stratford £10; to Thomas Combe his sword; to three of his old fellows, Burbage, Heminges and Condell, 26s. 8d. apiece to buy memorial rings. Similar small bequests were made to Stratford friends. Money to buy rings was left to Hamnet Sadler, perhaps his oldest friend, after whom and his wife Judith the twins were named; to William Reynolds, a kinsman of the Combes and a wealthy landowner; and to the brothers Anthony and John Nash, who had witnessed his purchase of Old Stratford land in 1602. To his godson William Walker, aged seven, he left 20s. in gold; and to his wife his second-best bed.

Whatever may have been Shakespeare's relationship with his wife during the thirty-four years of their marriage, this testamentary provision — an interlineation in the amended draft — gives no certain clue to it. Hotspur, not a patient man, likened a railing wife to a tired horse and a smoky house as tediousness beyond sufferance (*1 Henry IV* III i 160) and the immature Bertram declared war itself to be less strife-torn than 'the dark house and the detested wife' (*AWW* II iii 308): from which it must follow, to certain minds, that Anne was a virago and the marriage was unhappy. At least it endured, although in bourgeois society, where separations were rare and bore a stigma, this perhaps is not saying very much. That Shakespeare was consistently faithful to his wife is not the impression that his work has made on most of his readers. If it be true (and probably it is not) that every man in his life has one great passion, Shakespeare did not find his in Anne. On the other hand, this may have been a marriage of congenial temperaments, if not of true minds. The unusual reticence and detachment of Shakespeare's character possibly found a comforting response in the similar qualities of his wife. She seems to have been an undemanding sort of woman. Knowing that she could not accompany or help him on the long journeyings of the creative spirit, she wisely left him to travel that road alone, and gave him instead the solid unexacting companionship that such spirits need if the flame is to burn again. A man like Shakespeare could not have had an 'ideal', or even a normal, marriage in the way that the conventional world regards such things. At any rate, we have no grounds for saying that the family in New Place was not a happy one. Anne apparently expressed a strong desire to be buried in her husband's grave, but the sextons were deterred by the curse he had laid on any who should disturb his bones. The Latin epitaph composed for her — probably by John Hall, but at Susanna's instance — is conventional in form and sentiment but has an intensity often lacking in such tributes. It seems to issue from a deep and genuine devotion.

The interlineation bequeathing 'my second-best bed with the furniture' was the only specific mention of Anne in Shakespeare's will. The absence of further reference is a testimony to the trust and affection that prevailed in the family. Susanna and her family were leaving their house in the old town, near the church, and coming to live at New Place. Shakespeare was confident that Anne would be cared for to the end of her days. What he did not wish was that she should have any property of her own, because the manifest intention of his will was that the whole of his landed estate should be devised intact.

There is a difficulty here because it was the custom in some parts of the country, certainly in London, that the widow should have a life-interest in one-third of her husband's property. Local practice in Stratford is not known with any certainty. If it had been the custom there, Shakespeare's will would have been liable to challenge by an interested party, but he seems to have known, or assumed, that it was not. The lack of any specific provision of landed property does not argue a want of affection for Anne or an indifference to her material state; it merely protected her from the frailty and vulnerability of her sex. The Jacobeans had no faith in the ability of their womenfolk to transact business or look after themselves in a world where the widow was the prey of every man. Anne might be sixty, but in possession of any of her husband's property she would be worth the wooing. Gold 'makes the wappen'd widow wed again', and the widower too: here could have been an acceptable prize for some father with a clutch of motherless children. Unless it be that the partial life-interest was in Stratford so much the recognized practice that the will needed to make no mention of it, Anne would have gone to her new lord with no other dowry than that bed. It is surely reasonable to suppose that the arrangement had been discussed with her and had her considered approval. It would not have come as a rude surprise at the reading of the will.

The will made no mention of books, manuscripts and papers, but there was no reason why it should. Shakespeare made a few special bequests, such as a bowl to Judith and a sword to Thomas Combe, but in the absence of such provision any documents would have passed to the Halls as residuary legatees. His books he may have left in London for fellow-dramatists who would have more use for them than an overworked provincial doctor; if there were unfinished plays or poems, he is as like as not to have destroyed them. In his own will in 1635 Hall left his 'study of books' to his son-in-law Thomas Nash, but presumably most of these were religious or medical: Hall would not have had much taste for Shakespeare's reading. The inventory of the goods of Sir John Bernard, to whom what remained of Shakespeare's property eventually descended, contains an item for books 'worth £29 11s.', a respectable sum, and a further item for 'lumber at Stratford-upon-Avon', valued at £4. Fancy may dwell upon the possibilities here, but not very profitably.

Shakespeare did not long survive the making of his will. The exuberant

Ward (who, Nathaniel-like, made a note in his diary to remind himself 'to peruse Shakespeare's plays, and be versed in them, that I may not be ignorant in this matter') recorded that 'Shakespeare, Drayton and Ben Jonson had a merry meeting, and it seems drank too hard, for Shakespeare died of a fever there contracted'. It is possible. Drayton often visited Clifford Chambers, where the lady of the house had earlier been the object of his *Idea* sonnets. Hard drinking seldom leads to fever, but the visit to New Place of two old friends, the wine passed round the table and the re-living of past days through the enchanted veil of time and alcohol may have exhausted a sick man's waning reserves. Quiney's disgrace may have hastened his decline, and there was another family bereavement when on 17 April William Hart, Joan's husband, was buried in the churchyard. Shakespeare followed him eight days later. 23 April, supposedly his birthday, is accepted as having been also the day of is death.

He was buried before the altar, just within the chancel rail: a distinction enjoyed also by John Combe, so it may have been due less to literary fame than to the acquisition of property. On the flagstone over the grave was carved an inscription said in local report to have been written by himself:

> Good Friend, for Jesus' sake forbear,
> To dig the dust enclosed here!
> Blest be the man that spares these stones,
> And curst be he that moves my bones.

Baconians view this doggerel as typical of the crude versifier who could not possibly have written the plays. Like many medieval churches, Holy Trinity had a charnel-house into which the bones of the dead would be thrown to make room for new graves. Shakespeare would often have seen

> dead men's rattling bones,
> With reeky shanks, and yellow chapless skulls.
>
> *R*ʒ IV i 82.

At Elsinore the grave-diggers fetch limbs and skulls from the earth to make a space for Ophelia. In later years some other Stratford tithe-holder laden with municipal dignities might require to be buried in the chancel, and the grave of the long-dead poet would be broken up to give him room. Shakespeare determined to prevent this if he could, and it would seem that in spite of one or two near escapes, the curse has prevailed. He was not, however, buried in a vault but laid in the ground in a wooden coffin; so that if sacrilegious hands should ever remove the stone, there would be nothing now to see. All that was mortal of him must long ago have become one with the damp earth and the brisk-flowing Avon.

Susanna was not so fortunate. On her death in 1649 she was laid in the chancel between her husband and her son-in-law, but in 1707 her place was claimed by a tithe-holder named Francis Watts. The memorial stone was removed and her bones were thrown into the charnel-house. The inscription on her grave was, however, preserved by an antiquary, and in 1844 it was Watts's turn to have his memorial removed. A new stone was cut bearing the original memorial to Susanna, but her remains no longer lie beneath it.

Shortly after Shakespeare's death his family and friends commissioned a monument to stand above his tomb. The work was entrusted to Gerard Johnson, one of the four sons of Gheerart Janssen, an immigrant from Amsterdam. Since the family had their business near the Globe, they must often have seen Shakespeare in his lifetime, and it may have been through his kindly help that they had secured the commission to erect the recumbent effigy for which John Combe left £60 in his will. Two years earlier the Johnsons, or Janssens, had designed the tomb of the fifth Earl of Rutland at Bottesford, in Leicestershire, and this too may have a Shakespearean connection. But their labours on Shakespeare's behalf have given little satisfaction to his later admirers. The niche in which the bust is placed is a competent piece of Jacobean Renaissance, ornate by modern taste.[5] The bust itself has been repaired and restored more than once — Malone caused it to be covered with a stone-coloured wash. It has failed to commend itself as the likeness of the greatest of poets, and many people cannot bear to look at it. Presumably, however, it was acceptable to the family and to his old friends in the King's Men who came to see it shortly after it was installed. The poet himself has reminded us that

> there's no art
> To find the mind's construction in the face.
>
> *Macb* I iv 11.

There is a melancholy interest in tracing the gradual disappointment of the hopes which embodied, at least in its material aspects, the whole of his earthly striving. The Halls had no more children, but expectations were renewed when in 1626, at the age of eighteen, their daughter Elizabeth married Thomas Nash, son of Anthony Nash who received a memorial ring in Shakespeare's will. The Nashes were wealthy landowners in Stratford, and Anthony, as a tithe-holder, had been involved in the controversy over the Welcombe enclosure. Like so many sons of country gentlemen in that era, Thomas was trained as a lawyer, but on inheriting his father's wealth in 1622, he returned to Stratford to manage his estates. No marriage could have given a better prospect of fulfilling Shakespeare's intentions, for a son would have inherited considerable property from both his parents.

Unfortunately, there were no children at all, and it began to seem that

5 See *WS* II 182-5; Schoenbaum 308-13.

Shakespeare's estate might in the end devolve upon the heirs of Judith Quiney. Marriage and fatherhood did little to induce a sense of responsibility in Thomas, who in business was a feckless being. He ran his vintner's shop, the Cage, inefficiently. He was fined for allowing his customers to tipple and fined for opprobrious language, and the wine that he sold was sometimes suspect. He tried to sell the business but was prevented by his family, and by 1633 Hall and Thomas Nash were acting as trustees for his wife and children. As a councillor he was more successful, serving as constable and chamberlain, but he may eventually have left Stratford and lodged with his brother Richard in London. His death and burial have not been traced. As parents, too, the Quineys were unlucky. Of their three sons Shakespeare, the eldest, died in infancy, but Richard and Thomas, born respectively in 1618 and 1620, were growing into manhood and were of an age to marry and have sons of their own when in the winter of 1638-9 some infection swept through Stratford and carried off both of them within a month. Thereafter the Quineys' marriage may have slowly foundered. Although remembered in his brother's will in 1652, Thomas disappears from sight. Judith's burial is recorded in the church register ten years later, but she did not join others of her family in the chancel and her grave has not been found.

In the meantime the death of Dr Hall in 1635 had left Thomas Nash as head of the family, and he and Elizabeth, previously living at Nash House next door, joined Susanna at New Place. The coming of the Great Rebellion found Shakespeare's daughter obedient to her duty. In July 1643 the Queen of England passed through Stratford on her way to Kineton, accompanied by some 3000 men and an appropriate establishment of artillery, wagons and stores. Indigenous Puritanism was hostile to the royalist cause, but Henrietta Maria was received for two nights at New Place. Nash's contribution to the royalists at the outbreak of war was the largest to be offered by any citizen of the town.[6]

By the time of his death in 1647 Nash was regarding himself as free to dispose of his wife's property as though it were his own, and his will, while making generous provision for Elizabeth from his own estate, assigned New Place, the land in Old Stratford and the Blackfriars gatehouse to his cousin Edward Nash, with the instruction that they be settled on Edward's son Thomas. This was the sort of manoeuvre that Shakespeare's careful entailing had sought to prevent. (In 1625 the Halls had sold the tithe holding, but that was one of the 'leases' that they were free to dispose of as

---

6 Perhaps it is surprising that Susanna, 'wise to salvation' and for so long exposed to her husband's abrasive Calvinism, should have taken the traditional Anglican side. Much as we should like to know more about Shakespeare's own marriage, his daughter's may have been a fascinating story too.

conscience or inclination dictated.) Nash's will was cancelled in favour of a fresh settlement which left the estate successively to Susanna, Elizabeth and Elizabeth's issue; with the exception of the Blackfriars house, which seems to have passed at about this time to Edward Bagley, 'citizen and pewterer of London' and described as a kinsman of Elizabeth, by a connection yet to be discovered. In default of issue, Elizabeth was to dispose of her inheritance as she pleased. By now this was the only possible decision. Shakespeare's far-seeing arrangements had not been able to provide for the contingency of both his daughters dying without surviving children.

In 1649, a few weeks before the death of her mother, Elizabeth Nash was married again, to John Bernard of Abington Manor in Northamptonshire. Perhaps she was encouraged therein by a progenitive capacity proved in the eight children borne to him by his first wife, but once again she was to be childless. For the first years of their marriage the Bernards lived at New Place, but in about 1653 they moved to Abington. At the Restoration Bernard's royalist faith was rewarded with a baronetcy, and possibly a title was for Elizabeth some compensation for the failure of her better hopes. On her death in 1670 the direct line became extinct. She was buried, as she had been married, at the Bernards' family church at Abington. Her will left the houses in Henley Street to Joan Hart's grandsons and their heirs for ever. Throughout the eighteenth century the eastern house continued to be let, and the Harts occupied the western house, which they filled with dubious relics of their ancestor and exhibited to visitors. When they sold the property in 1806, this house was for a time a butcher's shop. Both houses were acquired by public trust in 1847.

Elizabeth further directed that on the death of her husband, which took place in 1674, New Place and the Old Stratford acres were to be offered for sale to Edward Nash, and on his refusing them, to her residuary legatee, Edward Bagley. In 1675 New Place was sold to Sir Edward Walker, Garter King-at-Arms, whose daughter married a Clopton and for a time restored the house to the family that built it. It was rebuilt in 1702 but fifty years later passed to the Rev. Francis Gastrell, who — according to Malone — thought that his assessment for poor rate was too high and pulled down the house to spite the citizens; having previously cut down a mulberry tree planted by the poet's own hands. Used briefly for a theatre and a ballroom, the site has since been laid out as gardens, and the foundations of the old house may still be seen.

Although Shakespeare's direct line became extinct little more than fifty years after his death, he had descendants by a collateral line. Of the three sons of Joan and Hatter Hart, Michael, the youngest, died in 1618 while still a child; William, the eldest, became an actor and joined the King's Men, dying unmarried in 1639[7]; but Thomas had four children. Three of these died without issue, so that even the collateral descent depended, as it were, on a single thread. But George Hart had seven children, and it is through them that people alive to-day may trace a connection, however tenuous and remote, with the family of William Shakespeare.

7   Reputedly he was the father of Charles Hart, who was apprenticed in the theatre to Richard Robinson, a boy actor in Shakespeare's time. He fought for the King and after the Restoration he joined Thomas Killigrew's company at Drury Lane, where he played such parts as Brutus and Othello. He is also said to have introduced Nell Gwyn to the stage, and to have been her first lover.

Chapter XI
Shakespeare's Mind

It is the witness still of excellency
To put a strange face on his own perfection.

MAN II iii 48.

1. The Ghost Writer.

The poet's curse on any who should disturb his bones has not protected him from intrusion of another kind. While the facts are few, and some of them open to contrary deductions, the whole body of his work is at hand to receive all the interpretations that interest and fancy can lay upon it.

But now he's gone, and my idolatrous fancy
Must sanctify his relics.

AWW I i 108.

Shakespeare's refusal of extreme commitment would seem to be an essential fact about him: as Hal said of Poins, 'never a man's thought in the world keeps the roadway better than thine'. But critics and commentators do not keep the roadway so easily, and over the years every kind of sectary, crank and moral deviationist has claimed his kinship and allegiance. Even in time of war enemy nations have identified themselves with the poet who is pre-eminently the poet of the English race. No doubt the present chapter, which seeks to discover his affections, his knowledge and his interests, will similarly be guilty of failing to keep to the middle of the road and will make inferences that are improperly subjective. Obviously, too, it must to some extent intrude upon a subsequent discussion of his artistic methods.

First it is necessary to look at the notion that he was not a dramatic poet at all, merely an actor who was able to command the services of an eminent Jacobean jurist. The first Baconian was Robert Greene, if by his 'upstart crow, beautified with our feathers' he may be taken to mean that Shakespeare was claiming credit for the plays of other and better men. Nearly a hundred years later a Restoration dramatist, Edward Ravenscroft, printed his adaptation of *Titus Andronicus* and found it necessary to explain his crude pillaging. 'I think it a greater theft to rob the dead of their praise than the living of their money', he said, but he felt no such guilt in the present case because

I have been told by some anciently conversant with the stage that it was not originally his, but brought by a private author to be acted, and he only gave some master-touches to one or two of the principal parts or characters.

Ravenscroft does add that he would be apt to believe this report because *Titus Andronicus* was 'the most incorrect and indigested piece in all his works; it seems rather a heap of rubbish than a structure'. Otherwise this is a classic Baconian statement of the 'private author' who took his play to the theatre and found a mendicant hack able to add 'master-touches' in the form of stage professionalism.

The Baconian fantasy was born of an unhappy mating between eighteenth-century severity and the more indulgent romanticism that followed it. David Hume, in his *History of England* (1754-9), regarded Shakespeare as 'a man born in a rude age, and educated in the lowest manner, without any instruction either from the world or from books'; and handicapped further by a 'total ignorance of all theatrical art and conduct'. Pope and Johnson, as we know, held similar views about an age that had 'more skill in pomps or processions than in poetical language', and the critics of the eighteenth century were forced to decide that Shakespeare was a freak. Hume thought that he was 'a prodigy' who had achieved immortality by the intermittent 'irradiations of genius' that visited him despite the imbecility of his technique. This was a notion that appealed to the Romantics, who exaggerated his lack of education and the lowliness of his birth in order to excite further wonderment at the miracle of his genius. Not only Shakespeare and his family but the whole of Elizabethan Stratford had to be downgraded in order to heighten the contrast between the man and his achievement. Inevitably it would in due course be suggested that as this unlettered peasant could not have acquired the knowledge and the wisdom to be found in his plays, the plays must have been written by someone else.

Bacon became the premier candidate because he was, so to say, available: a great deal of his work has survived, and when the Baconian fallacy was launched more was known of it than of most of the surviving verse, prose and drama of the age. The idea had even a certain speciousness. There are parallels of thought and phrasing between Shakespeare's work and Bacon's, as there are between Bacon's and other men's and between Shakespeare's and other men's. Noblemen did write plays, and they had to find select and courtly audiences for them since it was socially impossible for them to be shown on the common stages. Thus Bacon was supposedly driven to the shift of fathering his work upon a professional actor who already stood below the level of society's reproaches. In moderation, so long as neither Bacon nor any other nobleman is to be credited with the whole Shakespearean *corpus*, this is not wholly fantastic. Elizabethan dramatists undoubtedly were importuned by courtiers with a play in search of actors, an idea for a plot, or some choice verse to adorn the action. Shakespeare was always ready to save himself trouble and he liked to oblige. Perhaps on occasion men of divers worship did not importune in vain.

The Baconian industry, which went into production in America in the middle of the last century, will not be content with this: Shakespeare is a total impostor capable of no loftier poetic flights than doggerel composed for his own tomb or at the expense of Lucy and the Combes. With operatives also on the continent and among Shakespeare's own countrymen, the industry has generated periodicals and some thousand books, pamphlets and articles. It has sustained itself by anagrams, ciphers, rebuses and acrostics: the refuge of the desperate and the demented because they can be made to prove anything. Thus a telling anagram has been devised from *Love's Labour's Lost*, mistakenly supposed at the time (1910) to be Shakespeare's first play and therefore especially pregnant with hidden intimations. An anagram of Costard's *'honorificabilitudinitatibus'* (the longest word in the canon, is *'Hi ludi F. Baconi nati tuiti orbi'*: 'These plays, of F. Bacon's parentage, are preserved for the world'. Lovers of word-games will admire the ingenuity of this discovery and go on to construct their own. Other claimants do indeed exist, including the Countess of Pembroke, the seventeenth Earl of Oxford, the fifth of Rutland, the sixth of Derby, Sir Edward Dyer and Christopher Marlowe, whose proclaimed death in 1593, in circumstances admittedly furtive, was a cover for the deceit he was to practise for the next twenty years.

To assemble detailed arguments against anything as devotedly silly as the Baconian theory would be a waste of time: Baconians would not be convinced, and others have no need to be. The habit of the theatrical profession is surely evidence enough. In lines addressed to 'our English Terence, Mr Will Shakespeare' John Davies of Hereford mentions his having played 'some kingly parts in sport': that is, he identifies the actor with the playwright. It may be objected that by bribery or some other inducement Davies was persuaded to write what he knew to be untrue. But the conspiracy of silence would have had to embrace the whole theatrical profession and its fringe adherents: Shakespeare's own company, the boys, the hired men and the staff, together with all the rival companies and the rival dramatists, particularly Ben Jonson. If the theatre could guard the secret so closely that not a breath of it was heard for some 250 years, the profession was different then from what it has been since.

2. In His Own Age.

Certain facts about Shakespeare are beyond serious dispute. One is that although proverbially poets are dreamers, there was a strong prudential strain in him, expressing itself in a hunger for land and respectability. It mattered to him that he should acquire arms and property, and he worked hard to possess and defend them; although he showed little inclination to assume the civic responsibility which the ownership of property normally conferred. It may go against the grain to admit that great dramatic poetry was written to secure a provincial competence, but it is the only object we may be sure of. Almost from the start he was looking forward to the day when he could come home, and he made his first purchase in Stratford as soon as he had money to spend. It is significant that a house in London was the last of his investments, not the first. This sets him apart from most of his fellows, who made it their first business to settle themselves in London and bought their country and suburban estates afterwards.

In pursuit of these bourgeois aims Shakespeare worked extremely hard, and that is a further fact about him. His accepted output, within a span of about twenty years, consists of thirty-seven plays, two long romances, the sonnets and various shorter poems; in addition to his part in the staging of his own plays and the work which during his active association with the company he may have put into the work of other writers. For much of this period he was also an actor. The time spent in memorizing and rehearsing, apart from actual performance, was arduous; and touring, when circumstances required it, was an additional burden. We have a way of rarefying our poets, Shakespeare more than most, and of refusing to recognize the discipline which their art imposes on them. To satisfy the voracious demands of professional entertainment Shakespeare had to maintain a heavy, rapid and continuous output, and however copious his inspiration, he must at times have driven himself with no other impetus than a dutiful technique. It would explain the occasional carelessness, the loose ends and perfunctory finales, the apparent fits of boredom, lassitude and failing impulse. Dryden complained that 'he writes, in many places, below the dullest writer of ours, or any preceding age. Never did any author precipitate himself from such height of thought to such low expression as he often does'; and a royal critic would agree that he found much 'sad stuff'. But Dryden did not have to supply the continuous needs of an acting company, and the royal critic was not under the necessity of writing plays at all. The demand on Shakespeare could have been met only by a man unusually robust in mind and body, a man recognizably typical, in his physical endowment, of the brash and boisterous world he lived in. With the chameleon's aptness in taking colour from his surroundings, he may not have been easy to single out from the element he occupied. Sitting with actors in a tavern, he probably looked and behaved much like any other actor sitting in a tavern.

Contemporary references help to fill in the picture. The *Shakespeare Allusion Book* contains some two hundred references taken from the years 1591 to 1623[1], the majority commenting in general or particular terms on his work but many of them also revealing the impact of his personality on

---

1   The important ones will be found in *WS* II Appendix B.

those who knew him. The allusions to his work tend to be one-sided and unsatisfactory because they do not fully realize the breadth of his genius. They testify to the immense and enduring popularity of the two romantic poems and, in drama, of Falstaff, Romeo, *Titus Andronicus, Julius Caesar* and, judged as an exciting play of revenge, *Hamlet*. Contemporaries valued him for only part of his achievement. His lyric impulse excited them more than his profounder insights, and they wrote chiefly of the 'dulcet singer', the 'honey-tongued Shakespeare' who wrote so sweetly of 'rose-cheek'd Adonis' and 'fair fire-hot Venus'; Richard Barnfield referred to his 'honey-flowing vein', Heywood to 'mellifluous' Shakespeare's 'enchanting quill'. Richard Carew, striving to show that England could produce poets the equal of the great writers of antiquity, chose to match him with, of all people, Catullus. Carew wrote of Shakespeare, and Marlowe too, as writers of poems, not as dramatists, and for him 'the miracle of our age' was Sir Philip Sidney. Thomas Freeman's complimentary sonnet in 1614 found nothing more significant to applaud than *Venus and Adonis, Lucrece* and the early comedies based on classical models.

Two things prevented a more satisfactory appreciation of his work: the first that the two long poems, coupled with the lyric passages from *Romeo and Juliet*, were altogether too successful, and the second that his popularity in the theatre was a bar, rather than an inducement, to dispassionate criticism. The foolish gallant of the *Parnassus* plays was typical of those whose speech oozed 'naught but pure Juliet and Romeo' or the 'stately tropes' of *Venus and Adonis*, and sterner critics felt that Shakespeare should do better than dissipate his powers in loose enticements to venery.

> Making lewd Venus, with eternal lines
> To tie Adonis to her love's designs:
> Fine wit is shown therein: but finer 'twere
> If not attired in such bawdy gear.
> But be it as it will: the coyest dames
> In private read it for their closet-games:
> For, sooth to say, the lines so draw them on
> To the Venerian speculation.
>
> John Davies, *The Scourge of Folly.*

It is strange to find Shakespeare thus indicted as a purveyor of aphrodisiac poetry, but this was certainly his early reputation; and with people who liked to read poetry but lacked opportunity or inclination to go to the theatre, it probably continued to be his reputation. The unknown author of the *Parnassus* plays makes almost the same criticism as Davies:

> Who loves not Adon's love, or Lucrece' rape?
> His sweeter verse contains heart-throbbing line,

Could but a graver subject him content,
Without love's foolish lazy languishment.

2 Return 301.

Of course Shakespeare did have graver subjects, many of them, and to us it is baffling that this was not more widely recognized. Gabriel Harvey said that while *Lucrece* and *Hamlet* 'have it in them to please the wiser sort', it was in *Venus and Adonis* that the younger generation took most delight. A partial explanation may be that after 1600 the actors were more successful in preventing the publication of plays, so that fewer were available to be read, but it would in any case have been difficult for Shakespeare as a dramatist to efface the impression he had already made as a sensuous poet. In another passage John Davies showed how hard it was for even the best to live down the common belief that writing and acting for the professional theatre were pursuits unworthy of men of high aspiration:

Players, I love ye, and your quality,
As ye are men that pass time not abus'd:
And some I love for painting, poesy,
And say Fell Fortune cannot be excus'd
That hath for better uses you refus'd...
And though the stage doth stain pure gentle blood,
Yet generous ye are in mind and mood.

Microcosmos 215.

The initials W.S. and R.B. in the margin make it clear whom he had in mind, and there even seems to be a reference to *Sonnets* 29 and 37. Much as he admired particular actors, Davies despised the profession as a whole, and in a later poem he remarked again that in making them actors Fortune had failed to guerdon Burbage and Shakespeare 'to their deserts'. In an epigram on Shakespeare, addressed as 'our English Terence', he who played 'some kingly parts in sport', that is on the stage, Davies said that he was fit to be 'a king among the meaner sort'; and in the lines from *Microcosmos* quoted above, by 'generous ye are in mind and mood' he meant *generosus*: the qualities of Burbage and Shakespeare fitted them to be gentlemen but their profession forbade it. Himself a scholar and minor poet, Davies established himself at Oxford as writing-master to sons of the nobility, and he saw these things through their eyes. Theirs was the opinion that mattered, for they were the arbiters of elegance. This is valuable testimony, and it shows why Shakespeare's more serious work was unlikely to be adequately assessed by his contemporaries. It is true that Meres in 1598 praised him for comedy and tragedy as well as for his style (his 'fine filed phrase'), his lyric poetry and his 'sugared sonnets'; but Meres, who was soon to become a country rector and dominie, was not so much a critic as a man who enjoyed making lists.

Not even his fellow-dramatists, although they recognized his energy and success, knew that they had greatness in their midst. The Induction to *The*

Knight of the Burning Pestle brackets his work with *The Spanish Tragedy*, *Mucedorus* (a perennially popular comedy) and the prolific but pedestrian labours of Thomas Heywood. In the Epistle to *The White Devil* Webster commended his 'right happy and copious industry'. This bears out the Folio's tribute to his fluency, but Webster says the same of Heywood and Dekker. Beaumont declared that he had shown

> How far sometimes a mortal man may go
> By the dim light of Nature:

but this is an edged compliment because it implies that Shakespeare lacked art and learning, lights which shine more brightly. Only Jonson knew that he was dealing with a giant. In the Folio poem he acknowledged Shakespeare as 'the wonder of our stage' to whom all European drama was in homage:

> He was not of an age but for all time.
>   And all the Muses still were in their prime
> When like Apollo he came forth to warm
>   Our ears, or like a Mercury to charm.

In *Discoveries* (1630) Jonson was more critical because it irked him that Shakespeare, in his view, lacked classical discipline:

> ...he flow'd with that facility that sometime it was necessary he should be stopp'd: *Sufflaminandus erat*, as Augustus said of Haterius. His wit was in his own power; would the rule of it had been so too.

Another contemporary who came near to acknowledging Shakespeare's genius was William Basse, a poet, chiefly pastoral, who honoured him in an epitaph. Spenser, Chaucer and Beaumont need not huddle closer to make room for him in their tomb:

> Under this carved marble of thine own
> Sleep, rare tragedian, Shakespeare, sleep alone.
> Thy unmolested peace, unshared cave,
> Possess as lord, not tenant, of the grave.

He would have to wait for Dryden before he was again measured at his true stature. Milton's lines, written in 1630, are lamely conventional, proclaiming that Shakespeare needs no monument of 'piled stones' because his work is monument enough. Milton too makes the habitual reference to the 'easy numbers' that flow to the shame of 'slow-endeavouring art'.

On his personality those who knew him testify unanimously to his sweetness, gentleness, honesty and 'civil demeanour': no famous man has had so little evil spoken of him. Moreover, these words had other and deeper meanings for the Elizabethans than they have for us, and they signify much more than the rather insipid affability they might seem to suggest. All of them were essentially positive qualities. Jonson's 'honest' had a strong meaning that implied breadth and generosity of mind and a natural absence of any superiority or aloofness. Shakespeare's charm of manner must have been compelling and absolute. 'This is the flower that smiles on everyone': and of himself it would not have been said contemptuously as it was said of Boyet. His power of identifying himself with the mind and feelings of other people enabled him to be, not all things to all men, but that particular thing that each man would have him be. Rowe in his biographical sketch summarized a general opinion that has more authority than mere tradition:

> Besides the advantages of his wit, he was in himself a good-natur'd man, of great sweetness in his manners, and a most agreeable companion; so that it is no wonder if with so many good qualities he made himself acquainted with the best conversation of those times.

Men did not speak thus of Marlowe, who was boorish with his companions, nor of Jonson, who must always be the declamatory centre of any gathering, 'tossing or goring' his victims with the thrusts of his learning and contempt. In a well-known passage in his *Worthies* Thomas Fuller describes the 'wit-combats' in which the two contestants resembled

> a Spanish great galleon and an English man-of-war; Master Jonson (like the former) was built far higher in learning; solid, but slow in his performances. Shakespeare, with the English man-of-war, lesser in bulk but lighter in sailing, could turn with all tides, tack about, and take advantage of all winds, by the quickness of his wit and inventions.

It is a revealing picture. Shakespeare's mind could move nimbly because it was not anchored to particular creeds or modes of thought.

Perhaps for the same reason, it was not rancorous.

> No levell'd malice
> Infects one comma in the course I hold.
>
> *Tim* I i 47.

The amount of topical allusion in his plays is open to debate, but even those commentators who are always looking for it have to concede that there is not very much to be found. Possibly *Love's Labour's Lost*, first written for private performance, is a jest at the expense of Ralegh and 'the School of Night', but if so, it is too far detached from the victims to draw blood. The ruinous summer of 1594 is mentioned in *Midsummer Night's Dream*, and doubtless there are other references of the kind that have not been identified. In a profession that has always delighted in 'in' jokes, Hamlet's remarks on the little eyases, and the burlesque of Alleyn's style, were not the only references to theatrical affairs. Pistol, for instance, spouts tags from the older drama, and Shakespeare was always ready to have a dig at rival companies. Again, Essex's expedition to Ireland is mentioned in *Henry V*, but in very conventional, almost neutral terms, and the allusion comes in the Prologue, not in the heart of the action. A topicality of this sort is very rare. The directness of the reference to Marlowe as 'dead shepherd' in *As You Like It* (III v 82) startles by its unexpectedness, and anyhow it is complimentary. Unlike the majority of Elizabethan dramatists, Shakespeare did not use the theatre to make war on either individuals or groups. Apart from all the other arguments against it, the sad old legend about his vendetta with Lucy, or with William Gardiner, dissolves in the light of a professional habit from which he seldom if ever deviated. The third *Parnassus* play speaks of him giving a purge to Jonson, but its nature has not been discovered. Probably the writer supposed that he was part-author of *Satiromastix*, a Chamberlain's play by Dekker and Marston in which Jonson is untrussed and crowned with nettles. Shakespeare's work does not display the usual vindictiveness towards Puritan fanatics, affected gallants, purse-proud citizens, projectors, speculators or other sores of the commonwealth. If he did dislike these people, he administered to them the larger reproof of ignoring them. His tolerance was too wide to harbour animosities.

In praising his easy grace and gentle disposition, his contemporaries seem to have been unaware of the unusual strength and self-control that underlay it. He might be amiable and unfailingly courteous, but he would not be imposed upon. The people of Stratford found that they could not withold his just dues, or force him into transactions against his will, or interfere with his possession of his property. In London Chettle had to repent his hasty publication of Greene's malignity, and Jaggard found that Shakespeare was 'much offended' at having *The Passionate Pilgrim* passed off as his work. It is likely enough that as a shareholder in the company he was active in preventing the illicit publication of his plays. This streak of shrewdness was the complement in practical affairs of his inviolable independence of mind and character. There were limits to his easy-going companionship. With William Beeston as his source, Aubrey wrote that 'he was not a company keeper...wouldn't be debauched, and if invited to, writ: he was in pain'. In other words, he did not like rowdy parties, and if pressed to attend one, sent a polite message that he had a headache. With the example of such as Greene and Peele to warn him, he kept aloof from the excesses of the literary and theatrical world. Even when sharing the daily life of a company of players, he was never wholly of their fellowship, for he knew that one day he would leave them.

His friends may have found him, for all his charm, curiously elusive. It must have been almost impossible to corner him and wrest an opinion from him if he did not wish to give it. This restraint was both personal and artistic. In his drama he seems to have worked with the deliberate intention of concealing his personal views. He did not contribute to the abundant 'occasional' literature of odes and pamphlets that occupied most of his fellows; he did not join in the vilification and personalities that theatre folk find amusing; the age's follies did not move him to write epigrams, nor did its great events call for poetic celebration; his acquaintance in courtly circles did not receive from him the customary tribute of compliments and commendatory verses; and even his plays went forth, to reader and spectator alike, without apologies, blandishments, scoldings or petitions. He does not appear to have written letters: while he or his heirs might have destroyed letters written to himself, they could not have destroyed any that he had sent to other people, and none has survived. Nor was he in the habit, favoured by many, of corresponding with his friends in the form of polite little verses. Even his will, with bequests to his family and to eleven of his friends, has none of the affectionate extravagance of phrase in which benefactors like to indulge themselves: its wording is so matter-of-fact and undemonstrative that he might have been arranging to distribute bundles of driftwood among strangers. In his epitaph he makes no claims for himself but only asks to be left in peace. The man who attracted to himself so many expressions of warmth and friendship did not unpack his heart with words to say the like of others. Whether he loved or hated, he kept his counsel, and it is surely impossible not to see in this reticence a calculated intent. If we find him inscrutable, it is because he wished it so.

Eventually, therefore, and at some peril, we have to go to his plays and poems to see if we may discover there what he did not wish us to know. The personal experiences of his life, and his response to the temper and crises of his age, have been so assimilated and metamorphosed by his art that they have discarded the accidents of the present and the particular, but they cannot altogether escape enquiry. First, however, we have to assess the strength of his 'small Latin and less Greek'.

3. Shakespeare's Learning.

Jonson, a Latinist of Westminster School under William Camden, rightly regarded Shakespeare's scholarship as negligible beside his own, and in formal education Shakespeare was less learned than many of his fellow-dramatists who were university men or lawyers from the Inns. But even in his own lifetime — and no doubt Jonson started it and helped to promote it — the legend originated that he was quite startlingly ignorant. Partly it may have been his own fault, because he was the last man to make needless parade of knowledge or weight his conversation with ponderous evidences of his reading. Beaumont was meaning to be complimentary when he resolved to keep his own verses as clear of learning 'as Shakespeare's best are', but thanks to such loaded praise Shakespeare's lack of education has settled down to a long and vigorous life.

The tradition was handed on by Dryden, who was responsive to Shakespeare's genius but believed that 'he was naturally learn'd; he needed not the spectacles of books to read Nature; he look'd inwards and found her there.' To an extent this is true enough, so long as it is not taken to imply that

Shakespeare did not also read books. Augustan criticism was ruled by French conceptions of decorum, which included the doctrine of the Unities in its severest form. Elizabethan drama therefore was looked upon as barbarous in structure and feeling, and the mauling of Shakespeare's texts by Nahum Tate, Colley Cibber and others lasted through Garrick until the early nineteenth century. Speaking the Prologue to Dryden's *Troilus and Cressida*, the Ghost of Shakespeare is made to say this:

> Untaught, unpractis'd, in a barbarous age,
> I found not, but created first, the stage.
> And if I drain'd no Greek or Latin store,
> 'Twas that my own abundance gave me more.

An anonymous Prologue to his own *Julius Caesar* written in the same period says similarly:

> In country beauties, as we often see
> Something that takes in their simplicity,
> Yet while they charm, they know not they are fair,
> And take without their spreading of the snare;
> Such artless beauty lies in Shakespeare's wit,
> 'Twas well in spite of him what e'er he writ.
> His excellences came and were not sought.

This notion of Shakespeare as an artless Amaryllis of the theatre even had the authority of Fuller, whose *Worthies of England*, published posthumously in 1662, was begun when oral traditions were still available:

> He was an eminent instance of that rule, *Poeta non fit, sed nascitur*, one is not *made* but *born* a poet. Indeed his learning was very little, so that as *Cornish diamonds* are not polished by any lapidary, but are pointed and smoothed even as they are taken out of the earth, so *nature* itself was all the *art* which was used upon him.

Rowe, always a dutiful reporter of the prevailing sentiments of his own age, was accordingly able to conclude:

> We are to consider him as a man that lived in a state of almost universal licence and ignorance: there was no established judge, but everyone took the liberty to write according to the dictates of his own fancy. When one considers that there is not one play before him of a reputation good enough to entitle it to an appearance on the present stage, it cannot but be a matter of great wonder that he should advance dramatic poetry so far as he did.

Thus he 'lived under a kind of mere light of Nature'; and Rowe found *The Tempest* the least imperfect of his plays since 'the Unities are kept here with an exactness uncommon to the liberties of his writing'.

In 1767 Richard Farmer, Master of Emmanuel, published an *Essay on the Learning of Shakespeare* in which he maintained that although Shakespeare remembered enough to quote a few tags from his Latin Grammar, he had no first-hand acquaintance with either the writers of Greece and Rome or the modern European languages: 'his studies were most demonstratively confined to *nature* and *his own language*'. Passages which seemed to conflict with this view Farmer dismissed as the work of other hands. If he knew of it, he would therefore have endorsed the anonymous *Essay against too much Reading* (1728), wherein it was alleged that Shakespeare employed a 'devil' to look up his facts:

> I will give you a short account of Mr Shakspear's proceeding; and that I had from one of his intimate acquaintance. His being imperfect in some things was owing to his not being a scholar, which obliged him to have one of those chuckle-pated historians for his particular associate...And when he wanted anything in his way, as his plays were all historical, he sent to him, and took down the heads of what was for his purpose.

Remarkably, the chuckle-pated historian is still with us. In the recent Cambridge edition of the plays Dover Wilson has explained some of the textual and authorial problems by postulating a professional hack who at times was Shakespeare's 'particular associate': a crepuscular figure who consulted the sources, dug out the facts and even, when the master was bored or preoccupied, wrote some of the text. Much of Dover Wilson's fascinating editorial ingenuity was made necessary by his assumption that Shakespeare was not much inclined to do his own reading.

In fact Shakespeare's learning was much as one would have expected of the author of the plays attributed to him. It was well grounded in standard works, but in general it was casual, unpedantic, occasionally wide-ranging but as remarkable for what it lacked as for what it sometimes embraced. Dryden was right to say that his essential wisdom was not of the sort that comes from books, for

Learning is but an adjunct to oneself.

LLL IV iii 314.

No profit grows where is no pleasure ta'en.
In brief, sir, study what you most affect.

TS I i 39.

The man who devoted a whole comedy to pricking the bubble of bookish learning gained his own knowledge of mankind from watching and listening to men. Where Dryden was wrong was in implying that Shakespeare did not bother with books at all, that he was largely unread; whereas his work has evidence of wide selective reading and an easy familiarity with most of the intellectual concepts held by educated men in his day. His reading was not systematic, and he probably had small respect for the prizes attained by the continual plodders; but 'base authority from others' books' was always acceptable when his dramatic purposes required it. In his *Shakespeare's History Plays* E.M.W.Tillyard suggested that his learning was of the desultory, unacademic sort that Dr Johnson conjectured for Dryden himself:

> I rather believe that the knowledge of Dryden was from accidental intelligence and various conversation, by a quick apprehension, a judicious selection, and a happy memory, a keen appetite of knowledge, and a powerful digestion; by vigilance that permitted nothing to pass without notice, and a habit of reflection that suffered nothing useful to be lost... I do not suppose that he despised books, or intentionally neglected them; but that he was carried out, by the impetuosity of his genius, to more vivid and speedy instructors; and that his studies were rather desultory and fortuitous than constant and systematical.
>
> *Lives of the Poets.*

When Shakespeare's interest was engaged and the germ of a play was forming in his mind, his curiosity might be inexhaustible, and at times he would lay hands on any book, play or pamphlet that would satisfy it. Originality of thought, or even of phrase, was not expected of him, for the Elizabethans set little store by inventiveness and he was as free to plagiarize a speech or a sentence as to appropriate a plot. The true originality of his mind lay in the integration of ideas gathered from many sources and in his poetic gift of seeking new-found resemblances and expressing them in memorable verse.

Scholarly exploration of his sources[2] is inclined to suggest reading too voluminous and knowledge too encyclopedic to have been attainable in a busy professional life. Because a phrase, a sentence or an idea may be traced to some recondite original, we may never be sure that Shakespeare came by it in that way. He may have heard it from another, picked it up in conversation or conceived it for himself. Some parallels or derivations may be fortuitous, or alternatively they may be commonplaces. In *Shakespeare Survey 3* (1950) F.P.Wilson set out four possible derivations for Hamlet's 'There is nothing either good or bad but thinking makes it so'. Shakespeare may have been acquainted with all of these (and done some fairly esoteric reading in the process) or with none; he was quite capable of working out these things for himself. This particular thought was in fact a familiar assertion of the moral nihilism to which melancholy might reduce a man, and it was to be developed at some length in Chapman's *Biron's Conspiracy* III i 47sq. Again, Menenius's fable of the belly in *Coriolanus* appears in various forms in Livy, Aesop, Plutarch, Erasmus, Sidney, Camden and at least two other works by Shakespeare's contemporaries. In producing his own version of it, how many of these sources did he use?

---

2 Notably G.Bullough, *Shakespeare's Narrative and Dramatic Sources* and K.Muir, *The Sources of Shakespeare's Plays.*

Twelfth Night may be taken as an example of the numerous sources he may, or may not, have consulted in devising a plot. In part he was repeating his own devices: the mistaken identity of twins occurs in *Comedy of Errors*, and in *Two Gentlemen of Verona* a girl disguised as a page is intermediary between the man she loves and the woman he loves. The main source for *Twelfth Night* was an anonymous Italian comedy *Gl' Ingannati* (*The Cheated*), written in prose and performed at Siena in 1531. This has the basic plot of a disguised girl sent on a love embassy to a man who immediately falls in love with her; the girl's lost brother comes to town and the tangle is resolved much as Shakespeare resolved it. The play was frequently adapted, imitated and translated. As a play it appeared in a French translation by Charles Estienne; a popular English version, *The Bugbears*; an academic Latin translation, *Laelia*, acted at Cambridge in 1595; and two Italian imitations, both called *Gl' Inganni* (*The Cheats*). As a story it was one of Bandello's Italian prose romances, translated into French by Belleforest, and it was also used by Cinthio. Shakespeare's main source was probably the story of Apolonius and Silla in Barnabe Riche's *Farewell to Military Profession* (1581), which introduces the shipwreck not present in earlier versions; and in another story in this volume Riche has a husband who shuts his shrewish wife in a dark room and treats her as a lunatic. In the main the sub-plot, with the gulling of Malvolio, and Malvolio and Sir Andrew appearing as additional suitors to Olivia, was Shakespeare's own addition. Malevolti is a character in the original Sienese play. Malvolio's interruption of the revellers may have been suggested by an anecdote about Sir William Knollys, who in 1596 was made a comptroller of the royal household. At court the maids of honour 'used to frisk and hey about in the next room, to his extreme disquiet at nights although he often warned them of it'. Although a married man in late middle age, and known for his Puritan sympathies, Knollys was covetous of one of these ladies, none other than Mary Fitton, who led him on and brazenly fooled him.[3]

It is impossible to know how many of these versions Shakespeare consulted. Once the idea of the story appealed to him, he may have tracked down every available source — it is in one of the Italian imitations that the disguised girl takes the name of Cesare. But there is no discernible pattern in his methods of composition. Sometimes he relied on a single source, but more often on two or three at least; sometimes he had a source-play as a foundation, as in *King John*, *Henry IV* and *Henry V*, *Measure for Measure*, *King Lear*, and probably in other plays where such sources have not survived, but he seems never to have relied on these alone. Even when he more or less devised his own plot, as in *Love's Labour's Lost*, *Midsummer Night's Dream*, *Merry Wives of Windsor* — all first written for courtly occa-

3 See Chambers, *Shakespeare: a Survey*, 178-9, P. Alxander, *Shakespeare's Life and Art*, 135-6, K. Muir, *The Sources of Shakespeare's Plays*, 132-40.

sions — and *The Tempest*, he made use of characters and situations already familiar in story and legend, and some authorities are directly traceable, as Ovid in the story of Pyramus and Thisbe and Montaigne in *The Tempest*. The difficulty is to assess the extent of Shakespeare's personal reading and knowledge, because we are not to suppose that wherever a possible source is known to have existed, he made use of it. A large stock of classical learning, legend, history and romantic fiction was available to all, and Elizabethan writers plundered one another quite guilelessly. Shakespeare's mind was capacious and absorptive, and as Johnson suggested of Dryden, he had a happy memory and a powerful digestion — or the fortunate gift of being able to recall at need almost anything that he had ever read or heard. Often this process may have been subconscious. Richard Farmer was quite wrong to suppose that he was an unlearned man, but he had some wise words on his indebtedness to the men he met almost every day of his working life:

> Nothing but an intimate acquaintance with the writers of the time, who are frequently of no other value, can point out his allusions, and ascertain his phraseology. The reformers of his text are for ever equally positive and equally wrong. The cant of the age, a provincial expression, an obscure proverb, an obsolete custom, a hint at a person or a fact no longer remembered, hath continually defeated the best of our *guessers*.

In attempting to estimate his learning we should therefore be wise to adopt a cautious agnosticism rather than the certainty of a positive illumination: an attitude indeed commended by the scholars who have been most diligent in investigating his sources. With that saving reservation we may try to discover what were the chief intellectual influences on his work.

Elizabethan children went to church before they went to school, and the Bible and the English Liturgy impressed Shakespeare with their stories and the grandeur of their language. So too did the Homilies, official sermons to be read in churches on Sundays and Holy Days 'for the better understanding of the simple people'. They were directed also at simple or recalcitrant clergyman who might be incapable of preaching at all or might say the wrong things, and they stressed the Christian duty of obedience to constituted authority. Shakespeare was familiar both with the Bishops' Bible of 1568 and with the earlier Geneva version that probably held favour in Puritan Stratford. He knew the Apocrypha also, and quotations have been identified from forty-two books of the Bible. The characters most frequently referred to, directly or by implication, were Cain, the first man to secede from the human race, and Job, because we can but endure our coming hither and our going hence.

Shakespeare built on his grammar-school education, or its equivalent, by acquiring sufficient Latin to read works in the original when no translation were available. He knew Ovid well enough to be able to correct some of the mistakes in Golding's popular version. Professor Muir finds evidence that he had read in the original two plays of Plautus, Buchanan's *Rerum Scoti-carum Historia*, some Virgil, a good deal of Erasmus and possibly some of the plays of Seneca. There are errors in his classical mythology and his ancient history, but there are errors in his English history too, and his mistakes are never certain proof of ignorance. If frequently they were due to haste or carelessness — quite literally so: he did not care that Coriolanus died long before Cato was born — they sometimes enrich the artistic effect. He never hestitated to rearrange facts if it suited his dramatic convenience, and probably he was aware of most of the anachronisms that distress the learned. The whole of human history was spread before him as a single story. Strictly he should not have allowed Ulysses to cite Aristotle (*Troilus and Cressida* II ii 166), but human nature does not change and on matters of concern to humanity Ulysses and Aristotle may have had similar thoughts and conclusions.

His use of Latin and mythology was selective. From Plautus and Terence he learned something of the structure of comedy and the stock characters to be found in it, but he soon passed on to a style of romantic comedy more congenial to his own nature; Seneca, although always good for a sonorous aphorism or to reinforce a pessimistic mood, preached an indifferent fatalism alien to Shakespeare's usual thought; and the harshly forbidding conception of Nature in Virgil's *Georgics* is remote from the fertile countryside celebrated in the plays. His real affinity was with Ovid, with his frank delight in sex, his receptiveness to myth and legend and his abundance of good stories. The *Metamorphoses*, especially the first two books, he used more than any other work in any language, returning to it again and again for plots, characters, imagery and verbal inspiration. Probably he reshaped the average Englishman's attitude to Ovid. Arthur Golding, whose translation of the *Metamorphoses* was completed in 1567, had not approached his task with any expectation of sensuous enjoyment. He was an upright and religious man who translated many religious and philosophical works, including Calvin's sermons and Seneca's *De Beneficiis*. Medieval commentators had allegorized Ovid's meaning in ways that would have surprised him, and Golding's conceived the poem, this 'dark philosophy of turned shapes', to mean that the metamorphoses denote men's submission to carnal appetite, of which their transformation into beasts is an appropriate symbol. If men abandon themselves to lust and sin, 'What other kind of shape thereby than filthy can they win?' It was not exactly Shakespeare's view that the poem was replete with 'reproofs of vice in youth and age'. He found more rewarding things, as that (XV 75sq.) in the constant flux of Nature nothing is permanent but nothing is ever changed. His reflection on Time's revolutions in *Sonnets* 60 and 64, or in the debate between the King and Warwick in *2 Henry IV* III i, come almost verbatim from Ovid. Ovid retained his hold to the last, inspiring the account of the storm in *The Tempest* and 'Ye elves and hills...'

Rome made a deeper impression on Shakespeare than Greece. He may have been unable to read Greek. He used only a handful of Greek words, he mostly preferred the Latin form of the names of gods and heroes, and he was largely ignorant of Greek philosophy and art. In this he was typical of his age and time. Aristotle had so deeply influenced medieval culture that men used his ideas almost without being aware of it, but the Elizabethans knew more about Seneca and Julius Caesar than they did about Aeschylus or Pericles. Alexander the Great was the only Greek who fired their imagination like the famous men of Rome. In *Timon* Shakespeare allowed Athens to be governed by senators, and the Greek commanders in *Troilus and Cressida* have only a thin resemblance to their legendary originals. It is assumed that the appearance in 1598 of the first books of Chapman's translation of the *Iliad* drew Shakespeare's interest to the siege of Troy, but Homer had earlier been translated by Arthur Hall and there were two recent French versions if he had wished to consult them. His Greek commanders are singularly unHomeric, and this was his only use of a Homeric theme; Achilles is never mentioned in his drama outside this play, and Ulysses and Agamemnon very seldom. When midway through his career he came upon Sir Thomas North's translation of a French version of Plutarch's *Lives*, he ignored the Greeks whom Plutarch chose as parallels to his twenty-three Roman statesmen and wrote only of the Romans.

The story of Troy, on the other hand, aroused his imagination. It was Dido and Aeneas who would give place to Antony and Cleopatra in the realm where 'souls do couch on flowers', and their love that was used to transfigure the passion of the runaway Jessica. In Shakespeare's hands the themes of antiquity have this extraordinary potency to enrich a poetic creation. Hector, Troilus and Priam and his Queen have frequent reference in the plays, and they lend their quality to lesser men.

The great Duke of Marlborough reputedly said that he derived his knowledge of English history from Shakespeare's plays. If so, he only learned about the Tudors because all Shakespeare's history is contemporary. He read the chronicles, and probably he knew much more about his own country than appears in the plays, but it cannot be claimed that *Macbeth*, *King Lear* or *Cymbeline* give an informative picture of an earlier Britain. Shakespeare saw the medieval past in terms of rebellion and civil war, which he used as *exempla* to warn his own contemporaries of the perils of disunity. His play of *King John* ignored the constitutional conflict which later generations would find so significant. It was an appeal for national unity against the enemy without and treachery within. The two historical tetralogies have the same central theme, and their focus is on Elizabethan England. With medieval life and society Shakespeare did not much concern himself, and it would be difficult to find Faulconbridge a place in it or to realise that Falstaff was a contemporary of the Canterbury pilgrims.

Gower's *Confessio Amantis* was used at some stage during the compilation of *Pericles*, but Shakespeare's connection with this play, or its missing source, is uncertain and the groundwork may have been done before he handled it. He may have consulted Geoffrey of Monmouth for his two plays about ancient Britain, but in general he made surprisingly little direct use of medieval writers, Chaucer included. Good Chaucerians have been reluctant to admit this and have tried to refute or explain it. They say that Chaucer was primarily a story-teller and Shakespeare a dramatist, attitudes had changed towards the concepts of magic and courtly love, the Reformation had removed many of the superstitious and greedy ecclesiasts, and so on. It is not that Chaucer was not well known and influential among the Elizabethans, and here were two men of genius alike in their 'mere Englishness' and well matched in their wit and sanity and poetic artifice. Chaucer's influence on Shakespeare may perhaps have been felt most strongly in a harmony of thought and feeling, but the discernible and indubitable influences are few. There is nowhere a salutation to Chaucer, whose name does not appear in the canon, and the borrowings are miniscule: the Knight's Tale was a source for the Theseus plot in *Midsummer Night's Dream*, but so too was Plutarch and this is a small part of the play; *The Legend of Good Women* may have contributed to *Lucrece*; and there is *Troilus and Cressida*, in which Shakespeare was also influenced by *The Testament of Cresseid* (1593) by Robert Henryson, a dominie from Dunfermline. Professing to continue the work of 'worthy Chaucer glorious', Henryson makes Cressida the concubine of several Greek commanders and has her reduced by the angry gods to beggary and leprosy. In Shakespeare's play this fate is implicit in a sexuality not to be found in Chaucer, whose Criseyde is a kindly portrait of a bewildered young widow in an alien land, 'slydynge of corage'. She is not the bitchy wanton who in Henryson's poem was punished for being 'sa gigotlike'. Chaucer's Pandarus, too, is not Shakespeare's semi-impotent *voyeur*.

For *Richard II* Shakespeare used Froissart and possibly other French chroniclers, but for his histories he relied upon writers of the sixteenth century: Polydore Vergil, who approved of Henry V as the 'star of England' but saw the accession of the Tudors as a divine intervention; Edward Hall, crudely and uncritically Protestant but also a champion of the Tudor reading of history; Holinshed, an industrious compiler whose mood responded to his immediate sources; the compendious *Mirror for Magistrates*, weighty with political admonition; Warner's *Albion's England*, Camden's *Remains* and for its sympathetic interpretation Daniel's epic poem *The Civil Wars*.

Among modern languages he had at least a working knowledge of French, no doubt enlarged during his lodging *chez* Mountjoy, and since apparently he was familiar with certain Italian originals, possibly some Italian; but he would have had friends more fluent in these languages than himself and he may have depended on their goodwill and help for his occasional needs.

This is an uncertain area where scepticism is advisable. But it was to the story books, mostly available in translation, that he turned most often: Cinthio, Bandello, Belleforest and the English collections of William Painter and Geoffrey Fenton. He knew Boccaccio, and the *Orlando Furioso* and *I Suppositi* of Ariosto, and the work of a member of Southampton's household, John Florio, translator of Montaigne. All these assorted works were known to most writers of the time and they were a treasure-house of plots and sub-plots and incidental themes and characters. The earlier plays, some now lost, which Shakespeare sometimes used as groundwork were themselves intermediate sources derived from *novelle*, foreign plays or chronicles. He knew his contemporaries too, Lyly, Marlowe, Greene, Nashe, Peele, Spenser, Sidney and many more: the plays are full of echoes of contemporary plays and pamphlets — Nashe's *Pierce Penniless* in *Hamlet*, for example. In view of his professional position it had to be so. The King's Men had always to keep an eye on rival companies and their dramatists, and a sudden success would start an investigation that might lead Shakespeare to a source hitherto unexplored. He also acted in plays by Jonson and other writers who may have been more bookish than himself. The international popularity of the best-known myths and stories makes it hazardous to name precise authorities in particular cases. In *The Governor* (1513), a scholarly discourse on politics and education, Sir Thomas Elyot tells the traditional story of Prince Hal's being committed to prison for striking the Lord Chief Justice. The story had virtually passed into folklore, and of course Shakespeare knew of it. It was in his source-play and probably he found it there. But he may have had it earlier from *The Governor*, which had been a standard work for two generations, and the point is that this item cannot be taken as certain evidence that he had read *The Governor* or that he had not. It is a constant dilemma.

Undoubtedly, however, he was familiar with books of this kind. The age was rich in writers who compounded a moral philosophy from various elements drawn from medicine, psychology and ethics, and it has been argued that he was acquainted with the work of Timothy Bright, du Bartas, Pierre de la Primaudaye, Cardano, Thomas Crewe and others of this learned sort. So he may. He appears to have studied Bright's *Treatise on Melancholy*, Reginald Scot's *Discovery of Witchcraft* and a scholarly book of a different kind, Thomas Wilson's *Art of Rhetorique*. He was not averse from hard reading on theoretical subjects, and he mastered what he read. He is constantly surprising modern scholars by his knowledge of some of the advanced thinking of the age, a knowledge that is partly concealed by his deceptive skill in embodying it in poetic drama. Thus Hamlet's uncertainty in facing the possibly sinister manifestation of his father's Ghost was an orthodox exposition of current thinking on demonology. On this and similar matters Shakespeare wrote and thought like a man abreast with recent philosophical speculations, but he was so little doctrinaire that he would throw off a piece of advanced thinking side by side with some shop-soiled tit-bit of traditional folklore or rustic superstition. On many topics, where there was no immediate dramatic stimulus, he was content to be ignorant: but he wrote, apparently as a matter of course, of many doctrines that were only the possession of educated men.

He accepted the belief that matter was composed of four elements; he knew, and to some extent accepted, the theory of 'humours' and the results that may follow when they are not harmoniously blended; he believed that man was the centre of the universe, poised between angels and beasts and endowed with the godlike reason of the one to restrain him from the passionate appetites of the other. He accepted the notion of a Chain of Being wherein every created thing is linked with another in an ascending scale reaching to God and the angels; and he believed in the correspondences which join each plane of being in a fundamental unity, so that if the jackal overthrow the lion, rank fumiter will flourish where the rose once bloomed. He knew that the physical universe, the commonwealth and the soul of man were so indissolubly linked as parts of a single act of Creation that when one man slays another, the sun may be eclipsed and confusion suffocate the common weal: the sky dropped fire in presage of Caesar's fall, and at the sin of Macbeth the falcon was hawked at by the mousing owl. He believed in the Platonic doctrine of the music of the spheres, and he held that in some mysterious way each man's destiny, without loss of his individual responsibility, was governed by the stars. Above all, he recognized that order was Heaven's first law: that a harmonious balance in the community or in the mind of man was a reflection of a wider cosmic balance, and that unless men would accept the degrees and duties prescribed for them in the divinely-ordained hierarchy of the universe, chaos was come again. Shakespeare owned this vast body of thinking, primarily ethical in character, about the nature of man, his place in society and his relations with God and his fellowmen. His power to give it poetic expression in moments of dramatic conflict added a dimension to the men and women of whom he wrote.[4]

It is beside the point that some of these beliefs were unsound, that some of the components of the picture were mutually contradictory and that a complete world-synthesis was never achieved. What matters is, first, that the

4 The concepts mentioned in this paragraph are further discussed in the next chapter. For more detailed consideration of his learning, see J.A.K. Thomson, *Shakespeare and the Classics*, G. Highet, *The Classical Tradition*, Hardin Craig, *The Enchanted Glass*, Theodore Spencer, *Shakespeare and the Nature of Man*, E.M.W. Tillyard, *The Elizabethan World Picture* and *Shakespeare's History Plays*, A.O. Lovejoy, *The Great Chain of Being*, L.B. Campbell, *Shakespeare's Histories* and *Shakespeare's Tragic Heroes*, J.F. Danby, *Shakespeare's Doctrine of Nature*, R. Noble, *Shakespeare's Biblical Knowledge*, A.Hart, *Shakespeare and the Homilies*, V.Harris *All Coherence Gone*. The cautious reader will be aware of the tendency in these and other monographic studies to over-estimate the thoroughness of Shakespeare's reading and the exactness of his knowledge. Nor was Elizabethan thought as compact and tidy as some of these studies propose.

Elizabethans thought their picture to be true on the whole, even in face of Copernican doubts about their geocentric universe and the growing authority of opinions which challenged their optimistic view of man as the hub and purpose of it; and, secondly, that Shakespeare's acceptance of this picture puts him intellectually in the company of representative thinkers of the age. We cannot doubt his interest in science, metaphysics, psychology and — with the exception of theological debate — all the weightier topics that occupied the Elizabethan mind. In fact, when we find him casually satirizing the Ramist logic[5] which at Cambridge had lately toppled the monolithic Aristotle from his eminence, we may get to thinking him more learned than he was. The worst of errors is to forget that he was a poet. The carefree mastery of most of his material was a poet's mastery, not a scholar's. The brilliance and felicity of expression deceive the eye.

In many matters he was less knowledgeable than has been supposed. Although he was pre-eminently the poet of Nature and the countryside, drawing on them for a flow of imagery that seldom fails to touch the heart, his references to plants and animals contain frequent errors and he seems to have often depended on traditional lore instead of his own observation. When he does observe for himself, he is unsurpassable: as with the hare in *Venus and Adonis*, the eddy that he noticed as he stood on the Clopton bridge (*Lucrece* 1667-73), or 'his hoar leaves in the glassy stream' (*Ham* IV vii 168), a picture possible only to one who had actually seen the white underpart of a willow leaf reflected in the water. But he treated Nature as he treated books or historical facts: he was not interested in it for itself, but only as it prompted him to reflection on the ways of men. Thus the habits of the animal creation served him only as they approximated to the habits of mankind; and when he did not observe them directly, he often reported them wrongly, as in the famous excursus on bees in *Henry* V I ii, which he borrowed from Lyly. He had been wrong about bees in *Titus Andronicus* V i, possibly for the same reason, and he is frequently inexact about the cuckoo and the nightingale, birds common enough to be observed accurately by anyone interested in them but described by Shakespeare in the conventional phrases of country tradition. He writes of 'the gnawing vulture of thy mind' (*Titus Andronicus* V ii 32), and the image, however hackneyed, loses none of its power from the fact that vultures do not gnaw. None of his errors weaken the poetic force of the passages where they occur — often they need experts to detect them — and this justifies his way of working and reveals his attitude to all sources of information. They were matter for poetry, not for precise intellectual statement; and it is the poetry that has won him a reputation as an exact and exhaustive student of Nature.

5   As in the Gravedigger's reasoning in *Hamlet* V i 9-22, or Polonius on his 'foolish figure', II ii 97-104. The *Dialectica* (1543) of Pierre de la Ramée (1515-72) presented a new system of logic.

In his *Shakespeare* (1907) Sir Walter Raleigh made a rapid and illuminating survey (pages 35-7) to show how limited his knowledge was for a country-bred boy. He knew that the halcyon turns with the wind, that canker is in the rose and the lapwing runs close to the ground and sings when far from its nest, 'that the greyhound's mouth catches; that pigeons feed their young; that herrings are bigger than pilchards; that trout are caught with tickling...that the cuckoo lays its eggs in the nests of other birds; that the lark resembles the bunting'. It is fairly commonplace stuff, much of it accessible to a boy brought up in an urban civilization to-day. *As You Like It* being a pastoral play set in the forest of Arden, one would expect it to be full of natural imagery and observation, but Raleigh shows (page 126) that the illusion is created by poetry, with very little concrete reference. 'No single bird, or insect, or flower, is mentioned by name. The words "flower" and "leaf" do not occur. The trees of the forest are the oak, the hawthorn, the palm-treee, and the olive. For animals, there are the deer, one lioness, and one green and gilded snake. The season is not easy to determine; perhaps it is summer; we hear only of the biting cold and the wind.'

Although Shakespeare's images from falconry are so frequent and accurate that he must have taken part in it, he never uses the simile of the fish rising to the bait, and such common creatures as the otter, the water-rat, the squirrel and the dragonfly are all absent from his pages, as are common birds like the kingfisher, moorhen, woodpecker, heron, wood-pigeon and nightjar. No doubt he knew of them, but they had no particular place in folklore and he did not know them well enough to use them to illuminate an abstract idea. Although he rejected the popular belief that eagles are sucked to death by beetles, he endorsed the fallacy that the sea swells before a storm and that one fire extinguishes another; and he accepted from country tradition, or from the medieval bestiaries often consulted by Elizabethan writers, the toad that wears a precious jewel in his head, the basilisk that kills at sight, the pelican that feeds her young with her own blood, or the unicorn that may be betrayed with trees. He did not necessarily believe these fables, many of which are put in the mouths of characters naturally credulous, but he did not trouble to correct them.

When dealing with domestic animals whose ways he could study for himself, he was similarly content to use them as symbols of the unflattering qualities conferred on them by popular prejudice. Ape, dog, goose, ass, cat, 'creatures vile...of no esteem', were useful as illustrations of greed, servility, foolishness, obstinacy and various mischiefs. He found them matter for poetic decoration but seldom for sympathetic understanding. The common tongue, which 'robbed many beasts of their particular additions', was ready with these convenient symbols, just as today catch-phrases like 'drunk as a lord' or 'bald — or queer — as a coot' are used by people who have never met a lord or positively identified a coot. One of these symbols Shakespeare used so often that he has lowered himself in the thoughts of a dog-loving people.

The domestic dog, particularly the spaniel, had become a symbol of cup-board love, of the fawning adulation that expects to be rewarded with dainty gifts and then ungratefully moves on to the next hand-out. If a dog had a bad name, Shakespeare, carelessly looking for a resemblance, was the last man to spare him a hanging, and he could scarcely mention dog or greed or adula-tion or ingratitude without embarking upon the whole combined image. It has been inferred from this that he did not like dogs, unless they could make the noble music of the hounds, but the automatic recurrence of the image, which may well have been a commonplace, suggests that he used it without thinking. It was not his purpose to do justice to the nature of animals or to report accurately on their habits; they served him only for comments on mankind. But find a man whose dog is his companion and confidant, and the result is Launce's Crab.

An unhappy reference to the Bohemian littoral has brought Shakespeare's geography into question, and in the same play he located the Delphic oracle at Delos. But in general his geography is informed and accurate. He girdled the earth with an easy allusiveness and a richness of pictorial detail that must seem to originate in personal experience or long hours of study, but probably he picked up most of his information from the travellers who with their extravagant tales were always to be met in London. He knew well 'my picked man of countries',

> Talking of the Alps and Apennines,
> The Pyrenean and the river Po.
>
> *KJ* I i 202.

These ebullient gossips would proclaim in street and tavern their readiness to go

> on the slightest errand to the Antipodes that you can devise to send me on: I will fetch you a tooth-picker now from the furthest inch of Asia: bring you the length of Prester John's foot: fetch you a hair of the great Cham's beard: do you an embassage to the Pigmies.
>
> *MAN* II i 273.

Shakespeare often laughed at these harmless braggarts, but what he burles-ques at one time he has a way of using seriously at another. It was with gorgeous traveller's tales, of Anthropophagi and men whose heads grow beneath their shoulders, that Othello won Desdemona's heart.

Shakespeare knew enough of the sea and soldiering and the law to have persuaded some people that in early life he found a vocation there. That Protean mind was master of so many skills and activities that we can never be sure whether he is speaking from personal experience, or the stored informa-tion of his friends, or books that he has studied.

> He hath strange places crammed
> With observation, the which he vents
> In mangled forms.
>
> *AYLI* II vii 40.

Learning was useful to him only for the illumination that it cast upon the human scene, and he was blessed with the faculty of delivering it up at need. Touchstone perhaps put his finger on it:

> When a man's verses cannot be understood, nor a man's good wit seconded with the forward child Understanding, it strikes a man more dead than a great reckoning in a little room.
>
> *AYLI* III iii 12.

'Truly', Touchstone adds to Audrey, 'I would the gods had made thee poetical'. Shakespeare was poetical, and his imagination selected and transformed what he had read or heard. Perhaps something of this kind was intended by Jonson, Dryden and others who said that he was 'naturally learned'. His knowledge has been explained away by assertions that he had all his Ovid from Golding, which is demonstrably untrue; that he did not know, or need to know, French and Italian because he was able to use English versions now conveniently lost, which is possible but unprovable; that the scholarly references in the plays were generously supplied by better educated dramatists or by the ubiquitous playhouse hack. It could be so, and there is not enough positive evidence to allow anyone to be dogmatic. But whenever he handled a difficult idea, he almost always showed that he understood it, and his performance in scholarly matters does not have the casualness of his handling of chronology or of birds and beasts. The speech of Ulysses on degree (*Troilus and Cressida* I iii 83-137) is a classic text-book exposition, and its length, which is undramatic, suggests that the idea has conquered his imagination. He is more impressive, because the task is subtler, when he selects only a part of a significant idea or body of thought, using only so much of it as will advance a scene, or when he uses it for burlesque and yet shows that he understands it well enough for his satire to be accurate and fair. Touchstone (who was not so called without reason) is again useful here. His remarks on retorts and lies (*AYLI* V iv 71-109) — an interpolation necessary to give Rosalind and Celia time to get out of their manly garb — reveal some familiarity with the courtly manuals governing the etiquette of duels, and also sufficient of 'the forward child Understanding' to make Touchstone's commentary pertinent. There are far too many such passages, wittily and learnedly assimilated into the action, for anyone but Shakespeare to have been responsible for — at least — the vast majority of them.

4. The *Sonnets*.

We should be cautious in looking for personal history in the *Sonnets*. The evidence that they provide is artistic rather than autobiographical. Although they were known to Meres, who in his catalogue in 1598 referred to 'his sugared Sonnets among his private friends', the poems were not published until 1609, when Thomas Thorpe issued them along with *A Lover's Complaint*, a poem of 329 lines in which a girl narrates her submission to a professional seducer, and two sonnets, 138 and 144, that had appeared in a slightly different form in William Jaggard's pirated *Passionate Pilgrim* (1599). The likely date of composition is during the sonneteering vogue between 1592 and 1597. This is supported by stylistic similarities to be found in Shakespeare's two verse romances and in the plays written during these years, but both earlier and later dates have been conjectured. In 1899 Samuel Butler proposed 1595-8, and Dr Leslie Hotson, more formidably armed with Elizabethan scholarship, has agreed with him; but Dover Wilson, although obliged to admit that some of the poems were written in the nineties, puts others as late as 1600-06.[6]

Thorpe prefaced his volume with this inscription: 'To the only begetter of these ensuing, Sonnets, Mr W.H., all happiness, and that eternity promised by our ever-living Poet, wisheth the well-wishing adventurer in setting forth, T.T.' Succeeding generations have travailed ever since. On the assumption that 'the only begetter' referred to the man by whom the poems were inspired some, scholars have naturally chosen Henry Wriothesley, Earl of Southampton, the patron to whom Shakespeare dedicated his two long romances with a formal respect that may have been touched with personal affection. The inconvenient facts that a nobleman is unlikely to have been addressed as 'Master', and that the young man's initials were H.W. and not W.H., have been no impediment to the construction of certain notions about the relationship between them. Praise of the boy's beauty, 'the master-mistress of my passion', has disturbing implications, and it is appropriate here to dispose once and for all of allegations of Shakespeare's sexual perversion. The idea that the friendship of a man for a man was deeper and nobler than his love for a woman was a favourite theme in classical literature, as in the stories of Orestes and Pylades or Nisus and Euralyus. It had a vogue during the Renaissance, Lyly using it in *Ephues* and *Endimion* and Shakespeare himself in *The Two Gentlemen of Verona*. So far we are dealing with an attitude that may have been genuinely inspiring in ancient Sparta but had since declined into a romantic literary convention. On the practical issue Shakespeare speaks for himself. The astonishing ingenuity of his bawdiness has only become evident as scholars have discovered the Elizabethans' relish and capacity for double meanings. Understanding of such simple words as 'will' and 'die' brings new significance to

6   In the Cambridge edition of the poems. Other discussions may be found in L. Hotson, *Shakespeare's Sonnets Dated*, M.C. Bradbrook, *Shakespeare and Elizabethan Poetry*, E.K. Chambers, *Shakespeare Gleanings*, 111-24, C.F.T. Brooke (ed.), *Shakespeare's Sonnets*, R.J.C. Wait, *The Background to Shakespeare's Sonnets*, and the works of A.L. Rowse.

apparently simple statements. Shakespeare's instinctive exploitation of these rich possibilities shows him to have been exclusively interested in the relationship of men and women. If he had any deviant inclinations, they must have appeared in the constant flow of his sexual imagery, but they do not. The 'male varlet' Patroclus was in his sources and he gets little sympathy. Falstaff, it is true, 'if his weapon be out', will spare man nor woman nor child, but this is only a generalized tribute to his potency. Shakespeare does not make 'queer' jokes because he was not interested. In *Sonnet* 20 he is explicit on his relationship with the lovely boy. Nature made them different, and that was that.

Another candidate for the role was William Herbert, who became Earl of Pembroke in 1601. Dover Wilson, who supports him, has argued somewhat disingenuously that until he succeeded his father, he might have been addressed as 'Mr W.H.', but Thorpe's dedication was not written until eight years later. Chambers suggests (*WS* I 555-76, *Shakespeare Gleanings* 125-9) that Thorpe found 'To W.H.' on the manuscript that he had somehow acquired and, being unaware of Shakespeare and his friendships, added the 'Mr' out of his own misguided invention. As Thorpe had been in the printing business since 1584, such ignorance seems improbable. If these technicalities may be overlooked, there is quite a good case for Pembroke. Shakespeare may have been associated with his father's company in the confused theatrical years before 1594, and it was to him and his brother, generous patrons of the theatre, that the First Folio was dedicated in 1623. In 1595 a proposed betrothal to a daughter of Lord Hunsdon broke down through Pembroke's 'not liking' the match, and this would give point to the early *Sonnets* which remind Beauty of its obligation to propagate itself. Pembroke was not, however, as the youth of the *Sonnets* apparently was, the sole hope of his house, for he had a brother and a father living; and if the poems are to be taken literally, this is a weighty objection.

Alternatively it has been conjectured, and by Dr Alfred Rowse asserted as a matter beyond dispute, that 'Mr W.H.' was not the youth who inspired the sonnets but the person who passed the manuscript to Thorpe and so enabled it to be printed. Much here would seem to depend on the meaning of 'begetter'. 'Beget' was a word with strong Biblical associations, hardly appropriate for such a trivial act. Even if we accept 'begetter' as meaning 'procurer', the 'only' is questionable and 'our ever-living Poet' would not have wished eternity to a man who contrived a publication that he may not have wanted. Hotson has suggested as the procurer William Hatcliff, a Lincolnshire man who left Cambridge without a degree and went to Gray's Inn. Rowse has nominated Sir William Harvey, who was not a 'Master' but was the third husband of Southampton's mother. If the 'procurer' theory is to be accepted, the likeliest candidate would seem to be the printer William Hall, whose claims were advanced in 1898 by Sir Sidney Lee. At least he was in the trade and might reasonably have acquired the manuscript. But all this detective ingenuity may have been misplaced. Elizabethan publishers were notoriously careless and unscrupulous in their ascriptions and 'Mr W.H.' may never have existed. If he did exist, he has, like Anne Whately, kept his secret. Much more certain identification is necessary before it would be safe to regard him as biographical evidence about Shakespeare's life.

Thorpe, or someone, grouped the poems in a rough pattern. The first 126 were addressed to a handsome young man whom critics have assumed, although without specific evidence, to have been a nobleman, and the last 27 of these appear to have been written two or three years after the original sequence; 127 to 152 are miscellaneous, but most of them were addressed to a dark woman who had already appeared in some of the earlier sonnets; and the last two, derived from a Greek epigram, discuss the connection between eroticism and bathing. There is a further linking of themes within this pattern, the first seventeen urging Beauty to perpetuate itself by begetting offspring, and 78 to 86 reproaching the youth for transferring his favour to a rival poet. Other, smaller groups are linked by syntactical or stylistic devices, such as the repetition of certain words or rhymes. The collection is in fact more consistent in style than in the narrative, which with many reflective digressions loosely tells a story. It is impossible to know whether the poems were written in the order in which Thorpe printed them or whether the collection contains all the sonnets that Shakespeare wrote.

The identification of the rival poet (Chapman, Marlowe, Daniel, Drayton and Gervase Markham have been suggested) and the dark lady has proceeded with the same energy and ingenuity as the identification of the handsome youth and 'Mr W.H.' Rowse claims to have established beyond the possibility of doubt that the dark lady was Emilia Bassano, daughter of an Italian musician at the court. She was the mistress of the first Lord Hunsdon, the Lord Chamberlain and patron of Shakespeare's company. On becoming pregnant by him, she was hastily married to Will Lanier, another of the court musicians, but marriage and motherhood did not cure her of her coquettish ways. Rowse believes that in the period when the *Sonnets* were written, between 1592 and 1595, she held Shakespeare in an ignominious passion from which he could not free himself.

While the literary detection lavished on the 'story' of the *Sonnets* leaves us with uncertain answers, it is a fact that the sonnet sequence was a highly conventional art form with an acknowledged mood, rules and intention. The sonnet itself had been introduced from Italy by Wyatt and Surrey earlier in the century, and Sidney's sequence of *Astrophel and Stella* (1591), celebrating the relationship between himself and Penelope Devereux, started a fashion for exercises in this form. Drayton, Daniel, Spenser, Constable, Lodge, Barnfield, Giles Fletcher, Thomas Watson, Barnabe Barnes and Bartholomew Griffin were among the poets who served the fashion until it came to a sudden end with Robert Tofte's *Laura* in 1597. The convention was as rigid as in pastoral. The poet's 'conceitful quatorzains' were expected to encompass the Petrarchan themes of coquetry and the chase, the hunter's pursuit and the ambushes laid by the hunted. The lover was required to confess his wooing to be hopeless and his rhymes but 'the sad memorial of my miseries'. His desolation had to be expressed in modish conceits about the beloved's cruelty:

> The violet of purple colour came,
> Dyed in the blood she made my heart to shed.
>
> Constable, *Sonnets to Diana.*

The poet meanwhile lamented her remoteness and the anguish of separation. He invoked 'ungentle sleep [that] helpest all but me', but all the while consoled himself with the immortality which his 'world-outwearing rhymes' would confer upon them both. The renunciation of artifice, itself most artfully phrased, was another gambit in the game, for the ingenuity of his conceits was a measure of the poet's success:

> Many there be excelling in this kind
> Whose well-trick'd rhymes with all inventions swell.
>
> Drayton, *Idea.*

It is hardly to be supposed that within half a dozen years a representative selection of English poets were all plunged into the frustrating experiences that their verses proclaim; that the disdainful Cynthia, Coelia, Delia, Laura, Diana, Parthenophe, Phillis, Licia or Fidessa of their verses were all real. Critics do not seriously believe that Sidney was looking into his heart when he wrote his *Astrophel,* and it is absurd that Shakespeare, more than any other sonneteer, should be thought to have mused upon a personal experience. If he really did harbour an unnatural love for a young nobleman, and at the same time was inveigled and cheated by a slut, he is unlikely to have revealed this even in verses circulated (according to Meres) among his friends.

The sonneteering vogue corresponded to the vogue for verse romances that followed upon Lodge's *Glaucus and Scilla* (originally appearing in 1589 as *Scilla's Metamorphosis*). This lasted rather longer, attracting Shirley and Abraham Cowley in their younger days, and in the 1590s Shakespeare, Marlowe, Daniel, Drayton, Chapman, Barnfield and Thomas Heywood all took their part in it. Even if some of the sonneteers were drawing on personal experience, they had to keep the autobiographical element in the background because the presence of real feeling would have broken through the convention. The Elizabethan sonnet was a *tour de force* designed to proclaim the author's wit and artifice. In his novel *Jack Wilton* (1594) Nashe described the sonneteer as 'more in love with his own curious forming fancy than her face; and truth it is, many become passionate lovers only to win

praise to their wits'.
  They did win praise:

Report throughout Western Isle doth ring
The sweet-tuned accents of your Delian sonnetry.

Anon., Zepheria.

The *Parnassus* plays commended the fashion, approving particularly of
Drayton, 'sweet Constable', and 'sweet honey-dropping Daniel' who

doth wage
War with the proudest big Italian
That melts his heart in sugred sonneting.

2 Return I ii 241.

Like all exaggerated fashions, sonneteering also attracted some ridicule, but
even this was part of the convention. The poet would leave protesting for a
while and make wry fun of his own transports. Shakespeare's 130th sonnet,
'My mistress' eyes are nothing like the sun', is a violent example of this
occasional self-criticism, and the *Gulling Sonnets* of Sir John Davies were
conventional in form and spirit, however satirical their intention. No
genuine poet could labour indefinitely in the sort of artifice which 'heaven
itself for ornament doth use' without sometimes needing to cleanse his overheated bosom with a litte mockery.
  Even before the sonneteering vogue had established itself in England,
Sidney had complained of the extravagances of the Petrarchan manner. In
his *Apology for Poetry* he said that 'truly many of such writings as come
under the banner of unresistible love, if I were a mistress, would never
persuade me they were in love'. The bookish wooers studied their poetic
technique more closely than their ladies' eyes, and have thence 'caught up
certain swelling phrases' which do them the office of wooing. In the preface
to his sonnet sequence *Licia* Giles Fletcher confessed that 'a man may write
of love, and not be in love, as well as of husbandry and not go to the plough';
as indeed several poets did write pastoral on the barest acquaintance with the
realities of the rural routine. Rosalind was severe with Orlando when in 'the
quotidian of love' he addressed her with sonnets in the Petrarchan manner
(*AYLI* III ii, where she also reflects upon the sonneteering theme of Time).
Shakespeare is again satirizing the mode in *The Two Gentlemen of Verona*
when Proteus advised Thurio to

lay lime to tangle her desires
By wailful sonnets, whose composed rhymes
Should be full fraught with serviceable vows.

III ii 68.

It is easy, however, to be oppressed by the artificiality and to forget that poetry then was a highly formal art and pattern was of its essence. Courtly poetry, in particular, was hedged with conventional restrictions, and the sonnet was the most exacting of poetic forms. Even when they were strangling themselves with their own conceits, the Elizabethan sonneteers had something to say, and their common preoccupation with the interlocking themes of Time and Beauty produced some fine poetry of the second order. The couplet that opened Shakespeare's sequence expresses their main concern:

> From fairest creatures we desire increase,
> That thereby beauty's rose may never die;

or this, from *Sonnet* 65:

> Since brass, nor stone, nor earth, nor boundless sea,
> But sad mortality o'ersways their power,
> How with this rage shall beauty hold a plea,
> Whose action is no stronger than a flower?

For Renaissance poets *love* was often a symbol for their passionate apprehension of Beauty, and even in the struggle, unthriftiness and disappointment in which many of them passed their lives their dedication to beauty was absolute. Physical beauty fades and dies, but it must be born again. The war against Time, that 'ceaseless lackey to eternity', was the controlling idea of the Elizabethan sonnet.

This idea usually expressed itself in the plight of the lover importuning his 'unkind fair'. It derived from the courtly tradition which warned the poet that the response that he owed to Beauty must not degrade him to the level of the beast. The danger was lust. The love poetry of the Middle Ages had sought to avert it by evoking the powerful ideal of chastity, and the songs of the troubadours told of a love which should never be contaminated. A more recent tradition taught the need for a more comprehensive discipline: while his art should quicken the poet's faculties to respond to Beauty in all its shapes, it should also teach him self-restraint. It was possible for a doctrine of this sort to be at the same time conventional in its formal literary expression and sincere in its expression of personal feeling. *Venus and Adonis* exemplifies this. So far from being isolated from life, poetry showed men how to order their lives. Its function, as Sidney taught it, was pervasively ethical. Thus the sonneteers clung to the convention of their fair one's unapproachability. Bartholomew Griffin's *Fidessa* was not alone in being 'more chaste than kind'. The loved one's hard-hearted disdain, the remoteness of her station, her refusal to hearken to their insistence that her beauty was not eternal, sterilized their passion and preserved it from sin. Despite its erotic imagery, the symbolic world of the sonnets was essentially virginal;

and it was this that enabled Shakespeare to address his affection to a man. Convention demanded that the poets should lie sleeplessly on a bed of unrequited love, because if ever the fair one became accessible, she would no longer be worthy of the sort of devotion they gave her. Her surrender would have brought to an end the conflict which gave their poetry its purpose and meaning: the helplessness of Beauty before the deadly erosion of Time, and the glorious confidence that only their verse could give it immortality. In a sense, therefore, they did not of Beauty desire increase, for there would then have been nothing for them to write about.

Just as his plays cannot be judged in isolation from the drama of his age, so most of the false assumptions about Shakespeare's *Sonnets* have proceeded from the error of reading them independently of the brief but prolific fashion of which they were a part. If we must be looking for a 'story' or a slice of personal history, Emilia Bassano will do as well as anyone for the dark lady, or Hall or Hatcliff or Harvey will do for the 'only begetter' who was really a procurer. But there may have been no 'story'. The sonneteering mode may have attracted Shakespeare, as it attracted other poets, as a convenient medium for reflections on Time and Beauty and similar themes that were always close to him, and instead of looking for biographical details we may more profitably consider the *Sonnets* for what they reveal of Shakespeare's art and the focus of his interests.

His handling of the convention is orthodox in its representation of the unsatisfied poet who reproaches a lover, one in a higher social station, for unresponsiveness, for countenancing rival admirers, for wasting the gift of personal beauty by failing to have children, and so on through the accepted sonneteering gamut. But he changes the mistress into a man, an audacity which stands the convention on its head and at the same time enlarges its emotional and poetic range. He is audacious again, even outrageous, when in the poems addressed to the lady he denounces her as a wanton. He will use the fashion because artistically it is a challenge and it allows him to meditate on matters of enduring concern to him, but he does not take it very seriously.

On the other hand, the *Sonnets* were not an isolated exercise to be divorced from the rest of his work. They are relevant to the study of his development as a poet and dramatist, for he used them to make certain poetic experiments and to explore themes which he would amplify on later occasions. They have some relationship with his two erotic romances. (Number 26 is so similar in tone to the dedication to *Lucrece* that it has been adopted by those who favour Southampton as the 'only begetter'. It may be so; but it is just as likely that Shakespeare was amusing himself by self-parody, just as in his plays he allows comedians to burlesque the solemn transports of graver men, as, for instance in *Henry V* III i, ii). The *Sonnets* have an even closer kinship with two of the plays, *Love's Labour's Lost* and *Romeo and Juliet*, and simultaneous composition seems almost certain. Mercutio jests at the love that finds utterance in 'the numbers that Petrarch flowed in', and on his first appearance Romeo employs the familiar conceit of love as a set of contraries:

> Why then, O brawling love, O loving hate,
> O any thing of nothing first create:
> O heavy lightness, serious vanity,
> Misshapen Chaos of well seeming-forms,
> Feather of lead, bright smoke, cold fire, sick health,
> Still-waking sleep that is not what it is.
>
> I i 182

Shakespeare at that time delighted in oxymoron, which is not a difficult figure to achieve, and Juliet so expresses herself when she hears of Romeo's banishment for slaying Tybalt (III ii 72 sq.). Neither Shakespeare nor his audience saw anything inappropriate in the expression of feeling in elaborately figured language, and Romeo laments Rosaline's chaste inaccessibility in the manner of the sonneteers:

> She'll not be hit
> With Cupid's arrow, she hath Dian's wit:
> And in strong proof of chastity well arm'd,
> From love's weak childish bow she lives unharm'd.
> She will not stay the siege of loving terms,
> Nor bide th' encounter of assailing eyes,
> Nor ope her lap to saint-seducing gold
> O she is rich in beauty, only poor,
> That when she dies, with beauty dies her store.
>
> I i 214.

This was the period when Shakespeare was most in love with rhyme. The proportion of rhyme in *Love's Labour's Lost* is as high as 60 per cent (compared with an average of less than 10 per cent for his plays as a whole), chiefly because he used this play for experiments in the sonnet form. Seven quatorzains were introduced into the text, one of them written in Alexandrines, and numerous quatrains were combined with each other, or with couplets, in a way to leave no doubt that he was exploring the possibilities of this style for dramatic purposes. The spirit of this 'pleasant conceited comedy', as the title-page in the Quarto described it, corresponded to its form. It was Shakespeare's salute, half-mocking and half-admiring, to the vogue of Petrarch and the Euphuists. The tongues of nearly all the characters are conceit's expositors, and when Armado falls in love, he knows only one way to assuage his pain:

> Assist me, some extemporal god of rhyme, for I am sure I shall turn sonnet.
> Devise, wit; write, pen; for I am for whole volumes in folio.
>
> I ii 189.

The play's opening lines speak of Time's endless war on reputation and men's hopes of immortality:

> Let fame, that all hunt after in their lives,
> Live registered upon our brazen tombs,
> And then grace us in the disgrace of death:
> When 'spite of cormorant devouring Time
> Th' endeavour of this present breath may buy
> That honour which shall bate his scythe's keen edge,
> And make us heirs of all eternity.

Navarre and his companions resolve to seek enduring fame by their conquest of 'the huge army of the world's desires', but the inevitable encroachment of the outside world is symbolized by the arrival of the Princess of France and her ladies, and the four anchorites break their vows by falling most humanly in love. In the opulent speech (IV iii 327 sq.) in which Berowne proclaims that their real act of perjury was to make such vows at all, the love of which he speaks embraces more than woman. He is pleading for man's right to dedicate himself to Beauty in all its forms. Beauty, a dominating theme of the *Sonnets*, is his theme also.

Shakespeare was ready to turn sonnet, therefore, for ample reasons connected with his art, and we have no need to hunt for clues of a disturbing personal experience. The collection published by Thorpe differs from other printed sonnets in having no title, and it is not a sonnet sequence in the normal sense because it tells at least two stories and these are interrupted by by poems which reflect on matters not connected with the plot. The poems may have been written over a number of years and in many different moods, the plot — a very conventional one apart from the twists that Shakespeare gave it — being merely a loose framework for occasional meditations on a variety of subjects. Even the form is not absolutely regular: 99 has fifteen lines; 126, an *envoi* to 'my lovely boy', has twelve lines and is written in couplets; 145 has lines of eight syllables instead of ten.

Although he adopted Petrarch's invariable break between the octave and the sestet, Shakespeare used Surrey's form of a progressive movement of quatrains to state, repeat and illuminate the theme, which was then summarized in a final couplet. This form used seven rhymes, thus: *abab*; *cdcd*; *efef*; *gg*. The Petrarchan sonnet had only four rhymes, or sometimes five: the octave always went *abbaabba* and the sested varied *cdcdcd* with the occasional introduction of a third rhyme. This was the form used by Wordsworth and by Milton, Milton dispensing with the break in sense between octave and sestet and thus giving the poem a stronger unity. Shakespeare's structure lent itself to the Elizabethan enthusiasm for elaborate conceits. The necessary matter could be stated in the first quatrain, or even the first couplet, leaving two quatrains for the display of virtuosity. It is perhaps for this reason that few of the hundreds of Elizabethan sonnets, Shakespeare's included, attain the highest level. The form was inimical to great poetry. It was inimical particularly to two of the supreme characteristics of Shakespeare's dramatic verse, its intense concentration and the swift unimpeded flow of the imagery. Concentration is diffused when the point is made in the opening lines and nothing remains but to elaborate it; and the self-enclosed movement of the quatrains would not allow the images to stream into one another and obliterate the pattern of the verse. Sonneteering was well enough for Shakespeare at a time when much of his dramatic verse was still inclined to be static and he was content to delay its movement while he played with a seductive conceit until it died in its own too-much. It was an excellent form for the expression of feelings that were gentle rather than powerful, conventional rather than compulsive. It would never have served as a medium for passionate experience, and arguably the writing of sonnets hindered Shakespeare's development as a playwright.

Ultimately his sonnets are not love poems at all. A detached, ironic intelligence plays about the erotic convention and perfunctorily accepts its limitations. The poem that opens with the incomparable

> When to the sessions of sweet silent thought
> I summon up remembrance of things past...
>
> *Sonn.* 30.

windily fills its sails with sighs before it is done:

> Then can I grieve at grievances foregone,
> And heavily from woe to woe tell o'er
> The sad account of fore-bemoaned moan.

There is much stuff of this kind, and very few of the poems live up to the excitement promised in their opening lines. The collection derives its artistic unity less from the story that intermittently runs through it than from its dedication to the idea of Beauty, of Beauty corrupted by Time even as love is corrupted by desire. Time's 'thievish progress to eternity' takes with it the cloud-capp'd towers, the great globe itself and all that it shall inherit, because

> nothing 'gainst Time's scythe can make defence
> Save breed, to brave him when he takes thee hence.
>
> *Sonn.* 12.

In the *Sonnets* Shakespeare's musings on Time are weighted with a sense of overwhelming and irreparable loss. Only posterity can withstand for a while the fated return of all mortal things to their parent dust, and breed itself must in its season die.

The sonnet convention forbade consolation, except that which undying verse could give, and the note is of gentle defiance, seldom of hope. In his plays Shakespeare is not defiant, for the cycle of change, decay and death completes itself in renewal.

> And Winter, slumbering in the open air,
> Wears on his smiling face a dream of spring.

But in the *Sonnets* his meditations on Time are incomplete and unresolved. Only in 146, in many ways the finest in the series, did he resolve them into a satisfactory poem:

> And Death once dead, there's no more dying then.

Perhaps it was the sonnet mode that defeated him, or possibly the conflict was still too obdurate to be settled in his mind. At any rate he did not in the *Sonnets* submit Time to the metaphysical analysis that gives peculiar interest to certain speeches in *Troilus and Cressida*, nor had he yet attained the astonishing finality of his later lyrics, where a poetic solution seems to have been achieved.

> And therefore take the present time...
> For love is crowned with the prime.
> > *AYLI* V iii 32.

> What is love, 'tis not hereafter,
> Present mirth hath present laughter;
> > What's to come is still unsure.
> In delay there lies no plenty,
> Then come kiss me, sweet and twenty:
> > Youth's a stuff will not endure.
> > > *TN* II iii 48.

In the *Sonnets* Shakespeare makes Time's inexorable advance the occasion for some graceful poetry about Beauty and its passing. It is a common device of poets to treat their disregarded love as a symbol of a more general dissatisfaction, and under the pretence of addressing a loved one Shakespeare reflects uneasily on many things: on cold-heartedness and ingratitude, on his own status as a public entertainer, on the mysterious lameness — unlikely to have been a physical affliction — mentioned in 37 and 89, on the ambition and intrigue he saw around him in court and city, on lawyers, the influence of the stars, and lust's dominion. These were conventional poetic discontents, not necessarily his own, and in one of the poems he listed them in lines that anticipated Hamlet's world-weariness. The dutiful reference to the beloved in the last line shows how perfunctorily the supposed 'plot' might be treated.

Tired with all these, for restful death I cry,
As, to behold desert a beggar born,
And needy nothing trimm'd in jollity,
And purest faith unhappily forsworn,
And gilded honour shamefully misplaced,
And maiden virtue rudely strumpeted,
And right perfection wrongfully disgraced,
And strength by limping sway disabled,
And art made tongue-tied by authority,
And folly, doctor-like, controlling skill,
And simple truth miscall'd simplicity,
And captive good attending captain ill:
Tired with all these, from these would I be gone,
Save that, to die, I leave my love alone.

Sonn. 66.

This sonnet varies the general pattern by breaking through the usual division of octave and sestet and the separation of the quatrains, and some of the rhymes are carelessly forced. Except in the terse, epigrammatic phrasing that compresses a wealth of meaning into each line, it is not a great poem. Its interest lies in its summary of sonneteering complaints. Elsewhere Shakespeare moves less constrainedly among images that provide the constant background of the plays: pictures of the English countryside that make the senses ache with beauty and regret, and the homely, vivid images of daily life, the father with his child, the tired horse, the thrifty housewife chasing an errant hen, the grace of hawks and hounds, the damp climate, the craftsman at his bench; and beneath it all the intolerable pain of knowing that for each man none of this was eternal.

It may, however, be made eternal by those who in recognizing it and expressing it through their art may pass it on to the following generations. This is what Shakespeare and perhaps other sonneteers meant when they formally promised that the loved one's beauty should be preserved in their immortal verse. A poet of the present century, Walter de la Mare, has perceived their real intention:

Look thy last on all things lovely,
Every hour. Let no night
Seal thy sense in deathly slumber
    Till to delight
Thou hast paid thy utmost blessing;
Since that all things thou wouldst praise
Beauty took from those who loved them
    In other days.

We are the inheritors of those who perceived beauty in former times and had the genius to pass it on.

The *Sonnets*, then, may tell us something of Shakespeare as an artist but little about him personally. It is likelier that there was no dark lady at all than that he was the Bassano-haunted wreck promoted by Dr Rowse's researches, however 'rigorous'. They simply show him interested in the sort of things that always interested him, and his deep seriousness pervades even the most lyrical passages. None of his early readers looking, for example, at 129 or 146 could have doubted that one day he would write tragedy.

5. The Quality of Mercy.

In the last century Emerson declared that 'Shakespeare is the only biographer of Shakespeare... We have his recorded convictions on those questions which knock for answer at every heart.' Thus the plays have been held to reflect phases of his own life and suffering, and the random utterances of his characters have been regarded as personal confessions. Even critics of the eminence of Bradley and Chambers have accepted, within prudent limits, this attitude to his work. Bradley, albeit 'most regretfully', finds evidence of personal disgust with sex and alcohol, and a frustrating, unsatisfied relationship with a dark woman; while Chambers accounts for the unfinished *Timon of Athens* by the 'tempting' supposition that 'the waters closed over Shakespeare's head while he was still elaborating the play' (*Shakespeare: A Survey*, p. 276). From this immersion he reappeared in his right mind, but 'that the crisis took place is indisputable'.

It is most disputable. It is disputed, naturally, by the 'realists' of Shakespearean criticism who credit him with no feelings at all and see him as a catchpenny opportunist tied to the requirements of his company and possessing no more art than an inexhaustible facility for gratifying popular taste. More respectably, it is disputed by biographers like Sir Sidney Lee who insist upon the impersonality of his art: 'in his work it is vain to look for his biography'.

Here's my work: does work discover –
  What was rest from work – my life?
Did I live man's hater, lover?
  Leave the world at peace, at strife?
Call earth ugliness or beauty?
  See things there in large or small?
Use to pay its lord my duty?
  Use to own a lord at all?

Blank of such a record, truly
  Here's the work I hand, this scroll,
Yours to take or leave; as duly,
  Mine remains the unproffered soul.

                            Browning, *At the Mermaid.*

Actually Shakespeare proffered much: many of his convictions are recorded in his work, as Emerson said, although we must seldom expect to find them recorded directly. In the end one's response may depend on personal feeling, but it ought to depend also on the views one has about the nature of the creative process. Imagination is not a rootless thing, and every act of creation reveals something about the creator's mind. For example, Shakespeare's habit of closing his tragedies with no moral comment whatsoever must tell us something about him; so must his way of developing his chosen themes and his handling of the sources, what he omitted, added or transformed, what he softened or underlined in the re-telling of old familiar stories. If only because dramatic action is by its nature a sequence of cause and effect, the dramatist cannot wholly conceal himself behind his creations. A great artist is impersonal only in so far as he links the accidents of his individual experience with the universal of which they are a significant part.

On the other hand, it is unwise to try to explain his artistic development in terms of his life's story, and particularly unwise to read his life's story backwards into his work. The Shakespeare who emerges from such an operation is a man with a heavy load of sorrow, stricken with all the thousand shocks that flesh is heir to, and writing, it would seem, with no other purpose than to relieve the burden weighing upon his heart. Because the plays which he wrote between, approximately, 1602 and 1607 were touched with bitterness and disillusion, the reason is sought in some personal affliction that threatened his sanity and darkened his vision. It is variously found in his distress at the revolt and death of Essex, in which his friend Southampton was implicated; or in his disappointment with the new king and his drunken court; or in some shattering experience, probably involving a woman, which broke him in mind and body. But his infelicity had years too many. Men do not write *Othello* or *King Lear* or *Macbeth* when they are ill, and even *Troilus and Cressida* would have been quite a creditable achievement for an ailing mind. This acrid play does not have to mean that Shakespeare had become a Thersites seeing mankind degenerated into wars and lechery. It seems rather to have been, like the *Sonnets*, an exercise in literary de-bunking, its target being the popular heroic-romantic mode. On first looking into Chapman's Homer, Shakespeare did not feel about it as Keats was to feel.

Artistically, the identification of the tragedies and the problem comedies with his personal sufferings is untenable in the extreme form that has sometimes been proposed. The greater the artist, the more perfectly will his mind transmute the passion on which it works, and the greater, therefore, will be the separation between the heart that suffers and the mind that creates. Coleridge described a poet as the detached observer of emotion. His art is to beget a temperance amid the whirlwind of passion, and having tamed it, to present it, not in its crude reality, but to create an illusion of truth. The truest poetry is the most feigning because artistic truth is unattainable by a man who is too deeply involved in personal disaster to stand apart from it. It is not passion which makes art, but imagination, the power to create passion without actually experiencing it. Imagination is the refining agent whose action personal trouble frustrates.

Thus if Shakespeare's plays had been difficult to write because his emotions were in turmoil, they could not have been written at all. If only half of them had been resolutions of personal problems, there would not have been time to write them within the span of a single life. Only a man of strong nerves could have passed through the fires of suffering which Shakespeare conceived merely in his imagination, and we owe the great tragic period to his extraordinary balance of mind, his physical health and his power to detach himself from public and private cares. In part, it is true, his turning to tragic themes and disillusioned comedy may be explained by his professional obligations. Such matters were the new theatrical vogue. But although popular demand always had much influence on the direction of his interests, it can never explain everything about him. He wrote tragedy because his artistic development led him to it, and if it seems too much of a coincidence that he arrived there just when it was becoming popular in the theatre, it is well to remember that he set fashions as well as followed them.

The progression of his mood and his art was indivisible. The transition from 'golden' comedy to cynicism and tragedy was no sudden leap; it followed logically and naturally, just as the romantic comedy and robust melodrama of his early phase had in its time given place to the more meditative and sceptical mood in which the gayest comedy was flecked with shadows. To the artist as he matures time brings its gift of tears, and it was inevitable that Shakespeare should turn from the passive, theorizing world of Richard II and Hamlet to a world where the dominance of passion brought terrible consequences to guilty and innocent alike. He rose to his great tragic themes in the fullness of his powers. Nor was there at any time a fundamental change in his view of life. The difference between *Romeo and Juliet* and *Antony and Cleopatra* may be traced to a deepened experience, not to an altered vision. His awareness of evil, likewise, was not a sudden discovery of his tragic period, for he knew a good deal about human wickedness when he wrote his early histories and it is still present in the so-called serenity of his final plays when, according to subjective interpretations of his work, he had fallen into relaxed self-indulgence in the company of his grandchild. The revulsion from sex which pervades *King Lear* or *Sonnet 129* was implicit in the decorative stanzas of *Venus and Adonis*. Miss M.C. Bradbrook has pointed out (*Shakespeare and Elizabethan Poetry*, chapter vii) how *Titus Andronicus* crudely anticipates the agony of Lear: what was later set forth as experience and feeling was earlier related as mere doctrine and statement. Again, *Lucrece* was a heraldic lament in a traditional mode, but the anguish of Tarquin foreshadows the anguish of Macbeth. Tarquin knew the worthlessness of his conquest even before he had achieved it. Even the stagey villain Iachimo comes to life as he experiences a similar sense of guilt.

There is a fascinating continuity and consistency in the development of Shakespeare's mind and art. He never believed that evil could be finally cleansed from the world, but he found in the twin action of penitence and forgiveness the surest solvent of the misery it brings to men. This theme too, the cure as well as the disease, was present in his earliest work as well as the latest.

> Wilt thou draw near the nature of the gods?
> Draw near them then in being merciful:
> Sweet mercy is nobility's true badge.
>
> *TA* I i 117.

> By penitence the Eternal's wrath's appeased.
>
> *TGV* V iv 81.

He did not discover this conviction through any misfortunes that beset him after 1600.

In examining the plays for evidences of Shakespeare's mind and heart we should be mistrustful of direct statements torn from their dramatic context. A simple example will show how such statements have a way of contradicting one another:

> Here's a villain!
> Has a book in his pocket with red letters in't.
>
> *2 Hen VI* IV ii 96.

> Small have continual plodders ever won,
> Save base authority from others' books.
>
> *LLL* I i 86.

> My son profits nothing in the world at his book.
>
> *MWW* IV i 15.

> So, of his gentleness,
> Knowing I loved my books, he furnished me
> From mine own library with volumes that
> I prize above my dukedom.
>
> *Tem* I ii 165.

> Remember
> First to possess his books; for without them
> He's but a sot as I am.
>
> *Tem* III ii 99.

Again, Falstaff's appreciation of the tonic properties of sherry is at odds with Cassio's wondering 'that men should put an enemy in their mouths to steal away their brains', and such contrasts are numerous. But as has been suggested (see page 23), when a thought is frequently expressed by different men in different circumstances, it may be safer to regard it as Shakespeare's own opinion. He shows an unvarying attitude to music as one of the noblest of heaven's gifts to man and a symbol of the eternal harmony that should prevail in the universe, the commonwealth and the individual soul.

> How sour sweet music is,
> When time is broke and no proportion kept!
> So it is in the music of men's lives.
>
> *R II* V v 42.

Restless spirits like Cassius and Shylock dislike it, and this is a mark of their alienation from mankind; while Mistress Tearsheet's asking to be regaled by 'Sneak's noise' brings her within her creator's indulgence. But even with such recurring sentiments we should be cautious, as many of them were philosophical truisms or the statement of traditional beliefs like the nobility of the lion, the folly of the ass or the servility of the spaniel. The pedant being a standard butt of ridicule in the comic tradition, even the jests at schoolmasters may have been an automatic response. Shakespeare often wrote unthinkingly when looking for easy similitudes.

More convincing revelations of his mind and character may be found in the choice and shaping of his material. In *Measure for Measure*, for instance, he had four main sources: a tale by Cinthio and a dramatization of it, and Whetstone's two versions of his *Promos and Cassandra*. There are minor variations in these plots but in all of them the Isabella character tries to save her brother by submitting to Angelo's proposal, and subsequently she pleads for his life and marries him. Shakespeare alters this in various ways. First, he is careful to insist that Claudio's offence was not rape but 'most mutual entertainment' following upon 'a true contract'. Secondly, he makes Isabella a novice. We may not care for Isabella, but within the limits of the play her conduct is valid. The 'rancid chastity' which offends some critics is consistent with the mercy which the same critics applaud. Her religious vows committed her to both, and while she could plead forgiveness for Claudio's fault, her profession forbade her to obtain it by committing the same fault herself, and incidentally damning her brother if he consented to her sacrifice. Shakespeare then rescues her from her dilemma by the device of the 'bed trick'. She has been criticized for conniving at this, but she did so at the direction of one whom she accepted as her spiritual adviser; and once again Shakespeare is careful to insist that Angelo and Mariana were formerly betrothed. In his constant unwillingness to involve his characters in unlawful love there is a clear moral intention. A melodrama originally conceived in the savage spirit of Renaissance Italy has been elevated to a different ethical level, and on this level Shakespeare is able to develop the character of Angelo, begotten between two stockfish, a man 'unmoved, cold, and to temptation slow'. The bed trick, however unrealistic, is a wry comment on the blindness of sexual infatuation, and in the dark all cats are grey. Many of these changes, of course, were directed as much by Shakespeare's artistic compulsions as by his personal taste, and it is impossible to separate them; but throughout his work a study of his treatment of the sources will suggest his interests and the inclination of his mind.

This must, however, fall far short of a total revelation, and there is no more salutary warning against inferring overmuch from his choice of dramatic themes than the absence of any indication in the plays that the shrewd investor of Stratford had any interest in property or money. Shylock was a usurer and damned for it, and Timon denounces acquisitiveness, comparing the things that gold can buy with the loyalty and gratitude that are beyond its purchase.

> All gold and silver rather turn to dirt!
> As 'tis no better reckon'd but of those
> Who worship dirty gods.
>
> *Cym* III vi 54.

When Hamlet gibes at Osric as 'spacious in the possession of dirt', it is almost as though Shakespeare were trying to conceal a quality in himself, for he nowhere gives much approval to the prudential virtues he undoubtedly possessed. This stands him apart from most of his fellows, who were vehement in denouncing the covetousness and acquisition which they felt to be a serious social abuse.

> The first pure time, the golden age, is fled.
> Heaven knows I lie — 'tis now the age of gold —
> For all it marreth, and even virtue's sold!
>
> Marston, *What You Will* III i 117.

Shakespeare did not even rise to the mild indignation of Barnfield's *Lady Pecunia* (1598), a satirical poem on the power of money. Mostly he treats greed as venial, a subject for mirth rather than outrage. Although some of his heroines have wealthy suitors, it never occurs to them to marry for money; and although some of his young men — Bertram, Bassanio, Claudio in Messina — make enquiries about the fair one's inheritance, their true motives are romantic. Indeed the man of property treated offences against property as a jest: his thieves were but lightly rebuked, and their victims never had their money back. None of his characters showed the concern for material security that was so important to himself. We might believe that such outward things dwelt not in his desires, were it not that the facts show otherwise. If, therefore, Shakespeare was his own biographer, as Emerson claimed, he has left a considerable gap in the story.

On the other hand, he was not the mole in the cellarage urging others to action but remaining himself in the darkness.

Our poesy is as a gum, which oozes
From whence 'tis nourished.

Tim I i 21.

He was obviously a man of intense feeling. The verses about the hare and the snail in *Venus and Adonis* are commonly cited as proof of his imaginative sympathy with the least of creation, but proof in this matter is hardly necessary. All the beauty, the suffering and the gaiety of the world he could make his own, and all that 'smells of mortality' was worth the knowing. He did not conceal his impatience with pedants, precisians and all dogmatists who live by precept. He was deeply patriotic; he was not a prude; and he valued order and the preservation of degree above any untried nostrum for the betterment of mankind. Certain smaller inferences may also be gathered from his work, as that shipwreck was an event that profoundly moved him; or that, whereas he loved and understood music, architecture meant little to him and he expected painting to be merely photographic; or that, despite his preference for country over town, solitude did not please him — whenever he bids us accompany him to forest or island, it is because men are living there. Although his imagination could kindle to the glamour and heroism of war, he was always aware of its cost in blood and destruction. Even if at times he deplored the fortune that had made him an actor, his mind instinctively resorted to imagery of the theatre at times of crisis and emotional disturbance.[7] Great issues resolved themselves most easily not through speculative thought but through the medium of poetic drama.

We may even determine what some of those issues were. The most casual reading of his plays will show his concern, almost an obsession, about the clash of appearance with reality. The Duke in *Measure for Measure* excuses his relinquishment of office as a means to test men's true character and find out 'what our seemers be'. (Ironically, he makes certain discoveries about himself, as that he cannot do without power after all, because he never stops manipulating people, and that despite his self-sufficiency he has to fall in love.) Shakespeare's misgiving about appearances is such a commonplace of his drama that it would be cumbrous and unnecessary to demonstrate it in detail. The evidence is there to see. He felt so strongly about it that he devoted a whole play to it. It was only a comedy, *Much Ado About Nothing*, but it merits a brief examination because its artistic perfection disguises the seriousness of the underlying purpose.

The play is all about masking and overhearing, deception and self-deception. At the masked ball Don John fails in his attempt to show that Don Pedro is wooing Hero on his own behalf rather than Claudio's, and this causes him to embark upon a larger deception, to persuade Claudio, by means of overhearing, that Hero has been false on the eve of her wedding.

7 Chambers assembles a number of illuminating examples, *Shakespeare Gleanings*, 44-9. See also D. Masson, *Shakespeare Personally*, 181-5.

When denouncing her in the church, Claudio employs standard references to the falsity of appearance. Seemingly 'as chaste as is the bud ere it be blown', she is more intemperate than Venus. Her 'outward graces' conceal the thoughts and counsels of her heart, and Claudio departs in a welter of oxymoron: 'pure impiety, and impious purity'. Friar Francis then proposes a further deception, to let it be thought that Hero has died of shame and shock; and on this false report Claudio undergoes a somewhat lachrymose repentance and agrees to marry a surrogate bride, who of course is Hero.

Meanwhile — and the play is brilliantly constructed to alternate the 'good' and the 'bad' deceptions, along with the fumblings of the Watch — Beatrice and Benedick have been gulled into acknowledging their love. Beatrice could see a church by daylight, but she could not recognize her own feelings about Benedick and built an artificial barrier of wit and pride against him. Her self-deception is as evident as his, but it needs two further scenes of overhearing to break it down, and significantly the first of them is intro- duced by Balthazar's song bidding ladies sigh no more because 'Men were deceivers ever'. In the church scene the sudden shock of Beatrice's 'Kill Claudio' momentarily cuts through the artificiality of the comedy, and in the final recognition of their mutual love we realize that, paradoxically, deception has been a way to self-knowledge and a testing of character. Even Claudio may have learned something by it. At the end of the play he may be genuinely in love, instead of just deceiving himself about it. For the Watch ther is no such self-recognition, but they have made their contribution to the central theme. Dogberry is self-deceived about his own importance, and his malapropisms are the complement of the early wit-combats of Beatrice and Benedick, which were a way of masking truth. The Watch overhear Conrade and Borachio talking about Don John's conspiracy, and like everyone else in the play, the misunderstand what they hear. They are important to the action here, because if Dogberry's self-importance had not prevented him from telling Leonato concisely about the arrest of the thief called Deformed, the church scene, the main focus of the plot, need not have occurred.

Among other things, the play is a masterly feat of construction since it manages to retain suspense and interest even though the audience always watch it from the inside and are told in advance of every trick and turn in the plot. But the constant overhearing is a device useful for comic 'distancing', and it cannot have the impact of the swift tragic insights into reality and illusion in the later plays. All the great tragedies are built on deceits that now have more sombre implications. To Hamlet the court at Elsinore is just a sham, and in his disenchantment with it he sees it as a reflection of the greater world outside. Othello is deceived by 'honest' Iago, Macbeth by the juggling fiends that palter in a double sense, Lear by his carrion daughters. In his political plays Shakespeare shows what happens when power is divorced from merit, and always in his observation of mankind he finds an element of falsity, an alloy of baseness in the most resplendent virtue. Yet an outlook that might have been totally pessimistic is redeemed by the knowledge that also there is 'some soul of goodness in things evil', that the uses of adversity may be sweet and that subtle intelligence may sometimes be outwitted by honest stupidity. Shakespeare believed of men as Friar Laurence believed of herbs:

Many for many virtues excellent:
None but for some, and yet all different ...
For nought so vile that on the earth doth live,
But to the earth some special good doth give.

RJ II iii 13.

Such an attitude has not been explicit enough for critics with a weightier view of the artist's function. Of course Shakespeare was never as instrusive as Chaucer, who is constantly nudging the reader with authorial comment, so that critics of *The Canterbury Tales* have to be always distinguishing between Chaucer the pilgrim and Chaucer the poet.

Starting from the proposition that 'it is always a writer's duty to make the world better', Dr Johnson sighed over Shakespeare as an indifferent moralist who swept his characters heedlessly through right and wrong and was 'not always careful to show in the virtuous a disapprobation of the wicked'. In turning out plays for his company he 'sacrifices virtue to convenience, and is so much more careful to please than to instruct that he seems to write without any moral purpose'; and he even omits 'opportunities of instructing or delighting which the train of his story seems to force upon him'. Johnson required poetry to rise to the enunciation of 'general and transcendental truths', and he censured Shakespeare for letting 'his precepts and axioms drop casually from him' and leaving the admonitory lessons of wickedness 'to operate by chance'. It was this same supposed want of an integrated vision that led Matthew Arnold to complain, 'Shakespeare, you are as obscure as life is'. Arnold, like Johnson, wanted the poet to express a criticism of life, to become 'a complete *magister vitae*': he must 'begin with an Idea of the World in order not to be prevailed over by the world's multi-tudinousness', whereas Shakespeare — and 'those damned Elizabethans generally' — immersed themselves so carelessly in life's infinite variety that they failed to refer human action to any recognizable standards.

In a letter to his mother in 1863 Arnold said how gratified he was to have 'at last a chance of *getting at* the English public. Such a public as it is, and such a work as one wants to do with it'. As a professional playwright Shakespeare was certainly 'more careful to please than to instruct', and it is unlikely that he ever consciously sought to make the world a better place or that he wished to *get at* anybody. But the austere objections brought by Arnold and Johnson are not valid. His matchless power of identifying himself simultaneously with all the characters on his stage may give to his reading of life an illusory air of impartiality. But the absence of express condemnation is not absence of judgment, and judgment is always implicit. His self-identification with the torments of Macbeth, his understanding of all other sinners as well as Macbeth, neither condones Macbeth's crime nor remits the mortal consequences. He allowed Falstaff to defend himself so ingeniously against the charge of cowardice that at some tribunals Falstaff is periodically acquitted; but whether he was a coward or not, there is no defence of cowardice. Shakespeare recognized the existence of sin, and whatever mitigation he might in his compassion find for the sinner, sin remained and would bear its fruits. To say this is to say that Shakespeare was a moralist, that he had a point of view and that his point of view, on the matters of which he treats, may be discovered from his plays.

It is true that his reading of life will sometimes elude definition, because he was first concerned with turning human actions into poetry, not with prescribing codes of conduct or formulating systems of metaphysical thought. This has given a superficial plausibility to the notion that he was morally indifferent, for he brought all questions out of the cloudland of abstractions into the daily light of human discourse. He would insist upon looking at the details, and his 'law' consisted, in the English way, of case-law. He refused to be didactic, or to be much impressed by those who were; and he may have regarded any sort of explicit moralizing or formal reasoning as inadequate for the larger purposes of life. It is not surprising that Brutus's reasoned address to the Roman citizens is overwhelmed by Antony's appeal to the emotions of cupidity and revenge, and it is a significant revelation about the philosophizing Brutus that he should suppose his restrained rhetorical argument to be suitable to the audience or the occasion. We may be more surprised when Portia and Isabella, speaking passionately on Shakespeare's cherished theme of forgiveness, get a hearing but no assent. They gain their point in the end, and those who have disregarded them suffer for it, but the fact remains that they achieved nothing by mere eloquence. Nor did the Bishop of Carlisle, except to be put in prison for it; nor Ulysses, as the Greek commanders persisted in their divisions and Ulysses so far abandoned his own teachings on degree as to replace Achilles by Ajax as the army's champion; and it is unlikely that the Duke really persuaded Claudio to be absolute for death.

The plays are full of saws and instances and traditional aphorisms, but most of these are put into the mouths of fools or simple folk, or else of rogues who mask their crooked thought behind a glib sententiousness. Nor, as a rule, are the recipients grateful for this platitudinous wisdom. It is characteristic that Juliet's Nurse would stay all night 'to hear good counsel', but Portia's sharp 'good sentences and well pronounc'd', cutting short Nerissa's remarks on the advantages of the golden mean, comes as a rebuke, and she follows it with a 'sentence' of her own:

If to do were as easy as to know what were good to do, chapels had been churches, and poor men's cottages princes' palaces.

MV I ii 13.

Sententiousness is no more acceptable when offered by way of consolation;

He jests at scars that never felt a wound.

RJ II ii 1.

He talks to me that never had a son.

KJ III iv 91.

> I never yet did hear
> That the bruis'd heart was pieced through the ear.

Oth I iii 218.

At greater length, as befitted an older man, Leonato held forth on the emptiness of trying to 'patch grief with proverbs':

> 'Tis all men's office to speak patience
> To those that wring under the load of sorrow,
> But no man's virtue nor sufficiency
> To be so moral when he shall endure
> The like himself. Therefore give me no counsel:
> My griefs cry louder than advertisement...
> For there was never yet philosopher
> That could endure the toothache patiently.

MAN V i 27.

We find, then, a disposition in Shakespeare's mind to reject second-hand counsels and preconceived philosophies. He who coined many of the best-known aphorisms in the language doubted their practical usefulness. Although Johnson's statement that 'his works support no opinion with arguments, nor supply any fashion with invectives; they can neither indulge fashion nor gratify malignity' has proved to be an unhappy forecast of the future of Shakespearean studies, it is easy to see what he meant. Shakespeare wore no tidy set of opinions as a badge in his coat. He kept himself free from theories which entangle the imagination, from merely intellectual consistency and dogmas which inhibit the free play of the mind. Poets do not serve fashions, for their imaginative experience lifts them above creed and code and they do not have to assent intellectually to what they describe. Shakespeare allowed himself no perfectionist dream of unpathed waters and undreamed shores, for life's variety was too rich to leave time for the wooing of any single cause.

A plague of opinion! A man may wear it on both sides, like a leather jerkin.

TC III iii 265.

In some matters, however, he never changed his ground. Evil is always present in his work, and it gives significance to the largely trivial fables he brought on to the stage. He insists upon telling these stories in a way that forces his readers into an act of judgment: not into taking sides necessarily — that is often their unwisdom — but into sharing the struggles of his characters and attaining to some understanding of the issues at stake. A crude and barbarous Jew, a grotesque like the Jew of Marlowe and, probably, of the source-play that is lost, would have made a play, did indeed make several, but not for Shakespeare. He allows Shylock some of the attributes of our common humanity while allowing the other Venetians to treat him in the traditional way, as though he were utterly inhuman. There, quite simply, is *The Merchant of Venice*, which at least since Irving's time has been his principal 'problem play', and no one could say that the problem is not ethical. The sources gave him a mild and patient Lear who was the victim of unprovoked malevolence. Shakespeare so divides the moral responsibility that, although the evil of Goneril and Regan is hardly abated, Lear is in some degree author of his own sufferings. In order that there shall be no least excuse for Macbeth, the sensual, tyrannous Duncan of the chronicles becomes the honourable king whose virtues plead for him like angels trumpet-tongued. There is no evading Shakespeare when he is in this mood. He compels the reader to evaluate and judge.

The ethical seriousness of his plot-making is reinforced by the strong ethical bias of the imagery. He could scarcely mention bird or animal, tree or flower, without using it for illustrative comment on human beings. Nature always suggested to him a moral correspondence.

> Go, bind thou up yon dangling apricocks,
> Which, like unruly children, make their sire
> Stoop with oppression of their prodigal weight,
>
> *R II* III iv 29.

and this is followed at once by a further image of the 'too-fast-growing sprays' that spread untimely in the commonwealth. The course of true love brings to mind the smooth-flowing stream that

> Makes sweet music with th'enamelled stones.
>
> *TGV* II vii 28.

Youth wasting by dissipation suggests to Falstaff not a similitude but an obverse:

> For though the camomile, the more it is trodden on the faster it grows, yet youth, the more it is wasted the sooner it wears.
>
> *1 Hen IV* II iv 441.

The leafless boughs of a tree awaken memories of chancels stripped of beauty by Protestant zeal:

> Bare ruin'd choirs, where late the sweet birds sang.
>
> *Sonn* 73.

The movement of comedy may be interrupted by grave reflections sometimes inappropriate to the speaker. Hero, Margaret and Ursula are talking about the plot to make Beatrice and Benedick aware of their love:

> Whisper her ear, and tell her, I and Ursula
> Walk in the orchard, and our whole discourse
> Is all of her; say that thou overheard'st us,
> And bid her steal into the pleached bower,
> Where honeysuckles, ripen'd by the sun,
> Forbid the sun to enter; like favourites,
> Made proud by princes, that advance their pride
> Against that power that bred it.
>
> *MAN* III i 4.

This is not a thought likely to have presented itself to Hero's simple mind at any time, least of all at this particular moment, and Shakespeare has gone off at a tangent — almost, perhaps, without realizing it. He needed to picture a bower suitable for concealment, and at once it reminded him of the ambition and ingratitude of favourites who forget their benefactor. Instinctively his mind fastened on resemblances between Nature and the life of man: not for physical descriptions only, as when Beatrice, ducking below the hedge to be unobserved, suggests the lapwing running close to the ground, but for serious ethical comment. It strengthens the moral framework in which all his work is set.

If the vision of justice is to disclose the world as it is, the vision of mercy is aware of what it might be if men were different. Although sin is a constant presence in Shakespeare's world, and no one sins because of forces beyond his control, he never enquires into its origins; and although some power making for righteousness wages a not unsuccessful struggle against it, he never suggests that it will disappear. He left theology to the theologians, who in his day spoke with many voices on these matters, and concerned himself with the operation of sin in the hearts of certain human beings whom he chose to imagine. There is 'nobody but has his fault', as Mistress Quickly decided, though John Rugby's was no worse than an addiction to prayer. When Antony dies, it is the Roman Agrippa who says that 'a rarer spirit never did steer humanity',

> but you, gods, will give us
> Some faults to make us men,
>
> *AC* V i 32.

and if we would be otherwise, we must be created of other elements than we are. So Coriolanus seemed to a frightened general who had watched his approach to Rome at the head of the Volscian army:

> He leads them like a thing
> Made by some other deity than Nature,
> That shapes man better.
>
> *Cor* IV vi 90.

Shakespeare knew no such deity.

> The web of our life is of a mingled yarn, good and ill together: our virtues would be proud if our faults whipped them not; and our crimes would despair if they were not cherished by our virtues.
>
> *AWW* IV iii 83.

Shakespeare's specific, upon which his compassion ultimately depends, is that we shall act like men, show our kindred with the human race. Then even Parolles may receive indulgence:

> Simply the thing I am
> Shall make me live,
>
> *AWW* IV iii 369.

for 'there's place and means for every man alive'; and the kindly Lafeu later endorses it:

> Though you are a fool and a knave, you shall eat.
>
> *AWW* V ii 58.

Shakespeare saw in the obsessive dominance of 'blood' and 'the affections' (the words which to the Elizabethans meant the sovereignty of passion) the chief cause of the treachery and inhumanity which he regarded as the greatest of sins. Viola rated ingratitude above all the evils which corrupt the soul. It makes man 'unkind'. The notion of 'kindness' lies at the centre of Shakespeare's conception of virtue. It relates to the particular function of man as man, to the continued exercise of will and reason which are the attributes of his humanity and the sign of his superiority to the animal creation.

> Yet I do fear thy nature;
> It is too full of the milk of human-kindness,
>
> *Macb* I v 17.

where 'human-kindness' means that Lady Macbeth fears her husband is too much of a man — too little of a beast — to carry out the fearful project at which he has hinted. She fears that he may be true to his nature, whereby such a deed would be impossible. From the compunctious visitings of such a nature she herself terribly asks to be released: she would be unsexed, the milk of her breasts would turn to gall and she would become 'unkind', or less than human. This was the worst thing Shakespeare could say of anyone, implying as it did the voluntary abdication of specific virtues and a surrender to the universal wolf of appetite. In the form of *kindless* he uses it only of Claudius; as *unkind* (though this often has the shallower significance of modern usage, generally with reference to the heedless lover) it adds a special layer of meaning to certain sorts of behaviour, particularly behaviour tainted by treachery and ingratitude and the betrayal of trust. The sea-captain Antonio uses it of the youth he believes to be Sebastian; it is Worcester's rebuke to Bolingbroke for violating the pledges he had made to the men who helped him to his throne; Desdemona uses it of the breach between Cassio and Othello, when she thinks that Othello has been unnaturally stern and unforgiving; ironically, Lear uses it of Cordelia, until he learns that it belongs to his other daughters, of whom he can scarcely speak without likening them to wild beasts. It strikes with scarifying force in Antony's 'This was the unkindest cut of all': unkindest because it was delivered by the hand of friendship and trust. The penalty of unkindness is to be isolated from one's fellow-men. He who has shown himself to be less than a man is denied the blessings of humanity,

> As honour, love, obedience, troops of friends.
>
> *Macb* V iii 23.

Nature always seeks a balance, and the virtuous man is he in whom blood and judgment are finely commingled: not the calculating, passionless man, for that 'fitteth the spirit of a tapster', nor he whose obsessive desires yield to unkindness, but the man who is 'open and free': magnanimous, that is, temperate, brave and loving. In the mingled yarn of life such men are rare, and even they may be brought to ruin if they are perplexed in the extreme. Suffering will be the portion of most of mankind, and only love will redeem it. Poor unaccommodated man shall offer himself to mercy, not in some future world, because that's hereafter and is still unsure, but to the mercy he will find here. Compassion is the virtue that is more than kind. All the qualities which help men to resist evil in the world — courage, self-sacrifice, loyalty, forgiveness — are attributes of loving-kindness, and it is in his capacity for love and mercy that man may reach upwards to the nature of God. 'Let's exchange charity'. Where one is ready to forgive and another to repent, there evil fails.

> Upon such sacrifices, my Cordelia,
> The gods themselves throw incense.
>
> *Lear* V iii 20.

In the great invocations to mercy spoken by Portia and Isabella Shakespeare gives formal statement to his conviction, which grew more intense as the years went by, that a sinful world may be regenerated by the love which 'bears it out even to the edge of doom'.

Such love is quite simple. It is to be found in the kindly lives of men and women, more especially in the hallowed relationships of the family, the husband's cherishing of his wife and the mother's care for her child, the mutual respect of master and servant. It acknowledges the 'prerogative of age' and confers on men the quiet blessings of

> peace, justice, truth,
> Domestic awe, night-rest and neighbourhood,
> Instruction, manners, mysteries and trades.

Tim IV i 16.

Shakespeare is remarkably insistent on the preservation of these simple and fundamental ties, and when any one is broken, the consequences are usually dreadful. His implicit acknowledgment of the last six of the ten Commandments compelled him to surprising reticences which, superficially, were inconsistent with his enjoyment of bawdiness, cuckolds, irascible fathers, cutpurses and babbling gossips as subjects for dramatic comedy. Marriage out of wedlock did not strike him as amusing, and he took no pleasure in ridiculing women. His attitude to marriage and fecundity was almost one of reverence. This is not inconsistent with his dramatic practice because whenever he felt anything strongly, he would at some time or other make fun of it. To look at it through the eyes of a rogue or a clown was his way of testing it, and Parolles warning Helena against the perils of virginity, which is 'the most inhibited sin in the canon' and breeds mites (*AWW* I i 147 sq.), is but the complement of the first group of the sonnets, the pride of Hermione in her 'goodly bulk' and the satisfaction with which Shakespeare always brings his favoured lovers to 'a long and well-deserved bed'. The unspectacular virtues of *pietas*, from which mankind has drawn its deepest health and comfort, impressed him with their constant necessity. The reward he chose for the characters whom he loved and spared was not wealth or power but the blessing of 'one feast, one house, one mutual happiness', the promise of the procreant cradle and the assurance of the love that outlasts alteration. 'The quality of love stilleth our will and maketh us long only for what we have, and giveth us no other thirst'.

Few of his victims find no consolation, few of his sinners do not repent, and few are not forgiven. The silent obduracy of Iago ('Demand me nothing; what you know you know') refuses him the pardon which, if he had sought it, Othello was noble enough to have allowed him. Claudius and Macbeth wrestle with a tortured conscience, Angelo offers his life in expiation of his sin, Edmund tries to make amends. In comedy, where the invasion of evil but slightly darkens a sunny world, there is less for mercy and repentance to do, but Shakespeare insists upon it none the less, and two outsiders, Malvolio and Shylock, continue to exclude themselves by their refusal to seek it. Malvolio talks angrily of revenge and departs amid scorn, but it is significant that, even so, he is granted a second chance when Orsino sends servants after him to 'entreat him to a peace'; Shylock is sullen and unrepentant, and we need to move to moonlit Belmont for the assurance that the world is still sweet. Elsewhere the act of repentance may be hurried and perfunctory, sometimes taking place off stage, but the important thing is that it happens. Orlando's act of mercy, of 'kindness nobler ever than revenge', scotches his brother's evil intentions; Duke Frederick, marching on defenceless Arden in panoply of power, happens on 'an old religious man' and after some question with him is converted; Proteus, the conspirators in *The Tempest*, the outlaws in the Mantuan forest, all promise some sort of amendment; even Caliban will 'seek for grace'. It matters nothing that in comedy forgiveness is sometimes lightly bought — for Proteus no worse penance than 'to hear the story of your loves discovered' — the promise of amendment not always convincing. 'All's well that ends well' accorded better with Shakespeare's spirit than a strict 'measure for measure', and so long as love might be released to encircle the little world of his story, all ended well enough indeed. But when he is in his sternest mood, neither repentance nor forgiveness is ever perfunctory where there is much to be expiated.

6. Shakespeare's Religion.

Redemption by love is a cardinal doctrine of Christianity, but Shakespeare seems to have felt that redemption is brought about by man's individual action rather than by the efficacy of spiritual graces.

Elizabethan children were taken early to church, and whatever his later schooling, Shakespeare spent receptive hours at the Stratford church and, like other children, was instructed in the catechism before evensong on Sundays. The Prayer Book of 1559, the Homilies, and the Bible in the translations current before the Authorized Version of 1611, necessarily had a great impression on his style and ways of thought, and superficially the plays suggest an orthodox Christian believer with a wide range of verbal reference. He had a wide range of pagan reference too, but that is insignificant because many of his plays came from classical or pagan sources. We know that on at least one occasion he entertained a visiting preacher at Stratford, which was a duty —or a privilege, according to taste — that fell on prominent citizens in country towns, and they might be reimbursed for their hospitality. Lacking his father's intransigent spirit, he probably went to Holy Trinity equably enough, sat in his 'accustomed seat' (pew rights were jealously guarded and gave privacy from vulgar observation) and there thought his own thoughts about the matter provided. His interment in the chancel was his right as a tithe-holder and could not have been witheld even if, as Richard Davies wrote some two or three generations later, 'he died a Papist'. Davies is an unreliable source, and this is the sort of notion that might have grown up in a Puritan community where stage-playing was regarded as a typical Popish wickedness. The epitaph proclaiming Susanna to have been more pious than her father would mean only that she was stricter than he in the observances approved in Stratford. No doubt she was. An actor could never have seemed godly in the Puritan sense of the word.

To the externals of religion, by whomsoever professed, Shakespeare was invariably generous and respectful, and it is an astonishing fact about him that in all the events and circumstances of his drama it would be difficult to find any occasion when he suggests that religious beliefs were not sincerely held. This unwillingness to accuse the devout of hypocrisy, even if he thought them to be misguided, separates him from other dramatists and satirists of his age — and, of course, from Chaucer too.

When writing of the 'bare ruin'd choirs', or of the 'patines of bright gold' in the sky above Belmont or of the 'chalic'd flowers' in the song which Cloten orders to his heedless love, he acknowledges the potency of Catholic ceremonial. He understood the medieval doctrine of sacramental grace. Murder was doubly heinous because it took its victim unawares and rarely gave him time to receive absolution before he died. To the awfulness of fratricide and parricide Claudius committed the further sin of sending his brother to purgatory unabsolved,

> Cut off even in the blossoms of my sin,
> Unhousel'd, disappointed, unaneal'd,
> No reckoning made but sent to my account
> With all my imperfections on my head.

Ham I v 76

> He took my father grossly, full of bread,
> With all his crimes broad blown, as flush as May.
> And how his audit stands, who knows save heaven?

III iii 80

For the same reason Claudius shall not be dispatched while he is praying, for prayer has 'some relish of salvation in it' and Hamlet would not be properly avenged in killing him 'when he is fit and season'd for his passage'.

Shakespeare also softened or omitted much criticism or misrepresentation of Catholic behaviour that came to him in his sources. In *King John*, for instance, he suppressed the scene in the Friary at Swinstead (*The Trouble some Reign* I xi) where a nun is found hidden in a chest; and King John already has a fatal fever before he goes to Swinstead, whereas the source has a

monk poisoning him with 'the inwards of a toad' (II viii). Shakespeare's
friars are usually well-meaning if ineffectual, but in the argument to Arthur
Brooke's poem that was the main source of *Romeo and Juliet* 'superstitious
friars (the naturally fit instruments of unchastity)' bear much of the blame
for the tragedy, especially as for the purpose of their 'stolen contracts' the
young lovers make use of auricular confession, 'the key of whoredom and
treason'. Shakespeare is critical of Catholic doctrine only in his misgivings
about the cloistered life. To Hermia it is threatened as a penalty for filial
disobedience:

> You can endure the livery of a nun,
> For aye to be in shady cloister mew'd,
> To live a barren sister all your life,
> Chanting faint hymns to the cold fruitless moon.
> Thrice blessed they that master so their blood,
> To undergo such maiden pilgrimage;
> But earthlier happy is the rose distill'd
> Than that which, withering on the virgin thorn,
> Grows, lives and dies in single blessedness.
>
> *MND* I i 70.

The sentiment is to be expected in a comedy written in celebration of
wedlock, but the forcefulness of the language, especially in the potent image
of the rose, seems to suggest a personal conviction. There is the respect due
to the life of dedication, which is not lightly undertaken; but also regret that
any woman should deny the life that is in her body. We catch the echo of an
irreverent voice: 'It is not politic in the commonwealth of Nature to preserve
virginity... there was never virgin got till virginity was first lost' (*AWW* I i
137). Isabella feared that the 'privileges', or special regulations, of the
votarists of St Clare were not strict enough, but she was only put into a
nunnery to find the strength to resist Angelo, and she was released from her
vows easily enough when she was willing to marry the Duke.

Puritans were ridiculed in the theatres they sought to suppress. In *The
Puritan*, an anonymous play of 1607, Parson Fulbelly 'rails against players
mightily...because they brought him drunk upon the stage once'. They were
accused of being gluttons, catamites and hypocrites, and what especially
incensed the actors was their trick of twisting texts to suit their purpose.
Their literalness was held up to scorn, as when Nicholas St Antlings, a
young acolyte in *The Puritan*, will not steal, because Scripture tells him not
to, but he is quite ready to 'nim', which means the same thing. Eating pig on
a feast day is a sin, but Zeal-of-the-Land Busy in *Bartholomew Fair* found a
way of excusing it: 'We may be religious in the midst of the profane, so it be
eaten with a reformed mouth'. Because Angelo sinned in the intention but
not the deed, there may have been an appropriate Puritan irony in his
acquittal, but this is a serious study of a man goaded 'to sin, in loving virtue',

not a caricature. Malvolio's Puritanism is only one of his characteristics, and in fact his supposed abhorrence of 'cakes and ale' is attributed to him by Sir Toby rather than evidenced in his actions. Some critics have detected a Puritan priggishness in Cordelia's refusal to tell a lie even in charity, but her honesty is not in question. Shakespeare was remarkably restrained and forbearing towards the enemies of his profession. His fullest study of a Puritan is Sir Nathaniel, who abrogates scurrility, likes to quote texts and approves of the royal stag-hunt as 'very reverend sport, truly; and done in the testimony of a good conscience'. But this is an affectionate portrait crowned with as warm a tribute as Shakespeare could give to any of his fellow-citizens:

> a foolish mild man; an honest man, look you, and soon dashed. He is a marvellous good neighbour, faith, and a very good bowler.
>
> *LLL* V ii 584.

Unlike most of the dramatists, Shakespeare really understood the Puritan mind. The Duke says to Angelo:

> Heaven doth with us as we with torches do,
> Not light them for themselves; for if our virtues
> Did not go forth of us, 'twere all alike
> As if we had them not. Spirits are not finely touch'd
> But to fine issues.
>
> *MM* I i 33.

The core of the Puritan faith was election to salvation, and the duty of men so chosen was not to glory in their personal righteousness but to labour to build the City of God on earth. It was for this task that heavenly grace had redeemed them from the common fate of sinful man. In a simple poetic analogy Shakespeare has grasped the essence of the Puritan position.

Yet his very tolerance seems to imply certain reservations. Churchgoing probably appeared to him to be a commendable manifestation of social solidarity, something by which 'domestic awe' might be sustained. But despite his respect and understanding, his attitude to the religious beliefs of other men seems to hint at some personal detachment. The law of Christians enjoins two commandments, that they shall love God and love their neighbour; and unless the second is included in the first, it is not more than a kindly disposition of character. It is true, for what it is worth, that Puritan opposition to the theatre made it difficult for the drama to comprehend great religious issues, and that government prohibition forbade the players to involve themselves in doctrinal controversy. How far Shakespeare felt himself to be inhibited by this we do not know. But his characters do not have the Christian conception of sin as alienation from God (Claudius comes nearer to it than any); wherefore the mercy that is their nobility does not bring them into communication with God. The evil which permeates

Shakespeare's world is thick and palpable, and all the water in the ocean will not wash it clean, but essentially it is the evil that man commits against man. It is man who is offended, man who punishes and man whose forgiveness must be sought. Macbeth falls because humanity can endure him no longer. In the Elizabethan conception of the universe it was impossible for the heavens to be indifferent to men's acts, but in Shakespeare's drama the numerous invocations of heaven and hell and damnation have only a rhetorical resonance. When Lear and Timon arraign their pagan gods, it is for allowing men to be so wicked. These gods are impersonal forces that cannot be identified with the Christian idea of deity, and the beatitude that Lear ultimately achieves is not a Christian beatitude.

Marlowe was an atheist, but *Faustus* was a more Christian poem than anything of Shakespeare's. The agony of Faustus was the loss of God, and Mephistophelis had long ago warned him what that agony would be:

> Hell hath no limits, nor is not circumscrib'd
> In one self place; for where we are is hell,
> And where hell is there must we ever be:
> And to conclude, when all the world dissolves,
> And every creature shall be purified,
> All places shall be hell that is not heaven.
>
> V 121.

Hell, which is the penalty of sin, is severance from God. Macbeth, on the other hand, is concerned only with the retribution of outraged society, with the comforts due to old age that he will never receive. He does not fear God's judgment because he refuses to face it:

> That but this blow
> Might be the be-all and the end-all here,
> But here, upon this bank and shoal of time,
> We'd jump the life to come. But in these cases
> We still have judgment here; that we but teach
> Bloody instructions, which, being taught, return
> To plague the inventor; this even-handed justice
> Commends the ingredients of our poison'd chalice.
>
> I vii 4.

'We still have judgment here'; and when he is defeated, he babbles that it is the Witches who have deceived him.

Nor, again, do Shakespeare's characters console themselves with a Christian hope of immortality. When Cleopatra speaks of her 'immortal longings', Antony and Iras have lately said that when the bright day is done, we must sleep and surrender to the dark. The lethal baby at her breast, and the sexual imagery of 'the worm', imply the renewal of life on earth, but that is all. It is beyond knowing what Shakespeare personally felt about the approach of death and the extinction of the creative spirit, but in his drama it is the necessary end of life's journey: if it be not now, yet it will come, and the readiness is all. Under an immense variety of images he maintains towards it a consistent attitude which, for all the splendour of the poetry it aroused in him, was emotionally negative. Death is an enemy, for it is the ravisher of youth and beauty; it is terrible in shape and devours all that we hold dear; it is the hunter whose quarry never escapes, the wrestler who never loses. Life is a fever, an uneasy dream, death the physician and a gentle sleep. Life is a spark, fire, a candle, death the extinguisher. Life is a flower, death the frost that nips it. Death is a window closing, a veil descending, the darkness which falls when the bright day is done, the key which unlocks a prison — but never the key which opens the door upon a new life. It is the cancelling of a bond, something owed to God as one repays a loan. It is oblivion, a release from the world's troubles,

> that thing that ends all other deeds,
> Which shackles accidents, and bolts up change,
> Which sleeps, and never palates more the dug,
> The beggar's nurse and Caesar's.
>
> *AC* V ii 5.

> Better be with the dead,
> Whom we, to gain our peace, have sent to peace,
> Than on the torture of the mind to lie
> In restless ecstasy. Duncan is in his grave;
> After life's fitful fever he sleeps well;
> Treason has done his worst: nor steel, nor poison,
> Malice domestic, foreign levy, nothing
> Can touch him further.
>
> *Macb* III ii 19.

Between the poignant beauty of 'Fear no more the heat o' the sun' and the sardonic consolations of the Gaoler in the same play there is considerable difference in spirit but none in the conclusions reached:

> The comfort is, you shall be called to no more payments, fear no more tavern-bills...O! the charity of a penny cord: it sums up thousands in a trice: you have no true debitor and creditor but it; of what's past, is, and to come, the discharge.
>
> *Cym* V iv 60.

The longer expositions of the same theme, as in *Sonnet* 66, 'To be or not to be' or Vincentio's 'Be absolute for death', echo the same unChristian resignation. Death is an end, often a merciful end, but never a beginning.

> I am i' th' way to study a long silence.
>
> Webster, *The White Devil* V vi 204.

We should not let Hamlet's 'felicity' deceive us: he owed Denmark a death before the state could be purged of evil. Against the grinning tyrant Shakespeare could only tell the soul to be unafraid: 'And Death once dead, there's no more dying then'. He offered no promise of a further life.

He refused, in short, the comforts and inspiration of orthodox Christianity, even though the world of his creation had something of the true Christian assurance. Questioning neither degrees nor institutions, he assumed the social stability which religion had established and, if not itself put to the question, would maintain. The concepts of medieval religion held an imaginative power over him. In seeing man as a compound of God and beast, and in basing his drama on the interplay of man's divine and appetitive qualities, he was applying the experience of the great teachers of Christianity. He was religious in his respect for the impregnable individuality of each single man, in his refusal to label him and coerce him into conformity: 'but God is to be worshipped: all men are not alike'. In all that he wrote he honoured the Christian teaching that men shall love one another, bring one another to repentance and repay evil with good. Ethically, therefore, he stands among the great evangelists of Christianity: ethically, but not spiritually. He examined the Christian mystery and, presumably, found it good; but he seems to have rejected its full demands on the human spirit. He picked the flower but was indifferent to the soil from which it grew. If the world of his imagination was a good world, it was so by the power of love; but of the love which man can give to man, not of the love which he may receive from God.

Does nothing, then, lie beyond 'the thick rotundity o' the world'? Increasingly, perhaps, he grew to believe that there does but, like Virgil, he would not define it. His meditations on these matters will not be welded ino coherence; he seems to have kept his vision deliberately unfocused. There's a divinity that shapes our ends, and he rejected as inadequate, alike for tragedy and life, Gloucester's pessimistic view that the gods sport with men as naughty boys with flies. Beyond the blanket of the dark there lies a deified order, and there is more in heaven and earth than we dream of in our philosophy.

> And we have our philosophical persons to make modern and familiar things supernatural and causeless. Hence it is that we make trifles of terrors, ensconcing ourselves into seeming knowledge when we should submit ourselves to an unknown fear.
>
> *A WW* II iii 1.

'The world and life's too big to pass for a dream', and like Bacon, Shakespeare had rather believe 'all the fables in the legend, and the Talmud, and the Alcoran' than that this universal frame is without a mind.

'O, 'tis an accident that heaven provides', the Duke says on learning that Barnardine may be spared after all because conveniently the body of a dead pirate is available to sustain the pretence that Claudio has been executed. In the circumstances these words are ironic and bathetic, but in this strange, unfulfilled play Shakespeare appears to have conducted the experiment of allowing Providence to take over. After the characters have wrestled with their human errors and delusions, the Duke reappears in Vienna to distribute various arbitrary judgments and annexe an unexpected bride. There is a startling change in the character of the play, and neither morally nor artistically is it satisfactory. Shakespeare wrote his tragedies before he returned to his idea, and by that time he knew better than to make Providence the crude *deus ex machina* that Vincentio becomes.

The experiment was not forgotten, and the 'serenity' of the final plays is not just a critical cliché. Shakespeare emerged from the harrowing intimations of his tragic period with a strengthened confidence that the 'perpetual-sober gods' will not crack Nature's moulds and spill the unhinged planet into chaos; and this confidence is the more reassuring after the dreadful potentiality of evil and confusion he had lately faced. If evil did not prevail, possibly it was because there is an assured Providence watching over men. Human experience is valid so far as it goes; life is not just a general mist of error, nor the senses mere illusion. Thus although there is a world beyond our knowledge, it is not beyond our occasional perception; and the mere fact that Shakespeare kept his mental balance throughout his tragic explorations suggests that these perceptions were good. They are never explicit, but the verse of the final plays

> is no mortal business, nor no sound
> That the earth owes.

> *Tem* I ii 406.

The difficulty of the imagery, and the complicated syntax and the sometimes choking rhythms of the verse, convey a sense of timelessness and a mystery beyond human understanding, of a 'central peace at the heart of endless agitation'. Poets in this mood may not be sustained by unknowable truths but in brief illuminations they are able to

> take upon us the mystery of things,
> As if we were God's spies.

> *Lear* V iii 16.

Shakespeare never said clearly what he meant. There is a power, a directing mind, but he would not speculate about it.

> Let us be thankful
> For that which is, and with you [gods] leave disputes
> That are above our question.

> *Two Noble Kinsmen* V iv 152.

There is comfort in the intuition that behind the immediate and visible reality there is an absolute to which it corresponds: that, as was written in a modern poem by Kathleen Raine,

> Behind the tree, behind the house, behind the stars
>   Is the presence that I cannot see
>   Otherwise than as house and stars and tree.

So powerful is the transmutation of personal experience by the artist's vision that no reading of Shakespeare's mind and work is to be received as final and irresistible. To insist, on the other hand, upon the total impersonality of his work is a failure of the imagination; and to dismiss it as morally indifferent is to misunderstand the nature of art, which is, as Browning said, 'the one way possible of speaking truths'.

The present chapter has attempted to reach such conclusions as may legitimately be made from his work. This has involved, as was said at the beginning, some consideration of him as an artist, because there is always the danger that enquirers into his mind and character may forget that he was a poet and interpret occasional statements as a personal confession. If we happen to feel that he did suffer an enthralling and unhappy experience with a woman like Cressida or the Dark Lady, we shall feel it from the prick and heartache of his verse when he writes of baffled lovers. But his verse treats of larger matters than this. He seldom deals in direct statements divorced from his *personae*, and it is only when these begin to accumulate in different conditions that they acquire authority. Even *Sonnet* 129, seemingly an uncompromising statement of personal feeling, may have been only an explosive protest against Petrarchan sentimentality. Often his opinions may be inferred from things he does not say or conclusions that he fails to reach. His view of the pastoral life, for instance, is not discoverable from *As You Like It*, where he examines it through contrasted characters and gives no positive answer beyond suggesting that a romantic view is inadequate. He did not, like Jonson, force life into satirical patterns, chiselling at his characters until he had shaped them to embody predetermined notions. His characters were imagined from within, and certain things happened to them because of their being the men they were; but at the same time men like Mercutio and Falstaff had to be sacrificed to something that their creator needed to say which they could not say for him. It should be obvious, at least, that although he sometimes wrote hurriedly and expediently for the sake of quick theatrical solutions or the prejudices of his audience, he did not compromise when his highest feelings were aroused. He did not, as some of his critics have alleged, write just as the audience liked it. They wanted Falstaff to be Hal's companion in the wars in France, but despite an epilogue promising this, they did not receive it, for artistic reasons more powerful than any objections entered by the Cobhams. He did not handle the familiar tale of Hamlet and revenge as they were accustomed to seeing it on the stage. We may doubt whether many of them felt Cordelia should die or that it was a sufficient closing comment on all this great matter that the eldest hath borne most. Professional entertainer though he was, Shakespeare finally owed allegiance to no judgment but his own.

His work endures because he said significant things about men, commending those specific human virtues of fidelity, patience, love, courage and forgiveness which challenge the sway of passion and ease the burden of grief and sin. His strength lay in no deep speculative wisdom, nor in the exaltation of a spiritual vision, but simply in his sure hold upon the commonplaces of life, upon those daily reassurances which, because they were never so well expressed as he expressed them, were never so well thought upon as he thought upon them. He offers no promise of a redeeming happiness beyond the grave, where all is silent. His message is of life, and of the power that is in all of us to sweeten its corrupted currents before the bright day is done and we are for the dark.

Part V
Shakespeare's Art

Chapter XII
The Nature Of Man

How infinite in faculty.

Ham II ii 317.

The intellectual fashions which determined Shakespeare's habits of thought were still dominantly medieval. Neither the Humanists nor the Protestant reformers saw themselves as having initiated a violent breach with the past. They felt, rather, that they had reached the goal of much medieval striving and that they had restored ancient virtues in the teeth of recent wrongs. The Catholic world-order, attractive at a distance for its seeming harmony of warring elements, was in practice a loose agglomeration of ideas and principles that were never really fused but were liable to different degrees of emphasis at different times.

Thus the Humanism of the Renaissance was orthodox and conservative, and apart from the Anabaptist fringe, none of the sixteenth-century reformers said anything that had not been said many times before, and often said with the highest authority. Even the challenge to papal supremacy had a long and respectable history. Dogmatically, the Reformation put undue emphasis on certain selected doctrines that had formed part of the Christian faith since apostolic times, and in its origins the conflict looked like a simple domestic quarrel with an Augustinian monk challenging the flattening finality of the Dominican synthesis. As a product of the intense and violent energy of the medieval world, Renaissance and Reformation were not at once accompanied by disintegrating changes. These came later, with the forces which their success had released and put beyond ecclesiastical control. The Middle Ages ended when theology was no longer 'the queen of the sciences'.

This happened too late to influence Shakespeare's thinking. He belonged to a world where the novel was still silently absorbed into the familiar, and unity was still more powerful than change. The continuity of intellectual belief had yet to be disturbed, for the Renaissance had accepted a vast bulk of ossified doctrine about man, his nature and his place in the universe, a traditional amalgam of Christianity and pagan philosophy. This provided a cosmological system which, although complicated, inconsistent and uncertain in its details, was definite in outline and purpose. Its core was the assurance of the unity and intimate correspondence of the whole of God's creation. Beyond the imperfect world that is apparent to man's fallen sense there lies a spiritual universe perfect in form and function; and although the ideals and protypes are in themselves unknowable, men may guess at their nature by means of analogy, so that truth consisted of mankind's apprehension of this unseen world. It was to be apprehended by logic and intuition, not by the observation of phenomena, for this medieval cosmology was completely unscientific.

It was not, on the other hand, merely superstitious. It had evolved as a means of explaining and understanding life, it grew out of man's normal experience and his common needs, and it existed for his good. In assuring him of the interdependence of the spiritual universe, the physical creation (the macrocosm), the body politic and the individual soul (the microcosm), it gave him the confidence that all his doings were of concern to God. 'Even heaven itself must see and suffer ill', and at a mother's incest

> heaven's face doth glow,
> Yea, this solidity and compound mass,
> With tristful visage, as against the doom,
> Is thought-sick at the act.
>
> *Ham* III iv 48.

Man's conception of unity was unselective and various, after the medieval fashion, but it offered him a habitation that answered God's great plan, a tidy and comprehensive system in which everything had its place and nothing existed in vain. As an explanation of life it was at once Christian, rational and poetic, rejecting Faustian magic as firmly as it avoided deductive science. It was ethical, legal, physiological, religious and political, and it could not have satisfied man's needs if it had excluded any of these main approaches to life. It drew its potency from the ability of the medieval mind to embrace simultaneously various levels of knowledge and move, with the fortifying help of allegory, from one to the other, confident that the divine unity of all things physical and spiritual would ultimately resolve all ambiguities.

The fundamental principle of the universe was order, the cohesive power which holds together what is constantly threatening to dissolve. The fear that Nature would leave 'the observation of her own laws' expressed itself in contemplation of the dreadful consequences. The great speech of Ulysses (*Troilus and Cressida* I iii 78-134) expounds the Elizabethan view of the universe. 'The specialty of rule' is shown to have applications too wide to be merely political. Ulysses draws his parallels from the heavens, civil law, the elements, ethics and psychology, revealing all these as related parts of the same scheme. Disorder in the heavens produces a reflexive disorder in the sublunary world, the commonwealth and the soul of man; disorder in any one of these is the cause of disorder in all the others, and the performance by all created things of their appointed function is alone 'the stay of the whole world'.

This correspondence, or similitude, revealed the operation of order in the universe and the interdependence of all its parts. The Chain of Being, which linked all created things, linked the highest with the lowest and at once distinguished and united all the levels of existence. Since it was horizontal as well as vertical, it could be invoked to proclaim that as God is to the world, so is the sun to the heavens, the king to the commonwealth, the lion among beasts, the oak to the forest, justice to the other virtues or the soul to the body. If one of these primacies was overthrown, the rest must follow it to confusion, because harmony, which was an essential guarantee of order, required the proper functioning of every part in its allotted place. Obedience, respect, degree, status or calling were among the terms by which men stated their conviction that the specialty of rule must be preserved in all its applications. A few lines from Ralegh's *History of the World* express this central idea that is common to Shakespeare or Hooker or any thoughtful Elizabethan writer:

> For that infinite wisdom of God, which hath distinguished his angels by degree, which hath given greater and less light and beauty to heavenly bodies, which hath made differences between beast and bird, created the eagle and the fly, the cedar and the shrub...hath also ordained kings, dukes or leaders of the people, magistrates, judges, and other degrees among men.

In this traditional picture man occupied a central place.

> God first made angels bodiless, pure minds,
> Then other things, which mindless bodies be;
> Last He made Man, th'horizon 'twixt both kinds,
> In whom we do the World's abridgement see.
> Sir John Davies, *Nosce Teipsum*.

It was for the sake of man that the physical universe had been created. The goal of man's life is to know God, and God has revealed himself in two ways: first by the scriptural word and secondly by the creation. 'By His own word, and by this visible world, is God perceived of men'. According to the more optimistic view of human potentiality the Fall did not entirely obliterate man's reason. He bears still about him some remnant of vanished glories, and by means of the Law of Nature — which is the reason and conscience of God written in every human heart — he may apprehend through correspondences and analogies the ideal world from which he has separated himself through Adam's sin. He still has a special place in the universal scheme, thus described by Ralegh:

> Man, thus compounded and formed by God, was an abstract or model, or brief

story of the universal, in whom God concluded the creation and work of the world; and whom He made the last and most excellent of his creatures, being internally endued with a divine understanding by which he might contemplate and serve his Creator, after whose image he was formed, and endued with the powers and faculties of reason and other abilities that thereby also he might govern and rule the world and all other God's creatures therein. And whereas God created three sorts of living natures, to wit, angelical, rational and brutal, giving to angels an intellectual, and to beasts a sensual nature, he vouchsafed unto man both the intellectual of angels, the sensitive of beasts and the proper rational belonging unto man.[1]

This most excellent of creatures has the special attributes of reason and will: reason which allows him to distinguish between good and evil, and will which confers on him his unique endowment of choice. In the undelivered *Oration on the Dignity of Man* (1486) Pico della Mirandola contemplated a vast ladder of human potentiality, man being the only creature with the power to move on the Chain of Being, either upward to the angels or downward to an animal or even a vegetable existence. The choice is his alone, since God has not assigned to man any certain habitation or peculiar office, and whatever 'thou dost choose for thyself, the same thou shalt enjoy and possess at thine own proper will and election'. Other natural agents are not free: fire must burn, a plant must grow, rain must wet. Angels are beyond the necessity of choice, and beasts have not the capacity to choose, but man may sink to life's lowest levels or 'shall have the power, out of thy soul's judgment, to be reborn into the higher forms of life which are divine'.

The traditional view, less coloured than Pico's by the Humanists' short-lived optimism, warned that will, like reason, might be enslaved by passion. Either might be perverted by appetite to pursue an illusory good presented by the nearness and potency of the senses, as in the Faustian allegory. Will should be that upward aspiration which raises man to seek the ways of God, but when corrupted it degrades him to the mad pursuit of evil. *Wisdom*, a fifteenth-century Morality, declared man's soul to be 'both foul and fair':

Foul as a beast by feeling of sin,
Fair as an angel, of heaven the heir,
By knowledge of God, by His reason within.

Thus the traditional view was significant artistically because, whatever its scientific or philosophical defects, it allowed no evasion of personal responsibility. A man had no right to blame his failures on the pervasiveness of irresistible humours, nor to pity himself as the victim of inauspicious fate;

1 Quoted by Theodore Spencer, *Shakespeare and the Nature of Man*, 19. The first chapter of the book gives an admirable summary of the conventional view of man's place in the universe.

for neither stars nor humours could destroy him unless he shared in his own destruction by allowing his will or reason to be enslaved. ' 'Tis reason's glory to command affects'. The crux of Elizabethan ethics was the conflict of blood and judgment. Sin came into the world when man's faculties were corrupted at the Fall; but the divine nature stood revealed in scripture and the physical creation, and man's specific virtues would avail him, if he acted rightly, to master his affections.

Such, in outline, was the world-picture which the Renaissance took over from the Middle Ages and continued to elaborate and reinforce with affectionate ingenuity. Amplification of accepted beliefs was still the mark of an original mind. The method of the age was to lay down principles and enforce them by the citation of authorities and the furnishing of endless examples; so that a few simple axioms came to acquire a formidable authority by means of an aggregative process that was always adding fresh similitudes. The unity thus achieved was somewhat specious, but it held the imagination and it could be made to cover the full range of human thought and activity. The duty of obedience to authority was as firm in speculative thought and ethics as it was in politics, and the system was not easily responsive to a changing outlook in science, philosophy and religion. It was tenacious in its resistance to the discoveries of Copernicus, Bruno and William Harvey, and it seems that men were for a long time able to believe that Copernicus was right without seriously modifying their inherited notions about the universe. Eventually this quiescent conservatism produced a stronger reaction, and by the turn of the century a new cosmology became less flattering to man as it adapted itself to changing influences.

Whether or not he found its interpretation of life to be convincing, Shakespeare moved among the intricacies of the traditional system with familiarity and seeming confidence. Elizabethan thought and literary expression were in the main so conventional that it is seldom easy to discover the real feeling that lay behind them, and in some forms, such as court poetry and the Petrarchan sonnet, it is impossible. The inherited world-picture appears to have satisfied Shakespeare for the purposes of his art. For the writer it offered a satisfying stability and inclusiveness. The sense of finality that we receive from Shakespeare's work derives in part — but only in part: with a creative artist there is always a danger that influences of this kind will be exaggerated — from his acceptance of the interdependence of all the levels of being. Man is never viewed in isolation. He is treated always in his relation with the divine hierarchy, the physical universe and the world of animals and plants, all of which exist for his good and will, if he use them rightly, lead him towards his goal of reconciliation with God. This concept of the universality of man was common to all serious writers of the age. Some made a greater use than Shakespeare of certain features of the system, as Jonson and Marston with the composition of the humours or Chapman with the irresistible surge of passion, but no one treated all its dominant characteristics with such balance and comprehensiveness or gave it such perfect expression. The whole elaborate scheme took on grandeur, as in the hands of a great poet it always would. The pedantries became vivid and the fossilized bones awoke to new life as he proclaimed the immutability of the laws which govern mankind's being.

The habit of expressing an idea by means of similitudes and correspondences was particularly congenial to Shakespeare's art. As Shelley said, the quest of poets is to 'unveil the permanent analogy of things': 'their words are the echo of the eternal music'. Shakespeare believed that a valuable way to understand anything was to compare it with something else, and to watch for his use of correspondences gives a special excitement to the reading of his verse. To take only one example, the likening of the king to sun, rose, eagle, lion, cedar or other primacies is always adding an overtone of emotion. When Hotspur calls Richard II, whom he had helped to dethrone, 'that sweet lovely rose' (*1 Henry IV* I iii 175), the occasion becomes particularly moving and significant.

Again, in order and the due observance of function Shakespeare found the necessary laws for man's conduct of himself and his relations with his temporal sovereign and the gods above; and in conventional Elizabethan psychology he found an artistically adequate explanation of the weaknesses that bring men to ruin. However faulty in the light of modern knowledge, this psychology was sufficient for the uses of tragedy, and it produced more convincing poetry than the simplified, colourless parables in which medieval writers had accounted for men's fall from greatness. '*Deus quos vult perdere, dementat prius*' states in a crude way something that men have felt to be an important truth, and Elizabethan tragedy tried, with the aid of current physiological and psychological notions, to explain the madness that drives men to their destruction.

The traditional world-picture, then, provided Shakespeare with a framework for his reflections on human life, and in reading the plays we have to remember that its basic conceptions differed in many respects from our own. It rested on different assumptions, cherished different notions of virtue and, to a surprising degree, concerned itself with different issues. Thus although Shakespeare seems to be speaking directly to ourselves, as he has always seemed to be speaking directly to every generation, he speaks with important differences of emphasis. The Elizabethan cosmos was more intimate than our own, for its operations were purposive and inescapable. It postulated a divine scheme with man at the centre of it. For ourselves, on the other hand, science has withdrawn the physical universe into an indifferent remoteness where we can no longer feel that the stars control our destiny, if indeed we are able to think that we have any cosmic destiny at all. The stars no longer leave their courses at the news of man's insurrections. This is but another way of saying that our religious sense has weakened, and it is now possible, as it never was in Shakespeare's time, for the average man to go through life without ever feeling that the hour has come when he should patch his soul for heaven. The Elizabethans, believing that man's nature was universal and unchanging, and thus that all generations are in a sense contemporary, thought that human behaviour was consistent and predictable. In words to be used by Sir Thomas Browne, they would not have it that morality was ambulatory, for if God's laws are unchanging, so too is the conception of virtue. With the receding of this belief in an immanent universe and an immutable law man has lost his assurance of absolute virtue and has to make do with a shifting concept of a conditional good adapted to varying needs and occasions. Soil, climate, endocrinology, social legislation, political convenience and national emergencies determine it in a way which the Elizabethans would have found destructive of the order upon which the whole universe depends.

Thus Shakespeare and his contemporaries paid more attention than ourselves to problems of conduct and correspondingly were less interested in rights. Human rights, as many as sufficed, were implicit in the brotherhood of man to which the world-system daily testified. Despite the rigid classification of society, all men had duties consequent upon their participation in a common humanity. The modern abstractions of liberty and equality were as yet unformulated. Catastrophe and disaster were so much a part of the lives of men accustomed to the swift revolutions of Fortune's wheel that the Elizabethans had no expectation of the political rights and security to which we have attached so much importance. The freedom to which man might properly aspire was freedom from the bondage of passion and appetite, and the only 'standard of living' that he acknowledged was a moral standard. Whereas the modern world is moving towards complete irresponsibility of action and expression, the Elizabethans, in theory at any rate, esteemed only those qualities that taught men to be virtuous.

The system was not monolithic. The traditional body of doctrine had assembled itself snowball – fashion as successive generations added their contribution; and in the Elizabethan age, when it was still the dominant cultural pattern, it received further accretions as the new European Humanists amplified the older authors whose work they had absorbed. Thus in Shakespeare's lifetime the framework was enlarged to incorporate new speculations and discoveries in ethics, psychology and religion; and, faithful to its historic purpose, it even made tentative efforts to assimilate the conjectures of empirical science.

For a writer the existence of a recognized scheme of thought provided him with a convenient way of talking about people and life. It was a way that seemingly even the humbler members of Shakespeare's audience could accept and understand, and this was valuable because it solved the problem of communication. A key word or idea could be relied upon to promote the relevant associations. Shakespeare therefore could present in Hamlet a fashionable melancholic (although he is much else beside) in the confidence that most of his audience would recognize both the character and its implications; and as late as Leontes he portrayed a victim of passionate obsession. But the convention was never used mechanically. He never, for instance, absorbed himself like Jonson in the theory of humours, which he burlesqued in the person of Nym; and although he found in unregulated passion a partly adequate explanation of evil, he did not analyse its effects with the curious, almost pedantic exactitude of Chapman. Always there are local and personal reasons for the things that happen in his plays. His characters are men caught in particular circumstances, not puppets manifesting predetermined principles. It is not only passions that spin his tragic plots, and the histories have a wider purpose than merely to proclaim the duty of obedience. Personality is always breaking in, the ambition or weakness of a king that threatens political stability or the anarchism of a Falstaff that is destructively critical of social organization. Although the world-picture was always a part of his mental climate, Shakespeare used it when and how he needed it. Its alternating conception of man as angel and beast was important to a poetic interpretation of life. The final test of its value to him was the sort of poetry he was able to make out of it; and its hold on his imagination was strong enough to produce some of his richest and most subtle effects.

By the turn of the century, however, this world-picture was being assailed as too flattering to man and his society. There was nothing new in this as the Catholic world had never wholly discarded the idea that man's will and reason had been so corrupted by the Fall that unaided he was incapable of good. For a number of potent reasons this view was once more in the ascendant in Elizabeth's later years. The speculations of science, although but slowly and reluctantly absorbed into the general consciousness, were weakening the notion of a geocentric universe and so questioning man's claim to be the privileged darling of creation. With the eternal swing of the theological pendulum the determinist doctrines of Paul and Augustine were once more in favour, and the heresies of the miserable Gottschalk, a German monk synodically condemned at Quercy in 849, were established at the heart of Calvinist orthodoxy. In this darkening scene there was no possibility of that freedom of choice which the optimists allowed to man, for he had no hope of choosing rightly. The destruction of his faculties at the Fall was absolute. Calvin said that of man's reason, his specific virtue, 'a shapeless ruin is all that remains'. Nor could he be regenerated through society, because no human institution is proof against the sin of Adam. Only through divine grace could man aspire to salvation, and here God's choice had been effected 'before the foundations of the world were laid'. Calvinism even constituted a threat to the social order. Although Calvin himself was equivocal on the duty of obedience to the magistrate, Genevan missionaries taught that the ungodly ruler must be overthrown.

The doubts raised by science and religion found an echo in political and philosophical treatises. Machiavelli was the bogey-man of Renaissance

England.[2] Certain principles extracted from the *Discourses* and *The Prince* unduly restrict Machiavelli's powerful and enquiring mind, but these selected passages assert that human government, so far from being a divinely prescribed reflection of the celestial order, is founded on force and fraud. In propriety, therefore, his ideas were denounced, and a 'politician', specifically a Machiavellian, was 'one that might circumvent God'. But Machiavelli charmed as well as horrified. There was the disturbing suspicion that actual events, in contrast to the optimistic conception of government as the embodiment of virtue, proved him to be right. The fascination of his doctrines is attested by the number of references to him in Elizabethan drama and the popularity on the stage of the lawless 'politician'. His influence was more widely diffused than that of another critic of traditional optimism, the French essayist Montaigne, although Montaigne may have made a deeper impression on the thoughtful and the educated. His essays and his *Apologie de Raymond Sebond* led him to his doubting conclusion, '*Que sais-je?*' All knowledge is relative and the human reason is a fallible instrument. He found no immutable laws, no firm standards of belief or conduct, nothing universally agreed upon; if man has the faculty of reason, so too do animals, and in sense-perception man is the animals' inferior. This urbane, easy-going sceptic decides finally that if man wishes to rise above his wretched uncertainties, he can achieve it only by faith, by abandoning the brave folly of trusting to his own resources and throwing himself upon the divine mercy. Through Florio's translation Shakespeare seems to have known Montaigne quite well. Doubtless he enjoyed the entertaining paradox of a sceptical Humanist using Humanist methods to reach a fideist refuge.

Questioning of the world-picture gained a sharp edge from the practices and policies which men saw flourishing all around them. Many plays and *novellas* were based on semi-historical accounts of the savagery and intrigues that prevailed, often with papal participation, at the courts of Renaissance Italy, and Chapman was soon to dramatize similar and more recent treacheries among the nobility of France. Such works would be prohibited by modern laws of defamation, and some of them did promote complaint at ambassadorial level. The point is that they showed Machiavellian 'policy' in action. Here it has to be remembered that the system of correspondences, whose purpose was to reassure, would multiply doubt once it had been successfully threatened in any quarter. All the primacies would be endangered if Machiavelli's fox were to depose the lion. In this context the Massacre of St Bartholomew in 1572 had shocked the European mind. It was not just an assassination, which was common enough. The French government seemed to be attempting the mass extermination of its enemies,

2 For a discussion of Machiavelli's influence on Tudor thought and practice see M.M. Reese, *The Cease of Majesty*, 92-104.

and it gave the event a particular Machiavellian twist that the victims had come to Paris as wedding guests. When a civilized and Christian government sank to treachery of this kind, a new and incalculable force had been released in the sphere of human relations. The dykes had broken in the night. By all that men held traditional, this terrible deed should have been followed by reverberations in the planetary world and strange mutinies in the soul of man. Probably no one thought precisely on these lines. There was always a powerful element of allegory in the medieval system, and it is hard to decide where allegory yields to the intrusion of real feeling. But evil on this scale was felt to have cosmic consequences, and the Gunpowder Plot in England aroused a similar horror. Contemporary writings spoke of the king's escape in terms of a Messianic deliverance.

Copernican theory, Machiavellian 'policy' and Calvinism's loss of hope each gained additional force from the existence of the others. Donne was not alone in finding 'all coherence gone'. The new spirit of acquisitiveness, the trickery and exploitation practised by the race of 'projectors', seemed only to complement in the social order the lapse of the celestial spheres into 'an irregular volubility'. Mistrust of the new king deepened the disillusion. The miracle, as men saw it, of James I's peaceful accession had awakened unreasonable hopes. 'He is come that grace to all doth bring'. But the reality was different. He who claimed to be 'the great schoolmaster of the whole land' presided over a drunken, dissipated court, and the great issues of the time, financial, constitutional and religious, were not being settled. In growing bitterness the long Elizabethan debate continued.

Again we must not oversimplify and create an artificial substitution of Jacobean pessimism in place of Elizabethan optimism. Optimistic and pessimistic views of the world-order had existed side by side for centuries, and the young see things differently from the old. Humanism had always had its critics and its doubters, and Elizabeth's reign had seen too much of anxiety and tribulation to have been a period of uninterrupted hopefulness. No one had been more certain than Spenser that the world was running down, and his October Eclogue in *The Shepherd's Calendar* was gloomy even about the future of poetry. 'Tom Piper makes us better melody'. The fashion for pastoral drew its rather spurious vitality from an imagined picture of rural contentment far from the jostling struggle of court and politics.

It would be wrong, therefore, to imagine an era of hope suddenly replaced by disillusion. The last years of the Tudor century had gathered such a weight of unsolved problems that the country would have to work out new ways of settling them. The great Stuart contention lay just ahead. But for the space of a few years men seem to have wilted under the burden, and writers turned to testiness and cerebration. The Petrarchans fell silent with a very remarkable suddenness, and the new vogue was for satire.[3] The satirists

3   For some of the satirical authors and their works see Chapter V, note 2.

were solemn enough in their intentions. There was much talk about the 'sin-drowned world' and about wiping clean 'the snottery of our slimy time'. But they occupied a pulpit without a text. Lacking any constructive programme of reform, they revived the medieval device of personification, attacking abuses and individuals under the old abstractions of Avarice and Lechery. Even this could be a dangerous exercise. The young George Wither, an agreeable and inventive pastoral poet until he was 'changed' and became a Cromwellian officer, was imprisoned for his innocuous *Abuses Stripped and Whipped* (1613). Probably it was its own ineffectiveness rather than fear of sporadic government action that brought this satirical vituperation to a languishing end. Significantly, this was also the period when the dramatists waged their *Poetomachia*: when committed in public, theatrical cannibalism is seldom amusing. Jonson's comedy was degenerating from the subtle display of the quiddities of character into the laboured construction of puppets to embody exaggerated vices. After writing *Hamlet*, Shakespeare dropped his output to seldom more than one play a year. Although earlier authorship has been claimed for all three, it is likely that in the first years of the new century he wrote the three hybrids known as 'the problem comedies'. O.J. Campbell has suggested (*Comicall Satyre and Shakespeare's 'Troilus and Cressida'*) that these were his contribution to the satirical mode, which he found uncongenial. The characteristic of these comedies is the high proportion of thought — of hard intellectual wrestling — that has refused to resolve itself into poetic drama.

Before they could revert to their proper function poets would have to find a style appropriate to their new ways of thought. The important difference between the literature of the first decade of James and the last decade of Elizabeth[4] is a new mood of earnestness and concentration. The change is perhaps best exhibited in Donne, progenitor of the so-called 'Metaphysical' poetry with its achievement (as though Shakespeare had not been doing it all the time) of the condensed multiple image. The tight interweaving of mind and emotion was technically a demanding objective, and Donne himself seems to have found the brave *Progress of the Soul* too difficult to finish. On a less aspiring level than the Metaphysicals, other writers sought a more con-centrated form of expression. Of course the change was gradual and it was never all-embracing. At any time of transition there are always trivial writers unaware of what is going on, so that trashy plays continued to slide off the Henslowe conveyor-belt, minor poets sang the refrains of less urgent days, and pamphlets and sermons still employed Rhetoric's well-tried devices. But the abrupt termination of the sonneteering vogue is a fact of great significance. Many of its practitioners, along with poets and dramatists of the younger generation, now addressed themselves to the great questions of

4 For the main differences between Elizabethan and Jacobean modes of thought see F.P. Wilson, *Elizabethan and Jacobean*, U. Ellis-Fermor, *The Jacobean Drama*, especially chapters 1, 2 and 13.

the day without the excessive use of ornament. It was in this spirit that Shakespeare was exhorted to turn to graver subjects than 'love's foolish lazy languishment', although he already had. History attempted to become more exact and philosophic, and the exuberant old fictions drawn from fable and legend were discarded for the patient study of man's actual predicament. Rhetoric, with its lush arts of copiousness and amplification, was unsuitable for this new intensity of purpose, and in both poetry and prose there was a tendency for rhythms to be simpler and diction more natural. Hamlet's mother was true to her time in demanding more matter with less art.

The first notable work in the new fashion was the *Nosce Teipsum* of Sir John Davies (1599), a long philosophical poem setting forth the traditional doctrines of the Law of Nature, the immortality of the soul, the interdependence of the various levels of being, and so forth. Its content, therefore, was not new, and this sort of comprehensive re-statement of a conventional theory is usually a sign that the theory is having to fight for its existence. But as with Socrates, the injunction to 'Know Thyself' is not just an advice to individual self-examination; it demands an enquiry into the whole faculty and function of mankind. The poem was novel in the plainness of its style, austerely different from the rich and imaginative decoration of Davies's *Orchestra*, published some three years earlier. *Nosce Teipsum* is not a philosophical discourse that might have been written in prose, because it is unfailingly musical and the emotional control obtained through rhyme and a steady rhythm is integral to it. But Davies, who had already satirized the fatuities of the sonnet convention, seems to have decided to dispense with the devices of ornament and speak his meaning as plainly as he could.

Symbolically, the change in literary aim and method expressed itself in a more sceptical attitude towards the traditional world-picture. Its conventions did not disappear. They continued to be valuable as a statement of what man should be, and the ideal of stability was contrasted with what poets felt to be the reality of chaos.

> Knowing the heart of man is set to be
> The centre of this world, about the which
> These revolutions of disturbances
> Still roll, where all th'aspects of misery
> Predominate, whose strong effects are such
> As he must bear, being powerless to redress;
> And that unless above himself he can
> Erect himself, how poor a thing is man.
> Daniel, *To the Lady Margaret, Countess of Cumberland* (1603).

A new world-picture was being imposed upon the old, which never recovered its full authority. Mechanistic science was fatal to it. Change came with the dawning of a genuinely scientific outlook, of which the Jacobeans were uneasily conscious. They could not fully absorb its implications, but they knew that something had gone awry with their traditional beliefs. The telescope was an alarming invention, and it was no good saying that Galileo was wrong when evidentially he was so disturbingly right. Thus when Bacon wrote, in *The Advancement of Learning* (1605), that 'nothing parcel of the world is denied to man's enquiry and invention', or twenty years later, in *New Atlantis*,

> The end of our foundation is the knowledge of causes and secret motions of things; and the enlarging of the bounds of human empire, to the effecting of all things possible,

he was writing as a scientist, not as a moral philosopher. The conquests that he imagined were not the conquest of evil and the passions. Bacon's essays too, when the reader has penetrated beyond the language to the modest core of meaning, proclaim a somewhat utilitarian message. It would perhaps be a solecism to compare them in any way with the persuasions of Lord Chesterfield, but there is the same anxiety to give instruction in the matter of 'getting on'. The ethical sanctions are wearing thin, and ultimately knowledge and morality will be divorced from one another.

In imaginative literature the note was less confident because the gains were more doubtful. The transition was least noticeable in comedy, where the correction of manners had been the ostensible purpose since classical times. It was still a satisfactory medium for the examination of social ills. In the meantime the satirical impulse was finding a more effective outlet in the writing of 'characters' in the style of Theophrastus, and the recovery of classical models, in place of the personified abstractions of medieval denunciation, represented the recovery of a proper satiric mood. But it was in tragedy that the early Jacobean period achieved its most characteristic expression. Men were seemingly bound to the contemplation of their own wickedness and the certainty of dissolution: 'the long day of mankind drawing fast towards an evening, and the world's tragedy and time near at an end'. Such moods are ripe for tragedy but do not always produce it. Art sometimes expresses itself through a scornful hostility to the social order, as at the present day, or takes a frightened refuge in *contemptus mundi*. But Jacobean writers felt themselves to be deeply implicated in the fate of their civilization. Literature and life served one another, and the writer could not be indifferent.

The complaint of one of Marston's characters that the earth was become a Golgotha, 'the very muckhill on which the sublunary orbs cast their excrements' (*The Malcontent* IV v 107) epitomized the change to which the poets thought they had to reconcile themselves, and their work reflects their despair at the loss of the traditional supports by which they had been sustained.

And can there be worse sickness than to know

That we are never well, nor can be so?...
So did the world from the first hour decay,
That evening was beginning of the day,
And now the Springs and Summers which we see,
Like sons of women after fifty be.
And new Philosophy calls all in doubt,
The Element of fire is quite put out;
The Sun is lost, and th'earth, and no man's wit
Can well direct him where to look for it.
And freely men confess that this world's spent...
'Tis all in pieces, all coherence gone;
All just supply, and all Relation.

Donne, *The First Anniversary.*

Poetry lost the old assurance of the relationship between the visible and the invisible worlds, the correspondence between the reality apparent to the senses and the intuition of a spiritual reality behind it. Man might no longer be confident of a universe created for his illumination and sympathetic to his strivings. Only his immediate experience and his non-spiritual knowledge would avail him. Early in Tourneur's *Atheist's Tragedy* (I i 14) Borachio says 'There's nothing in a man above his nature'. These are words of resignation and defeat because they deny that man may learn anything of God through the universe that God has created.

Jacobean tragedy was thus an imaginative exploration of a world devoid of hope, devoid of any expectation beyond suffering and extinction. The sombre magnificence of Webster's two great plays seems to consist in his recognition of man's helplessness in the presence of evil, of life that is a general mist of error and its pleasures only the good hours of an ague. The dramatists for the most part refused the consolations of dogmatic theology and persisted in defiance. Their own vitality and creative splendour was no small argument against futility, and Jacobean pessimism was not effete: it required iron nerves to contemplate the desolation that these men imagined. A common impulse, too powerful to have been just modish, forced them to consider that their picture might be true and to wonder how man would conduct himself if it were. They stripped man of his lendings and turned him loose in a world empty of human-kindness or sacred pity. No facile sentimentality or meretricious happy-ending was allowed to ease the pain. Shakespeare's Gloucester, who was refused the insights granted to Lear himself, embodied this pessimistic view. The evils that he saw around him signified to him the determination of the unappeasable gods to bring down the universe and confound the wicked and the virtuous alike in a common destruction. When 'there's son against father' and father against child, there is no escaping 'the sequent effects'.

We have seen the best of our time: machinations, hollowness, treachery and all
ruinous disorders follow us disquietly to our graves.

Lear I ii 122.

But man had not lost his sovereign virtue of courage. The tragic hero would fill the spiritual void with the utmost achievement of which as a fallen creature he was able. If it was his lot to be driven helplessly forward by his passions, they should drive him to great extremes before they cast him without pity on the opposing shore. These lawless, ranting monsters were described in their outward aspect in the Induction to Marston's *Antonio and Mellida*, where the actor playing Piero was bidden:

> Thus frame your exterior shape
> To haughty forms of elate majesty,
> As if you held the palsy-shaking head
> Of reeling chance under your fortune's belt
> In strictest vassalage.

These were men for whose own good all causes would give way. Passion became its own excuse when they espoused blood against judgment and set themselves above the divine or moral law which they regarded as a broken pretence.

> Be free, all worthy spirits,
> And stretch yourselves, for greatness and for height:
> Untruss your slaveries: you have height enough
> Beneath this steep heaven to use all your reaches:
> 'Tis too far off to let you or respect you.
> Give me a spirit that on this life's rough sea
> Loves t'have his sails fill'd with a lusty wind...
> There is no danger to a man that knows
> What life and death is; there's not any law
> Exceeds his knowledge; neither is it lawful
> That he should stoop to any other law.
> He goes before them, and commands them all,
> That to himself is a law rational.
>
> Chapman, *Biron's Conspiracy* III iv 138.

In the sequel Biron, outwitted in his schemes, confronts the hangman with a confession of hopelessness that belies all these brave words:

> And so farewell for ever. Never more
> Shall any hope of my revival see me.
> Such is the endless exile of dead men.
> Summer succeeds the spring; autumn the summer;
> The frosts of winter the fall'n leaves of autumn:
> All these, and all fruits in them, yearly fade,
> And every year return: but cursed man
> Shall never more renew his vanish'd face...
> Strike, strike, O strike; fly, fly, commanding soul,

And on thy wings, for this thy body's breath,
Bear the eternal victory of death.

There the play ends. There is no message of comfort, no sense of continuing
life.

In other works defiance of the moral law may take different forms, as in
Ford's *'This Pity She's a Whore*, where a brother and sister find in the
strength of their passion a justification for incestuous love.

> O, how these stol'n contents
> Would print a modest crimson on my cheeks,
> Had any but my heart's delight prevailed.

II i 6.

> So where the body's furniture is beauty,
> The mind's must needs be virtue; which allowed,
> Virtue itself is reason but refined,
> And love the quintessence of that.

II v 18.

Their love ends in the destruction that is the inevitable outcome of these
Jacobean dramas. Man in the grip of passion invents his own reasons, as
Biron and Ford's Giovanni do, and tragedy narrowed itself to an examination of the individual's reaction, opinionated and defiant, to an overwhelming fate. In these studies of obsession the gods are at best indifferent
and more often are felt to be actively malevolent. Man cannot be said to
cooperate in his own destruction where he is doomed from the start and has
no chance to save himself.

Before very long, at about the time when Shakespeare was ceasing to write
for the theatre, the horror faded — or perhaps it became too terrible to
contemplate. Men seemed to resign themselves to the unfathomable
injustice of the cosmic process and turn aside to less exigent matters. It was
now that playgoing began to separate between the 'popular' audiences of the
Red Bull and the 'judicious' of the court and the private theatres. Both sorts
of audience now required their entertainment to be spiced with masque and
spectacle. The drama of Fletcher and Shirley has been condemned without
due acknowledgment of its virtues of sound construction, musical verse and
theatrical effect. These two poets in particular have had to bear the burden
of critical disappointment with the theatre's failings after the great age was
past. Romantic tragi-comedy became the favourite mode, and with it a
feature altogether new to English drama, the unexpected 'twist' in the plot.
In older plays the outcome is logical and predictable, giving a sense of order
and justice in human affairs. The new game, which often was not logical at
all, sacrificed authentic characterization to purely theatrical surprises of plot
and feeling. Written with wit, lucidity and decorous lyricism, these shallow
entertainments held attention on the stage, and after the Restoration they

were more popular than Shakespeare. They appealed to the philistine taste of Pepys, and even Dryden took them seriously. But they were damned by a complacent superficiality of thought and execution which even at this distance of time is hard to forgive. With mitigation for Massinger, who gave dramatic form to his interest in social and political questions, the drama was guilty of becoming evasive and irresponsible. It no longer reflected seriously on the problem of evil. Much of the verse was for decoration only, and true poetic drama yielded to cobbled contrivances of pathos, sentimentality and incident. In its avoidance of the great issues it prepared the way for the dulcet ineffectuality of Caroline poetry.

The contemporary conflict about the nature of man was a vital theme of Shakespeare's mature tragedy. In Gloucester's unseeing resignation, or the drive and egotism of Macbeth's ambition, or Timon's noisy defiance he gave voice to the new disillusion. This did not imply a radical change of outlook, because even in his early work, when he used the traditional optimistic picture in a fairly uncritical way, he was aware that it was not the only possible interpretation of life. Aaron and Richard III were sketches of the amoral individualist whose ambition was his only law, and Faulconbridge spoke unblushingly for 'commodity'. Throughout the histories he was reflecting constantly upon the hollowness of ceremony and the contrasting realities of public life. Sooner or later his art would have to determine the question whether man was all that he seemed to be, and in *Hamlet* he enlarged the scope of his drama to test the optimistic view of man and the universe by opposing to it the conclusions of a less reassuring experience. Whereas in earlier plays he had not gone beyond the doubts raised by the violation of order, in *Hamlet* he used the old melodrama of revenge to portray the agony of a finely sensitive mind as it realized that of the two views of man the pessimistic might be the true one.

Hamlet's speech and imagery show him to have been a Renaissance prince nurtured in the belief that man, by discourse of reason, might aspire to the angels' gift of understanding; but before the play opens his mother's hasty marriage to her dead husband's brother — canonically an act of incest — has tainted her sex and brought everything into question. Hamlet's very first remarks probe the difference between appearance and reality. He knows not *seems*. In the first of the four great soliloquies he states the orthodox conviction that because individuals are wicked, the physical universe and the commonwealth too are corrupt and sick. The uses of the world are flat and unprofitable, for it is possessed by things rank and gross in nature; and because of his mother's sin, and the sin he half-suspects in his uncle, heaven is thought-sick and something is rotten in the state of Denmark. The revelations of the Ghost complete his disillusion, and thereafter his language dwells on the contrast between what man professes to be and what he is.

Hamlet could not feel the contrast so deeply if his nurture had not taught him what a piece of work is man. In his first meeting with Rosencrantz and

Guildenstern he gives an incomparable statement of the optimistic tradition, made poignant by the dark convictions which have taken hold of him.

> What is a man
> If his chief good and market of his time
> Be but to sleep and feed? A beast, no more.
> Sure He that made us with such large discourse,
> Looking before and after, gave us not
> That capability and godlike reason
> To fust in us unus'd?

IV iv 33.

Reason, the noble, the sovereign, the godlike, is become a pander to the will; to be honest is to be one man picked out of ten thousand; and man, who should have the apprehension of an angel, is a miserable creature 'crawling between heaven and earth'. 'We are arrant knaves all'. Hamlet's superb capacity for generalization surrounds the accidents of his individual destiny with a universal significance. Against the ideal of his father's enlightened rule he sets the reality of the politician Claudius, and the contrast is so terrible that kingship itself is called in question. Against the ideal of his father's love for his mother he sets that same mother's lust, by which love itself has lost its sanctity. Recurrent images of painting, which hides ugliness under bright colours, or of disease and physical decay, particularly of ulcers filmed by seemingly healthy skin, give poetic reinforcement to the pervading theme of evil faintly disguised by insincerity and pretence. Finally, in the 'to be or not to be' soliloquy Hamlet's personal agony is transmuted into a cry for the predicament of all fallen humanity. It is ever a misunderstanding of his situation to call him an egoist, for the traditional ways of thinking bade all men regard the universal implications of a single act. As the play moves to its climax he attains to an emotional maturity in which he can see beyond the tragedy of his own experience.

His way to reconciliation is now clear. The Hamlet who returns from his adventures at sea is a more stable and a nobler man than the distracted youth of the early scenes. When Shakespeare tells us, in the sort of detail he seldom uses casually, that the undergraduate is become a man of thirty, the change is symbolic of Hamlet's new mental state. He has stepped out of the confines of the plot, and it no longer matters what happens to him or Claudius or anyone else. He no longer rails at the cursed spite that fated him to heal the wounds of a sick commonwealth, for his personal suffering merges into the scheme of things.

> There's a divinity that shapes our ends,
> Rough-hew them how we will,
> And there is a special providence in the fall of a sparrow

V ii 10.

It is a significant and consoling discovery because in the first shock of disillusion he had come to doubt the existence of order itself. The order that his sufferings have revealed to him is not the beneficent creation which the vaingloriousness of man had hopefully pictured, but his renewed conviction of a shaping Providence exalts his acceptance of his approaching death. Death to him signifies no more than the readiness to meet an engulfing silence. The change in his mood in conveyed not by what he says so much as by the way he says it. The firm, articulated rhythms of his speech tell of an assured purpose absent from the nervous, congested utterance of the earlier speeches; and because this new assurance is born of experience and not of theory, we may the more certainly believe in it. The accomplishment of his revenge (in purely theatrical terms almost an anti-climax) purges the human soul of lust and murder, just as the arrival of Fortinbras symbolizes the purgation of the commonwealth. But these goods, important as they are, matter less to us than the reaffirmation of some kind of world-order by a great and sensitive spirit who once had cause to doubt it.

The poetic vision which Shakespeare embodied in Hamlet remained constant throughout his tragedies. He surveyed the predicament of man in a universe sickened by corruption, but he refused to believe that the disease was fatal. He explored the pessimistic view of humanity — no man more terribly — only to reaffirm in play after play the positive values which assure to man a privileged place in a world created for his uses; and this without recourse to the standard teachings of Christianity. He was unimpressed, therefore, by the alternating resignation and defiance assumed by most of the heroes of Jacobean drama. Mere resignation was never offered by him as an adequate gesture for a being endowed with the infinite heritage of man. Courage is a splendid virtue, but all virtues become insufficient through excess and courage must be supplemented by the others of which man is capable. Gloucester's conclusion that men are to the gods as flies to wanton boys is an assertion of Senecan paganism that has to be contrasted with Lear's attainment of a superior wisdom. His losing of his eyes symbolizes a blindness of the heart for which his sufferings brought him no relief, and he dies, ' 'twixt two extremes of passion, joy and grief', no wiser than he has ever been. His passive submission to his fate loses the edge of virtue when he can learn so little by it.

In *Timon of Athens*, the most 'Jacobean' of his plays, Shakespeare made another study of a man who learned nothing by his suffering. This time it was the defiant type. It is unnecessary to regard the play as the distressed outpouring of a mind temporarily stricken, or as a morbid by-product of the vast effort of the imagination which begot *King Lear*, or in any apologetic or deprecatory sense. If we feel it to be unsatisfactory, probably it is because Shakespeare did not find Timon a satisfactory sort of hero. The sum of his ravings amounts to no more than the disillusion of a Thersites gifted with a civilized mind and haunted by the wrack of much that once was noble.

Apemantus, a Diogenes without a tub, at least is a cynic by conviction, whereas Timon only displays the peevishness of a spoiled child who has lost his toys. Pity and terror cannot be evoked when there is no grandeur in the central figure. Critics of the play are apt to forget, however, that Shakespeare expressly says at the beginning that a real tragic portrait is not being attempted. In a manner most untypical of him he provides in the very first scene an allegorical summary of the theme, the dialogue of the Painter and the Poet proclaiming that it was to be one of those time-honoured studies of a man hurled from prosperity to ruin, for no particular fault of his own, by the 'shift and change' of Fortune. As the Painter sententiously remarks,

> 'Tis common:
> A thousand moral paintings I can show
> That shall demonstrate these quick blows of Fortune's.
>
> I i 89.

This will serve for medieval Morality or a political handbook like *A Mirror for Magistrates*, but it is resistant to proper tragedy.

The play is Shakespearean in its chastisement of men guilty of false flattery and ingratitude:

> Most smiling, smooth, detested parasites,
> Courteous destroyers, affable wolves, meek bears,
> You fools of fortune, trencher-friends, time's flies,
> Cap-and-knee slaves, vapours, and minute-jacks.
>
> III vi 105.

The language here is forced and feeble, and Shakespeare always seems to be straining his powers to make poetry out of the sufferings that urge Timon to vituperation but teach him so little. Because there is no character in the play of sufficient understanding to make a contrast with Timon's hollow defiance, the mood of regeneration that envelops the great tragedies at their close is here absent. It is true that Athens is held to merit some purgation at the sword of Alcibiades, but Alcibiades, by his own confession a choleric man, is not an impressive agent of redemption. There is a strange lack of repentance. Ingratitude is rebuked loudly enough, but Timon's sufferings and his renunciation of society do not seem to make anyone aware of the sinfulness of it. The implication is that unless the victim of misfortune will learn something from his experience, no one else will.

Alcibiades and Coriolanus both marched upon a city that had banished them, but there is a radical contrast in Shakespeare's handling of them. Whereas Coriolanus had done the state some service and was banished through the political intrigues of his enemies, Alcibiades defied the Senate and tried to intimidate the civil power with military threats. There is majesty in Coriolanus's 'I banish you' and 'There is a world elsewhere', but

Alcibiades reacts to his sentence thus:

> Banishment!
> It comes not ill; I hate not to be banish'd;
> It is a cause worthy my spleen and fury,
> That I may strike at Athens...
> 'Tis honour with most lands to be at odds;
> Soldiers should brook as little wrongs as gods.

> III v 111.

This petulant threat to strike back suggests the gangster morality of Jacobean heroes and their immature conception of 'honour'. Alcibiades is an empty figure and Shakespeare does not pursue him. He appears only once more, in the company of some tattered soldiers and a pair of mistresses, before he is seen negotiating the surrender of Athens. One could have little confidence in a new social order of which this trivial person is to be the instrument. Coriolanus, on the other hand, has to make a truly tragic choice between honour and mercy. At first he will stand

> As if a man were author of himself
> And knew no other kind,

> V iii 36

and we recognize the Jacobean accent here. He will break 'all bond and privilege of nature'. In the end, however, he knows that the gods are mocking 'this unnatural scene', and it is by her talk of mercy, of behaviour that is natural and unnatural, and the bond between mother and child that Volumnia wins him over. Coriolanus still must die, but he has rejoined the human race; and with the pledge to 'unshout the noise that banish'd Marcius', Rome will be at peace again.

> Ne'er through an arch so hurried the blown tide
> As the recomforted through the gates.

> V iv 51.

In Iago Shakespeare made a study of the lawless individualist which, despite the extravagances implicit in the Vice convention, is subtler and more convincing than the bravura sketches attempted by other dramatists. Iago is an incomplete man. Intellect is the master of all his actions, and he is deficient in feeling and will, particularly in that upward aspiration that urges more exalted spirits to ride life's rough sea. He prefers to paddle in stagnant waters and make sure that they are muddy. Thinking himself to be incomparably clear-sighted, he early informs the muddle-headed Roderigo, in whom desire has to struggle with traces of a decent instinct, of his conception of the true nature of man. Man's only emotions are the appetites of the animal creation, and his reason serves to clothe appetites in a show of respectability. 'Virtue! a fig! 'tis in ourselves that we are thus or thus'. Iago is master of those base little passions by which most men may be moved. Although he is disgruntled at missing promotion, he is not really ambitious; money he regards as trash; and although he affects to believe that his wife is unfaithful, he would never drown himself 'for the love of a guinea-hen'. But he knows how to penetrate to the weaknesses of all his acquaintance — Roderigo's lust, Cassio's instability in liquor, Othello's quickness to anger and suspicion — and his malignity leads him to exploit his knowledge.

In this play Shakespeare shows the power of an evil man to involve all others in the corruption that constitutes his daily vision of the universe. It has often been remarked that Iago's mastery of Othello becomes so absolute that ultimately the two men think and speak and act as one. Othello descends to Iago's view of humanity, and his talk is all of goats and monkeys. His final vision of himself, broken and bestial and enslaved to passion, as the instrument of everlasting justice is a tragic revelation of his self-deception and of the change that has been wrought in him.

Yet Iago, the most densely evil of Shakespeare's full-length studies of wickedness, does not finally prevail. In an ordinary Jacobean play he would doubtless have been detected and punished — stabbed most likely, rather than brought to formal justice; but there would have been a vital difference in the manner of it. In Shakespeare his schemes collapse before the revelation of an inherent truth whose existence he has denied, and he learns in stubborn silence that his insight and realism, qualities that were his boast and pride, have failed him. In a warped fashion he personifies the Renaissance ideal of the subduing of blood by judgment; he sees so clearly through the hollow deceits of passion that he will never become their slave. But the superiority which this brings him denotes also an inferiority and a separation. His denial of blood and emotion is a denial of the normal attributes of a sentient being. It puts him, surprisingly, in the company of Sir Andrew, in whose liver is not to be found 'so much blood...as will clog the foot of a flea'; and Sir Andrew is something less than a man. Iago's failing, a serious flaw in one who regards himself as an acute analyst of human nature, is his inability to comprehend not merely the innate goodness of men nobler than himself but also the inconsistent and unexpected patches of virtue in those much his inferiors in capacity and intelligence. Othello's greatness of soul, the loyalty of Desdemona, even the doglike decency of the fallible Cassio, are virtues beyond his understanding. It is a master-stroke of Shakespeare to make him suddenly realize, when it is too late, that Cassio has a daily beauty in his life beyond his own previous perception. In the end he finds himself judged and discomfited by Emilia and Roderigo, creatures whom he has deceived and despised. Brabantio is the only man he judges correctly, and there is not much merit in that, choleric fatherhood being one of Shakespeare's most familiar targets.

Iago's world finally collapses when he is revealed not as a frustrated schemer, for his designs have succeeded terribly enough, but as a wicked man. Therein he is submitted to a standard of judgment that he has dismissed as the froth of deluded imaginations. He learns that it is not merely in ourselves that we are thus or thus. There are universal laws of which even Roderigo has some intimation; of which, indeed, in his successive attempts to conjure up a respectable motive for what he was doing to Othello, he has shown some fleeting intimation himself. The unemotional realist finds that his judgment of mankind has failed to cover all the facts. As he listens to Othello's last speech, he must know that his evil spell is broken and that his deadly strokes have not pierced his victim to the heart. If ever he should cease to love Desdemona, Othello had once said, then 'chaos is come again'. It is enough to unhinge his reason and carry him to irrational vengeance as the agent of a moral order he now denies. But with the proof of her fidelity the celestial order is restored, and Othello can begin to gather the broken fragments of his humanity, can speak again in language that befits a man:

> Here is my journey's end, here is my butt,
> And very sea-mark of my utmost sail.
>
> V ii 267.

Although 'this look of thine will hurl my soul from heaven', the vision of chaos has receded and 'we shall meet at compt', where all human acts are measured. His last words recover the majestic and sonorous rhythms which had charmed Desdemona in the days of their courtship, and his rich fancy is freed to wander for the last time among his cherished memories. At the sound of that voice Iago can only be silent, for it speaks of things of which he has known nothing.

The character of Iago was only one of the forms in which Shakespeare might have examined the crushing negations of the pessimistic view of human nature, but in whatever form he examined it he exposed it as inadequate and false. In *King Lear* the conclusions are hard to formulate, and perhaps no one has discovered what this gigantic creation really means. If its meaning is not too deep for comprehension, it is too complex to be restated in any language but that of the play itself. In the storm that rages in the old man's mind he finds the whole frame of things disjoined and Nature's laws subverted. We have here to contemplate a world so permeated by evil that order itself has disintegrated. Lear bids the forces of destruction let fall their horrible pleasure and invokes chaos to

> Crack Nature's moulds, all germens spill at once
> That make ingrateful man.
>
> III ii 6.

Yet, although it is hard to say exactly where it lies, this agony is enclosed by a grace and pity that elude human understanding. The great gods that keep this dreadful pother over our heads are not deaf to the voice that cries for the whole of stricken humanity. The world undergoes some ritual of purification that is only to be apprehended poetically; it resists any attempt to state it in terms acceptable to intellect. The protests of suffering and despair are stilled at last by the sound of a nobler music which scatters the evil and removes the pain. This music may not be described, but everyone may hear it.

In *Macbeth* the affirmation of good is easier to perceive. The symbols of evil and unnatural disorder are so clearly balanced by the landmarks of a peaceful world that their spell will not outlast the act of wickedness that engendered them. 'We may again give to our tables meat, sleep to our nights'. Macbeth is not wholly a wicked man. He does not relish the vision of evil as the more perverted Jacobeans do, and he is visited by compunctious imaginings which they would regard as the signs of a failing nerve. His tragedy is that ambition carries him into a darkened and disordered world from which he reaches vainly towards the blessings he has lost. His own act was confusion's masterpiece, and he is doomed in consequence to inhabit a world heavy with unnatural portents, where hostile banners flout the sky and the bladed corn is lodged and the pyramids slope to their foundations. It is a world where man is not born of woman and the forest advances in ordered array against the doomed castle. But 'fair is foul and foul is fair'. The images of continuing life stand in unemphatic protest against the disorders bred by a single act. Whenever Duncan is present or referred to, normality reasserts its sway and the dialogue underlines the kindly virtues of loyalty, honour and the family pieties. The Porter, too, sluggishly answering the knocking at the door, personifies the reaction of the human against the fiendish. There is a little point of rest again, bright in the surrounding darkness, when Macbeth holds a banquet and savours — or would, if his mind could shed its burden — the satisfactions that belong to kingship. The talk is of things solid and assured. The guests sit down according to their degrees, and the familiar words of *host, society, welcome, feast* and *cheer* remind Macbeth of the comfort he can never have. Because he always knows what he has lost — 'honour, love, obedience, troops of friends' — the evil that he has done is localized and 'good things of day' will lift their heads again when the night is over. The quiet assertion of kindness and tranquillity relieves the statement of an enveloping disorder, so that this is not a pessimistic, nor even a horrifying, play. Its recurring insistence on traditional values balances the evil, and there is no hint of final disintegration.

This, of course, is only one way of looking at the tragedies, which have a larger purpose than merely to weigh two contrasting views of mankind. But this conflict was in Shakespeare's day so crucial and pervasive that it gave poets and dramatists a convention through which they could debate man's destiny. Shakespeare's affirmation of a destiny favourable to man's higher aspirations was the more valuable for his having so pitilessly explored the pessimistic tradition by which many of his fellow-writers were momentarily overwhelmed. In the amplitude of his art he identified himself with both interpretations of life, and he rejected as inadequate that mood of negation and despair that caught poetry by the throat and silenced its characteristic utterance. In the 'unperfect' fragments that close the last book of *The Faerie Queen* Spenser was of the same mind in 'this so doubtful case'. The Titaness called Mutability has claimed dominion over all things in heaven and earth, over the planets, times and seasons, and finally over the will and mind of the gods themselves. But Nature herself escapes her sway because Nature, while seeming to change, preserves her constituent elements and her universal laws.

Then gin I think on that which Nature said
Of that same time when no more change shall be,
But steadfast rest of all things, firmly stayed
Upon the pillars of Eternity,
That is contrair to Mutability;
For all that moveth doth in change delight:
But thenceforth all shall rest eternally
With Him that is the God of Sabaoth hight:
O that great Sabaoth God, grant me that Sabaoth's sight.

The dark Jacobean mood should not surprise us when in our own day the clash of ideologies has confounded art with a similar attitude of frustrated impotence. Existentialism corresponds in kind to the Jacobeans' dance of death, their cult of extinction as the only reality. Now, as then, life's agonizing brevity has for the moment ceased to be a theme for poets since the nobleness of life is but to endure it. Shakespeare refused to surrender to these conceptions. Only in *Troilus and Cressida* did he conclude a play with the violation of a norm of order previously stated. Elsewhere the rebel powers arrayed against the soul fall back defeated, and the tragic victims are in some fashion reconciled with their destiny. The life-beyond offers them no certain compensation, but hope is reborn of their conviction that the stars shine still.

Chapter XIII
Character and Poetry

The play's the thing.

Ham II ii 633.

Shakespeare was not free from genius's obligation to take pains. Heminges and Condell said that he never blotted a line, and doubtless they had seen him go to work during rehearsal and improvise an effective speech in a few minutes. A professional needed to acquire that sort of facility if he did not possess it naturally. But like less gifted men, Shakespeare had to learn his trade, and there is a continuous development, of adaptation, experiment and rejection accompanied by an ambitious refusal to be content with the repetition of a successful formula. Even by 1594 he had shown sufficient mastery in three sorts of drama to have earned a living by no greater effort than a mechanical reproduction of what he had already done. But success in one sort of play was a spur to attempt next time something different and probably harder.

It is one of the paradoxes of a great artist that to be immortal he must first be of his own age. Shakespeare would not have been 'for all time' if he had not been a conscientious craftsman in current techniques and Elizabethan enough to accept the thought and conventions of the age and enter imaginatively into its concerns. Puck and Julius Caesar, Caliban and Hamlet were creations of a mind essentially Elizabethan. On the other hand, this does not mean that he absorbed contemporary ideas merely in order to furnish improving political *exempla* or fashionable case-histories of neurotic obsession. He used current theories in his own way without becoming the mouthpiece of any of them. No single convention, whether literary or dramatic, ethical or political, will provide a complete explanation of any of his work.

His plays do not have a single definable meaning, and probably they do not have a single definable purpose. As a rule they even refuse to fit into the categories appointed for them by their first editors, where, for convenience, they have remained ever since. The characteristic of medieval art was to achieve unity through an immense variety of detail, as in a tapestry; the artistic concentration which attains a single object by the omission of some elements, and the strict subordination of others, is a modern conception.

Thus the art which Shakespeare practised was large and multifarious, seeking to realize more than one end and achieving its unity by singleness of mood and impression. In medieval poetry all the possible meanings of a symbol were necessary for complete illumination; each meaning was true on its own level, and no one meaning excluded or falsified other meanings which it might seem to contradict. Life itself has many interpretations which do not invalidate one another. In the same way, Shakespeare's art, which concerned itself with individuals and not with orderly systems of conceptual thought, may yield several meanings without making any particular meaning untenable. Although readers may sometimes feel inclined to say to the whole tribe of critics, 'It shall to the barber's with your beard', this variousness ensures that almost all Shakespearean criticism shall be valuable in some degree. Just as it is never possible for all the facets of a diamond to catch the light at the same time, so no interpretation of Shakespeare will ever catch the whole of his meaning. But every critic, however laboriously he goes 'a-batfowling for stars', may add his spark of illumination, and thus help the reader to that act of recognition upon which so much aesthetic pleasure depends.

We have at the same time to bear in mind Coleridge's warning against the dogmatic theorist who 'fills his three-ounce phial at the waters of Niagara; and determines positively the greatness of the cataract to be neither more nor less than his three-ounce phial has been able to receive'. Shakespearean interpretation is endlessly complex, and it is not to be simplified by the isolation of certain elements. Each play is an imagined world poetically conceived, with its own postulates, language and climate, peopled by characters who have no existence outside it. Poetry is the agent by which these worlds become memorable, and the final response must be aesthetic.

Shakespeare seldom wrote of his artistic principles, but in *The Winter's Tale* he used the analogy of the grafting of plants to speak of an Art which 'shares with great creating Nature'. This Art, although made by Nature, is a means of improving it.

> Yet Nature is made better by no mean
> But Nature makes that mean: so, over that Art
> Which you say adds to Nature, is an Art
> That Nature makes...
>
> This is an Art
> Which does mend Nature, change it rather, but
> The Art itself is Nature.
>
> IV iv 89.

The statement is involved, more involved than it need be, and for her garden Perdita will have none of it. But Shakespeare was here insisting that Art, as the interpreter of Nature's laws and therefore a means by which man might fulfil his proper function, often improved Nature by elucidating mysteries which life itself left dark.

He did not come easily to the perfection of his mature style, and it is possible to watch him striving to bring poetry to the uses of drama and enlarge the scope of a play so that he may say more by the means of it. If we had no more of his work than *Henry VI*, *Comedy of Errors* and *Titus Andronicus* — if, that is, he had died of the plague in 1594 and left nothing else behind him — he would already have been assured of his place in the theatre. By that time only Marlowe had done more than this, and already Shakespeare had shown himself the wider in range and potential. The breadth of achievement in these plays, all now dismissed as the work of immaturity, is astonishing, and the qualities which unify them as the work of a single hand are as striking as the differences between them. The apprentice author is already adept in the three main sorts of drama. If Elizabethan drama had ceased to develop beyond that point — as with Greene, Marlowe and Kyd already gone, it easily might have done if Shakespeare too had died — the text-books would have had to say that Shakespeare had written one of the best farces of situation in the language; an exciting melodrama which incidentally was entered in the Stationers' Register as 'a Noble Roman History' and has some claim, by reason of its comprehensive if uncritical awareness of Rome's political institutions, to be included among his Roman plays; and the first attempt to turn the rambling chronicle play into a new dramatic species, a cycle based on a coherent pattern and an intelligible view of history. This was no small accomplishment for a beginner. The plays proclaim the advent of a new phenomenon, a man of the theatre who was also a poet, and a poet who was also a man of the theatre in a way that the University Wits were not. They are alive with an intense poetic energy, as yet over-rhetorical and diffuse but sufficient to create that unity of impression which is essential to good drama.

The young playwright was at this time oppressed by the models which he had imitated, but the first characteristic of his development was his easy escape from the shackling influence of learned or traditional forms. He soon learned how to handle things in his own way, and, when he made use of a popular tradition, to give it a wider application and a deeper significance. The Morality, the revenge play or the Italian romance were simply foundations or points of departure. His advance in dramatic technique was equally rapid, and here instinct was reinforced by the help and example of his fellows. What he learned as an actor was of service to him as a dramatist; and the formation in 1594 of a stock company with stable membership and a consistent policy assisted the evolution of a stagecraft that was a collective as well as an individual achievement. There is no need to particularize, for the performance of Shakespeare's plays, on stages quite unlike his own, gives daily evidence of his control over his medium. It is not just that he provided fat parts for the leading actors or rewarded the 'extras' with stray lines of flashing poetry. His plots unfold themselves with a sort of inevitability which, as Dr Johnson said, 'always makes us anxious for the event'. Leisured explanation alternates with speed and concentration in such a way that the actors should have no doubt what is required of them. Every sentence is a picture which imagines and directs the appropriate gesture and intonation. Thus the stage is always alive with movement and latent disclosure, and the action should never become static, because even when nothing is happening of immediate concern to the plot, the turn of a line, with its pauses, hesitations and accelerations, is always adding something to our knowledge of the characters and their situation.

The larger problem which Shakespeare had to solve when the theatres reopened in 1594 was how to turn dramatic poetry into poetic drama; not just a play written in verse, but a poetic idea conceived dramatically, with characters and incidents imagined from within. The force of this generating idea gives the play its life, and the playwright's other resources, of stagecraft, wit or musical expression, are necessarily subordinate to it. Compared with the epic poet or the novelist, the playwright is somewhat restricted. He has not their resources for personal descriptions or scenic beauties or the reflections which pass unspoken through the mind. Even his moral, if he has one, is not so easily made explicit. The devices which act as his substitutes — dumb-show, soliloquy, the lyrical description of a setting, messenger's speech or choric comment — are essentially undramatic. It is not that they are unrealistic, for theatre has always made use of certain conventions which have the odd effect of sustaining the illusion rather than dispersing it. But they impede the movement of the play and diffuse the concentration which it is the writer's duty to preserve. Everyone has to use them at times, even Shakespeare at the height of his powers, but the idea of the play best enforces itself through the words and actions of the characters. Unless a dramatist plans to abdicate his function in favour of musical and panoramic effects, his characters are the only proper means available to him.

To illustrate by an example, Shakespeare needs to end *The Merchant of Venice* on a note that will enable us to forget the trial scene and the bitterness and humiliation of Shylock. Men may become the evil that they fight, and not even Portia comes scatheless from this scene. Lorenzo and Jessica, who are asked to establish the change of mood, are not equal to it. Both have been shadowy and imperfectly realized characters and we do not know enough about them to feel safe in their company. They do not have it in them to accomplish a new mood from within, and so the dramatist has to do it from without. The famous passage about the sleeping moonlight does not proceed functionally from these two runaways, nor add materially to our knowledge of them, except that Jessica, like her father, has no taste for music. Portia follows with some rather ponderous reflections on the relativity of values, and then the strangely protracted business of the rings concludes a scene that in the theatre seldom achieves the final reconciliation proper to comedy.

Here the description of the moonlight is a clumsy, undramatic device. Lear's storm, on the other hand, exists through Lear's defiance of it. Whatever the stage staff contribute to it, and that should be as little as possible, the real storm is in Lear's mind and he and the storm are one.

The difference between these two scenes is the difference between dramatic poetry, decorative and external, and poetic drama conceived through a character's mind. It crystallizes the problem of making poetry integral to a dramatic vision, of harmonizing the thing said with the speaker and his way of saying it. If we try to simplify this by saying that it required Shakespeare to evolve a poetic style capable of giving lasting and individual life to his conception of character, this does not mean that the forging of character was either his principal object or his highest achievement. Although individuals occasionally insist upon outrageous self-assertion — Mercutio and Falstaff are the favourite examples, but there are humbler ones such as Barnardine — characterization was related to the working-out of the poetic idea, and at any moment it might be sacrificed to dramatic necessity. On the other hand, his characters are all that a dramatist has. Their speech and action and impact on one another, the whole sum of their relationships in the world they inhabit, are the means by which his vision becomes articulate, the means by which he is known to us.

In Shakespeare's early work, whatever period this may be held to cover, poet and dramatist are imperfectly fused. Both are labouring very hard, the dramatist shifting on to the poet tasks which are not properly poetry's tasks and the poet interrupting the dramatic movement with set-pieces and rhetorical reverberations ill suited to the stage. Such poetry often seems to be an end in itself, and it defers to fashions which the taste of 1590 regarded as the marks of poetic excellence, conceits and amplifications and well-tried antitheses. Shakespeare attacked the audience along a broad front, neglecting no approved weapon that might capture their emotions, and he was more concerned to stir them to a passionate response than to communicate an imaginative experience. The verse was striving for a weight and forcefulness which forbade subtlety. Even the lyric passages developed a self-regarding virtuosity which suspended the action. 'Bombast', which meant stuffing a verse with copious variations, packing it with artifice, was then a virtue in poets, and Shakespeare had to learn that it was not a virtue in dramatic poets. Probably it was a difficult lesson to learn because it meant the sacrifice of much that was pleasant and traditionally held to be effective. Aristotle himself had expected Rhetoric to 'discern all the available means of persuasion', and poetry that was richly garmented was believed to persuade through the pleasure that it gave. Shakespeare had to outgrow this conception, which was a commonplce of Renaissance art, before his verse could acquire the directness and condensation essential for great drama.

Thus the style of the early plays tends to be rhetorical and declamatory rather than dramatic. Forcefulness is sought, seldom happily, by a string of descriptive epithets and the forging of compounds, as in the rhetorically over-strained picture beginning 'The gaudy, blabbing and remorseful day' (see page 108). This particular line has acquired a modest fame of its own, but the adjectives accumulate without adding significance and some of them seem to exist only to fill up the line. The desired effect is blunted by monotonous excess, and the sterility of the passage is exposed when the Sea Captain briskly continues,

> Therefore bring forth the soldiers of our prize.
>
> *2 Hen VI* IV i 8.

Even in less earnest attempts at scene-painting Shakespeare is trying too hard:

> The day begins to break, and night is fled,
> Whose pitchy mantle over-veil'd the earth.
>
> *1 Hen VI* II ii 1.

This may be contrasted with lines already quoted, when Shakespeare had learned to link the setting of a scene with the speaker's emotions and the imminent action, and nightfall would find itself described as the thickening of the light:

> The west yet glimmers with some streaks of day:
> Now spurs the lated traveller apace
> To gain the timely inn; and near approaches
> The subject of our watch.
>
> *Macb* III iii 5.

Thus the scene is set for Banquo's murder, and there is an ironic contrast between 'the subject of our watch', who is to be killed, and the traveller hurrying towards a warm and friendly inn. A few lines earlier Macbeth's apostrophe to night is heavy with the darkness that has settled over his own mind:

> Come, seeling night,
> Scarf up the tender eye of pitiful day,
> And with thy bloody and invisible hand
> Cancel and tear to pieces that great bond
> Which keeps me pale! Light thickens, and the crow
> Makes wing to the rooky wood:
> Good things of day begin to droop and drowse,
> Whiles night's black agents to their preys do rouse.
>
> III ii 46.

We may notice incidentally how the broken, mainly trochaic rhythm of the second line, and the short sixth line, suggest a distracted mind by varying the dominant stress, but the importance of the passage is that it is functionally dramatic. The two extracts from *Macbeth* lose much of their power when quoted outside their contexts. Of the habit of assembling Shakespearean 'beauties' isolated from the context Dr Johnson remarked that it reminded him of a man with a house to sell who carried a single brick in his pocket to recommend it to would-be purchasers.

The men and women of the early plays are not much individualized, because the poetry will not permit it. In stiff, regular, mostly end-stopped lines they speak with undifferentiated voices of 'paltry, servile, abject drudges' or the 'empty, vast and wandering air', of 'lofty, proud, encroaching tyranny' or the 'always wind-obeying deep'. The epithets make no greater impression for being multiplied or wrought into compounds. The speakers' eloquence is further deadened by a couplet movement that makes their utterance over-formal. In Gloucester's speech in *2 Henry VI* III i 142-71 not merely is every line, with but two exceptions, end-stopped but the lines tend to fall together in pairs, as thus:

> Beaufort's red sparkling eyes blab his heart's malice,
> And Suffolk's cloudy brow his stormy hate;
> Sharp Buckingham unburdens with his tongue
> The envious load that lies upon his heart.

In this undifferentiated way of speaking the verse has not the subtlety to show whether a character means what he is saying. Here are two people lamenting Gloucester's death. Queen Margaret has to pretend that she is stricken by it:

> Might liquid tears or heart-offending groans
> Or blood-consuming sighs recall his life,
> I would be blind with weeping, sick with groans,
> Look pale as primrose with blood-drinking sighs,
> And all to have the noble duke alive.
>
> *2 Hen VI* III ii 60.

King Henry is genuinely affected by the event, and because he is here speaking in soliloquy we know that the feeling is sincere:

> Fain would I go to chafe his paly lips
> With twenty thousand kisses, and to drain
> Upon his face an ocean of salt tears,
> To tell my love unto his deaf dumb trunk,
> And with my fingers feel his hand unfeeling.
>
> III ii 141.

What immediately strikes us is that both characters, the sincere and the insincere, use the same overblown language and the speeches might be transposed.

The same incident of Gloucester's arrest and murder will illustrate another impediment to true dramatic writing, the prolonged, meandering conceit. Henry grieves that he is powerless to help him:

> And as the butcher takes away the calf,
> And binds the wretch, and beats it when it strays,
> Bearing it to the bloody slaughter-house,
> Even so, remorseless, have they borne him hence:
> And as the dam runs lowing up and down,
> Looking the way her harmless young one went,
> And can do nought but wail her darling's loss,
> Even so myself bewails good Gloucester's case
> With sad, unhelpful tears, and with dimm'd eyes
> Look after him, and cannot do him good:
> So mighty are his vowed enemies.
>
> III i 210.

It is not that the simile is indecorous, for England was shortly to have a monarch who would compare the House of Commons to a cow trying to cut off her tail; the tail being himself, the ordained of God. Nor, on this occasion, does it particularly matter that Henry's grief should find expression in language highly formal and not in the least individual to himself. The artistic fault is that the protracted lament, a favoured figure in bombast poetry, dissipates the emotion built up in the previous scene, when Gloucester stood at bay before his enemies.

For a while the fault grew more pronounced as Shakespeare's verse became more lyrical.

> Therefore, to be possess'd with double pomp,
> To guard a title that was rich before,
> To gild refined gold, to paint the lily,
> To throw a perfume on the violet,
> To smooth the ice, or add another hue
> Unto the rainbow, or with taper-light
> To seek the beauteous eye of heaven to garnish,
> Is wasteful and ridiculous excess.
>
> *KJ* IV ii 9.

It is excess indeed, and Shakespeare is often guilty of it. Poetry was still more important to him than drama, the way of expressing an idea more interesting than the idea itself or the character forming it. It is hard to feel that a man who speaks thus of grief has been wounded to the heart:

Beguil'd, divorc'd, wrong'd, spited, slain!
Most detestable death, by thee beguil'd
By cruel cruel thee quite overthrown!
O love! O life! not life, but love in death!

RJ IV v 55.

It is harder still to remember, as we must, that such writing was proof of a skill that was much admired. From the first Shakespreare was master of bright Apollo's lute and had the poet's faculty of translating thought into visual images; but as a playwright he had to free his verse from these seductive entanglements and bring his lyrical impulse within dramatic limits.

In the two romantic poems he liberally indulged himself in smelling out 'odoriferous flowers of fancy, the jerks of invention'. He allows himself twenty lines (1031 sq) in which to say that Venus could not bear to look upon 'the foul boar's conquest on her fair delight'. He thus describes a hand-clasp:

Full gently now she takes him by the hand,
A lily prison'd in a gaol of snow,
Or ivory in an alabaster band;
So white a friend engirts so white a foe;

VA 361

and thus a maiden's blush;

O! how her fear did make her colour rise:
First red as roses that on lawn we lay,
Then white as lawn, the roses took away.

Lucr 257.

For a dramatist, however, it will not do: partly because the theatre will not wait while such conceits proceed to their conclusion, partly because the imagery is too conventional, mummified almost, to carry the overtones that make character. In his dramatic maturity Shakespeare would say as much in a single line or a single compressed metaphor, but in his apprentice days he would toy with a conceit while the emotion that begot it perished and the dramatic moment slipped away. A palpable example is Julia's comparison (*TGV* II vii 24-38) of her love to a stream which 'makes sweet music with th'enamelled stones' if its course is not hindered but rages impatiently when obstructed. The boy-Julia no doubt made a pretty effect with it on the stage, but it is hopelessly undramatic and Lucetta receives it with a practical question which recalls Julia from her fancies and gets her down to business: 'But in what habit will you go along?' Julia is soberly reminded that if she proposes to pursue her lover in disguise, she will have to cut her hair, decide in what fashion her breeches shall be made, and submit to the indelicacy of a codpiece.

It would be wrong to attribute these extravagances entirely to the fashions of the age. Shakespeare cultivated them because he found them congenial, and if we are to regard *Love's Labour's Lost* as a magnificent bonfire after which he would abandon his poetic indulgences, at least their illumination filled the sky and the ashes never ceased to glow. He promised no more of his early self than that he would 'leave it by degrees', and he never left it altogether. Often it gave him matter for a May morning. If it is impious to find in Pyramus's invocation of 'grim-look'd night' a parody of the like invocations of Romeo and Juliet, the impiety comes from Shakespeare's own self-recognition. Similarly there is no doubt of a satirical intention in Demetrius's search for appropriate epithets with which to describe his love:

> O Helen, goddess, nymph, perfect, divine;
> To what, my love, shall I compare thine eyne?
> Crystal is muddy. O how ripe in show
> Thy lips, those kissing cherries, tempting grow;
> This pure congealed white, high Taurus' snow,
> Fann'd with the eastern wind, turns to a crow
> When thou holdst up thine hand.
>
> *MND* III ii 137.

The fairy love-juice helps to move the tongue to these conceits, but they will never be wholly confined to burlesque. The Spenserian fancy and the Euphuist's search for paradox and antithesis never wholly lost their fascination. The 'common proof' was another addiction. The particular persuasion that could be drawn into the orbit of a general truth was held thereby to double its potency, with the result that early Shakespearean oratory has a way of revolving round a platitude. Shakespeare kept his taste for aphoristic expression, but he learned to use it as a revelation of character: persons as different as Hamlet and Dogberry were much inclined to it. Again, the trick of plundering Aesop and Pliny for news of the wilder excesses of the animal kingdom imparts to the similes of the early plays a strange ferocity, suggestive of the exoticism the Euphuists tried to cultivate. This habit too was not discarded but disciplined, and images drawn from wild beasts were used not just to bombast out a declamatory speech but to mark the swell of passion. 'O tiger's heart wrapp'd in a woman's hide' is not the language of *King Lear*.

Shakespeare's work cannot be neatly divided into phases. He clung so obstinately to the fashions of his youth, subsequently wearing them with a difference, that there is no certain moment when he positively began to do this or ceased to do that. Methodical consistency belongs to the conscientious journeyman rather than the artist. Quite early in the plays we begin to hear voices which use poetry not just for ornament or declamation but as a means of expressing feeling in a manner peculiar to themselves. In the following lines the idea is amplified but there is also a personal accent:

The time was once when thou unurg'd wouldst vow
That never words were music to thine ear,
That never object pleasing in thine eye,
That never touch well welcome to thy hand,
That never meat sweet-savour'd in thy taste,
Unless I spake, or look'd, or touch'd, or carv'd to thee.

CE II ii 115.

One day this would became the lovely 'all your acts are queens' (*WT* IV iv
135-46), but already we may notice that the language is less affected and that
here the device of repetition speeds the verse instead of delaying it. Pace, in
the sense of a variety of speed, is the distinguishing quality we should look
for because it denotes the pressure of an individual voice on the traditional
style of poetic diction. Sometimes the movement will be slow and broken, as
in the Nurse's rumination on the age of Juliet and her own dead child (see
page 184). There has been nothing quite like this before. The Nurse is the
first of Shakespeare's characters to sustain a personal accent throughout
the play.

The development was only gradual. Shakespeare did not conquer the
whole of his territory at once, and when spontaneous utterance failed him,
he would fall back on convention, writing stylized verse and depending
upon the highly-trained actor to give it life by formal gesture and delivery.
But the individual tone is heard more and more frequently. It is heard for a
moment in Mercutio dying as it has not been heard in Mercutio living. It is
heard spasmodically in Richard III, whose terse, sardonic idiom stands out
from the conventional utterance of railing queens and sententious statesmen
until, with his objects attained, he too becomes declamatory. It is heard
more certainly in Faulconbridge and Hotspur, who, like Richard, pride
themselves on being plain blunt men. Richard 'cannot flatter and speak
fair', Faulconbridge ridicules the death-dealing boasts of the citizens of
Angiers and the Dauphin's preposterous conceits, Hotspur despises popinjay
courtiers, Welsh wizards, mincing poetry and the wives of comfit-makers.
There is significance in this, as though Shakespeare had come to realize that
too much poetic diction was inimical to drama. Others at the same time were
discovering that it was inimical also to science and psychology and even to
poetry itself, and the reaction was already setting in which would lead to the
intensity and condensation of the Jacobeans at their horrifying best.

Thus Shakespeare moved gradually towards a natural, realistic style.
Lucrece, compared with *Venus and Adonis*, is dramatic because here he is
attempting to probe the feelings of Tarquin and Lucrece and convey them in
unaffected speech. In the development of his art the interest (and surely
most of the beauty) of the *Sonnets* is in the imagery drawn from observation
and experience. The sonnet form was a tight discipline here, but nevertheless the theme and conception of these poems were more Petrarchan than
the style. *A Midsummer Night's Dream*, somewhat unexpectedly in view of

its subject-matter, is mostly forceful in its diction, the vigour of the dialogue often bursting through the shackles of metre and conceit. Finally, Hotspur and Faulconbridge fulfil themselves not so much in ridiculing the affectations of others (for Faulconbridge it was not a great success in a play containing the mannered lament of Constance and Arthur's agonizing conceits about the hot irons and the burning coal) as in their own freedom in speaking with voices that control the verse.

> Methinks my moiety, north from Burton here,
> In quantity equals not one of yours:
> See how this river comes me cranking in,
> And cuts me from the best of all my land
> A huge half-moon, a monstrous cantle out.
> I'll have the current in this place damm'd up,
> And here the smug and silver Trent shall run
> In a new channel, fair and evenly:
> It shall not wind with such a deep indent
> To rob me of so rich a bottom here.
>
> *1 Hen IV* III i 96.

Here, as in Hotspur's lines on the courtier who came to demand prisoners from him at Holmedon (I iii 29-69), Shakespeare has moved from the stiff rhetorical exchanges of the nobles who surrounded Henry VI. The lines have the proud quick temper of a human being, and under the pressure of his personality the verse structure almost collapses before the freedom of expression that he demands.

But neither Hostpur nor the Bastard is a complete man. There is a touch of the adolescent in them both, and Shakespeare could not achieve through them that way of writing which would lay bare all that can elate or perturb the human heart. He achieved this first, or the hint of it, in prose. During the period that separates *King John* from *Hamlet* (*Julius Caesar* being here the exception that foreshadows a later advance) his prose has a dramatic energy and concentration that so far he has seldom managed to achieve in verse. Shylock speaks prose: not always, but when he is most in need of words. 'Hath not a Jew eyes?... If you prick us, do we not bleed?'

> The curse never fell upon our nation till now; I never felt it till now; two thousand ducats in that; and other precious, precious jewels. I would my daughter were dead at my foot, and the jewels in her ear! would she were hearsed at my foot, and the ducats in her coffin!...no ill luck stirring but what lights on my shoulders; no sighs but of my breathing ; no tears but of my shedding.
>
> MV III i 89.

Prose is the medium of Falstaff, and of Prince Hal when he is in Falstaff's company — and when Hal is on the throne, he speaks verse on his public occasions but reverts to prose when he sheds, so far as he ever can, the robes of ceremony and thinks and talks like a man. Beatrice and Benedick duel and love in prose, and Rosalind speaks it both in her intimate gossip with Celia (here we should remember what Julia's Lucetta had to listen to) and when she bandies love with Orlando. Prose at this time was made to carry a heavier weight of thought and emotion than, in drama, it had ever borne before.

The office of poetry was correspondingly the less; and freed for the moment from its graver responsibilities, it began to acquire a speed and naturalism to which only a few speakers had hitherto attained. It has an unencumbered ease; it is colloquial; and in its new flexibility it registers the thrusts and hesitations, the latent fears and hopes, even the reticences, of the speaker's heart. No explanatory gloss is needed for these lines of Portia when Bassanio is choosing from the caskets:

> I pray you, tarry; pause a day or two
> Before you hazard; for, in choosing wrong,
> I lose your company: therefore, forbear a while.
> There's something tells me — but it is not love —
> I would not lose you; and you know yourself
> Hate counsels not in such a quality.
> But lest you should not understand me well—
> And yet a maiden hath no tongue but thought—
> I would detain you here some month or two
> Before you venture. I could teach you
> How to choose right, but then I am forsworn;
> So will I never be: so may you miss me;
> But if you do, you'll make me wish a sin,
> That I had been forsworn...

MV III ii 1.

This speech is poetic drama. It is a difficult scene for the dramatist because after the failure of Morocco and Arragon the audience know that Bassanio will make the right choice, and the undercurrent of sexuality, often in Shakespeare so much more potent than what is said on the surface, has made it obvious all the time. Yet the actual choice had to be made interesting theatrically. The speech lacks the colouring of imagery, and this want of overtones may somewhat diminish it; but within its limits this is the perfect language of drama, verse trimmed of its superfluities and growing naturally from its roots in mind and emotion. Prose would not do the business so well. It was only a stage in the progress towards an end, it could never fulfil the end of itself. In the formal structure of blank verse the iambic decasyllable established a norm from which the departures are immediately revealing; and all the possible variations — the shortened line, the extra syllable, the inverted stress, the parenthesis that disturbs the rhythm — are means to indicate the speaker's feelings.

Portia's lines need no stage directions and no special effort from actress or director. Gesture, movement and intonation are contained in the rhythm of the verse. As yet the mood does not always hold. Shakespeare was still travelling 'by degrees', and when Portia presently commands music, her speech is mannered and rhetorical. So too is Bassanio's when he reflects upon his choice, but as this is a highly formal occasion, it perhaps demands no less. Even so, it is not the vaporous declamation of an earlier style. The verse is supple and controlled, soberly attuned to its purpose, and the breath of passion gives it life:

> Look on beauty,
> And you shall see 'tis purchased by the weight;
> Which therein works a miracle in Nature,
> Making them lightest that wear most of it:
> So are those crisped, snaky, golden locks
> Which make such wanton gambols with the wind
> Upon supposed fairness, often known
> To be the dowry of a second head,
> The skull that bred them, in the sepulchre.
> Thus ornament is but the guiled shore
> To a most dangerous sea; the beauteous scarf
> Veiling an Indian beauty...
>
> III ii 88.

This is not easy verse. Even on the printed page it requires close attention, and in the theatre a sustained concentration which perhaps the Elizabethans were better able to give it than ourselves. The actor's task is becoming harder too, and passages like this make it easy to believe that this was Burbage's part. As Shakespeare's art developed, the shared labour of the three participants in the act of communication, the poet, the player and the audience, grew heavier all the time.

In our lazy way we are apt to miss a great deal through impatience to be with Falstaff in Gloucestershire.

> O God! that one might read the book of fate,
> And see the revolution of the times
> Make mountains level, and the continent,
> Weary of solid firmness, melt itself
> Into the sea! and, other times, to see
> The beachy girdle of the ocean
> Too wide for Neptune's hips; how chances mock,
> And changes fill the cup of alteration
> With divers liquors! O if this were seen,
> The happiest youth, viewing his progress through,
> What perils past, what crosses to ensue,
> Would shut the book and sit him down and die.
>
> *2 Hen IV* III i 45.

Warwick presently replies:

There is a history in all men's lives,
Figuring the nature of the times deceas'd;
The which observ'd, a man may prophesy,
With a near aim, of the main chance of things
As yet not come to life, which in their seeds
And weak beginnings lie intreasured.

III i 80.

The accents of Hamlet have been discovered in this scene. There is a hint of timelessness, of reference to a scheme of things removed from the immediate and the particular, that comes near to the atmosphere of the great tragedies. To explain this feeling we must not look to ideas and content, for the images in earlier plays have drawn likewise upon the world's spaciousness and bounty, but to the mode of expression. It is not yet Shakespeare's final style. Its rhythms are loose, it lends itself admirably to reflection and it responds at a touch to the pressure of emotion. But it is still too massive; it can still lapse at times into the rhetorical, still be poetic at the cost of dramatic intensity. Technically it lacks the suppleness, and emotionally it lacks the insistent intimation of the personal, which raise the great tragic speeches above our question.

                    So Caesar may:
Then, lest he may, prevent. And since the quarrel
Will bear no colour for the thing he is,
Fashion it thus: that what he is, augmented,
Would run to these and these extremities;
And therefore think him as a serpent's egg
Which, hatch'd, would, as his kind, grow mischievous,
And kill him in the shell.

JC II i 27.

Between the acting of a dreadful thing
And the first motion, all the interim is
Like a phantasma, or a hideous dream:
The genius and the mortal instruments
Are then in council; and the state of man,
Like to a little kingdom, suffers then
The nature of an insurrection.

II i 63.

Julius Caesar is not particularly well favoured by modern audiences but it seems to have been the watershed. The subsequent achievements of Shakespeare's style are too familiar to need illustration here. Gradually he had found his way to the perfect instrument of poetic drama, a speech that certainly was not prose and was not wholly verse but was something midway between the two which retained the musical and hypnotic power of poetry and yet sounded with the natural accents of the speaking voice. Ultimately it defies analysis, as great art always will. There is no saying why certain combinations of words on a page, certain arrangements of line and colour, a certain sequence of musical chords, should have the power to move us intolerably. The explanation may belong as much to physiology as to aesthetics. 'But the gift is good in those in whom it is acute', and we may be thankful for it.

Technically, little can usefully be said about Shakespeare's prosody beyond the fact that he exploited the blank verse line to attain all the variety it would yield him, with prose and rhyme introduced to give still further contrast and achieve special effects of their own. Attempts to identify his work by metrical tests were at one time plentiful and optimistic: they were to lay bare the secrets of disputed authorship and establish the precedence of the plays. But the conclusions were diverse and irreconcilable, and too much hope was built upon this sort of enquiry. It is useful for broad indications[1], but Shakespeare's work was too varied and experimental to permit positive inferences about such matters as dating, collaboration and revision. Shakespeare had no distinctive metre, no uniform style, any more than he had an unvarying way of handling history or comedy or tragedy. His hand is most surely recognizable when the blank verse line is no longer adequate for all that he needs to say and metre and syntax disintegrate under the overwhelming pressure of feeling.

One distinctive mannerism by which he may be identified is the 'doublet', the combination of two nouns, or less frequently of two adjectives, to suggest a third or a fourth. This is a crude way of describing a device which enabled Shakespeare to compress into two words a larger range of relevant associations. In the early plays these couplings seldom illuminate: nouns and adjectives accumulate only in order to give rhetorical weight to the verse. It is not until the middle, or prose, period, and particularly in *The Merchant of Venice* and *Henry V*, that they begin to achieve a deeper meaning. The rage is at its height in *Hamlet* and the problem comedies, but thereafter, although they never disappear, they become less frequent. *Hamlet* alone contributes, among others: 'dead vast and middle of the night'; 'perfume and suppliance of a minute'; 'the voice and yielding of that body'; 'the expectancy and rose of the fair state'; 'the gross and scope of my opinion'; 'the whips and scorns of time'; 'the morn and liquid dew of youth'; 'the teeth and forehead of our faults'. Among striking examples from other plays we may find: 'the force and road of casualty' (*MV*); 'grey hairs and bruise of many days' (*MAN*); 'this accident and flood of fortune' (*TN*); 'the vaunt and firstlings of those broils' (*TC*); 'the catastrophe and heel of pastime' and 'this captious and intenible sieve' (*AWW*); 'the fault and glimpse of newness' (*MM*); 'speculative and offic'd instruments' (*Oth*); 'loop'd and window'd raggedness' (*Lear*); 'the dark backward and abysm of time' (*Tem*). Shakespeare

---

1 See the tables in E.K. Chambers, *WS* II Appendix H.

overplayed the trick and in phrases like 'book and volume of my brain', 'best rank and station' or 'inaudible and noiseless foot of time' it contributed very little. But when the pairs of words combine the abstract with the concrete, the sensible with the intellectual, they enlarge the meaning with overtones which could not be expressed so economically in any other way. Some mysterious sleight-of-hand has dealt two metaphors and conjured a third out of the air. Although at first glance the device looks simple enough, no other English poet has been able to command it.

Then of course there is the pun: 'the fatal Cleopatra', according to Johnson, 'for which he lost the world, and was content to lose it'. The eighteenth century, failing to understand it, blamed Shakespeare's audience for making him condescend to it. But both Shakespeare and his audience admired it with the respect due to all the habitudes of medieval allegory; and it had also the intellectual prestige belonging to Rhetoric, which sought out words that stood at the centre of an infinite eddy of meaning. It was not until after the Restoration that the demands of exact science succeeded in investing words with precise and singular meanings. Dr Johnson was the first Englishman to make a dictionary because his was almost the first generation in which it would have been possible to make one. In Shakespeare's day the pursuit of words was made the more enchanting by the ultimate elusiveness of their meaning. A pun, after all, is the final crystallization of metaphor, which itself is a literary response to allegory.

The word-play in which the Elizabethans took so much delight might be intellectual or emotive. The intellectual kind Shakespeare exploited in the chop-logic of Launce and Speed and the wit-combats of *Love's Labour's Lost* and parts of *Romeo and Juliet*; and it was broadened by the fun to be had at the expense of rustics and foreigners who made 'fritters of English'. Along with this went some rather frigid punning that originated in Rhetoric, such as the play on 'hart' and 'heart' in Antony's funeral oration, or 'the half-achieved Harfleur' or Juliet's sustained conceit on *I, aye* and *eye* (*RJ* III ii 45). Modern readers miss much of Shakespeare's punning either because words have changed their meaning and pronunciation or because certain uses have become obsolete. We miss the associated meanings drawn from sports no longer widely practised, such as archery and hawking; or from coins (especially *angel, noble, crown* and *mark*) or the technicalities of music and the dance. Again, we are defeated by changes in pronunciation which prevent our discovering what Shakespeare was at. All these words were spoken in the same way: reason and raisin; not and note; nothing and noting; Rome and room; ache and aitch; tongs and tongues; Seville and civil; Ajax and a jakes. Shakespeare punned, therefore, much more frequently than we suppose, and he punned with an ingenuity that gave his audience the repeated pleasure of recognition.

The style of the Metaphysical Poets should, however, remind us that the function of word-play was not purely intellectual. To come upon Donne or

George Herbert worrying at a double meaning as a way of expressing his devotion to God is, to us, surprising and it may even be repellent. But such conceits were acknowledging the many-sidedness of truth, and they derived from the medieval conviction that the symbolical meaning of anything was as important, as persuasive and as *true* as any other meaning. They are not open to the charge of being mere artifice — although much art went into their making — because their hold upon the emotions lifted the thought into another dimension. A mark of Shakespeare's development was his use of word-play less for its power to stimulate the mind than for its power to promote feeling.

> If he do bleed,
> I'll gild the faces of the grooms withal;
> For it must seem their guilt.
>
> *Macb* II ii 55.

This famous pun has frequently been condemned as bathetic, but for its first hearers it did not dissipate the passion, it intensified it.

Shakespeare's apprenticeship in Euphuism had doubtless trained his eye to detect resemblances, but his inclination to write in this way was inspired by something profounder than technique. He found in it an outlet for the dualism in his nature which revealed the soul of goodness in things evil and the self-doubt concealed behind ceremony, which bade him create Iago as a complement to Othello, or Hotspur as a complement to Prince Hal and Falstaff as a complement to them both. The play on *gild* and *guilt* expressed the contrast between the bright face of things and the underlying evil. Shakespeare's mind worked instinctively in these contrasts. Even in the light-hearted mood of *Love's Labour's Lost* he apparently felt the need for the stabilizing influence of an opposite and found repose in a mannered antithesis between white and red. Later his mind dwelt upon the more elemental antitheses between light and darkness, sleeping and waking, love and hate, life and death; so that any word that contained within itself a double potentiality seems to have had a compulsive effect on his imagination. The ambivalence of his mind, with its apparent double-sightedness, reflected a comprehensiveness of vision which made it almost impossible for him to say one thing at a time. There was s constraint upon him to use double meanings when he could. The sort of word that attracted him was *boil*, with its implication of clean, healthy food and the opposite implication of disease caused by impurity of the blood. The contrast here is simple, and he was able to achieve a subtler range of implications with more complex words like *sense* in *Measure for Measure, honest* in *Othello* or *fool* and *nature* in *King Lear*. These are key-words in their respective plays, and their various uses offer a possible clue to interpretation. *Nature* in *King Lear* carries all the senses with which contemporary experience associated it, and *fool* has meanings ranging from guileless simplicity to wilful obstinacy, madness, ignorance and the seeming irrationality of the universe itself.

It is noticeable, again, how often in moments of stress and crisis his characters find relief in a play on words, as though the discovery of a resemblance would enable them to share the burden of grief. 'Ask for me to-morrow, and you shall find me a grave man'. Mercutio says, and Juliet achieves a pretty effect on Romeo's departure, a 'division' being also a swift passage of melody:

> Some say the lark makes sweet division;
> This doth not so, for she divideth us.
>
> *RJ* III v 29.

Constance cries, when Pandulph has excommunicated her:

> O! lawful let it be
> That I have room with Rome to curse awhile.
>
> *KJ* III i 179.

In the same way the dying Gaunt jests upon his name, and these are early and facile examples of an apparently instinctive habit which in later years would be strangely moving.

> I will o'ertake thee, Cleopatra, and
> Weep for my pardon. So it must be, for now
> All length is torture; since the torch is out,
> Lie down, and stray no further.
>
> *AC* IV xiv 44.

When Desdemona realizes of what Othello has accused her, she expresses her horror in a pun:

> I cannot say 'whore':
> It does abhor me now I speak the word.
>
> *Oth* IV ii 161.

Sometimes the concentration of meaning is so intense that various interpretations are possible, as in Hermione's

> For life I prize it
> As I weigh grief, which I would spare:
>
> WT III ii 43.

wherein *spare* can have the meanings of *part with, pardon* and *avoid*. The sentence may be paraphrased something like this: 'I esteem life as I esteem grief, as something I would willingly part with; but the one I would not destroy, and the other I would rather not meet'. Commentators have buzzed round it, and other paraphrases have been suggested. One will perhaps serve as well as another, not because it does not matter which is correct but because it is likely that all are correct. Shakespeare has brought word-play to a pitch where a single statement will dissolve into infinite shades of meaning.

Othello plays on *light* as he approaches his deed of darkness:

Put out the light, and then put out the light:
If I quench thee, thou flaming minister,
I can again thy former light restore,
Should I repent me; but once put out thy light,
Thou cunning'st pattern of excelling Nature,
I know not where is that Promethean heat
That can thy light relume.

V II 7.

The quibble is a means towards an imponderable significance. The image is exact, it is deeply emotional, and it releases all the conflicting forces of which the emotion is created. The contrast between light and darkness, life and death, usually suffices on the stage, but it does not exhaust the half-realized implications which the image sets running through the mind. The light is also Desdemona's fairness, 'that whiter skin of hers than snow', so pale beside that other darkness that is her husband's flesh. 'Thou flaming minister' is unusually strong for a burning torch, a minister being in a special sense an angel or messenger of God; and thus it may complement 'thou cunning'st pattern of excelling Nature', the perfection of Desdemona's mortal beauty. Yet 'light' must also carry its further meaning of a light woman, one who is easily faithless and seduced. The whole passage illuminates the conflict that ravages Othello's mind, where love and hatred, the desire to forgive and the sense of being an instrument of justice, carnal longing and an idealization of chastity are all struggling for possession of his broken reason.

Finally we may consider Shakespeare's most inscrutable play on words, the dying Hamlet's intimation of what lies beyond. 'The rest is silence'. No words are harder for an actor to speak because no words so surely reveal the power of poetry to liberate the imagination in search of countless overtones of meaning. 'Absent thee from felicity awhile' suggests that we may be about to go to the heart of Hamlet's mystery, but he eludes us at the last. These four words cheat us of knowing the manner of his felicity[2]. *Rest* may mean repose, but it need not. Hamlet may be telling us that death is a long silence, a nothingness, and man may find sleep there; or he may be saying that to man's questions about the future life there is no answer to be had; or that,

2 For a valuable discussion of the complex effects achieved by poetic drama see D.A. Stauffer, *The Nature of Poetry*, 154-88.

although he has divined the answer, we are not to have it from his lips. It may simply be that, with the fell sergeant's hand upon his shoulder, the greatest talker in literature must at last fall silent. Hamlet dies, and we do not know.

What began a few pages back as a discussion of the Elizabethans' inveterate love of punning has brought us to the distinctive mark of Shakespeare's mature style, its extraordinary concentration. In the compression and flow of the imagery nothing now is diffuse or ornamental or superfluous. The great tragic heroes compel attention because they bring their experience within the scope of ordered and musical expression. It is in this sense, rather than in the nature of the experience, that they speak for their creator, for his alone was the imaginative gift of reducing a multitude of sensations into a unity of effect and uttering them with a delight in their perfection of phrasing and rhythm. That is how poets become healers of mankind. Metaphor is the instinctive and compulsory act of the mind that investigates human experience; for thus, in relating the unknown with the familiar and perceiving the 'occult resemblances in things apparently unlike', it proclaims its unique discoveries. In those great moments when many elements are fused in a single act of illumination, so that their underlying unity is suddenly recognized, the poet reveals, according to Coleridge, 'the greatest faculty of the human mind'. He acts much as Nature acts when she merges the scattered features of a landscape into a single harmonious prospect. By the force of his imagination he becomes everything that he contemplates and intuitively grasps its essence, making 'the changeful god be felt in the river, the lion and the flame'.

Shakespeare thus used imagery as a dramatist, not as the lyric or epic poet uses it. To receive its full effect we have to consider the whole context: the quality of the image itself, the character and the occasion, the place and the time and the enveloping atmosphere. When thus considered, the progression of the imagery becomes something more than a way of unfolding a dramatic plot, it is the articulation of a vision of life. It routs the symbols of evil which he has bidden to his stage, and makes inexplicable joy of the pain that we have suffered in watching his characters in the net of their destiny. Their sense of musical delight as they reflect upon their experience, their insistence upon ordering this experience in patterns hitherto unperceived, distinguish his plays from the dramas of passion in which the Jacobeans wrote of man's angry defiance and submission. Ultimately, as Sir Walter Ralegh observed, they distinguish Shakespeare' style 'from all other writing whatsoever'[3].

---

3 So of course does his vocabulary. It has been estimated that he used some 21,000 words, of which 4000 were making their first recorded appearance. The Authorized Version has a vocabulary of about 6500 words, Milton in his poems 8000, including many Latinate uses. Perhaps even more remarkable than the fertility of Shakespeare's coinages is the range of topics and ideas that demanded a vocabulary of this size.

When the single condensed image will not suffice, the thought overflows into a stream of associated images. Often the flow is so rapid that the metaphors seem to be mixed; but what really happens is that each succeeding image treads upon another's heels and denies it space. A mixed metaphor is a transition too swift for speech to accommodate; or, as Lamb put it in a different figure, 'before one idea has burst its shell, another is hatched and clamorous for disclosure.'

> She should have died hereafter;
> There would have been a time for such a word.
> To-morrow, and to-morrow, and to-morrow,
> Creeps in this petty pace from day to day,
> To the last syllable of recorded time;
> And all our yesterdays have lighted fools
> The way to dusty death. Out, out, brief candle!
> Life's but a walking shadow, a poor player
> That struts and frets his hour upon the stage,
> And then is heard no more; it is a tale
> Told by an idiot, full of sound and fury,
> Signifying nothing.
>
> *Macb* V v 17.

In these lines several groups of images are woven into a single texture. The dominant image, suggested by *hereafter,* is of time, which runs through the passage: *to-morrow, day, time, yesterdays, hour. Word,* in the second line, presently finds echoes in *syllable, recorded, tale, signifying; creeps* at once suggests *pace,* which in due course is followed by *way, walking* and *struts;* in the meantime *lighted* is followed by *candle,* and *candle* by *shadow,* and from *shadow* Shakespeare's mind leapt instinctively to the *player* and his *stage.* Other groups are *died, death, life,* with which *shadow* too is associated; *petty, brief, nothing; frets, fury; fool, idiot.* As *dusty* may be connected both with walking and with the inevitable dust of the grave, there is no significant word in the passage that is not linked with one or more fellows. The technical accomplishment is dazzling, although the association of ideas in Shakespeare's mind was almost certainly unconscious and reflexive, and the elaborate pattern simply composed itself. We ought, finally, to wonder why this passage, so desolating in its content, has found its way into generations of anthologies and commonplace-books. It may be that its impact is less terrible than would appear. If we think of Othello's epileptic ravings and apostrophes to damnation, or of Macbeth himself when in a different mood he storms ineffectually at the 'cream-fac'd loon', there is no comfort to be had. But in the controlled rhythm of these lines and the succession and recurrence of familiar images there is that which belies their dreadful purport. Macbeth has supped full with horrors and come to a tortured rest:

There is no flying hence, nor tarrying here.
I 'gin to be aweary of the sun,
And wish the estate o'the world were now undone.

V v 48.

It is of his own life, and what he has done with it, that he speaks; but the same words speak also of the life he has lost and of all who are still glad of the sun.

'Time hath, my lord, a wallet at his back...' (*TC* III iii 145-70) is a speech in which Ulysses reminds Achilles that no man may rest upon his reputation; to keep it bright, he must never cease to deserve it. Here again Shakespeare is reinforcing a simple idea by a swift sequence of images each kindled by the one preceding it. At first sight the speech may seem to be one of those amplifications beloved of Renaissance poets, wherein a theme is elaborated in pretty convolutions. The difference lies in the quality of what is added to the theme. Each expansion of it adds to our awareness of the original idea and also of the man who is speaking and the man he is addressing. It underlines the action being proposed, and we shall remember these words when we see in what fashion Achilles acts upon them. Dramatically, therefore, the passage contributes to the ironic spirit of the play; and imaginatively it stimulates the individual spectator, who has to respond to beggars seeking alms, the iniquity of oblivion, the voraciousness of monsters, rusty armour hanging in the hall, a journey that becomes a pursuit and at length a battle with its trampled horses, and the host standing at his lighted doorway with his arms outstretched in welcome and farewell. A swift final stroke brings us back to the original image of a beggar touting for reward. Thus an idea has been brought to life by a series of pictures, each of them concrete and specific, and the audience are able to see the bubble reputation as, in a moment of self-identification with two of his characters, Shakespeare himself saw it. We are forced to live a particular experience when we might have been left in idle contemplation of a generalized sentiment.

Once Shakespeare had mastered this technique, metre became almost patternless. The blank-verse norm was perhaps so familiar to his audience that they unconsciously supplied the pattern for themselves when he departed from it, for as also with rhyme, expectation is an important factor in the listener's response to verse. Now the thought and the emotion create their own rhythms, through which they are the most surely apprehended. The poet seems to have heard a surge of music, or the accents of a human voice, more clearly than he heard the regular beat of verse, and he allowed the voices and their music to find their own appropriate expression. Increasingly the pressure of these thoughts and perceptions weighed upon his power of utterance, and we have almost to admit the paradox that the more perfect he made the instrument of his poetic drama, the less he was able to say all the things that *by its means* he might have said. The intellectual energy and abnormal sensibility of his characters sometimes overflowed the boundaries of normal speech, and then the result would be a dense and weighty obscurity which he refused to clarify by a debilitating diffuseness. In the theatre it is not easy for the actress to make it immediately clear what Helena is trying to say:

> The mightiest space in fortune Nature brings
> To join like likes, and kiss like native things.
> Impossible be strange attempts to those
> That weigh their pains in sense, and so suppose
> What hath been cannot be: who ever strove
> To show her merit, that did not love?

AWW I i 237.

As one reflection chased hard upon another, even as 'one fire drives out one fire; one nail, one nail', the rush of ideas was too turbulent for a character to stand back and say unambiguously what he felt. At moments of particular tension Shakespeare moved towards the modern technique of 'the stream of consciousness'.

> Affection! thy intention stabs the centre;
> Thou dost make possible things not so held,
> Communicat'st with dreams; — how can this be? —
> With what's unreal thou co-active art,
> And fellow'st nothing: then, 'tis very credent
> Thou mayst co-join with something; and thou dost,
> And that beyond commission, and I find it,
> And that to the infection of my brains
> And hardening of my brows.

WT I ii 138.

Upon this the following 'What means Sicilia?' is a fair comment. This is no longer language suitable for theatrical entertainment, and no doubt his fellows told him so. The explanation of the special style and tone of the final plays may not be, as has often been maintained, that he had said all that he wanted to say. It may be that he no longer felt himself to be in command of an instrument that in dramatic terms would permit him any further exploration of the human mind. The method of these plays is uniform. He establishes his plot as economically as possible (in *The Tempest* rather clumsily), employing for the purpose the heightened style of the tragedies, with its condensed imagery and the parentheses, anacoluthons and abrupt resolutions of the speaking voice; and then he withdraws to Wales, or the coastline of Bohemia, or the unlocated island, to write pure poetry. With important differences he returns to the manner of his earlier plays, where the poetry was often more exciting to a young man than the drama. The conflicts and struggles of his characters concern him less, and he seldom lifts their motives out of their subconscious minds. Instead we find the sensuous deployment of allegory and lyric, verse that runs smoothly within the decasyllabic pattern, and a renewed delight in the classical and mythological embellishments he had learned from Ovid. The tone is colloquial and the poetry is too carefully disciplined to impede the dramatic movement, but the mood is now formal and the characters seem to speak at one remove from life. Even the resolution of the plot is accomplished by means of a formal contrast between age and youth. Where in the past evil was dispersed, and the world regenerated, by the act of a great and suffering soul in attaining to wisdom and self-knowledge, the solvent now is the appearance of a younger generation to make a brave new world by calling their elders to repentance. Whether this really was the fabric of Shakespeare's final vision no one now can say. A veil seems to have fallen between him and his readers. We may no longer feel that we are standing at the surgeon's shoulder as he works, and we have to receive his reports at second-hand.

The depths and complexities of Shakespeare's art may be studied in many ways, and to study them in only one way is at once to be aware of the inadequacy of the single approach. It is possible to discover his genius in the terrifying veracity of his major characters, or in his unfolding conceptions of history, comedy and tragedy, or even in the agility of his stagecraft, his organization of the limited resources of the Elizabethan stage to achieve artistic ends seemingly beyond its scope. Some consideration must be given to these matters, but with the caution that ultimately it is the force of the poetic idea that gives unity and coherence to his art.

He turned to his advantage the inhibiting conventions of his stage. Much has been written of the absurdities of his plots, usually an amalgam of two or three sources, or of the liberties taken with time and place, or the huddled, perfunctory endings. He has been condemned for his facile use of the whole Elizabethan bag-of-tricks, including the lover in disguise, the nocturnal substitution, the ghost insistent for revenge, the wager on chastity, the real or assumed madness, the indisciplined clowning. But by bringing these time-honoured improbabilities within the control of a dramatic idea poetically conceived, he made them the unlikely vehicle of permanent truths. Once he had mastered the technical problem of finding for his characters an appropriate form of speech, all that was resistant in the medium could be overcome.

The mechanics of stagecraft, perhaps acquired as an actor, aided him from his first beginnings. Because there was no curtain, and characters had to walk down to the front of the platform, he introduced them in the middle of some exposition or argument and thus immediately involved the audience by letting them feel that they were intervening in a discussion. His characters use the Vice's technique of apostrophizing the audience and generate dramatic feeling by confiding their anxieties or their ambitions. The soliloquy, a regular device of his theatre to communicate attitudes or information, Shakespeare sometimes used to introduce an alternative course of action which is here debated although not pursued. The theme of suicide in 'To be or not to be...' is a case in point. By this means the audience are led to believe that events might take a different turn, that a character might behave unexpectedly; and in the unfolding of nearly all his plots there is a moment, whether indicated through soliloquy or other means, when it seems possible that the action may have a different outcome and the characters escape what has seemed inevitable. Shakespeare's plots are so familiar that we may easily forget that they do not have to end as they do.

As a playwright, then, he quickly learned to avoid flat statement and to rely instead on the thrust and counter-thrust of the dialogue. He took advantage of the swift changes of location possible on a stage not encumbered by heavy scenery, thus keeping the action brisk and varied: it has been calculated that 55 per cent of his scenes are less then 125 lines in length[4]. At the same time the indication of place was a means of indicating a mood. Nightfall, a lonely heath, the greenwood or a crowded street were conveyed rather by a character's reflections upon them than by a formal description of the surroundings, so that in a poet's hands scene-painting became the instrument of a larger purpose. Likewise the only sort of time with which Shakespeare concerned himself was dramatic time. Because Iago's poison must work quickly if it is to work at all, the play hurries to its climax; and conversely, Hamlet's indecision is allowed to impress itself through protracted dialogue and a succession of contrasted scenes.

His dramatic method was to begin with a postulate, rapidly and economically stated, which he at once forces us to accept. Even the opening line of a play seems to shut the door upon any world but this:

In sooth, I know not why I am so sad.

If music be the food of love, play on.

Old John of Gaunt, time-honour'd Lancaster...

Nay, but this dotage of our general's
O'erflows the measure.

Now is the winter of our discontent...

These inner worlds thereafter disclose themselves in obedience to the poetic idea with which they were created, and everything within them is controlled, coherent and inevitable. The poetic idea may be manifested in several ways — through the dominant imagery which establishes the mood and significance of the play, through the interaction of the characters and the rhythms of their speech, through the choice and balance of the incidents — but we should not expect to find intrusion from other worlds nor to make

4 Stagecraft is fully discussed in B. Beckerman, *Shakespeare at the Globe.*

comparisons with any of them. If of the Falstaff of *The Merry Wives of Windsor* we want to complain that 'This is not the man', it is our own fault for expecting that he should be, and Pistol and Bardolph share his decline. Probably most readers of Shakespeare have been tempted at one time or another to imagine some illegitimate transplants. King Henry VI, inapt for politics, would in comedy be a well-meaning friar whose schemes and counsels go harmlessly astray; Bolingbroke, politically efficient, would be boorish in a comedy, and in his later role as Henry IV, itself such a transformation in a different play, might in either comedy or tragedy appear as one of those heavy fathers whose sententious folly precipitates dire events; no Rosalind would submit to the fate of Desdemona, and so on. It is foolish speculation because the worlds of Shakespeare's plays are so privately enclosed that if necessary he will defy his sources and the facts of history to keep them so. Richard III develops naturally from the Gloucester of *3 Henry VI*, and there is some consistency in the progression from Prince Hal to Henry V. But Shakespeare owed no loyalty to his own precedents, and possibly he did not even notice the declension of the hard-headed Antony of *Julius Caesar* into the strumpet's fool. None of the transplants rather frivolously suggested above is as surprising as the conversion of the feckless, traitorous Aumerle of *Richard II* into the Duke of York who at Agincourt begs 'the leading of the vaward' and dies nobly in the field. 'From helmet to the spur all blood he was'. The inference is that seductive comparisons and seductive generalizations need to be resisted because each of Shakespeare's plays is self-contained and absolute.

To resist them altogether would, however, be an abdication of critical judgment, and the histories, at least, rest upon certain basic principles and assumptions. The sixteenth century saw the past as a mirror for the present, and accordingly believed that the study of history was valuable because it taught by examples. Nearly a hundred years after Shakespeare wrote his first chronicle Dryden held the same view, writing in his *Life of Plutarch* (1683) that history 'helps us to judge of what will happen, by shewing us the like revolutions of former times. For mankind being the same in all ages, agitated by the same passions and moved to action by the same interests, nothing can come to pass but some precedent of the like nature has already been produced'.

History was not as yet a very exact study. The sixteenth century had not wholly dispersed that cloudiness of historical perspective in which, for instance, artists of the Middle Ages were wont to depict Moses in the armour of a medieval knight. Shakespeare's audiences, similarly, were not troubled by seeing Brutus and Julius Caesar appear on the stage in Elizabethan costume. Facts being less important than the truths they might illustrate, and human nature being regarded as unchangeable, men were not much concerned to look for distinctions between past and present. Guicciardini, a Florentine contemporary with Machiavelli, wrote that although things might change their name and colour, 'the same events recur endlessly, and nothing happens that has not been seen before'. Much of Shakespeare's alleged anachronism therefore becomes intelligible by the standards of his age. There was nothing incongruous in having Ulysses, an ancient Greek, deliver the medieval doctrine of degree, and the Nine Worthies comprised representatives of quite different cultures, periods and race[5]. Men were unable, or unwilling, to grasp that conditions varied from place to place or that vast changes had been wrought by time. Thus Machiavelli blamed the collapse of contemporary Florence on the failure of her citizens to act like Roman republicans; and in Shakespeare's day the Puritans were seeking to reorganize the Church after the structure adopted by the scattered communities of the early Christians at a time of persecution. Puritan hostility to the theatre derived doctrinally from early Christian condemnation of the salacious spectacles of a pagan society that bore little resemblance to Tudor England or to its theatrical activities.

Renaissance writers displayed, however, a more mature interest in historical causation. They were looking for more sophisticated explanations than the wrath of God or the blind operations of chance, and Shakespeare inherited a philosophy of history which was limited and unselective but at least sought to explain events in England during the century that preceded the Tudors. It may even have been a Tudor fabrication, and its dogmatic ridigity has been questioned, but unmistakably the background for Shakespeare's history plays was the belief that England had to pay the penalty of civil war and the loss of France for the Lancastrians' sin in deposing and murdering Richard II. Sir Thomas More, Polydore Vergil and Edward Hall laid the foundations and Elizabethan poets — Daniel, Warner, Drayton, Davies of Hereford as well as Shakespeare — in various ways built upon them. The lesson was that rebellion was a crime with hideous consequences, and man's first duty as a citizen was orderly obedience to authority. The view that all history was contemporary history made this duty the more urgent. With Catholic conspiracy, Puritan intransigence, an uncertain succession and the threat of Spanish invasion, the Elizabethans had no difficulty in seeing the disorder of the fifteenth century as their own.

Pleas for unity, order and obedience occur too frequently in the history plays to have been accidental. Shakespeare felt the urgency of the times, and in the approved manner he used history as an *exemplum* to warn men of the dangers of rebellion. The destruction prophesied by the Bishop of Carlisle (*Richard II* IV i 114-49) duly took place, until the country's wounds were healed in the Tudor peace. While the usurper king is about to be tormented by the ghosts of his victims, Richmond's prayer on the eve of Bosworth has the confidence of a predestined deliverer. It closes with a quietness heard at

---

5 The nature of historical writing in the period is analysed in P. Burke, *The Renaissance Sense of the Past*.

no other time in this turbulent play:

> To thee I do commend my watchful soul,
> Ere I let fall the windows of mine eyes:
> Sleeping and waking, O defend me still!

R III V iii 116.

This conventional reading of history, familiar to all the audience because they encountered it also in the official Homilies read to them in church, gave Shakespeare a framework for the histories, but he was not constrained by any formula and he was free to examine men in their public relationships. It was natural that he should concentrate particularly on the ruler because history had not learned to interest itself in secondary or impersonal causes and it was on the ruler that the welfare of the community depended. The Renaissance attempted to treat the problem of government on scientific principles, and the age was prolific in manuals of statecraft basing their instruction on inferences made from the behaviour of rulers in the past. Still, however, there were religious overtones because man would always labour in vain if God chose otherwise. Even Machiavelli, resolutely anti-Christian, had to allow malign Fortune some part in man's affairs, and a providential interpretation of the past may be found as late as Clarendon's *History of the Great Rebellion*. After dealing in a spirit recognizably modern with various causes of the rebellion, he has to add that 'the immediate finger and wrath of God must be acknowledged in these perplexities and distractions'.

Shakespeare always acknowledged the hand of Providence in man's affairs, and there can be no doubt, either, that he knew and exploited the concept of history as a guide and warning to the present. The closing lines of *King John* were a specific address to the potential trouble-makers of the 1590s. But for purposes of drama he was less concerned with schematic interpretations than with the individual found in a certain predicament. In these undoubtedly political plays he was always aware of the conflict between the claims of the social order and the natural self-realization of the individual; and it may be a very limited world in which political good is an exclusive standard of reference. Always there is the voice of Falstaff, that great anti-Establishment man: 'Banish plump Jack, and banish all the world'.[6]

As his art developed in assurance and power, Shakespeare was able to look more closely at the character of the ruler, demanding to know why one succeeds and another fails. At first, it is clear, he was shocked to discover how much human weakness might shelter in the folds of ceremony, and to realize what this might entail in the ruin of the state. But this interest presently shifted to the ruler as a man: to the effect upon him of the shams of

6   See M.M. Reese, *The Cease of Majesty*, 333-9.

power and the dreadful responsibilities of office, to the consequences for the ruler himself as well as for the community. In *Henry V* he seems to give the answer to the question that had long occupied him: what are the qualities of the ideal king? The ideal king is one who accepts the discipline of responsibility and subordinates his personal affections to the people's needs. It was perhaps a rather hollow discovery after so long a time, and in a rather perfunctory play Henry himself is a rather bodiless man with no Falstaff to keep him company. The writing of history plays had concentrated his vision upon the individual heart and mind; but at the same time it was constricting because it obliged him to consider the individual only in a political context. His art was now ripe for tragedy.

The development of his comedy was simultaneously leading him in the same direction. His tragedies always follow a downward turn, starting with a man of high estate in apparent prosperity and showing his decline into suffering and death. The comedies move the other way, which is why most of them have been described as 'joyous'. At the beginning the characters are in difficulties, but after further entanglements and embarrassments the story ends in love and reconciliation. Often there has been tragic potentiality before this happy ending, and in due course Shakespeare would allow his plots to develop in obedience to their inner necessities.

Comedy as he found it had been attacked by Sidney because of its heterogeneous elements. The public liked to be entertained by romances of knights, sorcerers and fair ladies, preferably in a domesticated English setting, and they wanted also a generous measure of the antics of the company's clown. At the same time comedy was recognized as the scourge of human foibles and the schoolmistress of good citizenship. Thus the dramatist had a task resistant to good art, and usually he was content to serve up a romantic fable with a dash of social criticism and a liberal seasoning of farce. *The Two Gentlemen of Verona* is a fair example of Shakespeare's early struggles with this unpromising matter. The romantic convention, with its self-conscious cult of friendship, taxed his technical resources, and the clowning is a superimposed 'extra' alien to the mood of the play. A couple of Launce's speeches give a hint of what is to come, although it is unlikely that Kempe was satisfied to speak only what was set down for him. Technically, Shakespeare's problems in the next few years were, first, to assimilate the clowning into the plot, wherein he succeeded so well that before long clowns would invade history and tragedy without breach of decorum; and, secondly, to tone down the more preposterous demands of romance and fable, and devise the settings and a style of speech in which recognizable human beings could talk and act. His comedies would last, John Aubrey said, 'as long as the English tongue is understood; for that he handles *mores hominum*'.

The element lacking from *The Two Gentlemen of Verona* is the didacticism on which comedy habitually insisted. Any implied criticism is tolerant and gentle. Thurio's cowardice is kept at the level of a farcical joke, and no portentous conclusions are drawn about treachery in friendship or the proper behaviour of persons in love.

> Invest me in my motley; give me leave
> To speak my mind, and I will through and through
> Cleanse the foul body of the infected world.
>
> *AYLI* II vii 58.

This was not Shakespeare's way. In the play Jaques gets the worst of most of his encounters, and although his conception of the motley was in harmony with the mood of 1600, Shakespeare seldom thought it his business to cleanse the infected world. Except in *Troilus and Cressida*, he was only occasionally and incidentally a satirist. Very little of his work conforms to the classical definition of comedy as a corrective of absurdity, seeking to preserve the formal standards of society. In the Prelude to *The Egoist* Meredith defined comedy as 'a game played to throw reflections upon social life, and it deals with human nature in the drawing-room of civilized men and women': from which it would follow that laughter is primarily of the intellect, impersonal, lacking in sympathy and feeling, and apt to indulge in exaggeration and distortion to achieve its effects. Elsewhere, however, Meredith had to admit that Shakespeare's comedy had a larger scope. His characters, although they are of this world, 'are of this world enlarged to our embrace by imagination, and by great poetic imagination,...not grouped and toned to produce a comic exhibition of the narrower world of society'. In his two sonnets on *The Spirit of Shakespeare* he touched on a further conception of Shakespeare's comedy. It echoes with laughter which we feel to be the laughter of the earth itself,

> broad as ten thousand beeves
> At pasture...
> Thunders of laughter, clearing air and heart.

Shakespeare was not interested only in exploiting the absurdities inherent in all deviations from the common standard of social behaviour, although he could do it when he chose. There is a further province of comedy which brings into scrutiny men's virtues as well as their vices and looks interrogatively at their most cherished assumptions; and beyond that a further province still which offers an escape into laughter, a release from the weary and difficult business of living.

In the classic form of English comedy, the comedy of manners, Shakespeare did not particularly excel. He found it too restrictive, and left the humours to Jonson and Marston, to whom they were congenial. Although the social implications may be there for the seeking, his comedy was 'even to the world's pleasure and the increase of laughter' (*AWW* II iv 37). If he preached at all, it was to say that forgiveness and repentance will mend most of our troubles; and the form that his comedy mostly took was to bring lovers together after a chapter of accident and misunderstanding.

The progression was similar to that of the histories, moving from plays of situation to plays which allow the deployment and revelation of character. *The Comedy of Errors* and *The Taming of the Shrew* have been condemned as heartless, but here he was too busy manipulating his plot to be able to endow his characters with much humanity. In *Love's Labour's Lost*, too, the controlling idea is intellectual, and a single static situation is prolonged for the whole of the play. At first sight *A Midsummer Night's Dream* may not appear to have brought him much nearer to his ultimate purpose, for the characterization, except of the mechanicals, is as shadowy as the moonlit night. But the play shows an imaginative apprehension that brings disparate elements into unity by the force of a dominant idea. In comparison with any play that he had written previously, Shakespeare had marvellously enlarged his dramatic world. The nubile Athenians, the clowns and the immortals blend into a perfect harmony in which each group contributes to the controlling theme; and this theme — the demands of love and the response which men should make to it — belies the remote and dreamy atmosphere of the play in having a function that is acute and pertinent. Theseus and Bottom, the two realists of the comedy who take the world as it comes and have no faith in dreams and the fantasies of the lunatic, the lover and the poet, are taught that their vision is defective. As an incidental performance Shakespeare created a new dramatic species in presenting fairies as beings capable of a certain degree of domestication. There is a case for regarding Oberon as his first major villain. But the technical importance of the play lies in the handling of groups of contrasted, almost incompatible characters. By means of this new mastery comedy would blend into the historical scene to create the panoramic England of *Henry IV*.

First, however, in one of those leaps with which Shakespeare is constantly astonishing us, *The Merchant of Venice* will have compelled a serious moral judgment. This has not happened previously in Shakespearean comedy, and it means that the romantic convention has been modified to accommodate a real character. An authentic villain has found his surprising way into a love-story. The opportunism and ambition of modern actors have sometimes played false to Shakespeare's intention that the golden light of Belmont should soften the harsh issues raised by Shylock and his fate. It remains true, nonetheless, that a figure intended to be merely a symbol of an evil alien to the lovers and their world has by his very humanity raised issues that will not be silenced. Shylock remains an outsider because although he accepts his fate, he is not reconciled to it and there is no repentance; just as Malvolio too is unreconciled and makes his final exit swearing vengeance, leaving Feste with his sad little song about the rain that raineth every day.

Although none of them is ever again as desperately serious as Shylock, the persons of Shakespeare's comedy are increasingly sharpened and individualized. They stand out against the fairy-tale backcloth and remind us, many of them, that it is only by grace and choice of their creator that they are not persons of tragedy. If we prick them, do they not bleed? Evil is present in their worlds, and it fails, as ultimately it fails in the great tragedies; but because of a certain arbitrariness in Shakespeare's vision, it does not yet have tragic consequences. Inevitably, however, it will, and Shakespeare's poetry has found the music that will make bearable the suffering that it causes. When the exponents of the comedy of manners turn to tragedy, they are driven, as Jonson was, to take it from their books. We know them by their fruits, which are *Sejanus* and *Pizarro* and *The Mourning Bride*. True comedy and true tragedy are expressions of the same fundamental knowledge of life, and to achieve one is to be able achieve the other. In the development of Shakespeare's art comedy and history were forever converging upon one another, and together they were converging upon tragedy.

Medieval tragedy occupied itself mainly with the fall of great persons from high estate to low. The narration of the fall was by itself sufficient to engage the interest of both the poet and his reader. The concept of a blind and capricious Fortune had such a firm hold on the medieval mind that it was unnecessary to seek for any other cause of a man's decline from prosperity to ruin: the fickle jade marked her erstwhile favourites for destruction, and that was that. To avoid the impiety of seeming to arraign the ways of God, reference might be made to some sin or weakness of which the prostrate victim had been guilty in the days of his renown. Thus the sub-title of Lydgate's *Falls of Princes* (written 1430-8 but not printed until 1494) stated that the purpose of the poem was to show how great ones fell 'through the Mutability and change of unsteadfast Fortune, together with their most detestable and wicked vices'. This was prudent insurance, but the personal motivation was superficial. The pathos of medieval tragedy was contained in the fall itself, and lamentation over the fall was the accepted form of tragic statement. Somewhere behind this mutability in men's fortunes an eternal justice was believed to operate, and the innocent as well as the guilty were caught up in it, but little psychological penetration was shown in the rather perfunctory efforts to connect this justice with the moral shortcomings of famous men.

A Mirror for Magistrates was originally designed to continue Lydgate's work by warning princes against 'the slippery deceits of the wavering lady'. But it was the work of many writers, and additions were being made to it for more than thirty years after its first appearance in 1555. Some of the more thoughtful of these additions attempted to explore the question of individual responsibility. On the one hand the new psychology, more elaborate and comprehensive than older conceptions, was drawing attention to the physiological causes which might account for human actions; and on the other, religious reformers were preaching with renewed vigour the Christian belief that suffering was God's punishment for sin. The tragic interest accordingly began to shift from the fall itself to the fault by which it was occasioned; and then from the fault to the condition — usually the overwhelming of will and reason by some passionate excess — of which it was the consequence.

The recognition of new or revived fashions of thought did not, however, evict theories of longer standing, and the wavering lady retained to a surprising degree her influence over man's affairs. Late Elizabethan drama therefore had at its disposal a rich complex of tragic themes, and a dramatist was free to make his choice. He might avoid all pretence of motivation and exploit the possibilities inherent in the unpredictable turns of Fortune's wheel. But he also had a promising key to tragic action in the moral philosophy which warned against the disasters consequent upon the surrender of the pales and forts of reason to man's invading appetites; or in the semi-scientific dogmas about the proper blending of the elements and the prevalence of the humours he might find causes to account for the obliteration of the will by passion. The doctrine that suffering was the penalty of sin was not, except in casual references, assimilated into the drama, chiefly because religious subjects were prohibited. The scope of tragedy had been considerably enlarged nonetheless, for the tragedy of error had now taken its place by the side of the tragedy of circumstance. Interest no longer had to be restricted to the bewildered victim of arbitrary fate, as it was now possible to examine not merely the sort of error that had tragic consequences but also the reasons why men were betrayed into error. 'Esteem not my desires', says Chapman's Tamyra,

> Such doters on their humours that my judgment
> Cannot subdue them.
>
> *Bussy d'Ambois* III i 104.

But judgment cannot always subdue them, and the betrayal of men to passion by the irregularity of their humours became a favourite theme of Jacobean playwrights.

In his early chronicles Shakspeare was not much troubled about motivation. The characters endlessly likened one another to animals and behaved like animals; and when they fell, they blamed Fortune. Thus Edward IV, who had been guilty of treason, perjury, rebellion, cruelty and many other crimes, might have found in his defeat and capture some occasion to reflect that possibly it was these offences that had brought him down. The hour was ripe for a moral homily upon such lines if the dramatist wished it. But Edward bears himself vaingloriously, like one of Marlowe's champions, seeing no other cause for his overthrow than the malignity of Fortune and finding no other attitude than a proud acceptance of it:

> Though Fortune's malice overthrow my state,
> My mind exceeds the compass of her wheel.

What fates impose, that men must needs abide;
It boots not to resist both wind and tide.

3 Hen VI IV iii 46, 58.

Even *Romeo and Juliet*, a more thoughtful and concentrated play, takes its course in obedience to the inauspicious stars. It is true that the Friar sounds a deeper note when he warns the lovers that the haste and violence of their passion will undo them, but they do not heed him. The Chorus has said that 'the fearful passage of their death-mark'd love' is fore-ordained, and we are not surprised by Romeo's cry of 'I am Fortune's fool' when he has killed Tybalt.

This would hardly serve for mature tragedy, and neither would the belief that a man was unable to avoid the consequences of his physical make-up. Frequent allusions show that Shakespeare was familiar with this doctrine: so familiar, indeed, that his tragedy has been interpreted from this standpoint alone.[7] He would not, however, turn his drama into a psychiatrist's case-book.

> and bless'd are those
> Whose blood and judgment are so well commingled
> That they are not a pipe for fortune's finger
> To sound what stop she please. Give me that man
> That is not passion's slave...

Ham III ii 73.

In this same speech Hamlet was proud to say that his own soul was 'mistress of her choice', and it was evident to Shakespeare that 'slavery' of any kind was not a possible subject for real tragedy. Somehow, therefore, he would have to resolved the conflict between free will and necessity.

He never doubted that it was impious to ignore the stars. It was invariably the mark of a villain to insist that man is wholly master of his destiny, that ' 'tis in ourselves that we are thus or thus'. Edmund set out the matter with the wit usually allowed to men of his sort:

> This is the excellent foppery of the world, that, when we are sick in fortune — often the surfeit of our own behaviour — we make guilty of our disasters the sun, the moon and the stars; as if we were villains by necessity, fools by heavenly compulsion, knaves, thieves and treachers by spherical predominance, drunkards, liars and adulterers by an enforced obedience of planetary influence;

7 In *Shakespeare's Tragic Heroes* Lily B. Campbell summarizes contemporary works, medical, philosophical and religious, by which the drama may have been influenced at the turn of the century, She argues, learnedly and seductively, that all Shakespeare's tragic heroes were victims of some kind of passionate obsession, but it is difficult to feel that Shakespeare had no greater purpose than to exemplify the workings of Elizabethan psychology.

and all that we are evil in, by a divine thrusting on: an admirable evasion of whore-master man, to lay his goatish disposition to the charge of a star!

Lear I ii 128.

To speak thus is to blaspheme against Providence, and it classes the speaker with the Machiavellian individualists, men bloody, bold and resolute who gloried in their self-sufficiency even when it confounded them. Of such were Kyd's Lorenzo:

I'll trust myself, myself shall be my friend;

The Spanish Tragedy III ii 226.

and Marlowe's Jew:

Ego mihimet sum semper proximus;

The Jew of Malta I i 184.

and Richard of Gloucester:

I, that have neither pity, love nor fear...
I have no brother, I am like no brother;
And this word 'love', which greybeards call divine,
Be resident in men like one another
And not in me: I am myself alone.

3 Hen VI V vi 68, 80.

This insolent self-sufficiency fascinated the Elizabethans, even as it repelled them, by its audacious confidence. But it was at variance with their orthodox faith in a divinity that shapes man's ends, and this orthodoxy was expressed throughout Shakespeare's work by characters whom we recognize as good or as choric commentators. We have the testimony of Kent:

It is the stars,
The stars above us, govern our conditions;

Lear IV iii36.

or of Helena:

But most it is presumption in us when
The help of heaven we count the act of men;

AWW II i 154.

and particularly of Enobarbus:

I see men's judgments are
A parcel of their fortunes, and things outward

Do draw the inward quality after them,
To suffer all alike.

AC III xiii 31.

Thus there was a dilemma. To reject planetary influence altogether was to challenge the watchfulness and sovereignty of God; but a torpid fatalism committed the impiety of holding God responsible for the presence of evil and suffering in the world. The problem was resolved, so far as it ever could be resolved, by a compromise. Machiavelli had earlier pointed the way. As a political analyst and historian he was astute enough to equate Fortune with those impersonal forces in history which may overwhelm the individual if he does not perceive them and take his precautions.

> Many have held and hold the opinion that events are controlled by Fortune and by God in such a way that the prudence of men cannot modify them; indeed, that men have no influence whatsoever. Because of this they would conclude that there is no point in struggling over things, but that one should submit to the rulings of chance... Sometimes, when thinking of this, I have myself inclined to this same opinion. None the less, because free choice cannot be ruled out, I believe that it is probably true that Fortune is the arbiter of half the things we do, leaving the other half to be controlled by ourselves.

The Prince xxv.

He compares Fortune to a river which in flood carries all before it and makes resistance seemingly useless. 'Yet it does not follow that when it is flowing quietly one cannot take precautions, constructing dykes and embankments'. Fortune therefore is most to be dreaded 'where there is no force to hold her in check', and Machiavelli's conclusion is that in practical affairs the ruler who adapts his policy to the times prospers 'and likewise one whose policy clashes with the demands of the times does not'. By intelligent anticipation and adjustment the onslaughts of Fortune can often be resisted. It is important to be 'a child of the time'.

For the writing of tragedy it was likewise necessary to recognize the operation of an external fate that nevertheless left men free. The stars inclined but they did not compel, and their influence cooperated with man's inward qualities to guide his actions. This influence, moreover, was often propitious, and it was man's responsibility to collaborate with them when they were benevolent and resist when they were malign. 'Thou marshall'st me the way that I was going'; but the ultimate choice was free. Although each particular statement of the ambiguity might seem to veer to one side or the other, it was generally agreed that man prospered when his stars and his faculties worked to a common purpose.

There is a deep nick in time's restless wheel
For each man's good; when which nick comes, it strikes,
As rhetoric, yet works not persuasion,

But only is a means to make it work:
So no man riseth by his real merit,
But when it cries clink in his raiser's spirit.

Bussy d'Ambois I i 139.

By accident most strange, bountiful Fortune,
Now my dear lady, hath mine enemies
Brought to this shore; and by my prescience
I find my zenith doth depend upon
A most auspicious star, whose influence
If now I court not but omit, my fortunes
Will ever after droop.

Tem I ii 178.

Our remedies oft in ourselves do lie
Which we ascribe to heaven: the fated sky
Gives us free scope; only doth backward pull
Our slow designs when we ourselves are dull.

AWW I i 231.

It is with the same argument, twisting it for sinister purposes, that Cassius traps Brutus:

Men at some time are masters of their fates:
The fault, dear Brutus, is not in our stars,
But in ourselves, that we are underlings.

JC I ii 139.

The dramatist's problem was to find the balance or correspondence between fate and the individual that makes for effective tragedy. Misunderstanding of what Hamlet said and of what Aristotle said has led, in Shakespeare's case, to the unfortunate theory of 'the fatal flaw'. When regretting that the Danes' disposition to revelry has caused other nations to brand them as drunkards, and thus to undervalue their better qualities, Hamlet goes on to say:

So, oft it chances in particular men
That for some vicious mole of Nature in them,
As in their birth — wherein they are not guilty,
Since Nature cannot choose his origin, —
By the o'ergrowth of some complexion,
Oft breaking down the pales and forts of reason,
Or by some habit that too much o'erleavens
The form of plausive manners, that these men,
Carrying, I say, the stamp of one defect,
Being Nature's livery, or Fortune's star,
Their virtues else, be they as pure as grace,
As infinite as man may undergo,

Shall in the general censure take corruption
From that particular fault: the dram of evil
Doth all the noble substance oft put out,
To his own scandal.

I iv 23.

It is not an easy passage, and in some places the text itself is doubtful, but the argument is that one congenital defect may ruin a man's reputation: give a dog a bad name, and so on. Although Hamlet is not endorsing this view — it is merely, he says, accepted 'in the general censure', by the common opinion of mankind — the speech has given colour to the idea that Shakespeare's tragic heroes were victims of some vice or weakness in their natures which overwhelmed their greatness and led them to disaster. In *La Sagesse et la Destinée* (1898) the Belgian writer Maurice Maeterlinck said that 'None but yourself shall you meet on the highway of Fate. If Judas go forth to-night, it is towards Judas his steps will tend'. But the convenient dictum that 'Character is destiny', which has often been advanced as the key to Shakespearean tragedy, is true only in this limited sense: that when the stage has been set and our consent has been won to a certain arbitrary situation, when the characters are poised in conflict and the net is ready to be gathered about the victim, then the victim, because he is the man he is and has certain qualities that have been postulated, can no longer escape it.

Thus restricted, the thesis loses much of its force and interest. Nevertheless the 'vicious mole of Nature', or fatal blemish in a man's character, has been often been assimilated with the 'hamartia', or tragic error, of Aristotle's *Poetics*. It is necessary to remember what Aristotle was trying to do. Himself an inductive critic rather than a theorist, he was analysing for the benefit of his students the structural principles in the drama of ancient Greece. The nature of tragedy, he said, is to arouse pity and fear, and the eventual release of tension, the 'catharsis', is a source of pleasure. There is no tragic interest in the fall of an obvious scoundrel into the ruin that he deserves; and the fall of a saintly man, through no fault of his own, may create pathos but it does not stir us to pity and fear. The tragic hero, therefore, is not depraved, but nor is he 'pre-eminently virtuous and just'. He is a man whose misfortune' is brought upon him not by vice and depravity but by some error of judgment'. Aristotle's analysis of the error is somewhat ambiguous. It is not an accident, but it is devoid of any wicked intent; and yet it is sufficient to provoke the hostility of fate, so that we may feel that although he does not deserve what happens to him, yet he has contributed to it. This only seems to be a complicated way of saying that the tragic hero, being neither superlatively virtuous nor irredeemably debased and wicked, is an ordinary human being, fallible because he is human but essentially good, who runs into greater misfortune than he deserves. We cannot always foresee the consequence of our actions: and therein lies 'the pity of it'.

All this is some way removed from 'the fatal flaw'. Aristotle was not trying to uphold a system of retributive justice, for that would be mechanical and predictable and lacking in tragic power. He did not regard the tragic outcome as necessarily the penalty of error, nor even as a moral consequence. The 'hamartia' was an almost neutral act of causation; and although in Greek drama it often was a sinful act, Aristotle did not insist that it should be. It might be some incidental or trifling inadvertence, so long as it was sufficient to set the drama in motion and lead to the 'perepeteia', the unexpected reversal of fortune. Arguably the error, or one of the errors, in *Othello* was Desdemona's carelessness in letting fall the strawberry handkerchief when Emilia was on hand to pick it up.

What appears to happen in Shakespearean tragedy is that the latent forces of a hitherto impartial universe turn against a man who, before the play began, has seemed to be well-balanced and secure. Initially there is dramatic suspense because the outcome is uncertain, but under the pressure of events the hero's nature begins to work against him. His weaknesses reveal themselves, if we prefer to put it like that. Thereupon fate, or the universe, ceases to look impartially on those who have disturbed the balance. Circumstance no longer works haphazardly, but seems to consume and destroy the victim with implacable deliberation. There is no room here for moral judgment or a tariff of rewards and punishments according to desert. We are confronted simply with a combination of the man and the event, and it is beside the point that with a different man the same circumstances might have produced a different result. By a particular conjunction of character and circumstance — a conjunction valid in one world only; it is not the lot of all men everywhere, although in their agony the victims fear it may be — certain men are brought to face a universe that seems deaf to pity and justice and bent only on grinding its finest spirits in the dust.

Such spectacles would be unbearable in their nihilistic pessimism were it not that through the medium of Shakespeare's poetry the tragic victims rise to greater heights when the plot accomplishes their fall.[8] They never lose their humanity. Even when they are protesting against the 'cursed spite' of a hostile and unrelenting universe, they continue, by their acceptance of suffering, to be a part of it.

> Fortune knows
> We scorn her most when most she offers blows.
>
> *AC* III ix 73.

From the wreckage of both his public and personal life even Richard II, whose constant self-dramatization has been his greatest fault, rises to a

---

8 Perhaps this, rather than an Aristotelian catharsis, is the source of the pleasure which, however unexpectedly, spectators derive from tragedy.

dispassionate consideration of the human predicament. Hamlet's felicity is to have discovered that the readiness is all and that a sparrow does not fall unnoticed: the reconciliation is in the language, now so relaxed. Othello stops jabbering like a frustrated monkey; Macbeth's reflections on 'all our yesterdays' are not in their expression the ordinary reflections of a beleaguered gangster; Lear's final state is ineffable, but all his follies are dead.

It is only what is noble in them that concerns us at the end of the play, and the scattered generations have quickened to a poet's witness to man's unconquerable mind.

> Unbonneted he runs,
> And bids what will take all.
>
> *Lear* III i 14.

Great tragedy speaks of the infinite variousness and bravery of man as he fronts his destiny with unequal arm. 'Even here, virtue hath her rewards, and mortality her tears: even here, the woes of man touch the heart of man'.[9] The heart of the gods too, for upon such sacrifices the gods themselves throw incense. πάθημα μάθημα: in sorrow there is wisdom, and those who learn this wisdom may hope to be forgiven the act of self-determination which the gods found insolent.

> O sir, to wilful men
> The injuries that they themselves procure
> Must be their schoolmasters.
>
> *Lear* II iv 305.

Lear's discovery that the thunder will not cease at his bidding, that he is not ague-proof, is the outward expression of that access of self-knowledge which the outraged heavens seem to demand in expiation. No restoration of worldly satisfactions is to be hoped for, and full toll has still to be paid on earth, but the stain of evil will not spread. The tragedies close in reconciliation and renewal, and men who have erred a little and suffered greatly seem to vanish into the freedom that their souls have longed for.[10]

---

9   These incomparable words defy translation and sound better in the original:

> Sunt hic etiam sua praemia laudi;
> Sunt lacrimae rerum et mentem mortalia tangunt.
>
> Virgil, *Aeneid* I 461.

10   They correspond to those 'free spirits' who in George Eliot's novels fail to accommodate themselves to society's rigorous demands. By contrast, Greek drama was more concerned with the preservation of the social order than with individual hopes and suffering. Thus Orestes, who committed the sin of slaying his mother, could be acquitted and escape with his life: a consequence unthinkable in Shakespearean tragedy.

In these great plays Shakespeare has perfectly achieved the fusion of poetry and drama, and it is important to remember that this is what he has done, and not something else. Our own age, like the late Elizabethan, has a dominantly clinical approach to the riddle of human personality, and both our literature and our common speech have a precarious command of a semi-scientific jargon derived from the popularity of psychological studies. This casual similarity between the two cultures has caused some commentators to single out Shakespeare's power of characterization as the highest of his gifts, but it is a tempting doctrine in any age. A dramatist's ideas ultimately depend on the actor to give them flesh, and Shakespeare, as we know, wrote his plays with particular actors in mind. Whenever we have the good fortune to watch a great performance in the theatre, it is the individual character rather than his predicament that lingers in the mind. We are apt to remember X's Lear and Y's Hamlet rather than the total effect of the drama. The actor who 'steals the show' is always to some extent robbing his author.

Shakespeare was, as Keats described him, 'the mighty poet of the human heart', and we may be amazed by what he has to tell us about our hidden selves. But it has been the argument of the present chapter that this gift might have withered in him if he had not discovered in poetic drama the soil for its perfect flowering. Any competent talent can project an interpretation of character which, being created by intellectual energy, satisfies the mind of the reader as a sober, just and even a revealing analysis. But it needs the superior awareness of the poet to penetrate to the deeper, undisclosed sources of conduct and, by its action on the imagination, to show the inevitability of behaviour and situations which the mind may reject. Poetry not only discerns the reality which underlies our conscious being; its music works an enchantment which persuades us of the truth of the vision it reveals. To add that the thought is the word, that no revelation of truth has any substance until it has expressed itself in speech, is merely to insist upon the obvious.

Shakespeare's genius for characterization therefore had certain limits. The principal absolute to absolute veracity is that veracity and consistency of human conduct are not the highest aims of poetic drama. To observe what Aristotle called a true 'imitation' of life certainly enriches our experience, but the full apprehension of poetic truth may require us to exercise the imagination upon objects that are remote from life as we normally know it. Shakespeare was always able to meet the demands of naturalism or psychological realism when he thought it to be necessary, but he also knew that the essential truth about human beings may be conveyed by other means. Ultimately the characters and everything concerning them are conditioned by the poetic emotion.

Aristotle said that 'the life and soul of tragedy is the plot: character comes second'. Character is a man's quality, the thing he is, but it is what we do that decides our happiness or misery. In his more serious work Shakespeare seems always to have recognized this, but critics have complained that, particularly in the lesser plays, he would abandon his characters to the improbable exigencies of his borrowed plots. The freedom that they appear to enjoy in the middle of the play may be taken from them at the end, when the plot demands their adherence. In part this was what Johnson meant when he accused Shakespeare of sacrificing virtue to convenience; and other critics have followed Robert Bridges in maintaining that he deliberately ignored plausibility for the sake of immediate effect: 'It would seem that Shakespeare sometimes judged conduct to be dramatically more effective when not adequately motived'. It is true that the Elizabethan theatre would not have recognized the sort of realism and consistency demanded in most modern drama. 'Doubling', for instance, a consequence of large casts and small companies, would oblige a dramatist to dismiss characters just as they were coming to life; the intrusions of Rhetoric, enjoyed and expected by the audience, might force them into style and sentiments foreign to their habit; or it might be someone's lot to deliver a choric commentary, thus lapsing from realism into a purely symbolic role before subsequently becoming himself again.

Sometimes, again, Shakespeare's plotting was merely formal, as when he did not trouble to account for the emotional preferences of the lovers in *A Midsummer Night's Dream*. It seems not to have worried him that characters should be compelled by the plot to be paired with unpromising mates or be left victims of unmerited wrongs and humiliations. Such things offend against realism and would be objectionable if scrupulous characterization were the primary purpose of his drama. We may irritably wonder why he put up with these improbabilities, but it is unlikely that he was aware of any limitation. In old improbable stories and arbitrary refashionings of the past, undistracted by the actual and the immediate, he found the scope he needed for reflection upon the permanent problems that agitate mankind. His drama treats always of something larger than the present event; and his characters were a means for that reflection, not an end in themselves.

It has been proposed that Othello would have made no difficulty about killing Claudius, or that Beatrice would not have suffered as Ophelia did because she would have slapped Hamlet's face and sent him off to dress himself properly. This is misguided comment because it assumes that characters have an independent life outside their plays. The only thing that has an independent life is the play itself. The characters are not even independent within their particular worlds, for they affect, and are affected by, those who inhabit it with them. Shakespeare presents us with a group of people whose story is their interaction upon one another: Hal, Hotspur and Falstaff, for example, or Rosalind and Orlando, whose love is not only as they themselves see it but as it is seen by Jaques or Touchstone or Celia. It is Antonio's unexpected financial need that sets Shylock's vengefulness in motion; Angelo and Isabella, each of them seeking spiritual perfection, happen to be locked in a situation where each must fail. But of the life of these people outside their particular situations we know no more than Shakespeare thinks it necesary to tell us. We may enjoy guessing what we are not told, but we shall never say with certainty what was Hamlet's relationship with Ophelia before the play began. Or again what secrets were shared between Claudius and the Queen? How much did Gertrude know, how much did she suspect, was she too doughy and insensitive to suspect anything? To worry over questions which the dramatist deliberately left unresolved is to refuse the proper response to a work of imagination. Shakespeare's greatest characters touch life at so many points, sum up so much in their experience, that they do indeed take on the vesture of the universal, but we should not claim to know what they would do in different circumstances and the company of different men. All that Shakespeare says is that in a given predicament a certain person did thus and thus. Cleopatra died a Roman death because she was Cleopatra as a poet imagined her, not because this was the habit of royal whores everywhere. The play is always greater than the individuals who compose it, and it is the universalizing music of the verse which seems to bring their experience into kinship with the experience of all men.

Within these limits we are free to delight in the human portraiture which Shakespeare's liberality has given us. For character, finally, is the element in drama in which poetry and action meet and are united. Without it a play falls into melodrama or farce, and the verse becomes incidental decoration. Moreover, for a story to be touched to fine issues fine spirits must be involved in it. *Macbeth* is a great tragedy not because of Macbeth's situation but because it is Macbeth who is caught in it. We have to care about him before we can care what happens to him. This is important, too, for the quality of the poetry, for great utterance can only be, as Longinus wrote, 'the echo of a great soul' speaking in a great crisis. When, as sometimes happens, a fine passage falls short of sublimity — the last moments of Enobarbus come to mind (*AC* IV ix) or Claudio's revulsion from death (*MM* III i) or the grief of Troilus when Cressida betrays him (*TC* V iii) — it is through some lack in the speaker or his predicament. We do not sense a great nature behind the words, or possibly an occasion that should really move us. No man can become the embodiment of issues that are too great for his comprehension.

Shakespeare had only to imagine a man to become that man. The details seem to have been conceived at the same moment as the character, and it is hard to suppose Shakespeare often pausing to wonder what anyone was to say next. The very first words they speak, which seem to point to all they are and will become, show how intensely he visualized them from the start. How much of Hamlet is revealed in the acid word-play of his first disdainful sentences, and then in the hard, fastidious consonants of

'Tis not alone my inky cloak, good mother,
Nor customary suits of solemn black...   I ii 77.

Already the essence of Polonius has appeared in the pompous diction of his reply to a simple question:

> He hath, my lord, wrung from me my slow leave
> By laboursome petition, and at last
> Upon his will I seal'd my hard consent:
> I do beseech you, give him leave to go.

> I ii 58.

At any moment in a play a couplet or a single line may become a flash of illumination. A few words of Costard give life to Sir Nathaniel (*LLL* V ii 584); a few sentences to Davy (*2 Hen IV* V i 9 sq) give a worthier conception to Shallow; the dreamlike imagination of Richard II, with its dark streak of cruelty, shapes the terrible lines to Mowbray:

> The sly slow hours shall not determinate
> The dateless limit of thy dear exile.

> I iii 150.

In Octavia's

> The Jove of power make me most weak, most weak,
> Your reconciler!

> *AC* II iv 29.

a few simple words reach beyond the speaker's modest, unavailing character to the helpless destiny to which Roman 'policy' has appointed her. It is to the absent Cleopatra that they direct our thoughts, and to the inevitable outcome of the story.

By the sort of illusion that is possible to great art Shakespeare uses speech to suggest the attributes that lie beyond speech: a man's gait, the movement of his hands, the carriage of his body, even the scope of his imagination and the habit of his mind. An extraordinary power of self-identification created an instinctive propriety of utterance and mental process — and additionally, of course, told the actor his business. With Shylock, for example, Shakespeare had an especially difficult technical problem. In Elizabethan times there was not, as there is now, a mode of speech conventionally accepted as the idiom of the Jew. Yet Shylock's utterance had somehow to be differentiated from that of the Christians in whose world he was a sinister and alien presence. Shakespeare evolved for him a style and vocabulary that, although not distinctively Jewish, were not normal English; and these he made a window into Shylock's mind. Superficially Shylock distinguishes himself by his command of Biblical phrases and precepts, and he uses various words — *synagogue*, *Nazarite*, *Abram* (where others say *Abraham*), *publican* — which appear nowhere else in Shakespeare. For a less conscientious dramatist these external marks would have been distinction enough — and for Marlowe, if we look at his so-called Jew, more than enough. Shakespeare was not content with that. Shylock avoids the customary *interest* and *usury*, substituting *advantage*, or *thrift*, and *usance*. He calls an unbeliever a *misbeliever*, he uses the rare plural *moneys*, he *trifles* time where others waste it, an exact pound is an *equal* pound, and a pound of human flesh is not so *estimable* (valuable) as the flesh of 'muttons, beefs or goats'. This idiom is not realistic, for it is improbable that an Anglo-Jewish merchant in Elizabethan London spoke like that, but it is perculiarly his own and it establishes his foreignness. It is altogether different in kind from the few mangled consonants which sufficed to denote Shakespeare's Welshmen, for evidently there was for a period an actor who played these parts effectively and a few general indications were all he needed. Shylock was too unusual and complex a character to be left to the actor's unprompted imagination. His way of speaking had to be made the index of his whole range of feeling.[11]

Shakespeare's identification with Caliban was perhaps even more difficult as here he was dealing with a creature something less than human. An eighteenth-century critic, Joseph Warton, first drew attention to the methods used to convey Caliban's instinctive antipathies and preferences. When he wishes to curse, the generalized, largely meaningless execrations which serve human beings will not do for him. He is precise about the injuries he wishes to see inflicted, but with superb propriety he can think only in terms of what is abhorrent to himself:

> As wicked dew as e'er my mother brush'd
> With raven's feather from an unwholesome fen
> Drop on you both!
>
>   All the charms
> Of Sycorax, toads, beetles, bats, light on you!
>
>   *Tem* I ii 321, 339.

When, similarly, he wants to delight his new and favoured masters, he is incapable of imagining what they might enjoy. He can only offer them what he relishes himself, mostly things dirty and unpleasant:

> I prithee, let me bring thee where crabs grow;
> And I with long nails will dig thee pig-nuts;
> Show thee a jay's nest, and instruct thee how
> To snare the nimble marmoset; I'll bring thee
> To clust' ring filberts, and sometimes I'll get thee
> Young scamels from the rock.
>
>   II ii 171.

11 See Otto Jespersen, *The Growth and Structure of the English Language*, 206-8. The book devotes a chapter to Shakespeare's use of language.

He does not know the names of the sun and the moon, which he calls the bigger light and the less; and when he is urging his companions to move silently, Shakespeare gives him an image appropriate to his knowledge and power of understanding:

> Pray you tread softly, that the blind mole may not
> Hear a foot fall.

IV i 94.

His savage vision can picture no higher felicity than to pass his life in the service of Stephano, 'for aye thy foot-licker'. He speaks, too, in a grunting, monosyllabic rhythm, all harsh consonants, in which the words seem to come with painful labour from one not accustomed to communicate. Shylock and Caliban are extreme examples, but all Shakespeare's integrated characters are brought to life in this fashion, through their vocabulary and speech-rhythms and the imaginative range disclosed by the way their thoughts take shape. It is thus, and not by intellectual theorizing, that we are to know them.

'Simply the thing I am Shall make me live'. These men, like human beings everywhere, are ultimately mysterious. Their personalities are more than the sum of their dominant characteristics, and they are authentic because they will not be put into convenient categories. We should not expect human beings to be all of a piece. Medical science now knows more about the mind than was known in 1600, and its submissions have repeatedly confirmed the accuracy of Shakespeare's intuitions. On many of the occasions when he has seemed, through laziness or imperfect technique, to abandon his characters to the extravagant demands of the plot, he may have found a superior cause of their actions in the unknown depths unsuspected even by themselves. Modern psychology, in making us aware of the terrible acts that may be committed by a split personality, has taught us that this is only an extreme form of a not uncommon state in which the doer and his deed are loth to greet one another. Literary criticism is wrong to seek the 'hamartia' in some flaw in a character as revealed by his conscious actions when it should be sought, as a poet's intuition seeks it, in the unknown self buried below the surface. When Coleridge wrote of Iago's 'motiveless malignity', he meant that we should not be looking for a motive that will satisfy our normal expectations of human behaviour. That Iago himself made some attempt to explain his actions in this way only proved his unawareness of the subconscious forces that prompted him to evil. Even the pathological suspicions of Leontes, for which Shakespeare is held to have provided no sufficient motive, have been analysed by Freud as the ravings of delusional jealousy: a condition which proceeds from latent impulses unformulated in the victim's waking mind.

No doubt it is dangerous to carry too far the vindication of Shakespeare's story-telling by the tentative findings of psychoanalysis. One or two calamitous examples have shown already the anarchy to which the study of Shakespeare might be reduced if this process were unrestrained. It is nonetheless significant that although his sources gave him ponderable and adequate motives for the behaviour of, for instance, Leontes, Iago and Macbeth, he chose to deprive himself of this sort of motivation and leave their actions no longer explicable by the codes that society will recognize. 'Realist' critics argue that he did this deliberately because it was more effective on the stage; that in departing from his sources he was obeying not the superior instincts of an artist but the less scrupulous obligations of a professional entertainer. They may be right: calculations of this sort were never wholly absent from his mind. But titles such as *As You Like It* or *What You Will* suggest at the same time a certain detachment from the demands of his company and his public. Shakespearean criticism has given increasing weight to the notion that on occasions he refused the facile explanations provided in the sources because he sought the subtler motives revealed by a poetic exploration of the hidden springs of conduct.

If this be so, he found a means of reconciling his wayward plots with an account of human actions which, if we will accept his intuitions, we may find absolutely convincing. He did not always achieve this, and he did not always attempt it: it was perhaps the final perfection of his art. It leaves us with the assurance that what he tells us about mankind is the truth about mankind. He does not ask us to be content with one-dimensional sketches drawn after the arbitrary and transient standards of a particular culture, and he would not have us believe that men always behave in a manner that they themselves can predict. He presents man in all his obstinate contradictions, 'in doubt to deem himself a god, or beast', intermittently obedient to the promptings of a deeper, unknown self but finally invincible. Thus it is little wonder that for generations of his readers the contemplation of men in action has been the highest reward that the study of Shakespeare has to offer. Others are drawn into his imagined worlds by the potency of the emotional response he stirs in them; and others, again, because they feel they have been invited to participate in an act of judgment. Our common experience of Shakespeare is too various to submit to definition; but always it is poetry which conditions that experience.

Appendix A
Shakespeare's Company

In the First Folio of Shakespeare's plays the text is preceded by 'The Names of the Principal Actors in all these Plays'. There are twenty-six names:

William Shakespeare	Samuel Gilburne
Richard Burbage	Robert Armin
John Heminges	William Ostler
Augustine Phillips	Nathan Field
William Kempe	John Underwood
Thomas Pope	Nicholas Tooley
George Bryan	William Ecclestone
Henry Condell	Joseph Taylor
William Sly	Robert Benfield
Richard Cowley	Robert Gough
John Lowin	Richard Robinson
Samuel Crosse	John Shank
Alexander Cooke	John Rice

It is possible to name a number of other actors who appeared in Shakespeare's plays before 1623, such as Christopher Beeston, John Duke, John Sincklo, Thomas Pollard, Thomas Holcombe, Robert Pallant, and the boy actors John Thompson, Jack Wilson, Richard Sharp and John Edmans. Plainly, therefore, the above list was selective, and it is generally assumed that the twenty-six (from whom Lawrence Fletcher is conspicuously absent) were the men who had acquired shares in the Company by the time the Folio was published.

Very little is known of some of them, and the following notes, which are derived from Chambers, *William Shakespeare* I 57–91, II 71–87, are admitted to be speculative.

The patent of 1603 named Shakespeare, Phillips, Fletcher, Heminges, Burbage, Sly, Armin, Condell and Cowley. Three sharers had dropped out by that time, Kempe, Pope and Bryan. Chambers thinks that the three added in 1604 were Lowin, Cooke and Crosse; Crosse died or left almost at once (plague probably accounted for him) and was replaced by Tooley. The death of Phillips in 1605 made a vacancy for Gilburne, and by 1608 Underwood and Ostler had succeeded Sly and Fletcher. Gough had succeeded Gilburne by 1611. Cooke and Ostler died in 1614, Armin in 1615, Shakespeare in 1616, Cowley in 1619; and their places were taken respectively by Ecclestone, Benfield, Shank, Field and Robinson. Finally, Taylor replaced Burbage in 1619 and Rice replaced Field about a year later.

Kempe, Armin, Pope, Cowley, Shank and Robinson were comedians; so, at first, was Lowin, but he graduated later to heavier roles and played opposite Burbage. Bryan had some repute as an acrobat; Phillips was primarily a musician, and before long his responsibilities as the Company's business manager probably curtailed his stage appearances; Heminges succeeded him as manager and he too gradually gave up acting; Gough was possibly Welsh, in which case he may have played Lady Mortimer, Sir Hugh Evans and Fluellen; Taylor took over Burbage's roles; Shakespeare's name is not in any of the surviving actor-lists after 1603, but this cannot be taken as certain evidence that he gave up acting. Very few lists are extant and they are seldom complete.

Armin, Lowin, Ostler, Underwood, Ecclestone, Benfield, Shank, Taylor, Field and Rice joined from other companies, but of these Ecclestone, Field and Rice had formerly been with the King's Men before seeking further experience elsewhere. Gilburne and Robinson were boys with the King's Men, and Gough, Tooley and Cooke either boys or hired men, before they became sharers. Field, Ostler and Underwood were all boys of the Chapel Royal.

Field came from a well-known ecclesiastical family. His father was one of the most celebrated of Elizabethan preachers, and his brother, Theophilus, was successively Bishop of Llandaff, St David's, and Hereford. Nathan Field was a first-class actor and also a successful playwright, being the author of *A Woman's a Weathercock* and *Amends for Ladies*, and collaborating with Massinger and Fletcher. Armin too wrote plays, but not successfully.

Appendix B
The Order of the Plays

This is necessarily a controversial subject, but the order given by Sir Edmund Chambers (*W.S.* I ch. viii), although challenged in individual instances, is generally accepted. His conclusions were reviewed by J. G. Macmanaway in *Shakespeare Survey IV* and were mostly upheld in the light of recent evidence.

This is the dating given by Chambers. The symbols in brackets are the abbreviations used in this book.

1590 – 1	*2 Henry VI (2 Hen VI).* *3 Henry VI (3 Hen VI).*
1591 – 2	*1 Henry VI (1 Hen VI).*
1592 – 3	*Richard III (R III).* *The Comedy of Errors (CE).*
1593 – 4	*Titus Andronicus (TA).* *The Taming of the Shrew (TS).*
1594 – 5	*Two Gentlemen of Verona (TGV).* *Love's Labour's Lost (LLL).* *Romeo and Juliet (RJ).*
1595 – 6	*Richard II (R II).* *A Midsummer Night's Dream (MND).*
1596 – 7	*King John (KJ).* *The Merchant of Venice (MV).*
1597 – 8	*1 Henry IV (1 Hen IV).* *2 Henry IV (2 Hen IV).*
1598 – 9	*Much Ado About Nothing (MAN).* *Henry V (Hen V).*
1599 – 1600	*Julius Caesar (JC).* *As You Like It (AYLI).* *Twelfth Night (TN).*

1600–1	*Hamlet (Ham).*
	The Merry Wives of Windsor (MWW).
1601–2	*Troilus and Cressida (TC).*
1602–3	*All's Well That Ends Well (AWW).*
1603–4	————
1604–5	*Measure for Measure (MM).*
	Othello (Oth).
1605–6	*King Lear (Lear).*
	Macbeth (Macb).
1606–7	*Antony and Cleopatra (AC).*
1607–8	*Coriolanus (Cor).*
	Timon of Athens (Tim).
1608–9	*Pericles (Per).*
1609–10	*Cymbeline (Cym).*
1610–11	*The Winter's Tale (WT).*
1611–12	*The Tempest (Tem).*
1612–13	*Henry VIII (Hen VIII).*

Poems

1592–3	*Venus and Adonis (VA).*
1593–4	*The Rape of Lucrece (Lucr).*
1595–9	*The Sonnets (Sonn).*
1600	*The Phoenix and Turtle.*

Further reading

And so we leave you to other of his friends, whom if you need, can be your guides.
First Folio, *To the Great Variety of Readers.*

Any attempt to select from the massive store of Shakespearean scholarship is invidious, and it can only be claimed for the following list that the books mentioned should be reasonably accessible to readers and students. Some other books are mentioned in the footnotes, and a more comprehensive selection may be found in *Shakespeare* in Select Biographical Guides, edited by Stanley Wells (Oxford, 1973).

(a) Life and Background

M.C. Bradbrook, *Shakespeare, the Poet in his World.* Weidenfeld & Nicolson, London, 1978.

I.J.C. Brown, *Shakespeare.* Collins, London, 1949.

E.K. Chambers, *William Shakespeare.* Oxford University Press, London, 1930.

M. Chute, *Shakespeare of London.* Secker & Warburg, London, 1951.

H. Craig, *The Enchanted Glass.* Oxford University Press, New York, 1936.

J.H. de Groot, *The Shakespeares and the Old Faith.* 1946.

M. Eccles, *Shakespeare in Warwickshire.* University of Wisconsin Press, Wisconsin, 1961.

E.I. Fripp, *Shakespeare's Stratford.* 1928.

— *Shakespeare: Man and Artist.* 1938.

F.E. Halliday: Shakespeare: a Pictorial Biography, Thames & Hudson, London, 1956.

— *A Shakespeare Companion, 1564–1964.* Duckworth London; Penguin, Harmondsworth, 1964.

P. Milward, *Shakespeare's Religious Background.* Sidgwick & Jackson, London, 1973.

W. Raleigh, *Shakespeare.* (1907) Macmillan, London, 1950.

S. Schoenbaum, *Shakespeare: a Compact Documentary Life*. Oxford University Press, London, 1977.
J.S. Smart: *Shakespeare: Truth and Tradition*. (1934) Clarendon Press, Oxford, 1966.
E.M.W. Tillyard, *The Elizabethan World Picture*. Chatto & Windus, London, 1943.

(b) The Theatre and Acting

J.C. Adams, *The Globe Playhouse*. Cambridge, Mass., 1942.
B. Beckerman, *Shakespeare at the Globe 1599–1609*. Macmillan, New York, 1962.
G.E. Bentley, *The Jacobean and Caroline Stage*. Oxford University Press, London, 1941–68.
M.C. Bradbrook, *The Rise of the Common Player*. Chatto & Windus, London, 1962.
E.K. Chambers, *The Elizabethan Stage*. Oxford University Press, London, 1923.
W.R. Davies, *Shakespeare's Boy Actors*. Dent, London, 1939.
R.A. Foakes and R.T. Rickert (eds), *Henslowe's Diary*. Cambridge University Press, London, 1961.
A. Gurr, *The Shakespearean Stage*. Cambridge University Press, London, 1970.
A. Harbage, *Shakespeare's Audience* (1941) Columbia University Press, New York. 1962.
C.W. Hodges, The Globe Restored (1953) 1968.
L. Hotson, *Shakespeare's Wooden O*. Hart Davis, London, 1959.
B. Joseph, *Elizabethan Acting*. Oxford University Press, London, 1964.
R. Southern, *The Staging of Plays before Shakespeare*. Faber, London, 1973.
A.C. Sprague, *Shakespeare and the Actors*. 1944.
R. Watkins, *Moonlight at the Globe*. M. Joseph, London, 1946.
G. Wickham, *Early English Stages*. Routledge, London, 1963.

(c) Criticism, Sources and Influences

P. Alexander, *Shakespeare's Life and Art*. Nisbet, London, 1939.
E.A. Armstrong, *Shakespeare's Imagination*. London, 1946.
M.C. Bradbrook, *Shakespeare and Elizabethan Poetry*. Chatto & Windus, London, 1951.
A.C. Bradley, *Shakespearean Tragedy*. Macmillan, London, 1964.
C.F.T. Brooke (ed), *The Shakespeare Apocrypha*. Oxford University Press, London, 1918.
J.R. Brown, *Shakespeare and his Comedies*. Methuen, London, 1962.

G. Bullough, *Narrative and Dramatic Sources of Shakespeare*, Routledge, London, 1957 sq.

L.B. Campbell, *Shakespeare's Tragic Heroes*. Methuen, London, 1930.

— *Shakespeare's Histories*. Methuen, London, 1947.

E.K. Chambers, *Shakespeare: a Survey*. Sidgwick & Jackson, London, 1925.

— *Shakespearean Gleanings*. Oxford University Press, London, 1944.

— *English Literature at the Close of the Middle Ages*. Oxford University Press, London, 1945.

W.H. Clemen, *The Development of Shakespeare's Imagery*. Methuen, London, 1951.

J.F. Danby, *Shakespeare's Doctrine of Nature*. Faber, London, 1949.

M. van Doren, *Shakespeare*. New York, 1939; London, 1941.

U. Ellis-Fermor, *The Jacobean Drama*. Methuen, London, 1945.

B. Evans, *Shakespeare's Comedies*. Oxford University Press, London, 1960.

G.S. Gordon, *Shakespearian Comedy*. Oxford University Press, London, 1944.

A. Harbage, *As They Liked It*. Macmillan, London, 1947.

A. Hart, *Shakespeare and the Homilies*. Melbourne University Press, Melbourne, 1934.

A. Kernan, *The Cankered Muse*. Yale University Press; Oxford University Press, London, 1959.

J. Kott, *Shakespeare our Contemporary*. Methuen, London, 1964.

M.M. Mahood, *Shakespeare's Word-Play*. Methuen, London, 1957.

K. Muir, *The Sources of Shakespeare's Plays*. Methuen, London, 1977.

R. Noble, *Shakespeare's Biblical Knowledge*. SPCK, London, 1935.

C.T. Onions, *A Shakespeare Glossary*. Oxford University Press, London, 1953.

J. Palmer, *Political Characters of Shakespeare*. Macmillan, London, 1945.

— *Comic Characters of Shakespeare*. Macmillan, London, 1946 one-volume edition, 1962, *Political and Comical Characters of Shakespeare*.

E. Partridge, *Shakespeare's Bawdy*. Routledge, London, 1947.

M.M. Reese, *The Cease of Majesty*. Arnold, London, 1961.

I. Ribner, *The English History Play in the Age of Shakespeare*. Oxford University Press, London; Princeton, 1957.

A. Sewell, *Character and Society in Shakespeare*. Oxford University Press, London, 1951.

H. Spencer, *The Art and Life of William Shakespeare.* Bell, London, 1947.

T. Spencer, *Shakespeare and the Nature of Man.* (1943) Macmillan, New York, 1958.

M. Spivack, *Shakespeare and the Allegory of Evil.* Columbia University Press, New York, 1959.

C.F.E. Spurgeon, *Shakespeare's Imagery.* Cambridge University Press, London, 1939.

J.I.M. Stewart, *Character and Motive in Shakespeare.* (1949) Longmans Green, London, 1965.

D.A. Stauffer, *Shakespeare's World of Images.* Indiana University Press, New York, 1949.

J.A.K. Thomson, *Shakespeare and the Classics.* Allen & Unwin, London, 1952.

E.M.W. Tillyard, *Shakespeare's History Plays.* Chatto & Windus, London, 1946.

F.P. Wilson, *Elizabethan and Jacobean.* Oxford, University Press, London, 1945.

— *Marlowe and the Early Shakespeare.* Oxford University Press, London, 1953.

— *English Drama, 1485–1945.* Oxford University Press, London, 1969.

J.D. Wilson, *The Fortunes of Falstaff.* Cambridge University Press, London, 1943.

Index

Index